# HUGH GAITSKELL

# HUGH GAITSKELL

Philip M. Williams

Oxford   New York

OXFORD UNIVERSITY PRESS

1982

Oxford University Press, Walton Street, Oxford OX2 6DP

London Glasgow New York Toronto
Delhi Bombay Calcutta Madras Karachi
Kuala Lumpur Singapore Hong Kong Tokyo
Nairobi Dar es Salaam Cape Town
Melbourne Auckland
and associates in
Beirut Berlin Ibadan Mexico City Nicosia

First published by Jonathan Cape Ltd 1979
First published as an Oxford University Press paperback,
abridged and with new material, 1982

British Library Cataloguing in Publication Data

Williams, Philip M.
Hugh Gaitskell.
1. Gaitskell, Hugh
2. Statesmen—Great Britain—Biography
I. Title
941.085'5'0924    DA566.9.G3
ISBN 0-19-285115-2

Library of Congress Cataloging in Publication Data

Williams, Philip Maynard.
Hugh Gaitskell. (Oxford paperbacks)
Originally published: London: J. Cape, 1979. "First published as an Oxford University
Press paperback, abridged and with new material, 1982"—T.p. verso.
Bibliography: p.   Includes index.
1. Gaitskell, Hugh, 1906–1963. 2. Great Britain—Politics and government—1936–
1945. 3. Great Britain—Politics and Government—1945–1964. 4. Politicians—
Great Britain—Biography. I. Title.
DA566.9.G3W54 1982   941.085'5'0924 [B] 82-3633   AACR2
ISBN 0-19-285115-2 (pbk.)

Set by Macmillan (India) Ltd
Printed in Great Britain by
Richard Clay (The Chaucer Press) Ltd
Bungay, Suffolk

# Contents

## Epilogue

# Illustrations

*To My Mother*

# Preface

This is a book about the life and thought of one of the chief political leaders of post-war Britain, the most influential exponent of the democratic Socialist ethos. It sets the career of Hugh Gaitskell in the context of the political system and culture of his day. Dramatic though it was at times, his life is not merely interesting in its own right, or because of his national and international impact. Before 1951, his career throws light on the workings of government during the war and the subsequent Labour attempt to reconstruct British society more humanely and justly. In the long opposition years which followed, his activities afford an excellent window on the Labour Party, its characteristic methods of operation and its distinct traditions and pathology.

It is a political biography. I have avoided amateur psychology, and do not consider it appropriate for an outsider to explore Gaitskell's more intimate relationships while most of his family and close friends are still alive and entitled to their privacy. But I think I have omitted no important influences on his intellectual and political development.

I knew Hugh Gaitskell only slightly, just enough to form an impression of him as a man. In building up a picture of his personality and the development of his political views and style, I have been generously helped by his family and by friends from both early and late in his life. The book has benefited greatly from that, but its essential theme is the public life of a public figure.

From 1945 to 1956 he kept intermittently a diary about public events, which has survived. I have found it factually reliable and have quoted many brief extracts; the whole diary is to be published. A number of other private diaries have also been generously made available to me; so have some private letters to friends, one or two of whom prefer to remain anonymous; official papers have not.

A political biographer should show how the world looked to his subject, in order to explain why he took the decisions he did; and should assess as objectively as possible his proper place in the history of his country and his times. It is not easy to be both interpreter and judge. I have tried to understand and not denigrate his opponents, but political judgements cannot hope to command universal acceptance. Mine are those of an old sympathiser with Gaitskell's views and an old admirer of the man: better qualifications, no doubt, for the first role than for the

second. I began my task expecting to find my broad concurrence
tempered by many specific disagreements: those remaining are not
concealed, but I have been impressed at how often, on thorough
examination, his case proved stronger than I had anticipated. I have
tried to be a fair-minded advocate and an honest as well as a
sympathetic judge; others must assess the outcome.

*Oxford*                                                          P.W.
*January 1978*

# Note to the Paperback Edition

This abridgement uses the original text with a minimum of rewording
and rearrangement to preserve the flow of the narrative. It also keeps
the original chapter structure, except that the original first chapter has
been split in two to include new material (from Gaitskell's recently
discovered letters to his mother in 1926–28); Chapters 5 and 18
disappear as separate chapters and Chapter 19 almost entirely.
Consequently Chapters 2 to 4 are renumbered as *3* to *5*, and 20 to 27 as
*18* to *25*. There are a few substantive changes, as follows:

The first three sections of the original Ch. 1 now form *Ch. 1*, and the
last two form *Ch.2*; most of the new material is in *Ch. 2*, a little in *Chs.1*
and *3*.

*Ch. 5* now includes the first two, and *Ch. 6* the last two sections of the
original Ch. 5.

*Ch. 14* 2nd section, *The Leader and his Approach to Power*, was
formerly Ch. 13-iv.

Ch. 17 has been drastically rearranged, losing paragraphs to *Chs. 18*
and *22*, while *Ch. 17* 3rd section, *CND, and the Challenge from Cousins*,
was originally Ch. 18.

*Ch. 18* 1st section, *The Prelude: Foreign Affairs*, consists of
fragments of the former Ch. 17 and all that survives of 19; *Ch. 18* 2nd
and 3rd sections, *The Campaign: United We Fall*, and *The Inquest:
'Irreproachable and Unassailable'*, were formerly Ch. 20.

*Ch. 22* 3rd section, *Commonwealth Immigration, and Southern Africa*,
is drawn from the former Ch. 17-iv.

*Ch. 24* 2nd section, *Kennedy, Gaitskell, and Nuclear Weapons*, is
drawn from the former Ch. 24-vi and vii, and the rest of *Ch. 24* was
formerly Ch. 26; the parenthesis on p. 427 has been expanded.

*Oxford*                                                        P.M.W.
*March 1981*

# Acknowledgments

My first debt is to Baroness Gaitskell and to her husband's literary executors, the Rt Hon. Roy Jenkins and the late Rt Hon. Anthony Crosland, for selecting me to write his biography and giving me the run of Hugh Gaitskell's voluminous papers and his diary. Other members of his family have been very helpful, particularly his brother, Sir Arthur Gaitskell, his sister, Lady Ashton, and his daughter, Mrs McNeal.

My colleagues the Warden and Fellows of Nuffield College, Oxford, provided a very convenient and congenial environment, and as always I owe an enormous debt to my incomparable secretary Jean Brotherhood. My thanks to her and other friends for help with the proofs, and above all to Eleanor Brock who again complied the index.

Many people in politics, the Civil Service and elsewhere were generous with their time. I am greatly obliged to them all, and especially to those whose personal political views were different from Gaitskell's or from my own. In addition several of them kindly gave me useful original material which they allowed me to use. The letters to his mother quoted at the beginning of this edition, mostly in Chapter 2, were discovered when the main biography was already in print.

# Abbreviations

| | |
|---|---|
| AEU | Amalgamated Engineering Union (now the AUEW) |
| CLP | Constituency Labour Party, -ies |
| CND | Campaign for Nuclear Disarmament |
| EEC | European Economic Community (the Common Market; 'the Six') |
| EFTA | European Free Trade Association |
| ETU | Electrical Trades Union (now the EETPU) |
| ICS | Indian Civil Service |
| ILP | Independent Labour Party |
| IMF | International Monetary Fund |
| ITV | Independent Television |
| LSE | London School of Economics and Political Science |
| MEW | Ministry of Economic Warfare |
| NEC | National Executive Committee (of the Labour Party) |
| NFRB | New Fabian Research Bureau (amalgamated with the Fabian Society, 1938) |
| NUGMW | National Union of General and Municipal Workers |
| NUM | National Union of Mineworkers |
| NUR | National Union of Railwaymen |
| PLP | Parliamentary Labour Party |
| PPS | Parliamentary Private Secretary |
| SEATO | South East Asia Treaty Organization |
| SOE | Special Operations Executive |
| T&GWU | Transport and General Workers' Union |
| TUC | Trades Union Congress (and by extension its General Council) |
| UCL | University College, London |
| UNRRA | United Nations Relief and Rehabilitation Administration |
| USDAW | Union of Shop, Distributive and Allied Workers (formerly NUDAW) |
| WEA | Workers' Educational Association |

# Introduction

Hugh Gaitskell had led the Labour Party for exactly seven years when, almost on the threshold of 10 Downing Street, he was struck down by a fatal illness. His ministerial experience was very limited: a year and a half in junior office, two and a half as head of a Department, less than two at the Treasury, only one in the Cabinet. He led his party in but one general election: to a heavy defeat. Yet he was honoured at his death as no mere Leader of the Opposition had been before, and is still remembered with a respect by many opponents, and a devotion by many admirers, that is unmatched among his contemporaries.

His career was short but meteoric. He had sat in the House for only five years when he became Chancellor of the Exchequer, the shortest such parliamentary apprenticeship since Pitt; and for only ten when he was elected to lead his party, the shortest in modern times. Since Labour became a major party, he is the only leader chosen by a substantial majority – and the only one ever challenged subsequently for re-election.

The paradoxes go further back. Born to a family of soldiers and empire-builders, his strong sense of fairness and equality made him a Socialist. Unsuccessful in competing for scholarships to Winchester and Oxford, he became a university teacher, then a rare academic achievement. Undistinguished and unobtrusive at school, he was to be one of the most embattled and controversial of politicians. Keen on golf and literature as an undergraduate, he worked for the TUC in the General Strike; and the shy and sensitive public-school boy depended politically on the confidence and loyalty of trade-unionists, especially the miners who preferred him to a man of more dazzling gifts from among their own ranks. A Socialist, Gaitskell risked his political life for the American alliance; an admirer of the United States, he favoured a controlled economy; an ardent libertarian, he believed in strong disciplined political parties; the least insular of Labour leaders, he became the hero of the Party's Little Englanders. His public image was one of cold aloofness: it was less like his true personality than that of almost any other major political figure of the century. No 'desiccated calculating machine', Hugh Gaitskell in private was lively, warm and pleasure-loving. In public affairs his problems came from too much emotionalism rather than too little. He always detested trimming, and sometimes gambled to the point of recklessness for causes he thought right. Temperament made him seek drastic solutions, but reason made him mistrust extremes; and in rejecting the narrower values and prejudices of his class, he never became a vengeful apostate.

He led an argumentative and indeed fissiparous party in the difficult conditions of apparently unsuccessful opposition, and only at the very end did his reward come within sight. His turbulent reign as party leader illustrates the problems of one who tries to use his authority creatively, rather than merely registering conflicting pressures. Gaitskell was a leader of principle, and a committed educator. To become an effective instrument of 'conscience and reform', his party had to shake off the outlook of a band of propagandists without acquiring that of a mere machine to administer the existing order. He endangered his own position to make his followers face the implications and responsibilities of that difficult transformation. He insisted that the Party must attend to the concerns of ordinary people, and faced imperturbably, though not with indifference, the charge of betraying purposes which few of its voters had ever demanded.

His political style can be criticised as well as his policies. A passionate man himself, he often misjudged or offended the emotions of others. Thoroughly professional in equipping himself with the necessary skills for political leadership, he was not always an adroit tactician. Well aware that governments must act in circumstances which can rarely be foreseen, he could be pedantic about detailed policy-making in advance. Judicious and careful in weighing up the consequences of action, his final commitments were so wholehearted and so forcibly expressed that his attitudes were frequently misunderstood. Out of office, he would not propose policies he could not carry out in power; Harold Macmillan, who found his style as uncongenial as his views, said he missed all the fun of opposition by behaving as if he were in government.

He believed that the aim of political activity was to win power in order to govern according to clear values and principles. But the clarity and candour which impressed his admirers were sometimes found abrasive and divisive by others, for he would not bend before breezes of short-term sentiment in either party or electorate, and took great political risks when he thought principle required it. He lived up to his family motto, *Fortitudo et Integritas* – and sometimes seemed to be trying to impose it on the whole party. He sought to win power by convincing people through reasoned argument that his purposes and policies were right and relevant; for he despised the professional public relations techniques of exploiting the irrational, as well as more traditional forms of demagogy. Accused of elitism, in fact he paid voters the compliment of taking seriously their judgement, intelligence and capacity for idealism. Britain since the Second World War has rarely (if ever) found political leadership to match the quality of inspiration which, towards the end, Hugh Gaitskell offered.

# Chronology 1945–63

Offices held until new name shown; re-elections omitted unless challenged.

|  | 1945 | 1947–8 | 1949 |
|---|---|---|---|
| Foreign rulers | *Apr.* Truman |  | *Sept.* Adenauer |
|  |  |  | *Oct.* Mao |
| UK Prime Minister | *July* Attlee |  |  |
|   Foreign Secretary | *July* Bevin |  |  |
| Chancellor of the Exchequer | *July* Dalton | *Nov. '47* Cripps |  |
|   Leader of the House of Commons | *July* Morrison |  |  |
| Labour Leader | Attlee |  |  |
|   Deputy | Morrison |  |  |
|   Treasurer | Greenwood |  |  |
|   Shadow Chancellor |  |  |  |
|   Shadow Foreign Secretary |  |  |  |
| Main conferences (*Oct.*) |  |  |  |
| UK events: |  |  |  |
|   Labour |  |  |  |
|   Other political | *July* ELECTION | *July '48* Health Service | *Jan.* Lynskey Report |
|  |  |  | *Feb. '50* ELECTION |
|   Economic | *Dec.* US loan | *Feb. '47* fuel crisis |  |
|  |  | *July '47* convertibility |  |
|  |  | *Aug.* convertibility suspended |  |
| World events |  | 'cold war' | *Apr.* Atlantic Pact |
|  |  | *Feb. '48* Prague coup |  |
|  |  | *June '48* Berlin blockade |  |
|  |  | *June '48* Marshall Plan |  |

| 1950–1 | 1951 | 1952–3 | 1954 | 1955 |
|---|---|---|---|---|
| | | *Jan. '53* Eisenhower *Mar. '53* Stalin dies | | |
| *Mar. '51* Morrison *Oct. '50* Gaitskell *Mar. '51* Ede *Apr. '51* Bevan out | *Nov.* Churchill *Nov.* Eden *Nov.* Butler *Nov.* Crookshank | | | *Apr.* Eden *Apr.* Macmillan *Apr.* Butler |
| | *Nov.* Gaitskell *Nov.* Morrison | '52 Morecambe | *Nov.* Gaitskell | *June* Robens |
| | *Oct.* ELECTION | *Oct. '52* Gaitskell at Stalybridge | *Apr.* Bevan out of Shadow Cabinet | *Apr.* Bevan nearly expelled *May* ELECTION |
| *July '50* 1st arms programme *Jan. '51* 2nd arms programme | *Sept.* sterling crisis | Better terms of trade | | |
| *June '50* Korean War | | *July '53* Korean truce | *July* Indo–China partition | |

| | 1955–6 | 1956 | 1957 | 1958 |
|---|---|---|---|---|
| Foreign rulers | | | | *May* De Gaulle |
| UK Prime Minister | | | *Jan.* Macmillan | |
| Foreign Secretary | *Dec.* Lloyd | | | |
| Chancellor of the Exchequer | *Dec.* Macmillan | | *Jan.* Thorneycroft | *Jan.* Amory |
| Leader of the House of Commons | | | | |
| Labour Leader | *Dec.* Gaitskell | | | |
| Deputy | *Jan.* Griffiths | | | |
| Treasurer | *Oct.* Gaitskell | *Oct.* Bevan | | |
| Shadow Chancellor | *Jan.* Wilson | | | |
| Shadow Foreign Secretary | | *Nov.* Bevan | | |
| Main conferences | Margate | | Brighton | |
| UK events: | | | | |
| Labour | *May* Cousins, T&GWU Sec. | | | *Jan.* CND begins |
| Other political | | | | |
| Economic | | | *Sept.* Bank Rate up | *May* Bus strike |
| World events | *Feb.* Khrushchev's secret speech | *Nov.* Russians invade Hungary<br><br>*Nov.* Suez invasion | | |

| 1959 | 1960 | 1961 | 1962 | 1963 |
|------|------|------|------|------|
| | | *Jan.* Kennedy | | |
| | *July* Home | | | |
| | *July* Lloyd | | *July* Maudling | |
| | | *Oct.* Macleod | | |
| *Nov.* Bevan | *Nov.* Gaitskell<br>*Nov.* Brown<br>*Oct.* Nicholas<br><br>(Gaitskell pro tem) | *Nov.* Gaitskell<br>*Nov.* Brown<br><br>*Nov.* Callaghan<br><br>*Nov.* Wilson | | *Feb.* Wilson |
| (*Nov.*) Blackpool | Scarborough | Blackpool | Brighton | |
| | *July* Bevan dies | *Mar.* 5 MPs lose whip | | *Jan.* Gaitskell dies |
| *Oct.* ELECTION | *Apr.* Blue Streak ends | | *July* EEC talks | |
| | | | *Nov.* Immigration Bill | |
| | | | *July* Pay pause | |
| | *May* U2 crisis: Summit fails | *Aug.* Berlin Wall | *Oct.* Cuba missile crisis | *Jan.* De Gaulle vetoes UK in EEC |
| | | | *Oct.* India/China war | |

# PART ONE

# The Making of a Democratic Socialist

*'A life of Hugh is bound to be dull, because he was so damned blameless'*
(A colleague of HG in the 1930s to the author)

*'A man who had been biding his time, blossoming with the power'*
(A university acquaintance on HG in 1940–1)

# 1
# Searching for Values 1906–26

*'I always regarded you as a dreamer and not a do-er'*
(A boyhood friend when HG became Chancellor)

## Childhood: Homeless but Happy

Hugh Todd-Naylor Gaitskell was born on 9 April 1906 at 3 Airlie Gardens, Kensington, the son of an Indian civil servant. His family originally came from Cumberland, and derive their name from a local word which meant a sheiling (enclosure) for goats. His middle name came from his godfather who was in the ICS; he dropped the hyphen in boyhood. The Gaitskells included mercers, curriers, clergymen and a Whitehaven sea-captain. An older branch lived at Yeorton Hall near Egremont (from which Hugh's widow was to take her title); it was sold around 1870 to pay racing debts. Those relatives dispersed to California and South America. When Hugh's elder brother visited Medellin in Colombia for the International Labour Organisation in 1963, he was given the wrong key for his hotel room and found it belonged to Maurice Gaitskell, a distant cousin speaking only Spanish.

A younger branch moved to Bermondsey as distillers, and one of them, Thomas (who had once eloped to Gretna with an heiress), raised a regiment of Surrey Yeomanry in the Napoleonic Wars. Among its officers was his younger brother Henry, Hugh's great-grandfather. Most of Hugh's immediate forebears served in the regular army, often in India, and their descendants settled round the Empire. Henry's son, Colonel James Gandy Gaitskell, retired to Cheltenham. His own son Arthur, Hugh's father, went to a school for officers' sons there, and then to New College, Oxford. Arthur Gaitskell senior abandoned the military tradition, and joined the Indian Civil Service without taking his degree. Apart from occasional furloughs, he spent the rest of his short life in Burma, where he arrived at nineteen in 1889 – four years after annexation – and left in August 1914 as Commissioner for Settlement and Land Records in Rangoon. He then came home on sick leave suffering from sprue, a tropical disease from which he died in Scotland on 1 December 1915 at forty-five.

Everyone describes Arthur Gaitskell as a model of integrity, and he left a strong impression on his children even though they were not often together. He was a loving father to them by the standards of the day, particularly affectionate to his daughter; but his other juvenile relatives regarded with awe this good-looking, intelligent, serious and silent man, who gave up playing bridge because he was winning too much money at it. Responsibility and conscientiousness, devotion to the public service and the sense of an obligation to work for the less fortunate were qualities inherited by both his sons and translated into different circumstances and values; for Arthur junior, the difficult start and successful management of a famous peasant co-operative in the Sudan; for Hugh, workers' education and, later, politics.

There was another side to Arthur Gaitskell senior, whom the Burmese called 'Tiger Gaitskell'. In 1898, on his first furlough, he met on the boat to Japan the young daughter of the Consul-General in Shanghai, George Jamieson, who came from a farming family on Speyside in Banffshire. A poor but able youth, Jamieson had been encouraged by his village school-master to go on to Aberdeen University, and had risen to one of the top posts in the Consular Service, where he also became a distinguished Chinese scholar, as well as winning a prize – open to world-wide competition – for an essay on bimetallism. After a romantic pursuit to Scotland, Arthur Gaitskell married Adelaide Mary ('Addie') Jamieson. She was much younger than he was, and lived until 1956. Two of their three children were born in Rangoon: Dorothy Margaret (Jane to her brothers and Bunty to everyone else) in 1899 and Arthur in 1900; Hugh, nicknamed Sam, came five and a half years later.

Their mother was a very different character from their father: vivacious, charming, sociable and – from natural high spirits rather than social rebellion – often highly unconventional. She once embarrassed her husband by absenting herself from her own dinner party and, when a prominent leader of Rangoon society, she went out one night and mixed up all the street signs. Though quite conservative, and with a strong sense of social hierarchy, she made many Burmese friends when that was very unusual. She was devoted to her children, especially her sons, and when she came home to England their normal orderly life was disrupted; they were indulged with sweets and all discipline was thrown to the winds. To her Hugh owed the gaiety and friendliness which were so familiar to those who knew him well.

The family had many links with Burma. Harry Todd-Naylor, Hugh's father's cousin, whose Yorkshire gentry forebears had fought for Charles I, served out there as a Deputy Commissioner and became Hugh's godfather. At thirteen Hugh acquired a stepfather who was in business in Burma: Gilbert Wodehouse, first cousin of P. G., nephew of Graham Wallas the early sociologist, and schoolfellow of Clement Attlee. A third link was Hubert Ashton, Cambridge triple Blue and President of the MCC, who married Hugh's sister in 1927; after many years in the Burmah Oil Company he became after the war Conservative MP for Chelmsford and Parliamentary Private Secretary to R. A. Butler. Hugh was not indifferent to Burma (he was asked to read a book on it before publication in 1938) but the strong connections had – surprisingly – no apparent influence on his life, outlook or policy.

Separation from his parents possibly did have such an influence, though if so it should have had more impact on his brother and sister. The children had no home life in the ordinary sense. Their father died when Hugh was nine and for most of those years they were in different continents, together only when Arthur Gaitskell had his long leaves in England. Their mother came back rather more frequently, but apart from one exceptional year Hugh's entire childhood from the age of two and a half was spent boarded out with relations or at boarding schools. Hugh's life shows no sign of neurotic striving; 'entirely natural and straightforward,' wrote Maurice Bowra, who knew him from the age of eighteen, 'he lacked those inner conflicts which disturb so many young people'.[1] Yet, as Mrs Iremonger and others have shown, a surprisingly large number of famous leaders, notably British Prime Ministers and other prominent politicians, have had a childhood bereft of parents.[2]

Hugh spent his first winter in Burma, where a fine family photograph shows him in the arms of an aunt, with his parents and a dozen servants. Then his father came home on leave, bringing with him the child's devoted Indian nurse 'Mary Ayah', and they lived for fifteen months in Cheltenham. When he revisited it as a Minister after the war he thought the town attractive but found it 'still full of faint, early childhood memories, not particularly pleasant ones. Staying with stuffy relations and going to church in a stiff sort of way'.[3]

During school terms the three children went to live with their father's first cousin, Mrs Pike, in a large North Oxford house. 'Cousin May', who came from Achill Island where she was the local squiress, was kind but strict, and her household was disciplined and fairly puritanical. One pot of jam had to last a week; and there was much stress on truthfulness, good manners, and consideration for social inferiors. The austerities were tempered by Cousin May's daughter Kathleen, whom the children adored, and by a sprightly young nanny, who used to play with them and sing to them at bedtime: old Scots ballads for Bunty, music-hall songs for Arthur, and hymns for Hugh.

(He once startled a strange lady in the street by chanting to her from his pram: 'Soon shall you and I be lying/Each within our narrow tomb.')

For holidays they went to other relatives. Often they spent Christmas with their maternal aunts in rather grand detached houses in London, ruled by strange nannies. The older Gaitskell children felt themselves somewhat poor relations (they were given five shillings between them to buy presents for eighteen people); and Hugh, as the youngest of all, was much teased by his cousins. At Easter and some Christmases, they would go to their mother's aunt and uncle who lived at Kinermony, a farm near Aberlour on Speyside. Later in life Hugh often recalled those holidays: 'Some of my happiest memories are of night train journeys to Scotland, of breakfast in the train crossing the Forth Bridge . . . [and] playing for hours beside a burn that splashed down the hillside into the Spey.'⁴ Summer was best of all. Every year until 1919 George Jamieson, their only living grandparent, took the dower house at Brancaster Staithe on the Norfolk coast – the house that they thought of more than any other as home, where occasionally their parents or their mother would join them. They bicycled, fished and played with their cousins who stayed near by.

The Gaitskell children did not question the frequent separation from their parents, and their childhood was happy in spite of it. For the two older ones it meant a good deal of responsibility as well as more autonomy than was normal for children then; Hugh was the cherished baby of the family, relatively sheltered until he went to Winchester. Family relationships were warm when they were all together, and, with the parents so often away, the three children were deeply attached to one another. Arthur was always the leader and Hugh his devoted champion and follower. Nearly fifty years later he wrote to a friend: 'when I was a boy I loved my brother, no one else, and no one else would do'. Arthur was the more fiery and volatile, Hugh much more placid but also stubborn. Arthur, fearing to be late for school, would be driven frantic by Cousin May's table rules about finishing everything on your plate; Hugh, too young for school, would sit it out until a hotplate had to be brought for his meal, and sometimes he even won. Later, a game of bridge occasionally led to a row, with both the elder children marching off and leaving Hugh to play all four hands. Though their paths diverged later in life, the close relations between the three were never broken.

When Hugh was five, he, his sister and their nanny (Arthur was left behind) went out to Burma for a year, to the hill station at Maymyo where their father was posted. It was a great change from the relatively secluded life at Oxford, with other colonial children to play with, parties to go to and ponies to ride furiously. Mary Ayah returned to help with the children, while their parents pursued a gay social life. In 1912 the whole family returned and took rooms in Oxford for a few weeks. Arthur Gaitskell senior bought from the bicycle shop of William Morris (later Lord Nuffield) a temperamental motor-car, which disliked steep hills and would climb them only by zigzagging backwards – still possible when roads were quite empty. Then the parents returned to Burma. Cousin May had gone home to Ireland and the children stayed with her unmarried sister, Cousin Cis (Miss Todd-Naylor), at another North Oxford house. Hugh went as a day-boy to the Dragon School (known as Lynam's) from six to eight, and was a boarder from eight to thirteen.

Later he described the Dragon as a highly unorthodox and notably unconventional preparatory school.[5] C. C. ('Skipper') Lynam, the headmaster, was an ardent radical, devoted to the memory of Gladstone, who wore a red tie and seaman's jersey and concentrated on encouraging independence and self-confidence in his 200 pupils. Unlike Summerfields, the rival and more conventional Oxford prep school to which Harold Macmillan went, Lynam's admitted a few girls (unheard-of then) and the sons of local tradesmen as well as those of dons and professional people. Masters were called by their nicknames and formal discipline was little stressed, though classroom work was taken seriously. Everyone there then remembers it as a very friendly place. Hugh followed his brother and inherited Arthur's nickname, the Goat. Like Arthur, he and his best friend Charles Plumb (son of a bishop and later a civil servant) were favourites of the Skipper, whose tastes for loud ties and boating they shared. To one sporting friend Hugh was 'a nice little chap, quiet and unassuming . . . rather friendless'. But another had a stronger impression of him as 'the personification of decency', the natural arbiter in any quarrel between boys, and the leader in a protest against some injustice by a master. Later in life, too, his qualities were slow to reveal themselves to everyone.

He discovered quite young in various ways that his own situation, far from being typical, was one of exceptional privilege. Searching for early signs foreshadowing the future, friends later recalled some of his juvenile encounters with poverty; and he himself never forgot the friend's father who, hearing he was going to Winchester, told him: 'You don't know how lucky you are – only one boy in ten thousand is going to have the opportunities which lie before you.' It shocked him, he claimed, into 'the first awareness of a social problem'.[5] But at this tender age he was an ordinary typical little boy who showed no sign of becoming a fledgling politician (though there were a few at the school, and Hugh did come second to one of them, J. P. W. Mallalieu – son of a Liberal MP – in a public-speaking contest). Contemporaries commented, however, at prep school, Winchester and Oxford alike, that he was unusually unpossessive and behaved as a 'natural socialist', treating everyone as equal and everything as held in common.

## Winchester: Quiet Rebel

Hugh followed his brother to Winchester as he had to the Dragon School. He was never obviously unhappy but clearly found it much less congenial, though it left many enduring marks. The problems of adolescence were more than usually acute for him, for even the limited family life he had known was now wholly disrupted. His mother had stayed in England for four years after Arthur Gaitskell senior died in 1915, but then she returned to Burma to remarry. Then when grandfather George Jamieson died, the children lost the adult relative who meant most to them, and with whom they had often stayed in London and Norfolk. Bunty looked after Hugh at first, but in 1921 she also went out to Burma, returning periodically mainly for his sake. Arthur was at Oxford, and then went off to the Sudan in 1923, and for the first time Hugh was entirely alone.

Before the other two went abroad, the young Gaitskells had spent their holidays together. In 1919 they stayed in County Kilkenny with Protestant Irish family friends from Burma (where Hugh defied their hostess, whose temper was legendary, in defence of his brother who had spilt some water on the stairs – she astonished and relieved them all by bursting out laughing). After 1920 they discovered Exmoor – where Canon Wodehouse, father of their mother's second husband, had been a rector – and rejoiced in the contrast to the flat Norfolk countryside. About that time Hugh picked up dancing at a Christmas party; he always remained a passionate enthusiast for it, 'dancing himself to death like a dervish', as Harold Macmillan is supposed to have said. After Arthur's departure, Hugh sometimes holidayed with school friends, or invited one of them to accompany him to stay with his Martelli cousins at Brancaster. The Royal West Norfolk Golf Club, close to Sandringham, was an elite preserve which the youngsters had had to themselves during the war, but where they were not made very welcome after it; but at nineteen, against strong competition from his seniors, Hugh won the Prince of Wales Cup. He and his cousin George became attached to a red-haired local belle, Felicity Cory-Wright (a daughter of Sir Herbert Beerbohm Tree, she appears in a well-known poem of Rupert Brooke); years later, to his daughter, Hugh called her 'the adored of my youth'. He taught her children to play cricket (a game he never himself enjoyed). He acted with enthusiasm in charades, and showed considerable talents at pencil games as well as golf. His idealistic side was apparent too, and when he became Chancellor, Felicity – a staunch Tory – wrote 'I always regarded you as a dreamer and not a do-er'.[6]

At Winchester his career began inauspiciously, in the sanatorium with mumps before his official admission, and it continued without distinction. The intellectual star of the school in his day was his junior Richard Crossman, his classroom neighbour one year; the sporting heroes were the Ashtons, one of whom married Hugh's sister. Chatting to them once at a cricket match, Bunty vividly recalls Hugh saying, 'I hope all my friends see Claude Ashton talking to us'. He became a prefect in H House, Culver's Close, where the prefects' room contains a plaque in his memory ('greatly honoured . . . for his courage and integrity'). But he made much less mark there than Arthur, recently head of the house.

Winchester was a nursery for the professional upper-middle class, and has been called 'of all public schools the most aloof and intellectual'.[7] It educated rather fewer sons of old pupils and far more university scholarship winners than its leading rivals, and it instilled a strong sense of public service in its future judges, administrators, ambassadors and professors. A high value was placed on intellectual honesty, coherence and clarity, none at all on idle aristocratic eccentricity or commercial thrusting. After Hugh had left, when his mother wrote of her hopes for his 'great career', he replied: 'there is not, I believe, much chance of having a great career unless one is sufficiently egotistical. Winchester does its best to stop any Wykehamist from having a great career because it preaches the abnegation of Individualism and it generally succeeds.'[8]

Sometimes socially shy but always intellectually self-confident, Wykehamists have been stereotyped as high-minded, argumentative proselytisers – or as prim and dedicated prigs. Reinforcing his strict upbringing, Winchester's heavy emphasis on self-restraint helped Hugh to keep under firm control the strong emotions that seethed beneath a placid surface; so that an American who was a close friend at New College could call him 'a very thorough Wykehamist though superficially rebellious'.[9] That was only partially true, for his reaction against one side of Winchester was lasting. But in other aspects the discipline served him well in politics; and in many ways – his high-minded sense of duty, his notable courtesy and self-control, his rational style – he fitted the ideal mould.

Though far more conservative then than today, the school was slowly changing. One quite critical contemporary of Hugh's called it 'much less philistine than most of its contemporaries. Intellect was not despised as at Rugby or Harrow. You could reach the top of the school and be respected if you had a good brain, even if you couldn't lift a cricket bat off the ground.' Boys could now specialise in science or history as well as in classics; and there was an active cultural life, with flourishing musical, archaeological, natural history and debating societies, and crowded lectures on Italian painting by the headmaster, which inspired among others the future Lord Clark. Hugh was best at history, for which he won a prize. The Dragon School, which sent many boys to Winchester, heard reports of him 'working very hard, as usual'.[10] He played football with and other sports without enthusiasm, but (like Mrs Iremonger's Prime Ministers) he much preferred individual games such as golf and tennis. One terrible disappointment was to do badly through illness in a senior steeplechase he had been tipped to win. His fellows found him more serious-minded than most, notably fair and honest, unusually friendly to his juniors, and a relaxed and amusing companion. Only very occasionally did a streak of ruthlessness show. He was quite popular, without enemies; but no one ever expected great things of him. 'Quiet, gentle, charming and very honest . . . but one wouldn't look to him for any fireworks or leadership', was the view of a senior. The housemaster later wrote of 'a quiet, modest, studious and undemonstrative boy of whom no one could have predicted his future'; though as a prefect (by his appointment) he felt Hugh 'made his weight felt by quiet determination and a certain sweet reasonableness and sense of justice'.[11]

The houses (of about forty boys) were very self-contained, for juniors were expected to make friends only in their own house. Fortunately Trant's (as Culver's Close was usually known, after its founder) had and has a reputation for being 'more liberal, more grown-up and civilised' and less rigidly disciplined than any other. Plays were produced in alternate years, and Hugh's poetic and theatrical interests lasted all his life. Acting as a woman in Sophocles' *Antigone* (translated by his housemaster), he was stiff, awkward and over-rational; he sent his sister a photograph of himself, commenting (justly), 'Don't I look an idiot!' A group of seniors read papers on literary subjects, and occasionally invited some prominent public figure to talk, such as Lady Asquith or John Drinkwater the poet. Hugh was active in house discussions, with a strong taste for argument and a combativeness in it which surprised and puzzled his friends. His brother and sister had always found him 'slightly annoyingly the man who was right – annoying because he usually *was* right'. Now, a contemporary in the same house was exasperated by the mental agility with which he would 'frequently get the better of an argument, although he knew as well as you did that he was in the wrong!' Others remember his sarcastic, acid, inflammatory style, his bitterness about social inequality, and his liking for unpopular causes – defending trade unions, or criticising hunting, or attacking landlords or capitalists.

He was not explicitly political, though he himself believed that at Winchester his 'Liberal sympathies were quite evident'.[5] He is recorded as speaking three times in the school debating society, defending democracy in March 1923, and the next year supporting a vote of confidence in the first Labour Government – arguing that whatever the next one might be like, this one depended on Liberal support and was bound to be moderate.[12] He himself recalled only the third occasion, when in October 1923, soon after Italy invaded Corfu, he denounced Mussolini as a tyrant, an enemy of Britain and a likely architect of a new world war. His first political interest was in international affairs, and he was responsible for founding a branch of the League of Nations Union at Winchester. He later wrote – incidentally implying that he carried more weight than his contemporaries recall – that he had 'used his influence with the leading figures in the school – the popular games-playing element, school prefects, etc., – to induce them to join. This made it fashionable and before long it had a membership of over 100 – a quarter of the whole school.'[13]

His most distinguished scholastic performance at school was to win, against so formidable a competitor as Colin Clark, a prize for an essay on international arbitration offered by an old Wykehamist and rising young lawyer, Stafford Cripps. Hugh went to receive the prize at the donor's chambers, but Cripps was delayed in court and their brief conversation was conducted in a taxi to Paddington; the great man's remedy for the ills of the world turned out to be a union of the Christian Churches. It did not appeal to Hugh, who later told Maurice Bowra that he had abandoned religion in his last year at Winchester and never returned to it.[1] But despite his agnosticism, his internationalism and his egalitarianism, the family and school traditions were powerful; a close friend was surprised that when 'Tubby' Clayton of Toc H (a rest centre in France for troops on leave) preached in the Cathedral on patriotism, Hugh 'drank it in and days later still quoted passages'.

While retaining some Winchester values, Hugh rejected others quite violently. That was not obvious to his contemporaries, including one with whom he went walking every Sunday, who thought him a normal, friendly, happy schoolboy without obvious doubts about either society or the public schools. However argumentative with his regular companions, Hugh disliked scenes and did not obtrude his own opinions where they would be unwelcome. He was careful not to embarrass his Cheltenham aunt, or his personal friends at Winchester. But the closest of them all, Rupert Horsley, who came from the same free and easy prep school, recalls him as 'always on the side of the underdog' against the athletic extroverts, and as strongly critical of the school's intense pressure against 'bad notions'—things which 'weren't done'. Junior boys were required to learn, and were examined on, an elaborate private Winchester vocabulary (it even had its own dictionary); and they had to obey strict rules of conduct and costume, enforced by a very irrational system of punishments. 'I was terrified the whole of my first two years', said Horsley, 'terrified of offending against some unwritten law you didn't know about.' Boys from more illiberal prep schools were not so shocked by the system which, as there was no such thing as a good notion, encouraged cautious conformity—or else produced, as it did in Hugh, a strong reaction against authority and class prejudice and rigid convention. Later, in public life, he often both rejected and resented the pressure of an apparently monolithic Establishment (as in 1926, or 1931, or over ITV, Rhodesia or the Common Market).

Winchester exerted even stronger conformist pressure than most public schools, for it laid exceptional stress on communal life and abhorred individual privacy. Arthur had felt the strain during the war, and Hugh, who did not arrive till 1919, wrote later that his own undergraduate generation 'had experienced in an unusually intense fashion the pressures of the community on the individual'.[14] Two years after he left, he commented to his mother on the school's characteristic worship of the team spirit.

I must have argued over this question a million times. I may have felt that 'esprit de corps' feeling half a dozen times when I was at Winchester but not more. It is very much an illusion . . . firstly I don't think the ego is lost in playing for the side: secondly . . . I'm not at all sure that its such a good thing that he (*sic*) should be lost. The Co-operative Spirit is one which can be fostered easily enough . . . in the face of a common enemy whether its a nation, a school or a political party. But the esprit de corps for humanity as a whole which is clearly the only possible ideal in that line to aim for is non-existent and probably the best thing for humanity as a whole is the development of the Individual with as little harm as possible to his neighbours. I prefer this to the ideal of some patriotic Englishmen who consider it noble to let oneself be lost in a mob feeling and with a full esprit de corps feeling agree to things which one's intelligence tells one are outrageous. Thirdly and most important is the fact that at Oxford one has passed the stage when esprit de corps is supposed to make one unselfish.[8]

She had provoked that outburst by quoting a phrase of his father on the subject, and indeed a close friend of later years remarked that Winchester must have felt like 'his father put into commission'.[15] Others of that generation reacted too, and for the first time the school produced a crop of Socialist intellectuals and politicians: Colin Clark, Richard Crossman, Douglas Jay, D. N. Pritt, E. A. Radice.

Hugh's own revolt focused on a limited target with corresponding intensity. Eight years after leaving he wrote to his brother, with a vehemence which may partly have reflected the problems of a very lonely adolescence:

I believe that Winchester destroys, ties up, suppresses the natural vitality of almost all who go there. They remain unless some fortunate accident happens to them bound within the set of reflexes to which life at Winchester has conditioned them. You think you don't make friends easily – when did you begin not to, not surely until after the strain of the last gloomy years of Winchester. Nobody would have said that as a boy this was a characteristic of yours . . . The Wykehamist fear of not being a good citizen . . . prevented you from even considering what . . . you really wanted.[16]

That Hugh nevertheless exemplified so many of the school's less class-bound values was largely due to the one Winchester figure for whom he always kept an affectionate admiration, his housemaster Cyril Robinson. Unlike most public-school masters of the time, Robinson encouraged pupils to think for themselves and to question every established belief and practice. He founded the WEA in Winchester town and introduced the senior boys to its members; Hugh was probably a participant. Robinson was a superb teacher, 'interested in everything and anything', immensely keen and versatile and able to stimulate the same enthusiasm and intellectual curiosity in his pupils, to whom he 'opened horizons of all kinds'. Throughout his life, like many others from his house, Hugh looked back to his teaching and personality – if to nothing else at Winchester – with gratitude.

## Oxford: 'Heavenly Freedom'

In 1924 Hugh Gaitskell went up to New College, Oxford, then at an academic peak and attracting many of the ablest undergraduates. He made his choice for more traditional reasons: Winchester had a historic connection with New College, his father had been there and his brother had won a scholarship there. His last and worst disappointment at school was that he unexpectedly failed to do the same, coming down in General Knowledge. But he declined an exhibition at Hertford, and went to New College without an award.

Oxford was the critical stage in Gaitskell's development. Later on he was an intense pleasure-lover, regarding it almost as a duty to enjoy life to the full; but it was not until he shook off the constraints of the school that he really felt liberated. He wrote to his mother at the time, 'the idea of Oxford is to give the individual a chance after the crushing effect of the public school system';[8] and to a friend many years later: ' "To thine own self be true" was the great creed of my developing phase at Oxford. And I still believe it is the most important thing of all.' His total change of life-style had for two years no overt political content at all, but he was quietly working out for himself the personal values to which he adhered for the rest of his life. When the moment of decision came in the General Strike, he knew without a moment's hesitation which side he was on.

Long afterwards, he painted his own picture of the university scene:

Oxford in the middle twenties was gay, frivolous, stimulating, and tremend-ously alive . . . it was a brief, blessed interval when the lives of the young were neither overshadowed by the consequences of the last war nor dominated by the fear of a future one. Most of us sighed with relief and settled down to the business of enjoying ourselves . . . Politics, to tell the truth, were rather at a discount. We were in revolt all right – against Victorianism, Puritanism, stuffiness of any kind, but most of us weren't sufficiently bitter – or perhaps sufficiently serious – to be angry young men . . . [in] the heavenly freedom of Oxford [revolt] took the form of an outburst of scepticism, a mistrust of dogma, a dislike of sentimentality and of over-emotional prejudices or violent crusades.[14]

These recollections echo what he wrote at the time: 'I plead guilty to Sentimentality myself too but at least I am aware of it and make some endeavour to sift the true from the false emotion';[17] and again:

I know I'm inclined to accuse anyone who is emotional of being sentimental but I think it's so often true . . . I think sentimentality is implied in any kind of strong belief whether it be religion, patriotism, socialism or any thing like that – forcing oneself to believe in things for fear of living with no beliefs. I suppose I'm just the same in believing in the truth only.[18]

In his subsequent account, he continued:

We were, therefore, suspicious of general ideas, especially when these involved some mystical, collective, common good. We professed the happiness of the individual as the only acceptable social aim. As for personal values, truth was our supreme object and intellectual integrity was the greatest of virtues.[14]

A good-looking, curly-haired, friendly youth with a charming smile, unobtrusively intelligent and highly gregarious, Gaitskell deliberately broke away from the narrow clique of New College Wykehamists and made friends elsewhere in the college and – unusually for those days – in the university. He consciously rejected all pressures to conform, writing at the time:

I have given up the idea of going through life just adapting myself to other people: there have been plenty of attempts to make me shoot hunt and fish and do all that a gentleman should do, but the last two years being fairly independent I have followed what is more natural to me. And now I am not going to give up what I value to please others![18]

Years later he wrote to his daughter that there was a sharp split 'between the "hearties" who played games and were dull, & the aesthetes who didn't and weren't.'[19] By taste and by friendships he was close to the latter, soon adopting their conventions, abandoning the sober suit and flower in buttonhole for the fashionable wide 'Oxford bags' and even puce ties.

His tastes were literary and artistic, though not musical: 'The only success which would satisfy me in any way would be an intellectual or artistic one. Having no talents art is ruled out and the only thing left is for me one day to write something great.'[8] He read widely and discriminatingly. Housman was a favourite poet, Proust and D. H. Lawrence his most admired authors (he later read Lawrence's letters through twice over as soon as they came out); and he was sensitive to literary style, though his own was notable for precision and lucidity rather than elegance. As secretary of the Mermaids, the New College play-reading society, he broke with custom by bringing in modern authors like Ibsen and Strindberg; more frivolously, he kept up his liking for elaborate charades (a favourite pastime in school holidays) through another flourishing college society.

He made friends in many different circles, though (then, as later) he would not mix them up. He was to describe his first year as 'fairly normal – playing golf, making friends, amusing myself . . . I did not do a great deal of work either in my first or second year, but enjoyed myself at parties quite a lot'.[5] He played tennis frequently and cards occasionally, punted on the river and took long walks in summer, and went often to the theatre or cinema (though not to concerts). One ambition was to win a golf Blue; and he joined an exclusive dining club, the Gridiron. He had a little money, and he was anxious to break with public-school constraints and extend his social contacts. Years later he wrote to his brother:

I think it was your experiences at Winchester that stopped you getting what you might have done out of Oxford. You say Poverty interfered with your social life. Only a Wykehamist would allow it too [*sic*]. It is true that I was better off than you were but the fact that I joined the Grid was never of any importance at all. Plenty of well off Wykehamists joined too and because they remained Wykehamists never had a proper social life.[16]

Hugh was determined that artificial barriers should not restrict that. 'He had no sense of social distinctions, and this was not the result of intellectual conviction but the cause of it. He was a natural democrat who took people on their merits.'[20] While he regarded having a wide range of acquaintances as part of his emancipation, his more conventional friends thought some of the others distinctly scruffy. He delighted in the eccentricities of John Betjeman, whom he knew from the Dragon School, and he moved occasionally on the fringe of a homosexual set whose tastes were then quite prevalent among the aesthetes. At one of his first meetings with Elizabeth Harman (now Countess of Longford), they sat under a haystack talking about Oscar Wilde. Finding her sympathetic, he said: 'I'm so glad. If you hadn't thought that way, I don't think we could have gone on being friends.'

In practice Gaitskell spent much more time with girls than most undergraduates did. They were still new in Oxford, and even chaperones had not entirely vanished. But he sharply denied having been a ladykiller, saying that like most Wykehamists he 'was far too diffident and shy'.[5] Years later he told his daughter: 'emotionally it was chiefly romantic, divine, most pure calf love for women older than myself!'[19]

Though he was on the aesthetes' side of the great Oxford divide, he was not firmly in any one camp. He persuaded one friend to stand (successfully) for office in the Junior Common Room as someone acceptable to both parties, and light-heartedly told another (twice) that they qualified only as semi-aesthetes because they both disliked striped ties. He took one close friend – Jim Orrick, a Maryland postgraduate student of English literature who was years older than himself – for all-day walks on the Downs to cure him of being too thorough an aesthete. He seems to have been the sort of person to whom others took their troubles; and though no prig, he already displayed the conscientious prefect's concern for his friends' right development – which Orrick called long afterwards 'a passion for improving the human race, beginning with me'.

Among senior members Hugh's first close friend was Maurice Bowra. He had been up at New College with Arthur and was now Dean (later Warden) of Wadham, an overwhelming personality and for years one of Oxford's most prominent figures. Largely through him, Gaitskell met literary lions like Auden, Connolly, Day Lewis and Pryce-Jones. Bowra stimulated his frivolous, exuberant side (and also his lasting interest in and admiration for the ancient Greeks). Yet the influence was not all one way, for in the General Strike it was to be the undergraduate who altered the behaviour of the don.[20]

Even in those carefree first two years, there was a strong serious element. 'You could almost feel your mind unfolding,' said Gaitskell later;[21] and again: 'The great thing for me was the flowering of intellect and personality – much repressed at Winchester. Feeling oneself develop was exciting – also getting rid of a lot of adolescent shames.' It was a time of self-discovery in many ways, particularly in developing his own philosophy of life: 'We *did* think & talk a *lot* about morals including basic politics, but more I think *individual* morality, sex etc.'[19] He was never to change the fundamental outlook which he worked out then and immediately afterwards: 'out of all the confusion of adolescence values *do* emerge – at least they did for me – but not until I was in my early 20s. And on the whole I have stuck by them.'[22]

Absorbed in his personal intellectual and moral development, Gaitskell did not worry much about his future. Evidently he found his mother's aspirations for him either too conventional or too romantic, for he wrote to her that he had

very little ambition of any kind and indeed I find it very difficult to see the attraction of a great material success for instance in business; and yet I admit honestly that I should like to leave my mark and not just be one of the $99\frac{1}{2}\%$ obscure . . . one goes on acquiring knowledge about life by reading and thinking and above all by living and this seems a much more natural object than becoming a general or a millionaire or even a Lord Chancellor though I admit as I said before that I should like to be famous. The real trouble is that one simply is not either brilliant or lionhearted and there is no use now in trying to become either the one or the other. One must first understand oneself and one's limitations and then try and develop on the lines which are most natural to one . . . I am not and never will be either a healthy young animal or a Sir Galahad. If I was an animal at all I shouldn't be a Lion but only a rabbit or possibly a Roe deer.[8]

He did not concern himself with undergraduate politics. His brother had told him that the Union, the famous debating society, was a waste of time and so he never became a member. Though political clubs flourished, he was slow to join the Labour Club and took no active part. Even when friends with whom he had dined went on to a political meeting, he did not always accompany them. Nevertheless, his adventurous choice of an academic subject was a sign of the way his interests were moving. 'Modern Greats', now usually called PPE (Philosophy, Politics and Economics), was newly established; and when Gaitskell took finals in 1927 he had fewer than 200 predecessors. Many traditionalists had stoutly opposed its introduction, making its tutors and students determined to show that relevance was not incompatible with rigour.

Gaitskell had no time for metaphysics, and little interest in philosophy. 'I never really took to it,' he wrote long afterwards to his younger daughter.[23] About this time he wrote to his brother:

You seem to worry a great deal about things to which there never will be an answer – I mean Ultimate Objects, the Good, God etc.; as you know I never bother much about such things but try to confine myself to questions which can be answered in some way . . . : After all in spite of its philosophical unsoundness utilitarianism has a good deal to be said for it and serves as a good enough basis for practical affairs.[24]

In his first term he went for elementary economics to Lionel Robbins, who called it 'a subject deadly for both teacher and taught'. He would sit on Robbins's sofa reddening with suppressed mirth at the mild impertinences of his Australian fellow-pupil until his decorous Wykehamist reticence broke down in peals of helpless laughter. Later his economics tutor was the young, eccentric and stimulating Harold Salvesen, with whom he became friendly. In political organisation, he wrote essays for the Warden, H. A. L. Fisher; the treatment was competent, high-minded and far from radical. Yet, although the solemn and uninspiring subjects gave little scope for showing it, Gaitskell's outlook was already shifting.

Early in the summer of 1925, sitting on the Downs with their mother on his first home leave from the Sudan, Arthur was happily holding forth about his triumphs at polo and his dinner with the Governor-General when to his astonishment his young brother and devoted admirer told him forcefully that his life and values were altogether futile and worthless: a first challenge to his inherited imperialist attitudes which was to have a lasting impact on him. Hugh was just beginning to work out his personal outlook, and his reaction against the conventional assumptions, unquestioned by his family or their friends in Rangoon or Cheltenham society, gave him 'a predisposition to underdogs and socialists'.[9] After a visit to his aunt in the latter town, he exploded in a letter:

But Cheltenham my God! I scarcely realised that such people really still existed: a corner of the world for those who believe it wrong for anyone to think differently than they did in the '80s . . . chiefly, or notoriously, colonels . . . who have no powers of adaptability whatever . . . I naturally fume against such irrational, prejudiced, old-fashioned malicious nonsense as they talk.[17]

For he saw himself as 'quite obviously a product of the present and not the past generation' and as 'the most modern of the family', and he was determined to show that he had 'a personality, ideas and life of my own'.[17] Nor was his rebellion against the conformity of his elders confined to their imperial traditions; later that summer at Brancaster, he and his American friend Jim Orrick had an absurd but violent argument when Hugh, seeking to show his dislike of snobbery, wanted to write to a college servant as '– Nuttall Esq.'[9] A year afterwards, at the start of the summer term in 1926, Hugh tried in vain to explain his changing outlook to his friend Frank Pakenham, then an ardent Tory. Just a week later the change became a matter of public commitment when the General Strike provoked a dramatic break in Gaitskell's Oxford existence. It was the first major turning point in his life.

# 2

# Finding a Cause 1926–8

'*I object to the whole system of working & non-working classes*'
(HG, 1926)

## The General Strike: 'Betraying his Class'

The strike was a clash between the confused trade union leadership of a united working class, and a narrow-minded but determined government. The coal-owners were truculent, short-sighted and inefficient employers; the miners worked for poor pay in bad and dangerous conditions, and after years of bitter industrial struggle they preferred fighting to negotiation, were proud of their own solidarity, and expected workers in more vulnerable occupations to follow their lead without much question. Those workers, and a good many middle-class people too, had a bad conscience about them. The cautious, rather short-sighted leaders of the TUC therefore supported the miners in what they thought was an unusually large industrial dispute, and found themselves in a situation with no issue except capitulation – or the attempted revolution which they did not want, had not prepared, and could not have carried out. In contrast, the Government knew its own mind and meant to smash the trade union militants once and for all. The Prime Minister, Stanley Baldwin, was conciliatory in language but determined in resisting compromise moves by dangerous characters like the Archbishop of Canterbury, and skilful in presenting the strike as a challenge to the constitution. It was called off in nine days, but the miners fought on alone for six months. Winston Churchill, hitherto the most intransigent Minister, now tried to bully the colliery companies into accepting reasonable terms, but against the rapacious and vengeful coal-owners the Prime Minister's skill and determination evaporated.

In Oxford the strike and the Government's appeal brought an immediate response from the upper-middle-class undergraduate body. Class bitterness was then intense, and at a college ball the year before, the young gentlemen in their white ties and flowered buttonholes had been jeered by rows of angry workers shouting 'enjoy yourselves while you can, it won't last much longer'.[1] Many students went off to drive trains or act as special constables in order to defend the social order or save the nation from destruction, though many others did so rather in a spirit of fun or adventure. The Vice-Chancellor even contemplated conscripting the undergraduate population, and the hearties attempted to break up a rowdy protest meeting of the Labour Club (Gaitskell's presence is not recorded). But other senior members were, like the Archbishop, thoroughly unhappy at the bitter and divisive conflict.

Gaitskell had sympathised with the unions throughout, thinking it 'natural that the miners should object to a reduction of almost $\frac{1}{3}$rd of their wages'. He made up his mind decisively the moment the strike began, telling his mother,

I finally decided on not enlisting in the Govt Volunteers when the Govt abruptly broke off all negotiations . . . & in fact practically declared war on the strikers . . . If one joins the govt, be it only originally to maintain supplies, one is pretty well under orders & if things develop . . . it would be difficult to get out of what will practically be an Army.

Anyway I have offered my services through the University Labour Club to the Trades Union people in Oxford.[2]

As he was to put it much later,

the impact of the Strike was sharp and sudden, a little like a war, in that everybody's lives were suddenly affected by a new unprecedented situation, which forced us to abandon plans for pleasure, to change our values and adjust our priorities.

Above all we had to make a choice, and how we chose was a clear test of our political outlook . . . all my sympathies were instinctively on the side of the miners, the unions, the Labour Party and the Left generally. It was their cause I wanted to help.[3]

When Bowra protested that the strike would do the miners more harm than good, the undergraduate replied firmly that he would not 'desert his side just because it had miscalculated its means'; and impressed the don enough for Bowra to go round vainly lobbying in favour of conciliation.[4] Gaitskell wrote at the time that the owners seemed to be 'the most extraordinarily stupid and really unpleasant lot of men';[2] as Hugh Dalton remarked later, he found it 'impossible for any generous spirit to be emotionally on the side of "the masters" ';[5] and he had little tolerance for his many friends who saw matters differently.

When he sought leave to go off and work for the TUC, Warden Fisher refused, saying (according to Gaitskell at the time): 'Your arguments are well put and you have a strong case. But I have the power to prevent you going down and I propose to exercise it.' Furious, Gaitskell on his way out ran into Jim Orrick, told his tale, and asked what his friend meant to do. Nothing, replied Orrick, since Mr

Baldwin's pretence that this was a revolution was blatantly fraudulent; but had it been true, he would have felt obliged to support the Government. 'That's sheer vulgarity', cried Gaitskell, angrier than ever: and did not speak to Orrick for a month. It was their only quarrel.[1]

At G. D. H. Cole's house in Holywell, a dozen or so undergraduates had met to offer their services to the TUC. Gaitskell later described his enrolment:

What could I do? Precious little. Speak at meetings? God forbid! Organise? Absolutely no experience. Had I got a car? No. Could I by any chance drive a car? Yes, I had learnt the year before. Then perhaps I could drive John Dugdale's . . . as . . . he could not spare much time . . . I went off to the Oxford Strike Committee headquarters, got myself enrolled as a driver and received my instructions.[3]

With a paid-up trade union card as a papermaker, he drove undergraduate speakers like Evan Durbin and John Parker to village meetings around Oxford, carried messages to Didcot with John Betjeman, who thought it all a great lark, and maintained liaison with London by ferrying Margaret Cole to and fro and bringing back copies of the TUC paper, the *British Worker*. Returning at night, she recalled with alarm his disconcerting speed at the nine right-angled turns in Benson village, 'most of which we seemed to take on two wheels', since returning after midnight might involve being confined to college at night. Once he did arrive late, failed to climb in, and was fined £1 despite 'a fierce verbal protest to the Warden . . . that he was shockingly biassed'.[3] His contemporaries could absent themselves with impunity on the other side, and that injustice still rankled decades later.

Waiting about for hours in London, Margaret Cole took her young chauffeur to meet Labour personalities and intellectuals like R. H. Tawney, Harold Laski and Francis Meynell. (Tawney, whom he found 'the most charming man', was later to have a profound influence on him – but at the time merely remarked on his driving: 'How dangerous it is to let young men take charge of projectiles.')[6] The General Strike was an impressive introduction to the Labour Movement, reinforcing Gaitskell's developing outlook – although eight months afterwards he was to confess with his usual candour about himself that he had been 'guilty last May of "enjoying the General Strike because the idea of myself as a man of action appealed". This was only a small part of the business of course semi-unconscious.'[7] After it ended, he worked at raising money for the miners, locked out for another terrible six months, and was proud of extracting £8.10s. from his Tory contemporaries, including 10s. from an old schoolfellow, David Eccles.

'I must be getting quite notorious', he wrote to his mother; 'people I've only just met seem to regard me as a well-known Socialist – someone said to me yesterday "Of course you're going into Politics aren't you?" And yet I make no speeches and belong to no political set. It all arises from the fact that I stayed behind during the Strike.'[8] His family were appalled. One cousin said over dinner: 'What we can't forgive Hugh is betraying his class.' But his mind was made up, and he wrote to an astonished aunt: 'Henceforth my future is with the working classes.'[9]

Subsequently he came to see the strike as demolishing 'the absurd "myth" of syndicalism', and its collapse as a permanent warning that unplanned, emotional revolutionary activities led to disaster.[10] But at the time he was almost optimistic.

The only possible way out seems to me to be either (a) Nationalisation & then a General Election or (b) the General Election another govt. & some other policy. Otherwise there may be a Civil War. Let's hope not & certainly no one wants it except perhaps a few bloodthirsty old colonels . . .[2]

Looking back, he recalled:

It is wholly untrue that I deplored the strategy of the strike, I did not honestly think a great deal about it. I knew that once the chips were down my part was on the side of the strike. I considered the Government had behaved badly to the miners and that was that.[11]

His letters to his mother show how abruptly his views crystallised. Ten days after the Strike ended he wrote:

I acted as I did not with any Socialist bias but just from summing up the position as it was . . . However since then I have almost become definitely a Socialist – that is my mind has moved over very much to the left.

Not merely that I desire better conditions for the working classes but because I object to the whole system of working & non-working classes . . . You will be able to see my opinions taking shape from my letters. There is so much to be read, so many observations to be made, so much thinking to be done that I shall probably not definitely make up my mind for two years. No, it should be made up by the time I have left here [in just over a year].

If it is & I am quite sure of my position as a Socialist I shall probably try & get some sort of job on the W.E.A. that is 'Workers Educational Association' for obviously I should be more useful there than anywhere else.

. . . various ideas are coming out more clearly in my mind. I now understand the 'extremist' point of view . . . an extremist is afraid not of the oppression of the Capitalists that will only keep Socialism alive but of the gentle leading and enticement by the Capitalist of the working classes – he will lead them with a golden chain into the pleasant pastures of material enjoyment . . . I'm getting almost biblical . . . for the Socialist movement is founded really upon the highest Ethical considerations – it is essentially idealist & possibly I hope practical. You may receive more propaganda next week or possibly by then my violent interest in Politics will have waned.[12]

It never did.

## Studying with a Purpose

For Gaitskell the strike was no nine days' wonder. Its impact was immediate as well as lasting, and it transformed his Oxford life. He became determined to escape from the conventional middle-class career mould expected by his school and his family. That autumn he wrote:

I suppose one will never again be as free as one is now. Afterwards I'm afraid the horrible outside world seizes you and forces you to conform . . . I've got this odd sort of complex – it's almost a hatred of the rest of the world. For while despising their attitude completely – who wouldn't who had lived in Oxford? – one knows their power . . . added to that is the horrible feeling that I am almost bound to be a failure whatever I do – anyway not a success.

His reluctance to follow the family pressure to join the Indian Civil Service was reinforced a few weeks later by his visit to his elderly aunt, after which

3 days at Cheltenham made me quite convinced that I must make up my *own* mind about my life. It's too absurd to think of just doing what people of 70 or so want you to do i.e. the Army or the Civil Service or at *least* something respectable . . . they don't consider the existence of anyone outside it [their Cheltenham circle] . . . 'absurd to allow the miners extra wages' – 'they get quite enough as it is' – 'here are we taxed out of existence' (I wish they were, futile antediluvians).[13]

Consciously he set out to obtain first-class honours in order to acquire the independence that would allow him to choose his own future. Both in and out of term he now began working very hard to make up for lost time. Spending an industrious Christmas vaction with the family friends in Ireland, he rather resented their emphasis on grimy manual labour and the 'feeling that I was regarded as "a lily of the field" '.[14] In Oxford he was still able to enjoy himself, for he was good at organising his time, but his priorities were quite changed. He gave up serious golf, got down to his books by 9 a.m., and always seemed to be busy when friends visited his lodgings. Unlike most undergraduates he made no secret of his hopes of a First.

The direction of his work changed as well as the intensity. He chose as his special subject the history of the Labour Movement, finding in it the same romantic appeal that Pakenham, his room-mate, found in Irish Nationalism; one of his undergraduate essays on Chartism (finished at 4 a.m.) was published as a tiny book by the WEA in 1928. He also became active in a weekly discussion group for Socialist undergraduates which G. D. H. Cole, his tutor, inaugurated and presided over until long after the war. They took themselves very seriously, taking on the roles of Ministers in a Labour government, and trying to visualise and handle for themselves the practical problems of transforming society.

Cole was a good deal older than Bowra, and had a great influence on Gaitskell, who on first meeting him had found him 'almost the most striking personality in Oxford'.[12] In retrospect too, his pupil called him 'a wonderfully stimulating' tutor who 'treated one as completely adult – a research worker rather than someone to be pushed through an examination'.[3] Hugh learned much from him, culturally and aesthetically as well as politically. They went for long country walks together (though his brother and friends deny Hugh's own claim that it was Cole who taught him to like walking). Cole was an expert on wine, fine glass and poetry, and his public-school pupil with the aesthetic tastes was reassured to discover that 'you could be a Socialist without being a clodhopper'.[16]

In some ways the senior man became a surrogate father to Gaitskell, but again the influence was by no means only one way. In the summer of 1928 Cole wrote to his former pupil about the new book on Labour policy he was starting, which 'hasn't got far yet, partly because you will get into it, and my mind insists on arguing with you instead of the world at large. It is, in spirit, dedicated to you.'[15] Later, after a 'tremendous argument' one evening about Guild Socialism, in the morning Cole admitted himself convinced; Gaitskell was 'deeply touched and absurdly pleased'[3] by a reference to it in the preface. Gaitskell's impact on his tutor was not lasting, but Colin Clark, who knew them both well, wrote: 'By 1929, strange but true – I witnessed it myself – the roles had been reversed and Gaitskell was leading Cole. Gaitskell persuaded him to abandon his Guild Socialist ideas and turn his attention to ordinary parliamentary politics.'[17]

Friends who knew Gaitskell in his final year thought that as his political values crystallised, he was not only applying himself assiduously to academic work and developing new interests, but becoming fundamentally more serious. He remained as cheerful and amusing and attractive as ever, but Elizabeth Harman, who was in her first year at

Lady Margaret Hall and knew him well, could not believe he was the same Hugh who had taken a childhood delight in riding pillion on Arthur's motorbike, and had loved golf or punting. Now they endlessly discussed life and literature and art and sex, though not politics or religion. The teacher in him was coming out, and he was eager to improve his friends' taste in everything from dress to literature to personal relationships. Women, he held firmly–despite his own flamboyant ties–must wear sober and well-tailored clothes, nothing gaudy. Proust must be read in French–'and such was the force of his personality that you did it because *he* wanted you to'. Following his creed of self-realisation, he admired every sign of independence, unconventionality and escape from the normal way of doing things. Total realism and candour was his goal; he once wrote rather alarmingly, 'I'm watching myself and others at the same time to try and detect how they get away from Reality.'[18] The worst of sins was to 'dramatise the situation', but the changing nuances of a personal relationship must always be out in the open, never covered up–a characteristic not recognised at all by his male friends. That summer he took Elizabeth to a college ball where she met Frank Pakenham, her future husband; a year later Hugh planned–most unconventionally!– to propose to her at a dinner party for six in Paris, but it was not a success.

Hugh's sister had become engaged the year before to her cricketing celebrity, and he wrote congratulating her: 'I'm willing to forgive you for condemning me always to be known as Hubert Ashton's younger brother-in-law . . . I had my fortune told by Lady Morgan and am to have an unsuccessful life but two children . . . may you keep life for ever as a Romance and not a "Reality".'[19] The family came together in 1927 for the marriage, and for Hugh's twenty-first birthday. He celebrated with his Oxford friends at the Clarendon Hotel (no dinner jackets and a white woolly sweater for the host), and with his family in Venice, where he teased Arthur who had sent a telegram from Shepheard's in Cairo to meet at the Danieli–the two most expensive hotels in the Mediterranean. The brothers then went off on holiday to the Tyrol. Germany and Austria were Hugh's favourite foreign countries then, and–fearing French influence like most liberal Englishmen–he sympathised with the idea of *Anschluss* (union between them, assumed to be voluntary). He was there three times over the year 1926–7, 'climbing mountains by night in the Black Forest and watching the dawn rise from the top'.[19] He was in Italy too, and earlier in France which he liked less; and after his finals he went with Bowra on an Adriatic holiday, acquiring a lifelong love of that coast and especially Dubrovnik.

It was a good deal more foreign travel than was usual for undergraduates in those days, and Gaitskell was 'for his age and time, remarkably cosmopolitan'.[16] His many foreign friends included Victor Raul Haya de la Torre, the leading South American left-winger of the next generation, who spent some years in England. Yet Gaitskell shared, without the insular prejudice, the intense Englishness of the three mentors who, he claimed, later did most to influence his early development as a Socialist: Cole, Tawney and Dalton. Of Cole he was to write, starting with a sentence equally applicable to himself: 'However much on the intellectual plane Douglas was an internationalist, emotionally – and he never attempted to hide it – he was profoundly attached to England. He was not even a little Englander – really a little Southern Englander!'[3] Tawney once spoke in 1933 of his humiliation at seeing 'his fellow-Englishmen' in dreadful conditions in the Manchester slums before the war; when a friend remarked afterwards on his not saying 'fellow human beings', Gaitskell thought about it and said he too would have used Tawney's words.[20]

Committed but not sectarian, he shared lodgings that final year with two Conservatives, Frank Pakenham and Roger Nickalls, at 2 Isis Street near Folly Bridge; in 1952 Nickalls was taken back twenty-five years at hearing the familiar voice and characteristic phrase, 'It's not fair', in Gaitskell's first Budget broadcast as Shadow Chancellor. A young Fellow of New College of those days still remembers the excitement of his economics colleague realising that in an otherwise poor year Pakenham and Gaitskell might actually get Firsts. Both did, Pakenham without a serious viva, Gaitskell after a very long one indeed, in which he came up on the historical subjects at which he did best. Most of his examiners called him an excellent examinee who was rather lucky, but the economist, A. J. Jenkinson, was most impressed.

His mother was keen for him to join the ICS, but had reluctantly accepted that he need not do so if he took a First; and he would not budge when she tried hard, in a furious argument in the back of her son-in-law's car, to persuade him to change his mind and go to India after all.[21] Distressed as she was at his determination, she would have paid for him to stay on to do research. Cole had him to dine in Soho and offered to get him a scholarship to write a life of Feargus O'Connor, the Chartist leader. But Cole also proposed an alternative at which Gaitskell jumped: an adult education job in Nottingham. In his very first letter after the General Strike, Hugh had told his mother that if he did become a Socialist, he would try to get work of that kind. 'I think one gets paid enough to live on anyway.'[12] After Cole had made his two suggestions, wrote Gaitskell later:

I was tremendously pleased with this second idea. Having heard Douglas [Cole] talk about the WEA I had sometimes wondered if I could do this sort of job but thought it probably beyond me. Yet there I was being offered a start at once. I plumped for it, and on the strength of Douglas' recommendation, got the Nottingham post. It was my experiences there – especially in the coal fields – which were to turn me later towards active politics.[3]

### Nottingham: 'Seeking Something to Fight For'

Although working-class conditions shocked Gaitskell in Nottingham-shire, it was far from a depressed area. The town was prosperous in 1927–8, and the coalfield was one of the least badly hit. But with the owners pressing for district agreements, a breakaway union, led by the former district secretary George Spencer, tried to take advantage of the area's comparative profitability to work in collaboration with the owners at the expense of solidarity with their fellows in other coalfields. Miners who had been active in the strike, or had stayed loyal to the Notts Miners' Association, were victimised quite ruthlessly and persecuted in all sorts of petty ways. Bitterness was intense: 'to call a man a Spencer was like calling him a Nazi', said one loyalist many years later. Gaitskell wrote anonymously about it in his first published article, explaining the social background and the forms of economic pressure used, and concluding that the Spencer Union was too artificial to establish itself permanently.[22] (He wrote the article with the help of his unemployed miner friend George Keeling, who was desperately badly off; was paid three pounds for it; and without asking Keeling gave the money to the Miners' Federation. Yet a few weeks later Gaitskell, when his friend came to say goodbye to him just after he had drawn his last quarter's salary, tried to give or lend that money to Keeling – who refused.[24])

If Oxford had been intellectual emancipation for Gaitskell, Nottingham was the time of liberation from the personal constraints of colleges and landladies. He took a small two-roomed flat 'right in the centre of town above shops and offices and very convenient and nice . . . I have had it done up a good deal myself'.[23] The untidy establishment was entered through a small kitchen where he experimented disastrously with 'disgusting stews'. Until Christmas he shared the flat with his Oxford friend Jack James; afterwards he was able to put up occasional visitors, who recalled with distaste the squalid conditions, with unwashed cutlery from which to select a knife and fork, and none too clean sheets to sleep in.

His mood of bohemian revolt implied no conventional breach with his family, to whom he remained deeply attached. But he totally repudiated their values and style of life and those of his peers. When his cousin George Martelli left the Navy, Hugh was delighted; and on the day when University College Nottingham, acquired its charter, he refused to attend the ceremonies and took a girlfriend out for the day instead. (He was very attached to her, and twenty years later as a Minister wondered with wistful bewilderment why she did not write to him.) Now that he was in D. H. Lawrence country he became even keener on that author, trying (vainly) to arrange a meeting through James; he sometimes stayed up all night reading Proust; and the local *palais de danse* played a very major part in his existence. His one friend at the university was Sebastian Sprott, a young psychology lecturer, and in contrast to Winchester's litany of 'it isn't done', they both enthusiastically preached 'the virtues of scepticism'.

Gaitskell always felt depressed on starting a new job, and when he began at Nottingham the psychological strains were particularly acute. His family were scattered across the continents and his friends were living in a quite different world. He was far from confident that he could cope with the work. At first he found that while things were not going well, 'the process of making mistakes and discovering is painful but very valuable and I suppose I shall get better soon'.[25] He got little help from his colleagues, for few of them took him seriously and some were actively jealous of the shy, sensitive young public-school and Oxford Socialist. Gloomily he told his brother:

At first I was very depressed and felt that probably I was a failure but now I've ceased to worry – I am afraid I am just hardened and insensitive though for a time petty slights, not exactly personal ones, were very painful. It is not very satisfying because so many of the people are really too old to learn much & so many others . . . hope vaguely that if they sit there long enough they'll suddenly find themselves educated, others just don't bother to come . . . perhaps a lot of [my news] centres around the feeling and fact of stagnation . . . there are no proper library facilities. No one to discuss one's subject with, no one one wants to talk seriously too [*sic*] & a general atmosphere of depressed defeat. The University does seem to be full of people . . . who have ended up by staying here indolent & depressed & almost becoming provincial.[23]

In these first lonely and depressing weeks Gaitskell found some release with the other sex. He told his friends that Nottingham was the most libertarian town in the country, particularly uninhibited by class constraints, and he found plenty of girls from the dance hall or shops or railway booking offices to take out to dinner or on long country walks. His motto was 'act first and think afterwards', he told his brother, confessing after a few months,

I was afraid that my existence here was becoming too much sex without the essential intellect but I'm not afraid now of [that] . . . when I feel like treating the thing as an art and a game that's rather fun, like Swann before he falls in love with Odette. Probably after a few unsatisfactory evenings I shall settle down to work and then suddenly fall in love after I've forgotten all about it.[26]

He soon entered on his first mature relationship with a steady girlfriend, which was to continue for a time after his move to London. But for some years before and after Nottingham he rejected marriage as a bourgeois convention. At his last college ball he had been much excited by a lady who had left her husband – 'a thin stick-like haggard creature' whom he clearly saw as an early heroine of 'Women's Lib'.[27] In 1932 he assured his brother that marriage was 'becoming less and less essential in England'.[28]

Professionally, his start at Nottingham was not at all easy. With people of his own class, in familiar surroundings, he had acquired plenty of self-confidence in his last year at Oxford. At his first meeting with Hubert Ashton's father he cheerfully expounded the problems of India to a man who had gone out there forty years before.[21] But the assurance was backed by knowledge, mental agility and serious thought; at one dinner party at Bowra's where Gaitskell had a vigorous argument with a young coal-owner, he impressed his host (a stern judge) by his formidable controversial powers.[4]

At Nottingham it was a different story. The miners were a tough lot, who had had a very bad time in the strike. Half of them were unemployed, blacklisted by the owners. They were, as Gaitskell wrote later, 'naturally extremely bitter';[29] or as one of them put it, 'hostile and aggressive to everyone'. Gaitskell came from another class, had obviously never gone hungry, and gave at first a slightly effeminate impression; he had no experience of lecturing, and started off badly, 'tentative, hesitant and stuttering'.[24] Many years later he still shuddered at the memory. 'It *is* depressing', he wrote to his mother early on, 'to feel that the "students" are bored and that no one is learning anything or even interested in the subject. Indeed I sympathise with them. I don't see why anyone wants to learn Economics.'[25] For he was acutely conscious of the incongruities not only between his own background and that of his pupils, but also between their daily problems and the subjects he was supposed to teach them. His very first lecture was on Saving and Economic Progress. 'Looking back,' he remembered, 'I am surprised at my audacity. For I gave them . . . the full classical doctrine in which thrift . . . is crucial.'[30] Not surprisingly, they gave him a hammering.

He had to learn up banking and currency, which he had not previously studied, in order to persuade enough unemployed miners to take his class to qualify it for a grant. It was demanding in time and intellectual energy as well as emotionally, and the experience had a great impact on him. 'I am far less sensitive than I used to be', he assured his mother.

Yet in some ways this is a pity – hardening into a shell is not a very *good* process I feel.

It's disheartening when you say what seems very important to you . . . and it raises only a shadow of interest in other people. But it's also the realisation of one's own weakness – I cannot *make* these people read or write – they just won't though indeed that's due in no small degree to the fact that I have not acted in the way most calculated to make them do so.[31]

But Gaitskell was a stubborn man, and also a very patient and lucid teacher who took trouble to make his material relevant and interesting. He was, as Keeling put it, 'constitutionally incapable of a snobbish thought, word or deed'.[32] With his own love of frankness, he found the candour of his pupils refreshing, and he wrote to his brother that the miners were 'the nicest sort of people – indeed I like very much all the working people I have met . . . more honest and natural than the Middle Class who are always trying to be something they aren't & who are never quite sure whether they are saying the right thing.'[23] In 1927 victimised miners from the loyalist union did not often find well-educated middle-class young men coming to teach in their area and wholeheartedly taking their side, and he won their confidence because, as one of them said years later, 'he was so obviously sincere'.[32] He attracted 'fantastic loyalty and affection in the mining villages – they adored him'.[24]

He never forgot them, and the impact of that first contact with working-class life was profound. It 'brought him down to earth with a damned shock', said Keeling, and afterwards Gaitskell frequently told his friends how very deep an impression the conditions had made on him: 'He thought of poverty, inequality, unemployment and slums with emotion and spoke of them with heat.'[20] It gave a new and far more personal dimension to what had been an intellectual commitment. In that early, jaundiced letter he answered Arthur, who had 'rather offensively' rebuked him for 'grinding a Labour axe', by quietly insisting on the miserable conditions while vigorously rebutting any suggestion of the sentimentality which he so despised and distrusted:

I am as scrupulously honest as I can be and that is not difficult because I am so cold-blooded that I'm only too glad to calm the excitement of some of my pupils and induce them to revel in that doubtful pleasure the scientific attitude. I find to my surprise that on the whole its easier to excite one's moral indignation by reading 'The decay of capitalist Civilisation' by Sidney Webb than by hearing as I do at times that someone has been living on bread and beetroot or that the children have no shoes and very few clothes.[23]

Yet in their frequent long talks at this time about the shape of a Socialist society, Keeling described him as displaying an almost childlike nostalgia for the lost simplicities of Merrie England; and both Keeling the miner and Bowra the don characterised Gaitskell as a 'William Morris Socialist'. A society that was more just to human beings was essential, he told Keeling, even though it was likely to be somewhat less efficient economically. To his brother he wrote: 'Laziness is a vice but I think too much stress on efficiency is also one . . . [both] apt to create a feeling of dissatisfaction in one which spoils the harmony of one's existence.'

In the same letter he went on: 'there is far too much poverty and inequality . . . to remedy (without imagining that thereby you reach the millennium). It seems to be a question apart from one's own ambitions. It is simply a judgement.'[26] The reference to the millennium was typical. Discovering how the private owners treated their workers (and how short-sightedly they exploited the natural resources) convinced Gaitskell that the need to nationalise the mines was blatantly obvious; but even in those early days he never shared the common Socialist illusion that a change of ownership would end the workers' sense of alienation.[24]

Nottingham meant for Gaitskell getting to know working-class people as well as working-class conditions, and making the exhilarating discovery that the enormous differences of background and tastes between him and them did not preclude completely uninhibited human contact – with his girlfriends, or his washerwoman, who would occasionally drop in to tea to the embarrassment of visitors from Oxford, or the miners with whom friendships extended far beyond the classroom; they came to his flat, took him off to football matches, and went on camping expeditions with him. After a talk at an adult school where he could develop his own ideas, he wrote again to his mother in quite a different tone:

> the class turned up in a body to support me and indeed I needed their smiling encouragement. I talked in a rambling way about emotion, sentimentality, Religion, Morality, Sex . . . then question time – about 6 people got up in turn and denounced me as talking nonsense and generally disturbing the peace of their religious minds . . . 'believing where we cannot prove' provided me with a very good text . . . I *think* it was a success – of course I think I was brilliant and original; but it was a success in so far as it created any kind of sensation and also tightened my hold over the class, which is now going well, I think. They being young and socialistic were with me in the attack on superstition and hypocrisy.[31]

These new personal links with workers produced a great transformation in the shy young man, but he did not pretend to himself that he and they were really just the same; on the contrary, he was fascinated to find out how differently his new friends thought and felt and judged from his familiar upper-middle-class acquaintances:

> I am very interested in the question of 'class'. I would like to write something on it some time. It's quite extraordinary how important the thing is as a whole and historically though it does not exactly make my work difficult [*sic*]. But of course meeting so many people who have lived and do live so utterly differently from oneself is peculiar.[23]

Above all with his strong sense of fairness and justice ('a bee in his bonnet about it', said Keeling) Gaitskell was impressed by the intense and selfless loyalties for which mining communities are famous. All his life he was to preach the need for team work and solidarity in the Labour Movement, and the miners were a living example. A quarter of a century later, when he moved the third reading of the Bill to nationalise the mines, he referred to his Nottingham experiences – to stress not the economic misery, but the ruthless treatment of human beings. Often he said later that it was those miners who made him a Socialist, and he told the House of Commons: 'They taught me what economic feudalism was. They taught me what the naked exercise of arbitrary power meant. They taught me what it was to be victimised.'[33]

Gaitskell now had his mission in life: to use his excellent mind and the educational benefits he had acquired from his own class background to help people with fewer advantages than himself to struggle against the forces of power and privilege. The arena for that struggle was politics not adult education, though at this period his friend Orrick expected his engagement to take a different form. 'I thought he was going to be an agitator. It never occurred to me he would be a really serious politician.'[1] His upper-middle-class origins had seemed likely to prove a barrier in the Labour Party of the 1920s, but now that he had discovered how easily he could leap that barrier in making personal friendships, it did not look so insurmountable in public life. Indeed, he was worried at Nottingham that he might have, not too much money, but too little to be able to devote time to politics instead of earning his living.

It was his miner friends who urged him to make his first political speeches, who encouraged him to try to enter Parliament himself, and who asked him back to Nottinghamshire to make his first general election speeches in 1929. Hugh's very first venture was to speak with Keeling from a water-trough in the Derby Road, Nottingham; a more important occasion was the adoption meeting for a new Labour candidate, Seymour Cocks, in the small, smoke-filled ante-room of the Co-op Hall at Hucknall. Years later he called Hucknall 'a very ugly town for which I have a nostalgic affection'. He started the WEA class there himself, and the first one was held 'on a Sunday morning in the room which, having been the ladies' cloakroom the night before, retained a curious smell of tobacco and a rather strong scent'.[34] He always liked it best of all, and called its secretary 'the hope and comfort of my work (you can *watch* his intelligence growing – he is going to be really good, I believe)'.[31] He had four classes in all, which took him all round the county and to the Derbyshire border; on one of these expeditions he met in a miner's cottage near Worksop the rising young politician who was to do most to promote his early career: Hugh Dalton. Dalton found him 'very emphatic and delightfully un-respectful. He was out to change society from top to bottom. He was against all privilege and social injustice . . . for real social equality.'[35]

Gaitskell was a reflective man, making up his mind slowly but surely, and by no means sure of himself as yet in this new political arena. After several months at Nottingham, he wrote to his mother:

While I am not sure I believe much in myself as a Tutorial Class Tutor, yet . . . I shall remain semi-attached to the Working Class Movement. I am not sentimental about it but the industrial and class war on the one hand and the bad conditions on the other have confirmed me in my views on the present inequality of wealth. Perhaps I object most of all to the hypocrisy of the rich – almost any cloak will do to hide greed and property sense and ideals are poisoned and dragged down to do service to the avarice of the stockbroker or employer. And then too it annoys and amazes me how people complain about taxation . . . I think it extremely important that people should study economics and sociology and realise that it is possible to think of the community in general and not to judge the advantage of all from that of themselves; and realise too that *merit* (and who is to define that word?) plays a negligible part in the distribution of income.[36]

By then Gaitskell was far more at home in his teaching post. Though Nottingham widened his outlook in so many ways, intellectually he had at first feared it would have the reverse effect. For all his personal modesty, he was conscious of his own abilities; perhaps he was the more afraid of slipping backwards because his progress was so recent. 'I see tremendous danger of stagnating here', he had told his brother in December 1927: 'I went to London a few days ago. The difference is quite remarkable – there is so much more vigour and better taste and better intelligence and more personality in the atmosphere.'[23] But by the spring he was sounding much happier, more relaxed and self-confident, planning future research (unexpectedly, in Tawney's field of seventeenth-century economic history) and

doing a little lecturing and coaching and working on my own. All quite nice – I am playing a good deal of tennis and leading a *slightly* more sociable existence. I lecture at the Prison once a week which, in a way, is interesting, though there is nothing especially peculiar about the prisoners.[26]

By that time, however, he had already been offered and accepted a new job at University College London, where Noel Hall had just been appointed to revive the Economics Department. Advised by his former tutor at Brasenose (A. J. Jenkinson, the examiner whom Gaitskell had so impressed), Hall asked Gaitskell over lunch in Charlotte Street to come to UCL as his assistant. At first the young lecturer was reluctant.

Probably I shall refuse: I am fairly happy where I am and would prefer to do two years here. It's not as if I was *stagnating* here – I'm not . . . In London it's true I should be more in the centre of things, have much more work to do and probably learn a great deal, but I *am* interested in the Working Classes and just beginning to enjoy in many ways my contacts with them. In London I should have to teach for an exam and be far less free . . . Anyway it's exciting and restores my continually vanishing self-respect.[31]

But a fortnight later, after talking to Cole, he had already almost changed his mind.[37] As usual he scrutinised his own motives critically:

I think it is absolutely essential never to deceive oneself . . . it is true that the problem of self-cultivation v. self [*sic*] for the community does appear – personally I compromise – I go to London next year but hope to go on doing this work a little and at least write books which may be of some use – Of course I *want* to but that doesn't matter unless you're a puritan and religious which I am not.[26]

He was still determined to avoid conventional paths. He revisited Oxford twice that year, finding himself in February 'a little bored . . . out of touch with the intensely social life';[38] and then in the summer, when the undergraduate frivolities were in full swing, telling Elizabeth Harman most vehemently that the bubble had broken and he had nothing now in common with those who led that life.[27]

After making his decision to move, he wrote to his mother again:

as you say it is London and that makes all the difference. I am interested in my work here and shall probably supplement my London earnings by taking [a similar] class next year . . . Also I shall probably not become Academic for (a) I dislike the academics and their attitude and their bourgeoisieness (b) I am likely to continue my association with the Labour movement. I have seen enough of Working Class conditions, industrial war and Class war here to make it probable that on and off through my life – I am not religious enough to be permanently interested – I shall be taking part in the Working Class movement. However that may not interest you. The point is that the London job is a means not an end. I shall work hard and learn and learn and teach a little (as much as is necessary and usual) and then perhaps gradually move with Journalism and Politics keeping my lecturing job (one must live after all) at the same time. I am sorry in many ways to leave here so soon. I am interested in my work and also in the Social movement generally – if I stayed I think in a short time I would become prominent in the movement (finding as I do that I am more efficient and on the whole keener than most other people). However I want my learning and more solid background and . . . so I go to London. (How conceited this is! it is the alternative to complete self-abasement and depression.)[38]

Doubtless the ambivalent note reflects his usual uncertainty and unhappiness at the start of a new job – not only at Nottingham but almost throughout his life. Perhaps, too, he was unconsciously inclined to stress those of his motives and attitudes with which his mother would have some sympathy. Certainly he had neither the experience nor the confidence to recognise that the interests and contacts he would develop in the capital would lead to his becoming far more prominent in the movement than he would ever have been in the provinces. Yet for all his introspective agonising, it does seem that he did not yet fully realise how profound and permanent an effect his miner friends had had on him, or how decisively he would direct his energies into the political activities which were to dominate his life.

Some of those friends who knew him best were more perceptive about him than he was himself.

This tentative, shy, stuttering young man – this academic Socialist vaguely interested in helping the poor, became a real fighting politician. It really seemed to change his very soul . . . it was a complete and utter change in a human personality . . . he was almost unrecognisable when he went back to London . . . as if he [came] seeking something, and now he had found something he was going to fight for.[24]

# 3

# Aiming at a Classless
# Society 1928–34

*'I think life would be more amusing if one was ambitious'*
(HG, 1928)

### *'Low Bloomsbury': Bohemian Lecturer*

Gaitskell spent eleven years at University College London, arriving in a department of two, with only seventeen students, and ending as head of a staff of six. Overshadowed by the London School of Economics, their functions were mainly tutorial. Violent professional debate was raging over economic fundamentals, and the anti-Keynesian LSE professors objected to academic economists taking public stands on policy issues. Committed politically and concerned with the practical application of his subject, Gaitskell was somewhat sheltered by being in a separate institution.

Relations with both colleagues and students became unusually close at UCL – though not automatically, for UCL had a 'stiff and starchy' tradition. Gaitskell ignored it, taking trouble to get to know his undergraduates. He still felt himself to be a student, attending Robbins's lectures at the LSE to learn the technique. In his own lectures he was very shy at first, and stuttered badly. That soon disappeared. He always prepared his material thoroughly and organised it admirably, as he did his political speeches later on. He also had a humorous, lighter touch which he did not always retain later, but which at this period made him a popular after-dinner speaker. Years afterwards one student of his recalled:

It was as a tutor rather than a lecturer that Hugh Gaitskell excelled. He was in his element in the small discussion group . . . and, above all, in the private tutorial where students' written work was searchingly but gently criticised . . . .

What distinguished his tutorials from any others was the wide range of topics he would discuss with, and the genuine personal interest he showed in, his students . . . which . . . caused us to look on him not as a tutor only but as a friend as well. With whatever problems or even personal worries we went to him, we could always count upon a sympathetic understanding, helpful counsel, and not seldom, practical assistance.[1]

His teaching style in classes was unusually imaginative; a colleague in another department said he had a reputation as the best teacher in the college, and a junior lecturer found him in seminars 'a bit of an inspiration–very agile, very good at following undergraduate thought'.[2] Other former students liked him for special reasons of their own–the many Indians, or the Civil Service candidates whom he was responsible for advising, or the girls who found him 'a gorgeous dancer' and an attractive figure with his polite Wykehamist manners and his elegant dress.

The courses he was teaching integrated economics with other social studies in a way foreign to the modern specialised professional discipline. 'I am to confine myself to this "social side of Economics" by which is meant that I teach *more sociology* than anything else . . . Graham Wallas' subject–isn't it curious?'[3] The principal courses he taught at first were Comparative Social Institutions and Political and Social Theory (which included British Government). He was actively encouraged to work closely with the LSE sociologists and anthropologists. He made friends outside his own discipline with teachers of history and government, particularly M. M. Postan the economic historian–another new arrival at UCL, eight years older than Gaitskell. They argued frequently about Marxism and Russia (from which Postan had escaped). Another friend was John Macmurray, Professor of Philosophy. and the first person in Britain to study seriously the ideas of the young Karl Marx. He fascinated Gaitskell and Evan Durbin, helping them to sort out their ideas and evolve a moral basis for non-Marxist Socialism.

Durbin, the most intimate of all, was like Gaitskell an economist with friends mainly from other disciplines. They had known each other at New College, where Durbin was an active Socialist politician and Gaitskell thought him 'a bit of a prig and a puritan'.[4] He came to UCL a year after Gaitskell, and moved on after a year to the LSE. Until his tragically premature death in 1948, they were the closest of friends and the staunchest of political allies. They were very different, and Gaitskell loved teasing Durbin about the contrasts. Son of a Baptist minister who had become a pacifist in the First World War, Durbin had been brought up in the West Country Nonconformist tradition, and pulpit experience made him a far more accomplished speaker than Gaitskell. Durbin was earnest, Gaitskell light-hearted; Durbin reputedly lazy, Gaitskell energetic; Durbin rooted in the values of the lower-middle class, Gaitskell in revolt against those of the upper; Durbin a product of the radical-liberal tradition, Gaitskell a rebel against the Tory ethos; Durbin supplying the common sense ballast and applying with assurance a clearly thought-out philosophy, Gaitskell more tolerant but intellectually not so solidly anchored. Their friendship began in innumerable intellectual discussions, but soon concentrated on political thought and action.

Some friends realised that Gaitskell's heart was always in politics, and years later his brother wrote to him: 'I know how much this has really been the mainstream in your mind all your life.'[5] Yet other friends thought differently, and Hugh himself was somewhat ambivalent. Before coming to London he told his mother: 'I want to do internal [i.e. university] work for several years, learn one or two subjects really well – write at least one book and then either go back to Teaching or perhaps take to Journalism and Politics or perhaps just go on lecturing.'[3] As late as 1932 he wrote to Arthur:

Perhaps I am too complacent about myself and my life. Of course I have intense periods of depression, but I have never seriously contemplated any other kind of existence for it is so clear to me that I should only be more unhappy . . . I'm a real crusader about this kind of thing.[6]

As an administrator his early reputation was mixed; and he confessed later that the attraction of a don's life was its lack of discipline.[7] He never looked like making a major contribution to economic theory. His talents as an academic writer, like Cole's and Tawney's, were best displayed in economic and social history or in the lucid exposition of difficult arguments. He knew it, keeping up his WEA activities, writing mainly works of serious popularisation, and using his skills increasingly as a policy adviser to the Labour Party. His teaching was never just disguised propaganda; and though everyone knew his views, undergraduates and professors agree that he did not try to impose them. A respectable minority of his colleagues thought he could have risen high in the profession, but it was never the centre of his attention.

Apart from his formal duties, he played a very active part in numerous little discussion groups of colleagues and friends, which proliferated in university circles at that time. Durbin was a close friend of the psychologist Dr John Bowlby, and the two allies were concerned with psychology almost as much as politics. Postan led a group of economic and social historians who met for long walks in the country or over dinner; Gaitskell was much concerned with the attitude to Socialism of different social classes. He was a founder of Tots and

Quots, a small monthly dining club of scientists and intellectuals who debated 'the unity of scientific method'. Solly Zuckerman, another founder, believed that these discussions accounted for Gaitskell's later sympathy for scientists in public life; and his distrust for committed Marxists may also have originated there. Other groups, working out Socialist economic policy, are dealt with later.

In the brief period before these activities began, Gaitskell felt rather lonely as he so often did in a new job–though his Nottingham girlfriend came to stay for a short time. He spent Christmas of 1928 entirely on his own. He had found a large white-panelled flat in a Queen Anne house at 12 Great Ormond Street, which he took great trouble decorating; he was proud of his apple-green curtains, his carpets and chintz, and his original drawing by Meninsky. Penniless Oxford friends like Lionel Perry and John Betjeman stayed with him sometimes, and the Coles had his back room as a *pied-à-terre*. He and John Bowlby shared an excellent cook, and his students as well as friends came to lunch at the flat, in what was then an unheard-of gesture from a tutor.

His more frivolous activities centred on the Cave of Harmony at Seven Dials (later the Gargoyle Club) where he indulged his love of late-night dancing. At this time he was keen on radio entertainers, liked musical comedies even more than the straight theatre, and enjoyed the antics of his more outrageous friends; one evening in Trafalgar Square when Betjeman mounted on a lion to deliver a Socialist soap-box oration, Gaitskell was as delighted as their companion was embarrassed. He became a familiar figure in the Bloomsbury set around Francis Meynell, more actively political than those at the court of Virginia Woolf. He joined (though Evan Durbin never would) the 1917 Club in Gerrard Street, a cheap social and political centre–at a time when most clubs were expensive, socially exclusive and single-sex–where the impecunious young intellectual and professional Left met for lunch and gossip until it went bankrupt in 1931. Many scientists and actors joined, along with civil servants and poets; the prevailing life-style anticipated the permissive society of a later generation, and there was much overlap between the less earnest members and the Cave of Harmony crowd.

These young intellectuals met informally at Bertorelli's restaurant, with its excellent cheap dinners, and at the Fitzroy Tavern on the corner of Windmill Street, better known as Kleinfeld's, the most bohemian pub in London and a club for its large and devoted clientele. Originally the regulars had been mainly artists (headed by Augustus

John); later also writers, poets, journalists, dons, scientists and budding politicians, many of whom became famous. Most were hard up, but when anyone sold a picture or a story, everybody celebrated. Gaitskell was a frequent though not a regular customer at Kleinfeld's. To his staider academic friends at this time he seemed 'rather gay and fast with lots of girl friends and a *slight* touch of the enfant terrible'.[8] But at the Fitzroy Tavern the dashing blade of UCL was thought a quiet, gentlemanly, rather reserved young fellow, who was never drunk and never involved in the political arguments. Early in these Bloomsbury years, in 1930, he was depressed by a persistent toothache. A doctor friend sent him to Sir Thomas Horder, 'said to be the best diagnostician in London', who told him it was due to a small tubercular gland and successfully prescribed a long Swiss holiday.[9] That trouble never recurred, though a little later, as his political interests developed, some of his friends did wonder needlessly whether he was robust enough for so strenuous a life.

Foreign travel was very cheap, and unlike Durbin (who disliked 'abroad'), Gaitskell went to Europe often. At home he stayed twice in Scottish castles – in 1930 at Forfar with Burmah Oil friends of his mother, and in 1931 at Craignish in Argyll with Naomi Mitchison the novelist, and her husband Dick, a rising young Socialist lawyer. He went for twenty-mile walks, swam a good deal and acted in his favourite charades, once appearing as a Roman emperor in a bath-towel looking 'remarkably dissolute'.[10] He wrote indignantly to Margaret Cole, 'I will *not* be a character in one of Naomi's novels', but he did not entirely escape that fate.[11]

One of the best-loved people in those circles was Amyas Ross, who became Hugh's intimate friend. He had been a contemporary of Arthur's at the Dragon School and then at New College. In between he was an anti-war schoolboy with revolutionary views at Repton, where Victor Gollancz was a radical member of the staff. At New College he instigated a strike of college servants, and was a founder of the Oxford University Labour Club. Now he was a brilliant, impulsive, unpredictable entrepreneur of bright ideas, as well as an improbable WEA tutor in economics and a Labour candidate.

Between Evan Durbin and Ross there could hardly have been a sharper contrast in personality. Gaitskell's friends were as varied as his interests, and he always kept them in separate compartments: Bowra, for instance, complained that at Oxford, he 'was not allowed to meet' Durbin. This eclecticism was perfectly conscious. Gaitskell wrote to Cole in September 1928:

I can't change myself even if I wanted to – I can't honestly tie myself down either to one thing or one person or more, but to be true must be one individual with a number of contacts in different places reflecting the different parts of my personality . . . I may, as you suggest, find the one person in the world to combine my different selves into one. At the moment, however, she does not exist.[12]

He was to meet Dora Frost for the first time a few weeks later. In the spring of 1929, Amyas Ross was Labour candidate in a by-election in the Tory stronghold of St Marylebone, and she and Hugh were both among his active helpers. Their first encounter took place at Kleinfeld's when Hugh looked in to fortify himself before the ordeal of speaking at an outdoor meeting. At the end of 1950, Hugh Gaitskell the new Chancellor of the Exchequer dropped in at the Fitzroy Tavern to wish the proprietors a happy new year, and recorded in their visitors' book, 'This is where I met my wife.'

Dora was an old friend of Amyas and Peggy Ross. Her background was very different from Hugh's. Her father, Leon Creditor, was a Jewish writer and Hebrew scholar who had emigrated from Russia in 1903. He was a delightful man of saintly good temper, generosity and gentle wit, adored by his family. The Creditors first settled in the East End of London, where he taught Hebrew and wrote regularly for the only 'quality' Yiddish newspaper, the *Jewish Times*. He was devout and the three elder children, two girls and one boy, learned to speak and read Hebrew fluently; but though Dora enjoyed this, she was never religious. Their mother, uneducated herself but with five well-educated brothers, was ambitious for her son and daughters to acquire an education and a profession. Dora went to an excellent grammar school in Bow Road, and wanted to take a degree in English and French and go in for teaching. But she was ineligible for a grant, and was persuaded by her mother – much to her later regret – to switch to medicine. Just before her nineteenth birthday she married a young doctor, David Frost, who specialised in psychiatry and biochemistry. (It was he who called in Horder, his old tutor, about Hugh's gland.) Their son Raymond was about four years old when Dora first met Hugh early in 1929.

The friendship quickly took root. She was five years older than Hugh and soon became his confidante. They had many interests in common – in literature (especially modern fiction), in psychology, and not least in the Labour Party which Dora had joined at sixteen. She had no idea of going into politics, for she was happy with her job in publishing. When Hugh first came to London the Frosts were living in

Gower Street. Later they rented a big house just north of Regent's Park, where they let the top floor, often to young university lecturers; after giving up his flat, Hugh had a room there for a time before he went to Vienna. The Frosts had always each had their separate circles of friends, a style Hugh admired. His friendship with Dora flourished and grew closer over the years, and she discovered long afterwards that he had once said to Peggy Ross: 'If Dora were free I'd marry her.' But he was still strongly against matrimony, and if anyone had suggested that outcome to Dora at this period, she would have thought they were mad.

With Amyas Ross, Hugh's relationship was not merely political. The Rosses had just started a business in Soho Square, selling foreign prints, and in January 1930 Gaitskell discovered by chance that they were desperately short of capital – with plenty of orders but no petty cash to buy stamps to deal with them. After consulting Dora, he offered to put in £750. It was a generous gesture rather than an investment; he had never had much money of his own, and had just – disastrously – allowed another friend to risk most of it (£1,500) on the Stock Exchange, where it was rapidly lost.

The Soho Gallery sold, particularly to schools, good reproductions – at first principally of Impressionists and later of Old Masters. It organised school exhibitions, displays of original work and a loan club for pictures. Gaitskell rather prided himself on his knowledge of modern art; though he was never a genuine connoisseur, he gave a friend a Matisse long before they became fashionable, and he liked Van Gogh, Paul Klee and Picasso. But the Soho Gallery did not cater primarily for those tastes, and Gaitskell's main motive was to help a friend. His connection drew some lofty criticism from the artistic snobs of UCL – which he would meet by smilingly changing the subject. He became honorary chairman, and found the business experience useful and fascinating, though 'the worry and anxiety . . . [of having] all one's eggs in the same basket' could be 'very upsetting'.[13] Yet quite unexpectedly the gallery proved a great success, expanding its turnover in ten years from £500 to £33,000. Most of his loan was repaid in 1937, the rest – which he had waived – after the war in which the business, oddly, had boomed. He remained chairman until 1946, and sold his shares for £500 in 1952.

Gaitskell's speech for Amyas Ross in the St Marylebone by-election was his very first serious outdoor meeting. It began badly. But as he was struggling to interest a tiny handful of people in the naval estimates, a tramp began to heckle; the exchanges grew lively, and a respectable crowd of 200 gathered. When the speaker concluded triumphantly, the tramp came up to him: 'Well guv'nor, I reckon that was worth half a crown, don't you?' Gaitskell gave him 5s.[14]

All his early speeches were made on behalf of his friends, like Ross or Durbin or his Notts comrades. He was impelled into politics, too, by the hardship and oppression he had found among the miners. But he was also beginning to be attracted to it for its own sake, as he explained to his brother with his usual introspective anxiety to explore his own attitudes:

Personally I find myself concerned primarily with my own happiness (really non-unhappiness would be more accurate) and also to some extent with other people's. At least if you like to include it all under own happiness you can – it's certainly true that I'm not happy unless at least I successfully deceive myself into thinking that I'm doing something towards making other people happy.[15]

A few weeks later he exploded:

How I loathe the conceited ineffective snobbish rich! I suppose I have been insulted by them so often, and to be insulted by people one despises is intolerable. It is ghastly to think that people of our generation will be like that too – there is no doubt that equal education is essential.

He softened that tirade by adding, 'I hope you will be amused by this, as you are meant to be.'[15]

He was also aware, and suspicious, of another motive in himself. While still an undergraduate he had written to his mother about 'Another form of Dramatisation in which one pictures oneself in certain things – this must be avoided at all costs and things must be done for their own sake or not at all.' He went on to confess to having enjoyed his role as a 'man of action' in the General Strike, commenting: 'I'm again chasing reality and trying to sift genuine from false in myself and others too and I know that this matters.'[16]

Nearly two years later Hugh told his brother that he had revised his views on the subject:

one must have drama in one's life . . . this for me is rather revolutionary – I have always opposed dramatisation because of its hypocrisy. But now cynically I see that there may be much to be said for it . . . I think I have decided that I really do want to be a great man – this is not a burning passion – but rather that I think life would be more amusing if one was ambitious . . . By great I simply mean powerful, in the public eye, important . . . My motives may be mostly egoistical but because of a controlling altruism, my actions may lead to excellent results for society.

There is another point, perhaps the most important of all. I want to live at a higher rate, to exercise my vitality . . .

I am quite aware that I have no exceptional ability so that there really is no reason why I should be successful (except that *exceptional* ability really has little to do with it). But I want more vitality.[15]

With all his other outlets, he found that stimulus most of all in politics.

## 'Straight Out for Socialism'

During Gaitskell's first five years in London, from 1928 to 1933, the political situation changed dramatically, and among the young Socialist intellectuals, excitement and enthusiasm gave way to disillusionment and resentful gloom. At first the smug insular passivity of Baldwin's Conservatism was offset by optimism about the prospect of a new government. Hugh told his brother at the very end of 1928: 'I think that soon things will be more exciting here – the Conservative govt is such a fog – I hope it will be lifted altogether at the election.'[15] When Labour was returned he was overjoyed, as he wrote later:

The election of 1929 seemed to us at the time a wonderful, almost miraculous victory. We had done so much better than I (perhaps because most of my speaking had been in Marylebone!) had thought possible. We paid little, no doubt far too little, attention to the absence of a clear majority. It was enough for us that Labour was in power again, and for the first time held the largest number of seats. Our hopes for peace could be high, we would clear the slums – and, above all, tackle the unemployment[17] . . .

Then the world depression struck, and the Government stood helplessly by as the numbers out of work mounted steadily. Labour supporters soon became disillusioned. In the 1931 financial crisis, the Labour Party lost its three leading Ministers when Snowden and Thomas joined MacDonald's National Government as an emergency combination for a few weeks to save the pound. It promptly abandoned the gold standard, reduced unemployment benefit, and then went to the country; Labour was reduced to a miserable rump of fifty MPs and the Conservatives were installed in power until the war. Most of Labour's parliamentary leadership – for the only time in the Party's history so far – swung briefly to the Left in resentment and alarm at the defection of the leaders of the Labour Government, the electoral catastrophe brought on by its sterility, the demagogy of the other side, and then the advent of Hitler at the beginning of 1933. Even Clement Attlee was talking of emergency powers acts and local government commissars. That temporary mood influenced Hugh Gaitskell too. He was furious at the defections, he welcomed as thoroughly justified the naval mutiny at Invergordon in September 1931, and he was left stunned and bitter by Labour's electoral catastrophe. Concern that Labour would never be allowed to come to power democratically was so general at that time that even Hugh Dalton was talking of bringing the Durham Light Infantry to London to replace the Brigade of Guards; and long afterwards Gaitskell told a profile writer that it was 'the only time I have ever questioned the practicability of democratic Socialism'.[7]

His Left leanings were already apparent in his 1931 election speeches, and at an inquest on the results at Digswell Park in November a pencil note of the proceedings records laconically: '*Gaitskell* emphasised necessity for liquidating the opposition'.[18] Then, lunching one day in Bloomsbury in 1932, Gaitskell ran across for the first time for years his old Dragon schoolfellow Lance Mallalieu, now a pro-government Liberal MP – and treated him with blistering contempt for naively trusting the Tories. As usual, he had no truck with half-measures. He vigorously defended the Soviet regime against charges of dictatorship, he saw the Communist Party as just a bunch of impatient comrades, he talked freely to his friends of the revolution and the proletariat, the class war and the class enemy, and he struck more than one of them as temperamentally a natural revolutionary.

He and Evan Durbin, soon selected as Labour candidates for neighbouring Medway towns, had very different attitudes. Gaitskell said in his very first press briefing: 'The Labour Party must go straight out for Socialism when it is returned to power. But I do not believe in joining 'Left-Wing' organisations which are not part of the official Labour Movement. We cannot afford to have sectionalism at this stage.'[19] At Gaitskell's adoption meeting three days later, Cripps said Labour should not take office again unless it had a majority to introduce Socialism immediately. The new candidate entirely agreed, saying shortly afterwards:

The Labour Party had . . . tried to get better conditions out of capitalism . . . leaving the economic power in the hands of the same people as before . . . were . . . that policy to be pursued [again], it would have a second collapse much more serious than the first.

The only way in which Socialism could be got was shortly and fairly sharply . . . they should get the power, proceed with measures of Socialisation, and smash the economic power of the upper class. When they had the power he believed they would be in a position to carry into action measures which were essentially revolutionary . . . much better than by staying outside and trying to organise revolution.[20]

Five months later, Durbin was selected next door at Gillingham after a speech which put preserving political democracy as Labour's first objective, ahead even of Socialism and peace.

Throughout that year Gaitskell's speeches used strong language and struck a bitter note. Unemployment, he told his adoption meeting, could not be cured 'until they had got rid of the rich altogether'; slums, he said a year later, would remain as long as property-owners sat on the local council.[21] He set out his outlook more fully in a 1933 manuscript on wages policy. It opens: 'the destruction of this inequality, the creating and maintaining of a society in which it cannot exist becomes the essential and direct purpose of all Socialist activity'. The Labour Party was also obliged to offer answers to immediate problems, but in so inegalitarian a society that involved dangers:

Faced with this sentiment and lacking the support of a well nourished class hatred, many English Labour leaders have been inclined to put in the forefront . . . purely material advantages . . . Equality is degraded from its rightful place and allowed in, if at all, only when heavily disguised . . . [hiding] the essential aim of a Socialist party not only from the general public . . . but . . . from the members of that Party itself . . . [creating] a false sense of security and a blindness to the opposition and conflict which a redistribution of wealth involves . . . A Socialist party is different from other parties not because it offers a different mechanism for the same object, but because the object itself is different. Even economic planning . . . can exist without Socialism. Still more is this true of a particular monetary policy or the public control of an individual industry . . . the fundamental objective and criterion by which policy must be judged [is] the achievement of Economic Equality . . . without it Labour policy becomes merely opportunist, distinguishable only from the policies of other parties by the suggestion of attractive means to 'Prosperity', a greater humanitarianism, and, as some would have it, far less favourable circumstances in which to take action . . . A failure to advance in the direction of that ideal [of social justice] is bound to appear little short of a betrayal.[22]

Tawney's influence is evident in that equality (not public ownership) was already the centre of Gaitskell's commitment and loyalty. But the tone and style – the emotive terms, the suspicion of leaders, the warnings against compromise – are enduring characteristics of the Labour Left.

Gaitskell was never a trimmer, always a man for total engagement. Where Durbin already judged events in the light of a carefully worked-out philosophy, Gaitskell's was still fluid, and he reacted violently to dramatic incidents such as the General Strike, the collapse of the Labour Government, the repression of the Austrian Socialists. Politically inactive in Oxford, Gaitskell had missed the student socialist arguments about democracy and revolution, and so came to a considered position later than many contemporaries. But even in his left-wing period, he combined almost fanatical commitment with a contempt for wishful thinking, an insistence on rigorous rational argument, and a concern for practical results. Once he came to think through the means of achieving Socialism, he firmly rejected the hope of spontaneous revolution as a myth, the strategy of organised revolution as leading to the wrong end, the tactic of forming dissident groups outside the Labour mainstream as a futile diversion of energy, and the underlying Marxist analysis of society and history as false in theory and detrimental in practice.

Gaitskell's excellent short account of Chartism, written before the crisis in late 1928, discusses how the problems of power were faced by a radical movement frustrated by its impotence to influence the government. That weakness was cause even more than consequence of its factional divisions. Chartism, he wrote,

might have become purely proletarian – in which case there would always have been a tendency towards revolution – or it might have progressed by a middle and working class alliance – in which case a pacific policy was almost essential. In fact . . . the extremists undermined the case of the moderates and the moderates queered the pitch of the extremists. Nevertheless it is unlikely, even if their respective fields had been clear, that either could have succeeded.[23]

From this work he discovered that the revolutionary army was made up not of a growing skilled working class produced by the new forces of production, but of the shrinking labour force in declining and obsolete trades, with some déclassé individual allies – by no means the socially indispensable creators of wealth whom Marxist theory saw as the carriers of historical progress. He worried over that problem for years in those long discussions with historians about social classes and their role in history, and it was one major reason for his rejection of the theory.[24]

The dream that mass discontent alone could produce an unplanned, spontaneous, successful revolution had been doomed to failure in the nineteenth century, as he had argued in *Chartism*. The lesson was borne out, nearer to his own day, by the short-lived wave of syndicalist agitation before and just after the First World War. That agitation ended in disaster in 1926 when, partly because of the expectations it had aroused, the wholly unrevolutionary trade union leaders found themselves engaged in a hopelessly ill-considered challenge to the Government. Gaitskell had been unthinkingly loyal at the time of the General Strike, but once he did think about it his sympathy for the wretched condition of the miners did not predispose him to favour the self-consciously irrational doctrine which had largely contributed to their defeat. As an ultimate aim, Guild Socialism was more sophisticated, but even it, as he argued (successfully) with its main author and his own former mentor Douglas Cole, was 'both unrealistic and really directed to false aims. One must always, I said, come back to the happiness of the individual.' As a strategy, syndicalism was a recipe for disaster, the kind of left-wing movement expressing emotions without considering consequences which he always detested. Even in his own left-wing period he saw the General Strike as 'merely the last explosion of a firework which failed in 1921'. Later on he came to regard it as the most vivid and complete exposure of 'the absurd "myth" of syndicalism . . . of its emotional anti-rational outlook . . . contrast[ing with] . . . the ruthless logic and professional techniques of the Bolshevists'.[25]

That last alternative was equally unappealing for quite different reasons. One was his abhorrence of splinter groups, shown repeatedly in these years. Sir Oswald Mosley's revolt within the Labour Party had attracted many discontented young Socialists (including for a time Aneurin Bevan and John Strachey). Gaitskell, if ever tempted, reacted sharply as soon as Mosley left the Labour Party. His conviction of the need for unity, solidarity and discipline was just as strong in his left-wing youth as it was later when he became leader of the Party. He had not forgotten how the Chartists ruined their slender chances by frittering away their energies in fighting one another, or how after 1918 most European Socialist parties had been paralysed by disastrous splits. He was always wary of Communist efforts to divide the Labour Party in the name of Left unity, and he had far too acute a sense of power ever to be tempted into sects or sideshows.

He rejected the ends of Communism as much as the means. He had defended the Soviet Union enthusiastically, explained its faults as the product of Russian circumstances, and doubted the reality of dictatorship. But the great famine of 1933 came as an eye-opener, for he was never a man who allowed his faith to blind him to unwelcome evidence. He followed later developments closely, especially the purge trials, but continued to favour a defensive alliance with the USSR, and (unlike Durbin) never before the war equated Nazism and Communism. (After Durbin's death, he confessed to John Bowlby that he had been wrong about Russia and that Evan was always absolutely right.) But while he still saw their economic and social aims as entirely opposed, his notes for a speech on Fascism at Chatham on May Day 1935 contain the grudging words: 'It must be admitted that *politically* communism is the same.'[26]

Intellectually, too, Marxism did not tempt Gaitskell for long. In their very first conversation Postan was struck by 'the note of doubt he sounded every time he brought out a stock idea'.[24] Such a questioning mind could never be entrapped within a closed system of thought, and Gaitskell's examination of Marxism led him to repudiate it as old-fashioned, false and intellectually crippling. From his study of history, he rejected as untrue the class analysis culminating in inevitable proletarian revolution. In arguments with Marxist intellectuals, especially in Tots and Quots, he found them sterile and dogmatic purveyors of a 'hollow and boring' system of dialectics. Through following world events he came first to question the way the Soviet Union was developing, and then to discover in Vienna that Marxism did not aid but impeded his left-wing friends in assessing their own predicament. That experience both reinforced his emotional commitment to Socialism and anchored him firmly on the moderate wing of the Labour Party.

## Socialist Think-tank

During Gaitskell's left-wing period as well as later, he was busy preparing seriously behind the scenes for the practical problems which a Labour government would face: work which was the centre of his activity throughout the decade, and which has had no real parallel in the Party before or since.

Quite early in the disappointing life of the Labour Government, Cole had inspired a series of meetings of discontented intellectuals ('loyal grousers' as one of them put it) at Easton Lodge, home of the Countess of Warwick. Gaitskell was present from the start. From these gatherings eventually emerged two organisations with overlapping membership: the Society for Socialist Information and Propaganda (SSIP) and the New Fabian Research Bureau (NFRB). The first was a propaganda body, with an executive full of Gaitskell's friends, formed in June 1931 with Ernest Bevin as chairman. It lasted little more than a year, becoming absorbed – against the opposition of Durbin and Gaitskell – by that minority wing of the old Independent Labour Party (ILP) which stayed in the Labour Party when the rest left in 1932. The ex-ILPers insisted on replacing Bevin as chairman (thus reinforcing his deep distrust of intellectuals), and the new Socialist League soon became under Sir Stafford Cripps the main organisation of the Labour Left, until obliged to dissolve in 1937.

The NFRB, prudently kept separate at Cole's insistence, was a research organisation set up in March 1931 to take the place of the moribund Fabian Society (with which it merged in 1938). Attlee was chairman, Cole honorary secretary, and Gaitskell assistant honorary secretary, chairman of the economic section, and later vice-chairman of the foreign affairs group. He was efficient at administration, organising Cole's gigantic research programme, drafting reports and managing committees. It may have been owing to him and Durbin that, to discourage Communist attempts to capture it, the NFRB adopted a rule (still retained by the Fabian Society) that it would adopt no resolutions of its own on policy. He was good at smoothing over internal tensions, and soon became almost as influential as Cole himself. Years later Gaitskell wrote that the NFRB 'harness[ed] the intellectual energies of many younger socialists to the practical issues of policy confronting the party . . . brought them together and put them in touch with the older leaders . . . [many] who had been connected with it were members of the post-war Labour Government.'[17]

The NFRB was nothing if not ambitious. Its economic inquiries sprang from a double disappointment. The Labour Government had failed not only to move an inch in a Socialist direction, but even to govern effectively – tackling neither the long-term catastrophe of unemployment nor the immediate threat of financial panic. The aim was to organise serious thinking on both fronts. Gaitskell started off the committee on Socialist economics on a series of broad topics: criticism of the individualist organisation of resources; how far Socialism should employ, or abandon, the price mechanism; problems of efficiency and incentives, of saving and spending, of the direction of investment, of trade unions, wages and labour mobility, and finally of the conditions on which any form of private enterprise might be allowed.

The depression had brought new interest in the rapid remedies promised by monetary heretics like Major Douglas, the Social Credit leader. Gaitskell wrote a remarkably lucid and penetrating analysis of the doctrines of Major Douglas and three others,[27] and later, with Durbin and a colleague, carried out an official inquiry into Social Credit for the Labour Party.

The main theme of anti-Labour propaganda at that time was to stress the difficulties which a Labour government would face in dealing with the financial community (an implied restriction on democratic choice arousing no alarm in respectable circles, unlike suggestions forty years later that a government of the Right might face difficulties with the trade unions). In 1935 Gaitskell contributed to that debate, arguing in detail that a government which knew its own mind could easily overcome financial sabotage of all kinds, from a run on the banks to a flight from the pound;[28] and the subject remained for years a major preoccupation of his. To learn more about financial questions, Gaitskell belonged also, from 1934, to XYZ, a select dining club founded in January 1932 by the very few Labour sympathisers in the City, who became the anonymous advisers ('my experts') of Hugh Dalton, Labour's financial specialist and probable future Chancellor. The slightly conspiratorial title was chosen to protect its City members' careers – and twenty years later was to awaken the ever-ready suspicions of the Labour Left. It met in a pub over a City alley deserted by night, and produced memoranda and policy statements for the Party. Francis Williams, an early member, credits it with becoming 'a democratic Socialist "cell" which far exceeded in its success anything that the numerous much-vaunted communist cells of the time managed to achieve.'[29]

Problems of immediate policy also occupied Gaitskell, always linked to the central issue of unemployment. Again the NFRB was the main forum but not the only one. He wrote with Durbin a substantial manuscript on wages, but failed to get it published. Unlike many economists concerned about unemployment, he rarely joined those trying to influence government policy by collective letters to *The Times*, saying it was not 'my business to make the best of the National Government but rather to point out to everybody that their actions are neither morally nor economically justifiable . . . so long as we only do what the business world likes we shall never get anywhere near a classless society'.[30] He argued publicly that the Government's mania for economy was 'bound to intensify the depression . . . Yet it was just at this moment that the State would be right to spend the money to continue with its public works . . . this was the only way out of the depression.'[20] But elsewhere he wrote that such limited objectives were not enough: '[A] "Prosperity" policy [or] "controlled inflation" . . . need not involve in any way a diminution of inequality or an attack on the class structure. Such policies must therefore be supplemented or related to the true socialist objectives.'[22]

## Chatham: United Front Candidate

While busy on these back-room activities, Gaitskell kept up his WEA work as well. The college authorities encouraged him; and he himself told friends that he found it more rewarding than his university teaching. One colleague called him a brilliant teacher who gave the most lucid lecture she had ever heard; another (not particularly friendly) thought him as much superior to Crossman as a teacher as he was inferior as a lecturer. His students told a friend who stood in one month when he was ill that they thought him a future Chancellor of the Exchequer. Like many Oxbridge Socialists at that time, Gaitskell found it the most natural way to make contact with intelligent workers, and it helped later on in making it easy for him to meet trade unionists on friendly terms. It also contributed directly to his budding political career, providing his contact with George Dexter, WEA organiser for Kent and chairman of the Chatham Labour Party, through whom he first became a parliamentary candidate in 1932.

He had become quite an experienced speaker. In 1929 he had spoken in Notts again, making a good impression but perhaps foreshadowing a future weakness, for the miner friend who had asked him wrote afterwards telling him (cryptically) not to worry about the emotional side of a speech.[31] He spoke frequently also for Amyas Ross in St Marylebone. In 1931 he was again active on behalf of friends – for Dick Mitchison at King's Norton in Birmingham, and for Durbin at East Grinstead in Sussex against 'rowdy but good-natured Tory opposition'[4]. Even in those discouraging circumstances – a Conservative stronghold in a Conservative year – he impressed a critical academic colleague with his ability to arouse enthusiasm without descending into rhetorical nonsense. His vigorous left-wing appeal impressed Durbin's agent, Tom Baxter, who urged Gaitskell to put his name on the parliamentary panel.

That first step towards Westminster was relatively easy, though Socialist intellectuals of the previous generation – like Cole and Laski and Tawney – had rarely taken it. Many of Gaitskell's contemporaries did, but then found the next stage difficult; only one (John Parker at Romford) became an MP before the war. The Labour Party expected young men to work their way up from a hopeless seat to a marginal; when they were qualified to look for a winnable constituency, they had to compete with trade-union-sponsored candidates who appealed to the local party's soul, its pocket-book, and often its reverence for seniority also. Meanwhile young middle-class Socialists found it hard to combine earning their living with a Labour candidature. In business, particularly in the City, they dared not let their views be known; less intolerant professions, too, often considered the two occupations incompatible. Evan Durbin would not renounce his parliamentary ambitions and lost an Oxford fellowship as a result; Robert Fraser, another close friend, had to abandon his in order to keep his job on

Labour's own newspaper, the *Daily Herald*. Gaitskell was remarkably lucky: the first seat he fought had previously been won by Labour, and the second had been safe (except in 1931) ever since 1922. Meanwhile, University College gave him a base at the centre from which to operate.

Its tolerance was rather grudging. Its century-old charter flatly banned all political activity from college premises. After the 1931 election, when the left-wing students wanted to form a Socialist society, the Provost refused to lift the ban. The students were determined, and one evening Gaitskell went to tell his head of department that they were about to meet in his room to form the society. When Noel Hall said the defiance could not possibly be overlooked and the consequences might be very serious, Gaitskell answered: 'That's why I'm telling you.' Hall spent an anxious night, but next morning his junior considerately came in two hours earlier than usual to tell him they had met after all in a pub across the road. Though Gaitskell had second thoughts about risking his job for a pointless gesture, he took a leading part:

The formation of this Society owed a great deal to the backing and active support of Mr. Gaitskell. He presided at several meetings (if I remember aright he was its first president) and it was largely due to him that such prominent [speakers came] . . . as John Strachey and Stafford Cripps.[1]

The authorities agreed with reluctance to Gaitskell's standing at Chatham, and there were some mutterings about his taking time off to campaign in the 1935 election (though not from his students who, far from feeling neglected, often went to help).

The opportunity at Chatham came because Frank Markham, the Labour MP from 1929 to 1931, had followed MacDonald. In reaction against Markham, the local Labour Party was looking for a left-wing candidate, and for the one and only time in his life Gaitskell filled that bill. A strong left-winger himself, Dexter would have resigned the chair if anyone else had been selected.[32] The CLP interviewed one trade unionist and three dons (the others were Durbin and Colin Clark), and were so unanimous that Gaitskell's name was the only one put forward. At the adoption meeting, Dexter told the others that they had picked a future Prime Minister.

Technically Chatham and Gillingham were divisions of Rochester, and Chatham included middle-class parts of that town as well as the dockyards. There, wages were low—£3 a week was typical—and Gaitskell could never see how anyone could survive on it. The party

chairman during the 1935 election was a railwayman about to retire on
4s. (20p.) a week pension. At public meetings, collections of 6s. 7d. or
4s. 6½d. would be reported with pride. There was a combined Trades
Council and Labour Party (including the Co-operatives, which were
politically active locally) but no organised trade union domination. On
the contrary, there was some class tension between the aggressively
proletarian unskilled men, especially from the Workers' Union and the
Transport & General, and the numerous and able 'intellectuals'
(teachers, engineers and civil servants) who largely ran the Labour
Party. The former resented the latter and would not work for them in
local elections—and found no readier a welcome in the active local
Communist Party, dominated by schoolteachers. Some of the class-
conscious unskilled never quite lost their suspicions of Gaitskell's
cultured accent, but most party workers were quickly won over by his
regular activity, his friendliness, his interest in people and his
willingness to undertake tedious chores. Among the survivors, his
popularity has lasted for forty years and he is still spoken of with pride.
One of them called him 'the best candidate to work for we ever had',
immediately correcting herself: 'You didn't work for him, you worked
with him.'[33]

In the summer, he came every Friday night for three open-air
meetings where they had to get to the pitch before either the Salvation
Army or a business propaganda body, the Economic League. In winter
they met on Sunday evenings. Gaitskell carried their portable platform
round and then back to party headquarters at midnight. He was
punctilious and—for him—unnaturally punctual, frequently missing
his meals rather than be late. He managed to avoid talking like a lecturer
or over the heads of the audience, and no longer despised the tricks of
the public speaker's trade. As always he prepared carefully, showed
concern for the individuals he spoke to, and so was at his best in
personal canvassing or in his Saturday meetings with small groups. On
Sunday afternoons there were indoor discussion meetings at party
headquarters, followed by chats to more small groups of party faithful
to keep them satisfied and active.

The most distinctive feature of Gaitskell's candidature was his lavish
attention to the Labour League of Youth. On summer Saturdays he
went with them on midnight rambles, talking politics, and often ending
up with political chores into the small hours. On Sunday mornings they
had regular classes on Socialist problems. At twenty-six he was of their
generation but a little older, able to lead political discussions and offer
personal advice. His admirers proudly claim that that local branch was

reputed the best in the country, and say 'they worshipped him'. His interest in the LLY was as an educator concerned about his young friends, not because it offered an organisational spring-board. He played no part in it outside Chatham, regarding its activities as a diversion from serious politics, and knowing that an active and influential left-wing youth organisation would soon be curbed by Transport House; for he always disliked factional disputes, and thought his efforts best spent in the adult Party.[34]

In 1933 those disputes often turned on relations with the Communist Party, which was still pursuing its 'class against class' line, denouncing the social democratic politicians and trade union leaders as 'social fascists' and as the workers' most dangerous enemies: the same disastrous policy which had led the infatuated German Communists to collaborate tactically with Nazis against democrats, and to greet Hitler's advent to power as the last gasp of German capitalism before its inevitable collapse. The British Communists always sought to detach the Labour Party's following from its leaders through a 'united front from below', and found many Labour sympathisers – including Gaitskell – who saw them as merely headstrong, dedicated Socialists. They had an appealing cause in anti-Fascism, and in Chatham they set up a committee to enlist non-Communists, especially trade unionists, Labour and ILP supporters, and Jews. Gaitskell's two closest friends in the local Party were Dexter and Charlie Macey, both strong United Front advocates though loyally anxious not to let that campaign embarrass the candidate. Gaitskell warned Macey of the risks of being manipulated by the Communist Party;[35] but he was quite sympathetic to the campaign, and willingly spoke on the same platform with Communists.

The Chatham Labour Party was bitterly divided, for many leading members were very suspicious of the Communists. It came close to splitting, but Gaitskell kept friendly with both camps by concentrating on organisation and membership drives, leading a week's campaign of canvassing and open-air meetings at the height of the dispute. Already he differed from most left-wingers in his abhorrence of factionalism, and his willingness to subordinate his personal preferences in the cause of party unity and discipline. To minimise the damage to the local Party, he promised to respect the decision of the majority. When they decided to reject the United Front and ban appearances by the candidate on a platform with Communists, Macey and Dexter resigned from the Party.

The effect was soon felt. At Gaitskell's adoption meeting the main speaker had been Sir Stafford Cripps, the new flamboyant leader of the Labour Left; eight months later that other left-wing hero Harold Laski was 'not considered suitable'. Attlee (then deputy leader of the Party) came instead, and Gaitskell also spoke at the meeting: a last appearance before leaving England for a year abroad. Through Noel Hall, an adviser to the Rockefeller Foundation, Gaitskell had been offered a fellowship to Vienna – and the college expected him to give that offer priority over his candidature. His experience in Vienna was to prove as decisive as the General Strike and Nottingham, making him a lifelong and unshakeable supporter of collective security abroad and of parliamentary democracy at home.

## Red Vienna's Scarlet Pimpernel

Gaitskell took his holiday in Austria in the summer of 1933, before spending the next academic year in the capital. Vienna in the 1930s was a mecca for Gaitskell's political friends and for his professional antagonists, the classical economic theorists, as well as for its famous psychologists and philosophers.

In economics the Austrian school was the main inspiration of the orthodox resistance to Keynes, and Vienna produced many economists of world-wide reputation: among them Haberler, Hayek, Machlup, Morgenstern, as well as Mises in an older generation. In a badly paid profession in a poor country, they often earned their living by day and taught by night. In the coffee-houses – warm and well lit and supplied with leading European papers – the impecunious intellectuals would sit gossiping for hours over a cup of coffee. Many foreign economists visited Vienna, and their local colleagues made a fuss of them.

The advanced foreign students were among the chosen few invited by Ludwig von Mises to his private seminar or 'inner circle'. In this select gathering, Gaitskell noted (with some exaggeration, for argument was lively): 'there is no discussion. He is just incapable of it. There's one exception – the *English* are allowed to speak . . . but if any Austrian or German student raises his voice Mises shuts him up at once.' Gaitskell took advantage of the exception, volunteering almost at the first meeting to present – in German – a paper refuting Mises's own recent book arguing that a Socialist state could not have a rational pricing system. 'I was a little nervous for, of course . . . Mises is not exactly good at taking criticism. However, it went off better than I expected. He was very polite, and Haberler and Strigl both came firmly to my rescue.'[36] A visiting American economist recalls that Mises thanked the speaker only for his excellent *German*, though he himself had found the paper 'a quite convincing demonstration of a workable price system under socialism'.[37] It was a bold undertaking for a young man of twenty-seven, and after the ordeal was over Hugh wrote to his brother that he was 'feeling very happy and relieved and lazy'.[38]

Gaitskell found some individual economists (notably Haberler) 'absolutely first class', but professionally he was disappointed in Vienna: 'One is inclined to be lazy (which the Viennese certainly are) and to spend hours a day in coffee-houses . . . as a teaching and learning place Vienna is simply not to be compared with London.'[36] The teaching had no effect on his own views, except to make him react against it. But he took his work seriously, and professionally it was a fruitful period, inspiring his only substantial academic work. This was on capital theory, a fashionable subject among the Austrians, and considered important in studying the causes of unemployment. He eventually published in a German periodical what he called 'two rather extraordinarily high brow articles' on it, and fifteen years later (when he had just become Chancellor) was delighted when they were republished in a textbook edited by Oskar Morgenstern, a prominent ex-Viennese American economist. The exposition is so clear, in an area where clarity is rare, that after thirty years it was still heavily relied on in discussions of capital theory. He was among the translators of Haberler's theory of international trade; and he began translating a major work on capital theory by an important Austrian economist, Böhm-Bawerk, which Gaitskell's lucid and readable version would have made accessible to the English-speaking public. But the war and then political preoccupations prevented the translation ever being finished – as Böhm-Bawerk's own academic work had come to an end when he became Austrian Minister of Finance.

As in London, Gaitskell's life in Austria had its frivolous side. Red Vienna preserved a gaiety and liveliness sharply contrasting with both the grim ruthlessness of Communist regimes and the virtuous solemnity of much of the British Labour Movement, which he had once called 'that horrible strain of puritanism in us '.[39] Of all foreign cities the Austrian capital was his favourite, and though his London habits had not been austere, Viennese friends after seeing him at home commented on how much livelier was his life out there. In an early letter he wrote to his brother:

there is probably no place in Europe where the standard of women's looks is so high and their morals at the same time pleasantly loose. Not that I have so far had any great experience, but . . . if one had the inclination one's social life could be very well looked after here . . .

. . . most people here are quite crazily Anglo-Phil – they are in any case very nice to foreigners – so that one's path is really rather strewn with primroses.

God – But Vienna *is* charming – really absolutely unique – the whole atmosphere is quite peculiar. I know that if I were not attracted to Dora or if she were here, I should not want to go back to England. In the first place it is quite small – I live very much in the centre of the town and for the most part walk . . . one keeps coming across the most lovely buildings and squares tucked away quietly behind the main streets. Secondly it is very easy to get to . . . very good country . . . the last few days everyone has rushed off to ski . . .

Then it is so easy and cheap to amuse oneself in the evening. There are masses of dancing places and if one goes to the Viennese instead of the international ones it is really charming – everybody is so very gay – although most of them haven't a bean and can afford only a glass of wine . . . a mixture of charm, gaiety, kindliness etc.

. . . I have picked up a rather nice Viennese girl who . . . looks after children in one of the famous Vienna municipality (Socialist) kindergarten – she dances quite incredibly well and it's all nice and light and romantic and entirely without foundation which is exactly what I want . . . I am really too lucky, for Dora will probably be arriving here on Christmas Day.[38]

For Gaitskell's future outlook, the crucial impact of Vienna was political. Controlled ever since the war by a Socialist Party with two-thirds of the votes, one of the least healthy cities in Europe, once notorious for its tuberculosis rate, had been wholly transformed by democratic political action, and now provided post-war Europe's 'most exhilarating social monuments'.[40] The splendid new workers' flats offered not only collectively organised cultural facilities, but the physical and family amenities taken for granted by the middle classes. To the Viennese workers they were a source of immense pride. But the upper classes were grimly resentful at losing not only most of the empire, but even political hegemony in their own capital; and they and the lower-middle class now found their personal living space (above a bare minimum) attracting heavy municipal taxation to pay for housing the lower orders who had suddenly come to power.

Vienna brought Gaitskell into contact with a Central European Marxist tradition which was predominantly Jewish, and so doubly unfamiliar. Its revolutionary past was not far behind it. Elwyn Jones, coming out after the crisis, met a gentle, white-haired old Socialist who warned him that he would meet many extremists in Vienna; he told Gaitskell, who replied, roaring with laughter, 'Of course you realise he's an assassin?' (He was Friedrich Adler, who in 1916 had shot the Austrian Prime Minister.) The leaders still often used Marxist revolutionary language, though in practice they were firmly committed to democracy. That meant seeking power by winning a majority (they already had over 40 per cent of the national vote) but not blurring the sharp lines separating their own closed society from that of their political opponents.

The Republic of Austria was the politically disgruntled and economically precarious remnant of the old Habsburg Empire – a great capital and a rural countryside deprived of its industrial areas where the ethnic minorities lived. In 1919 the Allies had stopped the Austrian Socialists from carrying out the *Anschluss* with Germany, where Hitler now ruled, with the seizure of his Austrian homeland as his foremost objective. Two parties in the rump state had a very strong popular base, the Socialists among the Viennese workers and the Nazis among the peasants and middle class; but the much smaller conservative Catholic minority was in power, propped up by Fascist Italy. Members of the three parties did not mix much in their daily existence: each tried to provide for its followers, materially and culturally, throughout their lives. To the Viennese workers their party was no mere electoral organisation, but the equivalent at once of a church, a welfare state, a university, an army and a way of life.

Gaitskell was fascinated by the world of Viennese Socialism. He took long tram-rides to the suburbs on Saturday nights to learn about its history from his friend and teacher Karl Polanyi (whom he had met in London through Cole) over the minute dinners, one egg and one spoonful of spinach per head, which were all his hosts could afford. He sometimes attended editorial conferences of the journal of which Polanyi was foreign editor. Living at first in a centre for foreign students run by an eccentric Austrian Socialist, Dr Oskar Bock, and his English wife, Gaitskell extended his friendships quickly in party circles. Political commitment and social enjoyment were thus reinforced by the personal links which meant so much to him. Within a few months that entire world was smashed to pieces by Fascist artillery, and he saw at first hand the savage repression and suffering that followed from military defeat. The experience marked him for life.

The Austrian Party had proportionately the world's largest membership, and was proud of having preserved its solidarity – unique on the Continent – by avoiding both timid Social Democratic compromise and wild Communist adventurism. (During the 1920s Vienna was the headquarters of the 'Two-and-a-half International', to which the British ILP belonged.) But the Party kept its left wing within the fold only by renouncing coalition and going into opposition, leaving an army and police force which they felt sure would never fire on the workers. They organised their own private army, the *Schutzbund*, for protection not aggression – but it still alarmed the other side. Intransigence bred intransigence, and occasional muscle-flexing on the Left gave influence and a pretext to their extreme as against their moderate adversaries; while the 'mindless militarisation' of the Party, against the warnings of its best-qualified leaders, reinforced its separatist and isolationist tendencies.

At first the Socialists felt secure, believing as good Marxists in their inevitable victory. But their clerical conservative opponents, alone in power, gradually purged the armed forces which, in 1927, did fire on a spontaneous demonstration which had got out of hand. The Socialists' position weakened especially after 1933 when Austrian democracy was precariously wedged between mighty Fascist neighbours both north and south. Their leadership tried hard to avoid civil war, for they foresaw all the consequences of defeat – including the impossibility of escaping Nazi rule for long. But Chancellor Dollfuss, instead of compromising with them against Hitler, began from 1933 gradually but systematically to erode their positions of strength. Ten weeks before the climax Gaitskell wrote to his brother: 'One is witnessing the slow, very slow, depression and extermination of the socialist movement. Fascism in Austria is certainly milder than elsewhere but its existence can't be denied.'[38]

The likelihood of a clash brought tensions among Socialists. The leaders still hoped to strengthen the moderates in the government by avoiding provocations; they knew that if they struck first they would be condemned in the Western democracies; and they believed that the working class could fight effectively only if united in outrage against some blatant act of oppression – which Dollfuss carefully avoided. The younger generation feared that he was successfully whittling away the Socialist capacity to resist. Gaitskell knew everyone who mattered in both wings: 'As the danger of a confrontation drew nearer, Hugh became ever more involved. Sometimes he argued that he should after all be also working on his Thesis. Nobody quite believed that.'[41] But (as in Chatham) his close personal friends were among the left-wing opposition, including the Kulcsars, an ex-Communist couple who started before the clash a new undergound group named – after Lenin's paper – the Spark. In the endless arguments about revolutionary strategy he tried to warn his young friends that they were rash in overestimating their own strength, naive in imagining that a violent conspiratorial seizure of power could ever lead to democracy, and foolish in allowing hatred for the domestic enemy to blind them to the risk of total obliteration by the Nazis.[42] Nevertheless, when the clash came he seems to have thought their resistance might after all have succeeded. But after some final provocations from hotheads in the provinces (mainly Heimwehr Fascists, but also Socialists at Linz), the government struck first and ruthlessly, arresting the Party and *Schutzbund* leaders before they could even tell their men where the arms were hidden.

On the night of 11 February 1934 Gaitskell, returning from a lively party, saw machine-guns being set up in the streets. During coffee in the Bocks' dark sitting room next morning, all the lights went out; the general strike had begun. 'Blood will flow on the streets of Vienna tonight,' he said – for unlike the other English there, he knew that was the signal for the *Schutzbund*'s last stand. That day he stood with a visitor from the Rockefeller Foundation watching the government's artillery pound the prized new workers' flats; forty-eight hours later the military and political power of the Viennese workers had been crushed by the heavy guns. The Socialists mourned 1,500 dead and 5,000 wounded. Their leaders were in exile or gaol ( several were to be hanged); breadwinners lost their jobs, and families all their meagre possessions (down to underclothes). Occasionally starving children were rescued by Catholic charities – and put in convents. Execrated by most Austrians, the clerical-fascist regime survived the Nazi murder of the Chancellor in July 1934 but succumbed in 1938, after Mussolini lost interest in his puppet state.

As soon as the fighting ended Gaitskell threw himself into furious activity. From the *Daily Herald*'s Vienna office, where communications would not be intercepted, he telephoned to the Coles in London to alert British opinion; thanks to him the Labour Movement sent out Elwyn Jones to watch conditions in trials and prisons, Walter Citrine to represent the trade unions, and Naomi Mitchison to help, alongside the Quakers who had been doing relief work in Vienna ever since the war, to manage the hardship fund organised in London at Gaitskell's suggestion. Gaitskell got the Coles to arrange meetings for an Austrian economist friend who was in Britain to reveal what was going on, and tried to stir up public opinion at home through his journalist friends – G. E. R. Gedye, John Gunther, Vernon Bartlett, Philip Gibbs – and on his own Easter visit to England. He sent Transport House reports on particularly shameful cases of brutality and oppression, and promoted a petition to Dollfuss from foreign residents in Vienna, urging an end to the executions; eventually he and others persuaded the British authorities to intervene.

Personally, he kept in touch with distressed Socialist families in need of help – carefully, to avoid attracting police attention. He

was a leader, a counsellor, who constantly accompanied delegations into town halls and prisons. He was the organiser of innumerable secret meetings, of talks with clandestine Austrian Socialists, of activities to enlighten the public in the West. Gaitskell the courageous friend played an important part in kindling the spark of freedom into a flame so quickly among Austrian workers after the February days.[43]

He sheltered refugees (including Ilsa Kulcsar) in his own flat, and gave 'manifold assistance' to various clandestine groups:

An Englishman was almost beyond suspicion in those days. I remember running across Hugh one morning . . . in his shirt-sleeves, carrying a laundry-basket. 'I'm turning stoker,' he said. He was taking a load of compromising papers from [his] centrally-heated flat . . . to his former digs . . . where there were honest stoves to burn them in.[41]

Speaking German, but a foreigner, he kept contact between sections of the party, warned Socialist friends not to go home on nights when massive police raids were expected, and acted as courier to the exile capital of Viennese Socialism at Brno. Immediately after the fighting, on 14 February 1934, he accompanied three Socialist leaders to Prague by train and there met a young Socialist student, Josef Simon, who was to organise escapes (using professional pepper smugglers). He made frequent trips across the border to Brno and Prague, sometimes accompanying refugees by train, sometimes taking a wanted person out by car (each carrying the other's passport in case of arrest). He may have arranged false passports, especially for Socialist children. He was the first and a main source of funds for Simon to pay the smugglers and the families sheltering refugees; eventually 170 people, including some quite prominent politicians, escaped through that network. Back in London, he was very active in helping refugee scholars.

Gaitskell's activities can be known only in outline, for they took place long ago, and even at the time the less one knew what one's friends were doing, the safer for everybody. One British associate of those days thought Gaitskell very innocent and unsuitable for clandestine work. If so, he learned quickly. An Austrian who saw him at close quarters found him 'very active and resourceful, always very quiet and calm. I admired him very much because he seemed to take risks with equanimity'. Another, whom he met on many street corners to pass on names, addresses and money, called him 'an idealist and a good organiser. One could rely on his help.' A third, then abroad, remembered that 'Viennese friends told me at the time that Hugh was absolutely fearless and had an uncanny ability to unmask traitors and spies'.[42] A British friend said he was at his best in those days: 'ingenious and devoted and very brave'.[44]

For the second time in his twenties, Gaitskell had become emotionally wholly committed to a side which had miscalculated its means. He returned to England angry and frustrated at his own impotence, and seemed to his constituency workers for the first time capable of violence. He certainly approved of it in some circumstances, telling the Labour Party in 1935: 'Socialists should understand that it is their duty to do anything in their power directly or indirectly to assist the revolutionary opposition within fascist countries.'[45] He was always prepared to fight a domestic Fascist threat by any means necessary, and warned a public meeting in Chatham on May Day 1935 of the need, even with the 'Conservative' type of Fascism, for 'Clarity about ultimate possibility of need for Revolutionary action e.g. General Strike'. But pending that desperate last resort, his opening themes to the same meeting were: 'Our duty here – Maintenance of Democracy – The Tradition of Liberty – The Use of Political Freedom.'[26] Earlier, he had told the Chatham Party in his New Year message, 'I was a witness of two civil wars and their ghastly and tragic consequences, and I learnt, as never before, to value the freedom of British political institutions.'[46]

# 4

# 'A Proper Social Democrat' 1934–39

'Hatred of inequality and the Class Structure – the germ of all
Socialist feeling'
(HG, 1934)

## Constitutionalism and Collective Security

During 1933 and 1934 the Labour leadership (except Cripps) abandoned the vaguely revolutionary rhetoric in which they had briefly indulged, and with the great bulk of the Party set out again on the parliamentary road to power. More hesitantly, they also began renouncing the pacifism to which most Socialists had been emotionally drawn, and making a new commitment to collective security. Gaitskell participated in both movements – without the hesitation – and found himself in the mainstream of party opinion.

He returned from Vienna in the summer of 1934 bitter about the undeserved fate of his comrades; you could no longer joke with him about political matters, said Noel Hall, who provoked an explosion from him by setting an examination paper which treated Communism and Fascism as equivalent. Yet Hall also commented that it was not until after his return to England that Gaitskell became 'a proper social democrat'. The downfall of Austrian democracy had shown him that Socialists must choose. Its powerful enemies on the Right were strengthened by the Austro-Marxists' unwillingness to repudiate revolutionary aspirations clearly and unequivocally. That ambivalence was understandable in Vienna, for reasons which did not apply in England. There, Gaitskell now insisted, support for parliamentary democracy and rejection of revolutionary rhetoric must be absolutely specific. For, though both in Britain in 1926 and in Austria in 1934 the Left were victims far more than aggressors, in both countries the revolutionary talk of the previous generation had played a part in rendering the clash inevitable and in inhibiting the leadership from making the best of a bad situation.

In the six months after his return, Gaitskell debated these problems of political strategy in his usual way in a small group of a dozen friends

who went thoroughly into the risks of repression while the Labour
Party was in opposition, of sabotage after it won power, or of prior
Conservative moves to rig the constitution to prevent it winning; and
agreed – usually unanimously, occasionally with a couple of
dissenters – on the ways Labour would be justified in resisting.

Part of Gaitskell's revulsion from the Left was a change of attitude
towards the Communist Party. At Chatham he had been relatively
sympathetic. But in Austria the tiny CP had devoted its energies to
attacking the beleaguered Socialist leadership; and now, back in
Britain, Gaitskell was as impressed by their futility and irrelevance as
by their underhand methods. He agreed to the Socialist strategy
group's conclusion that Labour's case was best argued 'on grounds of
social justice and economic efficiency not . . . of class struggle'.[1] His
disenchantment with Marxism was directly derived from his Austrian
experience. Already sceptical on many grounds about the doctrine, he
concluded in Vienna that as a guide to practical action it was positively
harmful, diverting the faithful away from harsh realities into sterile
attempts to apply rigid, irrelevant categories. While he had no time for
the Communists, he found the moderate Marxists absurd. Once while
there, provoked by a passionately anti-Marxist Englishman, he is
recorded as having 'put the Marxist case'; but after his return 'In his
frequent conversational inquests on the Austrian Social Democrats he
invariably spoke of their Marxism as one of their afflictions'.[2] Contact
with their dogmatic British counterparts – as in Tots and Quots – only
made him more distrustful.

So thoroughgoing were his rejection of revolutionary Marxism and
his acceptance of constitutionalism that acquaintances from the NFRB
or the 1917 Club, or close but new-found friends like Douglas Jay,
could not believe he had ever taken a different view. In February 1936
Gaitskell (along with Eileen Power) paid an overnight visit to Beatrice
Webb and tried in vain to shake some of the misconceptions of his
hostess. Irritated that he had not read her recent eulogy *Soviet
Communism: A New Civilisation*, and that he did not believe that its
triumph in Russia would lead to a growth of Communism among the
British trade union rank and file, she recorded an unflattering portrait:

he is said to be one of the rising young men in the socialist movement. Like
Durbin he is fat and self-complacent; clever, no doubt, but not attractive; like
Durbin he is contemptuous of Cripps and a follower of Morrison and Dalton,
and, I think, he is anti-communist . . . Gaitskell altogether demurs to our view
that the young generation are going definitely communist. 'They pass through
a stage of communism; but they find that the working class are unaffected by

communist propaganda and they drift back to the labour party . . . [or] become . . . uninterested in politics' is his verdict . . . the professed Marxists don't count in the constituencies . . .

The Trade Union Movement is today, he thought, stale-mated as a progressive force in Great Britain as it is in the U.S.A. . . . with a mass of unemployed, strikes are of no avail. Political action of a reformist character – including municipal administration, was the one and only way according to Gaitskell: he was in fact an orthodox Fabian of the old pre war school. What is wrong about this group of clever and well meaning intellectuals . . . is the comfort and freedom of their own lives; they have everything to gain and nothing to lose by the peaceful continuance of capitalist civilisation.[3]

Vienna taught a harsher lesson, which rarely entered into the personal experience of British politicians: the impotence of good intentions and majority votes against superior force. The British Left, unlike Continental Socialists, had the false sense of national security of an island people sheltered from invasion for centuries. That sense was reflected in the different forms of pacifist illusion voiced by Lansbury, Maxton and Cripps; and in the insistence of the official Labour Party on continuing to register its hostility to the Tory Government by voting against armaments. Having seen for himself what the military triumph of evil entailed, Gaitskell had little patience either with those at home who talked glibly of violence without thinking out the consequences, or with those whose wishful thinking blinded them to the dangers of allowing the Fascist countries to acquire military predominance. He did not openly challenge party policy, which indeed he would have thought improper for a parliamentary candidate. But privately he was already persuaded that war was coming and that Britain must rearm.

As early as December 1933 he had written from Vienna:

politically everything is just too bloody . . . no one here seems to have any doubt that Germany is simply preparing for war . . . they naturally think our policy since Germany left the League completely mad – and so I'm afraid it is. I feel so ashamed of it and especially the way we have simply given everything up and gone back to a sort of shifting [sic] isolationism. Everything is just ghastly.[4]

Early in 1935 he publicly put the chance of a European war within five or ten years at more than two to one.[5] In 1935, too, his Chatham hostess Mrs Grieveson recalls Gaitskell and Durbin discussing in her sitting room when the European war would begin: one said 1938, the other 1939. In arguing with the Left, his first ground for supporting collective security was the need to defend the USSR against German attack – while his opponent claimed that British workers were being lured into a war solely to safeguard French predominance and 'the investments of our employers' when they should be building 'a free and happy socialist Britain'.[6]

Trying to wake up some of the younger denizens of this left-wing dreamland, in the summer of 1935 the Labour Party organised at Geneva a fortnight's summer school on foreign affairs. The director was a League of Nations official, Konni Zilliacus, with whom Gaitskell became very friendly at the time, though later on a target of his bitter hostility as a left-wing Labour MP. Among the 28 students were 13 future MPs and two future Foreign Secretaries, George Brown and Michael Stewart. The students lived in a large old Geneva house, went round the International Labour Organisation and the League of Nations, and attended outdoor lectures (though Ted Willis found another student much more absorbing than the lectures). The liveliest arguments were often informal: wandering round Geneva one velvety August night and finding a fruit stall open but unattended, they took some peaches and left some money – and, starting from this un-capitalistic confidence in mankind, argued long into the small hours over Socialist aims and how to achieve them. Willis attacked Gaitskell for his caution about the Labour League of Youth and the Communist Party, and was told they were quite irrelevant to the real problems of the Labour Movement and the trade unions – 'where power lies, and where my work lies'. When they next met twenty-five years later, Gaitskell greeted his rebellious student (long since expelled from both the Labour and Communist Parties) with no inquiry about his colourful political past, but by asking: 'Hallo Ted, how are you? Whatever did happen to that girl? . . . I wonder if we left enough money for those peaches.'[7]

Gaitskell wrote a thirteen-page summing-up of the proceedings, which condemned Labour's now discarded policy of a general strike against all wars as 'an invitation to the fascist aggressors'. The League of Nations, he said, should be seen as no longer a capitalist but an anti-Fascist combination, 'one-third socialist' now the USSR was in. (He recognised that in some countries Soviet defenders might be as unwelcome as Fascist invaders.) Though capitalism was largely blamed for both war and Fascism, the inference that nothing could be done till it was abolished was on many grounds 'both wrong and dangerous'. That approach offered Socialists no policy for the present day, when 'for most governments – especially those threatened with attack from Fascist neighbours – isolation is impossible, and so is unilateral disarmament'. It would lump together all capitalist governments, ignoring 'that there are degrees of temperature even in hell'; it would undermine collective security, the only hope of averting a war ending with 'civilization and capitalism (and Socialism) in ruins'; and it would not be understood by the man in the street. Finally, Gaitskell's note attacked Lansbury and Cripps ('certain Labour politicians who appear unwilling or unable to understand the policy to which their party is committed') and admonished Labour's National Executive: 'Greater discipline must be insisted upon among the leaders who speak on Foreign Affairs.'[8]

In March 1936 the Germans marched into the demilitarised zone of the Rhineland: the longest single step towards the Second World War, yet the hardest to challenge for a peaceful nation and party. Gaitskell favoured the Government's military staff talks with France, as a step towards a European pact of mutual assistance for all European frontiers – with Germany if she accepted the terms, otherwise without her. Three months later Gaitskell repeated these views in arguing against Cripps. 'If France and the U.S.S.R. went to war against a Fascist Germany, he would not be prepared to stay out just because Churchill was a member of the British Government that went to their assistance.'[9]

A few years later the Labour leadership, the Labour Left and the Communist Party (though not the semi-pacifist ILP) were all giving top priority to defence against European Fascism, and to foreign affairs over domestic. Hugh Gaitskell saw that need years earlier than most political figures on the Left – or elsewhere.

## Socialism Before the Deluge

In his own subject of economics Gaitskell was less prescient. He always favoured policies of expansion; but in economic theory, lacking self-confidence, he remained more orthodox than Keynesian until 1937, a year after the *General Theory* came out. The young Labour economists, like Keynes, attributed the trade cycle (in 1935) to changes in the relationship between savings and investment, and they named him as the appropriate economist to advise a future Labour Minister responsible for measures to restore prosperity. However, their detailed work on employment policy was a sophisticated analysis of traditional Labour measures rather than a new Keynesian approach. They also differed from Keynes in thinking that no expansionist economic policies could be carried out until the country's financial structure was changed, above all by nationalising the joint stock banks – in the early 1930s the main item of domestic controversy within the Labour Party. G. D. H. Cole was the main intellectual advocate of nationalisation; Attlee and Cripps supported it, but Dalton opposed it as economically unnecessary and politically dangerous. It was approved by Labour's Leicester Conference in 1932, but dropped from the 1937 'Immediate Programme'. Gaitskell stood with the Left, arguing for it in 1935 'with great ferocity'.[10] Moreover, one of his main points against the Social Credit spokesmen was that their plans could not be carried out without nationalising the joint stock banks (which they did not propose).

Bank nationalisation was discussed exhaustively in XYZ, which carefully assessed the need to take over major financial institutions and worked out practical means of doing so. The bill nationalising the Bank of England was drafted there; and Gaitskell and his friends gradually came round to the view (which post-war experience proved correct) that that was the only indispensable – though insufficient – prerequisite for economic expansion. The young economists were moving from the orbit of Cole the academic to that of the practising politician, and late in 1936 Durbin wrote to Dalton saying he no longer wanted nationalis-ation of the joint stock banks in Labour's Immediate Programme.[11]

Gaitskell was not an instant convert to Keynesianism, partly because its preoccupation with short-run macro-economic management con-tradicted the instinctive Labour presumption that the ills of capitalism were far too acute to be met by palliatives; and also because Keynes's approach avoided having to choose between capital and labour. But in 1936 Gaitskell still fully expected that a Labour election victory would open the struggle for power and not conclude it. Far from trying to temper Labour policies to what capitalists would concede, he spent much of his energies on considering possible undemocratic forms of resistance – from the anticipated financial panic to Conservative measures to strengthen the House of Lords – and planning how to counter them. The argument about bank nationalisation was entirely about power, and he renounced the policy only when convinced that effective power could be obtained without it.

Defeating financial panic in various forms remained a serious concern until the war. Weakness in coping with inflation was a longer-term financial threat to a progressive government. His worry about that threat was not due to special foresight about problems with the trade unions, for he was sure there would be none (and in his own time, rightly sure) and their bargaining power was still small; it arose instead from the crude lessons widely drawn from experience abroad, notably in France. It indicated no move to the Right, and he insisted that a

Labour government must at once 'take steps to reduce social and economic inequality . . . the major aim of Socialism'.[12]

Gaitskell was an active lecturer, remained a mainstay of the NFRB, and sat on various Labour Party advisory committees. While equality was always his fundamental aim, public ownership was his chosen instrument. In his first article in South Leeds after becoming its Labour candidate in 1937, he wrote: 'So long as production is left to the uncontrolled decisions of private individuals, conducted, guided and inspired by the motive of profit, so long will Poverty, Insecurity and Injustice continue.'[13] Soon afterwards, he supplied notes for lectures to the Labour League of Youth, in which he said social justice must mean ending the scandalous inequality which 'will exist so long as private ownership of means of production is general'.[14]

In a lecture in December 1935 he said four advantages could be expected from socialisation:

| | |
|---|---|
| 'Equality'. | 1. Through Public Ownership to lay the foundations of a classless society. |
| 'Internal Efficiency'. | 2. Through Coordination to remove 'internal' wastes and increase the efficiency of the industry. |
| 'National Planning'. | 3. As a necessary accompaniment to effective national planning, to eliminate unemployment, insecurity and waste. |
| 'Workers Position'. | 4. To improve the status and position of the workers. |

He opposed confiscation on grounds of both principle and practice, saying it was appropriate in a revolutionary situation but not in a democracy; but if compensation were paid, then the change of ownership would not lead to a rapid advance to equality, and consequently 'Socialisation as such is not Socialism'. He favoured workers having full control, if they wished, over workshop conditions, including discipline; but he opposed a syndicalist structure giving them power to raise prices or restrict output as they chose. Instead, 'What is needed is to get rid of the class distinctions' – and of spokesmen for capitalist interests at the top. As always, he based his views on a fundamental assumption: 'an underlying hatred of inequality and the Class Structure . . . [is] the *germ* of all Socialist feeling.'[15]

All these problems of Labour's political and economic programme and foreign policy were thoroughly discussed in a small group of close friends who met informally, perhaps as often as once a fortnight, in one or another's house or sometimes at the LSE, with Durbin as the moving spirit. Here Gaitskell was in strictly social democratic company, dedicated to strengthening the intellectual foundations of orthodox Labour politics.

These personal associations were reinforced when Gaitskell acquired a new patron, far closer to the centre of party power than Cole or Tawney: Hugh Dalton. Thirty years later Gaitskell was to call those three the men who most influenced his pre-war political development.[16] Dalton, who was universally regarded as a future Chancellor or Foreign Secretary, had an abiding, lifelong and selfless interest in encouraging able young newcomers and helping their careers—especially Gaitskell whom he privately saw, as early as November 1933, as a potential party leader in twenty years' time. The two men met first in a miner's cottage near Worksop when the younger man was teaching at Nottingham.[17] Both were upper-middle-class public-school Socialists who taught economics at London University, and were as interested in foreign affairs as in finance. Gaitskell, like Dalton's other young disciples, followed their mentor in party matters, notably over the leadership at the end of 1935—all favouring Herbert Morrison against Attlee and Greenwood.

The younger men also shared Dalton's contempt for Cripps, whose public posturings formed a striking contrast to their private (and radical) constructive hard work. No wonder Gaitskell told Beatrice Webb: 'The one hopeful institution in the labour movement is the Fabian Research Bureau . . . the younger men [who] . . . with Dalton and Morrison will be the intellectual leaders of the future.' She found him as scornful of Cripps's movement as of the man, dismissing the Socialist League as 'purely mischievous' but fortunately quite unimportant.[3]

Even when closest to them in his own views, Gaitskell had been wary of the quarrelsome factionalism of the Left and their endless revolts. Always a party man, in 1932 he told his selectors at Chatham that he had no use for splinter groups, and warned his friends who wanted a United Front with the Communists not to let themselves be used to split the Labour Party instead. He distrusted the sectarianism of the old ILPers, and vainly tried to guard against the Socialist League taking a separate line of its own. In 1935 he told Ted Willis he would have nothing to do with the factional disputes in the Labour League of

Youth, and he criticised the party leaders for insisting publicly on their own individual viewpoints on foreign affairs. All Socialist parties had always believed – in principle if not in practice – in the doctrine (now obsolete in Britain) that political action must be united and disciplined to be effective. Gaitskell's generation were the more conscious of the need for teamwork after seeing the harm so recently done by futile fragmentation: on the Left by Communists and ILP, on the Right by National Labour and New Party, and by the unpredictable Cripps who was consistent in nothing but his hostility to the leadership (within a couple of years he was to switch from preaching half-baked revolution and half-hearted pacifism to calling for alliance with anyone, however anti-Socialist, who would oppose Chamberlain).

By 1935 Gaitskell's position was thus clear. Politically the Labour Movement was moving away from pacifism and revolution towards collective security and constitutionalism, the Labour Left was busily discrediting itself, and the leadership was open to constructive suggestions on policy. Intellectually, he was becoming increasingly impatient with the Left's abstract theorising; in 1935 when Postan sent him an offprint on Marxism, he replied that he had lost interest in the subject and implied it was high time his friend did so too.[2] Personally, he was in touch with the party leadership through the friendship of a senior politician, and among his own generation he associated through Durbin with a group of intellectuals whose views were more orthodox and stable than his own had sometimes been.

After the war, he wrote that that group 'marked . . . the transition from the pioneering stage to that of responsibility and power'. His friends, he wrote, were – unlike Laski, Cole and Tawney –

not content to be merely intellectual advisers . . . separated too much from the main stream of the political movement because they did not accept . . . responsibility.

They broke away . . . from any kind of Marxist doctrine. They believed as passionately in democracy as they did in socialism . . . [seeing] the spectacle of Fascism rising on the Continent.

. . . They were not just interested in protesting against the ills of the present, they wanted to get rid of them in a practical kind of way . . .

. . . they were, before everything, realistic. They were not interested in Utopianism. They believed that if you accepted democracy as the best and only tolerable form of government, you had . . . to accept and understand [its] limitations . . . People had to be persuaded, and their views and emotions . . . taken into account.

They believed in making the economy more efficient; they believed in the possibility of full employment; they believed in social reforms which would gradually undermine the class structure, so that in due course a happier and more socially just society emerged . . . while accepting the ultimate emotional basis of moral valuation, they had great faith in the power of reason both to find the answers to social problems and to persuade men to see the right. They were for the pursuit of truth to the bitter end, through the patient and unswerving application of logical thought. They wanted no barriers of prejudice to obstruct the free working of the mind or blunt the sharp edge of intellectual integrity.[18]

## From Southern Marginal to Northern Stronghold

By the time Gaitskell went to Vienna the National Government had lost much ground in the country. Under Herbert Morrison, Labour for the first time won control of the London County Council in 1934; in the Medway towns they gained seven council seats. As always, the prospect of electoral success invigorated and unified the Party, restoring its confidence in itself and its leaders.

From Vienna, Gaitskell had kept in touch with Chatham by a regular correspondence with Mrs Grieveson, and on his brief visit home in April 1934. That autumn he officially attended his first Labour Party Conference at Southport as Chatham's delegate. Like Durbin earlier, he too now put the preservation of democracy in Britain first of his three political objectives, along with Socialism and peace.[19]

Since 1933 Durbin had been prospective candidate for Gillingham. Though next door to Chatham, it was very different: less hopeful (Tory in 1929), more of a dormitory suburb, and with fewer left-wingers – Durbin told his wife he would have been unhappy fighting Chatham. The two friends conducted many constituency activities together, each speaking frequently in the other's division, and writing jointly to the local press. (In the election they arranged to go together to a boxing match at the naval barracks, hunting sailors' votes; the unpunctual Gaitskell thought it an excellent idea but arrived very late – and met the Durbins, who had hated the whole thing, on their way out early.) They both followed the party line on foreign and defence matters, denouncing the Government for its betrayal of collective security, accepting military sanctions if necessary, repudiating 'one-sided disarmament' by Britain, but saying they would as MPs certainly have voted against increased arms estimates.

Parliament was dissolved in October 1935 and Gaitskell was plunged into the first of his six general elections. Besides his energetic local party, he had numbers of his students helping at weekends, several Austrian Socialist refugees who kept discreetly in the background, and many personal friends and relatives (including his Tory cricketing brother-in-law, and his mother who worked in the committee rooms and sat prominently on the platform, loudly announcing every now and then: 'I'm not a member of the Labour Party, you know.')[20] While Durbin fought 'a very candid, very educational, very W.E.A. type of campaign', Gaitskell was more effective – with a lighter touch, and rather more willing to play politics.[21] But he too was fundamentally serious, perhaps not bitter enough for the class-conscious unskilled workers; there was so little animosity in the campaign that he complained of the lack of heckling.

For some time he had been busily cultivating non-Labour personalities, particularly the many Liberals in the educational and Church world of Rochester; and he annoyed some Labour people by deciding on the very morning of nomination day to have several Liberals sign his first paper. He showed his usual talent for getting help from his influential seniors by attracting an impressive array of speakers for a first-time candidate: a prominent trade union leader, George Hicks, politicians like Cripps and Dalton, and intellectuals like Tawney, Cole and Laski. Privately he confessed to student friends that he had no chance of success; but at the count he was less philosophical, and became very wrought-up, saying later that the result was like a kick in the stomach.

| | |
|---|---|
| Capt Lionel Plugge (Cons.) | 19,212 |
| Hugh Gaitskell (Lab.) | 13,315 |
| Majority | 5,897 |

Gaitskell had polled 2,500 more than Labour had ever previously obtained in the constituency. He did a bit better than in other naval seats where Labour was strong, exactly the same as in similar seats in the south of England. His biggest disappointment was the total failure of his generation – apart from John Parker at Romford – to penetrate that stronghold of the elderly, the Parliamentary Labour Party.

A few weeks later Gaitskell told an NFRB inquest on the election: 'we had nothing to offer in time of boom, but . . . if another depression came, people would want big changes'.[9] He nearly became an MP in 1936, when he was runner-up at a by-election in the mining stronghold of Clay Cross, Derbyshire, close to his old Nottinghamshire lecturing ground. Had he entered the House then, he would certainly have been in the government in 1940 and (health permitting) in the Cabinet by 1945, with incalculable consequences.

Instead, after a year and then a term away, he had fences to mend at UCL. He decided not to stand again at Chatham, receiving in reply the warmest tribute a CLP in a marginal seat can bestow: 'the whole of the Party in Chatham would be pleased if you were offered a "safe" seat in the near future'. For domestic reasons he was not anxious to find a new constituency at once, for Dora was getting divorced. Even after that was settled and they were free to marry, he remained hesitant about a candidature. He found a letter from the agent in South Leeds ('a first rate seat') awaiting him on returning from his honeymoon in April 1937 – and had doubts about following it up since he 'had intended to concentrate on academic work and drop politics for the time being'.[22]

South Leeds had a solid working-class population employed in small engineering and textile factories and railway engine sheds. Labour's municipal leader in Leeds was a well-known pre-war housing reformer, the Reverend Charles Jenkinson, a parish priest from that constituency with a mission to demolish it. The area was largely self-contained and surprisingly isolated from Leeds north of the river. It had its own community life; Richard Hoggart wrote his paean of praise to traditional working-class communal values after growing up in the constituency.[23] Socialist Sunday schools still flourished between the wars, and every Sunday morning in summer 60 or 80 (occasionally even 200) people came to a Labour outdoor meeting on 'The Stones', in Cross Flatts Park in the centre of the constituency. The speakers were usually local councillors and party workers, quite often the MP, and occasionally visitors.

In 1904 Labour won some of its first municipal Leeds victories there, and in 1922 one of its first two parliamentary seats (out of six). The MP was Harry Charleton, an NUR engine-driver, who lost in 1931, and in 1935, owing to his age, won fairly narrowly. By the next election in 1939 or 1940, Charleton would be past the NUR retiring age for MPs, so the union would no longer sponsor him and subsidise the constituency. In 1936 George Brett, the secretary-agent, told Charleton that South Leeds would have to look for a new candidate, and the MP did not demur. But Brett, a forceful and intelligent man who was determined to choose a first-class candidate, did not add that he thought the CLP could if necessary afford to do without the NUR sponsorship money.

The local party invited several potential nominees to speak from The Stones that summer. Gaitskell, the only intellectual, was suggested by

John Parker MP, secretary of the NFRB and a friend of Brett's daughters through the University Labour Federation. Hearing well of Gaitskell from both Harold Laski and Hugh Dalton, Brett met him and took to him at once.

Gaitskell's competitors were all trade unionists, two of them from Charleton's NUR and one from the distributive workers' union. But NUR delegates (from all over Leeds) decided to send only one of their members, Tom Proctor, before the selection conference – so that South Leeds was forbidden by people from outside the constituency even to consider the other, Dai Jones. Naturally the locals were indignant, especially Brett, who distrusted Proctor, thought Gaitskell best, but would have been perfectly happy with Jones. From that moment the agent went all out for Gaitskell's nomination even though it would mean losing the trade union money on which his own salary depended – and wrote years later when Gaitskell became Chancellor of the Exchequer of his delight that 'all the risks I took to keep Bro. Proctor out [have proved] worthwhile'.[24]

He gave Gaitskell good advice before the selection conference on 3 September 1937. Gaitskell followed it, and won. Furious, the NUR claimed that the selection conference was invalid on a technicality. This powerful union, bitterly resentful of the constituency parties and probably joined by enemies of Dalton, persuaded Labour's National Executive to uphold the complaint. On 7 November a new selection conference was held. Before the voting, Gaitskell refused to offer to offset the trade union money, saying he wanted a choice on merit; only after his nomination was narrowly confirmed did he promise to pay £100 towards party funds and £200 to election expenses, enabling Brett to remain as part-time agent.

Worse embarrassment followed. Harry Charleton, when the constituency chose an unsponsored candidate, thought he could have remained as MP on new financial terms and complained bitterly at being asked to neither selection conference. He had no personal resentment against Gaitskell, but in his wrath at Brett and the local party he boycotted the constituency altogether for four years. Gaitskell had thus become candidate for a safe seat where the sitting MP would have nothing to do with him, but clung on at Westminster for eight years.

For the next two years of peace he was there regularly, and soon overcame his inauspicious start. Though a middle-class intellectual in a working-class constituency, chosen in competition with working-class rivals in succession to a working-class MP, he quickly attracted and always retained the enthusiastic loyalty of South Leeds. That was partly because he was so assiduous in constituency work, just as in Chatham – far more so than Charleton had ever been. He wrote regularly for the local party papers, and came regularly for canvassing, visiting the workingmen's clubs on Saturday nights as he enjoyed doing for the rest of his life, speaking from The Stones on Sunday mornings and attending the General Committee in the afternoons. The local party soon discovered his unassuming friendliness and pleasure in mixing with ordinary people and in constituency work. He would never stay in hotels, always with his agent or chairman (insisting on paying). He quickly became known, and quickly loved. When war came, he knew he could rarely visit and doubted if he could continue his financial contribution, but the Party was determined to keep him on; in 1945 he was ill at the moment of the election, but the selection conference knowingly renominated – unopposed – a candidate who might well be unable to campaign at all. Such was the reputation he had earned among his constituents in the twenty months of peace.

## Marriage, and Professional Promotion

Gaitskell's connection with South Leeds began at the very same moment as another lifelong bond, even more important: his marriage. The passionate friendship with Dora had ripened long before. The Frosts separated in 1933, and but for the 'utterly shameful and disgraceful' state of the divorce law – so Dora told the House of Lords much later – the Gaitskells would have married then or soon afterwards.[25] It was also in 1933 that Dora suffered a crushing blow when her publishing firm was taken over and she lost her cherished job. She went out to Vienna to join Hugh for the last five months of his stay there. On their return in the summer of 1934, he rented 24 Harley Road, an agreeable three-storey Victorian house near Swiss Cottage, shaken by trains which ran beneath the building. He was active in these years in helping to find jobs and asylum for persecuted refugee scholars, and he played his own part by sharing his house with friends from Vienna. Hugh and Dora went around together; she joined him in all the UCL outings, and saw much more of his political friends outside the Bloomsbury world.

Divorce still presented enormous problems. Until A. P. Herbert's Act of 1937, legal proceedings could be very slow, humiliating and precarious, and even afterwards it carried, for everyone involved, a stigma hard to imagine today. They wanted to avoid damaging either David Frost's professional career or Hugh's political prospects: very regretfully, Dora thought it unwise even to help Hugh in Chatham. By 1936, however, her divorce was under way, and when it was completed – without the difficulty or deceit they had feared – they were at last able to announce their forthcoming marriage to their friends at Kleinfeld's.

Hugh and Dora were married in the Registry Office in Hampstead Town Hall on his thirty-first birthday, 9 April 1937. Evan Durbin was best man, and only a few relatives and very close friends were present. They spent their honeymoon in Normandy and returned to Harley Road, where they lived until the war began. After all his scorn for bourgeois family life, Hugh was soon writing to a friend about to marry: 'As a husband of almost exactly 3 months standing and after a distinctly protracted engagement, I can confidently recommend respectability when one has reached the thirties!'[26] A UCL colleague noticed that Hugh 'carried himself better, looked healthier, life was . . . less full of devils around the corner'. The secure home life he had never known before had a tranquillising influence, giving him (said the same colleague) an impressive combination of 'ballast and buoyancy'.[27] The partnership was an exceptionally successful and happy one. Twenty years later, Hugh explained his change of mind about marriage in a letter to his stepson Raymond Frost, who had just become engaged:

I do think honestly you are wise to take the plunge. A bachelor's life is bound to become less and less satisfactory . . .

I agree too . . . about the advantage of having someone with whom one can share all one's problems & worries as well as one's successes & plans . . . someone on whose personal loyalty & affection one can always rely. Certainly in politics life would be very grim indeed without this.

Their domestic circumstances did not change much until a few months before the outbreak of war. Their enthusiasms continued – for convivial friendship, reading and walking; their literary tastes were so similar that Hugh soon left Dora to choose his non-political books for him. Throughout the gathering gloom of the 1930s, they escaped as often as possible for walking weekends in the Chilterns, the South Downs and Dorset, staying cheaply in pubs. Sometimes they met the Durbins, but joint holidays were not easily arranged – for Evan was a planner in advance, while the Gaitskells liked to dash off on impulse. Their favourite haunt was Abbotsbury in Dorset, from which they explored the Hardy country. In March 1938 they bought their first house: a cottage, Sweatmans, in the village of Milland just across the Hampshire border from Liphook; 'a pink washed house . . . reached through most lovely country . . . H. G.'s mother lives close by'.[28] It was here that Hugh developed his passion for gardening, at which he became expert.

About the same time his friend George Wansbrough, who was a director of Reyrolles, brought him on to the board of a subsidiary, the Eureka Vacuum Cleaning Company. Gaitskell was delighted to get the business experience, and his colleagues found he made many very useful and sensible contributions. His financial circumstances changed too, for he inherited a legacy from his aunt in Malta, Mrs De Burgh Griffiths, who died in April 1938 leaving some £14,000 to each of her Gaitskell nephews. Later on this money was shrewdly invested on Hugh's behalf by a friend in the City and multiplied several times over. Hugh's attitude seems to have been to ignore this personal capital. Certainly Dora was not aware until after his death how much it had grown: and it had little if any direct effect on their style of life. Another old acquaintance, who lived in the house for a couple of years, wrote when Gaitskell became Leader of the Opposition: 'He had an excellent sense of humour, and was economical in every-day matters: a good budgeteer'.[29]

As his wife, Dora could now take an active part in Hugh's political work. She accompanied him regularly to South Leeds, and wrote occasional pieces for the constituency Labour paper. But, contrary to what some of their friends suspected, she was not the driving force and did nothing to push him in the direction of a political career. She would have been happy if he had decided to remain as an academic Socialist; but she was equally prepared for the more exacting life of a politician's wife, and was to be Hugh's most enthusiastic ally in his chosen field. For the time, however, she was plunged into domesticity by the birth of their two daughters, Julia in April 1939 and Cressida three years later.

At this period Gaitskell also took on new responsibilities at UCL. On Noel Hall's departure in 1938, he was promoted to Reader and appointed to head the department jointly with his close friend and economic mentor, the Austrian economist Paul Rosenstein-Rodan. (They both forgot to attend a formal university dinner to celebrate their appointment.) In practice Gaitskell did all the administration, scrupulously carrying out the invidious tasks of hiring and firing with the utmost concern for individual feelings. Some colleagues and friends were annoyed that he was not offered a chair. His academic productivity had not been high, and with the strong competitive winds blowing from the LSE, there was still doubt about the future of economics at UCL. But it seems that the decisive factor was his unwillingness to give up his parliamentary candidature, which was not a statutory bar but was deemed by the authorities (as in other cases) to be incompatible with a professor's duties.[30]

Had Gaitskell returned to UCL after the war he was given to understand that he would have been appointed Professor. But it was never likely. He was an excellent teacher, who was anxious to do his best for his students, and who struggled and suffered with the difficulties of teaching a subject whose basic theory was in total flux, so that every lecture had to be revised afresh every year. But he lacked the mathematical equipment to go deep into economic theory, and was much happier writing works of serious popularisation like the short book on *Money in Daily Life* which he began for the new Labour Book Service. To one colleague he seemed just a nice ordinary competent economist, we all meet dozens of them'.[31] His academic career was respectable but not distinguished, and when he visited UCL not long after the war, he was surprised to find himself 'very unmoved'.[32]

Gaitskell in the 1930s was greatly appreciated by his friends, but those who claim to have foreseen his public eminence are very few. Casual acquaintances who had to do business with him sometimes found him rather priggish, though those who met him socially were often struck by his frivolous side. Eric Roll, a young economist who became very friendly with him at one weekend conference, was 'tremendously impressed'. Gaitskell seemed well established in both the academic and the political worlds, with lively cultural interests, and a 'glamorous young man . . . he took great care of his clothes, was elegantly dressed, good-looking with wavy hair, scholarly *and* worldly . . . not a drunkard but one who went in for worldly pleasures – dancing, the girls, food and drink'.

All his friends remark upon his considerateness, courtesy and charm, as well as his lively sense of humour. Often they stress how very speedily first acquaintance turned into real intimacy. The wife of one wartime colleague said: 'he had a wonderfully sympathetic understanding of people; unlike some of his clever friends, Hugh always made *you* feel clever too . . . he was like a magnet. When you were with him everybody felt sunny.'[33]

All competent politicians display a superficial warmth and a carefully cultivated memory for people, and Gaitskell did that too. But his interest in others was far more than a public relations device or a veneer of good manners, for he had a kind of 'fanatical gregariousness' about meeting new people and discovering their ideas and experiences. If he saw a young acquaintance with a girl, he would inquire about her next time he met the man – sometimes years or even decades later. Not only did his friendships ripen very quickly, they usually lasted for life; he never forgot those who had helped him when he was unimportant. Those who knew him well, however critical of his political weaknesses, remember him as a human being only with loyalty and affection.

Though polite in expressing his opinions, he was firm and very outspoken about them. But he did not obtrude his own aesthetic and other tastes on his friends. 'If you sat next to him at lunch,' said Noel Hall, 'the conversation lit up. He was so unobtrusive; he assumed you shared his pleasures and values . . . he was a very sensitive man.'[27]

Unlike Durbin at times, he was quite tolerant of disagreement. He enjoyed arguments but not quarrels, and on some sensitive subjects he protected his own integrity by silence. On religion he was 'totally uncommunicative – a very clammy clam' because he tried neither to pretend nor offend.[27] So the gap that later yawned between the public image and the private man exists even among those who knew him personally. Usually he was very open and uninhibited, a hater of humbug, with an 'incurable directness' and with strong emotions which he often showed. But in circumstances where he was not really at home he was armoured in an impenetrable reserve, a determination not to give himself away. Even intimates met that reserve occasionally if they differed from him on a subject like religion, or a great political crisis like Munich.

Privately he was introspective, and insistent on being brutally honest with himself, but he revealed these deep self-criticisms only to his beloved – and distant – brother. He was not arrogant, but was aware of his own abilities and without false modesty; occasionally he displayed his frustration and irritation with the elderly and ineffective Labour MPs of that period. He was rather attracted to the limelight and did not despise worldly success, but was much more concerned to try to influence events and policies. Many friends did not even think of him as a prospective politician, or as ambitious at all, and hardly any of them imagined he would rise so high in the political world – though he was publicly mentioned as one of Labour's potential leaders as early as 1939, in an anonymous study by a Conservative MP containing many very shrewd personal judgements on politicians of the day.[34] He was saved from most of the occupational faults of the political profession by the integrity which, when friends sum him up, is nearly always the first quality they emphasise.

He had thrown over the creed and values of his class and family, and to his colleagues like Hall 'his pride in his emancipation from his inheritance came flooding through'. His generation rejected conventional morality as humbug; but the same colleague saw no 'ambition in the sense of personal aggrandisement . . . [but he was] desperately ambitious as one might be ambitious to be a bishop, or St. Francis'.[27] For on fundamentals – courage, loyalty, integrity – he retained and reinterpreted the values of his upbringing. Where his military forebears had stressed physical courage, Gaitskell respected the same quality in moral and intellectual terms, fighting wholeheartedly for the side to which he committed himself. Loyalty to country remained, in the old-fashioned sense, but not to Empire. That was replaced by a new loyalty to the Labour Movement and its standards of collective action; years later he told his daughter that Socialism was his religion. In day-to-day struggles, too, he prized loyalty not to great abstractions but to persons, and felt a strong sense of solidarity with colleagues and allies who fought on the same side. First of all came intellectual integrity: a rigorous honesty in making up his own mind, a fastidiousness about candour in persuading others, an obstinacy about getting the argument exactly right, which could often infuriate – and sometimes inspire. To this personal moral code he adhered all his life, and he wrote twenty years later that he was 'much more likely . . . [to] be a failure than a sham'.[35]

## The Shadow of Hitler

Those first two years of Gaitskell's married life were overshadowed by the coming war. His own activities had already expanded beyond economic policy. He was vice-chairman of the NFRB's international section from 1934, did much of his speaking and lecturing on foreign topics, and wrote another unpublished book on the breakdown of the League of Nations.

It was a decade, wrote Quentin Bell, of 'mounting despair . . . unable to shake the complacency of a torpid nation, we saw the champions of war, tyranny and racial persecution winning . . . it was bloody to be alive and to be young was very hell.'[36] Gaitskell's reactions were identical. He wrote in the summer of 1938 that he felt 'continuously angry about the Chamberlain policy – especially in respect of Spain'.[37] Austria had succumbed to Hitler in March 1938, and Czechoslovakia – once the refuge for his Austrian friends – fell a year later. In those days he was never accused, as he sometimes was after the war, of showing too much sympathy for the men in power. 'The motive was not only stupidity and fear but *Capital's Class Prejudice and Economic Interest*.' That was one item of Marxist analysis which he still accepted, writing of Fascism as 'the last bulwark of Capitalism'.[14] Twenty years afterwards, he still recalled his impotent rage at 'the horrors of that time and the incredible obstinate stupidity of the crowd who were in power'.[38]

For him and for those who thought like him, Munich was shame and shipwreck. He thought that the mobilisation of the British fleet had deterred Hitler, yet Chamberlain had capitulated out of 'admiration for Fascism and hatred of Russia'.[14] His vehemence caused a temporary breach with Robert Fraser and severely strained relations with Evan Durbin, who saw no case for war with Germany over the Sudetenland. But Durbin was over-optimistic; and Gaitskell had good grounds for writing: 'I think events will do more to persuade you than anything I can say'.[39]

He told Durbin a week after Munich that democratic forces would collapse and friends of Germany come to power throughout eastern Europe. A German ultimatum to France would now find the victim isolated: 'Russia in my opinion would not move . . . Germany has achieved her goal of being able to fight a one front war.' In Britain the sacrifices required – including conscription – would be harder to get accepted, since Neville Chamberlain's policies had divided the country: 'while prepared to fight for the democratic ideal as such and for the ideal of collective security as such there is little to attract us in fighting merely to preserve the territorial integrity of the British Empire'.[39]

Three weeks after Munich Hugh Dalton called a dozen political friends to his flat to discuss foreign policy. Gaitskell was one of only four who remained resolute:

It would be fatal to oppose arms. Distinguish arms votes completely from foreign office votes. Concentrate on ARP [air raid precautions] and air defence. Expansionist monetary policy . . . Demand conscription of wealth. Scheme for large incomes . . . Our problem is how to combine a cunning foreign policy with moral uplift.[40]

The succinct summary conveys nothing of the atmosphere of desperation which oppressed Gaitskell and those who thought like him. A few days later he wrote to Durbin:

I suppose you just don't realise how deeply some of us feel this business nor how hopeless we feel about the future . . . struggling hopelessly and vainly against all that I most despise and detest . . . I can understand, you see, those who say that strategically we had to give way because of the arms position – I can understand the pure pacifists who will not fight for anything. But I cannot understand those who thought it *morally* right.[39]

On this life and death issue, Gaitskell now found some of his closest political friends taking a view he saw as disastrously mistaken, while some violent Tories – whom he had thought misguided or even malevolent – were on his own side. That made him feel more tolerant towards members of the other party. Yet though he recognised the anti-appeasers outside the Labour Party as potential allies, he did not join Cripps's Popular Front campaign to unite all Chamberlain's critics. Early in 1939 Cripps shocked Gaitskell's friends by arguing 'that of the two evils, imperialism and fascism, imperialism was the more abhorrent, and that a successful war against Hitler would . . . strengthen British imperialism'.[2]

It was not just a matter of rhetoric. The Popular Front spokesmen – including Cripps and Bevan as well as the Communists – were strong opponents of rearmament under the deeply distrusted Tory Government. Gaitskell knew that an armaments programme takes four years to develop, and unless it began at once, a better government would be unable to defend the country (let alone conduct a bolder foreign policy). Nor would there be a better government while the Opposition's foreign and defence policies remained so incoherent that the Labour leadership, and the Left even more, seemed to ordinary voters to advocate both 'standing up to the dictators' and denying weapons to the armed forces. From the spring of 1937 Dalton persuaded the Parliamentary Labour Party to abstain on defence estimates instead of voting against them, as the Left (and Attlee) still wanted to do. Gaitskell himself told his constituents: 'rearmament is also essential . . . the scandalous gaps in our defences have become a byword'.[41]

The need to make rearmament more acceptable led Gaitskell into a major effort to influence Labour Party policy. With the Nazi occupation of Prague in March, the Chamberlainites had at last recognised the menace and would soon have to break every pledge and precedent, and introduce military conscription in peacetime. Labour was likely to oppose that, for the semi-pacifists loathed it and the trade unions suspected it would lead to industrial conscription. Yet its opposition would discredit the Party, which had so long been demanding resistance to Fascism.

Gaitskell and his friends, encouraged by Dalton, did all that a group of political nobodies could do to persuade their seniors to take a more constructive course, suggesting that Labour should propose 'conscription of wealth' in return for accepting 'conscription of manpower'. With Durbin and Jay, he induced the principal leaders of the Opposition to put the idea to the Parliamentary Labour Party, which narrowly turned it down.[42] Meanwhile, throughout 1939 Gaitskell and his friends in XYZ were preparing much more drastic proposals to spread the burden of rearmament more fairly if war did come.

After Munich he ceased to believe that Russia would fight against Hitler, and in August 1939 he was 'among the very few . . . neither surprised nor unduly shocked by the Molotov–Ribbentrop agreement'.[2] Yet even with war inevitable, and all previous hopes submerged in the desperate struggle for survival, he did not feel that his activities had been futile. Twenty years later an old antagonist, Ted Willis of the Labour League of Youth and the Young Communist League, who had seen himself as a leading political spokesman of his own generation, told Gaitskell of his shock, on joining the army, at discovering that no one had ever heard of him. With better judgement, and more awareness that politics plays little part in the lives of ordinary people in ordinary times, Gaitskell was not surprised. But unlike Willis he did not conclude that the activity had just been pointless froth on the surface: 'You didn't waste your time. The generation that went into the Forces was quite different from the generation that went in in 1914 . . . politically *more* conscious and less like sheep.'[7]


Munich was the fourth great event in Gaitskell's early development. The General Strike had committed him to the side of the workers. The shelling of the Vienna flats had given him his lifelong loathing of repression and dictatorship (even in countries calling themselves Socialist). For his own inner security and stability, marriage was the decisive change. Now, over Munich, he advocated a course that to many ordinary people seemed likely to increase the risk of war which, led or misled by their government, they still desperately hoped to avoid. As he wrote to Durbin: 'Democracy certainly involves tolerance . . . but it requires many other things too – especially just now it needs people who have strong convictions and independence and courage to express what they believe without always wondering whether the electorate will like it.'[39] Once again, as in his breach with his family, this emotional and warm-hearted man was in disagreement on a major issue with people who were close to him, and had to choose between his public convictions and his private affections. It was an experience with which he was to become familiar, from which he suffered exceedingly, and through which he would emerge a far more formidable political leader than his friends had ever imagined.

There were already a few signs, as Douglas Jay realised after Dalton assembled his friends in his flat for their gloomy talk after Munich. Returning home in the Underground, Jay said to Gaitskell that, if that was how the saner half of the Labour Party felt, everything looked pretty hopeless:

He replied, with the utmost confidence, that a few of us would stiffen the Labour Party; that the Labour Party and Churchill would stiffen the country; that this country would stiffen France; and that we should then survive until Roosevelt joined in one day . . . it was spoken with such force, clarity and conviction that I was not merely reconvinced of the impossibility of acting on any other assumption, but travelled home astonished that I could have known someone apparently so well for five years without recognizing his extraordinary reserve of underlying strength – 'Will like a dividing spear', as John Strachey aptly quoted from Matthew Arnold after Hugh's death. To me it illuminated, once for all, what the next twenty-five years gradually unfolded to a larger audience.[42]

# 5

# Whitehall at War
# 1939-45

'*These old gentlemen with their optimistic twaddle can never win the war.*'
(HG, March 1940)

'*We've defeated the doctors—now we can smash the Tories!*'
(HG about his illness, 1945)

## The Ministry of Economic Warfare

Gaitskell's wartime role had been settled early, for German-speaking economists were few and in demand, and his old chief Noel Hall was active in recruiting them. In later years, Hugh often told Dora that he regretted having missed serving in the armed forces through being conscripted for Whitehall well before hostilities began; but with his rational outlook, he does not seem to have questioned a decision which so plainly made the best use of his skills. Long afterwards he recalled: 'I was put in a reserved occupation before the war and asked . . . to join the Ministry of Economic Warfare . . . on the very first Monday [I] turned up . . . as one of the founder members.'[1]

In September 1939 everybody expected the war to open with devastating bombing raids on London. Dora took Julia to the cottage at Milland, the first of several successive retreats in the country, which Hugh, visiting on his day off, found very overcrowded and depressing. He himself moved in to 20 Mecklenburgh Square as a paying guest of his old friends Eileen Power and her husband M. M. Postan, who had also been recruited into MEW. At first he feared that as a civil servant he would have to give up South Leeds; and though that proved unnecessary, his links with the constituency were now limited to letters to his agent and very rare visits.

MEW began life in the building of the London School of Economics. There were a few permanent civil servants on its staff, but the vast majority were temporaries from the City, universities or the legal professions. Most were serving for half or less of their previous earnings; but after a month Gaitskell learned that UCL would make his salary up to the full £800. He entered on his Whitehall task with high expectations and a sense of vast relief to be working actively against

Hitler at last.[2] But reality was often frustrating, and at first he found it 'all a bit chaotic', and 'difficult to get used to a subordinate position and all the red tape in matters where one thinks one knows better!'[3] His best language was German, but Noel Hall was in charge of German Intelligence; so Gaitskell was attached to the Neutral Countries section of the Ministry's Intelligence Department with the job of analysing the information about France. This introduction to Whitehall, he wrote later, 'did not seem very sensible to me: firstly because my French was, and still is, very bad; secondly, because I didn't think France was a neutral country'.[4]

After about a week Gaitskell took over responsibility for Belgium and Holland, Germany's neutral neighbours and a channel for her imports. 'Ships bound for neutral ports had first to be brought into our contraband bases and the manifests examined. Then we had to decide what was to be let through and what was to be seized. That was the Ministry's job . . . detective work done with the help of the famous black lists'.[5] At the start of the war the Ministry was also busy negotiating War Trade Agreements with the neutrals, restricting all their supplies to prevent them being shipped to Germany. He would himself have preferred a much tougher approach, rationing the neutrals instead of bargaining with them; and he knew what that might mean: 'I am frankly pessimistic about the war. It isn't going to be easy to blockade Germany properly – which I think is the only way to win the war – without risking a big extension of the war with many of the present neutrals drawn in on one side or the other.'[2] The work was demanding, never finishing before 8 p.m. It left Gaitskell frustrated as well as exhausted. The official historian of the blockade contrasts 'the offensive spirit and sense of innovation which inspired the group of enthusiasts which founded the Ministry of Economic Warfare' with the 'more conservative and cautious elements' from the Foreign Office and elsewhere.[6]

These internal frustrations were somewhat relieved by a palace revolution in December 1939, when Noel Hall became Director of Intelligence and Gaitskell once again stepped into his old chief's shoes, as Director of Intelligence with Enemy Countries. He was still bitterly critical of the Foreign Office people in his own Ministry. 'The temporaries,' he wrote later, found them 'a perpetual irritant to men who were mostly strongly anti-Munich and straining to impose a tough blockade'.[5] For serious interference with the trade of neutral countries might jeopardise their goodwill, which it was the task of diplomats to cultivate. Moreover, the appalling lack of co-ordination among economic Departments was the despair of those who took the war seriously. Gaitskell found a ready outlet for his impotent fury in his old patron Hugh Dalton, now the Labour spokesman on economic warfare, to whom he exploded: 'What can we do about the neutrals? The Foreign Office won't let us bully them and the Treasury won't let us bribe them.'[7] These contacts with Dalton were approved by his own Minister, Ronald Cross, but they were resented in other Departments. It was the first instance of Gaitskell's wartime professional dilemma: how to reconcile his zeal to use every channel to speed up the war effort with the need to keep the goodwill of a powerful routine-minded bureaucratic hierarchy. He managed that problem with surprising success.

Gaitskell partly resisted MEW's natural temptation to overestimate the immediate impact of blockade, which was later to harm its reputation and that of its Minister. In March he explained to Dalton that Germany would suffer less heavily from the blockade in this war than in the last: she could hold out indefinitely, and neither allies nor neutrals would remain convinced for long that we could win. Above all he was alarmed at the slow pace of Whitehall in the phoney war, the lack of urgency, and even the tendency in some high official quarters to conclude that, since the blockade was going badly, it might become necessary to make peace. A coalition government was essential, he told Dalton: these old gentlemen with their 'optimistic twaddle' could not win the war.[8] In the next two months the Norwegian fiasco so deepened his gloom that he feared it would be lost unless we pulled ourselves together. At breakfast on 8 May 1940, he wondered whether any preparations had been made if Hitler went for Holland and Belgium.[9] Two days later he had his answer – and, very soon, his coalition government.

The massive German attack made glaringly obvious the desperate need for new political leadership. On 10 May Winston Churchill became Prime Minister and asked for Dalton as one of his Labour colleagues, offering him the post he sought as Minister of Economic Warfare. Dalton summoned Gaitskell to his flat at midnight and told his young friend that he 'wanted him to be, in fact, a good deal more than a Private Secretary, more like a *Chef de Cabinet* in France. He should be fully in my confidence, and feel free to advise me on all questions, both of policy and persons. This invitation, after a night's reflection, he accepted.'[10]

## *Corridors of Power:* Chef de Cabinet

The appointment seemed to Gaitskell's friends an exhilarating piece of good fortune. He himself saw another side of it, telling a colleague that 'this is not really the job I want, but I feel I have to do it because I have a certain sense of loyalty to Hugh Dalton'.[11] He understood that a civil servant, snatched from the ranks to become the confidant and adviser of a Minister he knew well, might incur the suspicion and dislike of his former colleagues; and that the Minister's personality would not minimise friction either within his own Department or with others.

Hugh Dalton was fifty-two, a large man with hooded eyes, a loud voice, and rather too much vitality. He had done several great services to his party, notably in organising the back-bench revolt against the leadership's policy of voting against arms estimates, and in his lifelong preoccupation with spotting able young men and fostering their careers. Intellectually capable, politically astute but often abrasive, and a voracious empire-builder, he meant to extend the operations of the Ministry of Economic Warfare into adjoining fields cherished by other Departments – the Foreign Office, the War Office, the Ministry of Information. Within his own domain Dalton was determined, as he once put it, 'to divide or to educate, but in any case to rule'. [12] He expected quick, efficient, politically sensitive advice at the most improbable hours, and if it were slow in coming, or if he suspected official obstruction or opposition, his devastating temper would flare in a memorable scene. Gaitskell was now to serve this formidable master as confidential adviser, as buffer against the outside world, and especially as a channel of communication with the officials.

With the Germans in France, cargoes had to be checked not in the Channel as in the past, but in their ports of origin. That could be done effectively only with American consent, fortunately forthcoming. There were many difficulties, but Dalton's total dedication to winning the war overrode any consideration of foreign susceptibilities, humanitarian scruples, administrative routines or party politics, and the Ministry owed a great deal to him.

The prerequisite of such a policy was a reorganisation giving 'less power within the Ministry to the fearful and more to the bold'.[13] The Minister appointed two vigorous temporaries, Lord Drogheda and Noel Hall, as joint directors under the Director-General, Sir Frederick Leith-Ross. The men now running the MEW were kept furiously busy developing the new blockade system. They ate in the office, worked nights and Sundays and slept in bunks in the basement. Politicians, temporaries and career civil servants were thrown constantly into one another's company, soon came to know one another, and developed a strong and cohesive loyalty to the Department's personnel and policies.

Once Dalton had determined the main lines of policy and re-organised the Ministry to implement them, the blockade no longer required much attention from him. Within a month Gaitskell was telling him that he would soon have too little to do, and might take over economic general staff work from his Labour colleague Arthur Greenwood. But Dalton wanted the responsibility for running propaganda and organising subversion in enemy-occupied Europe – a job, he claimed, for a politician of the Left rather than a professional soldier. Gladwyn Jebb became his chief assistant for this work and – with his PPS Wilmot, and Gaitskell – one of the 'three attendant sprites' on whom Dalton relied for confidential advice.

Gaitskell found working for Dalton

exhausting, exhilarating and instructive. He taught me a lot, especially how to write Cabinet papers and draft letters. . . . He used to keep a 'prod list' on his desk so that he could follow up all the things he had started. . . . He had tremendous drive. He enjoyed power and getting things done. He was most impatient with difficulties . . . He could be exceedingly bad-tempered. He was apt to bully and shout at people. He got angry unreasonably when it was not really the fault of the officials. I found an easy way of dealing with this. I just shouted back . . . He liked this sort of encounter and respected people who stood up to him.[14]

Not many did. On another occasion when Dalton was bawling out a whole roomful of his staff, it was Gaitskell who interrupted him: 'Look here, Hugh, you are not to talk to civil servants like that – I won't have it.'[15]

This new self-assurance transformed Gaitskell's personality and astonished people who had known him well at UCL. One of them said:

Toughness, determination and ability shone out then – in that order – which I hadn't experienced before. He struck me then as quite ruthless, that I was seeing the real Hugh for the first time . . . He didn't strike you as being an ordinary Private Secretary but very much more. I never met another one like it in that department or any other. His bearing, the way he spoke, everything – he sloughed off a skin that had been a disguise. . . . But he wasn't unpopular – people admired his ability.[16]

Not for the last time, Gaitskell shouldered wider responsibilities not merely as capably as before, but much more so.

Dalton treated his trusted advisers, after his own peculiar fashion, as personal friends, and occasionally invited them to his rural retreat in Wiltshire. In September 1940, he and Gaitskell returned to London to find that the Ministry had been badly bombed in their absence. Just after the war began Gaitskell had written to Brett that he had 'given up worrying about Air Raids. London is very well defended and besides, I don't think we shall have anything serious for the present.'[3] Now a very different period was beginning, in which raids frequently occurred while the Minister's staff were working at night. His own temporary home was one of the first places in London to suffer. 'I have been having a rather exciting time,' he wrote to George Brett:[17]

The third night of the Blitz . . . they got a direct hit on nos. 30 and 31 Mecklenburgh Square – 10 houses down on our side: they were just rubble when we saw them the following morning. Finally, just to wind things up, they dropped a time bomb . . . the police ordered us out of the house in ten minutes [without even time to dress].

After Mecklenburgh Square was bombed he moved to Devonshire Place with Robin Brook, a banker and Jebb's personal assistant, who became a lifelong friend. All overworked and without their families, they spent little time at home; and Gaitskell struck some of his new associates as rather reserved, disinclined to gossip even about politics, and quite hard to get to know. He was largely cut off both from his family and from the close friends with whom he felt at home. One of these was the gentle and feckless Amyas Ross, who worked in MEW; sadly, he caught pneumonia after a car accident, and was found dead in his freezing, slummy flat.

With the invasion scare of the summer of 1940, Dora and Julia had moved to Jaylands, a house in Worcestershire which Hugh's sister had found. But though the house was 'reasonably comfortable', he found it 'very remote';[17] and he did not much enjoy the local society. Early in 1941 he took a house at Woburn, which he had to visit regularly since it was the headquarters of the propaganda activities for which Dalton now shared responsibility. Dora and Julia now moved there, and Hugh was able to see a little more of them. It was not much. One official who lodged in the house recalls that Hugh appeared only at breakfast (which Dora rose at 6.30 a.m. to provide) because the Minister kept him busy the rest of the day. The lodger was struck by his kindness to the children, and by the strenuous life he was leading: 'he could never have stood that pace without her'.

Woburn, wrote Dalton, was 'an active outpost in the Whitehall war'.[18] It was the headquarters for part of the 'Ministry of Ungentlemanly Warfare',[19] the second, clandestine area of responsibility which that restless Minister had now eagerly annexed. At first the Special

Operations Executive (SOE) had three branches. Gaitskell's main task was building up and dealing with SO1, which after some bitter political battles was to be absorbed into the Political Warfare Executive.

SO1 was controlled from London, and carried on secret propaganda to enemy and enemy-occupied countries from its country headquarters at Woburn. It was troubled by a series of distinct but overlapping conflicts. There were differences about the content of propaganda between Left and Right; personal rivalries among the propagandists, among the bureaucrats and between the two groups; and clashes between the staff and the Minister. There was departmental friction between traditional Whitehall Ministries and new wartime outfits; between the Foreign Office, which was 'slow to realise the importance of broadcasting', and the Woburn enthusiasts with their 'tendency to try to make foreign policy by means of propaganda';[20] and above all between MEW and the Ministry of Information, which had been left in charge of open propaganda. As a Labour Minister in a predominantly Conservative coalition, Dalton's position was weak, especially after July 1941 when Churchill made his own crony, Brendan Bracken, Minister of Information; and Dalton's abrasive personality did not win the loyalty of his senior officials.

Dalton wrote later: 'I owed much, in handling the many diverse and highly individual characters in SO1, to Hugh Gaitskell.'[18] Among them were Gaitskell's cousin George Martelli and his old schoolfellow Richard Crossman, whom he characterised to Dalton as 'brilliantly able, immensely energetic, and overwhelmingly ambitious . . . completely loyal, for the time being, to any Chief who he thinks will aid his ambition'.[21] Gaitskell's old Vienna acquaintance Kim Philby used to consult him, over sausages and mash in a Berkeley Square pub, about the political content of their propaganda; Philby felt that Gaitskell and Dalton would have liked to be more revolutionary, but were constrained by the Foreign Office. The personal assistant was kept busy smoothing over several internal rows: there was a bitter one in the summer of 1941 between SO1 and SO2 over a Middle Eastern appointment, and another between Woburn itself and the Minister's Whitehall entourage.

Friction between Ministers became worse when Bracken set out aggressively to regain the ground abandoned by his predecessor; SOE staff were not even allowed to talk to those from his Ministry. Dalton appealed for support to his party leader, writing to Attlee:

I am . . . faced by a combination of two Conservative Ministers and three principal officials, all of whom are anxious to reduce my influence over the new PWE to a minimum . . . There is a set being made in certain influential quarters, some political and some official, against Labour Ministers.[22]

This was not merely self-serving, for even after he knew he was to leave MEW, Dalton urged Attlee to see that SOE went to a man of the Left, like Cripps. But he could not threaten to resign over an obscure issue on which he would not carry conviction outside. At Christmas 1941 one of Dalton's staff presented his master with a book called *How to Get Rid of Bracken*, on which Dalton commented: 'the trouble is that it takes seven years, and then the bloody stuff may grow again'.[23] A month later the Prime Minister, bored by the constant rows, promoted Dalton to a new office.

The constant friction and manoeuvring between Ministers came as a shock to Gaitskell, who one day said innocently to Dalton: 'I had no idea that it would be all like this.'[24] But he loyally served his master's interests without becoming subservient to his whims. To one official, he was an indispensable check on the Minister's tendency to approve any wild scheme in order to win popularity among the staff. Gaitskell was influential partly because he alone in MEW dealt with Dalton's regular as well as clandestine activities. Always a hardliner on blockade policy, he argued strongly that concessions would certainly benefit the Germans rather than the captive nations; Churchill and the Cabinet warmly agreed. But Dalton was still complaining two months later of the need 'to be constantly vigilant . . . If the Foreign Office had had their way, the blockade by now would be leaking like a sieve'.[22] Yet, unlike many senior men at MEW, Gaitskell kept good enough relations with the Foreign Office for one of its officials whom he saw frequently to call him 'a perfect Private Secretary to a Minister'.

A *chef de cabinet* always fits uneasily into Whitehall, and 'Big Hugh's' personality did not help. But Gaitskell succeeded in interpreting the Minister to his officials, and vice versa, without arousing resentment. among his seniors against a junior suddenly thrust into a position of power. With new arrangements at Woburn, however, Gaitskell became 'rather bored' with a job he had never sought;[1] and hoped to move to an expanding Department active in the war effort.

In February 1942, Dalton's fortunes suddenly changed. Gaitskell had just been invited to become deputy to Leith-Ross to plan post-war supplies and food relief – as the second man in what became the British section of UNRRA. He went down to his mother's cottage at Milland to write out his resignation:

The telephone rang. Dalton wished to see me urgently. I saw him in London. He told me he was going to the Board of Trade and urged me to go with him. I told him I was about to resign.

It was a Sunday. We talked very late and drank a lot of whisky. Dalton said I could go as his 'personal assistant'.

Early in the morning I got up and went from the basement in the Ministry and wrote a note to Dalton, setting out my conditions: 1) the UNRRA job remained open for three months. 2) I was to go as personal assistant. 3) No more late nights with Dalton. He accepted my conditions.[25]

## *The Coal Scuttle*

The Board of Trade was the custodian of all the economic functions of the state that belonged to nobody in particular, the most sprawling and impenetrable tract of the Whitehall jungle. Gaitskell's first task was to map the territory and introduce the new President to the leading fauna in two very candid memoranda on the Board of Trade and the Mines Department, its subordinate Ministry.[26]

The President, if he is to be successful, *must* himself be prepared to go into the burning issues, partly because many of these are political, e.g. should tobacco rationing be introduced? Can we ration fuel? He will be met with excuses for inaction from so called experts, often really vested interests, and this opposition will have to be broken down. Moreover, not only must the President be in a position to judge the practicability of particular schemes for reducing consumption, concentrating industry, but he must also push them through if he approves and then keep an eye on the administration, so long as there is any danger of it going wrong.

The main memorandum was scathing about the leading officials. One or two were characterised as 'very able and energetic', but most were dismissed in such terms as: 'pleasant weak character: not much good'; or 'described as "wet" No. 1 in the Government Service'; or even 'One of the real enemies of the war effort'. The memorandum on the Mines Department was in similar vein, but called the statistician:

extraordinarily able . . . he is only twenty-six, or thereabouts, and is one of the most brilliant younger people about . . . he has revolutionised the coal statistics. The great thing about him is that he understands what statistics are administratively important and interesting. We must on no account surrender him either to the Army or to any other department.

His name was James Harold Wilson.

Over coal, party and class antagonisms still went deep; and though Labour was often defending the national interest, the Conservatives had an overwhelming majority at Westminster and their party leader in

Downing Steet. Twenty years of bitter strife and mismanagement were now taking their toll. Having won in 1926, the owners had imposed longer hours and lower wages, while British coal-mining became increasingly technically obsolescent. They resisted outside intervention, and after thirty months of war had made no serious attempt to improve efficiency.

This inefficient, undermanned industry, with its ageing and discontented labour force unable to produce enough coal, seemed ripe at last for reorganisation; meanwhile only rationing could ensure that limited supplies were fairly distributed. Every Minister on the Lord President's Committee accepted the first, and all but one the second. But the mineowners still hoped to avoid reorganisation and many Conservative MPs detested rationing; both urged the recall of miners from the forces instead. The Ministers accepted that too. Then all three proposals met a major obstacle: the Prime Minister. Alone, he successfully opposed any release of fighting soldiers. Aided by his party, he blocked rationing. Dalton eventually sacrificed that to achieve reorganisation; but though the owners lost some of their power to obstruct, Churchill absolutely vetoed nationalisation.

At several stages of Gaitskell's political life the miners played a crucial role. They had impelled him to join the Labour Movement in 1926; later on he made his reputation handling their problems as Minister of Fuel and Power, and he enjoyed their steady support both before and after he became leader of the Labour Party. It was as Hugh Dalton's assistant in 1942 that he made his first contacts with their leaders, and had his official introduction to their turbulent industry.

His first memorandum to Dalton set out the issues, including:

Problem of rationing. It must be done for all fuel, and there is a conflict of views. Opinion in the Board of Trade has been against, no doubt influenced by vested interest. Outside opinion in Whitehall is unanimously in favour. Can you ration fuel? This is the biggest question you will have to face, and you will have to go into it in great detail yourself.

Even more urgently, Gaitskell warned that the 'very grave' manpower situation needed the instant attention of the Lord President's Committee. Enough men were found from industry and the non-field forces to postpone that crisis, which in the end was unsatisfactorily met by training unskilled and unwilling conscripts (nicknamed 'Bevin boys'). Meanwhile, with labour short and stocks inadequate, Dalton and Gaitskell for three months concentrated exclusively on two problems: rationing fuel, and reorganising coal production to improve efficiency and regain the miners' confidence.

Already the miners' leaders 'regarded Hugh Gaitskell as an old friend and comrade. They always liked him to be present when we met'. Soon the mineowners came to ask for more money, and for the first time he met face-to-face the men whose conduct had so outraged him sixteen years before; 'never', he said, had he 'seen such a collection of hard-faced twisters', and he called their leader 'a pure Galsworthy type'.[27] In the losing battle for fuel rationing Gaitskell played a central role. He suggested using Sir William Beveridge, who devised a complex but (in Dalton's view) 'very clever and perfect plan'; his amendments helped make it 'a beautifully simple scheme'; and he, with Beveridge, remained its staunchest defender.[28]

It needed defending, for Gaitskell warned his master that 'through the press the vested interests are working like tigers against fuel rationing', and Dalton observed 'that the coal-owners are spending a lot of money trying to get rid of me!'[28] A decade later the official historian explained the storm as

the opposition of industrial and class interests – of all those who felt that the ration would be inconvenient . . . Fairly heavy sacrifices were being demanded of the middle classes and the larger houses . . . the rationing plan became a sort of unacknowledged test of the relative strength of parties and interests within the Coalition Government and in Parliament.[29]

It gave the Conservatives their greatest political victory of the war. The Left blamed the Labour Ministers for not arousing Labour back-benchers and the movement outside. But Dalton and Gaitskell, trying to do so through Brett, found the movement outside entirely sluggish. Nevertheless, Gaitskell was strongly against any concession. But the more experienced Dalton doubted if he could beat the big battalions of the majority party, backed by a Prime Minister who loathed all rationing schemes and had accepted them even for food and clothes only with the utmost reluctance. On 12 May he had 'a bathroom brain-wave!' Any Cabinet crisis on coal should focus on the whole problem, including reorganisation, where all the Labour Ministers would have to stand together.

This new conflict, probably the first in which Gaitskell and Aneurin Bevan were active on opposing sides, provided another instructive lesson in the realities of political power. Dalton and Ernest Bevin felt 'sure that if the owners lost control of the pits now, they would never get it back'. They were better prophets than Bevan, who predicted that if the pits were not nationalised in war, they never would be in peace.[30] When the compromise was accepted, Dalton commented: 'The miners' leadership . . . have learned the lesson that their traditional policy of "all or nowt" always ends in nowt.'[31]

Will Lawther told the next party conference after a year's experience of the compromise that Bevin and Dalton had done more for the mining industry than all their predecessors. But Labour critics like Bevan complained that if Labour Ministers had shown more 'energy', and Labour MPs acted 'more robustly', they could easily have won both the fuel-rationing and the reorganisation battles. That was soon disproved. In October 1943 Gwilym Lloyd George, the Liberal Minister now responsible for the mines, was backed by every one of his Regional Controllers when he told the War Cabinet that 'dual control' was working badly, and that the state should become the owner of the mines as long as the war continued. But Winston Churchill flatly refused to contemplate nationalisation, and explicitly threatened a general election on it.

No one took up the challenge. For once in a coal debate, Aneurin Bevan was silent. During the war, nationalisation of the mines was never again an issue. It was not robustness or energy that Dalton had lacked, but a sufficient power base. A politician concerned with achievement rather than gestures needed parliamentary and public support which in 1942–3 were not available for domestic disputes, and no robust and energetic agitation could replace the missing parliamentary majority. Gaitskell's experience under Dalton drove those lessons firmly home.

## Board of Trade Civil Servant

In June Dalton relinquished responsibility for coal, and in August the Permanent Secretary proposed that Gaitskell should take over a regular administrative post. Dalton tried instead to keep him as personal assistant for post-war reconstruction, but this time – to the Minister's fury – Gaitskell was adamant.[32]

Under G. L. Watkinson, the official in the Department whom he most respected, Gaitskell became responsible for 'half a dozen of the dirtiest jobs in the office . . . not unimportant but politically unexciting':[32] price control, retail trade, the film industry and, for a brief period, post-war reconstruction. Though the division's main activity was price control, it was by now a reasonably routine operation; so at first his main preoccupation was the retail trade. Dalton was sensitive to political dangers after his buffeting over fuel, and began a new policy of deliberate discrimination in favour of small traders. Gaitskell was actively involved, holding 'ticklish conferences' with the interests, being sent to 'nobble the National Chamber of Trade', and ingeniously selling Dalton's policies to the multiple stores which would suffer from them.[33] But again politics had triumphed over economic efficiency, for the retail trades kept too much labour; it was the biggest failure of the wartime Board of Trade.

With his departure from Dalton's private office, Gaitskell – in the words of a close friend –

disappeared as it were into a tunnel of steady, efficient, laborious administration . . . working on the same floor of the same building, I seemed to see less of him than at any time in the previous ten years or next fifteen . . . we were all so desperately busy with our own responsibilities in working hours, and with fire-watching and flying bombs out of them.[34]

At Easter 1943 Gaitskell agreed to work out schemes for his Minister to 'stimulate selected sectors of the Home Front.'[33] He was to find it a frustrating experience:

If you are interested in ideas and plans alone, it's quite fun, but of course it's far harder to get any decisions & when it comes to long run issues almost impossible. So one is apt to be very discouraged. One of the alarming things I notice is the very great gap between what I believe is the popular attitude to postwar – which is now much more socialistic & the attitude of the business men we have to deal with which is for the most part reactionary & capitalistic . . . there is such a very real struggle for industrial *power* . . . the Director class . . . are really much less concerned with maximising profits than with just exercising arbitrary power. They regard shareholders as a bore . . . and . . . the state as a menace. *They* want to be allowed to decide for themselves what is in the public interest.[35]

Businessmen were not the only opponents. Gaitskell represented the Board of Trade in talks on full employment in May 1944, and profoundly shocked the orthodox Treasury spokesman, Sir Wilfred Eady.[36] (The feeling was mutual, and in 1945 Gaitskell, at his first encounter with Dalton as Chancellor, warned him against Eady.) Gaitskell was also active over location of industry policies, and over anti-monopoly policy, where his draft working paper was compared to 'a tract on the drink trade written by a couple of teetotallers'.[37] In 1948, as a result of these discussions, the Monopolies Commission was set up; the talks also opened a long campaign by Dalton and Gaitskell to interest the Labour Party in consumer problems, especially resale price maintenance.

Of all his administrative tasks, Gaitskell was most fascinated by the film industry, with its exotic personalities, its crazy economics – for films tended to make either a loss or a huge profit – and its tangled problem of resisting American cultural domination without falling into insularity, or inefficiency, or British monopoly control. Gaitskell wrote Dalton's briefs and conducted 'quite tough bargaining' with the two principal interests. Less serious contacts included complimentary invitations to premières and private showings, dinners with Rank or Korda, and agreeable lunches with Vivien Leigh and Ingrid Bergman. Gaitskell made many lasting friends in the film world, and when he entered the House, Rank and Korda invited him to become vice-president and economic adviser of the British Film Producers' Association. He could not give enough time to justify a stipend, but he continued as an honorary vice-president until he joined the Government.

At the Board of Trade Gaitskell had at first as little family life as ever. The lease of the Woburn house ran out in February 1942, and he then arranged for Dora to go to stay with his mother at Milland for a few months. On 23 July 1942 his second daughter Cressida was born in a nearby nursing home, and they returned to their own cottage, to Hugh's delight. But he saw them only at weekends and the separation became increasingly galling, while the cottage was very cramped when he came. In March 1943, therefore, Dora and the children moved back to London. The Gaitskells rented the lower floors of 21 Well Walk, with another family living upstairs in the 'huge 1880 baronial house in Hampstead'.[35] The rooms were very cold, the ceilings very high, and the house very run-down. But the family was reunited and Hugh was now able to see more of them than before.

In January 1944 he wrote happily to Brett that Cressida was 'getting to the nicest age of all – which I put, so far, at 18 months to 3. Julie is as sweet as ever'. Less happily, he recorded 'a good deal of talk about the secret weapon and the bombardment of London from the French coast, but beyond making arrangements to send the family away if it ever starts and clearing the cellar, we are not taking it too seriously'.[38] Luckily, the children were away during a heavy raid a month later, which caused several local fires, and again at the end of the year when a flying bomb landed at the end of their road and smashed most of their windows.

Looking forward to the return of peace, he kept up his close relations with Dalton – subtly changing as Gaitskell acquired some of the administrator's attitudes towards politicians. When Gladwyn Jebb told

Dalton that Foreign Office officials 'spend all their time slaving away and then ministers either do nothing or do it all wrong', Gaitskell added 'that all civil servants in *all* Departments . . . often feel like this!'[39] Like many wartime academic recruits to Whitehall, he was happier there than as a don; and he found executive work, unlike Dalton's private office, 'wholly absorbing and satisfying'.[34] Cool, intelligent and rational in his appraisal of issues, good-tempered and skilful at managing men, to some old friends he seemed to have found his true *métier*.

Some regular civil servants had more doubts. Sir Herbert Andrew, then his subordinate and later a Permanent Secretary, felt that Gaitskell was too inclined to get into excessive detail and, as head of a Department, might not have reserved himself sufficiently for the broader issues: that criticism we shall meet again. But Watkinson, Gaitskell's immediate superior, whom he thought the ablest and most progressive senior man in the Board of Trade, had only praise for his work. He was effective and successful in dealing with other Departments, and the industry with which he had most to do – the film trade – was eager to secure his services after the war was over.

He was still impatient with the ponderous pace of Whitehall, which 'gives one the feeling of swimming in treacle';[40] and if the thought of an administrative career seriously crossed his mind, he did not entertain it for long. He had little time to think about the future, but assumed that he would return to UCL, who offered him a chair and allowed him to wait until the election before deciding. Early in 1945 he walked round Milland with a friend 'weighing the attractions of academic life and the occupational hazards of politics'.[41] He also had a renewed offer from Leith-Ross of a senior post with UNRRA, the international relief organisation. But that die had been cast in February 1942, when Dalton persuaded him to remain in the political race.

## South Leeds: Elected from a Sick-bed

While normal political activity was suspended during the war, Gaitskell did his limited best to keep up his links with South Leeds. But twice the constituency nearly lost him altogether: at the very beginning of the war, when he entered the Civil Service, and at the very end, when he was incapacitated at the time of the 1945 election.

At the outbreak of war, Gaitskell was worried that his Civil Service post would oblige him to withdraw. On 8 September 1939 he wrote to his agent that he could not make speeches, or do much as a candidate. But 'I do *not* want to sever all connection with S. Leeds'.[3] Evidently the executive committee were eager to keep him, and a week later Gaitskell wrote again appreciating their support. During 1941 one little local difficulty was cleared up at last when, responding to mounting criticism of the absentee MP, the Labour Party National Executive belatedly intervened and Charleton agreed to resume constituency activities. But two years later Gaitskell was still lamenting to Brett: 'There appears to me to be no prospect that he will resign.'[42] However, by the beginning of 1945 Gaitskell's parliamentary prospects seemed excellent: a safe Labour seat, a loyal constituency party with sound finances and its local squabbles settled, and a general election due before long. Then, at almost the last moment, the prize was nearly snatched from him by the only serious illness of his working life.

At the Board of Trade, as at the MEW, Gaitskell had continued 'grossly overtiring himself'. Political friends visiting Leeds told Brett so;[43] and Gaitskell referred to the load in several letters. Then, when Dora came to London one day in early March 1945, they went to the Gargoyle Club in Soho for their first evening's dancing for years. Hugh felt ill at the club, had a bad night and the next morning suffered a pain in his chest. The specialist decided that he had suffered a minor coronary thrombosis. He was promptly packed off for three weeks in bed with complete rest – he was not to write letters or even shave himself – to be followed by two more months away from work. Dora wrote to Brett on his behalf: 'one of the blood vessels supplying my heart is not functioning properly. . . . [it] happens quite often to older men but is unusual in someone of my age. I imagine it is simply the result of five years overwork and strain.' The doctors could not promise future immunity, only that the two months' rest would improve his chances. They discouraged him from fighting the election,

though not to the extent of positively forbidding me . . . To give up now would be a bitter blow and not only to me but to you as well who have helped me so much . . . I realise . . . that if I have to drop out, the Party must be given time to find someone to take my place, but I think it is reasonable to let me have just a week or two and perhaps more if the war does not go too fast.[44]

Brett's reply recalled that, after his own more serious coronary, 'my doctors would have had me pack up everything – they have an idea that politicians foam at the mouth & are always in a state of turmoil.' Gaitskell was now so popular with the local party workers that Brett 'was ready, if necessary, to fight the election without the candidate being there'. He welcomed Dora's suggestion of consulting Lord

Horder, who was experienced in assessing the strain of political activity.

On 11 May the party executive voted without dissent or abstentions to send a message of sympathy and continued support in the election 'if he can come to the constituency even although he can take no physical part'.[44]

Horder examined Gaitskell at Milland on 22 May, and reported that, given three months' limitation of effort, the patient could resume political activities. But he must stay away from South Leeds until the last fortnight, and appear only twice daily, and only once at an indoor public meeting. Gaitskell sent these terms to Brett on a postcard, and then – finding it still a strain to walk or even talk – went off to Sandown in the Isle of Wight for a short holiday. On 27 May the General Management Committee unanimously agreed to fight with Gaitskell even if he could not participate at all. That decision, wrote Brett, 'has never been questioned by anybody'. He added, 'we shall take great care of you & fight like tigers to win the seat'; and the candidate replied: 'We've defeated the doctors – now we can smash the Tories!'[44]

Gaitskell remained in the south for two more weeks, receiving almost daily letters from his agent and sending almost as many back. He wrote his election address in a couple of days, and urged: '*don't* worry too much about expense. I feel it will be a very close fight in S. Leeds.'[44] Cheating the doctors slightly, Gaitskell moved north nearly three weeks before the poll, but kept to Horder's conditions by staying outside the constituency. Brett had promised not to make the candidate work, but wanted him present at Attlee's two meetings on the 16th, and generally available to encourage the party activists. Gaitskell moved into South Leeds ten days before polling day and went round with a loudspeaker in the afternoons, appearing briefly before his one audience a night; he spoke for five minutes at the big rally in Leeds Town Hall before being whisked off by his protective supporters 'to another meeting'.[45] Fortunately it was a sedate campaign and he faced virtually no heckling.

His Conservative opponent was a Huddersfield solicitor, Brigadier A. M. Ramsden, who had fought in the First World War and held an anti-aircraft command in the Midlands in the Second; Brett described him as 'a decent sort.. . . I don't think he is really political'.[44] There was no animosity in his campaign, and he became a great admirer. Just in time for inclusion in his election address, Gaitskell was awarded the CBE for his wartime services, and his supporters underlined this in meetings, somewhat to his embarrassment.

Mild though the campaign in South Leeds had been, the sick man found it a very heavy strain. 'I was thoroughly alarmed in the last few days,' wrote Brett, 'but you came through splendidly.' When he retired to his mother's house at Milland a few days later, the pain came back, he had to return to bed under sedation for several days, and he feared he might need an operation. His wife, too, had been having a very difficult time, and when he returned to Hampstead at the end of the month, conditions were far from easy: 'We are in rather a mess here – everything very dirty and untidy. No help in sight. Dora very tired with a bad cold and the children coming back on Tuesday!'[46] But by then he knew he was Member of Parliament for South Leeds.

In 1945, because of the armed forces' ballots from overseas, the votes were not counted for three weeks after polling day. Gaitskell was now reasonably confident: 'My sober judgment is that after counting in the Forces we might get a majority of 5,000 which is quite good enough for me!' In fact his majority was twice that, with a swing almost identical to that in Leeds as a whole.

| Hugh Gaitskell (Lab.) | 17,899 | 1935: | Lab. | 15,223 |
| Max Ramsden (Cons.) | 7,497 | | Cons. | 14,207 |
| William Barford (Lib.) | 3,933 | | Ind. | 3,642 |
| Majority | 10,402 | | | 1,016 |

Ten days earlier he had written to thank George Brett:

Good advice, kindness, sympathy, encouragement – all have been showered upon me. And at the end, I know quite well it was *you* who were taking the really serious risks . . . you must now leave this particular ship to make its own way – having so to speak piloted it down the river to the open sea.[46]

# PART TWO

# Government and Shadow Cabinet

*'Such wonderful talent . . . such a difficult team worker'*
(HG on Aneurin Bevan, 1951)
*'He's nothing, nothing, nothing . . . The Party will sweep him away'*
(Bevan on HG, 1950 and 1951)
*'Achieving socialist goals under democratic conditions – the only thing worth talking about'*
(HG, 1958)

# 6

# The Ministry of Fuel
# and Power 1946–50

*'The most overworked man in Britain'*
(Herbert Morrison on HG, 1948)

## Back-bencher and Under-Secretary

Immense hopes were placed in the Labour Government which came to power in July 1945. The war had just ended in Europe, and was about to end in the Far East. Like most wars it had radicalised popular expectations, and distressed areas, dole queues and glaring social inequalities now seemed intolerable. The Conservatives suffered from this mood. Industry had been converted far more thoroughly to war production in Britain than in Germany or the United States, and could be reconverted only gradually. Besides losing her old markets, Britain had sold off foreign assets and incurred debts; so that exports paid for only a quarter of her imports, and investment income for only 2 per cent (as against 22 per cent before the war). To pay her way abroad, Britain had now to increase exports by two-thirds: a most ambitious target, achieved in only five years. To keep working during this dramatic recovery, Britain had expected that the United States would temporarily continue Lend-Lease supplies. But with the end of the war these were cut off almost literally overnight, so that Britain depended for her basic needs on hard and humiliating negotiations with a demanding American Administration, constrained by a hostile Congress. In those daunting circumstances, keen supporters expected the first majority Labour Government to carry out a domestic revolution, while Conservative opponents blamed it for austerities they knew to be inevitable. But by 1945 the Labour Party had much governmental experience and a new political self-confidence, and was singularly free from its inveterate factionalism.

In 1945 Gaitskell shared and expressed the euphoria. After the results were declared he participated in a motorcade round Leeds, and toured his constituency to thank his helpers. Next day he and Dora lunched with his friendly Conservative opponent, and he then returned to London for the first meeting of the new Labour MPs at the Beaver

Hall, commenting sadly on Morrison's 'frantic and rather absurd efforts to wrest the Party leadership away for himself . . . Ambition driving the most intelligent people mad as usual, I suppose'.[1] Two days later he attended Dalton's 'young victors' dinner at St Ermin's Hotel, where the discussion made him feel comparatively elderly and experienced. His own contribution stressed the need to deal with housing by giving skilled building workers higher priority in demobilisation; to meet any obstruction from the House of Lords by a well-timed general election; and to subsidise coal prices, as well as food and clothing, in order to permit the raising of miners' wages. Gaitskell was seriously considered for a parliamentary secretaryship to Cripps at the Board of Trade; but Horder advised him not to take office as yet.

When Parliament met, Gaitskell gave his maiden speech on the finance day, 21 August 1945, with hardly a Tory present: the only speech he ever declaimed beforehand to his wife. 'It went off well – as indeed it should have done in view of the immense amount of trouble I took in preparing it.'[1] Some of his colleagues later claimed to have seen him from that moment as a future leader of the Party.

Gaitskell no longer had the cottage at Milland which – to Dora's later regret – he had sold in July (characteristically refusing to maximise his profit – it fetched £2,400, and was resold two years later for £6,000). When the House adjourned he took the girls off for a holiday with the Durbins at their Cornish farmhouse, where the two new MPs spent hours writing in longhand to constituents, mostly about demobilisation troubles. In the new session Gaitskell, still careful about his health, played no conspicuous part. He sat on a Select Committee which proposed reforming parliamentary procedure by sending much more legislation to committees. His parliamentary commentaries in the *Leeds Weekly Citizen* condemned the Opposition for confusion, frivolity, and ignorance of the lives of ordinary people; singled out for particular praise three Labour Ministers – Shawcross, Cripps and Aneurin Bevan; and predicted a 'big future' for one back-bencher, Jim Callaghan. He displayed his familiar concern for consumers (over agricultural policy) and regretted Bevan's decision to let National Health Service doctors take private patients. Wisely, he himself spoke seldom, and only on subjects with which he was familiar: the administrative difficulties of price controls, and the bill nationalising the Bank of England which he had helped to draft, first in XYZ and then on the Select Committee. He defended the Government against the first Conservative censure motion, and also Dalton's Budget, urging 'a really hard blow at inheritance for the sake of social justice', and warning that pay-as-you-earn income tax might be dangerously damaging to the production drive. He was to return to both themes later.

He had nearly become Attlee's PPS in February 1946, and was being tipped for promotion in the press: he spent less than a year altogether on the back benches. Later, that was to prove a handicap in opposition and as leader, since his political experience was unlike that of nearly all his followers. But no such thoughts crossed his mind at the time, for he had decided early on to accept anything offered, however unattractive. A vacancy arose in May 1946, just after his fortieth birthday, for a Parliamentary Secretary at the Ministry of Fuel and Power. It was a crucial Department both economically – since Britain's industrial recovery depended overwhelmingly on the revival of coal production – and politically, because it was responsible for three of the first four industries to be nationalised. That strategic position guaranteed difficulties, and opportunities, to the Ministers responsible for it.

Gaitskell had short and undramatic interviews with the Prime Minister and Chief Whip, and then an unpromising telephone conversation with his new chief, Emanuel Shinwell, a veteran who had joined the ILP in 1903, before there was a Parliamentary Labour Party, and had entered the House with the Clydeside rebels in 1922. He had been Minister of Mines in 1929, later changing from the Prime Minister's leading admirer to the bitter critic who captured MacDonald's own seat at Seaham in 1935. Gaitskell had known him slightly since 1937 (through serving on a Labour Party committee on Empire trade, which he chaired) and thought him 'ravaged by suspicion'.[2] Shinwell had never trusted anyone, and was not about to start with the new young middle-class Labour MPs.

Other circumstances, too, were unpropitious. The Prime Minister was deliberately keeping the young Labour intellectuals out of the obvious economic and financial slots, and sending them to 'learn the facts of life' in dealing with the trade unions: a policy which irritated the miners, an important section of the Parliamentary Labour Party (PLP): 'I learnt later that a deputation had even gone to the Chief Whip about it. But it got nowhere, and fortunately I did not know what was happening'.[2] Finally, Shinwell heard Gaitskell's name before Attlee proposed it, when Hugh Dalton (whom he cordially loathed) boomed confidentially in a railway carriage full of northern MPs that Fuel and Power was at last to receive an urgently needed ministerial reinforcement.

Gaitskell's first weekend was busy, for the next three parliamentary days were devoted to the report stage of the coal nationalisation bill on which, he wrote later:

I . . . asked Shinwell to let me take some of the amendments. He agreed. I chose a few fairly simple but controversial ones and made, on the first, a successful maiden speech. This was quite easy as I was well briefed and the questions were not technical. But everybody thought it remarkable to be able to do well at such short notice![2]

A week later he wound up the third reading debate with 'a real Parliamentary triumph . . . that brought him congratulations from all the veterans'.[3]

Once his parliamentary baptism of fire was over, he soon discovered how awkward was the Parliamentary Secretary's position. He 'usually feels himself excluded from the important decisions . . . the Minister assumes the P.S. knows nothing about anything'.[4] In Fuel and Power the Parliamentary Secretary traditionally took charge of health and safety, and dealt with most parliamentary correspondence. Gaitskell fought long battles with civil servants, insisting that MPs needed replies to forward direct to their constituents, couched in human terms and not in bureaucratic jargon. He made six speeches in the House, one winding up on the Coal Bill, but most quite unimportant. Outside Westminster, he occasionally spoke beyond his departmental brief; housing was his main constituency problem, and like the Minister responsible, Aneurin Bevan, he wanted new houses built for durability and quality, not just cheapness. He visited many pits, talking to the workers and Coal Board staff. When speaking on the coal industry, he did not spare the old management, and defended the miners against 'white-collar snobbery'. For an able man who felt underemployed, it was a frustrating period. Then suddenly the humdrum life of the Ministry of Fuel and Power erupted into a great crisis, when the power stations were shut down for lack of coal, industry was halted, and 2 million men were abruptly thrown out of work.

For five winters coal stocks had been precariously low, and with the end of the war the demand for coal soared just as the reluctant miners were hoping to escape from the pits. Attlee and Morrison had been worried for many months. But Shinwell's ebullient temperament made him overconfident that his miner friends would respond to his exhortations, and predisposed to accept the optimistic advice coming from a senior official. Six months before the great shut-down he rashly said in public that everyone was expecting a fuel crisis except the Minister of Fuel and Power.

Gaitskell was put in an acutely embarrassing position. He had confidence in the advisers – Douglas Jay and James Meade – whose forecasts had so alarmed Attlee. But Shinwell mistrusted him both as a Wykehamist intellectual and as a protégé of the detested Dalton. He felt it would be improper and disloyal to gossip against Shinwell with political colleagues outside the Department, or to contradict the Minister in the weekly departmental meetings. Nor did his superior welcome private advice. Gaitskell wrote unhappily:

As an administrator, however, S. is hardly a starter. He has no conception at all of either organisation or planning or following up. Everything is done by fits and starts, and on impulse. The best you can say is that he contributes at intervals a kind of rugged force and drive which stimulates the officials . . . He will always try and evade an unpopular decision, procrastinate, find a way round, etc. Of course there often is a case on political grounds for this. But S.'s hesitations go beyond natural prudence and amount to sheer weakness and moral cowardice.[2]

On 3 January 1947 the Minister belatedly warned his colleagues of the risk of a breakdown of electricity supplies, after Gaitskell reported, on returning from Manchester, that the situation was far worse than had been thought. Then on 30 January came the worst snow blizzard for fifty years, inaugurating the worst winter weather for a century. Transport was blocked, the inadequate stocks soon exhausted. Yet the worried Cabinet was so little informed that on Thursday 6 February Dalton noted: 'coal and electricity supplies are in a pretty poor way. It will be a great relief to get through *March*.'[5] On the very next day, in a minor debate of the kind usually arranged for a Friday, Shinwell told an astonished House of Commons of the great shut-down:

Today, at this morning's Cabinet, [Shinwell] suddenly asks for permission to tell the House of Commons this afternoon that all electricity must be cut off from industry in London, South-East England, the Midlands and the North-West, and from all domestic consumers between 9 and 12 and 2 and 4 each day. This is a complete thunder clap, following on the usual rather hopeful tales we have had from this man during the past week.[5]

London's power stations were so short of coal that, unless it could be shipped in within three days, the Ministry feared that sewerage and water supplies would break down and the capital might have to be evacuated.

During the fuel crisis 'Gaitskell really emerged as a decisive force in the Department'.[6] He was an experienced administrator when urgent administrative decisions were desperately needed. He and the

Permanent Secretary (Shinwell played no part) spent all the first weekend drafting instructions for the 580 electricity undertakings when they reopened on the Monday. Attlee made him chairman of a committee of officials from eleven Departments, which met from 2 to 6 p.m. daily – including Sundays – for three weeks to apply these restrictions; all Permanent Secretaries had its minutes on arriving for work next morning. It decided which industries were essential, how much non-industrial users could have, and how the restrictions could gradually be relaxed. The secretary of the committee remembers no appeals against Gaitskell's decisions, but thought them unnecessary because he took such trouble to meet departmental views and revise burdensome decisions as soon as possible. Wigg, Shinwell's defender and no friend of Gaitskell, pays warm tribute to the Parliamentary Secretary's role in the crisis.

Gaitskell recorded later that:

the P.M. during and after the Fuel Crisis (and perhaps before) did not conceal his distaste for E.S. . . . criticising and questioning everything he said . . . through the Cabinet Fuel Committee, where these scenes used to occur, the Office of Minister of F. & P. was virtually put in commission.[2]

This Cabinet Committee under Attlee himself allocated the available coal to transport, electricity, and other major categories of users. Within 'general industry', it was assigned by a Fuel Allocations Committee, again composed of departmental officials and chaired by Gaitskell, who sent its minutes direct to the Prime Minister. Though its work soon diminished as the weather improved and stocks recovered, here too his chairmanship impressed both the officials and his political seniors.

On 1 January Gaitskell had become the first ministerial chairman of yet a third committee of departmental civil servants, again reporting direct to the Cabinet. This was an upgraded version of the wartime Materials Committee of officials, which was still meeting quarterly to allocate supplies of raw materials like steel, timber, paper, cotton and tin plate. Its new secretary wrote later that Gaitskell 'was the first and best of my chairmen'; his verdict was accepted every time, even by powerful figures like Aneurin Bevan. 'They obviously respected his judgment.'[7]

The officials took him more seriously after the fuel crisis, and his life became much busier. But relations with the Minister became more difficult than ever, for Shinwell knew that several senior colleagues wanted to get rid of him, and was in the worst of moods. Knowing that he was losing the confidence of the Prime Minister while Gaitskell was gaining it, he seems to have suspected his young subordinate of intriguing to take over his job. There was no truth at all in this, and Gaitskell himself wrote later that he would not have wanted to remain as Shinwell's Parliamentary Secretary, but never expected to succeed him.

Just before the fuel crisis, Gaitskell had wound up the second reading debate on the bill nationalising electricity with 'probably the most accomplished performance by a junior minister in this Parliament'.[8] The Minister delegated to him most of the committee stage, and Gaitskell's private secretary was struck by his self-confidence in selecting which amendments to deal with himself and which to leave to Shinwell. 'The difficult ones Gaitskell took. He went down very well with the committee . . . There was a sharp contrast between Shinwell's bluster and Gaitskell's . . . persuasive power.'[9] A sympathetic commentator described his style: 'He talks . . . quietly, unassumingly, without bombast or any . . . air of superiority. He never batters or bullies an opponent in argument, but rather meets him half-way . . . his allusive jokes and very gentle ironies go down well.'[3] That summer he was briefly left in charge of the Department, and relations had improved enough for him to persuade a reluctant Shinwell, against the Department's advice, to break a holiday to intervene and help settle a troublesome strike in Yorkshire.

Coal recovered quite quickly, but the fuel crisis was not the last of that appalling year. The Americans had insisted during the 1945 loan negotiations that sterling must be made fully convertible by 15 July 1947, a date which Keynes had vainly resisted as far too early. Within six weeks of 15 July, an immense run on the pound by all its foreign holders had wiped out most of the loan, and forced the suspension of convertibility. For years afterwards, fear of the threat to the currency posed by the sterling balances was to constrain British economic policy; immediately, the Cabinet at the end of August halted all currency allowances for foreign travel and abolished the basic petrol ration – of all the Government's unpopular measures, the one most infuriating to the middle class. That autumn marked the Government's lowest point in that Parliament.

The Cabinet was shaken by the disasters. Cripps and others plotted to replace Attlee by Bevin, but were foiled by the latter's refusal. Dalton reported Aneurin Bevan threatening to lead a left-wing revolt over nationalisation of steel. Gaitskell commented:

Bevan's head had swollen enormously . . . his bluff about resignation has been called . . . All the same . . . he still leads in the race for Labour Prime Minister in 1960! 'Very like LL.G. [Lloyd George]', says Evan. Yes, but I can't help wondering whether LL.G. was really quite so unscrupulous![2]

In August after an irritable PLP meeting, Gaitskell was surprised how often MPs for marginal seats 'are most unrealistic about the Left Wing character of the electorate . . . identifying their own keen supporters – politically conscious and class-conscious Labour men – with the mass of the people'.[2]

The austerities of 1947 changed his personal habits, for he gave up smoking when Dalton raised the tobacco tax, and imposed a spartan regime on his suffering household: electric fires were banned, and Raymond, when home from Oxford, hardly dared use an electric razor. In the previous summer he had moved from Well Walk to 18 Frognal Gardens, a big, rambling house with a private drive at the top of a steep Hampstead hill, which had once been the home of Sir Walter Besant, and was now to be Gaitskell's for the rest of his life. Various people, including his mother and his brother, shared it at different periods, and at this time he had as tenants Evan Durbin and two civil servants. When any of them wanted a bath, Dora had to use her own scanty coke ration to stoke the kitchen boiler, which Hugh sometimes made up at 8.30 a.m. before leaving for the office. In the country, at Milland, he had sold Sweatmans but still went to stay with his mother at Tuxlythe, where 'he chops his own firewood and gropes his way to bed by candlelight. His mother cooks breakfast by marsh gas . . . Milland has no piped water and the Gaitskells and I share supplies from the same meagre spring'.[10] At weekends in the early post-war months he worked hard on the weeds and bracken to create a productive garden and orchard. But in office the opportunities grew rare, and even in opposition he reckoned himself lucky to escape there on one weekend in four.

His private secretaries stood in some awe of his impressive intellectual equipment, but were reassured by his personal modesty – and by some signs of practical incapacity. A keen but not always successful photographer, he delighted them by seeking their advice on where he was going wrong. Even in public life his self-confidence came only gradually. Just before taking office, he wrote to the producer who had invited him to take part in a BBC Brains Trust:

As regards subjects, I feel profoundly ignorant of everything, but perhaps less so in the fields of economics, politics and social questions generally. As for your last paragraph, I am more than doubtful whether I shall enjoy the experience. In fact, at the moment it seems positively terrifying![11]

Pomposity was the last vice he could be accused of. A journalist covering one of his first meetings as a junior minister noticed how completely he was at home in the fish and chips bar afterwards. That meeting was in Chatham, for Gaitskell always tried to keep up links with old friends. In October 1947 he visited the South Yorkshire and East Midland coalfields and made sure of seeing his old Notts and Derby students. His last meeting of that tour was at Swadlincote, and the journalists came to it to photograph the new Minister of Fuel and Power.

## 'Unenviable Post'[12]

The ministerial reshuffle of October 1947 was long overdue and had been expected for weeks; Gaitskell found 'quite an unpleasant atmosphere' when he met the 'excited and jealous' MPs in the dining rooms at the House.[4] Besides winning Attlee's confidence as a committee chairman, Gaitskell had the strong backing of Dalton, Morrison and Cripps – and would have received the same office if the latter had succeeded in making Ernest Bevin Prime Minister. He picked up hints from associates, but was sceptical until summoned by Attlee, who

smiled and said in his clipped, muttering way, 'I am reconstructing the Government. I want you to be Fuel & Power'. I said, 'Oh! Well!' He said, 'It is not a bed of roses'. I said, 'I know that already.' Then I asked about the Parliamentary Secretary. They have given me Robens and I am pleased.[4]

He determined to give Robens a better deal than he himself had had.

With coal and electricity nationalised, Attlee had decided to leave both the new and the old Minister of Fuel and Power out of the Cabinet. Shinwell reluctantly accepted the War Office, but was furious at being the only Minister so demoted. He used George Wigg to inspire an editorial attack on Dalton in the *Daily Mirror*; and did not soon forgive his young successor. Neither he nor Wigg would speak to Gaitskell or Robens in the Westminster corridors, and all the civil servants knew of the bad blood.

Elsewhere, the new Minister met with a gratifying reception from his seniors. Ernest Bevin, fed up with Shinwell's bombastic speeches, advised: 'Don't speak for six months, don't say a bloody word, not even good morning.' The Foreign Secretary said that with 40 million more tons of coal, the extra exports would transform Britain's political position; and Gaitskell tactfully asked if he could come to Bevin for advice on the problems. 'He beamed about this and said, "Well, certainly, if the old war horse can help some of the younger ones he would be only too glad to".'[13]

Sir Stafford Cripps had just taken over from Morrison responsibility for co-ordinating economic policy: 'Cripps wants to run the thing with H. W., R. S. and myself as his lieutenants . . .[14] He is very friendly and very helpful so far. The only danger is of bees in his bonnet. There have been plenty in the past but certainly fewer and fewer in recent years.' But he was happier about personal relations than he was with the official machine:

The Cabinet Committee meetings which I have attended have been harmonious and friendly. The Big 5 are all without exception very well disposed to me and I think to the other young Ministers. There is no jealousy . . . Sometimes Cabinet Meetings [Gaitskell attended Cabinet for his own departmental business] horrify me because of the amount of rubbish talked by some Ministers who come there after reading briefs which they do not understand . . . A smaller Cabinet, mostly of non-departmental Ministers, would really be able to listen and understand more easily and hear the others arguing the matter out.[4]

After the first week Gaitskell wrote in his diary that 'becoming a full Minister is a great step and a great change. Much more so indeed than I expected earlier'.[13] Traditionally, that Department expected its political masters to know little and take official advice. In 1945 a new Permanent Secretary, Sir Donald Fergusson, reluctantly moved in from Agriculture to pull into shape this notoriously weak Ministry. He found

all the troubles that usually occur in a new Department . . . people whom [other] Departments could best spare . . . an enormous proportion of temporary staff . . . a great deal of favouritism . . . widespread disgruntlement, friction and inefficiency. It takes years of work to remedy such a state of affairs and endless patience.[15]

He had strong views on most subjects, particularly on the need for the new nationalised industries to be free of ministerial interference with their day-to-day work; and on the role of Ministers. They should deal with the big political, parliamentary and interdepartmental questions, stay out of detailed administration, and pay attention to the advice which would come to them through the Permanent Secretary. Hugh Gaitskell's outlook was very different for, unlike most new

Ministers, he knew the machine from inside. At his first meeting with the Ministry staff, he said that as an old civil servant he understood their concerns. From his wartime work in Whitehall, he thought much better of them than of either businessmen or Coal Board officials. And after seventeen months in the Department, he was familiar with its personnel and problems, and impatient to put his own ideas into practice. Hugh Dalton had taught him the importance of getting good civil servants, and he had himself seen how bad official advice had contributed to the failure to anticipate the fuel crisis. Fergusson sensed what was coming, and tried to warn his new Minister against unduly rapid and sweeping changes.

Most civil servants at Fuel and Power came to feel for Gaitskell much more respect and admiration, but perhaps less personal affection, than for Shinwell or Robens. But his private secretaries became warm admirers; Leslie Murphy, who served the longest, promised on quitting the Civil Service to return to Whitehall whenever Gaitskell wanted him. Some civil servants felt he was too impatient and short of time, or irritable with bad drafting, or unwilling to suffer fools gladly; others found him friendly though exacting, and much more considerate than many of his colleagues.

Gaitskell did not operate at all as the traditional civil servants expected: 'He found out straight away where the wisdom – such as it was – was to be found and insisted on going there directly without any intermediaries . . . and then he would by-pass the top people and disregard their advice.'[16] He ensured a hearing for the junior ranks, but at a price: he was a Minister fascinated, almost obsessed, with detail. To most (not all) of his civil servants then and later, this habit seemed a serious weakness. His immense capacity for work, and for absorbing complicated briefs, meant that it did not distract him from general policy; and it did help him to probe and assess the capacity of his advisers. But he carried it to extremes on almost every front. His civil servants were quite unaccustomed to a Minister who never thought it inappropriate or beneath his dignity to add up a column of figures. He was 'a ferret' who, when sent a file, 'instead of just reading the top [minute] would go through the lot and pick up things which officials sometimes hadn't intended to bring to his notice'. He had a grip on everything that was going on, but he risked both inhibiting the officials and imposing too much on them. 'He's another under-secretary and not my best either – he'll break the Department,' complained Fergusson early on.[9]

The Permanent Secretary would have preferred files going up to the

Minister to show only his own recommendations, without conflicting minutes. These clashing demands were reconciled by Murphy (who had been Fergusson's Private Secretary before becoming Gaitskell's). On some minor issues the Permanent Secretary had his way. On major matters, they mostly saw very much eye to eye; and where they did not it was the Minister who prevailed. These two powerful personalities soon came to feel the warmest mutual admiration. 'I really am blessed with a most admirable Permanent Secretary,' wrote Gaitskell after eight months as Minister. 'The more of I see of D. F. the more I like him. He is very shrewd and wise and yet not in the least obstructive . . . what an enormous difference it makes to my life'.[17] And Fergusson – who had worked for Sir John Anderson, Neville Chamberlain, Winston Churchill and Philip Snowden – was later to describe Gaitskell as 'the most efficient Minister I ever served'.[18]

## Petrol, Gas and Coal

The Permanent Secretary wrote to 'Dear Hugh' on his first day in office in October 1947, setting out both the immediate problems of staffing and policy and 'the major tasks that lie ahead over the next 2 or 3 years and the best way of tackling them both in the national interest and in your own interest'. Though it was essential to get more coal, the Minister should leave the Board to do its job: 'action by the Ministry will only do harm . . . [and] play into Horner's hands'.[14] (Arthur Horner, general secretary of the National Union of Mineworkers, was a leading Communist.) The other urgent problem was petrol for private motorists – inescapable politically because of the motoring organisations' furious campaign to restore the 'basic ration', and administratively because it provoked nearly two million applications for special treatment.

At the end of the war, demand for British coal was immense both at home and abroad. But the price for past mishandling of the industry's affairs now had to be paid: the National Coal Board took over an industry in desperate straits, with 85,000 fewer workers than in 1938, output 46 million tons lower, capacity and equipment badly run down, and productivity 10 per cent below the pre-war level. Though the Coal Board was criticised for failing to recover the output of a vanished past, its real task was to offset a downward trend which had begun well over a generation earlier.

Gaitskell was responsible for dealing with the immediate consequences of these long-standing problems. Everyone was clamouring for more coal: the domestic householder, cut to two-thirds of pre-war needs; manufacturing industry, which got only 85 per cent of its claims, the minimum to avoid economic disaster and unemployment; the booming electricity industry; and the insatiable export demand of a war-damaged Continent. Bevin had impressed on Gaitskell the immediate need for producing 40 million more tons. To regain any of the lost output quickly, the goodwill of the mineworkers was indispensable. Considering the generations of ill-treatment, the sellers' market they now enjoyed, and the wails of the middle class at austerity, the miners displayed astounding moderation and responsibility.

To demonstrate to the union that a new deal was intended, the five-day week was promised for May 1947, the miners undertaking that production would not fall. But the urgent need was to increase it. In October a new agreement was negotiated to lengthen hours again. With the five-day week an attendance bonus had been introduced, to be forfeited if any of the five shifts were missed. The union wanted only one-fifth of the bonus to be forfeit for each lost shift, but Gaitskell continued to resist this demand, which his Tory successors eventually accepted. His own solution—and Ernest Bevin's—was to exempt overtime earnings from income tax; but Dalton thought it administratively unworkable.

The Ministry of Fuel and Power had long suffered from appalling public relations. Gaitskell's realism and honesty at once created a good impression, and his candid approach soon earned him the confidence of the serious critical journals. Relations with the general public went less smoothly. Gaitskell, who set a good example in his own home, regularly called for fuel economy in his speeches. This led to the first celebrated gaffe of his public life, when he told a municipal election meeting at Hastings:

It means getting up and going to bed in cold bedrooms. It may mean fewer baths. Personally, I have never had a great many baths myself and I can assure those who are in the habit of having a great many baths that it does not make a great deal of difference to their health if they have fewer. And as far as appearance [goes]—most of that is underneath and nobody sees it.

As he wrote later, it was meant and taken simply as a joke. But Winston Churchill could not resist the opportunity:

When Ministers of the Crown speak like this . . . [they] have no need to wonder why they are getting increasingly into bad odour. I had even asked myself . . . whether you, Mr. Speaker, would admit the word 'lousey' as a Parliamentary expression in referring to the Administration . . . purely as one of factual narration.[19]

He received a few anonymous letters, and his old nurse, from whom he had not heard for thirty years, sent an indignant denial.

Those early weeks as a Minister were a difficult period. Hugh Dalton had to resign, after an innocent but monumental indiscretion – entering the House to introduce his autumn Budget, he had revealed its main outlines to a journalist he knew well, and they appeared in print before he had finished speaking, with the Stock Exchange still open; and Gaitskell felt depressed again by the 'no friends at the top' reaction of other politicians like Bevin and Cripps. In his own Department, Gaitskell recorded in his diary 'I am faced with a series of insoluble problems, one major administrative nightmare and much public criticism'. The last two reflected 'the perpetual, dreary row about petrol'.[20]

In August 1947, to the dismay of Fergusson who was on holiday, the Cabinet had abolished the basic petrol ration to which every motorist had been entitled. They hoped to save $36 million, and did not foresee the hurricane of middle-class fury blown up by the motoring organisations. Gaitskell loyally defended a hated policy not of his own making. But he did all he could administratively to reduce the odium. He took enormous pains to have letters answered promptly and sympathetically, and years later grateful writers still recalled the trouble he took. He decided that he would have to struggle against the Chancellor to 'get some sort of basic ration restored in the summer . . . The present thing is administratively a horror'.[20]

Before any general petrol ration could be restored, the black market had to be beaten. Measures against it were recommended by the Russell Vick Committee, and Gaitskell had a hard fight to force them through. But six months later he could happily record: 'I managed to persuade the Cabinet to let me give back some of the savings made beyond expectations from suppressing the Black Market.'[21] That transitional solution saved 250,000 tons a year over a crucial two years; and it greatly relieved the intolerable political and administrative strain.

That outcome lay far ahead. As 1948 began, Fergusson had sent him a friendly warning not to 'take on more than human strength can manage . . . you can't go on at the tempo of the last 3 months'.[22] But Gaitskell had no chance to relax. He wrote in his diary soon afterwards: 'The prospect ahead is pretty grim. Indeed, without Marshall Aid it is ghastly and there is no certainty about that. What will happen if there is a Republican victory and Taft is President in 1949?' Apart from coal production, the departmental outlook was 'horrible';[20] and even a few weeks later, when he appeased much of the hostility by restoring the petrol ration, he still found that

I am grossly overworked again. Everything is happening at once. The Gas Bill – now three days a week, mornings and afternoons in Committee; the new petrol scheme and all its repercussions; a crisis in the Coal Board; some horrible problems of coal quality and exports, and rather a heavy list of speaking engagements. And then finally the grim world oil situation with all its repercussions on our plans here.[23]

The Gas Bill should have been the least contentious of all the nationalisation measures, but it had become the target of a determined Opposition filibuster. The Government had sent the Gas Bill to standing committee without a guillotine resolution. That gave the Opposition a chance to block it for that session, after which it would have to start again – and so might again crowd out the hated Steel Bill. The Conservatives mounted a massive campaign of obstruction, producing over 800 amendments and even solemnly debating whether nationalisation should be spelt with an 's' or a 'z'. Their spokesman Brendan Bracken threw himself zestfully into the operation – until, just before Whitsun, the committee sat without stopping for fifty hours, through two consecutive nights, with only half-hour breaks for breakfast and with an all-night buffet outside the committee room door. It was a 700-year record, for there had been no single all-night committee sitting before. Gaitskell took a parliamentary question that afternoon, then went home to bed and slept for sixteen hours.

During these debates Herbert Morrison called the Minister of Fuel and Power 'the most overworked man in Britain'.[24] When the obstruction began, the new petrol rationing scheme was being mooted; as it ended, a long-developing crisis erupted in the Coal Board with the dramatic resignation of Sir Charles Reid, whose wartime committee had provided the technical case for compulsory reorganisation of the industry. Gaitskell was critical of the structure of the Board, on which Shinwell had insisted: only full-time members, with specific functional duties. He felt it blurred management responsibilities and provoked friction at every level from the Board downwards. Reid shared Gaitskell's views but not his patience, and resigned in a letter 'so plainly insulting to the rest of the Coal Board that I clearly had to accept it . . . in many ways I regret not having accepted his resignation months ago.'[24] Offstage noises came at the most delicate moment with a sudden burst of trumpeting from a familiar rogue elephant: the

Secretary for War, Emanuel Shinwell:

That man has entered my life once more to my considerable regret. He has started making speeches about coal . . . calculated to make trouble with the Coal Board . . . I sent a violent minute to the P.M. . . . [and he] promised to behave in future. Notwithstanding this, however, he plunged in far worse over the weekend and made an extraordinary speech more or less admitting the failure of nationalisation. This has caused great indignation in the Party.[23]

The unhappy legacy of the past meant that nationalisation faced special problems in the mines. The historic mutual suspicion between union and management affected organisational problems and appointments to the boards as well as industrial relations; and Conservatives, who had been so bitterly attacked for the failures of private ownership, naturally exploited these teething troubles. Gaitskell vigorously denounced their proposals in the House, warning that if areas had to pay their way, some would need to raise prices and close pits. Years later he wrote privately to an academic expert on nationalisation that the decentralised structure appropriate to gas would have been quite unsuitable for coal. 'Apart from anything else, the miners would never have tolerated it'.[25] 'The union's goodwill was indispensable for maintaining production: 'Reid would not matter at all if only output were better, but it has been very disappointing since Easter and I am now alarmed.'[24] Gaitskell was desperate to increase exports, which were still only one-third of pre-war; and when on 7 October 1948 he met the Board and the NUM he warned them frankly that, as the union's general secretary put it, 'further concessions to the miners must await increased output'.

The general secretary was Arthur Horner, a prominent Communist. But experience had made the other leaders of the union so anti-Communist that they mistrusted not only Horner himself but the Coal Board too, since its labour director was his friend and predecessor Ebby Edwards, who would deal with nobody else. Gaitskell became particularly friendly with the leaders from the northern coalfields (Sam Watson of Durham, Jim Bowman of Northumberland and Ernest Jones of Yorkshire) writing: 'the politics of the thing from now onwards will be an alliance between myself and them behind the scenes'.[26] Gaitskell toured the coalfields, speaking bluntly to large private meetings of managers and delegate conferences of miners. Nor did he get on only with his moderate allies, for in Scotland he found the Communist leaders 'surprisingly friendly'. James Griffiths, an old leader of the union and now his ministerial colleague, testified to his impact; and in May 1949 Gaitskell persuaded the NUM executive to continue the agreement for longer hours which they had adopted in his first days in office.

Gaitskell made an excellent impression on ordinary miners on his constant visits. He had no patience with middle-class censoriousness about the pitmen, and when mining executives complained about high wages, he told them there were plenty of vacancies at the coal face if any of them cared to apply. In South Wales, the miners at one pit (Penallta) threatened to boycott his visit, thinking he would be taken to an area dressed up for the occasion. Instead, he asked advice from the union lodge secretary, visited the most difficult section, and was afterwards told that his action had won the miners' complete confidence.

Like Aneurin Bevan, Gaitskell had no patience with the 'rather apologetic and timid attitude' of some of their colleagues to nationalisation, which let the Government's case go by default: 'This is not only politically extremely dangerous but also thoroughly bad for morale'.[27] No doubt he was referring to Shinwell, who had recently attacked as too high the very salaries he had when Minister sought to increase. For the same reason – maintaining morale in the industries – Gaitskell tried to avoid starting polemics himself, fearing that the violent Opposition attacks on the boards and their members made it even harder to attract first-rate people.

While Gaitskell sought and earned the workers' confidence, he knew that the ordinary consumer and voter had also to be convinced. Nationalisation would be judged, he told the NUM's annual conference at Whitley Bay, by six criteria: adequate supplies for industry; enough for exports; more for the domestic consumer; better quality; paying its way; and reasonable prices so that the consumer as well as the workers should gain from technical improvements.[28] By the end of his term of office, performance was improving. Output per man-shift reached the pre-war level in September 1949, far ahead of all other European countries. Production was rising, though not fast enough, and domestic consumption was well up, though still rationed for the sake of exports. Fatal accidents in 1948 were fewer than ever before, and fewer still in 1949. The miners had trebled their wages (while other wages had doubled); but prices had risen less than for many commodities, and the Board made a profit where the old owners took a subsidy (£27 million in their last year). There were still serious problems. But the Board succeeded in reversing the steady decline over which the companies had for so long presided.

## New Colleagues, and a Lost Friend

The constant crises of his first nine months had put a heavy strain on Gaitskell. His close friends had known he was exhausted and worried about his heart, and an alarmed Evan Durbin urged him to take a long complete rest at Whitsun 1948 so as to 'be fit for months and alive for years' – tragically ironical advice from one with only four more months to live.[29] But after that the pressures became less intense, and Gaitskell was able to lead a more relaxed life. He attended the wedding of Princess Elizabeth and Prince Philip (although 'I find it difficult to take these things seriously');[30] and a dinner at No. 10, with some of his younger colleagues, to meet the royal pair. He talked to her about fuel economy 'and she said that Queen Mary's house was the coldest she knew; she hardly ever had a fire anywhere. I asked if this was because she was spartan or because of the house, but she said, "no" – it was because of her national duty.'[23]

He was finding more time to meet colleagues. His fellow economic Ministers dined together each Thursday to chat and iron out minor departmental conflicts. Their host was Sir Stafford Cripps, the Chancellor, who dominated the Government's domestic policies. A vegetarian who symbolised austerity in material things, and a devout Christian, he enjoyed remarkable moral authority during three critical years. Gaitskell quickly developed immense admiration for him. He was no judge of men and he seemed unable to relax. But he had a very keen intelligence, patience, kindliness and, above all, 'courage which is closely combined in his case with superb self-confidence . . . Most of us, I think, are . . . always counting the political difficulties.'[31] As usual, Gaitskell's comments reveal a good deal about his own character.

These weekly dinners soon expanded beyond strictly economic business, for Cripps began inviting two of his pre-war allies. John Strachey was Minister of Food, and in the 1930s the most persuasive of Communist propagandists.

I reserve judgment about him. He is still, I think, much too inclined to abstract theory. At the moment he is a deflationist and rather anti-control . . . he is a very able negotiator, and fairly influential at Cabinet meetings – states his case forcibly though with exaggeration. Is he to be trusted? Probably not.[30]

Four months later Cripps introduced a second old associate:

last night Aneurin Bevan was also present and appears to have joined the group. I must say that Stafford is showing much more political acumen than I expected. He is obviously anxious to have Bevan as an ally . . . I could not help feeling that Stafford was surveying his future Cabinet. It would be surprising if he did not himself expect to be Prime Minister one day. But these things depend more on accident of age and health than anything else.[23]

A few weeks afterwards:

Personality is a funny thing. Bevan, of course, has it very decidedly. He is powerful, though maddening as well. But I feel pretty sure he will be Prime Minister one day and probably at that level will be a good deal better than now. I would not, however, have him as Foreign Secretary, he is much too unscrupulous and would involve us in much too much trouble with other countries.[17]

Barely a fortnight later, Bevan marred his triumphant inauguration of the National Health Service with a celebrated lapse, calling the Tories 'lower than vermin'. Gaitskell disapproved, without being unduly prim, criticising Bevan and his wife (Jennie Lee) who

now positively defend the policy of insulting one's opponents. 'Aggression is what will get us votes' – and suchlike nonsense. It would be much better if A.B. simply said that he was Welsh; he spoke as he felt, and sometimes he felt very strongly . . . Jennie Lee said she was worried about the fire going out of the miners because they were getting such a lot. I am afraid I have little sympathy with such attitudes.[32]

Gaitskell's relations with Bevan's friends were amiable, though he and Bevan did not always see eye to eye, for their style and temperament were altogether dissimilar – especially over foreign affairs, in which Gaitskell now had time to take an interest again. At lunch at the American Embassy to meet Kenney, the new representative of the Economic Co-operation Administration:

Nye typically opened his conversation with the gentleman on whom we depend for dollars by describing his experiences in the great San Francisco Dock Strike of 1933, and made it quite plain, quite pleasantly but unmistakably, that he held the lowest opinion of American Justice. (Mr. Kenney is a lawyer.)[33]

Yet on the major issues the future rivals were not far apart. Bevan was convinced that the American alliance was indispensable, while Gaitskell, its determined champion politically, was as firm as Bevan in resisting economic pressures from across the Atlantic. In Europe Bevan resolutely stood up to Soviet pressure – but went beyond any of his colleagues in demanding a guarantee to Yugoslavia against Russian aggression, and in arguing forcefully in the Cabinet for the relief of Berlin – blockaded in the summer of 1948 – by a tank convoy instead of an airlift.

Those events led to a review of British policy in Germany which

divided Gaitskell's friends. Dalton, with his violent national prejudices, was an unrepentant anti-German. On 22 December 1948, after
previous arguments, he reported an inconclusive Cabinet discussion:

S.C. said we ought to make up our minds whether we regarded the Germans as
still a danger, or as an ally in building W. Europe. E.B. said he was trying to
steer a middle course. A.B. said we ought to build them up as much as we could.
They were a better barrier against Communism than the French. I . . . spoke
sharply against the German danger.[34]

Outside Europe, the great issue at that moment was Palestine, where
Ernest Bevin's policy outraged Labour's Zionist traditions. Here
Gaitskell, in his moderate fashion, sympathised with the feelings which
at least once led Bevan to consider resignation. At a Cripps dinner,
'Nye came out quite openly against Bevin and seemed to be anxious to
start an intrigue to get rid of him. While nobody else joined in, I think
most of us feel fairly critical of the foreign policy.' When the House
debated it, sixty Labour MPs abstained. 'I think a good many . . . did
not realise they were really risking the fall of the Government. On the
other hand I must confess to some sympathy with their point of view.'[35]

Whatever his own differences with other Ministers, Gaitskell always
felt strongly the need – for decades appreciated by most Conservative
Cabinets and no Labour one – for solidarity in public and reasonable
mutual understanding in private. He had been indignant at Shinwell
for breaching the former convention, and was mildly shocked at
Bevan's contempt for the latter. After one Cripps dinner he wrote:

The Minister of Health [Bevan] . . . launched attacks on the Prime Minister,
the Lord President and the Minister of Defence, and of course on previous
occasions he has frequently attacked the Foreign Secretary. When this happens
everybody becomes embarrassed. Either you remain silent in which case you
feel 'pi' which is not a pleasant feeling . . . or you also say what you think,
probably in much more moderate terms . . . [and] feel rather a cad.
Stafford . . . revealed . . . that he had never had a private meal with the Prime
Minister since the Government was formed.[36]

Among his own generation, Gaitskell's closest friend had been Evan
Durbin, whose sudden death in the summer of 1948 was the saddest of
his bereavements. He and Dora had gone off on three weeks' holiday to
Abbotsbury, on the Dorset coast. On 3 September, after dinner,
Gaitskell learned from his private secretary that Durbin had been
drowned saving his daughter on a dangerous Cornish beach:

The feeling I most had was one of cold, as though I had had something stripped
from me and was exposed much more than before to the elements . . . Grief

affects people very differently. For me it is sort of chemical in its action. I find it impossible to control my tears . . .

I still cannot get it firmly into my head that he has gone. Every now and then I think about it again. I suppose one's personal loss declines as time passes, at least one will feel it less frequently. But the full loss to his friends and to the country will be there, sure enough. There is . . . nobody else in my life whom I can consult on the most fundamental issues, knowing that I shall get the guidance that I want.[37]

He was never again to enjoy the close companionship of someone of similar outlook and standing in the Party, with whom he could share all his burdens and battles in complete trust and intimacy. On becoming Chancellor he wrote sadly: 'It would be so much less lonely if he were here'.[38] Always inclined to do far too much himself, he might not have worn himself out so thoroughly if Durbin had survived. Much more emotional and impulsive than his friend, he might have been restrained by Evan's calmer advice from some of his more foolhardy acts. The close partnership of the two men would have been a good deal more than the sum of two impressive parts.

## Minister for Nationalised Industries

Gaitskell did not advocate public ownership on purely practical grounds, but he knew that practical arguments were indispensable to convince others. Early in 1949, with the experience of office, he set out his views on nationalisation to a student audience.[39] 'Not an *end* in itself,' say his notes. 'Our Socialism is . . . [aimed at eliminating] the *three* evils of individualism – *Inequality, Insecurity, Inefficiency.*' He referred also to:

(a) *Concentration of economic power exercised without responsibility*. Now much modified by (i) Govt. Controls (ii) Trade Union strength. It *still* counts.

(b) *Spiritual* aims – undesirability of concentrating on *material ends* . . . doubtful how far this changes except at top under nationalisation. All the same desire to serve community important . . . make *democracy* an end in itself and need to acknowledge this in our policy.

In Gaitskell's personal creed, inequality was the worst of the 'three evils of individualism'. But his ministerial responsibilities concentrated his attention on problems of efficiency. Managers had to be found for the industries who had the workers' confidence and were good at their job; they had to be given enough freedom to do it well, without being allowed to impose their own judgement on matters outside their proper sphere. The problem of relations between Minister and boards, where

Gaitskell had no useful precedents to guide him, was most acute in electricity. That of appointments to the boards was worst of all in the mines, where production directors drawn from the old management, and labour or welfare directors who were former union officials, were the carriers of generations of mutual mistrust. There were, Gaitskell admitted privately, 'too many people in managerial positions who are still strongly opposed to nationalisation.'[40] All the first chairmen of divisional boards came from outside the industry, partly to escape these suspicions and partly because no one from within it had experience of running a big organisation.

These considerations encouraged a peculiar vogue for appointments from the Services, of which Gaitskell approved. 'They have been brought up to believe in service and so, as it were, take to nationalisation.'[41] Moreover, a famous chairman from the armed forces might help to take the boards out of politics. Knowing that Hyndley (Chairman of the National Coal Board) might have to retire on health grounds, Gaitskell thought of choosing 'a really national figure . . . like Mountbatten or Montgomery'.[17] But Attlee and Morrison quickly disposed of this notion – to Gaitskell's relief when, at a Palace dinner six weeks later, he met the Field Marshal. 'How right the P.M. and Lord President were . . . But I fancy these traits – extreme egotism, lack of humour and being a bore – are not uncommon amongst successful leaders.'[32] Nevertheless when he had to propose a successor for Hyndley, Gaitskell's short-list was headed by Field Marshal Lord Alexander: 'a magnificent appointment from the figure-head point of view . . . His mere name is bound to stave off a good deal of criticism.'[42] In the end he persuaded Hyndley to continue until after the election.

Gaitskell was responsible for far more appointments to the boards of nationalised industries than any other Minister: counting only full-timers, about seventy. There was resentment against the appointment of Conservatives or former managers, especially opponents of national-isation, and also against high salaries. Gaitskell rejected these complaints.

Anything in the nature of political patronage in this sphere could only create insecurity within the industry and thoroughly discredit the Boards with the general public . . . If inefficient people are appointed on political grounds they will not work well . . . in practice some political concessions in this field have to be made. But we are always being pressed for more.[43]

At the Labour Party's Blackpool conference in June he was again 'worried by the failure of the leaders to defend nationalisation adequately. They are much too apologetic . . . this is thoroughly bad politics and quite unjustified.'[40] He urged a more robust attitude by Ministers over both appointments and salaries. Political discrimination would be wrong, and would have utterly 'demoralising and discreditable' results if a Tory government imitated it. Moreover, boards must pay enough to recruit good men. 'It would be quite disastrous to the whole national economy as well as to the success of the nationalised industries if our coal, electricity and gas industries were to be staffed by second-raters.'[44]

Gaitskell was always delighted to appoint able trade-unionists, but did not find it easy. 'I offered the job to [one] of the best NUM officials . . . but his wife almost had hysterics at the prospect of . . . moving so far up in the economic and social scale . . . How few people would expect this sort of thing to happen.'[45] But he flatly refused to appoint official spokesmen of the unions to run the industries in which their own members worked. Many unions did not want that, but the Communist Party – which controlled the Electrical Trades Union – took up the theme.

Gaitskell met their challenge head on, telling his colleagues, 'I regard the syndicalist tendencies now being encouraged by the Communists as exceedingly dangerous and requiring very firm handling.'[46] His mistrust of syndicalist militancy went back to the General Strike, which was in part the outcome of a generation's preaching by a dedicated activist minority. Later on he was to show interest in any practical scheme for workers' participation in running their firms; but in all the industries for which he was responsible, he was concerned both to ensure a fair deal for their workers and to protect the legitimate interests of the rest of the community. On price policy, for example, he privately warned the Labour Party: 'The real danger . . . is likely to be . . . that any surplus there is will be absorbed by wage demands which have no relation to the general situation of the country.'[43]

He clashed again with the ETU in December 1949, when a long-threatened unofficial strike at the power stations broke out just before the general election. Troops were put in at once when the strike began without warning. He thoroughly mistrusted the ETU, for

although it denounced the strikers officially, we are perfectly certain the unofficial elements are largely guided and controlled by the Communists as well . . . the Ministry of Labour . . . were concerned almost wholly with ending the strike; whereas we were concerned with smashing the strikers.
. . . the Government ought really to face up to the issue of Power Station

strikes, and decide whether they can afford to treat them as ordinary industrial disputes. In my view they cannot.[47]

Other governments were still asking that question a quarter of a century later.

The idea of autonomy for the boards was in theory accepted by the Labour Party, which had for years been committed to Herbert Morrison's conception of the independent public corporation. On the whole Gaitskell shared that view, as he told his colleagues in May 1949. However, Parliament held him broadly responsible for their record, and he had his own statutory responsibilities, which he had power to enforce by giving the boards a General Direction in the national interest. He should not use it frequently but he had done so on three recent occasions: to stop the National Coal Board fixing wholesale margins with the coal merchants and cutting off supplies to any who sold cheaper; to persuade them to sell anthracite to Canada for dollars when the European price was higher; and to insist on a higher charge for electricity in winter:

Some overriding consideration lying outside the strict responsibility of the Boards was, in every case, involved – the principle of preventing restrictive practice in coal distribution, the importance of exporting in the national interest to the right destination, the need to diminish the risk of load shedding and obtain the full assistance of industry in staggering hours.[48]

Though willing to issue a Direction, he had not needed to do so. He preferred frequent informal discussions with the chairmen. As he wrote privately a few years later:

It is true that in theory a Minister can exercise power without responsibility if he has a very weak Board. But . . . it is an extremely difficult thing, in my experience, for the Minister to get his way [surreptitiously] with the Board in a matter which they really object to.[25]

Gaitskell's successors did not adhere to these principles. Conservative Ministers set and later Labour ones followed a bad example of unavowed political interference. With responsibility blurred, and accountability impossible to enforce, the public corporations have attracted much justified criticism but have never, since those early days, been allowed to work as their originators intended.

His main battle on this front came with the electricity industry, as aggressive as any private firm in its determination to sell its product, though at peak hours power could not always be supplied. To the industry, this proved that its need for new generating plant deserved priority over competing claims for investment capital – while Gaitskell believed that consumers should pay the real cost of their demands (kept artificially low for years) through a surcharge at peak periods. His frequent clashes with Citrine as the chairman of the British Electricity Authority show the problems of that relationship: the more so because the latter had for twenty years been general secretary of the TUC and wielded far more influence than Gaitskell in the Labour Movement. Other Ministers suffered too; 'it's far easier to get cooperation out of ICI than out of Walter Citrine,' said one of them at one of Cripps's dinners. At Fuel and Power Gaitskell was a vigorous defender of the industry's legitimate investment interests; and at the Exchequer, when Citrine appealed against him to Attlee, it was the Chancellor who won. But the pressure was intense, so that a powerful chairman using all his influence and ingenuity was able to capture a disproportionately large share of investment resources.

On the consumption side, the boards were even more successful in frustrating ministerial policy. Gaitskell on taking office had at once to face the need to restrict electricity consumption in the home: otherwise industry and the unions would rebel against the voluntary load-spreading agreements which restricted their own supplies. He recommended a differential tariff, higher in winter, lower in summer, and so provoked an angry storm. 'This has always seemed to me common sense and I had no difficulty in getting it through the Cabinet.'[32] Citrine challenged Gaitskell to issue a General Direction to the Board – a legal power which had been used by no Minister then and very few since – to impose a most unpopular plan. It took almost reckless courage for the Minister to tell so powerful a chairman that he would; but when he did, Citrine agreed to comply. Citrine then announced a differential far too small to be effective, and sabotage by the area boards 'made it far more difficult to get it accepted by public opinion'.[49] Gaitskell still wanted to 'stand firm even if we do lose a few votes',[50] but the half-hearted scheme made too little difference to justify its unpopularity, and was abandoned the following winter. Commentators lamented for years afterwards the failure to adopt Gaitskell's policy.

Gaitskell liked to get his own way as much as anyone.

It is really very unsatisfactory having to deal with the Boards as though they were independent authorities with no special obligations to the Government. Yet if they choose that . . . without a major and public row there is very little the Minister can do about it.[51]

He remained above all concerned to preserve the morale of the boards:

even after leaving Fuel and Power. Against Herbert Morrison (of all people) he argued that concessions to public and parliamentary criticism would discourage their members and encourage Labour's political opponents.

We must avoid giving the Boards of the socialised industries . . . [and] even more . . . the public or Parliament the impression that we have lost confidence in the Boards . . . [or] we might find ourselves doing most serious damage not only to the reputation of the socialised industries, but also to their efficiency.[52]

It was not easy to draw the line between fussy political interference, damaging to the boards' efficiency, and timid political abdication, leaving them as autonomous state monopolies answerable to no one. Though doubtful about institutional checks, Gaitskell – with no precedents to guide him – developed as a Minister a successful middle course. When he left the Department Sir Geoffrey Vickers, one of the ablest members of the National Coal Board, sent him a warm tribute: 'you will be missed here . . . we have been properly hotted up, adequately backed up and sufficiently left alone . . . if you have set a pattern, everyone will owe you a lot.'[53] For Gaitskell approached the problem as a man deeply committed, both from conviction and for the sake of his own reputation, to making a new industrial experiment work successfully. As a practising politician, he knew that most Labour supporters as well as uncommitted voters would judge success by the kind of practical standards he had set for the coal industry at Whitley Bay. As a Minister, he was familiar with the difficulty of recruiting to run these enterprises the able men without whom they were sure to fail. As a Socialist intellectual, who had thought out his position with his usual thoroughness, he believed that nationalisation of these basic industries would contribute to Socialist aims, not directly by promoting equality, but by improving efficiency.

It was a coherent if rather narrow managerial outlook, understandable in a Minister struggling to overcome the teething troubles of new organisations by whose success nationalisation, and even the Labour Government, would shortly be judged by the electorate. He himself when out of office always tried to follow the line he would have taken in government; so he was shocked at the irresponsibility of the Conservative Opposition, and innocently believed that they could not expect to win the next election – otherwise they would not attack the boards so much.[54] As he exclaimed angrily in an election speech:

They have obstinately resisted all the Government's efforts to take the nationalised industries out of politics. They have shown bitter hostility . . . scoffed and sneered . . . belittled every achievement and magnified every weakness. How can you trust them . . . [after] such an orgy of slander . . . ?[55]

## Politics and Social Life

'An orgy of slander' was not too strong a phrase for the bitterness displayed on domestic matters by the Attlee Cabinet's opponents. Social tensions were acute, and much of the middle class bitterly resented Labour controls, Labour austerity and the very existence of a Labour government. A generation later a leading political correspondent wrote that he had 'never known the Press so consistently and irresponsibly political, slanted and prejudiced' as it was at this time.[56]

A fairly flourishing black market enabled many 'spivs' to make a dishonest living by evading the controls; the slender foundation for a shameful whispering campaign against Socialist corruption. It led to the Lynskey Tribunal of Inquiry, which reported at the beginning of 1949 on allegations against Ministers, civil servants and public figures who had had dealings with a flamboyant contact man, Sydney Stanley. Gaitskell (and Bevan) detested this method of investigation. He was himself departmentally involved, for one of the two men censured was the trade unionist George Gibson, a director of the Bank of England and chairman of the North-Western Electricity Board. His case greatly troubled Gaitskell, who read the evidence by and about him and believed he had behaved foolishly but in no way discreditably. He was saved from an unhappy dilemma – which might have had to go to Cabinet – by Gibson's own decision to resign. Gaitskell was 'very upset', and seriously considered speaking in the debate. 'I told the Chief Whip I cannot vote for the Government motion, and he accepted that. He did not want me to speak, but I warned him that I might if Gibson was attacked . . . I wish I was better at making up my mind on these difficult conscience issues.'[57] The great exposure of Socialist corruption ended with revelations of some dubious business practices, full vindication of the civil servants, and the ruin of an indiscreet trade unionist and an imprudent junior politician.

A supposedly respectable form of this unsavoury campaign was to attack Labour appointments as 'jobs for the boys' (in fact many fewer Labour politicians received paid public employment from Attlee after the war than Conservatives from Churchill during it). Gaitskell, who had been criticised by MPs on his own side for refusing to bestow political patronage, was one of the victims of slander by two BBC comedians, the Western Brothers. Senior Ministers very seriously considered legal proceedings, but the BBC and the comedians agreed to make an ample public apology.

By 1949 Gaitskell was no longer overworking and had time for holidays. At Whitsun he went on a strenuous expedition to the Lake District with Dalton, now back in office, and he and Alf Robens lost themselves and their wives in the neighbourhood of Langdale Pikes. In the summer an old 1917 Club acquaintance ran into him on holiday in Jersey, 'in shorts, climbing cliffs with the children and having a wonderful time . . . he was a very unstuffy person'. He was also meeting the Establishment:

There has been the usual run of social engagements, Buckingham Palace parties and garden parties, etc. The general feeling seems to be that the shadow of the coming election was visible. The parties seemed to be more Tory and less democratic than before. I do not think this is entirely imagination – all my colleagues seem to have the same opinion.[33]

That did not make him at all inclined to political compromise. In principle he remained a convinced egalitarian and privately at this time would argue seriously for complete, universal, Shavian-style equality of incomes. (As Chancellor he modified this to: no one should get over £5,000 a year[58]). Publicly, he told the Oxford University Labour Club that though the Government had done much to make incomes more equal, 'Property is still very unequally divided, and that is a problem which has got to be tackled [by the] taxation of inheritance on a still larger scale'.[59] Owing to flu, Gaitskell missed the secret conclave in the Isle of Wight where the Labour Ministers and National Executive met to discuss the future. Like Bevan, he strongly favoured an autumn election; unlike Bevan – and unlike most of the Party – he was far from sure that Labour would win by fifty seats. The complacent mood was soon to be shattered by a new dollar crisis leading to the devaluation of sterling, in which Gaitskell emerged for the first time in a central political role.

In the shadow of that mounting crisis, not yet realised by the man in the street, Gaitskell again attracted the unwelcome attentions of the press when the emotions that seethed behind his front of rational intellectuality broke through for the first time in public. On 6 July 1949 he was speaking to the NUM's annual conference at Porthcawl, three hours before the Chancellor was to make a statement in the House on the dollar situation. He suddenly dropped his script to talk of 'a moment of supreme crisis for the Government'. 'Mr. Gaitskell was overcome with emotion,' wrote one journalist; 'tears welled in his eyes, his voice faltered'; and another: 'for a moment he staggered as if he was about to collapse'.[60] As Gaitskell himself recorded 'tears came into my eyes and I had to stop speaking for a few seconds . . . From the point of view of the speech it was, I suppose, extremely effective. . . . I rather expected that the Chancellor or the P.M. might tick me off but . . . subsequent events have proved me right.'[33] As these events developed into a major crisis, Gaitskell – not yet even in the Cabinet – was given partial and temporary responsibility for the Treasury. As in the fuel crisis, but now on a larger stage, he rose to the challenge and played a decisive role which was soon to bring him to the Chancellorship, and eventually to the leadership of the Party.

## Minister for Energy

Gaitskell could be spared from his Department in the summer of 1949 because its work was completely under control. That meant much more than routine administration on the lines suggested by civil servants or boards of nationalised industries. Most Ministers of Fuel and Power before and since have been – as one senior civil servant put it – 'blown about by the industries'. Gaitskell, however, sought to represent the wider public interest, not the narrower perspectives of the industries themselves. That outlook brought him into conflict with some powerful forces: above all the oil companies, backed by the Foreign Office and by the Oil Division of his own Ministry.

Before the war, Britain had imported 82 per cent of her oil as finished products, nearly half of it from the Caribbean. Vital dollars could be saved by purchasing Middle East crude from new fields in the sterling area, if only the oil companies would refine in Great Britain instead of on the oil-fields themselves. Gaitskell vigorously promoted the policy, successfully fighting for steel in the Production Committee. By 1951 the new refineries enabled Britain to export more oil than coal.

The Ministry of Fuel and Power was anxious to keep the goodwill of the American companies, for the British Government had no statutory powers and could only coax them into home refining, or buying their tankers from British yards, or contributing in other ways to the British balance of payments. In December 1948, Morrison's NEC subcommittee on the next party programme also suggested nationalising oil distribution in Britain, and asked Gaitskell for his view – within three working days. For once his reply simply reproduced (with one trivial grammatical amendment!) a minute from Fergusson urging 'two overwhelming objections'. To take over the Americans' 40 per cent share of distribution in Britain 'would cause an uproar in the U.S.A., not only in itself but because of the effect it might have in encouraging other Governments to nationalise . . . The whole Marshall Aid Plan would be jeopardised . . . Americans would . . . regard it as threatening American as well as British command of oil resources and trade throughout the world.' Moreover, if British companies elsewhere 'were nationalised by foreign governments we should lose an immense amount of invisible exports. We cannot afford to risk this loss by setting an example of nationalisation'.[61]

Gaitskell clearly foresaw the danger for the British economy of dependence on Middle Eastern oil:

Should Russia over-run this area there would not merely be insufficient oil for Britain but for a large part of the rest of the world. And, even without Russia it is difficult enough. The Arab States are making difficulties about the pipeline because of the Palestine question. God knows when we shall really get our expansion programme going there, and how precarious it will all be even when the output is doubled as we plan in the next four to five years.[20]

But there was no simple way to replace dollar oil by sterling oil, as Gaitskell's detailed inquiries soon ascertained. When he left the Department, a prominent oilman called him 'the Minister who absorbed more quickly than any other the intricate problems of the oil industry'.[62]

That was not a euphemism for a man bemused by the experts or captured by the companies. Contrary to official advice, he kept up energetic pressure on the American firms, which operated in the sterling as well as in the dollar area, to switch the oil they sold to Britain to sterling sources. Under the loan agreement, which forbade discrimination, Britain would not be allowed to exclude oil which cost dollars. In the worst phase of the currency crisis:

Where it was expected that we could save 85 million dollars – we cannot without 'discrimination' save more than 30. But all efforts on my part to have this problem discussed and resolved have been blocked by the Foreign Secretary who is terrified of the reactions of the U.S. Oil Companies. I hope to return to the attack before long.[63]

And early the following year:

The Americans are being extremely tiresome . . . [over] the vested interests of the U.S. Oil Companies . . . American policy [is] to grant E.C. [European Co-operation] Aid in order to help us overcome the dollar crisis; but to resist like anything our efforts to do so if these involve displacing American exporters from overseas markets.[47]

In the long run, however, Gaitskell was successful, for the dollar share of British oil imports fell from 52.6 per cent in 1947 to 32 per cent in 1950 and – largely because of policies he had initiated – to only 19 per cent late in 1953, at an annual saving of £150 million.

Some supposed friends of Britain proved even more difficult than the Americans. The Australian Labour Government, 'extremely loyal and firm', had declined to damage sterling by de-rationing petrol, but the Liberal Opposition won the election and insisted on de-rationing. Gaitskell was angry. 'We have prepared what I regard as a rather masterly statement which . . . blackens the Australian Government as they deserve to be blackened.'[64] Meanwhile he was negotiating with Washington and in May 1950 – when he had moved from Fuel and Power to the Treasury – a compromise was reached: both British and American companies produced extra supplies, in return for de-rationing petrol throughout the sterling area. His immediate reaction was: 'I've got to say "Snap!" to this.'

The principles of Gaitskell's domestic fuel policy were that the industries should be co-ordinated to secure maximum efficiency at the lowest cost; and that the consumer should then choose the fuel he preferred at a realistic price. He had no love for controls for their own sake. He defended petrol rationing when it was most unpopular, but got rid of it as soon as he could. He thought Harold Wilson's 'bonfire' of controls in 1949 unwise, because it would have been more advantageous politically to drop them gradually over the year. But wherever possible the consumer should have a free choice. After six years of restriction Gaitskell allowed him to change coal merchants, against the wishes of the Coal Board.

He took more interest than most Ministers of Fuel and Power in the contribution of science, overruling Fergusson to bring in Sir Harold Roxbee Cox (later Lord Kings Norton) as Chief Scientist with executive powers. That was a unique position for a scientist in Whitehall, and it continued after Gaitskell's time; even in 1963 when Sir Burke Trend's committee reported, Fuel and Power was well in advance of other Departments. Like Dalton, Gaitskell was ahead of his time in attaching importance to 'quality of life' issues. On some environmental questions such as Oxford's perennial road problem, he was in the mainstream of the Establishment, telling Douglas Jay once in their official car from Hampstead to Whitehall: 'If they spoil Christ Church Meadow, I won't move the gas works!'[65] He disliked the open-cast coal programme, insisted that the ruined land must be restored, and would have abandoned the policy entirely had not Jay persuaded him that that was too risky. He was keen on smoke abatement and strongly supported his successor's measures on it; as party leader he once wondered if it would be a vote-winner.

Gaitskell was an excellent Minister of Fuel and Power. The command of and interest in detail was no bar to delegation; his Parliamentary Secretary had a full say on general departmental policies, but Gaitskell never interfered with Robens's handling of specific assignments; and he penetrated into detail without losing sight of long-term policy. In spite of his later reputation for obstinacy, he was eager to seek advice, and was not too stubborn to change his mind, as Douglas Jay induced him to do over open-cast coal. He would yield to argument, but not to political seniority or the weight of the Whitehall machine; Cripps so respected him that Gaitskell could tell one journalist: 'Sometimes we disagreed on something and it went to the Cabinet, but on more than one occasion when it got there he deliberately refrained from opposing me, and indeed sometimes supported me, feeling that as I was the Minister concerned I must really decide.'[66]

His decisions were his own, but he was skilful at winning assent to them without either offending or capitulating to those affected. He could stand up to the unions when necessary, but he still established excellent relations with the General and Municipal Workers, who were dominant in the gas industry; and Dalton – whose constituency was in the Durham coalfield – rightly told the Prime Minister that Gaitskell 'had done jolly well with the miners, who now much preferred him to his predessor'.[67]

By his civil servants he was universally respected – but less often called by his Christian name than Shinwell had been. A few of the older men resented his independence of mind, his willingness to seek advice from juniors, his determination not to be run by the industries. But others maintained stoutly that when he disagreed with his advisers he was almost always right. And however they found him as a person, all his civil servants recognised and admired his qualities: inordinate industry; businesslike habits; persistence and intelligence in dealing with other Departments; clarity of mind; incisiveness and decisiveness; drive; intellectual courage; and integrity. 'We get rare pleasure', wrote one who knew him well, 'out of seeing you take hold of all sorts of bowling.'[68] Apart from the concern for detail he approached the administrator's ideal of a Minister.

Outside the Department, his personality had made no great impression. The storm over petrol rationing had died down; and while the serious papers regarded him as a successful and competent administrator, readers of the popular press knew him best from a series of unhappy accidents – the baths episode, the Western Brothers 'joke', the tears at Porthcawl. In the House he had a few devoted admirers and much goodwill, notably among the miner MPs. Later on, as a party leader who worked far too hard, he was often accused of inadequate contact with his parliamentary followers; but as a Minister he kept in careful touch with back-benchers. He was courteous and persuasive in ordinary committee debates, and coped very successfully with the extraordinary challenge of the Gas Bill filibuster in 1948. Most of his speeches were lectures, well organised and thorough, informative and fair-minded, without much humour, sparkle or punch. But as one critical trade union MP shrewdly observed: 'It was always to your advantage when the Opposition went for you . . . severe tests . . . bring the best out of you.'[69]

Within a year, and with only five years' parliamentary experience, Gaitskell became Chancellor of the Exchequer. This meteoric success he owed partly to the exhaustion of the senior Ministers whose health was shattered by ten gruelling years in high office. He owed it partly to first-class administrative competence. His economic expertise was also a help. But above all he owed his promotion to his handling of a major crisis. Like the fuel crisis of 1947, devaluation in 1949 enabled Gaitskell to demonstrate his rare ability to meet a greater challenge even more successfully than previous lesser ones, and showed the senior men in the Government – Attlee, Cripps, Morrison and Bevin – his most important quality: his capacity for growth.

# The Treasury:
# Substituting for
# Stafford Cripps 1949–50

---

*'Being in the centre does . . . appeal to me'*
(HG on going to the Treasury, March 1950)

*'Opportunity is carrying you forward on a great wave'*
(Dalton to HG, September 1950)

---

### Devaluation: 'Vice-Chancellor of the Exchequer'

Four years after the end of the war, Labour Britain had made an impressive economic recovery. Exports (by volume) had risen from 50 per cent below the pre-war level to nearly 55 per cent above, and paid for 85 per cent of imports instead of one-third: the best performance in Europe. Industrial production by volume in the first half of 1949 was 30 per cent above 1938; and output per man-hour had since the war increased faster than in the United States. These achievements depended on strict controls at home, to direct resources into essential activities, and abroad, to check flights of capital and to use scarce gold and dollar reserves only for food and raw materials. But that involved discrimination offensive to the Americans' interests and ideology, and to the commitments they had extracted in return for Lend-Lease and the 1945 loan. After the loan agreement, sterling had for the moment seemed secure, as it did again once Marshall Aid was settled: 1946 and 1948 were favourable years. But in 1947 American insistence led to the disastrous experiment in convertibility of sterling, which dissipated most of the loan; and in 1949 a sharp recession in the US curtailed her purchases abroad, reduced the outflow of dollars, and at once revealed the precariousness of the pound.

The acute crisis which followed led to a sharp struggle over economic policy. Many, though not all, of the Government's official and financial advisers disliked the restrictions on trade and capital movements and were, like the Americans, eager to reintegrate Britain into the international economy. But with the gold and dollar reserves dangerously low, dismantling controls would make the stability of the currency dependent on the goodwill of foreign investors and bankers, strengthening domestic forces which were calling for severe deflation and heavy cuts in social services and food subsidies. Labour Ministers believed those expenditures desirable and necessary to retain trade union goodwill under the full employment which they were determined to preserve.

Nor did they believe, as did the foreign and domestic bankers, that the problem was due to inflation within Britain, curable by deflating the domestic economy. British costs and prices were not severely out of line; and it was not the United Kingdom but the rest of the sterling area which lost most dollars when the US recession reduced her purchases everywhere. The devaluation of the pound in September 1949, in the long run inevitable, was precipitated by the reluctance of foreigners who anticipated it to hold sterling. But devaluation was then a traumatic as well as a dramatic step. For some it reeked of immorality; for others it spelt national or party humiliation; for all it was a leap in the dark. In these debates Hugh Gaitskell was a central figure.

Gaitskell took on extra responsibilities at the Treasury in the summer of 1949. Cripps was away ill in Switzerland, and his duties were nominally taken over by Attlee, officially assisted by a youthful 'triumvirate': Harold Wilson, President of the Board of Trade; Douglas Jay, a junior Treasury Minister; and Gaitskell, still Minister of Fuel and Power. He took up these new duties at a time of crisis, when a recession in the United States was making dollars desperately short. His conduct made his reputation among senior men in Whitehall and in the Cabinet.

Treasury views were divided. Some officials found in the currency crisis an opportunity to press for sharp deflation. Gaitskell, while recognising the need for limited cuts in public expenditure, frustrated pressures for a more extreme course; a staunch defender of import and currency controls, he would have resigned if the Government had returned to convertibility. Other high officials saw devaluation as the only remedy for the dollar shortage. Once convinced, Gaitskell – still outside the Cabinet – successfully urged the policy on the senior Ministers and especially the sick and reluctant Chancellor. 'He took charge as the man who knew what needed to be done and was able to do it.'[1]

The US recession was reducing her purchases and therefore the flow of dollars, and no one could be sure how much Marshall Aid Congress would vote. The economic Ministers were determined not to deflate and as yet unconvinced of the need to devalue; they preferred to seek alternative supplies by making bilateral pacts which would discriminate against the United States. Bevin also endorsed those views, and was fairly hopeful of persuading Washington. Gaitskell in 1949 was gloomy about the Americans:

They want to force us to make all the effort to push our exports into the United States, and no doubt if necessary would say that we ought to deflate ourselves to achieve this. Nevertheless, if we were to succeed they would probably be demanding higher tariffs![2]

A week later he wrote:

we are at the parting of the ways. If we continue to aim at convertibility and multilateralism, I do not see how we can avoid deflation and devaluation now that the American slump is deepening. But if we do neither and go in for . . . trade discrimination in a big way against dollars and a great effort to replace dollar supplies with supplies from other areas, we risk the cutting off altogether of Marshall Aid.[3]

That was the context of his emotional reference at Porthcawl to 'a moment of supreme crisis for the Government'.

Gaitskell had wondered if that incident would damage his political prospects. Instead, a few days later he was for the first time brought into the very centre of policy-making as a result of the multiple illnesses which forced Cripps to take leave in 1949 (and to resign late in the following year). At the beginning of 1949, Harold Wilson would have seemed a much likelier successor. It was Gaitskell's leadership over devaluation which made him the preferred choice of both the Prime Minister and Cripps. In Jay's words, he

made up his mind clearly and decisively what needed to be done; convinced the doubters . . . and supervised all the arrangements . . . [persuading] those few who knew the facts that, if Cripps' health failed, Hugh Gaitskell was the only possible Chancellor . . . [and] determining the subsequent leadership of the Labour Party and so much else.[1]

Gaitskell wrote, in two instalments on 3 August and 21 September 1949, a full narrative of the crisis. This account is based on it, together with the recollections of other leading participants. Before Cripps's departure for Switzerland on 18 July the steady drain on the reserves became alarming. While Cripps and Bevin were still opposed to convertibility, Gaitskell was acutely worried by those Treasury officials for whom it was the main long-term objective, with devaluation and heavy deflation at home as the immediate steps. Bevin, records the diary,

> while opposed instinctively to any 'cuts' at home – he hates austerity – and opposed also instinctively to 'The Gold Standard' is also determined to rescue the world by successful negotiation in Washington . . . Undoubtedly, the danger is that these two most powerful Members of the Government on their own in Washington and advised by the Treasury, whose views are 'liberal' will agree to long term ties which will be eventually ruinous to us for the sake of some short term gain. They may indeed be driven to this because of the state of the reserves by the autumn.[4]

At one of these early July meetings, Cripps himself surprised Gaitskell by saying when the civil servants had left: 'One of my difficulties is that my official advisers are all "liberals" and I cannot really rely on them to carry through a "socialist" (*sic*) policy in these negotiations.'[4]

Devaluation seemed inevitable to Sir Edwin Plowden, head of the planning staff, and Robert Hall, director of the Economic Section of the Cabinet Office. By the end of June, Attlee and Morrison had broadly come round to their view, but Cripps and Bevin had not. As Gaitskell recorded: 'Harold Wilson now says he also favoured it then, but if so he certainly did not say so. . . . Others . . . thought . . . devaluation was just another way of reducing the standard of living of the working class.'[4]

Gaitskell doubted whether British exports to the dollar area would expand sufficiently to justify devaluation, and hoped to rely on discriminatory arrangements with other suppliers. In the next two weeks, the reserves fell sharply as world-wide recession damaged Britain's exports, and traders anticipating devaluation added to the pressure on the pound. After eighteen months in which the dollar deficit had steadily fallen, in the second quarter of 1949 it doubled and cost Britain £160 million in gold. With plenty of surplus capacity available in the export industries, Gaitskell and Jay separately but simultaneously decided that devaluation was inevitable.

On Monday 18 July Attlee, sitting next to Gaitskell on the Treasury bench, muttered: 'Oh, by the way, I am mentioning you in this statement.' It was the first time Gaitskell had heard directly that he was to substitute for Cripps. Jay lunched with him that Wednesday, and they rehearsed the arguments which had won them both over to devaluation, especially that 'the control over dollar expenditure was clearly much looser than we had supposed . . . The prospect of expanding exports to dollar areas was probably greater than we had at

first supposed . . . To delay devaluation might be exceedingly dangerous because as the reserve fell we should be completely dependent on
the U.S.A.'[4]

Within both the Treasury and the Government matters now moved
quickly. On the Thursday, Gaitskell and Jay first saw Harold Wilson,
who appeared to agree with them, and then easily won over Bevan,
Strachey and Strauss at one of their regular dinners. On Monday the
'triumvirate' met three leading Treasury officials, and went on to see
Attlee, Morrison and Dalton. They found that everyone now recognised that devaluation had become inevitable. The Cabinet met twice
that week but, as Dalton shows, the matter was not decided there.
Gaitskell criticised Dalton's 'very rosy view' that public expenditure
and the balance of payments were quite unrelated; some cuts in
spending, and therefore in taxation, would make it much easier to free
more resources to exploit the new export opportunities.

But on most matters they stood together against the Treasury:

H. G. and D. J[ay] come again to see me after this. H.G. says he'll resign if we
commit ourselves again to convertibility. They say there is still very heavy [*sic*]
from all official quarters 'to do something else' as well as devaluation . . . What
they all want is a slash in public expenditure on social services.

H. G. and D. J. both express distrust of H. W[ilson]. They don't know what
he's up to. They think he's currying favour with Bridges and Treasury
officials . . . it is agreed [in Cabinet] that P.M. should ask all Dept[al] Ministers
to cut down expenditure by, say, 5% . . . without undue publicity.[5]

There was a prolonged argument about the date of the devaluation.
To avoid international dislocation and resentment the Treasury
officials – backed by Harold Wilson – wanted to wait until early
September when Cripps would be in Washington for a regular meeting
of the World Bank and International Monetary Fund. Attlee was to
write to Cripps in Zürich, and they asked for the letter to set out more
strongly the case for waiting until Washington.

When the officials came back with their own completely redrafted
version, Gaitskell was appalled.

I exploded and made a scene. I said that they had gone far beyond the Prime
Minister's instructions; that I totally disagreed with their approach and we
must go back to the original draft by the Economic Secretary [ Jay]. They
crumpled up after this and we compromised by adding one or two
paragraphs . . . emphasising . . . the need for restricted Government
expenditure . . . this was the one passage of the letter to which the Chancellor
strongly objected.[6]

But Cripps was far from convinced devaluation was necessary. Until a devaluation is decided on, any finance minister has to deny that it would ever enter his head (for otherwise it would instantly become inevitable); and Stafford Cripps hated breaking his past commitments. The whole case would have to be argued out again when the sick Chancellor returned.

The Washington talks were now not far off. In Dalton's account (derived from Douglas Jay):

*In spite of all our Cabinet discussions and decisions*, the officials . . . put up a brief for Ministers, immediately before they were due to leave for W'ton, with all the old stuff about the 'need to restore confidence', and hence to make large reductions, including changes of policy, in public expenditure . . .

H.G. and D.J. fought this out. D.J. praised H.G. *most* highly. He acted as 'Vice-Chancellor of the Exchequer' and attacked the officials, both on intellectual grounds and on tacking on decisions already taken . . . If S.C. had had the wrong paper put up [or] the P.M. had weakened . . . the Labour Party [might] be breaking up as in 1931.

H.G. and D.J. saw eye to eye throughout. H.W. was away at this point, but D.J. doesn't trust him. He trims and wavers, and is thinking more of what senior Ministers – and even senior officials – are thinking of him than of what is right.[7]

When Cripps came back on Thursday 18 August Gaitskell sent him a ten-page memorandum on the case for devaluation, and a copy of a shorter note to the Prime Minister arguing for an election preferably in November 1949, possibly in the following summer, but not in between.[8] Next day, the Chancellor saw Bevin and the Prime Minister at Chequers, and Gaitskell and Harold Wilson were also invited. Gaitskell recorded:

It was a depressing occasion . . . the P.M. . . . sat at his desk doodling and listening to the argument. It was obvious that Stafford was quite out of touch . . . I was, of course, myself arguing both for devaluation and for the earliest date. H. argued strongly against the early date – although on the last occasion when we had met he had appeared to accept it. The Foreign Secretary swayed this way and that, and . . . treated [us] to a long monologue on . . . 1924 . . . 1931, etc. It was very hot and the room is a very small one. Bridges [Permanent Secretary of the Treasury] said little and was quite fair and objective.[6]

Bevin promised to support devaluation and Cripps reluctantly agreed, though insisting on waiting until Washington. Gaitskell went off on holiday to Jersey, returning for the Cabinet on 29 August which confirmed the decision to devalue and take strong consequential measures against inflation. Cripps and Bevin then left for Washington, where they settled on a devaluation of the pound from $4.03 to $2.80.

No one now doubts that the policy was right and inevitable, and Gaitskell certainly wanted a readjustment large enough to be quite clearly final. Following Cripps's return, the Cabinet met in secret on Saturday 17 September, using the back entrance to Downing Street. Cripps briefed Churchill as Leader of the Opposition, who complimented him warmly on a brave and correct decision but warned that 'I shall make the utmost political capital out of it'; his denunciation of Cripps for breaking commitments was so harsh that the Chancellor later refused to accept an honorary degree at his hands.[9] Next day, Sunday, after an impeccable operation combining full international consultation with total secrecy, the pound was devalued by 30 per cent.

## Cabinet Controversy, and the 1950 Election

The Government held together over the devaluation of September 1949, but the need to tackle the inflationary consequences soon produced ominous divisions. At the end of October Gaitskell wrote: 'Most people would say that things have not gone too well. We have produced our economy cuts and they have had a bad reception. The gold drain has certainly been stopped but the building up of reserves has been very slow. There is to be no Election until next year.'[10] Cripps threatened to resign unless economies of nearly £300 million were agreed, at which Bevan 'launched forth into a diatribe' with what Gaitskell thought rather dishonest backing from Dalton.[10] Dalton criticised Cripps's figure, while Bevan went even further, wanting economic affairs removed altogether from the Treasury. He 'thought S.C. would resign rather than give up his main proposals for economy. Others, including himself would resign rather than agree. One catalyst was a quick election.'[11]

Next day there was another battle over the detail of the cuts. The Foreign Secretary and Minister of Defence fought hard for the Service estimates. Cripps and Bevan, though old allies, clashed again – over the extent of inflationary pressure – and again both hinted at resignation. Cripps was thinking of a shilling increase in National Insurance contributions; Bevan was 'making it quite clear that he would have no interference with the Health Service'.[10] The result was a series of compromises, with cuts agreed at the rate of £280 million a year – half from government expenditure, and half from the capital investment programme, including £35 million off housing. The decision was poorly received, but Gaitskell thought the policies reasonable and the political outcome not too bad:

I do not believe this middleclass reaction at all typical throughout the country, and I doubt if we have lost much ground as a result, despite the terrific onslaught on the part of the press. Even papers like the Mirror, friendly to Labour, have been critical because they have failed to get any of the sensations which they love. How I detest them![10]

With its threats of resignation from Bevan if cuts were made in the health service and from the Chancellor if they were not, the 1949 Cabinet clash strikingly resembles the battle over the 1951 Budget. It provoked no less tension, for Douglas Jay found 'S.C. very messianic and A.B. very ideological about what are practical administrative questions not really lending themselves to either form of high emotion!'[11] Yet in this earlier conflict Bevan's antagonist was the man he admired as the best Chancellor Britain ever had, Sir Stafford Cripps.

Plainly, then, the 1951 clash was not simply due to the stubborn personality of Gaitskell, who in 1949 was not even in the Cabinet and played no important part. But his sympathies were already strongly with Cripps, as Dalton found:

He is now very frightened of 'inflationary pressure' and says that, if we don't deal with it, we shall have another dollar crisis in the spring. If this morning's clash came to a break, he would be with S.C. against A.B., and so he thinks would the country, and most of the Party. A.B., he thinks, should have been moved by the P.M. before now from a spending Dept. to, say, the Ministry of Labour, where he would do very well . . . he finds A.B. very difficult.[11]

Disagreement did not preclude friendly relations, and the Minister of Health was among the very few recipients of Gaitskell's two memoranda during the crisis. Gaitskell's diary records:

There is no doubt that Nye is really a natural witty and amusing conversationist. If his speeches are brilliant they are not the brilliance of carefully prepared, painstaking research, but something much more spontaneous. The remarks which he is famous for in public are equally made in private, as I have often heard at Cabinet meetings and similar occasions.

I think he is also a more profound thinker than he is sometimes given credit for. The other evening after a Group Dinner we drifted into a discussion about religion and philosophy. In this Nye started attacking religion, not as one might have expected on Marxist grounds, but far more on rationalist grounds – very sympathetic to me. It was a little embarrassing because of the Chancellor's religious views, but did reveal I think that Nye had really read and thought about these matters fairly deeply. I said to him afterwards, 'The other day you called me an "arid intellectual", and I wrote you off as a hopeless nineteenth century mystic but I am glad to welcome you back into the eighteenth century fold after your performance tonight'.

It is refreshing to find that one's colleagues can talk about these subjects in this way. We are all so busy as Ministers we tend to get into a terrible rut and talk shop. John Strachey said he had just finished reading Toynbee's great six volume history. I am really positively ashamed, amongst these friends, not to have read anything worth reading for such a long time.[12]

A few weeks later Gaitskell contrasted his problems with Harold Wilson with his pleasant relationship with Strachey and other colleagues,

with whom one can have that emotional and intellectual intercourse which is really the stuff of . . . friendship . . . such as Douglas [Jay] and Frank Pakenham, and even to some extent Nye Bevan . . . Frank . . . does not like Bevan and was rather horrified when I said that I thought Bevan would almost certainly be leader of the Party and therefore P.M. sometime.[13]

Gaitskell blamed the bad reception of the Government's cuts on the uncertainty about the election, causing delay which 'enabled the press to build up an impression that there were to be tremendously severe cuts. It is quite possible that it was deliberate policy on the part of the Opposition press . . . to make the whole plan appear a flop.'[10] The Cabinet discussed it for an hour on 13 October and decided to wait until 1950, as Attlee strongly urged. Bevan and Cripps dissented and Wilson was 'half against';[11] while Gaitskell, waiting outside, thought it 'a great mistake' when he was told.

Gaitskell celebrated the New Year with a great party – 'an enormous success' – for Hampstead and ministerial friends, though

I missed the highlight of the evening when Eva Robens . . . restive because of what she regarded as the phlegmatic behaviour of those present, looked hard at Harold Wilson and said, 'You come from north of the Trent, don't you? Surely you know how to behave!' and then proceeded to fling her arms around him and kiss him passionately, to his very great embarrassment. As he had previously been giving a lecture on why the ladies could not obtain nylons – which was full of statistics but all very sober, this incident gave great pleasure.[14]

At a rather dreary dinner party given by Cripps, after the dissolution, the production Ministers and their wives bet on the result and 11 of the 14 predicted a clear Labour majority of at least 70. But Gaitskell feared losses due to redistribution of seats, Liberal defections to the Tories, and a big swing against government interference in people's lives. He bet on a Labour majority of 30, won the pool, and preserved Cripps's cheque for 14 shillings as a memento.[14]

It was the only general election in which he was really active in South Leeds, for in 1945 he had been ill, and later he was everywhere in demand. He attracted national publicity only when he clashed with Churchill, who had committed the Conservatives to end petrol rationing as soon as possible. He did not enjoy it, feeling it 'impossible not to be bored with the sound of one's own voice long before the end. Indeed, if one were not bored it would only show what an intolerable character one was.' He thought the audiences showed both 'additional confidence in the capacity of Labour to govern, and . . . a collection of grievances . . . among the lower middle class and middle class.'[15] Austerity, petrol rationing and Aneurin Bevan's 'vermin' speech had indeed taken their toll in the commuter belt, where Labour's middle-class gains of 1945 were lost for twenty years. But there was no serious defection among working-class voters like those of South Leeds. The Gallup Poll found Labour drawing an even higher proportion of working-class voters in 1950 than in 1945, while the small parties and left-wing independents who opposed Labour candidates were decimated. Gaitskell found himself with much the safest Labour seat in the city and a result 'certainly quite up to my best expectations'.[15]

*South Leeds: Voting in 1945, 1950*

|  | 1950 | % |  | 1945 | % |
| --- | --- | --- | --- | --- | --- |
| H. Gaitskell (Lab.) | 29,795 | 61.1 | Gaitskell | 17,899 | 61.0 |
| B. H. Wood (Cons.) | 14,436 | 29.6 | Ramsden | 7,497 | 25.6 |
| E. Meeks (Lib.) | 4,525 | 9.3 | Barford | 3,933 | 13.4 |
| Majority | 15,359 |  |  | 10,402 |  |

Redistribution helped Gaitskell but severely – and predictably – damaged the Party as a whole: that had not deterred Churchill from denouncing it as Labour gerrymandering. Labour still polled 800,000 more votes than the Conservatives, a lead in votes which would have given the latter an overall majority of sixty-nine seats. But it gave Labour a majority of only five.

Beforehand, Bevan had thought the election quite likely to produce a weak Conservative government which 'wouldn't last long', and was dismayed at Gaitskell's prediction of a Labour majority of thirty, saying: 'I would rather not be in power at all'.[14] For in those days a working majority was supposed to be around forty, and a nominal but tiny majority was quite unprecedented. The prospect looked daunting, especially since many Labour MPs were tired and elderly. Gaitskell faced it robustly. At worst, a Conservative government after the next election would have a hard time and last only one Parliament; at best, fear of the Tories might enable Labour to recover Liberal votes, provided 'we can avoid giving unnecessary offence and quietly improve the economic position'.[15] World events were soon to dash any such hopes.

## Minister of State: The First Clash with Bevan

Gaitskell had early warning that if Labour won the 1950 election he would not return to Fuel and Power. Attlee meant to send him to the Treasury as Minister of State for Economic Affairs to help Cripps, whose health was still poor. Dalton had proposed his name, telling Attlee that a Treasury Minister needed 'not only keen intelligence or bright ideas, or diligence, or methodical adm$^n$, but power to resist high powered advice'. Dalton told Gaitskell and found that, though 'happy and reasonably comfortable' at Fuel and Power, he was now ready for a change:[16]

one is always in a way glad to leave a Ministry because you leave behind unsolved problems and some skeletons in cupboards and shed a load, and you walk into the other job with a free mind without . . . responsibilities for what has been done beforehand . . . being in the centre of the financial and economic policy does appeal to me.[13]

Years later Gaitskell told Malcolm Muggeridge that though it 'appeared to be a down-grading . . . I didn't mind that . . . I was pleased to be moved to a sphere I was very interested in'.[17]

In his first week he was laid low by flu, and wrote to one of his party workers in South Leeds: 'Just at present I feel in a thorough muddle and rather lonely and depressed. But this always happens in a new job & I suppose I shall settle down in time.' Before long he was showing, as a journalist noted, 'a quiet determination to run this most ancient department that shook some of its officials, . . . no administrative convolutions would deter him from getting to the bottom of a question.'[18] Again he disconcerted senior officials by his probing into detail, his disregard for hierarchy and protocol, his liking for long 'seminars' where a problem could be argued out.

As Cripps's understudy, Gaitskell was involved in the later stages of the Budget arguments, which brought the first rumblings of a great storm. For to Gaitskell's dismay the post-election reshuffle had not touched the Cabinet's most turbulent member. Bevan

certainly wanted to move and in my view it was imperative from the point of view of finance that he should be moved. Apparently under the influence of Bevin the P.M. decided he must go back to clear up the mess he created. It only means the mess will not be cleared up . . . It is a great mistake and one which may cost us very heavily.[15]

Gaitskell's view was not due to personal animosity. He was working hard (and successfully) to persuade Cripps to cancel the recent £35 million cut in Bevan's housing programme; and the Department to which he would have liked Bevan to move was the latter's own choice, the Colonies. The Minister of Health had exasperated his Cabinet colleagues by 'the mess he created' long before Gaitskell figured in the dispute at all.

The reasons went back to the beginnings of Bevan's great achievement, the National Health Service. When it was introduced in July 1948, no one could predict the demand. Understandably, the first estimates proved much too low and a large supplementary, nearly 30 per cent of the original estimate, had to be voted. In the Budget speech, the Chancellor warned that supplementaries had to be confined to rare cases such as a major change of policy; and specified that, failing economy in the use of the National Health Service over the next year, a special tax or charge might become necessary.[19] In May 1949 the all-party Select Committee on Estimates recommended 'such regulations as are practicable to prevent excessive or wasteful prescriptions'.[20] With the post-devaluation economy drive, authority to impose a charge for prescriptions was announced by the Prime Minister on 24 October 1949 and piloted through the House by Bevan himself on 9 December. It passed by 138 to 9. The 138 included 10 future Bevanites, among them Jennie Lee and Ian Mikardo, and 100 other Labour MPs; the opponents included only one Labour man, Walter Ayles. Bevan told the PLP of 'cascades of medicine pouring down British throats – and they're not even bringing the bottles back', and more sedately claimed in the House that since people knew of the 'abuse' of 'unnecessary expenditure' on prescriptions, the charges aroused little indignation.[21]

In March 1950, a year after the Chancellor's ban on supplementary estimates, the Ministry of Health presented one for nearly £100 million – about 37 per cent of the original estimate. By the Minister's own decision its presentation was delayed long after the Department knew it would be necessary, provoking an all-party protest against 'a serious impairment of the system of Parliamentary control'.[22] This was

Gaitskell's first appearance in the dispute. He successfully urged Cripps to insist that NHS spending must come under Treasury control like all other expenditure and that its total must be limited. He hoped to make Bevan face the choice between making economies or imposing charges. That did not succeed. 'As usual, there was a policy compromise because of the threat of Bevan's resignation and the unwillingness of the Cabinet to accept the principle of charging just yet . . . Personally, I think politically . . . cuts would have done us a lot of good.'[15]

The 'compromise' was negotiated, according to his own claim, by Harold Wilson. It fixed a generous ceiling, well above current expenditure, with measures to enforce it; and in return again deferred the charges suggested by Cripps in March 1949, hinted at by the Estimates Committee in May, authorised by Bevan's own Act in December, and again discussed by the Cabinet in March 1950. Nevertheless, the Chancellor knew that it had made a mockery of his statement a year before, and was determined that the estimate for 1950/51 – £34 million above the final total for 1949/50 – must really be 'a ceiling beyond which we must not be carried'.[23]

Bevan never meant to carry out his side of the bargain. As his biographer puts it, 'the charges . . . had been stopped and Bevan lived to threaten resignation another day'. He denied his colleagues' right to criticise his departmental expenditure in a letter to the Prime Minister. 'I do hope', he wrote a little petulantly, 'that I can have some peace to get on with my proper work without this continual nibbling.'[24] It soon became clear that he accepted the concession (no charges yet) but meant to ignore the counterpart (an effective ceiling).

His colleagues, however, were also anxious for the well-being of the services for which they were responsible. Already one-third of all expenditure on social services went to the health service; if Bevan were granted sovereign rights and a blank cheque, all economies must be made at others' expense. So Cripps was not speaking only for a parsimonious Treasury in his Budget statement that there could be

no excuse for exceeding the estimates in the coming 12 months . . . Any expansion in one part of the [Health] Service must in future be met by economies or, if necessary . . . an Amending Act will be introduced. It is not proposed to impose any charge immediately in connection with prescriptions, since it is hoped that a more easily administered method of economising in this branch of expenditure can be introduced shortly. The power to charge will, of course, remain so that it can be used later if it is needed.[25]

Above all the Cabinet would no longer rely on Bevan to enforce the ceiling. Like Shinwell after the fuel crisis, he had to put up with 'a barely sufferable indignity, the surveillance of Health Service finances by a special weekly Cabinet Committee, presided over by the Prime Minister'.[24]

When these decisions were being made, Gaitskell was still outside the Cabinet. As yet, Bevan was not hostile to him or even to the Treasury, and, wrote Gaitskell, 'has really given us quite good support on the general theory of preventing inflation.'[26] Even the health service conflict at first aroused no bitterness:

Relations with Nye have settled down again after the great row about the Health Services . . . his actual attitude on the essential points of policy is not nearly so far removed from Herbert's as it used to be. . . . Perhaps somebody really has told him that he nearly lost us the Election.

The thing I like about him is that one can have a terrific row with him in a Cabinet Committee and yet remain on quite cordial terms with a good deal of friendly back-chat. Another endearing characteristic is that he does not really make much effort to collect around him a lot of supporters in the Cabinet or Government, though his enemies would say that was only because he could not find any.[26]

The antagonism arose quite specifically from the attempt to enforce the ceiling on health service expenditure to which Bevan had nominally agreed. On the night the Prime Minister's committee was set up he had come home 'white with passion'; and his wrath fell on Gaitskell, whom Cripps had appointed as Treasury prosecutor. Exasperated above all by any mention of charges, he came to look on Gaitskell 'as the pedantic spokesman of the Treasury's most arid doctrines'.[24] From Gaitskell's side it was 'One of the more unpleasant jobs I have been made to do . . . a very wearing affair – always having to nag one's colleagues, and especially when they are as slippery and difficult as the Minister of Health.'[27] According to John Strachey, Cripps's dinners had already become tense occasions:

Aneurin Bevan began to lash Hugh with the fury of his tongue. Hugh would sit rather silent under it, occasionally replying with a dry, factual contradiction. When this had happened several times I walked away from one of the dinners with Bevan and asked him why he was doing it. 'Why', I said, 'are you going out of your way to make a rift between yourself and one of the really considerable men of the Government?' '*Considerable!*' Aneurin replied. 'But he's nothing, nothing, nothing!'[28]

## Minister for Overseas Finance

Most of the senior members of that Cabinet had held office for ten gruelling and anxious years. Early in 1950 Gaitskell assessed them all. Morrison had been desperately ill in 1947, but was now active again – prone to intrigue, but

mostly on the side of the 'angels', especially where public expenditure is concerned . . . [Attlee] seems to me to have more political sense than almost everybody else. Undoubtedly, too, his position in the Government is stronger than it has ever been . . . I think history will record that he was among the more successful British Prime Ministers.

Bevin was remarkably resilient, one day 'hardly capable of coherent speech and the next . . . shrewd, sensible, imaginative – all his old, best qualities'.[26] Cripps, now the champion of national unity, carried weight in the House, the Party and the country thanks less to his 'superb intellect' than to his 'moral strength and serene integrity'. Gaitskell later recalled 'often going to see him feeling depressed and worried over some difficult problem, and coming away with a wonderful renewal of confidence'.[29]

  Their co-operation could easily have been spoilt by the junior man feeling resentment at being neglected, or provoking it by aggressiveness. But no friction developed. Their relations turned out to be excellent, though quite unexpected. Cripps left technical and complicated matters to Gaitskell, and frequently took his advice. To the younger man's surprise 'in bargaining either with his colleagues or with outsiders . . . we all of us are nervous . . . lest he gives way too much. I find myself . . . having to stiffen him up on almost every occasion.'[26]

  The Budget of 1950 was unexciting. In the House Gaitskell attacked the Opposition for wanting total government expenditure cut, and more spent·on every separate service; and recognised as the major economic problem of democracy to hold full employment without inflation.

We must have some arrangement under which increased earnings, justified by an increase in output, are distributed among the various classes of workers. The Opposition . . . do not even want to contemplate this problem . . . How do they propose to get rid of it? We shall have an answer no doubt this evening.[30]

Before going to the Treasury, he had given his own anwer. In Dalton's account of it:

Don't rely mainly on financial controls to prevent inflation. Always keep demand just above supply, in order to hold full employment, and rely on *physical* controls – especially on total imports, capital export, building location and essential material . . . to hold inflation.[31]

But as Gaitskell knew, that strategy could be undermined by economic pressures from abroad.

In this connection, he was personally responsible for negotiating the arrangements for a new European Payments Union to which Britain could safely adhere. In doing so he was surprised to find some of the American representatives becoming staunch allies.

It is rather odd that after acquiring a reputation within the UK Government for objecting to so much of what the Americans were trying to do in Europe I should yet have been able to get on well with them. I think the explanation is that most of them had fundamentally the same outlook as I had. They were and are economist new-dealer types, and anxious to get the same kind of payments system going as we were ourselves.[27]

Before being wound up on the return to world-wide convertibility in 1959, the EPU had made a notable contribution to European recovery, and proved 'one of the major achievements of post-war European cooperation'.[32]

The episode had a lasting effect on Gaitskell, who had felt uncertain of the outcome. The talks undermined his deep suspicion of the Americans on economic policy, showing him that they could be invaluable allies for a Labour Britain. Towards the end he wrote to their representative, Averell Harriman:

on the really important issues we just naturally find ourselves thinking along the same lines. And since, like you, I believe that just about the most important thing in the world is for the United States and Britain to work along together, this experience has been wonderfully encouraging.[33]

It helps to explain his attitude to the rearmament gamble a few months later.

## *Korea and Rearmament 1950: 'The Maximum We Can Do'*

During the summer, Cripps's health deteriorated again, and Gaitskell and Plowden with difficulty persuaded him to go away for three months. 'Meanwhile, I have been left in charge, and in order to impress outsiders and officials, at his suggestion, have moved into his enormous room.'[27] Then on 24 June North Korean tanks invaded South Korea, and the crisis began which was to dominate Gaitskell's own Chancellorship: rearmament. On 26 July Washington urgently asked its allies how much, given United States assistance, they could step up their defence expenditure over the next three years. Britain – with the most stable political system and the most flourishing economy – held the key to the others' response.

Western minds were haunted by the Communists' behaviour in Eastern Europe: above all the Prague putsch, the threats against Yugoslavia and the Berlin blockade. In Washington, the National Security Council had recently forecast a world-wide Soviet offensive. Then came Korea, the first Communist military invasion of a neighbouring country since 1945, and within four days President Truman, with almost unanimous approval in Britain, had decided to intervene. Some people feared a Soviet march to the Channel, and others took very seriously the risk of another Communist satellite army attacking Yugoslavia, Scandinavia, West Germany or Iran; among these were Bevan, Crossman and the Yugoslav government.

Replying within ten days as requested, Britian on 4 August offered to spend on defence in the next three years – conditional on the promised American aid – an extra £1,100 million, of which the United States was asked to provide half. The three-year total would be £3,400 million. A later decision on Service pay raised it to £3,600 million.

The Korean War and consequent rearmament were to transform the British economy, British politics, and Gaitskell's career. For him, its first impact came through a humiliating Cabinet defeat over the extra £200 million for pay. Cripps's last official act had been to protest angrily to Shinwell about the Ministry of Defence making proposals without consulting the Treasury. Gaitskell argued the Service Ministers into compromising. But 'it was a bad Cabinet, flooded out with Service Ministers and Chiefs of Staff, so perhaps it was not surprising that I was routed'.[27] Three weeks later Gaitskell wrote to Dalton:

What annoyed me was that . . . I had persuaded Shinwell to accept a good deal less – so that the Chiefs of Staff (having I suspect got the ear of the P.M. in advance) really got a very weak sort of Cabinet to overrule this agreement – and that is bad. Politicians should keep on top! Also it is not a good thing that our colleagues should get into the habit of thinking that £15 million is just 'a ha'porth of tar'![34]

The move to the Treasury affected Gaitskell's private life, for he was now constantly conducting international negotiations, often abroad. Dora came with him to Paris for the final EPU meeting, when he amused the officials by getting sudden urges to dine in a garish restaurant, and to visit Montmartre. He found Geneva beautiful but 'very hot' and 'fiendishly expensive', and went off dancing and swimming and hunting for cheap cafés with his civil servants. International talks interrupted his 'entirely inadequate and improvised holiday' in the late summer, as he lamented to Dalton when he had to go to Paris for the regular World Bank and IMF meeting. His old patron had written that 'opportunity is carrying *you* forward on a great wave', and Gaitskell replied: 'Who wants to see these stiff-shirted bourbon bankers anyway when I might continue the marked progress I have made in surf-riding? . . . though the prospect of suddenly finding oneself . . . submerged by the succeeding wave is very real in each case!'[34]

On another official journey to Paris, he left at 6 a.m.:

I managed to wake in time, shave, dress and even have some breakfast, and then saw the car standing in the pouring rain outside, and found to my despair that I could not get out of the hotel. The doors seemed to be locked; it was pitch dark inside, and I did not know where the keys were. Everybody else was asleep. Finally in desperation I opened the dining-room window from the top – the bottom would not move – and clambered up and out – all in my best overcoat and black hat.[35]

Parliament was recalled on 12 September 1950 to pass the bill lengthening national service. The Prime Minister in opening the debate stressed that the rearmament programme was dependent on American assistance:

This great expenditure represents the maximum we can do . . . without resorting to the drastic expedients of a war economy [direction of labour and requistioning of premises] . . . we are reaching the limit of what we can do unaided without impairing our economic position . . . before we can decide the exact extent of our effort we must know what assistance will be forthcoming from the United States of America.[36]

Gaitskell spoke on the economic aspects, warning that the standard of living might well have to fall. He too took care to emphasise the dependence of the programme on American help, to qualify his forecasts and to reaffirm that the British people should not undertake 'burdens unduly heavy in relation to their resources' or to those borne by their allies.[36] 'I have never had more trouble with any speech,' he wrote. It was a great success, helping to establish him as Cripps's successor.

Tensions within the Labour Party were still muted, except for the few unhappy pacifists. Richard Crossman cautiously supported the programme. But warning notes were now appearing in *Tribune* (which had supported the Berlin airlift, the Atlantic Pact and the Korean intervention); and Jennie Lee suggested that Britain was doing too much and the United States too little. Across the Atlantic the view was naturally different, as Gaitskell was soon to discover when, at his own request, he went to Washington to put the British case on two rearmament problems: raw materials and financial assistance.[37]

Raw material prices were soaring as the Americans, pressing hard for a great allied rearmament effort, impeded it by their own purchasing programme, which was raising prices and creating shortages in Europe and especially in Britain. The seven United States agencies concerned were not brought together until December, and long delays continued because of 'the chaotic nature of the administration in Washington [and] the extraordinary fear the Americans have of giving any offence to the smallest possible power'.[38] By March 1951 a cumbrous organisation was at last in place – and raw material prices were falling from their peak.

The talks on financing rearmament proved no more satisfactory. In conveying the first United States approach in late July, the American Ambassador had given definite but not specific assurances of financial help. When His Majesty's Government responded by asking the Americans to pay half of the £1,100 million increase, 'They received our proposals very coldly and seemed to expect that we ought to be doing a lot more . . . They are curious people to deal with – nice, well-intentioned but, I think, often lacking in judgment.'[27] British politicians (and officials) normally served a government with a parliamentary majority which could fulfil any commitment it made; they found it hard to appreciate that no US Administration could do the same, and that no promises of assistance could be more than pious hopes.

The Administration could not deliver on its pledges, for Congress had severely restricted non-military aid. American public opinion was quite unsympathetic, for Britain's reserves had doubled – though still far too low, and threatened by worsening terms of trade. In Washington newspapers treated as blackmail the British warning that her rearmament must depend on the size of the American contribution, while US Treasury officials 'believe it is time that Britain chose between a suitable posture of defence and a continuation of her present high standard of living'.[39] As Gaitskell wrote, it was

a rather awkward situation. We had said in public that we would carry out this programme given substantial dollar aid. It was evident that the Americans would not be able to give us that aid. It was, however, equally apparent that some considerable speeding up in defence was necessary.[37]

The long-term prospects seemed somewhat more hopeful. During the tripartite discussions, Paul Nitze, Assistant Secretary of State, suggested that instead of the United States making bilateral grants to each of her allies, NATO should consider how far the defence burden was being fairly shared among the European countries and between them and the United States. Gaitskell returned from Washington reasonably optimistic:

the Americans probably start with the idea . . . that we ought to be able to carry . . . the £3,600 million programme without much financial assistance. We can, however, reasonably expect that they will be open to argument as a result of considering the whole question of equality . . . We may have . . . to adjust our ideas as to the form . . . [of aid], in particular as between military production and dollars . . . the former is greatly to be preferred.[37]_

Apart from business, Gaitskell enjoyed his first trip across the Atlantic – 'an event in anybody's life,' he wrote.

I felt quite boyish, the same as we used to when we went to Scotland as children, starting out on this trip . . . On arrival we found that our luggage was not there. We had been treated as so much VIP that they managed to put it on the wrong plane, and that meant waiting. So we decided to go into New York for lunch.[40]

He was struck by the number of black people , and by the 'endless streams' of cars delaying his Sunday afternoon flight on to Washington. He found the capital 'attractive . . . in its domestic architecture . . . big white Ministry buildings stand in a kind of park; and then the trees, mostly fully grown and just with autumn tints on them'. From Washington he had a bumpy, uncomfortable flight to Ottawa for talks with Canadian Ministers.

After three days in Canada Gaitskell took the train to New York, where he had little to do but enjoy himself. Returning to his hotel on the second night, he found a message to telephone the British High Commissioner in Canada. When the call was put through the voice told him to prepare for a shock:

I thought, 'Oh God! what awful brick have I dropped in Ottawa – are the Canadians going to claim that we have agreed to import far more?' Then he went on 'I have a message for you from the P.M.' I thought that he meant the Canadian Prime Minister . . . Then he read . . . that Stafford was not going back for a year and that after consulting with his colleagues, the P.M. wanted me to take his place. Would I agree to having my name submitted to the King? I can never think of the right thing to say . . . So I just said . . . 'Yes I will do it and I will send him a message myself soon'.

Unable to locate any New York friends to celebrate with, he summoned his official advisers (one of them from bed) to take advantage of his last few hours before the press arrived. 'A rather pathetic procession moved slowly up Broadway', the officials prudently dissuading the new Chancellor from entering each dubious establishment marked 'Dancing' and 'Girls', so that dissipation was confined to visiting a nightclub with a political cabaret. They were very short of money, and on finding that Gaitskell's whisky and soda had cost $10, Plowden forbade a second – to his master's chagrin when they discovered too late that the price covered several drinks. Next evening: 'My last night in New York while it was still secret was especial fun . . . I went with my friend, Jim Orrick and "did the town", the best part being dancing with his sister-in-law in Greenwich Village at a . . . most excellent cabaret of informal character.' He told Orrick of his promotion as they said goodnight, and went to bed at 4.30 a.m.; yet he was down for breakfast with a senior adviser who was catching a very early plane. The news broke that afternoon. 'I am getting quite used to being approached by journalists. It is rather like the novelette business of two detectives waiting for you. They step out and confront you, and . . . I gave them a quick message and was photographed – horrible photos – and had to pack.'

In his exhilaration on first hearing the news, he poured out to William Armstrong – Cripps's private secretary and now to be his own – his hopes for the rejuvenation of the Labour government with the arrival of his generation in positions of power. But by the time he landed at London Airport more sober thoughts prevailed, and when his own private secretary congratulated him he replied: 'No it isn't good news – it is ten years too soon.'[41] His first call was on Cripps, who was charming and did all he could to smooth Gaitskell's path; his next on Attlee, who advised reassuringly, 'don't worry, my boy, it may never happen'. As Gaitskell recorded it:

interviews with him are never very exciting or long. But I made sure that I really was to be Number 4 in the Government as Stafford had been. He warned me about Shinwell and Bevan, but told me that he was going to move Nye from the Ministry of Health to the Ministry of Labour – something I had been hoping . . . for a long time. But . . . he told me a day or two ago that there had been difficulties . . . So far everybody is being very nice but that will not last for long.[35]

# 8

# Chancellor of the Exchequer: Bevan and the Budget 1950-1

---

'*A high snow peak . . . a steaming tropical swamp*
(Dalton comparing HG and Bevan, April 1951)
'*One or other of us is not going to be a member of the government tomorrow –*
*I am not sure which it will be*'
(HG to the King about Bevan, just before the Budget)

---

## Unknown Chancellor

Because of Cripps's state of health, senior Ministers had known for months that a new Chancellor might be needed. Cripps himself insisted that Gaitskell must replace him both in office and as the fourth senior Minister, after the Prime Minister, Morrison and Bevin. Those senior colleagues also approved of Gaitskell and much preferred him to Bevan. Morrison, who did not think himself qualified, was content at the choice of a man too young, as it then seemed, to be a dangerous rival.

Gaitskell was only forty-four, the second youngest Chancellor of the twentieth century, with the least parliamentary experience of anyone since the beginning of the nineteenth. He had little standing with the Labour rank and file. Yet his promotion was well received in the PLP 'as a natural and inevitable step'.[1] The one really hostile comment came from the Beaverbrook press, pursuing a long flirtation with the Labour Left. The political correspondent of the *Daily Express* predicted that Gaitskell might 'crack emotionally under the strain of having to introduce a rearmament budget', and that the authority of the Treasury, asserted under Cripps, would now crumble if it were challenged.

Such challenges were not hard to foresee. Gaitskell learned that Harold Wilson was 'inordinately jealous, though in view of his age there is really no reason for it'.[2] The rearmament programme made friction inevitable between the Chancellor and the Minister of Defence, quite apart from the latter's personal antagonism. As Gaitskell wrote:

I have not had much trouble with any of my colleagues. Shinwell is the most difficult. Obviously my promotion over his head went very deep. He never loses an opportunity of picking a quarrel with me, sometimes on the most ridiculous grounds. In any case there are often very good grounds for it in view of the terrific defence expenditure.[3]

More ominous was the wrath of Aneurin Bevan, whose selection was opposed by senior Ministers and trade union leaders and, in Attlee's view, would not have carried confidence abroad.

Bevan had been restive for some time, and plenty of journalists knew it. He had stayed too long at the Ministry of Health, was unhappy with Morrison's policy of 'consolidation', and preferred rousing the Labour faithful to cosseting the floating voter. Such differences over political strategy become acute when a precarious government must soon face the electorate. As the party conference opened at Margate, a political correspondent drew attention to their 'duel for the future and not the present leadership of the party . . . the Minister of Health is man-oeuvring for support . . . [as] defender-in-chief of the social services, especially the National Health Service, against . . . the Treasury.'[4]

The battle lines were thus already drawn six months before the crisis over Gaitskell's Budget and three weeks before his appointment as Chancellor. That promotion touched off a major explosion, for Bevan had apparently expected Cripps to recommend him for the succession. When the appointment was announced, he launched a torrent of abuse against the Prime Minister in the corridors of the House. He sent Attlee a petulant letter expressing 'consternation and astonishment . . . it is impossible to give advice and counsel about Government policy when only a part at a time is disclosed to me.'[5] There followed 'a tremendous row with Clem', whose intended reshuffle had to be postponed.[6]

On becoming Chancellor Gaitskell retained his ministerial style. He did not move into 11 Downing Street but stayed in Hampstead, mainly because of the children's schooling. Again his civil servants found him fascinated by detail and determined to master all the complexities. Again he took immense pains with parliamentary questions, frequently siding with the critical MP against the office. Behaving more like a fellow-administrator than a senior Minister, he would spend hours talking with junior officials, or holding 'seminars' on the economic implications of policy. Senior and traditional Treasury men resented the time involved, and the questioning of the established policies of Whitehall's premier Department; at first some also found his manner brusque and imperative. But able younger officials saw matters quite differently.

As at Fuel and Power, he had already had months to get to know the senior officials. Again there was an early malaise:

the officials . . . have such a keen sense of their own independent departmental position as apart from serving me . . .

The machine can get so easily slack if you leave them alone. But if you harass them then they complain bitterly that you are interfering too much and not delegating, etc.[3]

Gaitskell knew that a Chancellor must not be submerged by minor problems. He delegated heavily to the Economic Secretary (John Edwards) and Financial Secretary (Douglas Jay), urging them repeatedly to refer upwards as little as possible. But the civil servants still felt he wanted to do too much himself. His insistence on redrafting major speeches was the despair of his advisers. He was bad at keeping appointments, seeing too many people and letting discussions run too long. Some shrewd civil servants – though not all – felt that he was too anxious to find the right economic answer, and so somewhat distracted from the Minister's role of exercising political judgement. But all thought him an exceptionally intelligent, courteous, clear-sighted and courageous chief. An unofficial historian of the Treasury writes that Gaitskell 'probably understood his job better than any Chancellor we have had before or since.'[7]

In long-term policy, Gaitskell told William Armstrong, the principal task of a Socialist Chancellor would be the redistribution of wealth; once that was accomplished, the philosophical differences between the parties would gradually diminish. His first and only Budget was designed to combat inflation by reducing consumption. But for his second he was planning a capital gains tax; and he frequently urged the need for Labour to think out its policy on the subject.

More immediately he was concerned, like later Labour Chancellors, with the pressures of trade unionists and of bankers. In his first major speech in the House he warned:

Higher incomes, unaccompanied by increases in production, will certainly lead to higher prices: and higher incomes in one group will lead to demands for higher incomes elsewhere, which, in turn, will lead to higher prices for everyone . . . We cannot by manipulation of personal income, get more out of the national product than is available . . . The Government must, as far as possible, so control through its budgetary and credit policy the flow of money as to reduce pressure provided this does not of course lead to unemployment.[8]

He was no less firm with the Bank of England, resisting its pressure for a higher bank rate and finding its spokesmen 'singularly bad at putting their case, and . . . usually wrong in their conclusions'.[9]

There was some departmental friction with the Board of Trade over monopolies, consumer grievances and resale price maintenance, and with the Ministry of Food which had overestimated Britain's bargaining position in negotiations over Argentine meat; Gaitskell had repeatedly tried to persuade them to settle, but loyally took responsibility for their thoroughly unpopular policy. (His wife impressed the housewife's resentment on the Chancellor by keeping him on fish, which he did not like.)

There were faint tremors of the coming domestic earthquake:

Outwardly Nye Bevan is quite friendly again, and at least he gives a much more honest view of things than Shinwell does. I do not really feel with him that he is insincere and for long going to take a view simply because of his personal likes or dislikes.

Harold Wilson is probably still exceedingly jealous, but I must say I have had no great difficulty with him. But all this is rather premature because the real struggle will come when we try and settle expenditure policy and get nearer to the Budget.[3]

Prospects of a peaceful settlement of that coming struggle were not improved by the end of Marshall Aid – formally on 1 January 1951 but in fact six weeks earlier. Knowing that Britain's balance of payments surplus made this inevitable, Gaitskell made the best of it by ensuring maximum publicity for her impressive economic improvement. Aid was to be restored if the situation deteriorated seriously: a commitment never fulfilled.

## Korea and Rearmament 1951: 'To the Limit of the Resources under our Control'

Marshall Aid was ending because of Britain's rapid recovery, but also owing to new burdens on the United States arising from her own and allied rearmament. For by December 1950 the Communist Chinese had entered the Korean conflict, in which the US was to incur very heavy casualties. General MacArthur had driven back the North Koreans in September, advanced beyond the 38th Parallel and then, to Britain's dismay, approached the Chinese frontier, where he was thrown back in disarray by a massive Chinese offensive on 24 November which nearly drove the United Nations forces out of Korea.

After Truman's supposed hint that the atomic bomb might be used against China, Attlee flew to Washington on 4 December 1950 for a famous meeting, at which they differed sharply. Both had so far hoped to conciliate China and keep her out of the Soviet orbit. But the

Americans – engaged in a desperate war, and with the Republican hawks strengthened in Congress – now urged the UN to declare China an aggressor and to prepare sanctions against her. The Senate voted for that (the 'Brand China' resolution) with no dissenter, the House of Representatives with only two. Since American support was vital both to economic recovery and to balance Soviet military power in Europe, the British Cabinet disagreed over whether the United Kingdom could risk a break with Washington.

Gaitskell played a major part in this controversy. The British Government feared, he wrote on 10 January 1951, that if the Chinese were bombed or blockaded they would retaliate by seizing Hong Kong and attacking Indo-China and Malaya. 'The awful dilemma is that if we cannot restrain the Americans then we have to go in with them in China, which nobody wants, or desert them . . . [with] very serious consequences in their participating in European defence.'[10] Bevin's policy had been to try hard to moderate the Americans, but in the last resort accept their proposal. Then on 25 January the Cabinet, with Bevin away ill, were told they 'must assume the resolution would be put in an unpalatable form'. The Foreign Office Minister of State, Kenneth Younger, wanted to vote against the United States. Gaitskell proposed abstention – which was also preferred by Attlee, Morrison and Jowitt. But Younger said it was really no different from an adverse vote, on which course the majority decided. Gaitskell was appalled. It meant opposing all the white Dominions, and 'would enormously strengthen the anti-European block in the U.S.A. It might lead to their virtually coming from Europe [*sic*] which would, in my opinion, be the end for us.'[11] Discovering next day the dismay of the Treasury and Foreign Office officials, which they felt sure Bevin would share, Gaitskell privately warned the Prime Minister that he might have to resign if the decision was maintained: a very bold stand for a young Minister with no popular following.

Events at once made it pointless, for Washington agreed after all to consider an amendment (inspired by the British Ambassador) which deferred discussing sanctions till after a new attempt to conciliate China. The Cabinet agreed to vote for the resolution if the proposed amendments were accepted, and if not to let Attlee decide; Gaitskell felt confident 'he would not go further than abstention'.[11] The United States did agree to delay any decision on the sanctions, and the amended resolution was voted by 44 to 7.

The American Administration was still under heavy pressure from the Republican hawks to break free from European entanglements and fight an all-out war in the Far East, which President Truman publicly called 'a gigantic booby-trap'. But the Department of Defense insisted on bargaining American commitment in Europe against European acquiescence in immediate rearmament, including that of West Germany. Any Administration sympathy for Europe's needs and difficulties was soon swept aside by the impatient and suspicious congressional Republicans. The Korean invasion was taken, contrary to the advice of the State Department's Russian experts, to show a new Soviet willingness to use armed force to achieve her objectives;[12] and against NATO's 12 divisions the Russians had 175, with 27 (plus 60,000 militarised German police) in East Germany alone. On 6 December 1950, during Attlee's visit, the American joint chiefs of staff sent out a general war warning to all NATO commanders. The British War Office warned the Cabinet early in the New Year: 'war possible in 1951, probable in 1952'.[13]

In this mood of crisis German rearmament was reluctantly accepted 'in principle'. The main opposition came from the French, but the British Government was unhappy too, and divided over Germany as well as China: 'there is to some extent the same cleavage', noted Gaitskell:

The anti-Americans . . . will not admit now the Russian menace. This leads them to oppose a lot of things which the Americans want to do . . . [like] re-arming Germany [and] to follow opinion in the Party which certainly is pretty anti-American, and still rather pacifist . . . personal ambitions and rivalries [are] at work. H. W. is clearly ganging up with the Minister of Labour, not that he cuts very much ice because one feels that he has no fundamental views of his own, but it is another voice. The others on Bevan's side are very genuine. Jim Griffiths for pacifism; Chuter Ede because he is anti-American and Dalton because he hates the Germans.[11]

Differences in the Cabinet turned on foreign policy, not on the need for the West to rearm, where Britain still held the key. Continental recovery was far behind hers, and political stability and determination were far less. Without a British lead, there would be no significant European contribution and no hope of convincing Congress or the American public to help defend the Continent while still fighting in Korea. No financial aid would come unless Congress voted for 'burden-sharing' – as it never would if Britain balked at faster rearmament.

The American soldiers sought from Britain a programme costing £6,000 million in three years, which was endorsed by the British chiefs of staff, and apparently accepted in principle by Shinwell, the Minister of Defence, in Washington just after Gaitskell became Chancellor. At the NATO Council in Brussels in December 1950, Bevin announced the British Government's decision to rearm faster. On 29 January Attlee told the House of Commons that the Cabinet had decided on an expansion from £3,600 million to £4,700 million over the next three years.

In August the Government had already agreed to raise defence spending by £1,100 million over three years; now it proposed to double that expansion. The earlier proposal had depended on American help, but by December it knew that aid would come only slowly and uncertainly through 'burden-sharing'. The extra load on British resources had trebled in six months, and the share of GNP going to defence was to rise from 8 per cent before the crisis to 14 per cent after it – a proportion exceeded in NATO only by the United States. No longer did the Prime Minister warn of reaching Britain's economic limit; instead he promised 'to carry out this production programme to the limit of the resources under our control'.

In early January Gaitskell had recorded 'something like a panic developing about our defence programme . . . the atmosphere becomes more and more like 1940'. In this mood the Cabinet accepted the £4,700 million programme on 25 January with little dissension: less, over a decision which would have repercussions and provoke controversy for years, than over that crucial UN vote on the 'Brand China' resolution. Gaitskell's diary describes the atmosphere:

We got the rearmament programme through however rather more easily than might have been expected . . . It was expected that Bevan would put up a lot more resistance. I never thought so myself . . . We were committed to some acceleration – we could hardly start arguing with the Chiefs of Staffs about what was essential and what was not essential. Both the President of the Board of Trade [Wilson] and Minister of Supply [Strauss] made some effort to resist it, partly I think on political grounds (they are linking up with the Minister of Labour) and partly just as an alibi in case the programme could not be fulfilled or exports dropped catastrophically.[11]

G. R. Strauss, then Minister of Supply, confirmed Gaitskell's account:

I went to see Aneurin Bevan and said: 'This is much too big . . .' He made sympathetic noises but I was surprised he wasn't more enthusiastic . . . I made a speech against it to the Cabinet. Nye never opened his mouth, or if he did he didn't say anything worth saying. Only Harold Wilson and I were against it.[14]

Wilson's biographers say that Bevan dissuaded him from resigning in February over the raw materials situation; though at the time Strauss found him, as well as Bevan, lukewarm.[15]

In the Cabinet, Bevan merely cast doubt on the military intelligence estimates. Many of his colleagues – whom he had never previously left unaware when he seriously disapproved – have testified that he did not challenge the programme until two months later. This is confirmed by Attlee, Dalton, Freeman, Gordon Walker, Shinwell, Strachey, Younger (present on 25 January 1951), and both Gaitskell's and Attlee's private secretaries. (These recollections must be treated with caution: Strauss forgot Gaitskell's active part, Wilson forgot Strauss's, and Shinwell and Younger forgot Wilson's.) His general unhappiness had often been leaked to the press; but those familiar rumblings foreshadowed a coming battle over paying for rearmament, not an attack on the policy itself as unnecessary, undesirable or impracticable. Besides, Bevan did not just silently and reluctantly acquiesce; shortly before the programme was agreed, he at last accepted his long-suggested transfer to the Ministry of Labour, which was directly involved with it. (Gaitskell expected that he would there maintain 'his reputation of being radical in everybody else's Ministry except his own. He will probably be more cautious about wages policy and the direction of labour than he has ever been in the past.')[9] At his own request, Bevan wound up the defence debate on 15 February 1951; and he made a categorical public commitment to the full rearmament programme, which Attlee and Gaitskell were careful to avoid. Attlee said: 'If the programme is fully achieved, the total defence budget over the next three years . . . may be as much as £4,700 millions . . . limitations on production . . . may make it impossible to spend this sum within that period.' Gaitskell used identical words.[16] But Bevan made no such qualification: 'we do beg that we shall not have all these jeers about the rearmament we are putting under way . . . We shall carry it out; we shall fulfil our obligation to our friends and Allies, and at the same time we shall try to . . . give mankind another breathing space.'[16] Many agreed with Gaitskell that it was one of Bevan's best speeches, and it won acclaim even from diehard Tories.

Nye gave one of [his] most brilliant performances . . . glittering with striking phraseology . . . What a tragedy that a man with such wonderful talent as an orator and such an interesting mind and fertile imagination should be such a difficult team worker, and some would say even worse – a thoroughly unreliable and disloyal colleague. Will he grow out of this? Will he take on the true qualities that are necessary for leadership?[17]

On 9 March Ernest Bevin was at last moved from the Foreign Office and replaced by Morrison. Because of Bevin's precarious health the Prime Minister had had time to consult widely about the succession. Attlee would have liked to appoint a trade unionist; but Bevan was never mentioned. He had thus been passed over for both the senior offices, despite his ability and standing in the Party. He doubtless feared his support for rearmament would alienate his following, and that by resigning he could mobilise them against the 'disastrous and accelerating drift to the right'. From 9 March, wrote Leslie Hunter, he was looking for a pretext to resign;[18] and many of Bevan's colleagues concurred. Bevan became more critical in Cabinet after Morrison's appointment, and in discussions on rearmament 'the superficial cordiality between Gaitskell and himself . . . rapidly disappeared'.[19] But according to Wilson's biographer it was only after the die was cast that, persuaded by his two fellow-resigners, he broadened the issue beyond teeth and spectacles and 'became a Wilsonite' about the defence programme. For his disappointment coincided with a long-foreseen crunch: the rearmament Budget.

## The Cabinet and the Health Charges

The Budget was presented on 10 April 1951, and within a fortnight Bevan, Wilson and Freeman resigned. Gaitskell recorded the developing crisis in two long entries in his diary upon which the following account is based. He knew early on that he would have to find between £100 and £200 millions, and at first hoped to get half from economies. But since old age pensions had to be increased, he soon discovered that simply to hold the social services bill constant would involve very drastic cuts in the health service, entirely eliminating free dental and optical services. The Ministers responsible, Hilary Marquand for Health and Hector McNeil for Scotland, quickly dissuaded him from that. When he informed Attlee, Morrison and Bevin of his modified plans, he met 'no adverse reaction' on health charges but 'no enthusiasm at all' on tax increases. 'The P.M. said, "Well! We shall not get many votes out of this."'[20]

During February the health service estimate had to be settled. The previous amount was £393 million; the Ministry wanted £30 million more; Gaitskell persuaded Marquand to try to keep within the old figure, provided the Prime Minister's committee on health service finance were told and accepted the consequences, which they did. In mid-March they approved Marquand's scheme for keeping within the ceiling by imposing some dental and optical charges, and also the prescription charge authorised in Bevan's Act of November 1949. Gaitskell asked Attlee to convene a further *ad hoc* meeting of interested Ministers, particularly Bevan, to give them early warning. There the Prime Minister did not defend the proposals of his own committee, which Bevin now joined Bevan in attacking; anxiety was felt about the prescription charge rather than teeth and spectacles, but a majority backed the Chancellor. Both he and Bevan hinted at resignation. That evening McNeil promised to go with Gaitskell if necessary.

The four senior Ministers met on Tuesday 20 March, and Ernest Bevin proposed compromising on £400 million for the health service. Knowing that that meant no prescription charge, Gaitskell at once accepted providing all others did. Morrison agreed and so (in writing) did Attlee. Next day, the Prime Minister entered hospital with an ulcer. On Thursday 22 March the Cabinet spent an hour and a half on health charges. Bevan again threatened to resign, and indeed to walk out of the meeting, though he was persuaded not to. Although the Home Secretary, Chuter Ede, and Jim Griffiths 'were a little doubtful, all but Bevan and Wilson concurred . . . the decision was a perfectly clear one – to proceed with the preparation of the Bill on the lines of the Bevin compromise.' The main clash came 'between Shinwell and Bevan when Bevan began to attack the arms programme in the middle of the discussion': the first contemporary reference to Bevan opposing rearmament itself.[21]

Over the next fortnight other features of the Budget were being decided and Gaitskell was preparing his speech. There were constant appeals to him to compromise with Bevan, and by him to Morrison to call another meeting of Ministers to settle the matter. Morrison would not do so, and Gaitskell found it an agonisingly lonely period.

Bevan went public on 3 April, telling a Bermondsey heckler that he would not remain in 'a Government which imposes charges on the patient'. To Gaitskell and others it seemed 'a blatant threat'. He exploded to Dalton: 'Nye's influence was very much exaggerated . . . If we didn't stand up to him, Nye would do to our party what L.G. had done to the Liberals. It would, he thought, do us good in the country to make a stand on this.'[22] But that intemperate mood soon passed.

On Monday, April 9th, my birthday, I went to the Cabinet . . . There was little comment on the Budget as a whole, what there was being favourable . . . But there was another very long discussion on the Health charges . . . Bevan himself did not raise [any other] objections . . . Of course, everybody was aware . . . [and resented] that he had deliberately put himself in a position . . . to say . . . he was forced to resign.

During the discussion that morning I did not say anything about resignation myself.

Apart from the two dissidents and George Tomlinson, Minister of Education, who was willing to pay any price to keep Bevan, everyone agreed to reaffirm the Easter decision; Ede, who liked Bevan's arguments, was put off by his threats. But the repeated appeals to Bevan made him more intransigent, and at lunchtime the meeting adjourned until 6.30 p.m. That gave time to consult Attlee in hospital, and allowed Gaitskell to go home for a birthday party. His private secretary recalled:

The girls had made an enormous cake and were tremendously proud of their father about to introduce his first Budget, which he knew – and no one else did – might never happen at all. In the end he broke down completely and had to leave the party altogether – and I almost broke down too.[23]

At 5.30 Gaitskell went to tell the King about the Budget and the clash with Bevan:

He said, 'He must be mad to resign over a thing like that. I really don't see why people should have false teeth free any more than they have shoes free'; waving his foot at me as he said it. He is, of course, a fairly reactionary person. As to the rest of the Budget the King did not comment on it and never does. So I left him, saying, 'Well! it looks as if one or other of us is not going to be a member of the Government to-morrow. I am not sure which it will be'.

Meanwhile Morrison and Whiteley, the Chief Whip, had visited Attlee, and when the Cabinet resumed, 'Morrison read out a message from the P.M. which . . . urged the Cabinet to stand by me.' This evening meeting lasted till 9 p.m.: 'This time, though very quietly, I . . . said that it would be impossible for me, having had a Cabinet decision in favour of this just before Easter, to have it reversed at the last minute. I said that if I resigned I would make no trouble whatever and would always support the Party.' Dalton confirms his promise 'to go quietly, and not to attack the Government afterwards. This is a high moral attitude compared with Nye.'[22] Again only Tomlinson voted with the two dissidents.

Before the vote Tomlinson suggested retaining the £400 million ceiling but omitting the charges – precisely the formula which, a year earlier, Bevan had nominally accepted from Cripps but made no effort to observe. Gaitskell resisted it as a dishonest dodge to avoid the charges – without which the health Ministers knew they could not keep within the ceiling. But Morrison liked the formula, kept bringing it up, and put the idea to the Prime Minister, who was to see Bevan and Wilson at 10.30 a.m. and the Chancellor afterwards.

Gaitskell had worked on his speech at home with his private secretaries until 1 a.m. on Budget day, Tuesday 10 April. Ten hours later

I went along to the hospital [where] . . . he had been kept fully in touch with everything . . . he tried to get me to accept some form of words . . . which [Bevan and Wilson] would accept, to the effect of a ceiling of 400 millions and if charges were necessary then they would have to be passed. But I had made up my mind that I would announce the charges and I refused to give way. I offered my resignation several times, and I thought as I listened to his arguments that he was going to accept it . . . Finally, he murmured what I took to be 'Very well! You will have to go.' In a split second I realised he had said 'I am afraid *they* will have to go.'

Just then the Home Secretary [Ede] and Chief Whip came in . . . knowing the Home Secretary was very much a wobbler, I felt very depressed. However, there was no need to be. The . . . P.M. . . . turned to the Chief Whip and said, 'Well, Willy can we get this through the Party?' 'Not the slightest doubt if there are no resignations – No difficulty at all.' They both expressed the view that they thought Bevan wanted to resign in any case.

Gaitskell then offered to drop his proposal for the charges to come into force at once, so that the bill need not be retrospective and could be delayed a little. His three hearers thought it would make no difference, but at the very last minute Morrison decided it might.

Gaitskell told Dalton next day: 'Up till noon he hadn't known whether he was going to make a Budget speech or not. He had twice offered to resign, and not to attack the Government.'[22] After a quick lunch in the Treasury with his wife, Gaitskell walked across to the House escorted by his PPS and private secretary – and found Morrison coming out of the chamber to urge him to make the change after all. He 'struck out the [relevant] sentence at 3.28 p.m. . . . [and] began to deliver the speech'.

As usual on Budget day, the House was packed. Gaitskell was wearing an outsize red carnation given him by Felicity Cory-Wright – the flower was the old symbol of the Austrian Socialists, who were touched that he wore it. He began at a tremendous pace. Churchill intervened to tell him to take his time, and his speech lasted 133 minutes, but it won universal acclaim. He 'rose a comparative tyro', wrote one Tory paper, and 'sat down an acknowledged star'. An academic study writes of 'a *tour de force* in analysis and exposition' which 'stands out from those before and since'.[24]

The content had a more mixed reception. Gaitskell earned Labour congratulations and Opposition criticism by not cutting social services, and by laying almost all the fiscal burden on the better-off. Rearmament involved spending on defence nearly £1,500 million in 1951/52, an increase of over £500 million. The Chancellor's tasks were to find the real resources for defence production; to finance the programme without inflation; and to prevent excessive strain on the metal and engineering industries on which the main burden would fall. Gaitskell's plans, more precisely set out than those of any predecessor, were to be spectacularly frustrated, through circumstances which could not be foreseen, by a great balance of payments crisis. No future Chancellor gave hostages to fortune by taking the public so fully into his confidence.

The extra resources needed for defence were expected to come mainly from an increased Gross Domestic Product. The new government expenditure would slash the Government's big contribution to savings. To stop consumers having too much to spend and draining away resources, the new Budget must therefore close an emerging inflationary gap, calculated at £140 million, between total savings and total investment. Gaitskell filled it entirely by raising more revenue, over half from income tax (with measures to ease the burden on wage-earners).

The metals and engineering bottleneck was crucial for exports, investment and now rearmament. Purchase tax was doubled on major consumption items competing with defence; and civilian investment was discouraged from absorbing these scarce resources by suspending 'initial allowances'–the most damaging long-run feature of the Budget, which Gaitskell himself said he hoped could soon be reversed.

The Chancellor had conceded nothing to the Conservative clamour for cuts in government expenditure which, with prices rising fast, would have meant big changes in policy. Half that expenditure was for defence or interest on the National Debt; £1,615 million for social services; less than £400 million for other domestic items. That was already, despite rising costs, well below the previous year's figure; the social services were not, but their expansion was limited to the £26 million increase in their estimates–so that with the £20 million increase in pensions, estimated expenditure on all social services was up by nearly £50 million. Food subsidies were unchanged.

Those measures followed closely the recommendations of *Tribune*, which had advocated increased old age pensions, national assistance, and perhaps family allowances – to be paid for by higher direct taxes on unearned incomes and distributed profits, and by heavier purchase tax on luxuries.[25] It differed with Gaitskell on only one item; but for that it did not forgive the Chancellor. The health service was to keep within a ceiling of £400 million, having only £7 million more instead of the £30 million for which its Ministry had asked. Since hospital costs were rising and standards should not be reduced, the difference was to be made up by charging half the cost of false teeth and spectacles, which would bring in £13 million in 1951/52 and £23 million in a full year. (Children were exempt from both, and expectant and nursing mothers from the former; those in hardship would be reimbursed from national assistance; dental treatment was not affected.) At this point in the Budget speech a lone 'Shame!' came from Jennie Lee, listening beside her husband in the shadows behind the Speaker's chair. 'Bevan, red in the face and breathing like an angry bull . . . was standing as inconspicuously as possible'; he walked out when Gaitskell finished that passage.[26] His wife's 'muffled cry' was, in Michael Foot's words, 'the only hostile demonstration Gaitskell received that afternoon'.[27]

## The Parliamentary Labour Party

Bevan and his wife were entirely isolated. The Budget of April 1951 was warmly and enthusiastically received in the PLP, even by his sympathisers. All the parliamentary correspondents confirmed Dalton: 'the Party are very pleased & the Tea Room is full of his [Gaitskell's] praise . . . it is practically all one way'.[22] Chuter Ede, very often a critic, told Gaitskell: 'This is just what the Party wanted. It will make all the difference.' Stanley Evans spoke of the 'tonic effect on my Party. Indeed, I do not remember the PLP being so perky, united and harmonious for a long time'.[28] In the debate, 20 out of 28 Labour back-benchers applauded the Budget and not one attacked it. Detailed criticism fastened not on health charges, but on the conditions – meant to discourage early retirement – attached to the increased old age pensions. Four Members regretfully approved the charges and three did not. But the three all welcomed the Budget, one of them calling it 'one of the best . . . for years . . . can be defended from any angle'.[28] Even on its slender majority a united Cabinet could have carried it with no difficulty at all. The charges began a long crisis, but not because they provoked any spontaneous revolt in the Labour Movement, in the PLP or even in a dissident minority. Their impact demonstrated the individual influence, and was due to the individual reaction, of one man alone.

That reaction was delayed. On the morning after the Budget most commentators expected Bevan to take the escape route he had left himself at Bermondsey by claiming that part-payments for dentures and spectacles were not 'charges on the patient'. He told the PLP amid applause 'that he had decided not to take a certain course'. In Cabinet next day, Wednesday, he and Wilson tried again to get the charges postponed. Glaring at the silent Gaitskell, Bevan exploded as they dispersed, 'Why should I have to put up with these bloody absurdities?'[29]

There were two efforts at compromise. Three trade unionist Ministers – Griffiths, Isaacs and Tomlinson – revived the 1949 idea of increasing the national insurance contribution in lieu of the charges; both Bevan and Gaitskell refused. At the Cabinet on Thursday 19 April, Bevan said he would resign on the third reading. Dalton recorded 'a general impatience in the Cab with this continual nerve war – first he threatened to resign before the Budget, then on Budget day, then if the charges were brought in, then he wouldn't vote on a second reading & now this.'[29] But when Shinwell suggested announcing that the charges might be temporary, Bevan replied 'that would make a great deal of difference' – and Gaitskell agreed to say they need not be permanent. Bevan threw a note across the table to Wilson, 'We've got them on the run.'[30] That afternoon Shinwell put up a formula, 'should not be permanent'; Gaitskell changed 'should' to 'need not necessarily'; and the paper was handed to Bevan:

He read it and tossed it aside contemptuously, calling it 'a bromide'.

He then went on to say that he would not be satisfied . . . [unless we] left it open whether the charges ever came into force at all. He followed this up with a long and rather excited statement that the arms programme could not be carried out . . . I gather he had this impression from a meeting of the Defence Production Committee which had taken place that day.

I said that of course if there were to be a complete change in the Defence programme we should need a completely new Budget . . . but until . . . [then] I was not prepared to budge on the Health Bill. Shortly after there was a Division and we did not see Bevan again. He had, however, been asked by the Home Secretary to produce an alternative form of words, and in fact never did so.

Exasperated by Bevan's renewed intransigence, the leading Ministers – Morrison, Gaitskell, Ede and the Chief Whip – now decided that the Prime Minister must be informed.

Meanwhile Gaitskell had made a successful Budget broadcast and winding-up speech in the debate. But Bevan, busily lobbying against the bill in the tea-room, where he was never normally seen, had infuriated Ede, the Leader of the House and his former sympathiser. The final straw was that evening's *Tribune*, savagely attacking Gaitskell personally as well as the Budget. It probably swung several Ministers away from compromise: notably Dalton, who called it 'a most wicked publication'.[29] Among them was the Prime Minister. In his hospital bed on the Friday afternoon, listening to Ede, Attlee finally said: 'Well, we cannot go on like this. He must behave properly if he is to remain a Member of the Government.' He then sent what he called an 'ultimatum' that he hoped to hear before the weekend that Bevan would loyally accept and carry out government decisions. Next day Bevan resigned.

*Tribune*, founded by Cripps in 1937, was edited by Bevan during the war and then, when he took office, by Jennie Lee and Michael Foot – the only two of his associates who wanted him to resign. Loyal to the Government while Bevan was a member, it had lately been restive. Its financial state was always precarious, and a few days before the Budget Foot thought it would have to close; he foresaw, however, that Bevan's resignation might 'save' it, offering it 'new opportunities, a new lease of life'.[31] He therefore approached Lord Beaverbrook, with whom he had formerly been friendly. That Tory magnate was happy to supply the sinews of factional war within the Labour Party by keeping *Tribune* alive, unknown of course to the constituency activists who read it. He had often hired away its talented left-wing journalists to run his own right-wing press empire; and when his manager objected to the use of *Daily Express* funds to pay the subsidy, he retorted: 'Where would we get our recruits without *Tribune*?'[32]

This was the journal which, on 20 April 1951, ended several years of reasonable harmony in the Labour Party and reopened the fratricidal civil war which has lasted on and off ever since. Its editorial claimed that not since 1931 had Conservatives so warmly applauded a Labour government. The charge was false, for only the *Daily Express* leader-writer (a Beaverbrook-Bevanite?) cynically applauded Gaitskell for taking Tory measures. Where *Tribune* wanted more government expenditure at home, the entire Opposition press clamoured for less – while also condemning the Chancellor for overburdening the better-off. So did Conservatives in the House. Reactions from the Press were similar: 'Almost any cut in expenditure would have been preferable'

(*The Times*); 'Niggling, tinkering, juggling . . . mediocre' (*Mail*); 'The middle and upper classes are bearing a disproportionate share' (*Scotsman*).

*Tribune*, however, denounced 'the Gaitskell dictate' as 'contemptible', 'timid and squalidly inadequate', and 'another 1931'; twice accused him of having 'deserted Socialism at the moment of crisis'; and compared him directly to the former Labour Chancellor Philip Snowden. To its readers Snowden was Judas: the Chancellor who allied with the Tories, slashed working-class standards, accepted a peerage and turned bitterly against his lifelong associates. Yet from start to finish Gaitskell had the support of *Tribune*'s own founder, Stafford Cripps, whom Bevan regarded as the best Chancellor Britain ever had.[33]

On Saturday 21 April, eleven days after the Budget and just after the *Tribune* assault, Bevan sent the Prime Minister a resignation letter which, as Attlee tartly replied, 'extended the area of disagreement a long way beyond the specific matter'.[34] Bevan had known quite well that teeth and spectacles were too narrow an issue to resign on, telling a sympathiser who said so, 'Don't you worry, I'll broaden it all right.'[35] Harold Wilson and John Freeman, Parliamentary Secretary to the Ministry of Supply, soon followed him. Both had been worried for much longer about the scale of rearmament, and both advised him to base his dissent on that. Yet Bevan hesitated to the end, for only his wife and his future biographer pressed him to go.[36] At the last minute he urged even Wilson and Freeman to remain. It is said that in the end Wilson proved the most resolute of the three.

Bevan's resignation speech on the Monday was preceded, to the delight of the House, by a parliamentary question from George Thomas on the perils caused by straying sheep in South Wales. Gaitskell wrote mildly of Bevan's 'extraordinary performance, totally lacking in any understanding of what people expected, [which] turned opinion even more sharply against him – on top of the Tribune article'. Moving far beyond teeth and spectacles, Bevan criticised the British rearmament programme as impracticable, and the American programme as a greater threat to the West than the Russians themselves, for it risked mass unemployment and imperilled even 'the foundations of political liberty and Parliamentary democracy'. He turned to denounce the Budget for not restraining inflation, and for having 'united the City . . . and disunited the Labour Party' in the interest of the USA. He attacked the Treasury for having too many economists, 'and now we have the added misfortune of having an economist in the

Chancellor of the Exchequer himself'. He charged Gaitskell with political dishonesty, arousing furious Labour resentment – for he knew Gaitskell could not reply since personal statements are not debatable:

the Chancellor . . . said that he was now coming to a complicated and technical matter and that if Members wished they could go to sleep. They did. Whilst they were sleeping he stole £100 million a year from the National Insurance Fund . . . so that the re-armament of Great Britain is financed out of the contributions that the workers have paid into the Fund in order to protect themselves.'

Bevan went on to attack the health charges as the first pebble of an avalanche that would sweep away the welfare state – and to explain why he had set an earlier pebble rolling himself. 'I had to manoeuvre, and I did manoeuvre and saved the 25,000 houses and the prescription charges.'[37]

When he sat down a moment later, wrote Michael Foot: 'not a touch of warmth alleviated the universal coldness. No single cheer greeted his peroration.'[38] Bevan's was the only resignation speech for thirty years or more to show no regret at the breach with old colleagues; and though he drew sympathy and attention at first, he lost both by the boast about his own 'manoeuvre' and the personal attack on Gaitskell.

Harold Wilson next day covered similar ground without bitterness or personal invective, and won much more sympathy. Freeman made no statement, but wrote to both Attlee and Gaitskell. He told the Chancellor he stood with Bevan, but that 'breaking up the government on such a narrow issue appeared to me the height of folly' and that he had worked wholeheartedly against a split; he hoped their good relations would continue, and was delighted 'to see . . . how clearly the mark of greatness sits upon you'.[39]

The party meeting next day opened with 'restrained' statements by Wilson and Freeman. Gaitskell then rose to a 'pretty considerable ovation' which he attributed to resentment against *Tribune*. On his friends' advice he ignored the personal attacks and defended himself calmly. He denied knowing (as Bevan had charged in the House) that the amount allotted to defence spending was already 'unrealisable' – though he was so innocent of the new standards of controversy that he would not repeat that denial publicly lest it damage the Party. He warned that if raw material shortages did occur they would hamper civilian as well as defence production, add to inflationary pressure, and so require a tougher Budget not an easier one. He sat down to tremendous applause.

Bevan made things even worse for himself by following this with a shocking outburst of bad temper which was evidently a revelation to many people in the Party. He almost screamed at the platform. At one point he said, 'I won't have it. I won't have it.' And, this of course was greeted with derision. '*You* won't have it?' called other Members of the Party. Of course in the Cabinet we have had this on [*sic*] a number of times but they had not seen it before.

Other eye-witnesses were less restrained. One spoke of Bevan as hysterical and almost screaming; another, Dalton, as 'soon quite out of control . . . sweating & screeching, & seemed on the edge of a nervous breakdown'.[40] Dalton and Ede, MPs in 1930, were both reminded of Mosley; in winding up from the chair, Ede said so.

Bevan had greatly overestimated his own influence. Gaitskell, whose political antennae were not always sensitive, had underestimated it immediately after the Bermondsey speech. His friends soon corrected that mistake: Dalton told him he thought too much of the electorate as a whole rather than the Party, and Callaghan warned: 'Oh! Boy, these temperamental Celts!! Wilson doesn't matter either way – Nye does.'[41] Gaitskell listened to them, quickly recognised Bevan's strength outside the House, and by May thought the rebel might well win within the Labour Party – and so condemn it to opposition 'for years and years'. But the Bevanites wholly misjudged the mood of the PLP. Bevan himself, unlike Gaitskell, brushed aside Callaghan's friendly warning that his rival was stronger than he thought, exploding: 'The Party will sweep him away!'[42] He predicted to Dalton that the bill would fail: 'The Party will be a rabble, and you won't carry it.'[22] His resignation brought a new bitterness into the debate on it. But its second and third readings, on 24 April and 7 May, were both unopposed. In the one division in committee, the Government won by 262 to 3; Harold Wilson, Barbara Castle and other future Bevanites voted with the majority, but there were thirty or forty abstentions. 'It was a humiliating spectacle to see the Labour Party quarrelling while the Conservatives looked on and laughed'.[43] In 1951 angry quarrels in the PLP were unfamiliar: a different world.

The bill included a time limit, which had been offered to Bevan without changing his mind, but might have altered Wilson's. There was as yet no feeling in the constituencies. Both the TUC and the trade union MPs – especially the miners – felt more anxious to shield old age pensioners from rising prices than to keep dentures and spectacles free. On pensions there was real, widespread and spontaneous feeling among back-benchers. Where only three of the twenty-eight who spoke in the Budget debate criticised health charges, a majority pressed for the higher pensions to be paid earlier. Gaitskell saw the trade union group and 'found that the pensions were the only thing they were worried about. They were quite solidly behind me on the teeth and spectacles'. Ministers feared the Opposition would support a pensions revolt, and the Whips 'all said that the feeling was very strong in the Party as a whole'. Gaitskell agreed to pay the increase to those who had retired, but not to those who would reach 65 later and could stay at work: 'the Trade Union Group accepted it with much gratitude. . . . I had always expected this and indeed said in the Cabinet and the Party Meeting that if there were any more money available I would not have put it into the Health Services but done better for the pensioners.'[43] That would both give help to the neediest, and respond to working-class preferences. But it was not Bevan's priority; and his approach to the crisis is sadly illuminated by his biographer, twenty years later, calling Gaitskell's remark a gratuitous provocation.

## Merits and Politics

Any case for giving way to Bevan on health charges in 1951 would have rested entirely on a political calculation. It was not that he held a more principled view than his critics, or championed a policy to which all Socialists had long been devoted, or had convinced the Labour Movement that the health service should be exempt from normal financial constraints, or could avert a threatened Tory 'avalanche' sweeping away the welfare state. It was that, like Joseph Chamberlain in 1886, he was a commanding political figure, capable of raising a revolt large enough to split his party for years. Bevan might not have resigned if his great achievement had been left untouched, and no serious revolt would have been likely without him; so that his colleagues, however good their case and bad his behaviour—indeed just because it was likely to be bad—might have been wise to let the rogue elephant have his way, if by doing so they could have avoided civil war in the Party.

The calculation depends on hindsight about troubles which occurred later on in opposition. Gaitskell's whole case was that Labour had to prove itself a responsible party of government—an opportunity the Party was soon denied by electoral defeat, so that the future he envisaged was unattainable in 1951. Thus, even if Bevan had had his way over health charges and remained, it might have made very little difference if, as seems likely, he would have rebelled in any event as soon as Labour went out of office.

Two conceptions of the Party's future were in conflict. Bevan foresaw Labour's defeat with equanimity, and indeed would have preferred that to victory by a majority he thought inadequate. Gaitskell already saw Labour as a reforming party of government, not as a movement of impotent protest; he was not at all defeatist about the next election, believing it could be won if Labour proved its competence in running the country. He saw his own stand as essential to demonstrating that conception of the Party, telling Gordon Walker early in the struggle: 'We must show that we administer responsibly.'[44] After it was over he thanked a supporter in his constituency:

it really meant a great deal to me – coming from you who are not only one of our best people in S. Leeds but also know such a lot about the Health Services. It has been a very heavy strain – emotionally as well as intellectually – fighting this battle and letters like yours just make me feel that it *was* worth while taking all the risks and facing all the brickbats and beastliness.[45]

Gaitskell was well aware of the personal aspect of the contest: he was a young man, junior in his party and suddenly promoted to high office, whose authority as Chancellor would soon vanish if he retreated under fire, as commentators had expected when he was appointed. Nine years later he summed up to George Brown: 'It was a battle between us for power – he knew it and so did I.'[46]

Bevan's discontent had been well known for months, especially since he had been passed over for both Exchequer and Foreign Office. Yet if he was simply looking for a pretext to resign, it is hard to explain his prolonged hesitation. He must have found it unthinkable that Gaitskell ('nothing, nothing, nothing') could prevail over health charges where Cripps had given way. After losing the battle at the Easter Cabinet, Bevan at Bermondsey publicly threatened resignation; if he could not be Chancellor, he would show himself more powerful than the Chancellor. When that failed, he felt he would be stronger outside than in, and it was time to go.

Bevan was uninhibited in expressing his personal feelings. When the Cabinet accepted Ernest Bevin's compromise, he protested that 'his own personal position would be rendered impossible; his prestige would be undermined . . . It will be known that he has been overridden.'[47] After several such outbursts Dalton wrote to the absent Prime Minister: 'Hugh's . . . attitude to resignation, as compared with Nye's, was like a high snow peak compared with a steaming tropical swamp!'[48] Big men have big faults – which can alone explain why the legitimate policy dispute provoked such vituperative ferocity, and why Bevan aroused such resistance in his colleagues.

It was only reluctantly that the Cabinet supported Gaitskell, the junior and far less powerful figure, and his unpalatable proposals. The majority against Bevan did not exist until his miscalculation, intransigence and bullying created it. At first several colleagues sympathised with his dislike for health charges. But they also recalled the repeated postponements in Cripps's day, when Bevan's ceilings were disregarded while other Ministers had to cut their estimates. Later Gaitskell won their approval by showing loyalty and goodwill, accepting Ernest Bevin's compromise, and promising that if he resigned he would make no difficulties for the Government. But Bevan provoked them by seeking to force their hand in public – so that Chuter Ede felt it would be intolerable for Cabinet majorities of 18 to 2 to be overridden because 'X' was one of the 2.[49] Bevan was, wrote Dalton, 'determined to bend the Cabinet to his will or break it . . . He showed, [colleagues] thought, unbearable conceit, crass obstinacy and a totalitarian streak.'[50]

Clement Attlee was not affected by this atmosphere, for he had entered hospital three weeks before the Budget. He was regularly consulted, and whenever obliged to decide he supported Gaitskell. But his physical absence permitted not a timely intervention from Olympus, but – in his usual style – a calculated detachment until events dictated an apparently ineluctable outcome, only four hours before Gaitskell was due to bring in his Budget. No one could suppose a Prime Minister (least of all one with a single-figure majority) would accept his Chancellor's resignation so late. Expecting and hoping to the last that one man would give way, Attlee must have known much earlier that in a crunch Bevan would be the one to go.

Attlee's tactics were faulty, for as the dispute dragged on it became harder to settle. At the very start, Gaitskell might have given way under strong pressure; if not, he would have resigned alone and at a much less disastrous moment. But Attlee, who had chaired the Cabinet Committee, tried neither to reverse its decision nor to defend it; and once Gaitskell had accepted Bevin's compromise and won Cabinet endorsement for it, he would not himself retreat, and he would no longer have resigned alone.

Bevan was the more frustrated and resentful of the two, but the less determined either to win or resign. Having failed in private persuasion he publicly challenged his colleagues: so that later, when Attlee could no longer let Gaitskell go without open capitulation and grave loss of prestige, the last hope of keeping Bevan was by insisting that the Cabinet decision of 22 March must be upheld, while offering to save his face. Instead, Attlee waited until the last moment for someone to crack – thus minimising both his personal involvement in the quarrel and his chance of solving it.

Even after Budget day all Bevan's colleagues were still hoping to extricate him from the embarrassment they thought he had put himself in at Bermondsey. Only after he rejected Shinwell's compromise did even Chuter Ede insist to Attlee that Bevan must play with the team or go. Measuring the exasperation of his colleagues, the Prime Minister could see at last where the balance of forces lay.

Gaitskell was expecting soon after Bevan resigned that he would organise revolt at the October party conference. Such a revolt could be defeated with 'strong and firm' leadership from the Prime Minister, but Gaitskell now knew better than to count on that; and if Attlee sought to compromise and patch things up, 'then I think we shall probably lose. I cannot carry on the fight alone. I have not the standing or the experience.' In the event, Attlee remained non-committal. By the summer Gaitskell and Morrison thought 'that the P.M. has taken a very weak line about Bevan. He is very careful not to come out fully and firmly in the open against him, nor has he really given in our view much lead to the country on rearmament, though it was he and Bevin who initiated the new programme.'[51] Attlee blamed Morrison as acting Prime Minister for the resignations, became 'pretty cool' towards Gaitskell, and did not welcome their good relations. In May, Gaitskell had summed up:

Although I . . . [knew] it would be a hard struggle I did not think it would be quite so tough. I suppose that if I had realised that there were so many things which could have meant defeat, I might never have begun; or at least I would have surrendered early on. If Ernie had not suggested the compromise; if some of the Cabinet had been more frightened; if Bevan had played his cards better; if the Budget speech had not been a success; if the Broadcast had been a flop; if I had not won the battle decisively in the Party meeting. If any of these things had not happened it might have meant failure . . .

All the same, with all the risks I think I was right. I said . . . [once] to Hugh Dalton, 'It is really a fight for the soul of the Labour Party' . . . I am afraid that if Bevan [wins] we shall be out of power for years and years.

# 9

# Chancellor of the Exchequer: The Economy 1951

*'He probably understood his job better than any Chancellor before or since'*
(Sam Brittan on HG, 1970)

## Inflation, Incomes and Iranian Oil

Gaitskell's last six months in office were dominated by the repercussions of the Western world's rearmament. Bidding against each other for raw materials, the NATO countries contrived a wild commodity boom which first threatened Britain's precarious wage and price stability, then provoked a sudden balance of payments crisis – making the Labour Government vulnerable in the Party to the Bevanites, and in the country to the Conservatives. In the November 1951 election, the latter won more seats than Labour but fewer votes.

From the moment he became Chancellor Gaitskell had been concerned about inflation. He was afraid that his Budget might have been too mild, not too harsh; and he rejected higher food subsidies as adding to the inflationary danger. Thus prices rose, pressure for wage increases mounted, and two years of trade union restraint were ending. He spent much time and thought on proposals for linking wages to the cost of living, or to productivity; but he concluded that they all involved great risks and difficulties and would be acceptable to neither side of industry. In the first five months of the year consumption, far from falling, was 5 per cent above that of 1950, and by the summer Gaitskell was worried. In late July he restored some controls consumed in Harold Wilson's bonfire, limited bank advances, and proposed to forbid increases in dividends in order to encourage 'reasonable restraint in the field of wages'.[1] This met 'most furious and violent abuse from the Right wing press . . . However, I am certainly a good deal tougher than I was, and it is just as well because I am in a very much more exposed position – detested by the Left and now very much out of favour with the Right.'[2]

In September 1951 Gaitskell engineered an invitation to speak to the TUC at Blackpool. He warned that disastrous inflation was inevitable if incomes rose faster than productivity, and appealed for moderation in wage claims in the interest of the export drive. He said that life was 'thinner, poorer, harder' than necessary because production was 'cramped and held back by fear . . . fear of the machine . . . fear of the lost job, fear of letting unwanted men go . . . fear of better methods, fear of letting someone else share in the work.' He used unpalatable and as yet unfamiliar figures to show that subsidies could not be financed from higher taxes on the rich, or wages increased at the expense of dividends. But that made it all the more necessary for the Labour Movement to attack inequalities of property.[3] Congress voted, most unusually, to print and circulate the speech, and Gaitskell hoped it had cemented his relations with the trade union leadership.

On 1 May 1951 the Iranian Parliament, which Gaitskell thought 'corrupt and incompetent', passed a law scrapping the British concession and nationalising the oil wells and refineries. It threatened to be costly in dollars, since that was the main source of oil under British rather than American control; and it might well tempt Iraq to seize her own oil, or Egypt the Suez Canal. The Cabinet was divided. Herbert Morrison and Shinwell called loudly for a show of force. Gaitskell was much more cautious, but wrote: 'The rest of the Cabinet . . . do not realise how serious the loss of the oil would be .'[4] But the British Chiefs of Staff, who knew that no action was possible without the United States, kept reassessing their resources and their advice – from 'extremely warlike' to 'outright appeasement' and back.[5] President Truman sent Harriman out to mediate, and Gaitskell met his old friend secretly in Paris and urged the dangers of an outright Iranian victory or an Anglo-American split. (The Americans wanted Gaitskell himself to go out, but he could not be spared.) By September, when Morrison again wanted to use force, Gaitskell was clear that Britain must not break with the United States, and that except to save lives the use of force would be illegal, immoral and politically unwise.

## The Balance of Payments Crisis

In the first half of 1951, the balance of payments looked healthy; the reserves reached a post-war peak on 30 June. But in the second half of the year the British economy had both the biggest trade gap and current-account deficit for any half-year, and the biggest deterioration between one half-year and the next, that it had ever experienced. The Government and its advisers had little warning of the coming storm, for the situation changed with catastrophic suddenness, reflected only belatedly in the statistics. A bad trend in the third quarter turned into a catastrophe when the RSA (the Sterling Area countries other than the UK) suddenly and without warning vastly increased its dollar purchases, and turned in a dollar deficit instead of the expected surplus.

Gaitskell was quick to seek international action on the long-term problems, though without much success. In July he took measures to limit dollar imports, to cut some food rations and to tighten control over steel and other allocations. But as he wrote years later, 'the change in the situation was anticipated, but not the speed with which it took place'.[6] Late in August, 'I found to my dismay that . . . the dollar deficit in the third quarter would be at least 500 million dollars . . . [and] likely to continue . . . unless energetic steps were taken.'[7] After speaking to the TUC in Blackpool in the morning of 4 September 1951, and attending Cabinet in the afternoon, he flew off that night to the United States.

Gaitskell had two tasks: first in Washington, negotiating privately and directly on Britain's behalf; then at the NATO Council in Ottawa, becoming Europe's spokesman in publicly challenging extravagant American assumptions. He was surprisingly successful in both. 'My first job was, of course, to impress on the Americans the seriousness of the dollar situation which was developing so that they could consider giving us various forms of help. As usual, it was necessary to tell the same story to different Ministers.' On his return he told the Cabinet that the Americans had been, 'As usual, "taken by surprise" at our account of our troubles, but terrified of Congress, and, in any case, won't settle anything till after an election'.[8] There were pressures to resist from various US politicians and agencies, each with its own objective which would have made Britain's situation worse. Gaitskell made no progress over the violent and damaging oscillations in the Americans' raw material purchasing policy. The US Treasury was not at all friendly; John Snyder, the Secretary, suspected Gaitskell's intentions, blocked him from seeing the President, and would not let the IMF be used – as the British wanted – to help nations in exchange difficulties.

Fortunately the Departments directly concerned soon came 'to understand and take seriously our economic plight'; the State and Defense Departments and the European Co-operation Administration were friendly and helpful. In particular Gaitskell was impressed by Dean Acheson, the Secretary of State, 'a sensitive and cultured man' with whom he argued constantly over the Americans' insistence that European rearmament was still inadequate, and their refusal to talk about 'burden-sharing'. Gaitskell, as he told Dalton on his return to London,

said that we could not, as U.S. were pressing us to do, go beyond £4,700 million (rearmt in 3 years) and could only reach it, if certain conditions as to supply of materials, etc., were fulfilled. Other European countries were doing much less than we, both absolutely and in relation to their paper programmes. French and Italians were very weak and mendicant. H.G. asked whether U.S. Treasury screened demands of Armed Forces, as *we* did. He gathered not. He urged them to.[9]

According to Acheson, Gaitskell told them that Britain's balance of payments deficit would amount to $1,000 million, half of it due to the frantic United States purchases of raw materials driving up prices, and much of the rest to the diversion of manufacturing resources from exports to arms. He concluded: 'The British were already behind in their own program for 1951; the increased requests of General Eisenhower were out of the question. Not only was it impossible for them to do more, but they could not long continue the present rate of rearmament.' The Administration's attitude to 'burden-sharing' now changed abruptly. 'Thoroughly convinced', Acheson got President Truman to authorise a full review of the economic capacity of the NATO countries.[10] (The French wanted the inquiry conducted by three experts; and the Americans suggested that the three should include Gaitskell, and serve in a personal not an official capacity – a remarkable move to allow him to represent Britain even if her government changed.) Eventually 'burden-sharing' was to ease Britain's difficulties – but too late to help the Attlee Government.

Far from rigidly insisting on an impossible programme, Gaitskell did more than anyone else to persuade the Americans to scale down their objectives.

I had once more explained [to Harriman] the gravity of the dollar situation and made it plain, as I had done on several previous occasions, that if they did nothing about it we should not be able to carry through the defence programme – we should have to give priority to exports. I never, of course, said anything of this kind in public.[7]

But he was outspoken, courageous and influential where he thought public criticism appropriate. From Washington he flew to the NATO Council at Ottawa, where Acheson demanded simultaneous increases in military and civilian production. Gaitskell replied bluntly that the United States, by refusing to contemplate the slightest cut in her own civilian consumption, was cornering available world supplies and stopping her European allies from getting enough to increase their production. Flatly contradicting General Eisenhower's call in Paris for a 'burst of speed', he urged the need over a long period for strong defences and a 'steady pull', since

> it was absolutely out of the question for us to do any more unless we were to have a war economy both internally and in our relationship between each other. I criticised Acheson for appearing to suggest that we could have guns and butter as well. This was one of the things which continually irritated me – a sort of ganging up between the Americans who always wanted promises of tremendous programmes for Congress and the mendicant Europeans who would promise anything so long as they thought they could get some dollars. However, I think . . . [we] made a considerable impression . . . even before we left Ottawa the Americans . . . had all begun to talk of screening down the military requirements.[11]

After two days in New York, Gaitskell returned to Britain and a worsening economic crisis, caused – as he told the Cabinet – by '(1) Lesser U.S. buying of wool, rubber and tin; (2) Increased U.K. purchases, not for re-armament – (3) Persia.'[12] The sales and prices of raw materials were dropping at a disastrous moment. For the sterling area countries had been selling at the top of the market, and now began to spend the proceeds; normally they offset the United Kingdom's dollar deficit with a surplus, but now they aggravated it with an equal deficit of their own. Moreover, controls were insufficient over capital exports to the sterling area, especially Australia and South Africa.

Gaitskell had to explain the crisis publicly in the context of an election, called by Attlee in his absence. On 3 October 1951, in the Chancellor's traditional Mansion House speech, he gave a frank account of the state of the reserves, the heavy impact of adverse price changes, the difficulties of the engineering industry, and the need for the defence burden to be more equally shared within NATO. As R. A. Butler made clear, the speech was based 'on the best information then available';[13] and the policies announced by Butler after the election were (except for the bank rate) in Gaitskell's words 'exactly what we would have done'.[14]

## The Defence Burden

The balance of payments crisis imposed cuts in the defence programme, which Labour prepared and the Conservatives implemented. Those cuts naturally reinforced the Bevanite view that the original programme had been mistaken. Gaitskell had ardently supported it in public: and in private perhaps too ardently for a Chancellor of the Exchequer. But its initiators were Attlee, Bevin and Shinwell; and responsibility was shared by Bevan, Wilson and the whole Cabinet.

Its critics made three distinct assumptions. One view was that the policy was unnecessary and even dangerous: that opinion, never held by the Bevanite Ministers before they resigned, gradually came to predominate in their camp. The second view was that the programme, however desirable, was impracticable and might seriously damage the British economy; Wilson and Freeman had held it throughout the ministerial discussions but Bevan not until the very end. Third, the critics (after they resigned) took for granted that the economic costs of agreeing to an excessive programme outweighed the political costs of refusal. There were other confusions. The situation changed rapidly during 1951, and Ministers' actions show that they had much more in common with their critics than either would admit; but their speeches do not, for they could not risk the international repercussions of saying so.

The first assumption cannot be conclusively disproved. We cannot know how far Western rearmament dissuaded the Russians from asserting their overwhelming conventional military superiority. They neither marched across Europe nor encouraged their satellites to pick off exposed salients; but then, by 1952 and 1953 the vacuum was not quite so tempting. No responsible administration could prudently disregard such formal warnings as 'war possible in 1951, probable in 1952'; only a dozen years before, men like Gaitskell had despaired to see their predecessors neglecting similar dangers. Had they known in 1951 of Stalin's paranoia in his last years, their alarm might have been even greater.

Conversely the political perils of the American alliance were unconvincing. Rearmament never did endanger Western democracy as Bevan's resignation speech predicted it would. Allied or not, Britain would suffer from any dangerous tendencies in American foreign policy; but a breach with the United States in 1951 would only have increased them, for the danger of American adventurism lay in the Far East, not in Europe. That danger was much reduced when Truman (three days before Bevan resigned) courageously dismissed General MacArthur. But the Republican Right were still wedded to an Asia First policy, and would have been reinforced if Europe had refused to contribute to her own defence.

The economic argument was much stronger, especially when the incoming Conservatives cut the programme back after ten months. But that decision is not conclusive. The cut was made in response to a situation which British rearmament had not caused and which the Bevanites had not foreseen: for many of their predictions were not borne out. The programme was sometimes said to be physically unattainable for lack of essential raw materials and machine tools; sometimes to be economically unwise, leading to mass unemployment, wrecking the balance of payments, and endangering Britain's hard-won economic recovery; and sometimes to impose too great a strain on one crucial sector, metals and engineering.

The Government always recognised that the programme would require raw materials and machine tools from abroad. Officially it was conditional on these supplies – a reservation for which Bevan perhaps disingenuously claimed the credit – and Attlee and Gaitskell carefully said so in their speeches though, curiously, Bevan did not. The possibility of a cut was always present in the minds of Ministers who stayed, as well as those who resigned. As Morrison's journalist confidant put it:

In public, ministers were forced to show an inflexible determination . . . [so that] Congress would vote the necessary supplies. In private, they knew that if the Americans failed to deliver the goods, it would be the rearmament programme and not the British economy which would suffer. And Bevan knew it too.[15]

Genuine economic dangers had to be weighed against the political risks of refusing to step up the defence effort. No defence plans could either be effective or appear to be so without American participation. The North Atlantic Treaty secured that on paper, but it would be without substance until the United States sent more troops to Europe and appointed an American supreme commander for NATO. Today, after decades of continuous, active and sometimes clumsy American involvement in Europe, we forget how hard it was for the Administration to persuade public and congressional opinion to accept a policy so contrary to American traditions. It had no hope of success without signs of similar seriousness in Europe, where any response was known to depend on a British lead. In January 1951 the British Government whittled down the proposed three-year programme from £6,000 million to £4,700 million. Had they instead refused any significant increase at all, the consequences might have been very grave: similar refusal by other allies; rejection of the European commitment by Congress and American opinion; and a vacuum across the Elbe tempting the Russians to believe that the United States (just as in Korea before the attack) had lost interest in Europe's fate.

For a responsible government such risks had to outweigh equally hypothetical economic losses. So on 25 January the Labour Cabinet – with no talk of resignation from Bevan – resolved to carry out the £4,700 million programme 'to the limit of the resources under *our* control' – while warning the Americans that their resources also would have to contribute to it. Even if Ministers suspected that the US assurances would not be carried out, they could neither be sure in advance nor say so publicly. In conditional acceptance they chose the least damaging response.

When Bevan issued his challenge in April 1951, the programme was less than three months old. The production Ministers, far from suggesting that the original figures were unrealisable, told Gaitskell that these 'were still the best available estimates'.[16] Commodity boards had just been set up to plan raw materials distribution; Britain would not have got better treatment from them by abandoning her commitment. The burden-sharing exercise, assessing the economic load on each country and the compensation for those worst affected, was still only a promise – and one which was dependent on the Americans considering the European programme adequate. Any economic gains from a cut-back in April might be offset by losses through reduced offers of assistance in both raw materials and finance.

While the Bevanites pointed with relish to any signs of production falling short, these only increased Gaitskell's worry about inflation. For civilian goods as well as armaments would be held back by shortages of raw materials, worsening the inflationary pressure. Failure for economic reasons to fulfil the defence programme, far from releasing more for social services, would require a tougher Budget – either heavier taxation or real cuts in domestic spending. To this argument the Bevanites found no satisfactory answer.

In the end extra defence expenditure over the first year fell short by £120 million, far less than the Bevanites' proposed £300 million cut. No doubt a smaller programme would have meant less industrial dislocation than the large one did. Bevan had predicted mass unemployment in industrial areas by the middle of 1951. Yet in August, Gaitskell still feared that inflationary pressure had been underestimated 'partly because the impact of the defence programme . . . has been rather greater than we allowed for. At any rate, the level of unemployment has fallen sharply to the 1945 figure'.[2]

Within the whole economy, engineering was the sector crucial to defence production. There the critics' case was strongest. Rearmament would absorb metal goods and leave an export gap, which it had been hoped would be filled by textiles; by the end of 1951 these were clearly performing disappointingly – the first signs of the decline of the woollen industry. At first engineering carried the increased burden, quite unexpectedly keeping up its 1950 level of exports. Its main competition came from West Germany, whose factories had no defence orders to fulfil. The main economic drawback of British rearmament was that loss of an export opportunity – ironically, partly due to the Bevanites and other opponents of German rearmament. By the end of 1951 this acquired new importance for reasons neither they nor anyone else had foreseen. Gaitskell's export target was met, not pushed far out of reach by defence demands as they had expected. The strain on the dollar reserves came largely from the rest of the sterling area; the United Kingdom contribution to it was not through low exports but high imports (largely for stockpiling, which was in part for defence). Its full dimensions were not apparent until the autumn.

The critics had foreseen the new situation though not the reasons for it. Gaitskell warned the Americans privately that Britain could not fulfil the programme without a bigger contribution from them, and publicly that they were expecting far too much from Europe. But his public statements were constrained both because he was friendly to the Americans and because he was a responsible Minister seeking concessions, and therefore needing their goodwill. The Bevanites profited politically by ignoring these constraints – and gave Ministers a useful argument in Washington (just as the Communist threat was an invaluable dollar-earner for the French and Italians, and an implacable Congress often convenient to the US Administration). In the September talks Plowden warned Harriman, ' if you let [the Chancellor] down now you will be playing straight into Bevan's hands. Moreover, don't imagine that if the Labour Party lose the Election it will help at all . .'. Bevan may capture the whole Labour movement in opposition.[7]

Had Labour won the election, they would have benefited as the Conservatives did from the turn of the economic tide. Certainly they too would have spread the British defence programme over an extra year. The political as well as the economic situation had changed: Congress had authorised the United States commitment, the Administration had agreed to a slower pace, and the European countries had undertaken (though not carried out) their own defence programmes. Alarms about Soviet intentions were less urgent, as Churchill – presumably reflecting intelligence reports – said in December 1951. The cut was made when the economic case for it had become far stronger, and the political and military cases against it no longer relevant.

In the next decade, reluctance to abandon overseas commitments was to play a major part in Britain's slow economic decline. In 1951 Britain took some economic risk to continue in a Great Power role which, as Gaitskell knew, could not indefinitely be sustained. He wrote in 1952: 'in our military and political association with America we generally try and hold a status which . . . [implies] a 2 to 1 power ratio but just does not fit the real ratio of − say − 7 to 1 . . . we find it a heavy burden to carry'.[17] Yet at that time and relative to her neighbours Britain still really was a Great Power whose abdication might have had far-reaching consequences. The Bevanites were right about the long-run need to cut commitments, wrong to ignore the immediate danger of abandoning them prematurely.

## Last Days in Office

Gaitskell, Morrison and Shinwell were at the Ottawa conference when they learned to their dismay that the Prime Minister had decided to go to the country. Now a national speaker, Gaitskell was to be kept busy electioneering in Scotland, the Midlands and London. His faithful local party ran the campaign, as in all later elections, with the candidate arriving only for the last few days. Redistribution had made South Leeds safer than ever and, even without a Liberal, his majority was hardly dented.

| | |
|---|---|
| Hugh Gaitskell (Lab.) | 30,712 |
| Winifred Brown (Cons.) | 16,493 |
| Majority | 14,219 |

But a tiny national swing against the Government brought the Conservatives back to power, though much more narrowly than he had expected. Their majority was only 17 seats, and few observers thought they would retain power for thirteen years.

When Gaitskell became Chancellor he was a competent departmental Minister little known to the public, and his qualities were appreciated only by a few in the Cabinet and Whitehall. A year later he had become an international figure. He was inexperienced and had minor failings, from chronic unpunctuality to pernickety redrafting. But he was a quick learner, rapidly improving in handling the press or the House of

Commons. He did not simply follow the rules, either in policy or administration. On behalf of the Arts Council his old schoolfellow Sir Kenneth Clark wrote: 'You have been in the past, and may again become, our chief protector.'[18] Nor would he always submit to 'precedent and the awful Whitehall logic about endless repercussions'.[19] He knew his own mind, understood and tried to overcome the difficulties of applying his policies, was effective in persuading Cabinet and Parliament, and was always willing to take responsibility.

Abroad, where he had no pre-Treasury experience, he proved a skilful negotiator, so that the Americans wanted him as British representative both in Iran and for the burden-sharing inquiry. Having decided that the United States was indispensable to British and European security, however awkward her economic policies, he defended the alliance without flinching from the political costs. But while never condemning the United States publicly for letting Britain down, he worked hard behind the scenes to limit the economic burden without straining relations with Washington; and he succeeded, though too late for his own government or party to reap the benefit. 'A brave and very responsible man, who had been misled but would not defend himself because he thought his country's needs should take precedence.'[20]

At home, his bitter dispute with a formidable colleague split the Labour Party for years. Yet his proposals were at first warmly welcomed on the government benches. There would have been no revolt but for the resignations, and then no bitterness but for the tone adopted by Bevan and his journal. No one else thought the health charges justified a split; Gaitskell may have been too stubborn about them, but he was not acting at all like Snowden in 1931, or 'deserting his Socialism in time of crisis', or 'dismantling the welfare state'. Nor can he reasonably be blamed for the balance of payments crisis. For its causes were largely outside the UK and overwhelmingly outside his control; its development was wholly unforeseen and unprecedentedly sudden; and it was met by measures prepared under his auspices.

Politically, he plotted no manoeuvre to drive out Bevan, whom he had rather admired; on the contrary, the clash seemed likelier to terminate his own ministerial career. But it was not he who alienated his colleagues, for he never personalised the conflict in Cabinet; he always promised loyal support from the back benches if the decision went against him; and though for the first time he faced bitter personal hostility, yet in the hope of healing the split he carefully refrained from replying in kind to his opponents, and would not give the struggle within the Labour Party priority over that against the Tories.

Gaitskell was in politics to achieve the power to put his ideas into practice, and had no patience with those (familiar on the British far Left and the American far Right) who would willingly see their opponents taking the decisions affecting men's lives, rather than infringe the purity of the Opposition's party principles..When one Treasury adviser once asked how he could stand his intolerable life, overworked all week and speech-making or fence-mending at weekends, Gaitskell replied: 'I love it. It's the power.'[20] Yet when he thought it necessary he did not hesitate to put at risk both the office and the influence which he properly prized so highly. But when the Government fell, he could not have imagined that only three of his Cabinet colleagues – Patrick Gordon Walker, James Griffiths and Harold Wilson – would ever hold office again.

In the three great controversies of his Chancellorship, Gaitskell's judgement may be challenged over health charges, over rearmament, and over the balance of payments. But no reasonable critic of his policies would deny his outstanding political honesty and courage (qualities less rare among politicians than cynics maintain, but not universal). Once again Gaitskell, confronted with wider responsibilities, in Attlee's words 'rose to the occasion splendidly'.[21] In the perpetual parliamentary reassessment of political reputations, he was for the first time being discussed as a potential leader of his party and of the nation.

# 10

# Opposition Front Bench
## 1951–4

---

*'A desiccated calculating machine'*
(Bevan on an unnamed rival, 1954)

*'We must earn their respect and gain their confidence'*
(HG on the voters, 1952)

---

## The Labour Coalition

When the House met in November 1951, Hugh Gaitskell sat on the
Opposition front bench, which he was to occupy for the rest of his life.
The Labour leaders had both to mobilise their forces against the new
Tory Government with its narrow majority, and to meet a vigorous
assault from their own dissidents, concentrated against Gaitskell. The
dispute partly diverted his attention for the next four years, under
Attlee's leadership, and for two more under his own in 1959–61. We
must therefore examine the structure and traditions of the party
through which both he and his critics worked.

In origins and organisation the Labour Party is the political wing of
an industrial movement. The emotions of the faithful are stirred by
myths and memories older than the Party, reflecting uphill struggles
against employers and sometimes the state itself. Conservatives and
Liberals were organised from above, to mobilise support in the country
for an established parliamentary leadership. But the Labour Party was
built up from below in protest against a Parliament unresponsive to
working-class concerns, as an alliance of the trade unions with the
societies of Socialist propagandists. It took the form of an elaborately
structured federal coalition, on to which the Parliamentary Party, born
in 1906, had to be awkwardly grafted.

While the Labour Party was developing into the alternative
government of the country, its federal structure remained but the
components changed. The (Marxist) Social Democratic Federation
withdrew very early on, and its various Communist and Trotskyite
successors have normally been excluded. The Independent Labour
Party, which once assembled most active British Socialists, declined in
the late 1920s into a small sectarian Left opposition, half revolutionary

and half pacifist, and broke away in 1932. The Socialist League organised the dissidents in the next five years, then dissolved itself under threat of disaffiliation. Thus the Socialist societies, except for the Fabians, disappeared from the coalition, while after 1918 local Constituency Labour Parties (CLPs) took their place.

The unions still provided the big battalions, dominating the annual conference with five million votes to the CLPs' nearly one million (in 1950); by long-standing custom (not rule) affiliated organisations cast their votes as a block, so that six large unions alone could outvote the rest of Conference. Between conferences the Party in the country is represented by the National Executive Committee (NEC), elected by Conference each year in 'divisions': 12 representatives of the unions, one of the Socialist societies, seven of the CLPs, five women, and the party treasurer. Since 1937 the first three divisions have elected their own representatives, but all affiliated organisations could still nominate and vote for the others. The party leader, chosen by the PLP, served *ex officio*. Thus in 1950 18 of the 27 NEC members were chosen by trade union votes.

Since 1922, Labour has been either in office or the official Opposition. Its front-benchers were its best-known spokesmen, expressing its views in Parliament, and forming the team which would govern the country if Labour won an election. Yet the PLP chose only one representative on the NEC, the leader (though individual MPs were always elected by the divisions). The two bodies – the NEC, representing Conference, which settled party policy, and the PLP leadership, representing Labour voters and views in the House and the country – each had a claim to legitimate authority. Conflict between them might embarrass the Party in its battle for public support, as when Winston Churchill in 1945 suggested that the NEC might unconstitutionally try to dictate to a Labour Cabinet (incurring a memorable rebuke from Attlee). Various devices were adopted to prevent clashes: an item could become party policy only if Conference voted it by two-thirds; the election manifesto was drawn up jointly by the NEC and the PLP; and the timing of its implementation was left to the latter. But the only real safeguard was a common outlook among members of both bodies.

For most of the Labour Party's history up to the 1970s, harmony was maintained because the front-benchers and the trade union majority generally agreed. The parliamentary leaders were responsive to the needs of government and to the ordinary voters; the secretaries of the big trade unions were concerned with the influence of their organisations on public policy, and with the standard of living of their members. Political and industrial leaders had more in common with one another than either had with the ardent ideologists among the constituency activists (for whom that was further proof that the industrial 'bosses' were out of touch with their members). The union leaders were natural defenders of a party constitution which ensured their own predominance in Conference; while the constituency parties had ensured since 1937 that, besides the principal PLP leaders, a few left-wing critics – Cripps, Laski, Bevan – sat on the NEC to act as a ginger-group.

The leaders could usually rely on a majority of the Parliamentary Party, for few MPs believed internal dissension or left-wing policies would help to defeat the Conservatives. But they could ignore neither their active constituency workers nor the electoral damage done by open disputes, so that a revolt in the local parties or the unions put the PLP under effective pressure. In those days, however, trade union leaders faced few political demands from the mass membership, and resisted those of unofficial activists. Experience of industrial battles and negotiations had taught them the need for solidarity, for acceptance by minorities of unwelcome majority decisions; and in politics too they preached loyalty to the leadership, and sustained it in Conference and on the NEC. Often they were blunt men, trained in a hard school, who had little patience with tiresome rebels in union or party.

Structure and traditions allowed rival tendencies to control different segments of the coalition. Critics were strong in the constituency parties where many besides the perpetual malcontents instinctively felt that the leaders needed an occasional prod. The front-benchers had to accommodate their policies to a political and economic situation which they could not control, and to the need to win over uncommitted voters if they were ever to implement those policies. But the Labour Party was always receptive to rebels against a leadership which they accused of lacking determination or vigour or Socialist principles.

These systematic critics ranged from the Communist Party, whose small but dedicated forces were important in some trade unions, to the impatient idealists, far more numerous but often less effective. Those temperamental rebels were given to utopianism and wishful thinking, certain of their own unblemished rectitude, suspicious of all compromise and all authority. They never forgot the temptations of power that afflict some front-benchers, or recognised the temptations of purity to which critics succumb – as Aneurin Bevan in the 1930s warned Jennie Lee: 'Yes, you will be pure all right. But, remember, at the price of impotency. You will not influence the course of British politics by as much as a hair's breadth. Why don't you get into a nunnery and be done with it?'[1]

Their outlook reflected the old radical, provincial, Nonconformist tendency to see Westminster politicians as willing victims of the aristocratic, or the parliamentary, or the Whitehall embrace. All those suspicions were so stimulated by the trauma of 1931 that even a generation later the most influential figure in the Labour Movement was said to be the ghost of Ramsay MacDonald. Of course many active constituency workers passionately wanted their party to come to power, and usually gave the leadership the benefit of the doubt. But every election defeat brought Labour's deep-rooted opposition-mindedness to the surface, allowing the PLP minority to blame the leaders for excessive moderation, and present themselves as the exclusive guardians of principle – even as simple rank and filers, keeping a watchful eye on the careerists at the top. But they too were politicians, disagreeing with the leaders perhaps on the extent of necessary compromise; perhaps on electoral strategy, wanting to rally the active party workers and not worry about the floating vote; or perhaps aiming at a change of leadership, and meanwhile seeking status and prominence as constituency representatives on the National Executive.

The front bench faced such opposition from the ILP in the late 1920s, and from the Socialist League and the Popular Front campaigners in the 1930s. But from 1939 to 1951 dissent had generated no sustained attack on the leadership or its policies. As the elections of 1950 and 1951 showed, the Attlee Government retained its solid working-class following, absorbing or wiping out all the splinter groups on its Left – Communists, ILP and Common Wealth. Yet the responsibilities of office had entailed supporting some unpopular policies, especially over defence where Labour's pacifist tradition had deep roots. Once out of government, with the leaders' prestige eroded by defeat, many CLP activists were relieved to revert to a more familiar stance.

Bevanism thus revived a tradition which had seemed to be disappearing. To Gaitskell and his associates, it threatened not only their policies and their own positions of leadership, but also Labour's prospects of power. Before the war, Labour's criticisms of Chamberlain's appeasement policy were discredited by its votes against defence estimates; now as the Bevanites came to question any need for rearmament at all, Gaitskell feared they would threaten Labour's credibility as well as Britain's security. As he wrote in 1952:

An Opposition that is continually taking the easy line . . . may evoke much enthusiasm among its own supporters, but it is most unlikely to win the confidence of the electorate as a whole. And even if it does, its failure to live up to what was said earlier will soon lead to its downfall.[2]

Frequently in his first year out of office he warned against demagogy, pointing out the

extraordinary contrast between what the Tories now say and do as a Government and what they preached and promised when in Opposition.

We do not intend to follow this very bad example . . . If we [do] . . . we may temporarily enlist the support of some sections or interests and we may enjoy a shortlived emotional satisfaction, but we shall certainly suffer in our reputation with the country and weaken our chances of getting back into power.[3]

The argument was sharpest on foreign affairs and defence, but was not confined to them. For Labour was still a rather new party needing to establish its credentials as a serious instrument of government. Uncommitted voters, Gaitskell wrote, 'are interested not only in policy but in whether we shall govern the country honestly, efficiently and in a truly responsible manner . . . By our bearing we must earn their respect and gain their confidence.'[4] But as Roy Jenkins once put it years later, 'Fighting Opposition or Alternative Government?' was a false dilemma for Labour, since it was easy to be neither and difficult to be both, but impossible to be the one without the other.

## Revolt at Westminster: A Party Within the Party

Labour had been in office for eleven years. The ex-Ministers who dominated the Parliamentary Committee (or Shadow Cabinet) were concerned to defend their own records and sympathetic to their successors' problems. But in November 1951 many MPs wanted more aggressive opposition, and hoped to disengage from some governmental policies which were unpopular among party workers in the constituencies. So, though the Bevanites were few in the PLP, they found much sympathy when they sought to push it towards the Left – but none when they divided it by pursuing, at Westminster and in the weekly press, a bitter feud against the front-benchers.

The problem of leadership was in everyone's mind, for Attlee's successor would have to be chosen before long. Morrison, his deputy, had neither his backing nor that of the unions, and handled foreign affairs badly in opposition as in office. Bevan had plenty of sympathisers, and on the whole behaved moderately until 1954; even so he often alienated them by emotional outbursts, as he had in 1951. In 1954-5 he forfeited their goodwill by his sustained intransigence; and his friends' unrelenting vendetta against the leadership did him further harm. Though Gaitskell made bad mistakes too, by 1955 both his rivals had thoroughly discredited themselves and gave him a very comfortable victory.

His insistence on responsible opposition proved a heavy political handicap. In one early PLP argument over the Chancellor's economy cuts, he himself spoke (as he admitted) rather pedantically, and Bevan won great sympathy with a moderate and effective reply. 'Bevanites pushing', wrote Dalton. 'Weak opposition. H.G. not sufficiently combative against the Tories.'[5] In the House next day Gaitskell did better. But he would make no concessions to demagogy. As he insisted soon afterwards to a trade union audience: 'We should never stifle the still small voice that whispers to us: "yes, but what would you do if you were the Government now?" That is something precious, that voice . . . the conscience of an Opposition Party, and we should cherish it.'[6]

At first even the defence controversy was subdued. The Bevanites argued against taking dollar aid for the rearmament programme lest political dependence follow. Gaitskell refuted their case in a long memorandum to the Parliamentary Committee, arguing that it would bring quite small economic benefits but large political drawbacks, leaving Britain even more dependent on America. The PLP twice voted heavily against it. But the Government's cuts in the defence programme revived the Labour quarrel. Churchill especially annoyed Gaitskell by going 'out of his way in the most mischievous manner to pat Bevan on the back . . . to stir up trouble in the Labour Party'.[7]

Hoping to restore unity, Gaitskell refrained from starting polemics himself or even answering those directed against him. He defended his own record vigorously, and even appealed to his critics to call off the vendetta for the sake of the Party. While believing that Bevan would be satisfied only by the party leadership, Gaitskell nevertheless hoped he and Wilson might 'work their passage' back to the front bench. But seeing the Bevanites as a small minority, he would not make large policy concessions to them; and he did insist that once the PLP had settled its tactics, all MPs must support the decision – as they always had in Socialist parties everywhere. For revolts or ostentatious abstentions were still very rare; there had been only a couple of peacetime cases in twenty years. Front-benchers who were more flexible on policy than

Gaitskell were often even stronger than he over enforcement of majority decisions.

After long arguments, no Bevanite stood for the Shadow Cabinet. James Griffiths came top with 195 votes and Gaitskell third with 175, far ahead of Dalton and Shinwell. But Wilson would still have liked to return to the front bench, and in some moods so would Bevan – who was violent in private, but was active in neither the House nor the PLP.

Since the disaffiliation of the ILP twenty years earlier, there had been many differences of opinion among Labour MPs but no organised group seeking to use the differences to raise mutiny – or revolution – in the ranks. The Bevanite caucus therefore provoked great resentment, especially when on 2 March 1952 they carried Labour's divisions to the floor of the House by rebelling on the Service estimates – the very question on which the Party had discredited itself before the war. The Shadow Cabinet (against Gaitskell's wishes) had put down a rather absurd amendment approving the defence programme but attacking the Government's incapacity to carry it out; the Bevanites' substitute proposal was turned down heavily in the PLP. Next day, defying a three-line whip, they abstained on the Labour amendment and then voted against the estimates.

Most Labour MPs were enraged. Open rejection of majority PLP decisions in opposition was unheard-of. Every Labour candidate had signed the PLP's standing orders, which forbade voting against those decisions and allowed abstention only on grounds of conscience; but since 1945 these had been suspended. Now the Shadow Cabinet recommended that they should be reimposed; every MP should promise to observe them; and the rebels should be censured. That was a compromise, for the Chief Whip William Whiteley, a Durham miner, had wanted the rebels to lose the Labour whip at once. But a new faction – nicknamed the 'Keep Calm' group – sought both to limit the Bevanites' revolt and to check any strong action against them. They proposed a compromise resolution merely restoring standing orders, and carried it easily, 163 to 74.

The Keep Calmers had averted an open and immediate clash, but they had also convinced dissidents that open rebellion was quite safe, ensuring a continuing public struggle within the Party. When it broke out again bitterly in 1960, most of the surviving ex-mediators reappeared not as Wilsonite compromisers but as staunch Gaitskellites. Like Bevan in the Cabinet, his friends on the Left constantly alienated their would-be sympathisers.

They paid the price eventually in the choice of a successor to Clement Attlee. In 1952 Attlee was sixty-nine, a taciturn man with public-school and military values, few friends and no personal faction. He was respected by his opponents, and admired by his followers as the leader who had brought Labour to power and carried out its policies. To his colleagues he was preferable to any rival, for he was skilled at balancing between strong personalities and conflicting tendencies. He had enjoyed the prestige of the Premiership, and the massive backing of Ernest Bevin. But now Bevin was dead and the Party out of office. Faced with a bitter internal feud, he preserved his own position and the Party's unity by giving no lead at all.

His likeliest successor seemed to be his deputy Herbert Morrison, five years his junior and the other survivor of Labour's inner cabinet. A shrewd, cheerful cockney who understood the British electorate, a superb organiser, master of the London County Council in the 1930s, a courageous wartime Home Secretary, and then a most effective leader of the House of Commons, he was the natural beneficiary of Labour's strong sense that great service deserves great reward. But he could be a ruthless party manager, and he had made many enemies. His vision was narrow, and his naked ambition appeared unseemly even to hardened colleagues. The trade unions had no love for him, the Left detested him, and even his friends thought him ultra-cautious about the floating voter. He suffered too from Attlee's personal dislike, and from his own catastrophic performances on foreign affairs. Gaitskell respected him as honest and courageous, 'the nearest we have to a Scandinavian Socialist leader', who 'really understands the working of democracy'.[8]

In the spring of 1952 Attlee told his journalist friends: 'I'd go at once if I thought Morrison could hold the party together, but I don't think he can. He is too heavy-handed . . . I may have to hang on for a bit and see.'[9] About the same time several anti-Bevanite ex-Ministers had the leader to dine at the House to persuade him to intervene more actively. As one of them, Gordon Walker, recorded: 'Attlee was rather casual. Bevan would fade out as a menace: it had often happened before. The thing was to give him time . . . suddenly Attlee said that no one ought to be P.M. after 70 . . . We should give our mind to finding the next leader.'[10] He then departed abruptly, leaving the others recalling that his birthday was in January – only eight months away.

Gaitskell wanted to persuade Attlee to stay for four or five years, provided he would take the lead against Bevan. But if Attlee would not lead, then he should go quickly. Instead the leader suddenly announced that he hoped to go on into the next Parliament. But when he lunched with the ex-Ministers at the end of July:

> We all said we could not attack Bevan without leadership. Gaitskell said that it all turned on whether Attlee would make a strong speech about the Party in the Party. . . .
>
> Attlee did not commit himself at all. He . . . had been advised by 'people close to the rank & file' not to attack. Bevan would hang himself in time.[11]

In the House of Commons Bevan did seem likely to 'hang himself in time', and Attlee's technique was quite effective. Elsewhere it was a different story.

## Revolt in the Constituencies: Morecambe and Stalybridge

Attlee's advisers proved as wrong about party workers in the country as they were right about the MPs. Gaitskell was almost alone in speaking out in defence of the rearmament programme with unpopular forthrightness, and was soon recognised as Bevan's chief antagonist.

At the 1952 party conference at Morecambe, the Bevanites used the elections for constituency representatives on the NEC – hitherto a contest among individuals seeking to influence party policy – for an organised factional campaign to discredit the parliamentary leadership. Sensationally, they took six of the seven seats, while other left-wingers lost votes. Morrison came slightly and Dalton badly behind the winners. Gaitskell was next, doing far better than Shinwell (a member of the Executive till 1950); but with only one-third of Bevan's vote and half that of Wilson and Crossman. Thanks to Labour's fondness for familiar faces, the Bevanites now had a permanent institutional base within the Party.

At the time Dalton called it the worst conference 'for bad temper & general hatred' of the past twenty-five years; afterwards, younger men thought it the worst of the next twenty-five. Arthur Deakin, giving his 'fraternal' address from the TUC, furiously denounced the Bevanites against 'Vesuvian' interruptions; he was angry at Attlee's silence and very nearly said so. The weather was wet and blustery, the accommodation poor, the hall too small. Labour had never been to Morecambe before. It has never returned since.

Morrison accepted rejection with dignity, winning a tremendous ovation when he promised to continue to serve loyally. His defeat and the violence of the galleries produced a reaction, as Crossman had feared, both in the conference and among Labour's supporters in the country. Bevan's following among Labour voters fell to 22 per cent (against 51 per cent for the leadership), and among party members to 40 per cent (against 48); only 11 per cent of the voters and 22 per cent of the members welcomed Morrison's defeat, which 40 and 55 per cent respectively deplored.

The leadership thus still had far more support in the electorate and even in the Party than its critics, and it had carried its policies. But, unchallenged among the activists, the Bevanites had scored a spectacular success; and Gaitskell feared that if Attlee's tactics of silence continued to prevail, the morale of their opponents would collapse. When the results were announced, he told a journalist: 'There is only one thing we have to do in the next few years, and that is to keep the Labour Party behind the Anglo-American alliance.' Since the Bevanites so willingly pandered to anti-Americanism and neutralism, he wrote: 'it is clear to me now that we must fight. The worm must turn'.[12] Before the conference he had cooled down local party workers in Leeds who urged him to pull no punches against the Bevanites. Now they begged him to speak out. He consulted no Westminster colleague. But on Saturday morning he came to the *Leeds Citizen* office to draft 'what was for me an unusually violent speech . . . a call to battle'.[8]

Gaitskell found 450 people waiting for him in the small old-fashioned theatre at Stalybridge, and warned them to expect a shock. He condemned the 'gross political ingratitude' and 'blind stupidity' of rejecting Morrison. He alleged that many resolutions and speeches were promoted by the Communist *Daily Worker*:

I was told by some well-informed correspondents that about 1/6th of the Constituency Party delegates appeared to be Communists or Communist inspired. This figure may well be too high. But if it should be one-tenth, or even one-twentieth, it is a most shocking state of affairs to which the National Executive should give immediate attention.

He welcomed the Morecambe policy decisions, which all loyal Labour supporters would now accept. He protested that the CLPs had been badly misled by the Bevanite press pouring out 'a stream of grossly misleading propaganda with poisonous innuendoes and malicious attacks on Attlee, Morrison and the rest of us'. To reply was not

endangering the unity of the Party. For there will be no unity on the terms dictated by *Tribune*. Indeed its . . . vitriolic abuse of the Party Leaders is an invitation to disloyalty and disunity. It is time to end the attempt at mob rule by a group of frustrated journalists and restore the authority and leadership of the solid sound sensible majority of the Movement.

If we don't or can't do this we shall not persuade, and shall not deserve to persuade, our fellow citizens to entrust us once again with the Government of the Country.[13]

The hitherto silent audience gave him a loud round of applause at the end.

The speech was injudiciously phrased. The much-resented words 'mob rule' were not meant to attack the delegates themselves, but Gaitskell was entirely to blame for not making himself clear. Communist infiltration was indeed a danger, and the Communists themselves emphasised that many Bevanites were far more anti-American than their leader; but Gaitskell was most unwise to publicise a very exaggerated estimate which he neither publicly endorsed nor privately believed.[14] The 'frustrated journalists' were particularly indignant at becoming targets themselves. Kingsley Martin, editor of the *New Statesman*, threatened to sue for libel. Gaitskell replied with appropriate caution, and Martin then said he would publish the correspondence. But, when Gaitskell justified his charges with a long dossier of quotations, Martin conveniently ruled that publication would bore the readers.[15] However, when writing to critical rank and file Labour workers sick of the bickering politicians who damaged morale in their local parties, Gaitskell always replied most patiently. A local secretary from Somerset, who urged 'the likes of you' to go out to the backwoods to make your 'suicidal speeches', was astounded and delighted when Gaitskell accepted this as an invitation to speak.

Everyone wanted to end the feud, and no one but the Bevanites thought it could be ended on their terms. As Gaitskell said, they had no idea how much resentment they had aroused, or how others saw their activities. Where Michael Foot had found the past year 'exhilarating', to Clem Attlee it was the unhappiest of his long leadership, and to Jim Griffiths it had almost caused the Party 'irrevocable harm'.[16] When Parliament reassembled, Crossman found 'the atmosphere . . . worse than I have ever known it . . . such hostilities in the air that you sweated before you got hot'.[17] Dalton sadly noted 'More hatred, and love of hatred, in our Party than I can ever remember.'[18]

A chorus of respected Labour voices now endorsed Gaitskell's remedies for the trouble: Griffiths, the one leader without enemies; Morgan Phillips, the cautious secretary; Dalton and Strachey. Even Attlee at last abandoned his silence:

What is quite intolerable is the existence of a party within a party with separate leadership, separate meetings, supported by its own press . . . I say . . . 'Work with the team. Turn your guns on the enemy, not on your friends' . . . The most brilliant player on the left wing [would be] no use if he . . . put the ball through his own goal.[19]

At the PLP meeting on 23 October 1952, Crossman reported Morrison saying: ' "Considering what Gaitskell had had to put up with for a year, he couldn't blame him if he didn't choose his words quite right." This produced an enormous round of applause for Gaitskell.' From the chair, Attlee, having at last made up his mind, demanded a vote – as a question of confidence – on disbanding unofficial groups and ending personal attacks; declined to call the Keep Calm leaders; refused any postponement; and succeeded by 188 to 51 with a dozen abstentions.[20]

Gaitskell promptly welcomed the PLP resolution; and Bevan, overruling some of his closest friends, decided to co-operate. 'To continue the Group now is to perpetuate schism,' he told Crossman: 'If you were to continue the Group in these conditions and I were the Leader, I would have you expelled. The Group is intolerable.'[17] To show independence, Bevan stood against Morrison for deputy leader, polling more than expected (82 to 194). To show reasonableness he then stood for the Parliamentary Committee of twelve. A new electoral system had been devised by Attlee to avoid plumping by minorities. On the first round Gaitskell, despite Stalybridge, again came third with 179 – four more than in 1951. Bevan was twelfth with 108, and on the second ballot again twelfth with 137, so that he would have been elected under either system. Wilson polled 91, but other Bevanites far below the group's strength.

The mood was transformed at once. Even in Bevanite constituencies, Crossman found that 'Attlee's counter-attack has been extremely successful' and the 'whole atmosphere has changed'.[20] At Westminster:

Mysteriously, and with astonishing rapidity, the mood of the Parliamentary party has changed. The Bevanite and anti-Bevanite feeling has melted away and . . . everyone is rather shamefacedly aware that both sides are on the same side after all . . . this couldn't have happened if there had been real fundamental issues of policy dividing the two sides . . . the enormous desire of the Labour Movement for unity, and therefore the enormous fear of any contestant of being blamed for disunity, [is] at least a partial explanation.[21]

Gaitskell conceded privately that the Stalybridge speech was badly worded, but he always maintained that in the long run his stand had been necessary and healthy for the Party. It affected his own position too, for Arthur Deakin mistakenly thought he had found a true hatchet-man of the Right. His enthusiasm was both to promote and to embarrass Gaitskell's career.

## A Solid Bastion: South Leeds

Gaitskell's West Riding base influenced his political attitude. His working-class constituency kept him in touch with grass-roots opinion and confirmed his own suspicion of the far Left. But it was not typical of a city where Labour politics were turbulent, and social and geographical divisions sharp. North of the river were the business and civic headquarters, the university, the prosperous residential areas, the flourishing Jewish community. South Leeds always felt neglected, kept distinct by distance and poor transport – especially Middleton which, with its miners, became part of South Leeds only in 1948. With their fierce sense of identity and deep-rooted working-class culture, Labour voting was still an expression of local as well as class solidarity; in some areas canvassers did not knock on doors but rang handbells to bring whole streets to the polls.

Always a safe seat except in 1931, after the war South Leeds was impregnable to Tory attack. Gaitskell's assiduous attention to it was due not to political prudence but to temperamental thoroughness and feeling for the people he had gone into politics to serve. As back- or front-bencher, Chancellor of the Exchequer or Leader of the Opposition, his monthly weekend visits had top priority even if he had to fly back from abroad; he is said to have missed only once in his whole parliamentary career. Usually he came up by train, writing a speech on the way. He lodged (and insisted on paying) with a local supporter, generally his agent: Brett or Goodwill at first, George Murray after 1950. At election times, needing space and quiet, he went further afield, staying with Mrs Duffield, Brett's daughter (he amazed Mrs Duffield by going to bed on whisky and chocolate biscuits); and later in North Leeds with his prosperous friends the Gillinsons. They provided an escape from endless politics, and the opportunity to meet Leeds writers and artists such as Terry Frost. But he always felt guilty at being out of the constituency.

Usually he held Saturday 'surgeries', and brought his agent or a local councillor along to help deal with constituents' problems. Among the commonest were pensions and military service matters, and especially complaints against landlords or property companies or estate agents, since local housing was appalling; at one time he had fifty letters a day. That was local council business, but an MP's intervention could sometimes speed things up. If he could help he would take endless trouble; if not he would say so straightforwardly. Early in the evening he would relax, often watching a cowboy film on television, and then tour the workingmen's clubs where he was completely at home. He might see more people on Sunday morning, then have a good traditional Yorkshire lunch at the Goodwills' or the Murrays'. The general committee met on Sunday afternoons for his convenience, and he often caught a tea-time train back to London. Whenever possible he came for social events, and in September 1953 he spent a full week canvassing the area, which he always enjoyed. He would linger chatting with the housewives so that fellow-canvassers would find themselves two or three streets ahead and have to slow down. But his party workers knew that 'you could always find him when you wanted him'; and that at election time voters would say, 'Oh yes, we know him well, he's been here to tea.'

These working-class people never understood the notion that Hugh Gaitskell found it hard to mix with or talk to ordinary folk. 'He was pleasant, friendly, you never felt he was talking down to you. The whole division was fond of him . . . the sort of approach that encourages people to talk helps a person who is perhaps a bit nervous, draws people out . . . not necessarily about politics', said a woman trade-unionist. 'I never met anyone so brilliant and yet so friendly,' echoed a shop steward. 'It's very difficult to find people with the level of intelligence he had and yet who had so obviously the common touch and who was so ready to learn from things he had done wrong himself.' To a third party worker 'He didn't seem an intellectual, he was down to earth, never up in the clouds about realities, it didn't matter what company he was in, he was just the same to the people who knew him . . . He talked with you, he didn't talk down to anybody.' The Middleton miners seemed a closed and impenetrable group to other trade-unionists in the constituency, but not to Gaitskell: 'he was their idol', said their spokesman. An occasional young lower-middle-class left-winger never felt at ease with him and doubted if others did either – though readily admitting it was not for want of effort on Gaitskell's part, and affirming that he was 'a much-respected man'. But nearly everyone else used words like 'loved' or 'adored' or 'worshipped', often carefully denying that these were euphemisms for deference.[22]

Solid Labour constituencies, with no real electoral contest, often have weak local parties. South Leeds was active but narrow, without much of a women's section or a youth movement. Gaitskell was attentive to the fairly small devoted band, mostly councillors, who ran it for years. He always showed appreciation of their work, kept in close touch, gave them a good time when they came to London or to a party conference, and often quietly helped with their family problems. In

1961 he suggested and paid for an annual dinner-dance for the 100-odd collectors of subscriptions; it was a huge success, and the constituency has held one ever since. His reward was unshakeable personal loyalty, buttressed by the intense if rarely displayed local pride of good Yorkshire folk who knew they were sending Britain's next Prime Minister to Parliament.

Gaitskell never had to worry about their backing. In 1952 they made him a delegate to allow him to stand for the National Executive. Before Stalybridge they were keener than he to denounce the Bevanites; after it they gave him a unanimous vote of confidence. In 1954 he was unanimously nominated as party treasurer. They unanimously congratulated him over Suez (not to be taken for granted in a working-class area where feelings ran high). They disavowed his policy only once, when he attacked Clause Four, which they reaffirmed by 17 to 12 – though a personal vote of confidence in Gaitskell was at once passed by 30 to 2. Over the defence battle in 1960, South Leeds supported its member throughout, and became a bastion of the Campaign for Democratic Socialism.

Like so many local Labour parties, in NEC elections South Leeds was amiably tolerant and frequently voted for representatives with whose views it disagreed. Gaitskell did not try to influence its choice, though he called it 'absurd' that the NEC was chosen by people who had no idea of the 'real relative merits' of the candidates.[23] Even in 1960 South Leeds endorsed Gaitskell's policies but supported five of his opponents (and two more in the women's section) for the NEC. In 1961 it rejected all seven.

Though Gaitskell was meticulous in telling his local party about current Westminster controversies, that sympathetic audience gave him something of a holiday from factional politics. For Labour's internal battles had little echo in South Leeds. The harmony was rarely disturbed – in the late 1950s by a couple of middle-class ex-Communists who had left the CP over Hungary, and occasionally by a youthful left-winger who grew up in South Leeds but soon moved on to redder pastures. The rest of Leeds was very different, for Trotskyists were already active there. There were moves to proscribe them in 1954 and in 1959. During the 1960–1 battles Gaitskell was twice the target of ugly demonstrations. In the university, where the far Left had its headquarters, Gaitskell had a few good friends, although he never had much to do with the place. He had excellent relations with the Leeds unions, especially the engineering shop stewards; astonishingly, though not a member of the AEU, he once presented their annual award of merit when their president Bill Carron was ill.

As South Leeds was geographically separate, socially homogeneous, fiercely self-contained and suspicious of outsiders, the quarrels of the rest of the city rarely penetrated there. Local people, asked why they had so much less political strife than their neighbours, always explained that they were entirely a working-class party, and that all the university lecturers lived north of the river. No wonder, perhaps, that Gaitskell once wistfully wished the constituency formed a separate borough of its own.

## Shadow Chancellor and the 'Butskellite' Myth

When a moderate Conservative succeeded a moderate Labour man at the Treasury in November 1951, *The Economist* light-heartedly invented a composite Chancellor-figure. 'Mr Butskell' became a target for those in both parties who advocated polarisation politics. Gaitskell and Butler agreed in favouring a moderate electoral strategy, in disliking violent abuse of opponents, and in treating issues seriously. Both were respected by people exasperated at the barren aspects of party conflict. But his economic training, his emotional temperament and his 'unquenchably Socialist' opinions were alien to Butler.[24] Gaitskell's actions were sometimes reckless. He prized loyalty to colleagues highly. In private he put the same views to everyone, and in public he sought to convince people by freely revealing his mind and motives. The two personalities had little in common.

There was rather more justification for the concept of Butskellism, for they agreed both on Keynesian economic techniques and on maintaining full employment. But they differed on the role of monetary policy; on the incidence of budgetary burdens and benefits; on convertibility of sterling; and about the distribution of wealth. Gaitskell always insisted on the need for investment, constantly reiterating that better terms of trade brought Britain only a precarious surplus, which must be devoted to industrial investment not consumption. His main parliamentary successes were in leading united Labour attacks, year after year, against the class bias of Butler's budgets. Abroad, where Butler gave priority to convertibility, Gaitskell defended exchange controls and the sterling area (foreshadowing later arguments over the Common Market).

Poor Mr Butskell: a short life, wrecked by schizophrenia.

By 1954, many of his own wing still thought Gaitskell too rigid to be a coming party leader. As in 1951, Bevan's errors in polarising the Movement and personalising the issue again unwittingly built up Gaitskell's stature. In April 1954, quite suddenly and with no warning even to close friends, Bevan reopened Labour's civil war. The next twelve months were the only post-war period in which he normally followed the advice of his irreconcilable rather than his moderate friends. During that year he finally destroyed his chance to lead the Labour Party.

# 11

# Foreign Affairs and the
# Disintegration of Bevanism 1954–5

*'I don't see how one can have strong loyalties . . . and continually refuse to
do any of the dirty work'*
(HG, 1955)

*Indo-China and German Rearmament: Bevan on the Offensive*
Labour conflicts in these years were over attitudes to rearmament, and
to the United States. The Bevanites had accepted the original defence
programme in 1950, but by 1952 they were becoming critical of any
rearmament at all. Gaitskell argued that it was inducing caution in
Moscow, and thought their outlook dangerous, for he feared that any
dictatorial regime might exploit a tempting military vacuum.

Without American power the Central European vacuum could not
be filled. Gaitskell was therefore alarmed by the growing hostility
towards the United States, which by 1952 the Bevanites were
exploiting. He pointed out that defence cuts and independence of the
United States were incompatible: we would become more dependent
on her and less able to affect her policy. He attacked those who 'seem to
face both ways. They declare in favour of alliances like NATO . . . but
always demand cuts . . . playing up to the . . . pacifists, neutralists
and fellow-travellers and fanning the flames of anti-Americanism.'[1]
Privately he attributed the hostility partly to real differences with the
United States; and he was exasperated when the new Republican
Administration and Congress abandoned burden-sharing, treating aid
as an expression not of solidarity among allies but of American charity.
But he rightly emphasised British resentment at the changing power
relationship, and perceptively predicted that it might soon be echoed
on the Right.[2]

As in 1950–1, suspicion of the United States was most evident over
Germany and over the Far East. In Indo-China the war against the
French was coming to its climax in early 1954. The Americans wished
to form a regional defensive alliance modelled on NATO; the British
Government and Opposition were both willing, provided it was
acceptable to the Asian Commonwealth countries. But when Attlee on

13 April 1954 appealed to the receptive Foreign Secretary to ensure that any alliance should include Asians and reject colonialism, Bevan seemed to 'almost trample on his diffident leader' in his haste to get to the dispatch box and denounce the treaty as a surrender to American pressure.[3] When the Shadow Cabinet met next day, Bevan announced that he would leave it after Easter. Gaitskell recorded:

We then went upstairs to the [PLP] meeting . . . and Clem . . . to our astonishment, proceeded to speak with the utmost vigour and indignation about A.B.'s behaviour on the Front Bench . . . I have often wondered whether Clem did this deliberately, knowing that it would provoke A.B. into an immediate resignation.[4]

Bevan at once declared that he had already resigned. Downstairs, ' "What a wonderful Easter egg!" said a Tory at the tape.'[5]

Harold Wilson as runner-up was entitled to Bevan's vacant Shadow Cabinet seat, and accepted it in the name of party unity. Bevan told Crossman that was 'gross personal disloyalty' and 'would be the end of Wilson's political career'.[6] But Bevan's resignation had enraged the Right of the Party and the great bulk of the middle-of-the-roaders. Since the United States did not intervene in Indo-China, it baffled his followers in the country; and at Westminster he had done himself 'incalculable harm'.[7]

Bevan took a far more serious step when he deliberately decided to divide the industrial as well as the political Movement. On 6 May 1954, learning that the party treasurer Arthur Greenwood was dying, he resolved to stand for the post against Gaitskell – expecting to lose but hoping that his opponents would 'split every union and expose Deakin and Tom Williamson by making them prefer an intellectual like Gaitskell to a miner like me'.[7] He would give up his safe seat on the NEC, where – since the majority were against him – he had no interest in trying to shape Labour policy.[7] To him the Party was still a battleground, not an army fighting the Tories for power: and its institutions were not forums for comrades to agree on strategy, but enemy forts to be conquered. Just before Greenwood's death he had told his friends that

an electoral success would be disastrous until it [the front bench] had been completely changed as the result of a mass movement in the constituencies . . . Nye said twice that he didn't care one halfpenny about the Labour Party in its present form, and also mentioned MacDonaldism in close connection with Harold.[8]

Bevan attributed his defeats to a conspiracy of bureaucratic leaders frustrating the rank and file, and hoped by polarising the Movement to undermine their power within three years. It was an error of judgement. His first attempt alienated his own following in the constituency parties instead of Gaitskell's in the industrial wing; his second forfeited instead of attracting support in the unions. For most ordinary party supporters wanted to heal the split rather than widen it; they put Labour's interests before those of the party within the Party. In that mood it seemed natural to them for Labour's financial spokesman to seek a place on the NEC as treasurer – but not for a rival leader to abandon a safe Executive seat simply to keep him out. They feared that Bevan would willingly disrupt the Movement from top to bottom in order to win control of the rump.

When Greenwood died on 9 June, Deakin promptly proposed to nominate Gaitskell for treasurer; and Gaitskell was surprised to hear later that Bevan would stand against him. His victory was not predetermined by the trade union steam-roller; in July he still thought he might well lose the Engineers, the Miners and the election.[9] Two days later he won both nominations. The Bevanites claimed with little cause that his success was a blatant defiance of the rank and file. Strife was acute in the AEU, where the executive's right to nominate was now contested for the first time. But recriminations about undemocratic wire-pulling could not apply to the Miners, Bevan's own union, whose executive made no recommendation. Their delegate conference chose Gaitskell by 505,000 to 233,000.

For propaganda purposes the struggle for nominations continued, but the AEU and NUM votes would clearly be decisive. Bevan had plenty of time to drop out and return to his safe seat in the CLP section. He did not do so. Gaitskell concluded that 'he cannot retreat of his own volition. So a story is invented to cover up his action, that he intends to go on challenging the power of the block vote, and run against me year by year. Maybe he will. But I am pretty sure this was not his original intention.'[4] At the same time as he abandoned the NEC, Bevan bought a Chiltern farm. Crossman felt that he did so as 'a reinsurance against failure'.[10] The failure was to be resounding.

The treasurership vote was to coincide with the debate on the rearmament of West Germany, the very issue where Bevan was strongest. In office, Dalton and others opposed it, though Herbert Morrison was less reluctant. Gaitskell, wrote Dalton in 1951, was 'always very careful to balance bet[n] H.M. & me on this'.[11] But while some of his colleagues shunned, in opposition, policies which they had

accepted in office, Gaitskell – typically – moved the other way. When
the Conservatives brought up the treaties for ratification, the Labour
Party was so closely divided that the NEC abandoned normal collective
responsibility, and in the PLP the leadership's majority fell in
February 1954 to only two.

Gaitskell wrote to one Labour MP: 'I have never been a fanatic
either way. It has always seemed to me a profoundly difficult
issue . . . The military side is probably less important than the
political and psychological.'[12] But as usual his balanced view did not
preclude an active commitment once he had decided. He argued that
only military occupation could prevent Germany rearming; but since
the Americans would not co-operate, that was bound to fail – with
disastrous results: 'to start on it without carrying it through . . . would
create a fire of German militarism . . . which might be impossible to
control'.[13] He fought the 'most dangerous illusion' that the West could
accept Russian terms for neutralising Germany, which risked both
American withdrawal from Europe and Russian control of all
Germany. At the Labour Conference at Scarborough, he was willing to
compromise to avert defeat, but he found that the union leaders might
not agree. Attlee opened the debate by saying that emotional hostility to
Germans was natural but irrelevant, like American emotional hostility
to the Chinese who had killed their soldiers in Korea. A few unions
switched, and the official policy was carried by 3,270,000 to 3,022,000.

Thirty years later the high passions and alarming predictions seem
much exaggerated on both sides. The early 1950s passed with no
German troops and no Soviet drive to the Channel. The Russians did
not stop negotiations or launch preventive war; and the new German
army did not undermine democracy as the critics confidently expected.

Gaitskell was elected treasurer at Scarborough by 4,388,000 to
2,032,000 for Bevan, winning between a third and half of the CLP vote.
In the constituency parties section Bevan had again misunderstood the
people he claimed to represent: instead of finishing Wilson's career,
they elected the defector in first place, while Anthony Greenwood – not
identified as a factional candidate – gained sensationally and finished
third.

Bevan reacted furiously to his defeat. He denounced the new NUM
president Ernest Jones by name for misrepresenting the miners: 'He
had better learn to behave himself. That is blunt.' His next target was
unnamed. We now know, he said, that 'the right kind of leader for the
Labour Party is a desiccated calculating machine who must not in any

way permit himself to be swayed by indignation . . . [at] suffering, privation or injustice . . . for that would be evidence of the lack of proper education and absence of self-control'.[14] Those present were not sure whether he meant Attlee, as the context suggests, or Gaitskell as was later supposed; Gaitskell himself was doubtful. The speech went down badly, and Bevan's conduct in defeat was compared adversely with Morrison's two years before. Gaitskell was not surprised by it. 'It is quite wrong to think of him as a scheming careful plotter. He schemes only at intervals, and his actions are determined far more by emotional reactions, particularly anger and pride, than anything else.'[4]

Immediately after Scarborough Gaitskell publicly predicted that the narrow decision would be accepted and that the German rearmament controversy was over. Surprisingly, he proved right; and only two years later Bevan was privately 'accusing the Germans of trying to blackmail us into defending them without their doing their share'.[15] There was one final splutter in November 1954, when the Government brought to the House of Commons the treaties on rearming Germany within NATO. The PLP accepted them by a majority of fifty (as against only two in February). But feelings ran deep and dangerous, and everyone knew it; so that when in the Shadow Cabinet Callaghan proposed that Labour should abstain, to his surprise Morrison and Gaitskell at once supported him.

Every Labour candidate was pledged to accept majority decisions of the PLP. Its standing orders allowed MPs on grounds of conscience not to vote for a party decision, though never to vote against one. The Bevanites were warned that they would be expelled if they divided the House. But no reminder or appeal or persuasion could deter 'half a dozen pacifists, egotists and crackpots' – as Gaitskell described them – from calling a division.[16] The PLP withdrew the whip from them (though not for long) and the press at once denounced Labour for excessive discipline.

Herbert Bowden, the Deputy Chief Whip, was sure the Bevanites wanted to establish a precedent for unpunished defiance and so make the standing orders unenforceable. Gaitskell told several critics that not to withdraw the whip would have reduced the Party to a rabble and played into the Bevanites' hands. An opposition must convince the electorate that it could form a stable government:

Moreover, while we all admire a man who follows the dictates of his conscience, I cannot myself agree that the man who puts his own views first and the loyalty to the group second is necessarily right, or better than the man who sacrifices his own point of view for the sake of the group.[17]

It was a view congenial to those in the majority rather than the minority. Before long, in March 1955, Labour's disciplinary crisis was to reach its climax over Aneurin Bevan himself.

## The Bomb, and the Bevanite Break-up

During these early Opposition years, Gaitskell co-operated regularly with three groups of political associates – later adding the moderate Bevanites, to whom he gradually drew close. First were his own political generation of ex-Ministers: James Griffiths later became his respected deputy leader, Alf Robens and Sir Frank Soskice his trusted advisers, Patrick Gordon Walker after 1959 his unofficial chief of staff. Dalton, more senior and not politically in that set, also remained influential. A second group comprised the young MPs whom Gaitskell encouraged in the Dalton tradition. Crosland and Jenkins were economic specialists on the Finance Bill team; so was Jay from an older generation; the better-known Wyatt was not. The link to this group was personal friendship. Lacking status outside Westminster, these allies could not share Gaitskell's burdens (e.g. on the National Executive). They had a common Oxford background and a similar intellectual and political outlook, though each disagreed with Gaitskell at times. They were close because he found them congenial companions, with whom he could relax and enjoy himself, and because they all displayed the two qualities he valued most: courage and loyalty.

That was true too of the third group, his allies in the trade union movement. On its political side there were two of his Leeds neighbours: Alice Bacon, a member of the National Executive; and Charlie Pannell, later a leader of the trade union MPs along with George Brown. Beyond Westminster the most prominent were the general secretaries of the two great general unions, Arthur Deakin and Tom Williamson. Until his death on May Day 1955, Deakin dominated the industrial movement by the force of his personality and the power of his union. He was one of those vigorous, boisterous, extroverted and intolerant working-class characters whose bullying and crudity are readily excused by intellectuals who like their politics, but never forgiven by those who do not. He was the chief of a group of trade union leaders who, in the precarious economic situation after the war, had used their great bargaining power with restraint – resisting a militant or dema-gogic minority who challenged that policy. They had a bad press on the Left and their heritage has been ostentatiously repudiated by many of their successors. Yet they improved their members' real standard of living substantially, without imposing the arbitrary injustice of inflation on the poor and weak; and they allowed the Attlee Cabinet to reconstruct the economy and lay foundations for lasting prosperity on which future governments failed to build.

The closest of all to Gaitskell, and a crucial figure in all the crises of the 1950s, was Sam Watson of the Durham miners, the uncrowned king of the county. The miners' union was an old federation of districts, in which the Communists had a secure foothold in Scotland and South Wales. The struggle against them in the NUM was perpetual, and since 1926 the suspicion of them among other miners' leaders was profound. Watson was quite a different type from Deakin: a personal friend of Bevan as well as Gaitskell, keen on adult education, a man of broad interests and great intellectual ability. He was Gaitskell's staunch ally both in the union and on Labour's National Executive, where he was chairman of the international sub-committee. No power-seeker, he repeatedly refused to move from Durham to London. Like Pannell and Alice Bacon, he began as a valued political supporter and became an intimate friend.

Conflicts in the unions were often bitter and neither side was always scrupulous about means. Over their own problems, the union leaders expected help from Labour politicians who were normally their allies.(When Gaitskell as party treasurer sought higher subscriptions from them, the general secretary of the TUC told him that 'the best way to get the Unions to pay up was to make it clear to them . . . that the Labour Party Machine would . . . [help] against Communist candidates at Union elections'.[18]) The trade unionists in the PLP and on the NEC usually voted with Gaitskell against the Bevanites, and when they called on him in turn for support, he did not feel they should be left to fight disagreeable battles alone. That sense of solidarity and obligation was to lead him into his worst blunder: his backing – after great hesitation – of the move to expel Aneurin Bevan in March 1955.

Bevan's Scarborough outburst in October 1954 provoked a hostile reaction among Labour MPs; and his subsequent absence and failure to lead did him immense harm. *Tribune* harmed him too by its violent denunciation of Deakin: 'Bevanism', said Harold Wilson, 'would be far better without *Tribune*.'[19] At the end of 1954 the *Daily Mirror* planned an article on 'The Flop of the Year: Aneurin Bevan'. So, at the New Year, Bevan tried to retrieve his position by reviving the argument over German rearmament – although the German Socialists and the International had now accepted the policy, and even its former Shadow Cabinet critics like Dalton strongly resented efforts to reopen the old divisions. Attlee on behalf of the Shadow Cabinet moved that Bevan's conduct 'makes a farce of Party Meetings and brings the Party into disrepute', and carried it by 132 to 72.

Within a week of this formal warning Bevan led another spectacular revolt – against Labour's acceptance of the hydrogen bomb, of which he had himself approved only a fortnight earlier.[20] On the morning of 24 February, a few hours before censuring Bevan, the PLP debated the government announcement that Britain would make the H-bomb. Attlee had already approved, and so did Crossman and some other Bevanites. The Shadow Cabinet knew their views when it proposed a motion of censure (on a three-line whip) which, however, explicitly accepted the H-bomb as a deterrent to aggression. In Bevan's absence the morning PLP approved the motion with very few dissentients.

Bevan met his friends again on Tuesday 1 March for their weekly lunch. At the very end he said he could not vote for the Labour motion. That evening Crossman persuaded him to do so, but next day, 'Jennie . . . had changed his mind again . . . he left fairly determined to lead a new split. In the House he met George Wigg, who . . . swung him back again. We went into the debate together, and as we entered the Chamber he said to me, "I'm still completely in two minds which I should do." '[20]

He had neither attended the PLP meeting on the subject nor tried to raise the question with the front bench in the five days since then; instead, he embarrassed Attlee on the floor of the House as he had over his SEATO challenge just a year before. The White Paper said the alliance would retaliate with nuclear weapons against an attack even by conventional forces. Neither the Government nor the Opposition leaders were willing to specify the circumstances, telling the Russians just how far they could safely go: when asked to do so, Attlee would not reply. So Bevan repeated the question, making three separate attacks on his own leaders, and then led sixty MPs in ostentatious refusal to vote for the censure motion. But a dozen old Bevanites refused to follow his lead, and one, Crossman, wrote to a bewildered party worker that Bevan, who 'had no moral scruples about the H-bomb . . . seemed almost deliberately to pick a quarrel with Clem Attlee . . . [for] a most unconvincing reason.'[21]

## Painful Epilogue: 'If thy Nye Offend Thee, Pluck it Out'

Labour MPs generally were indignant at Bevan's disruptive activities. In 1952, after losing in the PLP, he had instigated the first mass abstention in the lobby. At Westminster he had repeatedly offended his colleagues, and in the country both he and *Tribune* had kept fanning the flames of Labour's internal feud. Recently he had challenged Attlee on the floor of the House over SEATO, resigned from the Shadow Cabinet in a fit of petulance, declared war on the union leaders when he failed to win the treasurership, and tried to reopen the German rearmament wound as soon as it began to heal. Within a week of being warned for that, and without even attending the meeting which decided party policy, he had again challenged the leader in public and staged an open split in the House. No one defended his conduct, and when on 7 March 1955 the Shadow Cabinet held a special meeting to discuss the issue, it was Ede and Callaghan – no stern disciplinarians, and both opposed to German rearmament – who insisted that Bevan must forfeit the party whip.[22]

Withdrawal of the whip – expulsion from the PLP – was a sanction for misdeeds at Westminster, imposed by vote of all the Labour MPs. But only the National Executive could expel from membership of the Labour Party, and then the victim could appeal to Conference – as Cripps had vainly tried to do in 1939, and Bevan might do successfully in 1955. If a rebel MP was not expelled from the Party, losing the whip would relieve him of his promise to observe the obligations imposed on Labour MPs while leaving him the right to stand for any party office. Gaitskell therefore warned his Shadow Cabinet colleagues that it would be foolish to deprive Bevan of the whip unless they were both willing to expel, and able to carry both NEC and Conference. He advocated strong censure instead. But Attlee was the aggrieved party, he concluded, and the leader's view should prevail. The majority view was strongly for withdrawing the whip, and in the end Gaitskell voted for that course. 'I do not recall throughout this that Attlee said anything. Certainly . . . [nothing] heard by the Committee generally.'

Bevan and his irreconcilable advisers hoped that 130 MPs would sign a round robin of protest, but had to drop the idea after a discouraging canvass; and hoped too that their six NEC members would threaten to resign, but found no enthusiasm for that. Crossman told Bevan bluntly at one of their lunches: 'you were wrong last week and everybody knows you were wrong except the people in this room'.[23] Nevertheless, as the Shadow Cabinet knew, many MPs would vote for withdrawal of the whip only if the leaders made it a matter of confidence. But at the PLP on 16 March Attlee carefully avoided hinting that the issue was one of confidence, though when specifically asked if it was, he replied, 'Yes, necessarily so' – in a voice so weak that half the meeting could not hear him. An amendment to censure Bevan was lost by only 124 to 138, and Attlee's motion carried by 141 to 112:

exactly the result Gaitskell had expected, because he foresaw Attlee's hesitancy in putting the case. Gaitskell concluded, and his trade union friends concurred, that Bevan could not be expelled unless, on being asked for assurances about his future conduct, he refused to give them.

Attlee now busily set about disclaiming responsibility. He saw Gaitskell and Robens, complaining at being made 'the spearhead of a policy in which I did not believe'. They both protested that he had never made his disbelief clear at the time; for had he done so, their own attitude would have been different. Gaitskell suggested that Bevan's membership might be suspended for six months – a period which would be up before Conference – in order to deny him a clear victory. Attlee considered the idea but rejected it. The trade union leaders had been willing to settle for that, but both Deakin and his ally Williamson now publicly called on the leader to take a firm stand. But protests against expulsion came from 150 local parties, and many MPs were very unhappy. Some of Gaitskell's close friends – and his wife – told him he was going much too far. On 21 March Crosland, Jenkins and Wyatt jointly wrote to say they had frequently voted for the Shadow Cabinet while doubting its wisdom, but could no longer do so out of loyalty and contrary to their own views; and warned him that no one could lead the Party unless, like Attlee and unlike Morrison, he enjoyed solid support from people in the Centre who had opposed withdrawing the whip.[24]

Now the affair became entangled with Gaitskell's job as treasurer. In that capacity he was asking the unions to agree to higher affiliation fees, raising the income of the Party by 50 per cent. They negotiated over dinners at the St Ermin's Hotel in Victoria, and the next was on Monday 21 March. There the union leaders agreed to raise the fee; Deakin and Williamson had already offered to affiliate their unions to the Party on a much higher membership. They also initiated, and others supported, a call for Bevan's expulsion even against Attlee's wishes. Gaitskell did not conceal either from the leader or from the Bevanites that his own attitude was influenced by his need as treasurer to keep the unions' goodwill; he said so to Attlee on 17 March, and was reported by Crossman as saying: 'Many of our big backers were asking why we hadn't acted three years ago.'[25] The more lurid versions alleging decisive financial pressure can, however, safely be discounted.

At this St Ermin's dinner Gaitskell made up his mind that he must keep solidarity with his trade union allies. Morrison and Dalton agreed to support expulsion even against Attlee, and for the first time Gaitskell became fully committed, finding a mover and seconder and canvassing the trade union members – who complained that Attlee should lead, not they.

On the other side, Crossman invited Gaitskell round for a drink and tried to change his mind, warning him that he was appearing to be 'a stooge for big forces outside'. Gaitskell denounced Bevanism as 'only a conspiracy to seize the leadership', which his host denied. Allegedly he found parallels between Nye and Adolf Hitler as demagogues; he admitted 'minor differences' such as Bevan's concern for parliamentary liberty! Gaitskell was bitterly critical of Attlee, thought Bevan's influence would wither in the wilderness, and concluded that the main Tory issue in the next election (Who leads Labour?) would be undermined if Bevan were expelled, and underlined if he were not.[25] (His own account omits Hitler, and the silly analogy, though it was in his mind, was not his considered view.) After one great row with Bevan – probably this one – Gaitskell was escorting a friend to an XYZ ladies' night in the House when Bevan passed them on the stairs and she made a very derogatory comment. 'It was the only time Hugh ever ticked me off. He said, "Helen, that's not the way to talk about a great man and a great politician" – although he was fighting him. He really gave me a lecture.'[26]

Next day, Wednesday 23 March 1955, the NEC met. Attlee said Bevan might claim that his expulsion was a breach of parliamentary privilege, which Sir Frank Soskice (consulted by Gaitskell) thought 'inconceivable'. Attlee proposed that Bevan should be seen before the final decision, and Gaitskell said that would ensure no expulsion. They exchanged sharp words over the meaning of the PLP's vote. Trade union members of the NEC on both sides were under pressure from their unions; and Attlee won by 14 to 13.

Bevan was seen by a sub-committee of eight, of whom three had voted for expulsion and four against (plus the chairman). He very reluctantly agreed to clear his statement with Attlee, and to offer a 'really abject apology' which at first infuriated the Bevanite irreconcilables;[25] but even they had seen it to be necessary by the time he met the sub-committee on 29 March. There, Gaitskell recorded, he was quite unrepentant:

There was a general effort to keep the temperature down. In accordance with this I said very little. Most of the questions came from Jim Haworth and Jack Cooper . . . The only time I did intervene nearly led to a row. I said, 'Would you agree that it was a bad thing for the Party if members attack the leaders, and if so, will you agree not to do this in future?'

He said, 'I refuse to answer that question. It is a trap.' . . . in general he evaded every question of this kind.

The NEC voted to endorse the action of the PLP and to 'note' Bevan's assurances; and because of the news of an imminent election, Bevan regained the whip at once.

Gaitskell had expected that. He summed up succinctly and accurately: 'nobody has really come out of it very well'. Attlee had lost support on the Right, Bevan in the PLP as a whole, and he himself in the Centre, where he was again suspect as a rigid right-winger after a year in which he had begun to shed that reputation:

> most of my friends think I was very foolish to allow myself to be 'framed' as the 'Chief Prosecutor' . . . I don't see how one can have strong loyalties with people like George Brown and Alf Robens, not to speak of the T.U. leaders, and continually refuse to do any of the dirty work for them and with them . . . my own position is no doubt weaker . . . [but I] cannot regard that as the only thing that matters.

All the protagonists had shown very poor judgement. Bevan's behaviour so outraged everyone that even the irreconcilable Bevanites did not defend him at the time; and Keep Calmers felt he had been hopelessly wrong. Attlee was hailed as the saviour of the Party from a disaster principally of his own making; for no one would have suggested expulsion if Attlee had opposed it from the first. For the third time in four years he abdicated the responsibility of leadership by allowing matters to rot before showing his hand. Gaitskell always saw that the worst of outcomes was to fail in attempting extreme measures: unless both NEC and Conference would vote to expel, it was a mistake to withdraw the whip. He put the right alternatives, then – as he himself recognised – made the wrong choice: 'undoubtedly had I foreseen, as I should have done, where Clem's original attitude would lead us, I should have thrown my weight on the first day against withdrawing the Whip'. But Attlee was not exclusively to blame. The Shadow Cabinet hardliners should have been warned by their own assessment that they could not carry the PLP convincingly without a collective threat of resignation. Most Labour voters opposed expulsion, and if the MPs themselves were doubtful, the leadership would fail to force it through – at the cost of widespread resentment.

Both sides had their conspiratorial interpretations. The Bevanite view, that Attlee would be the next victim after Bevan, was the exact reverse of the reality. If Bevan had gone, Attlee's position would have been unchallenged; the leader was criticised only after he struggled to save Bevan, and then mainly for vacillating while others were committing themselves to unpopularity on what they thought to be his behalf. Conversely, Gaitskell exaggerated the cohesion and organisation of Bevan's supposed conspiracy, and helped the disintegrating Bevanites briefly to patch up their deep divisions. But though they all opposed the expulsion, after Easter their Tuesday lunches were never resumed, and Bevanism was no more.

Crossman had been right to warn Bevan:

Your strategic aim is fantastically over-ambitious: my own is limited to trying to restore a proper balance between Right and Left in the Party . . . your general line in the last few months has taken you further from effective power and nearer to the danger you mentioned of becoming a Jimmy Maxton.[27]

That reference to Maxton, the lovable but futile ILP rebel of the 1930s, gives a clue to the attitudes of both Bevan and his opponents. The idea of a Labour Party which could not accommodate Aneurin Bevan seems absurd today, as it would have done in 1951 or 1959, given his record over the previous few years; but after 1954/5 even his admirers feared he was becoming a perpetual dissident, effective at disruption, but with nothing to offer a Labour Party preparing for power.

His critics thought that Bevan in the wilderness would either fade away like Maxton, or return chastened to the fold. Expulsion had never been a political death sentence for Labour MPs (except for four who seemed indistinguishable from Communists). Nearly all the rest came back in time; and after rejoining they were not penalised but often held high office: for instance, Cripps, Bevan and Strauss who suffered expulsion in 1939 over the Popular Front; Ellen Wilkinson who renounced to avoid it; George Buchanan the former ILP MP. Those who merely lost the whip have all regained it before the following election. Except for fellow-travellers, the NEC used expulsion as a sanction not to destroy rebels politically, but to enforce on them minimal standards of co-operation with party colleagues, on pain of going it alone in an electoral climate deadly for independents. As that climate has changed since, parliamentary discipline has loosened considerably.

Thinking of Maxton and Cripps, the leadership doubtless underestimated the unpopularity of Bevan's expulsion. But he was very lucky to escape so lightly. The NEC majority wanted him out but never all voted together. A newspaper strike saved him from humiliating public dissection of his apology. Above all Churchill's retirement heralded an early election, and persuaded Labour to close ranks. The electoral drawbacks of expelling Bevan were not wholly clear, but the attempt to expel revived the harmful impression of Labour's disunity and quarrelsomeness – mainly but not only owing to Bevan.

An unsuccessful move to expel, disillusioning Labour activists without reassuring floating voters, was the worst possible prelude to the election campaign. Yet for Labour's longer-term health that may have been the best outcome of the clash, for it brought about the change in Bevan's conduct which the threat of it was meant to achieve. He was never again to follow the advice of the irreconcilables who had led him so close to disaster. Gaitskell too learned a lesson: using mistaken tactics in a vain effort to obtain a dubious objective, he had harmed himself with his closest friends, with uncommitted MPs, and with Attlee. The 1955 election therefore reopens the forgotten chapter in Gaitskell's life in which he conscientiously conciliated the moderate Left – a course he had begun earlier, only to be diverted by Bevan's outburst. The expulsion crisis put an end not only to Bevanism, but to Gaitskell's Stalybridge period too.

# 12

# Leader by a Landslide 1955

---

*'I am a socialist because I want to see fellowship . . . [while preserving] the
liberties we cherish'*
(HG at Conference, 1955)

---

## Party Treasurer, and the 1955 Election

During 1955 Gaitskell's position in his party was dramatically
transformed. He began it as a respected politician of high intelligence
and great courage, who seemed too rigid for party leadership. Over
Bevan's expulsion, the doubts crystallised so sharply that Gaitskell's
prospects of leading the Labour Party might well have been destroyed.
Yet only nine months later he was chosen to do so by a margin far more
impressive than in any comparable contest. During 1955 he broadened
his base in the Party; improved its organisational efficiency; co-
operated increasingly with the moderate Left; and proved that he could
appeal effectively to Labour's rank and file, satisfying (as he did for four
years) their overwhelming demand to end the feuding.

The first step was his election as treasurer in 1954. The office offered
plenty of scope for useful work, for 'the job of Treasurer has simply not
been done for ten years'.[1] Just before the TUC in September 1955, the
executives of eighty affiliated unions agreed to his proposal to increase
the affiliation fee from 6*d.* to 9*d.*, raising the Party's income by 50 per
cent and allowing it to start remedying the worst organisational
deficiencies. Through this and other financial activities, Gaitskell
gained personal political benefit too. They gave him closer contact with
the union leaders, for purposes cherished by constituency party
workers, and aligned him with the moderate Bevanites on the
Executive. That co-operation was soon to extend beyond organisation
to policy.

In the 1955 election Gaitskell played a major part on television. In a
broadcast on the cost of the Labour programme, he said: 'he was not in
the least worried about the financing of it if production went up steadily
. . . saw no reason why they should put up taxes and hoped . . . to
reduce taxes on lower incomes.'[2] Nothing in the reception of his
argument in 1955 forewarned him of the devastating Conservative

counter-attack when he repeated it as leader in 1959. In a straight fight against the same opponent, he marginally improved his share (65.2 per cent) of a smaller poll:

| | |
|---|---|
| Hugh Gaitskell (Lab.) | 25,833 |
| Winifred Brown (Cons.) | 13,817 |
| | |
| Majority | 12,016 |

Though the Conservatives increased their majority in the House, 1955 was the only post-war election defeat which did not swing Labour to the Left. Gaitskell thought the lesson was clear. He warned that Labour must never become 'a sterile dogmatic group, living on our own illusions', and emphasised the need to 'understand those whom we wish to carry with us, and adapt our approach to them accordingly . . . *Our local parties must be truly representative of the ordinary Labour voter.*'[3] It was, he wrote, 'the most important subject of all . . . to make the constituency parties keep in closer touch with Labour supporters in general and the electorate as a whole . . . [and] not relapse into isolationism again'.[4]

## Margate, and the Demise of Mr Butskell

When the new Parliament met in June 1955, Hugh Dalton, the enthusiast for youth, retired from the Shadow Cabinet and so shamed his contemporaries into following his example. Hoping to postpone a leadership election, he astutely excepted Attlee from this pressure, for every delay would diminish Morrison's chances and Dalton wanted Gaitskell to be the beneficiary. For the new Shadow Cabinet, in a smaller PLP, Gaitskell won his biggest vote, 184 – two behind Griffiths, the only other to exceed 150. Wilson was fifth with 147, and Bevan seventh with 118.

For the treasurership, the Miners' delegate conference again proposed Gaitskell. Two of the 'big six' unions, the NUR and USDAW, had supported Bevan in 1954; both now switched to the incumbent. Many constituency party voters also appreciated Gaitskell's work as treasurer and were fed up with the feud. Half their votes now went against their former idol; Bevan polled only 1,225,000 in all, to Gaitskell's 5,475,000. His campaign against the bosses had detached not their rank and file, but his own.

On 10 October 1955 the party conference opened at Margate. Gaitskell had displayed his inexperience at the previous night's demonstration, with a front-bench kind of speech which was received with impatience. Then on Tuesday afternoon, after the treasurership announcement, 'a time-bomb went off with a shattering explosion. It was the fearful noise of Mr. Bevan blowing his top at what was comically called a private session. As every window was open and the loudspeakers on, even the quiet fisherman at the end of the pier could catch every word.'[5] Gaitskell made his platform début that afternoon in a debate on the nationalised industries. Saying their achievements had been insufficiently publicised, he corrected that mistake with all too plentiful statistics down to nett ton-miles per engine-hour – until a wry sentence delighted his bored audience: 'You even need a calculating machine to work it out!' Suddenly spotting Bevan laughing with his friends at the back, Gaitskell dropped his notes and changed his tone. We have to persuade the voters, he said, that nationalisation was relevant to a better standard of living, economic security, greater equality and planning. But the need to do so did not affect the quality of his own convictions:

I am a Socialist and have been for some 30 years. I became a Socialist quite candidly not so much because I was a passionate advocate of public ownership but because at a very early age I came to hate and loathe social injustice, because I disliked the class structure of our society, because I could not tolerate the indefensible differences of status and income which disfigure our society . . . because I hated poverty and squalor . . . Pay people more if they do harder, more dangerous, and even more responsible work; pay people more if they have larger families. But the rewards should not be, as they still are, dependent upon the accident of whether you happen to be born of wealthy parents or not . . . I am a Socialist because I want to see fellowship, or if you prefer it, fraternity . . . [while preserving] the liberties we cherish . . . over the world as a whole.

These to me are the Socialist ideals. Nationalisation . . . is a vital means, but it is only one of the means by which we can achieve these objects.

He wound up by quoting Clause Four of the party constitution in order to distinguish the end, namely 'To secure for the workers . . . the full fruits of their industry', from 'the common ownership of the means of production which is the means'.[6]

Aneurin Bevan, 'red-faced and furious' at the back of the hall, muttered 'sheer demagogy, sheer demagogy'.[7] But even *Tribune* wrote that 'After [Gaitskell's] performance, perhaps public ownership will cease to be a wall between Right and Left';[8] Attlee was enthusiastic; and the applause of the delegates lasted three times as long as for Morrison. One American observer noticed that 'the ovation he received was universal and not partisan. It was the first time in his career that Gaitskell had been so applauded.'⁹

It was largely his achievement that the Margate mood changed in mid-week, so that delegates dispirited by a bad start went home in good heart. Once again he had risen to an occasion and demonstrated new capacities with which his friends would not have credited him. Moreover, the new alignment survived the conference. As Crossman noted, when the new NEC met,

There is no doubt whatsoever that . . . Gaitskell is ready to work with us, and there is a new centre of the Party forming, which is trying to create a policy and a leadership not subservient to the Unions on the one side or appeasing Bevan on the other. There is no doubt, however, that if Herbert succeeds Clem in the near future, he will fight this new centre for all he can.¹⁰

Gaitskell's triumph at Conference was soon followed by another in the House. That was the last of a series of clashes with Butler, whose chickens were now coming home to roost. In February 1955 Butler had checked demand, restoring hire purchase restrictions and raising bank rate to its highest level for over twenty years. Less than eight weeks later, he expanded demand again in his Budget. In May the Government was re-elected; in July he imposed new restraints on credit and capital expenditure; in October he was forced into a crisis Budget. The deplorable record was a gift to Gaitskell, who gained stature with every speech – as Morrison quite failed to do.

Gaitskell's criticisms were summed up in his attack on the pre-election April Budget. He claimed that Labour had restrained consumption to build up exports and investment – both now booming in other countries but stagnant in Britain:

When the Government came into power, . . . [it had] the opportunity to construct on a sound basis an even more flourishing export trade, an adequate surplus for investment abroad, reasonable gold reserves, and, above all, a high level of home investment . . . this opportunity has been missed.¹¹

Butler was giving nearly £140 million in income tax reliefs, mainly to companies and well-off individuals. But rising consumption depended precariously on better terms of trade. Those criticisms were echoed elsewhere at the time, and confirmed by all later critics. When the Chancellor restricted credit and capital expenditure in July, Gaitskell accused him of 'deliberately deceiv[ing] the electorate', and drove him to admit that the 'fundamental causes' were 'that we have been consuming too much at home'.¹²

To that excess consumption his April Budget had given a stimulus. Gaitskell had warned that the Conservative electoral prospectus was fraudulent and the bills would soon have to be paid. Early in October Butler spoke at the Mansion House of more restrictions to come, and his Shadow charged him with the 'biggest act of political deceit since . . . 1935'. Gaitskell was furious too at the injustice: 'to cut back the spending of worse off people to cure a crisis mostly caused by too much spending by better off people is intolerable.'[13] The autumn Budget withdrew £38 million from companies and £110 million from individuals – almost exactly the amounts each category had received in the spring. But instead of reversing his income tax concessions, Butler imposed purchase tax on household necessities (for the first time for a decade, or in some cases ever), raised postal charges, and severely cut capital expenditure by the nationalised industries and local authorities. Gaitskell saw nothing changed since April: 'There is no new element. The . . . dangers were pointed out to him again and again, but he remained obstinately complacent'. The point of the April Budget, said Gaitskell,

was not the incentive to people to produce more, it was the incentive to vote Conservative . . . He has persistently and wilfully misled the public about the economic situation and he has done it for electoral reasons . . . having bought his votes with a bribe, the Chancellor is forced – as he knew he would be – to dishonour the cheque . . . He has behaved in a manner unworthy of his high office. He began in folly, he continued in deceit, and he has ended in reaction.[14]

Labour was delighted, and the Tories deeply embarrassed. Not without malice, Wilson then urged an immediate censure motion – to be moved by Herbert Morrison. Everything had been said already, and the deputy leader's long ramblings came as a sad anticlimax.

The Opposition kept up a prolonged campaign against the Finance Bill, and the struggle had far-reaching repercussions. Gaitskell's assault finished Butler as Chancellor; as Roy Jenkins perceptively predicted, he never introduced another Budget and Harold Macmillan soon replaced him as the dominant influence in Eden's government. On the other side, it affected the leadership. The close collaboration between Gaitskell and Wilson was suspect to some senior trade-unionists in and out of Parliament. But Attlee told the Chief Whip that with those two in harmonious alliance, he could safely retire at last.

## Attlee Takes His Time

Gaitskell did not campaign for the party leadership, and was indeed reluctant to stand in 1955. It was not false modesty. He had considered standing for deputy leader in 1953 if Morrison did not; from 1954 he was talked of as the next leader but one; and he hoped to replace Morrison as deputy leader when the latter succeeded Attlee. Yet when supporters appealed to him 'to dish Bevan by settling the leadership once for all', he answered that he would play no part, and he consented to stand himself only after Morrison's parliamentary reputation and performance collapsed. In September he still said firmly that he would not split Morrison's vote; he might have to reconsider if drafted by a great many MPs, but 'I don't think that likely';[15] and just before the Margate Conference, he told the Chief Whip that Morrison should have his turn. He changed his mind only when 'with the greatest difficulty he was persuaded that Morrison might well be a loser, and, even if not so, a played-out and inadequate leader';[16] and that Bevan's only hope lay in Morrison's failings.

Bevan had wrecked his chances by quitting the Shadow Cabinet in 1954 and by his intransigence in the subsequent year. As Attlee told Crossman: 'Nye had the leadership on a plate. I always wanted him to have it. But you know, he wants to be two things simultaneously, a rebel and an official leader, and you can't be both.'[17] Many of Bevan's followers knew it. A few, like Crossman and Wilson, now thought Gaitskell far preferable to Morrison; most did not, and these now, as Leslie Hunter recalled, 'began, with that unanimity which so oddly marked their opinions long after their group had been disbanded, to discover that "poor old Herbert" was getting a raw deal.'[15]

The party conference helped to crystallise opinion, and the Chief Whip even told Gaitskell that Morrison was slipping so fast that Bevan might win. On Friday 14 October, Gaitskell drove Harold Wilson home to Hampstead after they had broadcast together, and in a side-street in Soho Wilson promised to support Gaitskell as the only possible leader now that Bevan had ruled himself out – provided he would seek 'accommodation not constant confrontations; which he took very well'.[18] That same weekend, Robens said in Manchester that Attlee would retire in ten days. On 25 October the *Daily Herald* published a curiously equivocal denial from Attlee in Malta. Morrison's lamentable failure in the censure debate suddenly eroded his remaining support, and in early November, under pressure from more and more MPs, Gaitskell decided to stand when the time came. Roy Jenkins recalled:

He only swung because he was convinced by me and others that Herbert's position was very *weak*. Then he said: 'I must see him alone and tell him' . . . He came back in a state of high euphoria, saying it was terribly easy because

Herbert was euphoric too, and said: 'Of course, my boy, you go ahead if you want to, you'll be out on the first ballot'.[19]

Gaitskell 'thought Herbert would just about get it, but . . . anything might happen in the next month or so'.[20]

Morrison refused to recognise the decisive factor – the PLP's determination to settle the issue by choosing a younger man. That factor meant that if Gaitskell did not stand, another contender of his own generation was likely to appear; so that without helping Morrison, he might wreck his own prospects of succeeding later. He still did not think the contest imminent, and refused to canvass support in the PLP as all but two of his friends wanted him to. They did so instead, led by Dalton, who revelled in political intrigue and operated (so his wife said) 'like elephant going through jungle – clumsy, trumpeting but sly'.[21]

Bevan as well as Gaitskell gained from the collapse of Morrison's prestige. Moderate Labour MPs became alarmed that in a straight fight Bevan, backed by the Left, the Miners, the Welsh and Morrison's many dedicated enemies, might even win; while if Morrison won, four years under a leader so far past his best would demoralise his own wing, to Bevan's great benefit.

By the time the House met, the Bevanites' preference for Morrison over Gaitskell was widely taken for granted. It was encouraged by others, as one acquaintance testified.

I was one of those whose advice Nye Bevan sought . . . [on how] to counter Hugh Gaitskell's bid for leadership . . .

I pointed out to him that he . . . [should] support . . . the older man in order to defeat Gaitskell. Then, when Herbert . . . [went,] he should have a straight fight against Gaitskell, which, by that time, he might win.

He did not contradict me, but remarked upon the difficulty of . . . support[ing] the enemy whom you really wished to defeat . . . we parted amicably.

This adviser to the champion of red-blooded Socialism was James Stuart, Chief Whip of the Tories whom Bevan had called 'lower than vermin'.[22]

## Defeat of the Unholy Alliance

On 3 November the hatchet was solemnly buried. The two old enemies met over a drink in the smoking room. It was understood that Bevan would offer Morrison his support in return for second place and eventually the Foreign Office. For Morrison based his strategy on picking up Bevanite votes at the second ballot; and the Bevanites desperately needed Morrison to split their opponents on the first round.

On the morning of Wednesday 7 December, Attlee, without trying to warn Morrison, announced his retirement. That night Morrison and Bevan dined together. Nominations were due by 11 a.m. on Friday, and on Thursday afternoon their last desperate manoeuvre was mounted. Bevan told the press that he would willingly accede to the proposal of ten elderly MPs that the younger men should withdraw and give Morrison an unopposed return. The ten sponsors included four Bevanite sympathisers; and also Morrison's most ardent supporters, Shinwell and Stokes. Several signatories were astonished to see their names in print. Public pressure was no way to persuade Gaitskell, but his enemies doubtless hoped his refusal would cost him votes.

Their misjudgement was complete. The reputations that suffered were those of his two opponents, cynically allied after years of mutual hatred. Twenty MPs came up to Gaitskell on the Opposition front bench to urge him not to withdraw. James Griffiths summed up: 'It was altogether too Machiavellian and created cynicism, and finally decided many to turn and vote for Hugh Gaitskell.'[23] The latter's press statement said that despite his high regard for Morrison, he felt the Party should choose. When voting ended at noon on Wednesday 14 December, virtually every available ballot was cast: Gaitskell had 157 to 70 for Bevan and only 40 for Morrison – by far the most convincing victory any Labour leader has won (Those elected by more than 60 Labour MPs were Attlee, Wilson, Callaghan and Foot, who went to more than one ballot, and MacDonald who won by five, in a straight fight). It was partly a tribute to his own hard work and his recent efforts at conciliation; partly a reaction against his opponents, reflecting Bevan's contempt for party unity and for the Labour MPs, and Morrison's dismal performance; and most of all a sign of hope that the dreary feud could be ended by settling the leadership for many years. R. H. Tawney wrote: 'The decisive majority . . . made me feel a stronger confidence in the future than recently I have. And, on more personal grounds, it was a great pleasure to know that one whose courage, in addition to other qualities, I admire is to be in command.'[24]

Gaitskell had reaped the reward of years of hard work, arguing assiduously and persuasively in the PLP and in the House itself. His vote surpassed most prior estimates. He carried the northerners and over two-thirds of the Scots, and cut into Morrison's London base. Almost all the trade union MPs supported him. The Centre of the Party, so suspicious of both intransigent groups, had recently come to

1. Hugh Gaitskell (*left*) with his undergraduate brother, Arthur

2. With his family at home in Frognal Gardens, Hampstead, just
after becoming Minister of Fuel in October 1947

3. With Sir Stafford Cripps at a Press Conference on petrol rationing in 1948 – the most unpopular policy of Gaitskell's time at Fuel and Power

4. With Herbert Morrison (*left*), Prime Minister Clement Attlee, and Sam Watson (*right*) in Durham, 1949

5. A clutch of Chancellors at a dinner in May 1952: (*left to right*) Hugh Dalton, Rab Butler, Winston Churchill, Hugh Gaitskell, John Anderson and John Simon

6. (Above) Reading to his children, 1950

7. (Left) Outside the employment exchange at Bellshill, Lanarkshire, 1958

8. Welcome back. Returning from Moscow for the election, Gaitskell and Bevan are greeted by Barbara Castle, Chairman of the Party, Jim Griffiths, deputy leader (*left*), Ian Mikardo and Bert Bowden, chief whip (*behind*), and Alice Bacon (*right*)

9. With housewives in his Leeds constituency

10. 'Fight and fight again.' Gaitskell strongly opposes nuclear disarmament

11. Catastrophe? With George Brown and Harold Wilson, visiting
the Prime Minister during the Cuban Missile crisis in 1962

12. With his wife in their garden

see him as a conciliator; so that only three years after Morecambe, most constituency party representatives on the NEC voted to be led by the author of the Stalybridge speech. Bevan, who had always dismissed the Labour MPs as irrelevant, in June 1955 suddenly discovered that they mattered after all. He had waited too long.

Gaitskell's response was impeccable. He thanked the Party and said how humble and responsible he felt. Then he made a moving appeal to the man whose hopes had been so cruelly extinguished. Saying the Movement needed Morrison's services, he begged his senior not to resign the deputy leadership. But Morrison had made up his mind beforehand – without waiting for Shinwell's call, 'Don't take it, Herbert.' Bevan's reaction, as usual, was ambivalent. Gaitskell did his best, saying as soon as Morrison walked out: 'Nye, we haven't got on in the past, but if you will accept this vote, as I would have had to accept it if it had gone the other way, I promise you I will not be outdone in generosity'.[25] Bevan replied offering congratulations and support, and wishing Gaitskell 'higher office'. Those first seeds of reconciliation took a year or two to flower, yet on the very next day, 'Nye was already busy finding out if he stood a chance of being elected Deputy Leader . . . despite the fact that only a fortnight ago [he] had been talking of walking out of the Party if Gaitskell was elected.'[26] He contested the vacancy in order to show his willingness to serve under Gaitskell; and his high poll again showed the MPs' eagerness to end the feud.

At the Gaitskells' usual noisy and crowded New Year party in the rambling Frognal house, Attlee sat quietly in a corner with perhaps 100 people milling about in the big room. Suddenly he called for silence and offered a toast: 'To the Leader of the Labour Party!' Blushing furiously, Gaitskell rushed in from the next door room to thank him: 'I'm very touched, Clem. I wasn't expecting anything like that.' *Sotto voce* but not quite inaudibly, his predecessor muttered: 'You'd no right to, either!'[27]

A few years later Gaitskell gave his own assessment in a letter to a friend who thought his triumph astonishing:

It isn't really. It was forecast over 20 years ago that I would be Foreign Secretary or Chancellor. The leadership came my way so early because Bevan threw it at me by his behaviour. Ask yourself about the Labour Party now – if not me then who?

Qualities? Perfectly ordinary ones – intelligence, hard work, capacity for getting on easily with people – and –which is what always surprises people – some moral courage. Of course there are great weaknesses – don't I know it! But the whole subject is boring.

# 13

# Labour's New Champion

*'Compared with Attlee I am a furnace'*
(HG on his alleged coldness)

*'It is much more likely that I shall be a failure than a sham'*
(HG, 1959)

## The Man and His Friends

Hugh Gaitskell was forty-nine, the youngest party leader that twentieth-century Britain had yet seen. He was one of the least known to the public, for his rise had been very rapid: it was only ten years since he had entered Parliament, eight since he had become a Minister, five since he had joined the Cabinet. He was also the least understood; his personality was less like the public impression of him than that of almost any other front-rank political figure. Having been actual or Shadow Chancellor, he could not shake off the label of the desiccated calculating machine: 'about as big a misjudgment', wrote a very old journalistic friend, 'as anybody could make of a man, most of whose political weaknesses came from too much emotionalism'.[1] It was equally inappropriate to the private individual, who enjoyed life thoroughly, was an enthusiastic dancer, found official functions boring, and never would subordinate personal friendships to political advantage.

Physically Gaitskell was not particularly imposing: a well-built energetic man of medium height, with curly brown hair, blue eyes, a fresh complexion, and no very prominent features for the cartoonists to seize on. Rebecca West had once cattily said that if he entered a room with someone else, eyes turned to the other person; and Gaitskell himself apparently felt he lacked presence. He was never obsessed with politics like some of his colleagues. He liked going to the theatre and opera, and his literary tastes extended from Shakespeare to P. G. Wodehouse and Simenon. On holiday he went back to old favourites like Proust, Hardy and his wartime discovery, Henry James; and all the great Russians, Tolstoy, Chekhov, Turgenev, Dostoevsky. He kept up with new novels which Dora used to select for him; and his range impressed a friendly publisher. Like so many politicians he enjoyed Trollope, but his reading was less confined to history and biography than that of many colleagues. Most of all he adored poetry, invariably reading a little every night before going to bed. Shakespeare's *Sonnets* came first in his affections, and then Yeats, though he had nineteenth-century favourites too. There was great excitement when he found a copy of Meredith's sonnet sequence *Modern Love* in Norman's Hampstead secondhand bookshop; in 1959, he wrote quite a long comment on an analysis of it by an Oxford undergraduate friend of Julie's.

His home life was happy – especially so, in the view of some MPs, for a prominent politician. Yet during the week he saw almost nothing of his family. Domestic weekends were rare, often only one in four or seven. He loved his garden, especially his irises; and once replanned it, turning all the lawns into flowerbeds and vice versa. He worked at it strenuously, and said gardening had ruined more men than drink. In less energetic moods he was fond of listening to great jazz singers like Ella Fitzgerald and Billie Holliday; he was once buying records in Oxford Street with Cressida, who had gone off for more, when to his mild embarrassment a lady MP entered the cubicle where the new Leader of the Opposition, alone, was cheerfully dancing to the music. He was a great fan of both Greta Garbo and Mae West. Though for years he had no television set either at home or in his room at Westminster, in the constituency friends arriving to talk politics might be firmly shushed until the end of the Western he was avidly watching.

The Gaitskells lived comfortably but not extravagantly in a prosperous, cultured suburban environment. They ran no car when Hugh was in office, and bought only one new one during the next eleven years; a Wolseley acquired before the 1959 election, number VLX1 – a happy symbol, said someone, for 'Vote Labour X'. The house was always full, with Hugh's mother and stepfather living there; and an old schoolfellow Charles Plumb and his wife on the top floor. Hugh was not allowed to help in his years of overwork and eminence; Dora did all the cooking and ran the household and family affairs with a daily help and a friend to garden twice a week. Hugh confessed to conservatism only over food and women's clothes: 'I like good roast beef, best English sausages, potted shrimps, apple pie, ginger cakes. And it always takes me time to adjust to any new fashion – especially in hats.'[2]

The girls went to school first at King Alfred's on the edge of the Heath, a co-educational school with an old if somewhat muted progressive tradition; and then to Queen's College, a day school in Harley Street, from which Cressida later transferred to North London

Collegiate at Edgware. Middle-class Labour politicians of that generation often sent their children to private schools; it seems to have aroused little domestic argument or public criticism. But Gaitskell found it embarrassing. He called it a transitional problem which parents must decide in the children's interests:

I don't think it reasonable to criticise parents for doing that . . . [or] inconsistent to say we wish to . . . not be faced with this extremely difficult choice . . . we ought to have such a good state system of education that in fact private schools just didn't come into the picture . . . But . . . unless you happen to have a very good state school fairly near it is difficult.[3]

Gaitskell was most scrupulous over financial matters great and small. On becoming leader, when the Co-operative Societies still wished to pay him the agreed retainer for chairing a committee of inquiry into their affairs, he declined because he would have much less time for it. When he consented to sign an election article for the *Mirror*, written by a member of its staff, he insisted that the fee must go to the Labour Party. He set an example to other ex-Ministers from economic Departments by avoiding any entanglement with business, turning down all offers of directorships or consultancies, and declining a gift of shares worth £30,000 from his old Nottingham friend George Keeling, the ex-miner who had become a wealthy manufacturer. During the early 1950s he was not particularly well off, kept quite a careful eye on expenses, and was glad to earn a little extra by his articles and lectures both abroad and at home: in 1954 he wrote to a friend of 'the 101 things one has to do, some for money, mostly for nothing'.[4] But (unlike so many Bevanites who accused him of lack of principle) he would never take money from Lord Beaverbrook. Subsequently he was economical more from upbringing than necessity, for later in the decade his financial situation improved substantially.

Election to the leadership limited but otherwise did not much affect his home life. The Gaitskells entertained from time to time and were excellent hosts. Hugh still kept his diverse friends in compartments, mixing them up only occasionally at a big party. There might be a lunch or an evening for trade union leaders, a foreign ambassador and his wife, or a visitor like Adlai Stevenson or Kwame Nkrumah, with interested political colleagues. But he would not use his home as an annex of his office, and he always insisted that politicians were human and needed some private life. Few of his guests at Frognal Gardens were there because of their political status; and those parliamentary colleagues who came were those he found congenial rather than those he calculated could be useful. Most Labour Premiers have entertained little, and Crossman thought that with Gaitskell in Downing Street and Chequers, social life would have been skilfully used to smooth over tensions in the Party. Some close friends felt he did not use it enough, and some touchy political associates felt they deserved more frequent invitations to Frognal Gardens. But grumbles against the 'Hampstead set' reveal the social weaknesses of Labour personalities rather than the political weaknesses of the party leader.

The close personal friends of the 1950s were not, as his opponents supposed, the secret inspirers of his political outlook; that had been fixed long before he met them. They were not a kitchen cabinet of the all too familiar kind, or a substitute for the professional staff he lacked until 1959, for their talents and interests did not lie in that direction. Nor were they sycophantic courtiers hoping to ingratiate themselves – for this monarch was entirely surrounded by candid friends. They were simply young like-minded individuals with whom he associated in Parliament, and whom he admired for their intelligence, culture and character. Anthony Crosland practised astringent intellectual puritanism and preached unabashed libertarianism and private enjoyment – a combination particularly attractive to Gaitskell as it recalled his own youth. Roy Jenkins, cultivated and urbane but also politically courageous, seemed to Gaitskell to show sounder judgement and was also an attractive companion. The leader was aware of their weaknesses and occasionally not quite sure of their seriousness. But he insisted on the primacy of personal relationships, and would not give them up when they later became, as he knew, a political embarrassment. 'Kings who had favourites were never popular', he wrote privately in June 1960, listing among the sins which were held against him 'kicking against the pricks of loneliness – in other words wanting to continue to have friends – real ones . . . I put that as something I want especially to try & keep.'

Gaitskell's mother, Mrs Wodehouse, died suddenly and painlessly on 14 October 1956. She was, wrote her cousin who had been 'proxy grandfather' at Hugh's christening, 'one of the gayest and at the same time the kindest person that I have ever met . . . I think the parson thought it [the christening ceremony] was a little too frivolous.' Hugh owed to her much of his zest and vitality, and they had been far closer latterly than in his youth, when they were usually separated, he in England and she in Rangoon, an enthusiastic social leader of the local community. During and after the war she was home again, and Hugh's career gave her an interest in politics she had never shown before: from a non-voter she became a Labour loyalist, called her son 'the Minister' even to close friends, and frequently attended the House of Commons. She had a flat during the week in his Frognal Gardens house, and he was often with her at Milland.

Her death marked a double break, for besides the sadness of the bereavement itself, it cut his last link with that village, to which for twenty years he had occasionally managed to flee. He had disposed of his own house, Sweatmans, in 1946 (without making any profit on it). But he had retained thirty acres next door to his mother's, with a picturesque but condemned old cottage farmhouse called Maysleith, which he had bought in 1941 hoping to renovate it or build on the site. In 1954 he sadly abandoned the idea, and two years later, just before she died, he sold the land (again for no more than he paid for it). Apart from Milland, he and Dora liked to escape for weekends to Abbotsbury in Dorset, or Washington in Sussex, or to stay in Kent with old friends like the Balcons or the Brooks. They played a lot of croquet, and in the evenings indoor games like L'Attaque: 'he always knew all the rules, he was frightfully good, he was always *determined* to win'.[5] Real holidays, in the summer, were entirely carefree but by no means inactive, for he believed that expeditions made a vacation seem longer. He was keen on swimming and boating, exploring all the local scenic beauties and historical attractions, and – as always – making new friends. In the early 1950s the Gaitskells were particularly fond of Pembrokeshire; later they went abroad – to Italy and Yugoslavia – partly for the sake of privacy. On holiday he was always totally relaxed, forgetting his public responsibilities and cherishing the rare opportunity to see his family.

As a guest the Leader of the Opposition is much in demand, and Gaitskell rather enjoyed his social activities. He had always found parties irresistible, especially if they included dancing; he and Dora liked good food and wine and conversation; he would flirt light-heartedly for an evening with a pretty woman. He wrote to his daughter at Oxford in 1958:

You know what a pleasure lover I am. So you must not expect a puritan outlook from me! Pleasure is not only all right but good so long as it is not too selfish or too undermining of one's capacity to do whatever it is one *can* do . . . if you have too much of it (in the crude sense) you react against it & look round for a little monasticism.

He and Macmillan were about to be given honorary degrees at Oxford (by accident on the same day), and though he found stuffy official functions tedious, he was looking forward to staying with Bowra and to 'lots of junketing'.[6] He perhaps felt it was a side of life he had neglected, and seems to have consciously striven to make up for lost time. He was confident in his own integrity, and imprudently indifferent to the reactions of others.

His gregariousness was not at all confined to London society, for he was happy too with accidental acquaintances – hitchhikers to whom he gave a lift, neighbours on a flight, people in a railway waiting room. Staying with friends in a village, 'he charmed everyone, he was so interested in everybody . . . whoever he was talking to was the only person in the world for him'.[5]

He never forgot people he had known long before he became famous. He had not been a close friend of Eric Cash, the party secretary at Chatham, but Gaitskell went out of his way to help when Cash asked his advice twenty years later. At an export promotion conference in the 1950s, he spotted the civil servant who had been his secretary on the Materials Committee eleven years before, and deserted the dignitaries to go and chat. He was concerned about his political colleagues simply as people, and sat for two hours in the hospital when Crossman's wife was dying, in case he might be needed.

The Winchester motto is 'Manners Makyth Man', and Gaitskell was renowned among friends and opponents alike for his courtesy and considerateness. As a civil servant and Minister, he had earned goodwill for 'doing the unpleasant thing in a pleasant manner'.[7] As a party politician he often astonished peevish correspondents on both Left and Right by the patience and thoroughness of his replies. 'His gift of getting along with all kinds of people', wrote one journalist, 'is his main political capital.' Emanuel Shinwell spoke of his 'inordinate and phenomenal politeness'; and the Liberal leader Jo Grimond said he had 'the best political manners of anyone I have known'.[8]

Now and then he could be insensitive. A young Fabian official (an admirer and later a valued supporter) was upset when Gaitskell said publicly that the many misprints in his Fabian pamphlet were not his fault (after he had been late with the proofs). When after many talks Kenneth Younger finally gave up his Grimsby seat, Gaitskell after only perfunctory regrets at once inquired whether Crosland could win it. But more typical were the Labour candidate in 1950, harassed by criticisms of the Government's fuel policies, who was impressed by the Minister's understanding of the questioner's worry as well as by the thoroughness of his answers; the close Jewish friend in Leeds whom he phoned on the night of his Suez broadcast to reassure her that he was not turning against Israel; the inexperienced author of another Fabian pamphlet on which he performed necessary and devastating surgery with extreme kindness.

He was insistent on maintaining the dignity of his office as leader. He declined to speak on a Liberal motion at the Oxford Union, or indeed at all except against one of the four senior Conservative leaders: 'If I were to debate against Macleod who is Minister of Labour – very pushing –it would *downgrade* the whole party.'[6] Even for close colleagues, a summons to Gaitskell's room at the House had some flavour of an invitation to the headmaster's study. Back in 1945 he had rather disliked his supporters' exploitation of his wartime CBE in the campaign; but as leader he made sure that the letters followed his name on the report of the Co-operative inquiry. Crossman even wrote once of his 'naive self-importance'.

Off duty he was quite different. One lady who had known him since the 1930s thought of him as one of the very few politicians who 'never turned into a balloon'; another, a later but closer friend, said much the same:

He had *absolutely* no side at all. I've never in my life met anybody else who wasn't altered by his position . . . who didn't get a tremendous weight of importance on their shoulders. It was a completely individual characteristic of Hugh . . . at the dinner table he would sit completely silent while two other people were talking about a subject that he knew about and they didn't. He was absolutely unassuming . . . he was a very good listener and he didn't have that thing of getting the conversation round to him, unlike anybody else.'[9]

When he first visited the United States as leader of his party, the official American brief described him as 'Totally devoid of pretentiousness and self-importance'; and he insisted on flying tourist to the dismay of his wealthy trade union sponsors. In Milan, the Congress for Cultural Freedom allotted him an expensive luxury hotel, from which he and the family promptly moved. Meeting new acquaintances at the annual Anglo-German encounters at Koenigswinter, he would introduce himself quite naturally, never expecting them to know he was Leader of the Opposition.

On holiday abroad he valued privacy above all. He would ask friends to suggest good cheap obscure restaurants in France; and on official visits he eagerly escaped from constraints, and dismayed his younger companions by his nocturnal energy and enthusiasm. Leslie Hunter recalled:

One week-end he had left home at dawn, flown to Copenhagen and spent the whole day at an extremely tricky meeting of the Socialist International. It was followed by an official dinner which broke up about midnight. My wife and I were sneaking off when Gaitskell caught us and demanded to be taken somewhere to dance. For the next three hours he was giving brilliant expositions of 'jive' and 'bepop' with a crowd of youngsters . . . though some years younger than Gaitskell, I felt balding and middle-aged beside him in this company. He was very much at home.[10]

As Leader of the Opposition, doing far too much himself and with a jealously guarded timetable, he found it far harder to keep spontaneous contact with ordinary people. Political opponents on the Left therefore reproached him with being cold and remote – at which he once privately protested: 'Compared with Attlee I am a furnace'. But he did his utmost to keep in touch with the working-class roots of the Party. He was always welcome and at ease in the flourishing workingmen's clubs of the West Riding; he enjoyed and drew strength from meeting ordinary Labour supporters on provincial tours, and in time he became much more relaxed and spontaneous in those surroundings.

It was not an impression he always managed to convey from the platform or the television studio. People brought into direct contact with him, after knowing him only as a public figure, were struck time and again by the niceness of the man:

he tends at a distance to create an impression almost wholly different from that he does in his direct personal relations.

His friendliness, warmth and humour are veiled by distance. The intellectual ability and integrity, the logic and power of objective judgment, communicate. But not the emotional fire that gives them life.[11]

## The Politician and His Style

Gaitskell worked himself far too hard. He managed his time better than he had as Chancellor, no longer letting his appointments run later and later during the day. But he still would never waste a moment, and did everything at the last possible minute – notably catching trains, which he always ran recklessly close. On the way to a meeting he would compose his speech, and in a slow question time he might write a newspaper article. If he had his secretary in Leeds he would dictate correspondence to her in the car. (Sometimes he drove up, and in his careful way he worked out the least time-consuming route – that later adopted for the M1.) Friends warned him constantly to slow down, drop trivial engagements, run a marathon not a sprint, conserve his energies for the long haul. The worst strain, emotional as well as physical, came later when his leadership was threatened; but from the start he took on much too much.

One typical week, about a year after he became leader, began at 10.15 on Monday morning with a study group discussing policy for the nationalised industries. He lunched with Leslie Murphy, his former private secretary, to talk about the oil industry where Murphy now worked (it was soon after Suez). In the afternoon he attended three sub-committees of the National Executive, and went on to a trade union dinner. On Tuesday and Wednesday there were four more sub-committees, an all-party committee on broadcasting, an appointment with a trade union leader, meetings of the PLP and the Shadow Cabinet – the House was sitting – and a Downing Street dinner for the Crown Prince of Iraq; the previous evening the leader had dined with the Government's Chief Scientific Adviser, his old friend Sir Solly Zuckerman. On Thursday he met in turn a Transport House official, a journalist, the Prime Minister of Malta, a Manchester civic dignitary, and the parliamentary lobby; he lunched with the editor of the *Manchester Guardian*, and dined with Crosland. On Friday, when he did not have to be at Westminster, he had three long morning appointments (one with a difficult Co-operative Commission member), spoke that evening at a meeting of a London local party, and afterwards, accompanied by Dora and Julie, had dinner with an MP. Both the previous and the next weekend were fairly free; on the Saturday he was dining with an economists' club in Oxford, and visited Crossman's nearby farm on the way. Most weekends were busier than that, but sometimes the week itself was broken up by provincial rallies and meetings, short trips abroad, and receptions for distinguished foreign visitors – or interrupted by a call on the Prime Minister, a session of the independent Co-operative Commission, or a meeting of the House of Commons Privileges Committee.

Correspondence was substantial. Constituency cases were no longer a flood as they had been just after the war, but they still generated about twenty letters a month. Routine mail flowed in from the general public, and from people concerned with current problems. Some problems attracted enough attention to be filed separately: for instance prisoners in Hungary, crisis in Cyprus, Labour's big policy-making exercise, reform of the Co-ops, affairs of the Socialist International, politics in Scotland. Apart from all these, he would receive on average more than one letter a day of a serious kind. Over half of those came from a variety of sources – foreign ambassadors or British diplomats, Transport House officials and local Labour worthies, prominent foreign

Socialists, British journalists or academics or former MPs, an occasional Gaitskell relative, or a professional organisation with a problem. The rest were from parliamentary colleagues, discussing an item of domestic policy, writing informatively from abroad about the situation in a foreign country, giving advice or praise or criticism about his handling of that week's parliamentary crisis (if it were a serious one, there would be twice as many letters from MPs). He was scrupulous in replying, and also in sending condolences to the sick or bereaved.

His tiny staff were also worked hard. On a senior level he had no one until 1959, when John Harris came for the election campaign. Harris stayed on afterwards as personal assistant, public relations adviser and link-man with the press. Gaitskell's PPS was normally a fairly elderly trade unionist MP (he briefly had two PPSs towards the end) and was used as a sounding-board for opinion in the PLP but not much for substantive matters. The leader took advice on specific subjects from the Shadow Cabinet colleague or Transport House official concerned, and sometimes even accepted their drafts. But his confidence in party headquarters was limited, and in particular those who differed from him politically found him hard to work for, feeling he would never leave them alone. Indeed, his redrafting itch was a trial to everyone, and a serious misuse of his time and energy, though it did usually lead to genuine improvements. He had a secretary as Leader of the Opposition, Mrs Skelly, whom he inherited from Attlee and who came from the Labour Party staff; she found him 'a marvellous boss who gave you a job to do and left you to get on with it'. But when asked about Suez being a specially hectic time, she replied that she could not remember a period that wasn't. Gaitskell's wife felt exactly the same.

Some people thought him a worrier, and everyone remembers his fussiness over detail. Yet he would deal easily with several problems in quick succession, switching his orderly mind from a major academic lecture to a constituency visit and then to a personal letter to a fretful colleague. Off duty, he forgot his problems at once and relaxed completely. And he never worried in the least about his capacity to carry the responsibilities of government. In his day Conservative leaders still felt born to rule, and their supporters saw Labour administrations as passing aberrations. Even on the Labour benches those feelings were widely shared. Attracting natural critics and gadflies, used to opposition and its familiar outlook, the Labour Party had developed deep-seated psychological reflexes which still operated when it astonished itself by winning an election. Defeatism and opposition-mindedness were so widespread that a sympathetic Transport House official thought Gaitskell the only Labour leader who genuinely felt far better qualified to run the country than the men in power.

Yet he was born, one profile-writer wrote, with one skin too few. As he wrote about the daughter of a Hampstead friend: 'I quite understand her being sensitive to aggression from others. This one has to overcome, and does in time, though it is a painful process.'[12] He cared a great deal about his friends and their opinions, and took immense time and trouble to explain his own views to unknown correspondents. His thin skin, and his consciousness of his own ability and integrity, help explain his occasional unwise concern at attacks in the press – which he himself once attributed to his knowledge of his own inadequacies. Most political leaders react irritably to the media – Kennedy and Johnson no less than Wilson and Heath (to say nothing of Nixon); and Gaitskell would sometimes write an enormous letter to the offending journalist, both correcting error and explaining the rectitude of his own stand.

He was a thoroughly professional politician, who used the public relations salesmen but kept them in their place. After one favourable interview which he found 'rather nauseating', he promised his daughter:

Above all, you need never worry that I shall be 'merely the man they attempt to put over' . . . the one thing that matter[s is] 'to be oneself'. I have never changed my mind about that and I really don't have any fears that I ever shall do. It is much more likely that I shall be a failure than a sham.[6]

He kept his sense of balance, and never shared Bevan's intense suspicion of advertising men and all their works. Indeed he welcomed their technical help in campaigns, and overcame the Labour Party's deep distaste for public opinion research. Again unlike Bevan, he saw that mastering television technique was now indispensable to a politician, and patiently spent many weary hours in rehearsal. But he detested the whole notion of manipulating personalities in order to improve the 'image' of public figures, and would never dream of lending himself to such an operation. The party leader traditionally read the lesson in church on the morning before Conference; Gaitskell, because his friends knew he was not religious, was most reluctant even to attend – though once persuaded, he characteristically sought advice on how to read the lesson.

Gaitskell was quite a shrewd judge of character. He leaned towards indulgence, particularly perhaps with women; though when he met Jacqueline Kennedy at the zenith of the Camelot myth, he thought her shallow and superficial. He felt serious doubts about endorsing as a Labour candidate a businessman of acceptable views and excellent sponsorship, who later acquired a wider but mixed reputation as an MP. The chairman of a pro-Labour popular newspaper found Gaitskell 'a most difficult, buttoned-up character'; many political colleagues must have regretted not having made the same impression on Cecil King when he promptly bared their private confidences to the nation in his famously indiscreet memoirs. In Transport House, as earlier in Whitehall, Gaitskell generally picked good advisers; and some doubts about his judgement reflect the disappointment of Labour MPs whom he did not favour, and their resentment of those he did. The younger politicians whom he encouraged – despite charges of cronyism – later made their own way to the very front rank under a Labour leader with no personal inclination to help them. But friendship alone gave their views no extra weight in Gaitskell's mind, and when colleagues trusted in one field advised on another, they would be told firmly: 'That's not your subject.'

His highest priority was his conviction that people should be themselves. He assured the worried young daughter of his Hampstead friend that not being too sure of her political views was 'a sign of political integrity – almost the most important quality in public life'.[12] That did not impair his dedication to his own fundamental values. Their emotional roots had been part of him always; their intellectual foundation, solidly laid before the war, did not shift after it. But when this committed man dealt with others who had a different commitment, his touch was not always assured. He gave great weight to what he called 'the mysterious but vitally important quality of judgment . . . the highest, the most important quality of all, which means very largely knowing what other people are thinking and feeling and how they are going to behave'.[13] (Bevan too regarded it as a Prime Minister's most crucial need.) Yet he was very resistant to pressures, which he often failed to anticipate. Despite – or because of – the strength of his own emotions, he easily misunderstood or disregarded the emotional commitments of others. So, having always believed in public owner-ship just as one desirable means to accomplish Socialist ends, he failed to foresee either the number or the intensity of feeling of those who saw in it the essence of Socialism.

He prized intellectual honesty highly, and was conspicuous among public men for his willingness to face rather than fudge difficult issues, and to explain his reasons candidly. After he accepted an illogical compromise motion on bomb tests in 1957, he agreed with his fellow-Wykehamist Kenneth Younger that 'a Winchester education is a grave handicap for this sort of operation, by making one attach too much importance in *all* circumstances to intellectual clarity and consistency!'[14] As his troubles mounted in January 1960, he wrote to a friend:

> I still tend to assume that people are rational & that if you go on telling the truth as you see it you convince them. You once lectured me on the need to dissemble, but I never really learnt the lesson. Someone said to me the other day that Macmillan obviously loved saying one thing and doing another – and I'm sure that's true & no doubt in politics the corkscrew is really what you need. It's no use being superior & goody goody about this, when it's really just that you can't do it that way.

One friendly journalist wrote during the 1959 election campaign: 'I have never known him soften the uncomfortable truth to win the easy approval of his audience.'[15] Applied to Gaitskell, that sweeping statement was less rose-tinted than to most political figures; but he too was well aware that politicians must simplify their message to reach a large audience, and that 'It's no use trying to go on being 100% academic when one is in politics.'[16] Over the years he condoned a few party propaganda statements at which the pure searcher after truth would have jibbed. Crossman, the eager practitioner of psychological warfare, records them all with reproachful surprise – reflecting Gaitskell's personal reputation rather than ordinary political standards. He was probably the 'prominent Bevanite' who told Henry Fairlie in 1955 that Gaitskell lacked 'the toughness or capacity for self-deceit which was needed in a party leader'. Soon after Gaitskell's death he said with intent to shock: 'At last we have a leader who can lie.'[17]

Crossman too was a Wykehamist; indeed their relationship was always warped, as Crossman (typically) recognised, by his own far more glittering record at the school. After supporting Gaitskell for the leadership, he wrote:

> I do know Gaitskell better than most people and realise how wrong people get him. He is not a cold man, but a person of competence with an enormous lot of rather vague emotions, which lead him often to burst into tears, a man not at all sure of himself outside his special subject, a man who felt himself a hero and a St. Sebastian when he stood up to Nye and, most serious of all, someone who takes a moralising and reactionary attitude, which is almost instinctively wrong

in my opinion, on every subject outside economics. But he is also an extremely honest man and a sensible man, with the kind of mind that will take advice, who might become a very good Leader.[18]

Gaitskell was indeed more 'moralising' than Crossman over Suez or immigration, but hardly more 'reactionary'. The casual dismissal of 'a person of competence' reflects some contempt for an utterly different intellectual style. Crossman could instantly justify by dazzling in-tuitions each rapid shift of political front; what the diarist saw as Gaitskell being uncertain and not knowing his own mind was rather his insistence on thinking things through before making it up. When he had done so, his views were far more stable and solidly based than Crossman's, and he was most reluctant (perhaps too much so) to sway with short-term political breezes. Whatever tactical problems that style entailed, it was much likelier than Crossman's to inspire confidence.

In pointing to Gaitskell's sense of becoming a martyr to duty, Crossman drew attention to an attitude apparent later as well as earlier in the new leader's career. At the start of 1951 Gaitskell had thought it likely that he not Bevan would have to resign office; subsequently, feeling himself much too junior to carry the burden of fighting the Bevanites in the country, he expected them to win control of the Party unless Attlee spoke out – an improbable event which occurred only after Gaitskell had again risked his own political life at Stalybridge. More than once in 1960 and 1961 he thought the next party conference might well be his last as leader. Nor was he buoyed up (like so many of his enemies) by any zest for that kind of battle, for he loathed faction fights among supposed comrades almost as much as he suffered from the hatred and misrepresentation directed at him personally. His attitude was far removed from the Left's myth of an arrogant politician, who would make no move until assured of victory by the big trade union battalions, and who was driven by 'cold and methodical ambition for Party power'.[19]

Gaitskell was more convinced about his own judgement than Crossman supposed. As leader he did not entirely lose his inner doubts, but they had less and less effect on his actions as his self-confidence grew. The emphasis on his strong emotions was better justified, for he had deep feelings about people and the tears did flow easily. But on public affairs those emotions were not in the least vague, but precisely directed and singularly consistent over the years. He had no sympathy at all for those left-wing enthusiasts who regretted the past with its simple choices – when ordinary human beings were miserable and frightened, but some political activists could satisfy their hunger for emotional thrills. 'His nostalgic remarks about the 30s frankly shocked me,' Gaitskell wrote to his daughter about one such writer. 'It was a horrible period and you were lucky not to be alive then!'[6] Nor had he much sympathy for those who thought emotional drive a substitute for serious intellectual effort. When his friend Dr Rita Hinden wrote that 'Socialists must be visionaries', Gaitskell asked what she meant: if idealists, he agreed; if utopians, he dissented. A party 'either in power or on the verge of it' could not conduct itself like 'a pioneer hoping to convert people to a general point of view but not concerned with any immediate practical problem'.[20]

Gaitskell was passionately committed to working out in an intellectually respectable way the practical political means of realising his objectives, and then to persuading people to support them by means of rational discourse. His enemies called him an elitist; it was the very reverse of the truth. Ten years after his death, David Watt commented that his were the only parliamentary speeches of the period which still read well, because they were 'the product of a calm belief that people are quite capable of understanding sophisticated arguments and responding to them'.[21] As the country's prospective Prime Minister, he remained a dedicated teacher, determined to educate and not merely cajole, anxious that people should not only do the right thing but do it for the right reason. After an interminable discussion with a group of Durham miners, he replied sharply when a friend reproached him with taking so much trouble over people who were going to vote Labour anyway. 'It's not trouble, it's the whole point of our party, that we do try and see their point of view, that we do argue the toss, that we all go forward together.'[22]

## A Civilised Populist at Home, a Liberal Realist Abroad

For Gaitskell, always an educator, the party leadership provided (as Theodore Roosevelt said of the American presidency) a 'bully pulpit'. Before his election, in the same Margate speech which impressed the delegates with the sincerity of his Socialism, he had already called for serious thought about Labour's fundamental aims, concluding: 'Let the clear fresh wind of hard and fearless thinking blow through our minds and hearts.' Now he had the opportunity to try to make his followers face reality as he saw it. In private he insisted on analysing situations with intellectual rigour undistorted by political calculation. In public he revealed the results of that analysis much more fully than most leaders, particularly in pressing for policies which did not merely reiterate old slogans but related to genuine contemporary needs. As a journalistic admirer wrote in 1959: 'He is an enormously persuasive speaker – a surgeon, not a butcher – and he inflicts no unnecessary pain. But the incisive surgery is there to let out stale political flatulence and let in the fresh air of thought.'[15]

The need to win democratic consent for Socialist policies was Gaitskell's fundamental premise. Since his ethical priorities were equality and freedom, he decisively rejected the revolutionary road – as a short cut not to the Socialism in which he believed, but to a society without equality or freedom and bearing no resemblance to it. But if only democratic means could attain his objectives, the implications were inescapable. Those who rejected the democratic road to power were deadly enemies; and he did not take very seriously those who accepted it but ignored the constraints it imposed. Opponents must be fought but not gratuitously outraged: their reasonable grievances should be heard, and essential changes made in a way that minimised hostility. Oppositions must resist the dangerous temptations of irres-ponsibility, and avoid making promises or advocating policies which could never be carried out. Above all, unconvinced voters must be persuaded of the relevance of Labour policies.

The need to win over ordinary voters made Gaitskell wary of anything hinting at a return to post-war austerity. That did not stop him keeping up, even in these golden years of affluence, his Cassandra warnings against subordinating British economic growth to de-flationary international pressures or sacrificing long-term investment to immediate consumption. (Indeed, Harold Macmillan accused him of 'always entering horses for the Calamity Stakes, but they get scratched one after the other before the race starts':[23] a gibe sounding better then than it does today.) Those warnings fell on the deaf ears of those who had never had it so good. But they reflected economic caution, not sympathy for the 'squeamish' attitude to material progress of some of his friends: 'People do want a higher standard of living, and I do not see why we should not accept this. Certainly if we fail to accept it there is precious little chance of getting ourselves accepted by the electorate.'[20]

That populist strand in his make-up helped Gaitskell in his relations with the unions, though like every Labour leader he had to make some unwelcome concessions. (He would have liked the National Executive to propose safeguards for the liberties of unpopular individuals and minorities; but, as he had feared, the unions proved very cautious and he did not press the point.) He made a few courageous speeches on the difficulties of reconciling free collective bargaining and full employment without inflation; but it was a long-term problem which could best be tackled in government, and he would not make it a major theme. On industrial matters he was always careful of trade union feelings, and once defended Frank Cousins at serious political cost.

On the basic problems of policy expressing Labour's aspirations towards a classless society, Gaitskell's outlook emerges throughout this narrative. Rather than recapitulate at length here, this section concentrates instead on the other problems which the leader of a progressive party must face from time to time, where minor incidents often reveal significant attitudes. Gaitskell displayed an unusual combination of views, for he frequently showed strong populist sympathy with the values of working-class voters – as well as the familiar concern of the affluent middle-class progressive with humanitarian and libertarian causes, issues affecting the quality of life, and a liberal approach to problems of race and international affairs.

Public ownership had never been the central tenet of his Socialism, but it was quite false to infer that he was against it. Six months before his death he told the ETU that people who thought so 'couldn't be more wrong. I was responsible . . . for nationalising three industries [and am] very proud of that. But you've got to have the political basis for doing it'.[24] As leader, he sought new approaches to old objectives. Conventional nationalisation of entire (usually unprofitable) industries under a public corporation had been severely – if not constructively – criticised from both Left and Right. But the state might have to make up a deficiency of investment capital due to redistributive taxation, and it should then acquire corresponding control. This concept, the germ of the National Enterprise Board idea, briefly won the unanimous support of Labour's National Executive.

Just after becoming leader, Gaitskell published an essay on 'The Ideological Development of Democratic Socialism in Great Britain'.[25] The latest writers given thorough treatment were Cole, Tawney, Dalton and Durbin. Jay was mentioned as an interpreter of Keynes, and four other economic books were given a short footnote; Strachey as a Marxist, and Laski as a writer influential outside Britain, were quickly dismissed. (Crosland's *The Future of Socialism* came out a few months later.) He explained how the British tradition differed from the Continental: Marxism much weaker, trade unionism much stronger, the ILP influenced by Christian Socialism, the Fabians by Henry George. But he concentrated on the issues of his own generation. The egalitarian goals expounded by Tawney, he wrote, could now be approached more directly by Dalton's fiscal plans than by nationalisation (which in a democracy entailed compensation). For planning the whole economy, Keynes's ideas and the experience of the Second World War had transformed Socialist views; though there must be limits – not yet resolved – to government control and redistributive taxation in a mixed economy. Discussing the Left, he showed little sympathy for pre-war writers like Harold Laski who were ambivalent about political democracy. The war and its aftermath, he concluded (rather optimistically) had confirmed Durbin's ideas, cleared up 'the old confusions', and established the democratic tradition in British Socialism far more solidly than in the 1930s.

He was much more sympathetic to G. D. H. Cole and to ideas of workers' control. As Minister of Fuel he had fought against Communist efforts to exploit syndicalist feeling, but out of office he was sympathetic to the 'influential minority [who] are undoubtedly keen about industrial democracy'; though participation could not be compulsory, he stressed 'the importance of providing the opportunity to participate for those who want it'. As party leader he thought of starting a pilot scheme in the Post Office, where the unions were traditionally favourable. In 1961, he spoke of oligarchic control of industry as among the aspects of modern society crying out for reform.[26]

Throughout his life, however, equality rather than public ownership had always been the driving force of his Socialism: an emphasis which emerged in the choice of subjects for his floor speeches at the 1953 party conference – taxation and public schools – which surprised George Brown. He chose them not to win votes but because he thought them important, trying persistently to persuade an unreceptive National Executive, and telling the editor of the *Guardian* in 1961: 'The public schools were a source of snobbery and social evil. He had believed that all his life . . . gradually and with the maximum consent . . . in the end they must abolish the public schools.[27]

Here he was responding not to the working-class majority who were quite indifferent, but to another audience to which he was sensitive: the younger university generation who would be the opinion leaders of the future. He was concerned at Labour's failure to develop a strong youth movement like some Continental Socialist parties which he knew well, such as those in Germany or Austria; and in 1959 he set up a Party Youth Commission to find ways of improving its appeal. He feared that as prosperity eroded class consciousness, young people were 'repelled by what they feel to be the fusty, old-fashioned working-class attitudes of the people who run the Labour Party. How can one meet the demands of these young people without seeming to betray all the ideals of the old people?'[28] The Commission's brief was not mainly political (though it was the first to recommend votes at eighteen, which Gaitskell promised to support). But he aimed much wider. It was to study the problems of the 15–25 age group, and how the government, local authorities or voluntary groups could encourage sport, drama and the arts. Anthony Greenwood was responsible on the Executive, but Gaitskell was active in recruiting members – preferring prominent sportsmen, writers, musicians, actors and artists of broadly Labour sympathies to Greenwood's politicians. Gaitskell's old pre-war opponent Ted Willis was a member, and commented that the leader appreciated, well before most people, the new outlook of a younger generation enjoying financial independence and personal mobility, understanding

that there was a new sound in the air, that old values were breaking up, and a new shape was coming to the world . . . He said, 'It's never going to be the same again with young people, and I want this reflected in the Labour Party.' I was very impressed, I hadn't even myself thought of it that way before.[29]

Following that precedent, and with the same audience in mind, Gaitskell set up in 1962 a similar Advertising Commission. Again he tried to strengthen its authority and broaden its appeal by attracting well-known people who were sympathetic to Labour as well as publicly committed supporters. He chose as chairman Lord Reith, creator of the BBC and high priest of the improving paternalism Gaitskell deplored in other contexts – though he did worry about repercussions on the current television controversy, making elaborate inquiries about Reith's political views and state of mind. Some of his choices thought it a misdirection of effort. But he had confessed much earlier that there were 'some aspects of the affluent society that I find rather unattractive . . . something rather nauseating and humiliating about those [television] advertisements . . . [where] people are regarded as sort of objects on which the ad. men can get to work.'[30]

The New Left, who were somewhat obsessed by that problem, had by then achieved intellectual prominence. Gaitskell fought them on foreign and defence policy, and had no sympathy with their more esoteric preoccupations. He thought some of their ideas

pretty lunatic – though I should not mind that if only they recognised a 'division of labour' and did not go on talking as if they were our main opponents. I suspect, however, that while some are genuine 'thinkers', however muddled, others are ex-communist & trotskyist politicians with more than their fair share of aggression.[6]

But he willingly consented to speak to them privately, and shared the wider anxieties they reflected:

the younger generation at the universities . . . hate the growing influence and power of advertising and . . . feel insulted and humiliated that their desires and wants are being dictated to them regardless of how real they are . . . I understand and sympathise with them. But I have to point out the limits of what can be done, how most people do not yet seem to feel the way they do, how cheap newspapers have to depend on advertising, etc. Nevertheless, I am glad they are worried . . . If this sort of worrying was not going on the Labour Party would lose something very vital to its character. [30]

Gaitskell's concern for majority views was not just vote-catching. On many matters he shared the instincts of his working-class followers rather than those of the progressive intellectuals. Even when his own sympathies were with the latter, he was often made cautious by his awareness of popular feelings. So, when 'moral' issues came up in Parliament, he usually took a liberal but not a crusading stance. He always voted to abolish the death penalty, but was not passionate about it, gave it a low priority and would not have endangered Labour's programme for its sake. He favoured reform of the homosexuality laws, and privately assured the Government that if they acted Labour would make no party capital out of it; but that was as far as he would go. He was most reluctant to interfere with the pleasures of others. In 1949 he assured a Winchester contemporary, a keen huntsman, that on those grounds he would oppose a Private Member's Bill against blood sports. Ten years later, defying the old Nonconformist temperance tradition so strong in the Labour Movement, he persuaded the Party to agree to revise the 'moth-eaten laws' on licensing. A supporter of the police, he was shocked when younger friends once suggested attacking them in an election campaign.

As a politician he knew that independent television was popular, and he would never join the Establishment's cultural crusade against it. As early as 1953 he told Crossman, who had asked if the next Labour government would reverse the newly proposed policy: 'No, and anyway it's a pity we didn't encourage the BBC to lease out time to commercial companies.'[31] A decade later he would not be bounced by Labour's broadcasting spokesman Christopher Mayhew (normally his staunch ally) into supporting the latter's proposals for separating the control of independent TV programmes entirely from the sale of advertising time.

Mayhew's plan had strong Labour support, and it was unanimously adopted by the Pilkington Committee on broadcasting, which reported in June 1962 praising the BBC and criticising the independent companies. But while Gaitskell was quite willing for an experiment with the plan, he was among the experienced Labour broadcasters who were not sure that it would work; also he was not at all convinced that BBC programmes were always better. The press had accused Pilkington of wanting to suppress the most popular programmes, and he wanted to shield the Labour Party from that charge – but 'electoral considerations [were] not dominant' in his mind, and he was quite willing to back Pilkington and lose votes on it if the Party so decided.[24] But while he had no love for the advertisers at all, that did not convert him to Pilkington's specific proposals:

For example, the Pilkington Committee do not want to cut down advertising; personally I would like to see less of it. The Pilkington Committee want the B.B.C. to raise all its money by licence fees; I am not at all sure about this. The Pilkington Committee on the whole defend [newspaper?] ownership of shares in Television Companies; I very much doubt that they are right . . . I do not much like the idea of the fourth channel going to Commercial Television at all.

He reacted strongly against the committee's 'very indifferent' arguments, and above all against its elitism: 'I have seldom been more irritated. The priggish, arrogant, puritanical tone dominates the whole Report.' He warned Mayhew that 'we must beware of imposing our own middle class and intellectual concepts on the workers'.[32]

That warning went much deeper than mere opportunism. Years earlier, he had had just the same private reaction to the draft of a philosophical book by his worthy 'do-gooding' friends in Socialist Union. They overemphasised quality-of-life issues, he wrote, in a way 'terribly reminiscent of Fabian drawing-rooms. It is school-marmish in its flavour. It suggests the refeened middle-class lady holding her nose against the vulgarity that she sees round her. I had hoped we had got away from this kind of thing.' When they exhorted ordinary people to perform civic duties, he demurred:

I get impatient with those who think that everybody must continually be taking an active part in politics or community affairs! The vast majority find their happiness in their family or personal relations, and why on earth shouldn't they! There will always be a minority who are genuinely interested in social activity and social work. They can get on with the job.[20]

He reacted similarly to their unhappiness about affluence, and was anxious for people to enjoy more of its fruits. He pressed for the Labour programme to include setting up a consumer research organisation.

Among his first acts on the National Executive was to sponsor the consumers' back-bench champion, Elaine Burton, in her effort to make shoddy goods the theme of one of the earliest party political broadcasts. There was opposition from the other lady members of the NEC, and from Wilson and Crossman, and Miss Burton wrote later to Gaitskell: 'I know full well that it is only through you that we have the chance of putting this over to the public.' The broadcast was a triumph, drawing the best response yet recorded. Years later, Gaitskell remained an enemy of resale price maintenance; and one of his last business letters pressed Transport House for policy proposals, especially on hire purchase, as 'a pretty good vote-puller'.[33] But again the electoral impact was not his only concern, for he told his puritanical Socialist Union friends in 1955:

I just cannot share this Gandhi outlook . . . If people have more money to spend they may, it is true, gamble or smoke or drink it away. But a lot of them will also enjoy nicer holidays, which is a very good thing for them. We really must keep under control, and pretty strict control, the area within which 'the man in Whitehall knows best'.[20]

That outlook made him a libertarian, sympathetic to practical proposals for protecting the individual against bureaucratic abuses. He raised the problem at the 1959 party conference, and welcomed the remedy – the appointment of an Ombudsman – soon after the Whyatt Committee suggested it two years later. Gaitskell also, despite the extreme caution of his chief adviser, supported the National Council for Civil Liberties' proposals for the treatment of civil servants who became suspect in security cases.

Populism was not philistinism. Gaitskell was much more sensitive than most politicians – and much earlier – to quality-of-life issues. As Minister of Fuel he had shown an interest in environmental problems which was to persist, notably in his continued enthusiasm for town planning. As Chancellor he had actively encouraged the arts, and he did the same in opposition, where Anthony Greenwood, the front-bench spokesman, found him very sensitive on all aesthetic matters. Far from having a vote-catching motive, he wrote that his main aim was 'to build up public opinion behind the idea of more State aid and support'.[34]

While Gaitskell opposed attempts by superior persons to impose their own tastes and preferences on the ordinary man, he firmly resisted popular prejudices against supposedly inferior people – whether over Suez, or coloured immigration, or colonial problems (to which both he and Bevan gave a prominence which some trade union MPs resented). In the electorate, Gaitskell's leadership on these questions both extended Labour's appeal to the liberal middle class, and alienated some of its working-class support.

When he became leader, foreign affairs replaced finance as his main single preoccupation; for his accession to the leadership coincided approximately with the Indian summer of the British economy, in which prosperity produced electoral complacency and the political waters were ruffled by fewer of the economic squalls in which he had made his reputation, but by more typhoons from distant oceans. Prime Ministers, prospective or actual, had now to deal with the problems of the emergent Third World countries in such crises as Rhodesia or Suez. Labour leaders faced special problems, for different sections of their followers traditionally sympathised with Zionism, regarding Israel as the progressive homeland of an oppressed people; with the Soviet Union, still seen as a Socialist state; or with pacifism, given a new lease of life by the fearful prospect of nuclear war.

Gaitskell's international outlook showed his familiar fundamental values and balanced appraisal. His approach was set out fully in the Godkin Lectures at Harvard after a year as leader.[35] Welcoming Anglo-American co-operation in defence of freedom, he warned in the friendliest tones against many past and indeed future American mistakes. He rejoiced that the Eastern European revolts of 1956 had shown that indoctrination and terror could never produce 'a robot-like race in whom the desire for freedom itself had died'. But his suspicion of Communism gave force to his rejection of the crude and strident anti-Communist crusaders; and, while wanting NATO strengthened, he was most sceptical about similar alliances elsewhere.

Even in Europe he opposed the Bonn and Washington hard line over Germany; he was always sympathetic to Yugoslavia; and he favoured demilitarising all Central Europe. For the Polish and Hungarian risings of 1956 had shown, first the unpopularity of Communism there, so that disengagement was unlikely to mean Communist control of West Germany; second, the trouble the satellite countries were giving the Russians; and third the risk of a new East German eruption provoking West German intervention. Contrary to the claims of the Labour Left, Gaitskell had not changed his mind about the dangers of a disarmed and neutral Germany – and was under no pressures of party politics, for no one but Denis Healey had ever suggested disengagement to him.[36] Instead he was thinking in a new international context, in which the Russian occupation of the satellite states was bringing them less advantage. He hoped that demilitarising these countries – Poland, Czechoslovakia, Hungary, and both East and West Germany – might change that context further, since without Soviet troops their domestic balance of power would be transformed. (Like most people, he expected international détente to bring relaxation within Communist countries, not tighter controls.)

In Asia, he doubted China's alleged aggressiveness, and favoured her admission to the UN despite strong American hostility. Denying that international Communism was monolithic, citing Ho Chi Minh as a Communist ruler likely to remain independent of his powerful neighbour, condemning Western military intervention in Asia, and warning that democracies would never fight long wars of repression, he demolished years beforehand the whole rationale for the Vietnam disaster:

The Western powers suffer in these areas from the taint of 'colonialism' . . . the technical and psychological problems associated with land fighting in Asia can hardly be exaggerated, if the local populations are indifferent or even hostile . . . A great deal turns on the attitude of the local populations as well as their governments . . . the political front is the really vital one and . . . the value of a military alliance itself turns largely on its political consequences.

Critics of decolonisation

gravely underestimate the immense force of nationalist feeling . . . [and ] the advantage which communist propaganda has if it is working together with such nationalist feeling. Finally . . . [a] democracy cannot for long maintain a policy of complete repression in its colonies without the people of that democracy themselves deciding to abandon the struggle. And . . . public opinion in the rest of the world . . . will declare itself against policies of this kind.

He repudiated both the connection between economic *laissez-faire* and political freedom, proclaimed by the ideologues of the American Right; and the view that all neutralism was immoral, as the Secretary of State, John Foster Dulles, so often preached. The Third World countries, Gaitskell explained, were attracted to neutralism because of their colonial past, their remoteness from recent European experience with totalitarianism, their reluctance to spend heavily on defence instead of on urgent economic development, and their desire, which should appeal to Americans, to assert independence by breaking with 'wicked power politics'. They should be given economic aid 'without expecting a flood of appreciation or attaching to such help any military strings . . . [solely so that] they can enjoy the same opportunities of economic progress as . . . [us] on a stable and democratic basis.' Aid should enable these countries to raise their standard of living without such stringent restrictions on current consumption as to provoke revolt and destroy any hope of democracy (he was thinking no doubt of India). Mainly because of the impact on these countries, he was against Britain joining a European political union or the embryo Common Market unless one day the Commonwealth disintegrated, leaving Britain only an offshore island.[37]

He thus managed without wishful thinking to discuss foreign affairs in an idealistic and principled perspective and, without offending his American audience, to put to them a distinctive approach, which on most matters commanded very wide support in Britain. There were obvious exceptions: at home, among the nationalist Right (then vociferous because of Suez) and the fellow-travelling Left (then reticent because of Hungary); abroad, with respect to the Middle East and the United Nations. But on world affairs Gaitskell's outlook was generally welcomed far outside the Labour Party, as well as by most people within it.

Gaitskell would not truckle to popular prejudice or abandon his own principles in order to extend support or seek consensus, either in external or domestic affairs. Shortly after entering Parliament, he was asked on a BBC brains trust what he would like on his epitaph, and replied by specifying the qualities of character he most valued: kindness, courage, vitality, living a full life, integrity. As a Minister he hoped to disprove the sad old comment that there is no friendship at the top. Before his election to the leadership, he praised in a private letter the virtues he saw in his own circle of close political friends: intelligence, intellectual honesty, loyalty, judgement.[38] And a couple of years later Arthur Allen, his trade unionist PPS, wrote to him:

Let me first wish you both a very Happy New Year . . . You deserve happiness in that you work wholeheartedly for the good of others and have done so for many years even when there could not have been any reward in prospect for so doing . . . There was a time when the ethical ideals of Socialism carried compulsion in the hearts and minds of sensitive people like yourselves; a time when not to serve those ideals would have been rank treachery to your innermost thoughts . . . I still think hearts can be stirred to react against injustice and minds enlisted to promote the good. That is why I am so glad that you, Hugh, have become the leader of the Party . . . You have qualities of heart and mind incomparably superior to so many of those with whom you of necessity must associate. That is the reason why it gives me so much pleasure to do the little I can to help you. We must make you Premier. It is so desperately important that guidance of our affairs should be taken out of the hands of cynics.

By the way, I didn't set out to write like this at all.[39]

# PART THREE
# Leader of The Party

*'First of all his job is to keep the Party together . . . second to listen to other people . . . thirdly . . . to tell them what he thinks'*
(HG, 1957)

*'The atmosphere is full of suppressed hysteria and neurosis – not so suppressed either'*
(HG, 1960)

*'That leadership issue is once for all out of the way'*
(Crossman closing the 1961 Conference)

*'To unify the party and carry the country'*
(HG on his aims, 1961)

# 14

# Brief Honeymoon 1956

*'We can perhaps count on Mr. Gaitskell to lean rather more to the Left than is strictly necessary for party purposes'*
(Daily Telegraph, 1956)

*'Our present leadership is not only more intelligent but also much more flexible than the Attlee regime'*
(Ian Mikardo, 1958)

## Healing the Wounds

Gaitskell was elated at winning by the most convincing majority in Labour's history. But his sudden transformation from factional spokesman to party leader left many doubts about him, especially outside Westminster. Labour activists were accustomed to opposition not government, disposed to criticism more than construction, often receptive to utopianism and wishful thinking, and uneasy with a leader who had only briefly been a back-bencher and never a rebel. Always suspecting their own front bench of caution, compromise and careerism, they were liable to mistake the trumpetings of *Tribune* and the sneers of the *New Statesman* for the voice of Socialist purity.

In his twenty years of leadership, Clem Attlee had handled the Left cautiously. In office he had taken an unpopular stand occasionally, but in opposition he rarely risked his credit by standing up to dissidents. His successor was described by one commentator as 'Left-inclining with almost undignified speed'; another thought that he 'more than any alternative leader, may be able to hold them together'; a third expected him to 'attempt to do deliberately what Mr. Attlee appeared to do intuitively, that is, to lead the party from the centre'.[1]

During his first Parliament as leader Gaitskell met those expectations. He set out to reunite the Party in two ways: first by healing bruised personal relations, then by working out a new and broadly acceptable policy. In dealing with other politicians he was neither naive nor neurotically suspicious. He gave them the benefit of any doubt, though he was indignant when he felt his confidence betrayed. But he did not bear grudges, and was so unsectarian in choosing his colleagues that Leslie Hunter could write of him in 1958 heading 'a predominantly left wing team'.[2] During those forgotten early years he was strikingly successful within the Party; outside it, critics felt he gave too little weight to the Opposition leader's role as a national as well as a party spokesman. In 1958 a writer compared him to Attlee, adding:

Gaitskell has within his own party drawn together many loose ends of discontent. But can he do the same for the country?

His ability to compromise is famous in the Labour Party. But Britain needs leadership, not compromise.

Too often Gaitskell has seemed the leader who follows.[3]

Since he led a party not an army, its members had to be convinced not commanded. Before 1959, skill in accommodation was the aspect of his leadership most emphasised alike by himself and by his critics on Left and Right. After eighteen months, a BBC interviewer brought up 'the commonest criticism of your leadership . . . that you don't really lead them – that you wait to hear what they want and then say it'. Gaitskell replied that a leader had several tasks: 'to keep the Party together . . . to listen to what other people say . . . to tell them what he thinks . . . but he's jolly well got to take into account what people's thoughts and views are; and frankly anything else would not be tolerated in the Labour Party'.[4] Even his old critic Ian Mikardo found his leadership 'not only more intelligent but also much more *flexible* than the Attlee regime [and] ready to give way . . . to a clearly-expressed view of the back-benchers . . . with good grace.'[5] Conservative critics made exactly the same points. One wrote: 'He has united his party behind an agreed policy, certainly. But he has united it by following . . . Never once, since he became leader, has he ever risen above party, or ever given a hint that he would be capable of rising above it.'[6] Another even claimed: 'We can perhaps count on Mr. Gaitskell to lean rather more to the Left than is strictly necessary for party purposes'.[7] Then, over Suez, he encountered real hatred from many Conservatives – who mistakenly attributed his opposition to partisan calculation. In 1959 an old Beaverbrook-Bevanite confessed: 'from the party point of view he has acquitted himself magnificently . . . he has established an ascendancy that Attlee never accomplished.'[8] He was thus seen as a brilliant party leader, skilful at reconciling a quarrelsome following, unassailable since he led from left of centre; but prone to pay too high a price for unity, and too willing to yield to pressures from the ranks behind him.

In the late 1950s – a time of general prosperity felt to be insecure – party unity proved a necessary but not sufficient condition for electoral victory. In 1959 Gaitskell fought an impressive personal campaign arousing immense enthusiasm among party workers – but Labour was decisively beaten. That defeat had a great impact, dividing his leadership into two sharply contrasting periods.

## The Leader and His Approach to Power

The commentator was correct who described Gaitskell's early style of leadership as one deliberately chosen, for his instinctive conception was quite different. At the age of twenty-two, in his youthful study of Chartism he had condemned the men who gave no positive lead of their own, claiming that 'the people must be asked what they wanted to do . . . A belief in democratic principles was doubtless behind the support of a few for this policy, but for many it was only a cloak under which they might escape for a time from their too responsible position.'[9] Now he had to reconcile his belief in those principles with the opportunities, and the constraints, of his own responsible position.

His confidence in the rationality and decency of ordinary people assured him that they could be convinced by good aims and a good case, and his fundamental commitment to democratic methods required the Labour Party to convert a majority before it could come to power and start to carry out its objectives. He could become impatient with those who ignored that necessity and its implications. Forgetting his own inexperienced and passionate youth, he wrote in 1958 to his daughter at Oxford:

Many of your friends do not understand about *democracy*! . . . or the practical problems of achieving Socialist goals under democratic conditions. Yet it is the only thing really worth talking about . . . The difficulty, if anything, is that [Labour's programme] is probably still too radical for the electorate.[10]

A few years later he told a trade union audience that most of the trouble in the Party came from those impatient with the need to convert marginal voters. Yet that need was 'basic', for 'without power we can do nothing; we can only win power when we have the confidence of our fellow-citizens'.[11]

Far more introspective than most of his political colleagues, Gaitskell was fascinated by power, irresistibly attracted to it, yet always conscious of its fragility and elusiveness. He suggested more than once that friends should write a book about it, because real power did not exist. In a television interview in 1961, Malcolm Muggeridge said that he himself looked on power as 'a dreadful thing, a dangerous thing', and asked, 'Do you feel frightened of this, uneasy about it or avid for it?'

Gaitskell replied that power was far less freely exercised than most people believed:

Certainly not avid for it, but . . . [your] whole conception . . . is a wrong one . . . from personal experience . . . [it is] extraordinarily limited . . . [as] a Minister, you can make certain appointments, and on the whole they rest with you, but you know the care you have to take . . . that the right balance in a particular board or council is preserved, that the right sort of people are put on, that they are going to succeed, [so] that you don't think 'I am controlling a benefit' at all, indeed very often you're much more concerned as to whether the persons are going to accept the jobs . . . you do not decide [policy] on your own, except to a very limited extent, you have to persuade people . . . you've got to take [your officials] into account, you probably have to persuade your colleagues.

Not even the Prime Minister had

personal absolute power, he's got to think of all his colleagues, you can have a revolt after all [like Eden] . . . In forming your Cabinet again you would have to take so many things into account, but above all the question of success, of whether you were going to succeed as a government . . . [a] complex of personal relations to consider, the whole question of how you can keep the team working together, it may be a word you dislike but . . . it does mean something . . . the idea of I decide, a sort of dictatorial power, nobody questions my decision is complete nonsense in my experience.[12]

Of course Gaitskell was ambitious: men who are not rarely go into politics, let alone succeed there, and Gaitskell had never been concerned to preach the word without seeking the power to apply it.

Being a practical politician and wanting to get results rather than satisfy emotions, he accepted the inevitability of working in a team . . . he was interested in the winning of power in order to get things changed. He was contemptuous of those who seemed more concerned with the emotional satisfaction of expressing minority views.[13]

He saw nothing wrong with ambition in the service of principle. The Labour Party, he told his daughter, needed

people with integrity & ability & common sense plus the ordinary good qualities of loyalty, courage & honesty. It's better to ask whether people have these qualities rather than whether they are careerists. Ambition doesn't matter (& is to be expected anyhow) so long as people have the other things too.[10]

But the object of getting into power was to put principles into practice, and he had no respect for colleagues or opponents who sought it as an end in itself, or simply as the culmination of a personal career. He hated the cynical view of politicians as men who subordinate self-respect and ordinary human decency to its obsessive pursuit, and when the behaviour of others appeared to fit that stereotype he found politics utterly distasteful.

## Labour Harmony, Tory Disarray

Twenty turbulent years had passed since the Party had last systematically formulated its policy. Its recent manifestos had reflected no serious long-term thought, proposing to nationalise one group of industries in 1950, none in 1951, and a different list in 1955. Conference then agreed that a new policy should be worked out over three years. Gaitskell had favoured the conception, and was now to preside over the execution. Although he always mistrusted broad professions of principle unsupported by practical plans, his enthusiasm for precise policy-making was surprising, for he knew very well that the record of a government counts far more electorally than any Opposition proposals. Yet it was under him that Labour in opposition went furthest in working out detailed policies for government. They made no impact at all on the electorate.

In January 1956, his first month as leader, Gaitskell consolidated his front-bench team, improved his Transport House contacts, and established personal relations with the press and BBC. For several months he reverted to keeping a detailed diary, beginning dramatically with a call on the Prime Minister on New Year's Day to propose (unsuccessfully) the recall of Parliament to debate Egypt's acquisition of surplus British tanks. He spoke at half a dozen receptions and conferences, attended over a dozen party committees and talked to twenty-five prominent colleagues. He also saw individually most members of the Shadow Cabinet, to urge on them the need for more teamwork and less back-stabbing and intrigue. He had a dozen official engagements (largely diplomatic), saw several journalists, and had four sessions with photographers and three exhausting rehearsals for his first television appearance as leader. His one weekend at home was broken by a lunch with Dalton and a party at the Attlees' Chiltern home.

Day-to-day parliamentary opposition was already taking a new form. Attlee had made the main change immediately after the 1955 election, under pressure from Gaitskell and his new allies Wilson and Crossman, by introducing the modern Shadow Cabinet organisation with members responsible for (and confined to) specific departmental functions. Despite its serious drawbacks, it did have advantages in promoting effective teamwork. That style of opposition reflected Gaitskell's personality, but all his successors have retained the system.

When the House of Commons met on 24 January 1956, the PLP had to choose a deputy leader to replace Morrison. Bevan contested the election, polling 111 and losing by only thirty to a strong rival, James Griffiths. Many MPs were again signalling their anxiety to end the quarrel – and many more did not do so only for fear that Bevan would soon shatter the new unity. They were nearly right. Bevan reopened the wounds two days later at Manchester: 'If the Labour Party is not going to be a Socialist Party, I don't want to lead it . . . When you join a team in the expectation that you are going to play rugger, you can't be expected to be enthusiastic if you are asked to play tiddly-winks.'[14] The whole speech was clamouring for martyrdom, but Gaitskell ignored it. He took that decision entirely on his own. He told a friendly journalist that he would not 'allow Mr. Bevan the luxury of becoming a storm-centre again. He . . . is not going to prevent the PLP from getting on with a serious job of work.'[15]

Gaitskell did not exploit his patronage, but used it for conciliation. The posts vacated by the new leader and deputy leader went to Wilson, who took over from Gaitskell as Shadow Chancellor, and to Bevan himself. Griffiths had shadowed the Colonial Office, a post which Bevan had long coveted. Gaitskell made the offer after Bevan's Manchester speech. As the leader recorded:

He said 'I would have liked Foreign Affairs . . . The only difficulty about the Colonies is that I really know so little about them.' This is a very rare admission from Mr. B! . . . We are giving him every possible chance . . . an interesting [job] with plenty of Parliamentary scope, with travelling . . . that he can really get his teeth into. If, despite this, he refuses to work in the team, and goes on behaving as he has been doing recently, sooner or later he will simply get himself out of the Party. But whether he will do that, or whether after all he will settle down, we cannot yet say.[16]

For once party leadership seemed more of a problem for the Conservatives than for Labour. Eden's apprenticeship had been as prolonged as Gaitskell's was brief, and the new Prime Minister had no experience of running a team. In domestic policy he had never held any responsibility; even abroad he appeared to be losing grip. After a critical Middle East debate in March 1956, when Gaitskell thought Eden made an 'almost pathetic' winding-up speech, Ian Waller correctly predicted that by 1957 Harold Macmillan would replace Eden in Downing Street.

Eden had already been bitterly attacked editorially in the *Daily Telegraph* – influenced, it was said, by Lady Pamela Berry, wife of the editor-in-chief. She had never met Gaitskell, but cornered him at a reception in the Fishmongers' Hall to demand insistently:

'Tell me, Mr. Gaitskell, is it possible to get rid of a Prime Minister in peacetime?' I said, 'It is extremely difficult if he doesn't want to go. But you can, of course, make life so intolerable for him that he becomes ill and cannot carry on.' 'You aren't suggesting that I should murder him?' she said.'[17]

But Eden's personal unpopularity was not the Government's only weakness, for the last instalment of Butler's economic legacy was now coming due. Macmillan, the reluctant new Chancellor, introduced the fourth deflationary package in twelve months. It made an easy target for the Opposition. In the House, Gaitskell left the opening assault to his colleagues, commenting:

Harold [Wilson] and Douglas [Jay] both made outstanding speeches . . . If we can only make the Party understand that they should attack on themes where the Party is most united and the Government most vulnerable, and not attack on the opposite occasions, then I think we shall continue to do fairly well.[18]

That glimpse of the obvious speaks volumes for the tactical problems facing Labour leaders.

Gaitskell quickly earned newspaper praise as 'the most effective Parliamentarian for many a long year'.[15] Feeling themselves more useful, the mood of Labour MPs improved, and so did that of the constituency parties, and Crossman could therefore write: 'a new young leadership is actually taking over and the old men are actually moving to the sidelines. . . . just at the moment when the Tory leadership is showing every sign of disintegration.'[19]

## '*The Night of the Long Spoons*' and the '*Mush of Unity*'

The first attacks on Gaitskell's leadership arose from a visit of the Soviet leaders to Britain. Stalin had died in 1953. Malenkov, a deputy premier, came over in March 1956, charmed his hosts by his open-minded frankness, and was evidently impressed by his first contact with the West. Gaitskell spent five hours with him, and Malenkov delighted his hearers by favouring a Soviet guarantee of Israel's frontiers and by agreeing that a nuclear war would obliterate Communism as well as capitalism. And Khrushchev told Gaitskell later: 'You seem to have made a great impression on him'.[20]

Malenkov was soon followed by Khrushchev the new First Secretary, and Bulganin the new Prime Minister. With them, relations were very different. Not yet mellowed by experience, Khrushchev pursued intransigent policies in the crudest style, revelling in the destructive power of his nuclear weapons, which he insisted would wipe out capitalism while Communism would survive. Gaitskell had forty minutes with him in private, and intended to seek the release of social democrats imprisoned in Eastern Europe. But the moment never came, for there was an earlier explosion at Gaitskell's warning that good relations could never be achieved through Communist front organisations or fellow-travellers. Khrushchev reacted furiously, attacking Labour's foreign policy and saying he found Tories much more congenial.

The Labour Party gave a dinner for the Russians, who knew the imprisoned social democrats would come up in questions. Khrushchev, as Gaitskell recorded, spoke 'for an hour . . . [with] vehemence, almost brutality . . . it was pretty frightening.' Crossman wrote eighteen months later: 'I will never forget . . . [Khrushchev's] couldn't-care-less suggestion that we should join the Russians, because if not, they would swat us off the face of the earth like a dirty old black beetle.'[21]

Gaitskell raised Labour's questions, but was carefully conciliatory and sought no immediate answer. But Khrushchev at once said offensively: 'If you want to help the enemies of the working class, you must find another agent to do it', then rushed out in a furious temper without shaking hands. Next day, before leaving, the Russians invited Gaitskell to Moscow and departed 'with continual handshakes and general cordiality'. It was superficial, for Khrushchev nursed his resentment for years. Shinwell and a handful of MPs wanted to apologise, but Gaitskell said Labour had done itself good by standing up for its principles, and won great applause. Only the *Daily Express* and *Daily Worker* attacked Gaitskell, and the latter abused Bevan equally. But it was the end of the honeymoon, and a few mutterings now began against Gaitskell's leadership.

In the autumn of 1956, Gaitskell attended his first party conference as leader. Bevan returned to the National Executive by winning election as treasurer at last—by 3,029,000 to 2,755,000 for George Brown and 644,000 for Charles Pannell of the AEU. Frank Cousins, appearing at his first conference as the new Transport Workers' secretary, promised he would maintain that unity and not tell the Labour Party how to do its job; Gaitskell found him 'profoundly ignorant of the real issues', much too prone to talk without thinking, and obviously hungry for power. But the leader felt that personally 'he and his wife were extremely friendly to us. And he several times went out of his way to show that he was entirely on my side'.[22]

Gaitskell himself presented the new policy document *Towards Equality*, and told the delegates that it was the aspect of Socialism he had cared about most for thirty years. His speech changed the minds of delegates previously convinced that the PLP had chosen the wrong man. They gave him a tremendous ovation, and he came beaming to the rostrum: 'Thank you, comrades. We take that as a pledge between us.' It was a moment of triumph not repeated until his final conference six years later. In the new mood, not even foreign policy and defence divided the Party, and the old battle lines were dissolving into an agreed compromise amid what Jennie Lee called a 'mush of unity'.[23] Gaitskell's leadership thus seemed accepted, successful and secure when, on the very eve of the recess, there erupted his first major challenge: the Suez crisis.

# 15

# Suez 1956–7

'You "spoke for England" – for England's real & best self'
(Lady Violet Bonham Carter to HG, 1956)

'The Rt Hon. Jellyfish'
(Daily Telegraph, 9 October 1956)

## Colonel Nasser's Rhineland?

In early 1956 Gaitskell's speeches in the House on the Middle East had pleased all sections of the Party, and even of the House. By the summer, the West was taking alarm at President Nasser's ambitions. On 19 July the United States abruptly withdrew her promised support for building the Aswan High Dam to promote Egyptian economic development. A week later, without notice or negotiation, Nasser seized the Canal installations, increased Canal dues, and threatened to imprison foreigners who tried to leave their jobs: as Bevan later remarked: 'if the sending of one's police and soldiers into the darkness of the night to seize somebody else's property is nationalisation, Ali Baba used the wrong terminology'.[1]

Gaitskell heard the news in 10 Downing Street, of all places, at an official dinner for the King of Iraq. On Monday 30 July 1956, the Shadow Cabinet met and

there was some anxiety about our going too far in a bellicose direction and it was felt important that we should stress exactly what our attitude was to nationalisation, as contrasted with the breaking of international agreements or concessions . . . Jim Griffiths and I went to see Eden at my request . . . I was a little concerned lest he might suppose that we would back force as a Party in the same way as the [Tory] Suez rebels . . . I said that this was not the case . . . He confirmed . . . [that he favoured] international control of the Canal under the United Nations, I think, with the hope that Nasser will accept this. I said 'What happens if he doesn't? Do you then use force?' Eden said, 'Well, I don't want to take that hurdle yet.' I had already made it plain, I may say, that I doubted whether we could support force merely on those grounds.[2]

The Shadow Cabinet met again on 31 July, and agreed with Gaitskell that it was unwise to attack the Government when Labour could so easily be 'framed as unpatriotic and'. . . irresponsible'. He saw three MPs – Benn, John Hynd and Warbey – whom he found much too pro-Nasser and equivocal about Israel. ('Tony Benn . . . talented in many ways, a good speaker and a man of ideas has extraordinarily poor judgment. He is the last person in the world I would go to for advice on policy.') He reassured them 'that although I thought that action was necessary against Nasser, force could not be used and should not be used unless there was real justification for it.'[2]

Gaitskell's views did not shift. Britain had a major legitimate interest in the Canal, for most of her oil came through it and nearly half the ships using it were British. While nationalisation alone gave no justification for imposing an international solution by force, the manner in which Nasser had acted showed he had an ulterior aim: to score a prestige triumph over the West and so promote the expansion of Arab nationalism – or the aggrandisement of Egypt. Gaitskell never believed in the Third World right or wrong, or approved of ambitious military dictators just because their skins were dark; and his sympathy for the Israelis, felt by most Labour people since the 1930s, had been keen since his visit in 1953. But any action to block Nasser's expansionism needed American backing. So did the economic pressure which he hoped would bring Nasser to the negotiating table. That policy might have worked in 1956, when Britain and France enjoyed the goodwill of most other countries and particularly the United States; it had no chance in 1957 after the invasion had isolated them totally.

Gaitskell at first approved of Eden's military precautions, though he soon became alarmed at their scale. But he thought an attack on Egypt, in defiance of the Commonwealth and the United States, would be inconceivably reckless – especially after the assurances he believed he had from the Prime Minister. The emphasis of his speeches therefore changed with the situation: on 2 August he sought to prevent his own party becoming Nasser's apologists; on 12 September he concentrated on averting an immediate naval confrontation in the Canal; on 4 November, after the British and French ultimatum, he denounced their 'criminal folly'.

The first debate was on Thursday 2 August 1956. That morning Eden saw Gaitskell alone and, as Gaitskell later came to feel, misled him:

I pressed him once more about the use of force. There was not disagreement on the military precautions . . . I went into the House of Commons and told John Strachey that Eden had said that force was to be used only if Nasser did something else, and we agreed that that was satisfactory.[3]

Twenty minutes later Gaitskell rose to make a speech quite consistent

with all he said later, yet which was to lead to his being widely charged
with trimming for partisan reasons.

He said that the seizure of the Canal was objectionable because a
single state should not have sole control of an international waterway;
the manner of the seizure undermined all confidence in Egyptian
assurances; and it was plainly 'part of the struggle for mastery in
Middle East', calculated to raise Nasser's prestige so that 'our friends
desert us because they think we are lost, and go over to Egypt . . . It is
all very familiar. It is exactly the same that we encountered from
Mussolini and Hitler in those years before the war.' Iraq and perhaps
Jordan were at risk at once, Israel later. Gaitskell urged a conference of
the 1888 signatories, to include Russia and Egypt. But it was settled
British policy not to use force

in breach of international law or, indeed, contrary to the public opinion of the
world. We must not, therefore, allow ourselves to get into a position where we
might be denounced in the Security Council as aggressors, or where the
majority of the Assembly were against us . . . we must be sure that the
circumstances justify it and that it is, if used, consistent with our belief in, and
our pledges to, the Charter of the United Nations and not in conflict with
them.[4]

The reception gave no immediate hint of the coming storm. 'I was
a little embarrassed by far too much praise from the Tories
. . . Presumably they did not listen to the last part of my speech.'[3]
Gaitskell should have known that his pre-war analogy was far more
memorable than the cautious unremarkable sentences at the end
expressing his reservations about using force. No phrase-maker, he
thought of his whole balanced argument and not of the selective
reporting. He was walking a political tightrope, trying to discourage
both British bellicosity and Egyptian intransigence.

I would have spoken even more plainly in the debate had I not been so anxious
to avoid any appearance of disunity . . . I tried to make it as plain as I could
that we could not support force, except as permitted by the U.N. Charter –
without giving Nasser encouragement that he could disregard any idea of any
international solution.[5]

Gaitskell did not know that the Cabinet had already agreed to use
force unless a negotiated solution was quickly found. He later felt
personally betrayed, believing that the Prime Minister had deliberately
misinformed him; at the time of the debate 'it never entered my head
that the Government would do what they finally did'.[6] That evening,
however, he learned that the Foreign Office were telling journalists that

Egypt would face an Anglo-French ultimatum and invasion. He was incredulous until he saw the morning papers, but then 'I sat down and wrote to Eden a letter in my own hand . . . not [to] assume that the Labour Party would support the policy of force . . . repeating what I had [previously] said to him . . . much more emphatically in the letter. We then went off to Wales.'³ In it he wrote:

I deliberately refrained from putting the hypothetical question in public 'Was it proposed to use force to compel Nasser to accept the International Control Scheme?' For I felt that it might embarrass you to do so. Had I said in my reply to my own question that we could not support such action, it might, I felt, have gravely weakened your chances of achieving a settlement . . . up to the present, I cannot see that he has done anything which would justify this.⁷

Both the Conservative press and Gaitskell's Labour enemies later propagated the myth that he had supported Eden's policy of using force, but changed his mind because of a Labour revolt. Yet Gaitskell said exactly the opposite in the House itself, and then, before any breath of Labour criticism reached him, gave Eden three separate private warnings. After the debate both his Chief Whip and his own press officer told Eden that Labour would not support a policy of force – but the sick Prime Minister chose to see only what he wanted to see.

Bellicose briefings from No. 10 and the Foreign Office now filled the press, where Conservative papers claimed the full support of the Opposition. Prominent Labour supporters were alarmed by the misleading press reports of Gaitskell's views, and on 9 August the Party's deputy leader and general secretary therefore circulated his speech – stressing the UN passages – to MPs, candidates, unions and local parties. Gaitskell shared the alarm himself, for Eden's reply to his letter of 3 August gave no assurance about force, and Gaitskell now suspected that the military preparations were not merely precautionary. From Wales, he sent the Prime Minister another letter, his fourth note of misgiving and anxiety, and he cut his vacation short to return to London on Sunday 12 August. On Monday afternoon the Shadow Cabinet unanimously endorsed his speech of 2 August, reiterated his warnings against using force, proposed reference to the UN Assembly and supported a UN control scheme. Gaitskell wrote:

To my particular astonishment Nye Bevan himself was very much in agreement with me . . . He was in no doubt about Nasser being a thug . . . [or] about the need for international control . . . [He] opposed . . . a reference to . . . internationalisation of waterways, . . . [calling it] 'a great mistake to say anything at the moment which would embarrass the Americans' . . . the meeting could not have been more harmonious or friendly.[3]

Next morning Gaitskell, Griffiths and Robens again saw Eden, Lloyd and Salisbury, the Lord President. 'We did not get very far with them . . . [but] they certainly were left in no doubt about our views on the whole situation.'[3] On 24 August Gaitskell saw John Foster Dulles, congratulated him on proposing his international control scheme at the recent conference, and repeated that half the country would not support the use of force. (The Secretary of State then warned Eden that he was misjudging British public opinion, and Eden again rejected the warning.)[8] Gaitskell also argued to the French Ambassador: 'we had to so conduct ourselves to get world opinion more on our side . . . it can only be an advantage to have been to the United Nations, whatever the exact outcome.'[9] But at the end of the month he still did not believe that Eden meant war. In newspaper interviews he condemned both extremes: 'Nasser is an ambitious military dictator . . . But, so far, what he has done does *not* justify armed retaliation.' If Nasser refused to negotiate, the West should boycott the Canal and prepare for a long economic struggle.[10]

The Gallup poll showed the UN line to be popular, and it helped avert a Labour split; for a majority of the TUC General Council's international committee were behind the Government, and millions of trade unionists had served in Egypt during the war, seeing mainly the parasitic hangers-on around the army camps. But Gaitskell, who often stood with the working-class populists against the intellectual Left, wholly rejected their feelings of hate and contempt for Egyptians. Whatever the political consequences, he would not play to that gallery.

## Lull before the Storm

The crucial issue was whether or not to use force to impose international control on Egypt. A scheme was agreed in August 1956 by the conference of eighteen user nations, mostly small and some from the Third World. But when President Eisenhower publicly renounced the use of force, the Egyptian President felt he could safely break off the talks. The UN now became a field for tactical manoeuvre. The British and French Governments proposed to go to the Security Council, expecting a Soviet veto and intending then to attack Egypt. Dulles feared that would oblige the United States to choose between her allies and the Third World countries, and suggested instead a new Suez Canal Users' Association to control the navigation. Hoping to commit the United States to oppose Egypt, Eden reluctantly accepted this plan, implying to the recalled Parliament that escorting warships would force the convoys through if necessary. Gaitskell at once protested at the threat; so that his speech on 12 September had quite a different emphasis from that of 2 August. For, while he still reaffirmed all his old criticisms of Nasser, a Leader of the Opposition who foresaw a catastrophe now had a plain duty to expose the new dangers.

Gaitskell warned that the talk of war found no support except in France. Joint Anglo–French action, opposed by the rest of the world, would mean disaster. If the threats were bluff, then Britain faced 'the greatest diplomatic climb-down in our history' and Nasser's prestige victory would be enormously magnified. The Government should state now that they would not use force against the Charter, and would take the dispute to the UN – 'not just to go through formalities so that we may thereafter resort to force . . . [but for] a further period of negotiation'. If the users' association was a device for provoking Egypt to obstruct the ships, would the United States act with us?[11]

Eden still refused a pledge not to use force contrary to the Charter. Winding up the second day's debate, Gaitskell was told of Dulles's press conference statement that the United States would not 'shoot our way through the Canal', and repeated the words of the Secretary of State: 'Is he prepared to say on behalf of H. M. G. that they will not try to shoot their way through the Canal?' In a tumultuous and passionate House, Eden replied in the last five minutes of the debate, apparently giving the assurance demanded. 'I have never seen', wrote one level-headed Labour MP, 'a clearer or more outstanding victory of Opposition over Government.'[12]

After the debate Gaitskell believed that at least for the moment they had drawn back. 'I may be too optimistic but my feeling is that we are probably over the hump now. Certainly the danger of immediate war provoked by trying to break through the Canal seems to have been averted.'[13] He knew that public opinion was uneasy, that the moderate Conservatives were mobilising, and that senior Ministers were struggling to restrain the fire-eaters. He had to try to influence the Cabinet against its reckless course, without seeming to criticise his own country. Just before his first party conference as leader, Crossman wrote: 'He has seen the dangers of getting ourselves tagged as simply a pro-Nasser, anti-British party. He has made great efforts to get the Left and the Right of the Party working together, with some success, and his own speeches have been really very good.'[14]

When Conference debated Suez on its opening day, 1 October 1956, the speeches were so strongly pro-Nasser that it seemed Gaitskell must follow or be overwhelmed. He rose 'to an extremely perfunctory welcome . . . [but] seized upon the most tactful approach apparently by instinct, and thereby turned the political tables in a trice'.[15] He urged the delegates to concentrate on the central question, and not play the Tory game by sounding unpatriotic. Reference to the UN must not be a formal prelude to an invasion, but an opportunity to negotiate and to bring economic pressure on Egypt.

Whether Colonel Nasser was right or wrong, the rights of canal users, the right of self-defence, and the question of precautionary measures, are issues thrown in to muddy the water and confuse . . . *the* crucial issue of the use of force . . . we have had no clear undertaking from the Government that they would only use force in accordance with the Charter . . . I wish I could say even now that the danger is entirely over.[16]

It was a triumphant handling of a most awkward situation, reversing Attlee's usual reception: 'tumultuous applause at the beginning of his speech, and polite clapping from the faithful at the end'.[15] Crossman was impressed: 'It's a real test for a new, untried, suspect Leader to have to start by rebuking and educating the Party, and I thought he did it extraordinarily well.'[17]

## Invasion: 'Criminal Folly'

Gaitskell had turned a nasty political corner, but the real crisis lay ahead. The danger of war was not over, and the die was apparently cast in that very week. Gaitskell did not discover that the Cabinet fire-eaters had regained their ascendancy. He was emotionally drained, and distracted from public affairs, by his mother's death on 14 October. Rationally, too, he was convinced and indeed insistent that no British Administration would embark on so crazy an adventure in 1956. Official advisers, he clearly assumed from his own governmental experience, would oblige blind or self-deluded Ministers to face reality.

He was too orderly an administrator and too far-sighted a politician to conceive of a sick but stubborn Prime Minister rigorously excluding all unwelcome news or views. For Eden's colleagues 'were perplexed by decisions taken outside the Cabinet in the Suez Committee';[18] naval plans were concealed from the First Lord of the Admiralty; very few officials were kept informed; advisers seemed reluctant to report bad news; the Foreign Office and legal experts were deliberately not consulted; the British ambassadors concerned were kept in the dark; communications with Washington were cut (the Embassy was kept vacant for the crucial month); the angry Commonwealth countries were told nothing. Eden and Macmillan relied on intuition to predict the response in those capitals, wantonly closed off any means of testing their own wishful thinking, reassured their worried colleagues – and then, after the invasion, expressed pained surprise at the furious reactions they had inexcusably misjudged.

The wounds were self-inflicted. Eden boasted of rejecting normal international consultations precisely because they would generate pressure against the project. Astonishingly, he did not see that a long-drawn-out military operation would also generate such pressures (especially in a Washington irritated at the secrecy and enraged by the timing, on the very eve of the presidential election). Whatever its morality or wisdom, the attack was sure to fail unless it presented the world with an instant *fait accompli*. But the military refused to use paratroops alone; and seaborne forces would take six days from Malta. The shrewder soldiers knew these military constraints made political failure inevitable. But, self-insulated from any unwelcome advice, the politicians crashed ahead.

Yet, though Eden would not rule out using force to impose internationalisation, he had privately thought it impossible without a new forcible act by Nasser. By 16 October, however, the French had persuaded him that after a pre-emptive strike by Israel against Egypt, French and British forces could 'separate the combatants' by seizing the Canal. The 'hypocritical and disingenuous ultimatum', as Randolph Churchill called it,[19] was ostensibly to justify an emergency peace-keeping intervention. It deceived no one outside Britain, and finally hamstrung the military operation itself. For the British Government, fearing exposure, had to reject Israeli offers of help; and when Israel and Egypt stopped fighting, it had to accept its own cease-fire proposal before it had attained its real objectives.

At 4.15 p.m. on Tuesday 30 October the Prime Minister – once the champion of internationalism and advocate of bipartisanship – gave the Leader of the Opposition fifteen minutes' notice of the Anglo-French ultimatum. Gaitskell obtained a short debate that evening, in which Healey from the back benches made the first strongly critical Labour speech. The leader's own comments were more cautious, but impressive for moderates: two years later an anti-Suez Tory MP said to him: 'I don't think there is a single word you would wish to change in it. It is pretty remarkable because you had very little time to prepare it.'[20] Accepting the Government's version – a surprise Israeli attack on Egypt which must be halted at once – he argued that Britain should propose in the Security Council, first an Israeli withdrawal and then prompt redress of her grievances. He probed how far the Commonwealth and the United States had been consulted; and asked what the Government would do if it proved (as it did) that the Israeli forces were still too far from the Canal to threaten it. Receiving no promise to delay military action until the Security Council met, and assuming that the invasion would be immediate, Labour divided the House.

Next day brought no assurances, no invasion, but an Anglo-French veto of an American resolution in the Security Council – which Gaitskell condemned as

an act of disastrous folly whose tragic consequences we shall regret for years . . . irreparable harm to [our] prestige and reputation . . . a positive assault upon the three principles which have governed British foreign policy . . . solidarity with the Commonwealth, the Anglo-American Alliance and adherence to the Charter of the United Nations.

The Security Council was paralysed by the veto, but in the Assembly the invaders would face a hostile two-thirds majority, perhaps alone. No others would believe the 'transparent excuse' for a long-planned policy of force, particularly ill-timed at a moment of hope in Warsaw and Budapest. Gaitskell called for a denial of collusion with Israel; and appealed to the Tory dissidents, particularly Butler, against this 'reckless and foolish decision' which would arouse a wave of hatred against Britain, and which Labour would oppose 'by every constitutional means at our disposal'.[21]

Next day, Thursday 1 November, the Prime Minister condemned the Opposition for not supporting British soldiers going into action. But he did not even know the rights of those soldiers if captured, for he was unable to say whether the United Kingdom was at war. Nor had Ministers any news of the many British civilians in Egypt whose lives were now in jeopardy. For the first time for over thirty years the Speaker had to suspend the sitting for half an hour. Next day it became apparent that the oil supplies and free passage through the Canal, which it was Eden's stated aim to preserve, had both been lost before a single soldier landed. Moreover, while world attention was centred on Egypt, the Russians seized their opportunity and sent their tanks back to Budapest to destroy the new National-Communist government of Hungary.

Most exceptionally, Parliament met on Saturday morning, 3 November 1956. Gaitskell, who hitherto had hoped and believed that the Government would abandon its disastrous course, now declared: 'There is only one way out, and that is a change in the leadership of the Government. Only that now can save our reputation and re-open the possibility of maintaining the United Nations as a force for peace. We must have a new Government and a new Prime Minister.' Only the anti-Suez Conservatives could achieve that. 'I ask them to do their duty.'[22]

Sir Anthony Eden broadcast that evening, and Gaitskell claimed the right to reply. The Prime Minister tried hard to deny it, and allegedly planned to take over the BBC by legal manoeuvres which the directors and staff successfully resisted. The BBC, which then decided such disputed cases, accepted Gaitskell's claim to reply to Eden after a great row with Downing Street and some delay. His broadcast on the Sunday was therefore prepared in utter chaos at very short notice.

It attracted a record audience. He said the Government argued that Britain and France had to act because the UN was too slow; if so, that was due solely to their own veto. Otherwise it would have reached an early decision, which Britain could have offered to help enforce by providing part of a UN force. That would genuinely have separated the combatants – but would not have given Britain control of the Canal. Instead we had gone to war against Egypt, split the Commonwealth and the country, imperilled all that we claimed to protect, and forfeited our own moral standing in the world at the very moment of the Russians' savage aggression in Hungary. We should at once abandon the invasion, accept the UN's cease-fire resolution and welcome its force on the Arab-Israeli border. But that required a new Prime Minister.[23]

Orthodox Conservatives were enraged by such a broadcast, coming when the troopships were approaching Port Said. To many officers aboard – who alone were allowed to listen – it seemed virtually treasonable. But other people saw it as redeeming Britain's ruined reputation. One Labour MP reported that view from British diplomats in the Middle East; another, in India and Pakistan, was told everywhere that only the broadcast had kept those countries in the Commonwealth. Conor Cruise O'Brien watched it on television in an Irish pub.

A crowd accustomed to be cynical both about politicians and about Englishmen, was deeply moved by Gaitskell's controlled and genuine passion and by his power of argument. Most understood the political and moral courage which it took to make such a speech at such a time. A tram-driver lowered his pint. 'You can't beat an Englishman', he said, 'when he's straight.'[24]

The broadcast delighted the Government's opponents (and was cited for years to justify political talks straight to camera, without tricks). But it was not directed to them, for Gaitskell concluded by appealing again to Conservatives who were also 'shocked and troubled . . . our purpose too . . . rises above party . . . we undertake to support a new Prime Minister in halting the invasion of Egypt, in ordering the cease-fire, and complying with the decisions and recommendations of the United Nations'.[23] The appeal was counter-productive, and rallied waverers to Eden. Gaitskell seems genuinely to have misjudged the likely reaction of the dissident Conservatives. Yet if he had omitted his appeal, the outcome would have been the same. Those unhappy men were alarmed by Eden's policy – but also at the prospect of a general election or a Labour government, to one or both of which the overthrow of Eden must, without Gaitskell's pledge, inevitably have led. To most Conservatives that would have seemed a betrayal of both party and country, and the dissidents naturally shrank from it. They welcomed any excuse to give Eden another chance. Gaitskell provided a pretext by making his appeal – and would have provided another by not making it.

It might well have been otherwise if – as Gaitskell probably hoped – a senior Minister had resigned to lead the revolt and offer troubled Conservatives an alternative leadership. But Monckton decided not to resign, since he neither wanted the Opposition to come to power nor believed in Labour's notion of 'a kind of rump of the Tory Government led by Butler, which they would support. This could not last'.[25] Butler too thought the appeal was specifically addressed to him, and Gaitskell apparently tried to reach him (whether successfully or not is unclear) through PPS channels. (Gaitskell's PPS was to tell Butler's: 'tell your boss that if he intends to strike he must strike now'.) But neither Butler nor his PPS recalled any communication.[26] Butler asked many friends soon afterwards whether he should have resigned; but did not do so.

Plainly the Opposition would have benefited from any change of government in such circumstances – though most people on both sides expected Labour to gain anyway. But no one could have done more than Gaitskell to demonstrate that he opposed the invasion not from party or personal ambition, but from his clear obligation to speak for the horrified half of the British people. His denunciation expressed the political character of a lifetime. As a consistent internationalist, who had founded a schoolboy branch of the League of Nations Union, and made his very first speech against Mussolini's attack on Corfu, he was appalled when his own country was rebuked as an aggressor threatening international order. As a militant democrat, he was furious that its government was helping the Russians escape any political penalty for their outrage in Hungary. As a mature politician who tried to foresee the consequences of his own acts, he was dismayed when others headed straight towards predictable disaster: for Nasser's fall would not have enabled a viable but docile Egyptian government to be formed, or the Canal problem to be solved, or Israel to be made secure, or French rule to be preserved in Algeria.

Suez was one of many episodes in Gaitskell's career showing his characteristic shift from cautious judgement to total, even reckless commitment. The invasion ended any need to discourage Nasser as well as Eden, and any hope of satisfying simultaneously both Labour's militant trade unionists and Jews, and the bulk of the Party. The act of 'criminal folly' imposed a new priority: no longer to warn against the folly but to condemn the crime. The warnings were in retrospect unquestionably justified, the condemnation still remains violently controversial. Gaitskell represented a long British tradition of pacific, often moralising internationalism, which repelled some normal Labour supporters but appealed to many people beyond Labour's ranks. In that tradition, Gladstone had denounced the Bulgarian atrocities and Lloyd George the Boer War; in 1956 there were Conservatives too who took the same side.

Government supporters of course thought Gaitskell's vehement opposition ill-judged, but were silly and petty to assume it concealed party calculation or personal ambition. Yet so they did, the more virulent of them accusing him of time-serving, political cowardice and even treason. Many felt that a Leader of the Opposition, whatever his own doubts, had a duty to hold his peace and support the Government when British troops were going into action. Gaitskell did not share their view, or expect their fury: another instance of weak antennae. But the Government's case was so threadbare and unconvincing that all sections of the PLP, a few Jewish MPs apart, at first applauded his handling of the affair. Still warmer tributes came from those outside the Labour Party for whom he had spoken. Three will suffice. 'Nothing aroused my own contempt more', wrote Sir Edward Boyle, 'than the personal attacks on yourself . . . I don't see how the case against the Government could have been put better than you put it.' Commander King-Hall in his influential *Newsletter* praised the Labour leaders' fulfilment of 'their duty to speak and struggle for a cause greater than any political party issue'. Lady Violet Bonham Carter, Asquith's formidable daughter, sent before the broadcast 'a line of passionate personal gratitude for your magnificent speeches during this week. It was not for your party only you were speaking – you "spoke for England" – for England's *real* & best self.'[27]

## National Humiliation – and Tory Popularity

The high drama intensified over the next few days. On Sunday 4 November 1956 at 2 a.m., the General Assembly passed a resolution to send a UN force to Egypt. Eden, who later claimed credit for the UN action, considered accepting the force provided it included Anglo-French troops – which the Afro-Asians vetoed. By the end of the afternoon the British Government, stiffened by the French, had decided to invade: yet when the paratroops were already on the tarmac with their harnesses on, London was still asking how late it could order a twenty-four-hour delay.

At dawn on Monday 5 November, the troops at last landed. That afternoon the Prime Minister told the House incorrectly that Port Said had fallen. Rightly doubting whether the cease-fire was general, Gaitskell stressed that if so the Government had achieved its ostensible objective of ending the fighting, and should at once withdraw. Israel, like Egypt, now agreed to stop hostilities, depriving Eden of his cherished fig-leaf. So the British Cabinet, to the dismay of the French, halted the operation at midnight on Tuesday (election day in the United States) with the troops still seventy-five miles from Suez. The pound was under pressure, and Washington, by preventing Britain borrowing from the IMF, drove Harold Macmillan – Chancellor of the Exchequer and Eden's strongest supporter – to insist on an immediate cease-fire. Gaitskell spoke that night at the Albert Hall, and the packed audience gave him 'an ovation such as few party leaders can expect even after a great election victory'.[24] At the end the Pakistani High Commissioner came up to him to say: 'Thank God for your speech, you have saved the Commonwealth.'[28]

The next six months showed the humiliating cost of offending the rest of the world by a display of vanished power. In December the British and French troops were withdrawn, after Washington would not let them be used as a bargaining counter for a Canal settlement. Eden, so used to warm bipartisan public approval, suddenly faced bitter attack and the ruin of his policy; his health finally broke under the strain, and after a brief escape to Jamaica he resigned at the New Year. The Conservative kingmakers mysteriously concluded that while Butler's equivocations over Suez disqualified him from the succession,

Macmillan had qualified by advocating with equal ardour first invasion, then cease-fire and withdrawal.

Most people opposed military action beforehand and even at the time; but a plurality, though never a majority, approved of it afterwards. Eden's popularity—like Kennedy's after the Bay of Pigs—grew as his policy visibly collapsed. His frustrated followers eagerly hunted scapegoats. 'The Americans come first with the Labour Party a close second', wrote Gaitskell.[29] The crisis had stirred deep emotions at Westminster, where the House of Commons was more disorderly than for decades. Gaitskell, like all political leaders who condemn the catastrophic military adventures of their governments, met the most virulent hostility. He was accused simultaneously (if inconsistently) both of hysterical revulsion against Eden's policy and of calculated exploitation of it. The first charge was false as well as the second; twenty years later the impression made by his speeches is not of hysteria but of an always courteous tone expressing forceful argument and acute prediction. But he was a sensitive man and by no means impervious to the hatred, which even made him wonder whether his effectiveness as Leader of the Opposition had been permanently impaired.

In the country, Suez did his reputation some harm—though not where he could explain his case in person. He held his own among his own supporters, but lost half his former Conservative admirers; and the number thinking him a bad leader nearly doubled, owing probably to rather non-political people influenced by the newspaper attacks upon him. For Suez had one strange by-product: an extraordinary press campaign praising Bevan at Gaitskell's expense (the Beaverbrook press began it). Yet, far from reviving their conflict, the crisis consolidated their rapprochement, for the former rivals worked harmoniously together throughout. Early in October Bevan intimated that an offer of the shadow foreign secretaryship could lead to a reconciliation—in a private feeler, giving Gaitskell six weeks to respond without loss of face. Gaitskell knew that in both big foreign affairs rows—first the Russian visit, then Suez—Bevan had supported rather than embarrassed him; and Alf Robens, Attlee's choice for the post, had performed disastrously in the September debate. Robens volunteered to resign if the leader wished, and Bevan was chosen to wind up—very successfully—the Suez censure debate on 1 November. So 1956 ended with Bevan as Labour's foreign affairs spokesman.

When Eden resigned, Harold Macmillan took over the leadership of an unhappy party at an unpopular moment, with the Conservatives in a violently anti-American and resentful mood, British foreign policy in ruins, and the economy hard-hit. The new Cabinet seemed so precarious that Macmillan told the Queen it might last only six weeks.[30] In restoring Conservative unity and morale he displayed brilliant political leadership. Yet a government with a majority of sixty could have been brought down only if the Suez Group of Tory rebels had combined with the Labour Opposition, as he himself evidently feared. But Gaitskell knew that the diehards who loathed him would never upset their own government to bring him to power. After the final humiliation in May 1957, when the Government advised British shipping to return to the Canal on Nasser's terms, the Opposition carefully worded their motion to avoid alienating the Suez Group. Yet only fourteen Tories abstained.

The folly of the fire-eaters was thus exposed. The show of military force had demonstrated Britain's political impotence, and in doing so had destroyed a negotiating position which had once been quite strong. Before the invasion Gaitskell had expected to settle the Canal dispute reasonably by talks, for he believed that Nasser's situation was weak and, once Egypt came under economic pressure, time would be on the side of the West. That policy depended on solidarity among the users and goodwill in the United States: assets which the fire-eaters had dissipated by May 1957. But in the previous autumn it might have succeeded. Gaitskell was not making reliance on the UN a substitute for a British policy. He always saw the UN as a useful forum for negotiations, but it was only after the invasion took place that he insisted on compliance with UN resolutions. By then Eden's folly had changed the problem, lost any chance of a satisfactory settlement, and destroyed British influence in the region as Nasser could never have done: in Kenneth Younger's words, 'No one wants her backing . . . and no one asks her views.'[31]

Suez was Britain's last imperial fling, both displaying and accelerating her decline. In default of the military power she could no longer wield, Britain might still have exercised considerable political influence; Suez undermined it both in the Middle East and generally. The Government's policy thus led swiftly to the total disaster Gaitskell had foreseen. But the blunder was advantageous to its perpetrators (Eden apart), and as Macmillan rightly judged after the debate of May 1957, his government was secure for the rest of that Parliament.

# 16
# Into Partnership with Bevan
# 1956–7

'. . . *an almost pathetic anxiety to lead the party in whatever direction it wishes to be led*'
(Tory journalist on HG, 1957)

## Nationalisation: 'Industry and Society'

When Harold Macmillan became Prime Minister in January 1957, the crisis within the Conservative Party was acute. He was brilliantly successful at keeping his followers loyal by soothing their prejudices, adopting a studied traditional manner, and facing away from the direction in which he meant to go. Before long, Harold Wilson was admiring his skill at holding up the banner of Suez while leading the retreat. Gaitskell, in contrast, was 'disdainful of Macmillan's fondness for doing everything behind a smokescreen';[1] that contempt perhaps helped shift his own political stance after his 1959 defeat. But in his first Parliament the style baffled and infuriated him.

During these early years of leadership, Gaitskell gave priority to conciliation within his own party. He was active preparing the three-year programme of policy statements, working through the National Executive. Where the Labour Party usually tears itself apart over plans for its next government – and so reduces its chance of implementing them – these statements were endorsed in an unusual atmosphere of concord. But as Gaitskell wrote in 1961: 'If there is one thing that the 1959 General Election result shows, it is surely that unity is not enough.'[2] That defeat was to put at risk all his patient efforts to reunite the Party.

Gaitskell was not at his best in the House in the early months of 1957, and slipped back within the Party. Enjoying the psychological advantage of every Prime Minister, Macmillan used mocking badinage or wounding disdain to provoke the derisive back-bench jeering which made Gaitskell wonder if he should continue. But fortunately Bevan had decided to settle for influence rather than status, and to give priority to the common purpose of ousting the Tories. He made those priorities clear at Labour's 1957 conference, over both nationalisation and nuclear disarmament. His decision that co-operation was both necessary and tolerable was indispensable to Gaitskell's success.

The expected early election reinforced the pressure for unity, on which Gaitskell could play thanks to his ability, essential to anyone trying to lead and educate the Labour Movement, to feel, and be felt to be, part of it – at once the class-mate and the invisible tutor'.[3] As the party conference met at Brighton, one political correspondent condemned Gaitskell for 'an almost pathetic anxiety to lead the party in whatever direction it wishes to be led'. As the conference ended, another said that he had in two years 'transformed Labour's policy in all essentials to Gaitskellism . . . Brighton has left him with his personal authority at its peak.'[4]

The main domestic disagreement was on public ownership, about which Gaitskell's ideas were worked out by 1953, and set out in *Socialism and Nationalisation* in 1956; very similar views were more thoroughly developed by Anthony Crosland. Frank Cousins and Aneurin Bevan stood with Gaitskell, who was opposed by Herbert Morrison and the right-wing intellectuals of *Socialist Commentary*.

Gaitskell thought the main contemporary role for public ownership was to generate investment resources to replace those diminished by redistributive taxation: either by nationalisation, or by new competitive state enterprises, or by buying up particular firms, or expanding nationalised industries into new fields. It could contribute to equality if the state acquired shares in lieu of death duties or through a capital levy or simply through purchase, so that the community benefited from the mounting capital gains. All these ideas appeared in the Party's new policy statement, *Industry and Society*. It was drafted by a very representative working party, and the National Executive accepted it unanimously.

The policy was imprecise, facing in all directions and hoping to please all sides: precisely the kind of intellectually inglorious but politically convenient compromise of which Gaitskell was later supposed incapable. The document promised, ambiguously, 'to extend public ownership in any industry or part of industry which, after thorough enquiry, is found to be seriously failing the nation'. In the words of *Socialist Commentary*, it gave the Party 'a mandate to do about public ownership whatever it may happen to like when it is returned to office.'[5] Thirty-two trade union MPs wrote a critical letter to one Labour journal and Herbert Morrison attacked the document in another. Then, with NEC elections due shortly, Barbara Castle and Ian

Mikardo discovered that the policy they had approved was another betrayal of Socialism by the right-wing leadership. Gaitskell told Crossman: 'if they can't stand by a document which they have helped to draft in the National Executive, he wouldn't trust them in a Cabinet'.[6]

Inevitably, the Left assumed that Gaitskell's only aim was to bury public ownership. They were wrong. All his associates privately favoured nationalisation for one industry or another: and Gaitskell himself, though cautious about going beyond the agreed line, privately agreed over aircraft and chemicals, and publicly spoke of it for 'machine tools and perhaps aircraft production'.[7] His real aim was to secure a reasonably free hand without provoking a split, to conceal the differences of purpose behind an acceptable formula, and to defuse a divisive issue. After the policy was safely adopted he wrote:

Candidly, I doubt whether the public ownership plan is a positive and saleable proposition. I look on the whole thing rather in a negative way. If we had gone wrong here we could have lost millions of votes. Our positive attraction to the electorate is going to be far more through superannuation, housing and education.[8]

At the party conference at Brighton, flat rejection of the document was moved by Jim Campbell, general secretary of the NUR – then a moderately left-wing union. But Bevan undermined the critics by refusing to associate with them, and by conspicuously applauding Gaitskell's speech. Privately, he told Gaitskell he did not want a 'shopping list'; and he helped to persuade Cousins not to oppose on principle. Harold Wilson proposed the document from the platform. Morrison's attack on it was backed by the equally disgruntled Shinwell. Gaitskell in reply again underlined that the statement did not preclude further 'old-style' nationalisation. Cousins told Crossman he was satisfied, and the policy was carried by 5,309,000 to 1,276,000 – with half the constituency parties voting for it, and only one big union (the NUR) against. 'Shopping list' nationalisation had been buried for a long time.

Gaitskell had devised a policy which Wilson proposed, Bevan commended, *Tribune* accepted then repudiated, Morrison and *Socialist Commentary* denounced, and on which many years later Tony Benn founded his new model Socialism. Depending on the political and economic circumstances in which it was introduced, everyone could hope to deflect it in his own direction. Gaitskell did not despise such devices to keep his coalition together, and could afford them when his leadership was secure. He was to discover in the next election that the price paid for them was high, and after it that the unity bought by them was short-lived.

## The Bomb at Brighton: 'Naked into the Conference Chamber'

For the Labour Party, defence always provoked even sharper disagreement than nationalisation, especially in the nuclear age. In 1957 the Conservatives were no more united on it. A new Defence Minister, Duncan Sandys, adopted a strategy of total reliance on the nuclear deterrent, sweetened by ending conscription; he claimed that volunteers would suffice, which his predecessor denied. Another senior Minister, Lord Salisbury, resigned when the Archbishop of Cyprus was released from detention; the Prime Minister, worried about the coming capitulation over Suez, wrote privately, 'What a blessing he went over Makarios!'[9] But the vigilant press was more concerned with exposing ideological splits in the Opposition.

In 1955 Attlee had dodged the issue of the H-bomb: he favoured making it, opposed testing it. The price of that absurd compromise had now to be paid. In March 1957, Britain announced a series of tests at Christmas Island. The health hazards were just becoming known, and the Labour Party was thrown into turmoil. Labour's defence specialists saw no point in making a bomb which could not be tested, but many others were appalled that Britain too should poison the atmosphere and perhaps spark off more tests by other countries. On Monday 1 April the House debated Macmillan's wide-ranging talks with President Eisenhower in Bermuda, intended to restore the relationship shattered by Suez. The Prime Minister skilfully diverted attention from Salisbury's resignation two days earlier (which he did not even mention) and from Suez (so contentious within his own party) to the nuclear issue. His long statement minimised the health dangers; and he challenged Gaitskell to say whether in office Labour would stop the tests, abandon the bomb, and so accept both permanent conscription and military inferiority against Russia. Inhibited by the division in his own ranks, Gaitskell replied that only a government could decide but that Labour would not unilaterally stop tests.

A week later he wrote privately: 'I blame myself for not understanding sooner how strong the feeling in the Party was.'[10] For the PLP was deeply troubled, and Gaitskell knew he could command only a small majority. Christopher Mayhew proposed a compromise which the Shadow Cabinet recommended: to call for a temporary suspension of the British tests while appealing to the super-powers to cancel theirs.

The plan – a precursor of the 'non-nuclear club' – was approved by acclamation. Gaitskell wrote candidly to a friend:

The H-Bomb is an almost impossible subject for us . . . It is impossible to reach a real logical conclusion without splitting the Party. So I am afraid we just have to go on with compromises of the kind we had last week. It is perfectly clear that the Party much prefers this . . . to . . . a resumption of the trouble of a few years ago and . . . they are perfectly right.[11]

Gaitskell was as conciliatory in 1957 as he was to be combative in 1960. But the sequel shows that the later and far more serious conflict could not have been fudged with a formula. Conservative morale revived and Labour's declined. Opposition MPs became more critical of their leader and Government back-benchers more enthusiastic for theirs. Crossman wrote: 'That debate turned out to be the moment when [Macmillan] consolidated his leadership and stopped the collapse of the Tory Government . . . the beginning of the turn of the tide for the Tories.'[12] Outside the Westminster hothouse, the Gallup poll found increased Labour support for testing and a 10 per cent jump in approval for Macmillan.

Never a unilateralist, Bevan discovered in September 1957, in long talks with Khrushchev in the Crimea, that British renunciation of the H-bomb would make no difference to the Russians. He returned to Britain just in time for the party conference. At Brighton over the weekend he tried in vain to get the unilateralists' motion modified, believing both that if a Labour government came to power he could help to check the proliferation of nuclear weapons, and that a unilateralist party could never win an election.[13]

Bevan's decision at Brighton entailed no renunciation of his former principles (though that did not save him from bitter and furious reproaches from his old admirers). When replying to the debate, he spoke of sending the next Foreign Secretary 'naked into the conference chamber . . . to preach sermons . . . Do it now as a Labour Party Conference? You cannot do it now . . . All you can do is pass a resolution [and create] a diplomatic shambles . . . you call that statesmanship? I call it an emotional spasm.'[14] The resolution was massively defeated by 5,836,000 to 781,000, and Crossman summed up this

monumentally successful Conference . . . the Bevan-Gaitskell axis . . . is now securely and publicly established . . . [they] have strengthened their position with the electorate at large by curbing the Party extremists . . . Seen from the inside, it has, of course, been a complete victory for Hugh.[15]

Gaitskell himself wrote to a friend: 'Naturally, I am very happy about the whole thing . . . it could scarcely have gone better.'[8]

# 17

# Macmillan Ascendant
## 1957–9

*'The Labour Party needed a tranquilliser. He provided one.*
*But . . . now . . . a tonic is needed'*
(Labour journalist, 1957)

*'Mr. Gaitskell is . . . going through all the motions of being a Government*
*when he isn't a Government. It is bad enough having to behave like a*
*Government when one is a Government'*
(Harold Macmillan, 1959)

*'Our party decisions are not dictated by one man – whether the*
*leader . . . or the general secretary of the T&GWU'*
(HG, 1959)

## Labour's Precarious Unity

In domestic affairs, Gaitskell as Opposition leader faced a dilemma in 1957–8. The Government was resisting wage claims in the public sector. If he defended the unions, he would risk his public support; if he opposed them he would alienate many of his own followers – above all Frank Cousins, the new leader of the largest union in the country, which included the London busmen who were in dispute. The Opposition rightly suspected that senior Ministers and Conservative back-benchers both welcomed the conflict: the Minister of Labour Iain Macleod had indeed been overruled, for the Prime Minister privately thought that 'nothing could suit us better' than a strike.[1] Since the busmen could not win, Cousins was opposed to calling one. But he would not defy the busmen's leaders: a course that seemed democratic to him, but which the General Council saw as an abdication of responsibility.

Gaitskell knew the strike was bound to fail when the General Council disapproved of it. Yet he knew also that Cousins had and the Cabinet had not tried to avert it, and privately thought them both to blame;[2] and he valued Cousins's goodwill for an expansionist government of the future. He criticised the Government's handling of the dispute at Glasgow on May Day weekend, and the Shadow Cabinet decided upon a censure motion. That was imprudent, for Cousins was not a popular figure. Macleod saw an opportunity, and theatrically proclaimed his 'scorn and contempt' for Gaitskell's Glasgow speech.[3] Though Gaitskell replied effectively, he was vulnerable because of his current reputation as a leader too preoccupied with the Party's internal problems; and the ground thus lost in the House could not be regained in the country since the strike was doomed to failure. Gaitskell knew that he had suffered: 'we lost a lot by supporting the strike and got no kudos within the TUC because they hate Cousins'.[4] Indeed, Macmillan believed that his government's recovery in the country dated from the defeat of the strike.

Gaitskell was an unrepentant Keynesian, influenced by his experience in office, who remained confident that inflation need not be the price of economic expansion. In 1958 the stop-go cycle was new, and he believed that the Conservatives had repeatedly mismanaged the economy. Just before the bus strike, he arranged a party political broadcast intended to show that Labour and the unions could agree that higher wages should match productivity so that they were not eroded by inflation.

Later that year at the Scarborough Conference, the major union leaders warmly commended the Party's economic policies. Cousins thanked Gaitskell handsomely for his support in the bus strike, and obscurely blessed the policy. Gaitskell wound up the debate: 'we shall not attempt a wage-freeze, but we do not want a wages spree either . . . our policy can create a climate in which the unions would . . . work with the Labour Government so that [real] wages and productivity go up together'.[5]

Labour's new unity was sealed at Scarborough, where on Sunday at the pre-Conference rally Bevan gave a famous pledge: 'The movement should realise that the leadership of the Party has been settled and the gossip should stop. Hugh Gaitskell is there, elected by the Party, and he commands the loyalty of us all.'[6] Gaitskell won his tribute from Frank Cousins, and his biggest conference ovation so far. That week transformed the mood, and the delegates departed 'in much better heart than even an optimist could reasonably have expected'.[7]

Gaitskell's leadership was thus unquestioned. It was an extraordinary transformation, and with Bevan's indispensable help he had accomplished it in a very short time. There was no serious conflict over the new, detailed policies hammered out during his first three years as leader; Denis Healey and Sydney Silverman were even able to celebrate their agreement on foreign policy. But to avoid alienating either Labour enthusiasts or floating voters, the domestic policy statements too often reflected Gaitskell's 'painstaking compromises'. They were quite sensible, but made no public impact. An independent Conservative journal wrote of:

the shifty appearance given by the party's *persona*. In trying to bring the disparate elements of the Left into a coherent party, capable of offering a stable alternative government, Mr. Gaitskell can claim to have been surprisingly successful; but the end-result is unappetising . . . in the process of trimming its sails to catch what few fitful breezes are now blowing it has lost its soul.

This is not the fault of its leader. Mr. Gaitskell was appointed Lord Attlee's successor to do a job which, in the main, he has succeeded in doing: fusing the party's discordant elements.[8]

## Doldrums of Affluence

The Labour Party was enjoying an interlude of comparative peace, in which most commentators agreed that Gaitskell seemed in his style of leadership, as a sympathetic Labour journalist put it, 'the passive instrument of an instinct for survival within the Labour movement – the reflection and symbol of a need to compromise . . . the Labour Party needed a tranquilliser. He provided one. But . . . now . . . a tonic is needed.'[9] Yet the party worker's tonic might repel the uncommitted voter. The Conservatives were not popular, but Gaitskell's personal rating was also unimpressive; Liberals not Labour were benefiting from the Government's unpopularity. Grumbling about Gaitskell's leadership was no longer on Left-Right lines, but reflected the volatile moods of politicians bored with opposition in a dull and listless Parliament.

Part of the leader's task which Gaitskell originally found awkward was the Party's organised provincial tours. But though ill at ease at first, he soon became less aloof, finding the tours a refreshing escape from the Westminster hothouse, and welcoming contacts with the ordinary people who kept the constituency organisations going. These visits helped – though a more flamboyant man might have done more – to remedy his old problem that his personality had made little mark in the country. For that purpose television, though still a novelty, was already the principal medium. Gaitskell took endless trouble to master the technique, welcoming television exposure because 'the image people have of me [from] Tory propaganda – has hitherto been pretty different from my real character. I long to say . . . how the Press always tries to make one either inhuman or too human whereas in fact one is merely human.'[2] But he was not corrupted. To one adviser on broadcasting, Gaitskell wrote: 'Of course, I wholly agree with what you say both about my not changing my public personality (you need not worry about this – I would not tolerate anything of the kind) and also about the much more profound dangers in the techniques of public persuasion.'[10]

In the House, Gaitskell paid a price for his rapid rise. The Conservative whips noticed that on parliamentary business he was much less able than Attlee to commit his followers to decisions they would accept. The withdrawal or disaffection of many leading veterans proved a severe handicap. Because he lacked influential colleagues with solid backing in the Parliamentary Party, the weight of leadership fell very heavily on Gaitskell's own shoulders. In crises, therefore, he had neither time to consult nor powerful associates to deliver solid support. *The Times* political correspondent pointed out:

> Mr. Gaitskell cannot lead his party by economically winning over, or falling into line with, lieutenants who would bring their troops with them. More than any of his predecessors, he has to win over the party as a whole, and that is difficult and laborious work in a sudden crisis that sets the rank and file in turmoil.
>
> How often Mr. Gaitskell must pray for the boon of a second Ernest Bevin.[11]

In spite of Dalton's purge, the Shadow Cabinet was still elderly and uninspiring. Able men left politics in frustration, and few of those who stayed seemed to share the leader's undoubted will to win. In terms of parliamentary tactics, some Labour initiatives were unwise, and Macleod told a Tory rally: 'Mr. Gaitskell, leading his party with all the dedicated drive of a bumble bee, is a jewel beyond price for us.'[12]

The Prime Minister was particularly effective at exploiting Gaitskell's difficulties, playing on the Conservatives' distaste for him by offensive and wounding phrases. Relations were bad between the two men, who seemed to typify the political 'bishop' and the political 'bookmaker', and who at this period had no mutual respect. Gaitskell thought that Macmillan 'cheated at politics',[13] and trusted the Prime Minister so little that he tried to avoid meeting except in the presence of the Liberal leader Jo Grimond. Macmillan thought Gaitskell tiresomely stuffy and 'responsible': 'The trouble about Mr. Gaitskell is that he is going through all the motions of being a Government when he isn't a Government . . . The whole point of being in opposition is that one can have fun and . . . be colourful.'[14]

The Prime Minister was not only a splendid performer on the screen, but also enjoyed the appurtenances of power and the sympathy of the press – which praised him (and later Wilson) for the skill in party management for which Gaitskell was condemned, and gave the Prime Minister six times as many news stories as his adversary. In the opinion polls, Macmillan was rated a good Prime Minister by over half the respondents. Labour supporters stayed loyal to Gaitskell, but in the whole electorate only 40 per cent thought him a good leader, and a Tory paper wrote that Macmillan 'outshines Mr. Gaitskell as a lighthouse does a glow-worm'.[15] From October 1958 to September 1959, the Conservatives scored at least 38 per cent in nine polls out of twelve while Labour (which had never dropped below that level from losing office in 1951 to the beginning of 1958) attained it only once.

Gaitskell privately expected a small Labour majority until early in the spring of 1959. He gave a simple answer to one common complaint:

I certainly would like a sharper differentiation in the public mind between ourselves and the Tories so long, of course, as this is to our electoral advantage and not to the contrary. The Tories undoubtedly try to blur the distinction whenever they think we produce proposals which are popular . . . [and] try to sharpen the distinction when they think our policy is unpopular.[16]

To another criticism he replied:

the way we present our policy must be geared to the need to win over marginal voters (if we did not do this we should not be worthy of our jobs) . . . [but] we are [not] just concerned with vote-catching . . . the Labour Party is [no] more or less respectable today than when I first joined it over thirty years ago. It is . . . no longer a pioneering minority. But it is still inspired by the same ideals . . . in which for my part I still whole-heartedly believe.[17]

Then, in that election summer, Gaitskell's achievement in reuniting his quarrelsome followers began to fray, just as Macmillan had hoped, over the great issue of nuclear weapons.[18]

## CND, and the Challenge from Cousins

The H-bomb was an awesome problem which was to change the course of Labour politics. In 1957, after the Brighton Conference, Gaitskell had discouraged moves to specify Labour's attitude, writing: 'It is really quite impossible in opposition, and on the limited information available, to work out a detailed defence policy.'[19] He knew that the 1957 compromise was no substitute for a policy: 'I have never regarded the suspension of H-bomb tests as more than a starting point. Obviously, the main problem is getting an agreement on nuclear weapon production.'[20] But he hoped to avoid either firm commitments or bitter arguments over matters which might look quite different when serious decisions needed to be taken. That hope proved untenable when the bomb evoked the greatest and most sustained movement of public opinion in post-war Britain.

At New Year 1958, Anthony Greenwood, with Gaitskell's warm encouragement, attended a private meeting – which launched the Campaign for Nuclear Disarmament. At Easter 1959, Frank Cousins was spotted in Trafalgar Square at the end of the CND march. Then on 4 June the annual conference of the most loyal and cautious of unions, the NUGMW, voted for a unilateral British ban on the manufacture or use of the H-bomb. The result was perhaps accidental, and in August it was reversed. But it revived the public dispute over defence policy and set off or speeded up a flurry of political activity. For changes in the international situation were already affecting Gaitskell's attitude, and the Labour Party National Executive was already considering a TUC request for further talks. The NUGMW resolution made a new policy more urgent, and a British moral initiative more politically desirable. Technical and political developments both pointed to the 'non-nuclear club' idea, which Gaitskell had never ruled out.

That idea was the germ of the future non-proliferation treaty. Britain was to promise to give up her own bombs if all other countries, excepting the two super-powers, agreed not to make or acquire them. Gaitskell, though sceptical at first, had carefully avoided a public commitment against it at the Scarborough Conference; and the risk of new countries acquiring nuclear weapons had grown rapidly since. On 24 June Labour's support for the non-nuclear club was announced at a press conference.

Cousins was thoroughly sceptical. Gaitskell, Bevan and Brown all spent hours with him trying in vain to bring him round to it, though Gaitskell was sure that Labour's conference would approve the new policy whatever Cousins did. Finally the two men tried once more to agree in an exchange of confidential letters shown to no one else. But Cousins was not to be appeased, and the T&GWU's biennial delegate conference in the Isle of Man opposed official policy on both nationalisation and defence, specifically rejecting the non-nuclear club. The leader was not surprised, believing that 'Cousins was a demagogue . . . throwing his weight about so that he could make his power felt . . . anxious to show his strength.'[21] Gaitskell knew that the country would resent a union leader seeking to change the defence policy of the alternative government. To defy Cousins would therefore help Labour electorally; and Macmillan knew that too.

Gaitskell replied on 11 July 1959 before a hundred people in a cold wind at Workington. He admitted that other countries might not join the non-nuclear club, but said the best chance was now, before they had made bombs and acquired stocks. The unilateralists must decide whether or not they intended Britain to stay in NATO. If not, their policy was honest but 'escapist, blind and positively dangerous to the peace of the world'. If so, then we must play our part loyally. He also met Cousins's challenge directly:

The problems of international relations . . . will not be solved by slogans, however loudly declaimed, or by effervescent emotion, however genuine . . . our Party decisions on these matters are not dictated by one man whether he be the Leader of the Party, our spokesman on Foreign Affairs, or the General Secretary of the Transport & General Workers' Union. They are made collectively . . . we should argue out and settle ultimately in our Conference the great issues of policy. But it is not right that a future Labour Government should be committed by Conference decisions one way or the other on every matter of detail for all time . . . A Labour Government will take into account the views of the Conference . . . but Annual Conference does not mandate a Government . . . This has always been understood in the past, and it must be clearly understood again today.[22]

A week later he was asked on the BBC: 'suppose the Conference carried a resolution in favour of unilateral nuclear disarmament, a tremendous issue of policy, would not that bind a future Labour Government?' He replied: 'I think that would, yes.'[23] He was not asked whether he would lead a Labour government so bound, and commentators assumed he would not.

Cousins was a decent, honest man with passionate convictions about the bomb, and an uncomplicated faith in traditional Socialist ideas. For two years he had gone slow on both issues in the interests of party unity. Yet now he dramatically broke with the leadership on both questions, only a few weeks before a general election. Some of his personal characteristics were peculiarly antipathetic to Gaitskell: a muddled mind, a tendency to self-deception, a reluctance to face the unwelcome implications of his own actions. He convinced himself, and told his union delegates, that his own three main points had already been put forward as Labour Party policy. (That was quite untrue.) He would not admit the consequences of his policy either for defence or for the Party. He denied that it entailed leaving a nuclear-armed NATO, and refused to say whether he would wish America to renounce nuclear weapons when Russia had not done so. He insisted that he was not splitting the Party; and when reminded that Gaitskell and Bevan would resign if they lost at Conference, he replied confidently, 'That has nothing to do with the issue at all.'[24]

By the beginning of 1959 this powerful, awkward, insecure man was feeling isolated and harried. The London bus strike had been a costly disaster. His General Council colleagues distrusted, feared and even hated him. Influenced by Michael Foot, he muttered privately that he might 'break with them [the parliamentary leaders] for good and teach them a lesson';[25] and he and especially his wife complained of not seeing enough of the Gaitskells socially. In his new mood, Cousins accepted all the old suspicions of Gaitskell's motives – and not only over defence. The 1959 T&GWU conference unanimously rejected the policy of *Industry and Society*, calling for old-fashioned nationalisation instead; 'You are a good Socialist', Cousins was told in a telegram from Shinwell and even from Morrison, who were showing a sudden new enthusiasm for the old policy. His own switch on nationalisation reflected his disillusionment over defence, where he had grounds for resenting the way the new compromise had suddenly been formulated, and apparently (like the suspicious Left) saw it as a hypocritical device for clinging to the British bomb, relying on France to ensure that the non-nuclear club was never born. As Crossman lamented, Michael Foot was now calling

for a fight to the death and the campaign to go on throughout the election . . . [although] only a fortnight ago, he regarded the non-nuclear club as a real advance. But, as so often happens, anything which is accepted by the Establishment becomes unacceptable to the opposition within the Labour party . . . At least these two [Gaitskell and Bevan] have faced the issue with intellectual honesty and have worked out what is pretty well the best policy they can. What is depressing is that they get no credit from their closest colleagues or from the Left for doing so.[26]

It was a special case of a Labour leader's perennial problem – how to appeal to his own enthusiastic followers without alienating the rest of the country. Gaitskell had been accused, in venomous personal attacks which did great harm both to the Party and to him, of giving way to pressure over Suez. He had to guard against allowing that charge to be revived. Moreover, he knew that the Left would accept no compromise for long, while he would pay a high price elsewhere for conciliating them momentarily; and when they revived the quarrel, it would be harder to defend the essential positions from which he would not shift. Above all, neither he nor Bevan would allow a powerful union leader to determine government policy.

Cousins now felt that his Socialist conscience required him to use his power as Deakin had, but for ends he saw as better ones. His duty was to prod the laggard leadership, and theirs was to attend to him. But Deakin had expected the leaders of the Party to lay down policy and had then offered his staunch support for it; his successor was trying to invoke his power as a trade unionist to insist on a change of defence policy by the alternative government of the country.

Gaitskell too had strong convictions on the issue. He too had other motives: he believed as in 1951 that he was in a struggle for power; his leadership might be threatened or nullified by concessions interpreted as weakness; and appeasement of Cousins would shock public opinion and gravely damage the Party. But above all he thought appeasement wrong in principle. Gaitskell did not interfere with the way the unions were run, and expected their leaders to leave the politicians to formulate policy: especially when he believed the stakes were the security of the country, and perhaps the prospects of peace.

After three years of uniting the Party by conciliatory leadership, he now surprised many commentators and colleagues by demonstrating, on the very eve of the election, that there were concessions he would never make. It was a risky decision. Henry Fairlie, an old admirer turned critical, was impressed. 'Mr. Gaitskell has grown in the past year. He is assured and confident and fit for power.'[27]

# 18

# Turning Point: The 1959 Election

---

*'The 1959 election shows that . . . unity is not enough'*
(HG, 1961)

---

## The Prelude: Foreign Affairs

As the election approached, the prospect of power seemed to recede. In the spring of 1959 the Conservative leader underlined his chosen theme of 'Peace and Prosperity' by adroitly removing Labour's most popular cards: economic expansionism, European disengagement, and Summit talks among the Great Powers. Symbolising a sudden new flexibility in British foreign policy, Macmillan visited Moscow in February 1959 wearing a white fur hat to delight cartoonists. In April 1959 'the most cautious of Chancellors was responsible for the most generous Budget ever . . . an object lesson in the dangers of trying to go too fast'.[1] In July Cousins issued his challenge; and in August Eisenhower arranged his European tour to give his ally the maximum help and news coverage. Rejection at the polls might, as Gaitskell knew all too well, jeopardise his leadership of the Party. For many of his colleagues were 'carefully preparing their positions to blame others for the defeat' if it came.[2]

When Macmillan dissolved Parliament, his rival was in the Soviet Union, for Gaitskell was a great traveller. Always fascinated by the problems of foreign countries, he felt particularly at home in the United States, where all his life he had a powerful appeal (not confined to the liberal Democrats to whom he felt closest). His other favourite country was Yugoslavia; and he also kept a strong interest in relations with the New Commonwealth. In the Socialist International, too, he was much more active than any previous or subsequent Labour leader.

His long-planned visit to the USSR was fixed, after many delays, for the end of August 1959. Dora, Aneurin Bevan, the Healeys and a few others accompanied him. As always, Gaitskell's greatest impact was face to face. After their three days in Leningrad their escort (a local party leader) told Edna Healey: 'You know, I'd never seen Mr. Gaitskell or met him; I've read a lot about him; I know now that he's a really good man – that he wants the sort of things that I want.'[3] One day, they returned to their Moscow hotel to be told that Macmillan had announced the election for 8 October. They flew straight back to London, where Gaitskell had an electoral briefing in the VIP gents' at Heathrow.[4]

## *The Campaign: United We Fall*

The 1959 election gave the Conservatives their biggest post-war victory, and began the break-up of the two-party United Kingdom. For the first time for thirty years the Liberals gained votes. Labour made progress in Scotland and Lancashire while declining elsewhere, and won over middle-class voters while its working-class supporters were falling away. It was also especially striking in the disjunction between the campaign and the results, with the apparent trend reversed at the very end. Conventional wisdom was upset. Normally the campaign benefits the party in office; only in 1959 did the Opposition gain. Normally enthusiasm among party workers is said to bring out stay-at-home voters; in 1959 enthusiasm was exceptional among Labour activists, but the marginal electors defected. Normally the Conservative effort is the better organised; only in 1959 was it clearly outclassed.

Gaitskell was directly responsible both for the main blunder of that campaign, and for its general appeal. Normally, failure at the polls undermines the standing of a party leader. But his performance was so universally acclaimed that he enhanced his reputation even in defeat.

When Parliament rose on 30 July, he expected to begin in six or seven weeks the election campaign which might carry him into Downing Street. It formally opened nine days after his return from the USSR – just in time to appear on television on his first night back, rescuing a disastrous party political broadcast. Next morning he spoke to the TUC at Blackpool, using it as a spring-board for his campaign. A week later came Labour's first election broadcast, on which his chief opponent wrote: 'The Socialists had a very successful TV last night – much better than ours. Gaitskell is becoming very expert.'[5]

Unlike Attlee, Gaitskell carefully prepared his major speeches for his gruelling campaign trip: fifty meetings in eleven days, which drew enormous crowds and a passionate response. At Labour headquarters Crossman, the campaign committee chairman, recorded:

The Gaitskell boom has been rapidly swelling. How strange political leadership is! . . . I can watch the godhead emerging from the man . . . The leader emerges from the husk of the ordinary politician . . . Up till a week ago it was assumed that a Labour defeat would all be blamed on Gaitskell and the Labour propaganda. Now Gaitskell is superb in the public eye, and second only to Gaitskell is the brilliance of the Labour propaganda.[6]

Transport House began to believe they could win; and among Conservatives who suddenly saw the election slipping from their grasp were the Prime Minister, the Chief Whip, and the previous and current party chairmen.

Gaitskell spoke mainly on domestic problems, knowing that a sceptical electorate had to be convinced of the practicability of Labour's policies. At Birmingham on Saturday 26 September 1959 he contrasted the Tories' present caution with Butler's boast before the last election of doubling the standard of living in twenty-five years. That, said Gaitskell, was quite a practicable aim if the economy expanded steadily so that a Labour Chancellor could count on substantial extra revenue. The speech had an excellent reception, and that night Gaitskell told Roy Jenkins he expected to win.

Now Gaitskell learned – or thought he did – of a forthcoming massive Conservative scare that Labour would increase income tax by 2*s.* 6*d.* (12½p.) in the pound. Urged by John Harris, and without informing the campaign committee (though he did consult his Shadow Chancellor), Gaitskell promised at Newcastle on the Monday night that in normal peacetime conditions a Labour government would not increase the rates of income tax. The Conservatives pounced at once. Macmillan challenged Gaitskell to extend the pledge – 'queer for an ex-Chancellor' – to other taxes. Then, at the daily Transport House press conference on 1 October, a journalist picked up an old handout saying Labour would reduce purchase tax on essentials – and Morgan Phillips told him that it was indeed a Labour Party commitment. Gaitskell was furious, and it gave him his one sleepless night of the campaign. For the income tax pledge was now clearly transformed into a liability, fuelling the raging fire of Tory criticism of Labour's and his own orgy of mass bribery.

Gaitskell had taken no sudden decision to turn the election into an auction. The financial arguments, like the policies themselves, had been put forward for years and had never produced the slightest reaction. In the 1955 campaign Gaitskell already claimed that expansion would provide the extra revenue for domestic reforms. In January 1959, before the Budget, he was publicly hoping both to carry out reforms and to reduce income tax. After it was cut in the Budget, he again said publicly that over a full Parliament the programme could be paid for without putting taxes up again.

He had calculated the costs with his usual thoroughness. His fault was naivety not cunning. He knew himself to be a man of integrity, and believed the public knew it too; so he thought he could enhance Labour's credibility by staking his own high financial reputation. Stop-go was new, and politicians were not yet derided for thinking they could manage the economy better than their opponents; Gaitskell certainly believed what he said. Indeed his failure to foresee the storm was partly because he had said the same so often before without trouble. But a pledge from the prospective Prime Minister at the height of an election was bound to have a vast resonance, and a politician of his experience should have foreseen how it could be exploited by his opponents. His antennae had failed him badly.

Politicians on both sides instantly saw it as a big mistake. The Transport House professionals thought at once that the election was lost. The Conservatives' counter-attack now concentrated on Gaitskell himself, for his performance in the campaign had finally convinced them that he not Bevan should be their target. Labour were now suffering for failing to publicise their policies before the campaign began. Far from being last-minute bribes to catch votes, the pensions increase, the redistribution of purchase tax and the argument that revenue would expand with the economy were all themes sounded for years. Yet the attacks on them revived many latent doubts and suspicions. Most Labour candidates felt that the tax pledge did harm. Gaitskell himself came to think that, while the Conservatives would have won anyway, it had been 'a very grave mistake' and had probably brought them their increased majority.[7] Others on both sides (including Lord Butler) thought it made no difference and prosperity was decisive. The opinion polls showed that the Don't Knows went steadily up and the Conservative lead steadily down until the final weekend; but quite likely the doubtfuls would never in a time of affluence have risked voting Labour, and the pledges merely gave them a pretext for playing safe.

Gaitskell had begun the campaign thinking victory unlikely. But by the final Sunday, when he learned of the coming Gallup findings showing the major parties neck and neck, he felt confident, and that night he wrote out his Cabinet list. He spent the last days in South Leeds, where, in a three-cornered fight, he had a smaller share of a higher poll and a majority down by 500:

| | |
|---|---:|
| Hugh Gaitskell (Lab.) | 24,442 |
| John Addey (Cons.) | 12,956 |
| J. B. Meeks (Lib.) | 4,340 |
| Majority | 11,486 |

At the local count in Leeds Town Hall, John Harris gave him the gloomy news – that the Conservatives had won, and by a bigger majority. At 1 a.m. he conceded the election in an unprecedented gesture that infuriated Aneurin Bevan. It was the worst disappointment of Gaitskell's public life, a profound shock very deeply felt. Yet the grace with which he swallowed the bitter pill earned him immense credit from admirers and opponents alike. Indeed it was at the moment of defeat that Gaitskell's personality most impressed the country, and established his claim to national authority.

## The Inquest: 'Irreproachable and Unassailable'

For the first time in a mass electorate, a political party had gained seats at four successive elections and won a majority in three successive normal parliaments. The pendulum had stopped, and the uncommitted voter evidently recoiled from electing a Labour government. Worse: defections were greatest among the young. Labour had only 10 per cent of middle-class people aged 18–24, while 35 per cent of working-class youngsters preferred the Tories. In private Gaitskell did not pretend it was a minor setback, but saw the causes as deep-rooted. Everyone agreed on the principal reason: it had been a safety-first vote. Labour's gains came only from Scotland and industrial Lancashire, with their high unemployment. Elsewhere, Conservatives still received credit for affluence, and in the prosperous South and Midlands, 'Don't let Labour ruin it' was a potent slogan.

Those alarms were reflected in scepticism about inflation and the costly Labour programme, crystallised by the tax pledges; and also in fear of back-door nationalisation of the '600 companies', which Bevan thought had been very damaging. But very few Labour candidates believed that the Party had suffered because of its policies. Labour supporters, indeed, were enthusiastic. Regional organisers and correspondents from many areas confirmed Morgan Phillips's reference to the 'magnificent response from our workers everywhere' and his tribute: 'There was much praise for the campaign and the leadership.

Such expressions as "brilliant", "the best campaign in history", and so on were frequent.'[8]

Gaitskell's leadership, despite the income tax pledge, was overwhelmingly rated an asset. He thus became the first and only leader of the Labour Party – perhaps of any party – to add to his reputation in a heavy election defeat. The point needs stressing, since the mistake he was about to make is otherwise incomprehensible. No one put forward the familiar excuses for Labour defeats – poor propaganda, decaying organisation, indifferent leadership, an impression of endless fratricidal strife; instead Barbara Castle publicly testified to Labour's 'good programme, better organisation than we have ever had and brilliant leadership by Hugh Gaitskell'.[9] Privately, too, she sent a warm tribute. Crossman underlined the contrast with the Party's customary 'hunt for the scapegoat', saying every candidate he had met was 'inspired' by Gaitskell's leadership, which alone had 'prevented a catastrophic landslide' sweeping away up to 100 seats instead of 20, including everything south of the Trent.[10] At this time, as an experienced American journalist was to recall two months later,

Hugh Gaitskell was receiving from his followers from Left to Right an acclaim and devotion and support which no Labour leader had been given in decades. Whatever the proportions of the election defeat, Labour was unanimous that it had a leader, and that his handling of the campaign had been masterly and his inspiration superb.[11]

Gaitskell had expected to be vulnerable if the election was lost, but was reassured by his reception. The press were sure that whoever was blamed, it would not be he. Henry Fairlie told his readers that within the Party he was 'now irreproachable and unassailable'.[12] J. P. W. Mallalieu, once a bitter Bevanite, wrote in his column that apart from the income tax pledge, 'Gaitskell's leadership . . . inspired the party . . . there is no possibility of a personal challenge to Gaitskell.'[10] He could hope that his advice would be received as coming not from the suspect chief of a discredited faction, but from the trusted leader of a united movement. That mood was not to last.

# 19

# Clause Four 1959–60

---

*'It is [not] prudent . . . that all forms of private property should live under perpetual threat'*
(Aneurin Bevan, 1952)

*'It was never an issue of principle; it was an issue of presentation'*
(HG, 1960)

---

## Enter the 'Hampstead Set', with Boomerangs

Gaitskell maintained that a major reappraisal of the Party's basic outlook and strategy was properly a matter for Conference. He meant to use the established machinery to persuade his followers of the need for a bold solution, and Conference would provide the best platform. He failed to foresee the speedy disappearance of the goodwill which the campaign had generated. After a lost election the rank and file often blame the leader; and his influential colleagues suddenly perceive, instead of a man about to appoint a Cabinet, a vulnerable politician and a shaky balance of power. Gaitskell had known that a reaction against his leadership might follow a defeat, but the acclaim for his electoral performance had created a mood of false security.

He himself did a little, and his friends much more, to foster that reaction: though not, as the Left assumed, by any deliberate attempt to alter the nature of the Labour Party. But left-wing paranoia was so familiar that he and his associates should have been far more wary. He was to pay a high price for his unwillingness to interfere with his friends' activities.

Gaitskell's farewell party for Dalton on the Sunday after the election was not the planning session for grand political strategy assumed by the Left, but a 'desultory talk' among very tired men on an 'unbelievably superficial' level.[1] There was no evidence, no agenda and no attempt to plan. Dalton's account shows Crosland almost and Harris completely silent:

D. J. [Jay] started off with a great oration on the moral of the election defeat. He wanted (1) to drop 'nationalisation', (2) drop the Trade Unions, (3) drop the name 'Labour Party' . . . (4) drop the principle of political independence, & make agreements, even up to merger, with the Liberals . . . I said I thought this was rather wild, pouring out the baby with the bathwater & throwing the bath after them . . . Others too were more cautious than D. J. . . . H. G. said little in front of so many. He is . . . resolutely, but cautiously revisionist . . . Party Constitution might be revised, some new formula on public ownership substituted for 1918 text . . . Pary Const$^n$ might also be changed by having Nat[1] Exec elected by Unions (local parties represented regionally) . . . and Parliamentary Party, with shift of authority towards Parliamentary Leadership. But any such changes will take time & need most careful handling. H. G., very wisely, listens more than talks to groups like this.[2]

Privately, Gaitskell was against most of the suggestions, especially Jay's.

That Sunday morning, 11 October 1959, Jay said he might write a piece in *Forward*. In it, as a last-minute afterthought, he was tentatively to suggest dropping steel nationalisation. Gaitskell did not instigate the article, or see the text, or agree with the content; yet nothing could shake the Left's conviction of a Frognal Gardens plot. Crossman knew better. Their protests, in his view, prevented not a retreat from nationalisation, which had never been likely, but the chance of constitutional reforms favoured by himself, Morgan Phillips, Jim Griffiths and Aneurin Bevan – as well as Gaitskell.

That same evening, Gaitskell and Crosland both dined with Woodrow Wyatt. Clause Four was discussed; Crosland warned that revising it would cause far more trouble than it was worth, and Gaitskell insisted that the leader's duty was to try to 'shape' the Party – which must show that it was intellectually honest and was facing the present, not bound by nostalgia for the past. Wyatt's favourite remedy was an electoral pact with the Liberals, but Gaitskell thought they could not deliver their vote. In Gaitskell's own area, the West Riding, they were close to the Conservatives on economic and social questions, and he seriously underestimated their penetration by youthful radicals elsewhere. As the Labour debate developed, his distaste for the pact grew.

Gaitskell's reappraisal was sweeping, covering also the Party's institutional structure, which all the leaders thought in need of reform, and the distribution of personal responsibilities, which was to arouse serious friction. On the night of Tuesday 13 October, he stayed with Crossman and

talked to me at length from 6 to 11 and then again in the morning when he could get a word in after our walk round the farm and discussion of cows. So he must have had six hours. First of all he made it clear that in his view we couldn't afford to lose the next election again . . . 'Douglas Jay and Roy want to drop all nationalisation. I am not in favour of dropping iron and steel and road haulage. That is why I propose a complete rewrite of the constitution, defining our aims in modern terms and introducing a federal structure, with indirect election for all. This means the Parliamentary Party will elect its representatives as the trade unions do, and the constituency parties will elect rank-and-file members, as they will be forbidden to choose MPs.' I was at first very surprised by this constitutional reform, but he told me that Morgan [Phillips] had long ago recommended it and Jim Griffiths was keenly in favour. Nye Bevan also had concurred during lunch . . . and had shown no signs whatsoever of wanting to lead a Left attack on moderate policies. I said . . . any constitutional reform or moderation of our attitude to public ownership should not split the Party, and . . . Nye must have the veto. Hugh looked a bit surprised but, on reflection, saw this was sensible.[3]

Gaitskell's mind was not settled, for he feared that the trade union leaders might be left in a backwater, that weakening the link with the unions might therefore do more harm than good, and that strengthening the PLP might make Conference quite irresponsible.

Crossman also proposed changes on the front bench, suggesting Harold Wilson for Shadow Leader of the House of Commons. Gaitskell was also inclined to shift him to another Shadow office, and during the election there had already been reports that Wilson knew he might not be Labour's Chancellor. Never a trusting man, Wilson called on Crossman on Thursday 15 October 1959, 'furious at the suggestion he should be promoted to Leader of the House. He regarded this as a conspiracy to chase him out of the Shadow Chancellorship . . . I told him it was his duty to go and see Gaitskell about it.'[3] The proposal – Crossman's own – was for a parliamentary and organisational chief of staff, as Morrison had been for Attlee, combined with the shadow leadership of the House. It was not at all what Gaitskell had intended. For he talked freely to Crossman next Sunday, 18 October, about making Wilson Shadow Foreign Secretary: because he was too unpopular in the City, was not a good enough economist, and 'wouldn't take the tough decisions'.[4] That was no demotion; but soon Crossman was blandly saying that indiscreet talk about moving Wilson had been 'Gaitskell's worst post-election blunder'.

Wilson now thought that Gaitskell meant to replace him (and later said that but for this affair he would not have agreed to stand for the leadership in 1960).[5] Gaitskell told Alastair Hetherington that he had quite failed to reassure Wilson, who 'was afraid that his succession to the deputy leadership – and so to the leadership "say fifteen years hence" was in jeopardy.' The editor had just suggested that Gaitskell could probably safely go abroad for a month at Christmas, since Harold Macmillan also would be out of the country. 'Yes', was the reply, 'and Harold Wilson will be out of it too.'[6]

Gaitskell did reshape the Labour front bench, promoting talent without offending the older men. Of the twenty newcomers, five (all later in Wilson's Cabinets) were still in their thirties: again an unusually young team for a Labour Opposition. Gaitskell thought highly of them, saying privately that, given the chance, everyone in the Shadow Cabinet could have taken a good university degree.

On 21 October Gaitskell met the PLP for the first time since the election and received a standing ovation. But the prestige he had acquired in the election was already more tarnished than he realised. He stayed in the background, appealed for a friendly hearing for everyone, made no excuses and invited criticism. The debate was quite good humoured, but it showed that there was no chance of Jay's line being accepted. For in two weeks the unwonted fraternal harmony of the election campaign had been dissipated, and Gaitskell's friends had greatly harmed their own cause – not by secret intrigues but by ill-judged public statements. Ideas which might have been acceptable were now discredited by association with those that were not. The old Bevanites reverted to factionalism, defensively as they felt; and, far more dangerously for Gaitskell, Jay's article re-awoke suspicions of the intellectuals among the trade union MPs, and affected – however unfairly – their attitude to the leader himself.

By the time Gaitskell came to speak out at the Blackpool Conference he had lost much of his room for manoeuvre. In stormier waters and a much worse climate, he was persisting with a familiar style of leadership which he soon had to abandon. The *Observer* noted:

He has become increasingly obsessed by one thing – the imperative need to keep the party united . . . Like Clem, he would . . . keeping resolutely to the middle way, show that he was the honest broker . . . On October 8 . . . it looked as if he could do anything he liked. . . . the atmosphere is no longer quite the same. Mr. Gaitskell now has his critics . . . He can hint, he can beckon and he can point; but the day seems to have passed when he could insist and command.

But at least he knew from those PLP meetings

that the weight of opinion among Labour M.P.s is overwhelmingly against Mr. Jay and that [it] would invite disaster . . . to steer the conference too fast and too far . . . He knows with certainty . . . exactly what is expected of him and what his audience will bear. It will be surprising if he gets an emphasis, a gesture, or a tone of voice wrong.[7]

If he provoked a storm, it was not for lack of warning.

## Ends and Means

Unlike many participants in Labour's debate in the autumn of 1959, Gaitskell saw the danger that refusing any change could lead the Party to disaster, for another defeat would be final. He saw 'very strong underlying forces working against us. The problem is how to deal with these without splitting the Party. It is not an easy matter.'[8] But too many people would not face the danger: not just left-wingers but many who simply disliked change, and more who knew that change was necessary but would not risk their popularity with the activists by discussing it openly. Gaitskell was dismayed at their 'political cowardice', especially over the status of nationalisation – not in Labour's immediate policy but in the Party's conception of its own ultimate purpose.

Gaitskell never repudiated nationalisation where it could solve a real problem: a few months after this he called for public ownership of urban building land. But he wanted both to demonstrate that Labour reached such specific decisions on merits, not just for the sake of nationalising; and also to clarify its long-term aims. In the shorter run he rejected no remedy as unpalatable, but many as either irrelevant or clearly unacceptable within the Party. He envisaged no substantial revision of Labour policies, for he both believed in them, and knew that it would look like 'cynicism or opportunism' to jettison them because of the defeat. But he thought it essential to improve the Party's image and modernise its appeal:

I see no reason whatsoever [he said on the BBC] why we should have any doubts about the basic principles . . . we still believe . . . in equality and freedom at the same time, in equal opportunity, in a fair deal; in . . . behaving decently and honourably to other nations . . . they're eternal things . . . But how they should be . . . interpreted and expressed . . . [for] a modern generation, that always needs reappraisal, I think.[9]

The nationalisation question seemed to provide the opportunity. The official election inquest reported that its unpopularity was due not to the steel proposal, but to 'general uncertainty as to the Party's intentions'. *Industry and Society* had talked imprecisely of measures to be taken against leading firms which 'failed the nation'. Its ambiguities had helped to win assent within the Party, since everyone could interpret it to his own taste; but they also permitted business and Conservative progaganda to exploit it, as Gaitskell, Wilson and Bevan all agreed.

In this context, Gaitskell fastened upon Clause Four, Section Four, of the party constitution. Adopted in 1918 – before full employment, the welfare state, the growth of trade union power or widespread affluence – it proclaimed Labour's aim as

To secure for the workers by hand or by brain the full fruits of their industry, and the most equitable distribution thereof that may be possible, upon the basis of the common ownership of the means of production, distribution and exchange, and the best obtainable system of popular administration and control of each industry and service.

In principle, Gaitskell throughout his life thought of public ownership as not an end, but a means to the true Socialist objective of a just, egalitarian, classless society. In practice, he told a worried constituent in 1952: 'Some of my friends have also suggested that the clause you refer to is no longer appropriate, but for my part I do not think it is very important either way.'[10] Just before becoming leader, he had referred to Clause Four which 'speaks of obtaining for the worker the full fruits of his labour on the basis of common ownership, the emphasis is really on equality'. On his election six weeks later, one commentator suspected 'that he would dearly love to release the Labour party from the pledge' in Clause Four.[11]

In 1956 Anthony Crosland published *The Future of Socialism*, emphasising *inter alia* the growing importance of managers as against owners. Gaitskell's PPS remembered his master often expressing serious doubts about the relevance of Clause Four. But Gaitskell would not repudiate it publicly, insisting instead 'that public ownership, though we propose to do it gradually, nevertheless is necessary to achieve the ideals in which we believe'.[12] He did not change that view in 1959. The view he did change was the one he had put to his worried constituent seven years earlier: that nationalisation would be a long, slow process and so 'we can leave unanswered the question of what might be eventually left to the private sector'.[10] In the Labour Party of 1959, very few people envisaged nationalising the whole economy in their lifetime; and now he wanted them to say so. Three years later a careful survey of CLP leaders found that fewer than half wanted Labour to move Left on 'nationalisation and national planning'; even among those who did, many no doubt still favoured a mixed economy.[13]

That was in a new climate in which even Conservatives were calling for planning – in contrast to 1959.

His decision astonished both friends and opponents, for Clause Four had played no part in the election. Though it was (and is) on every Labour Party membership card, the Conservative *Speakers' Handbook* did not mention it; indeed it is said that Central Office, having no copy of Labour's constitution, had to go out and buy one after Blackpool. But it did symbolise an approach to nationalisation (and even to politics generally) which had done great harm. Jim Griffiths, the retiring deputy leader, admired and disagreed with Gaitskell after their 'series of long talks' beforehand about Clause Four.

Once he made up his mind there was no calculation of the consequences to himself . . . Integrity, absolute integrity, this was the essential quality of Hugh Gaitskell's character . . . He knew . . . that Clause Four was an article of faith to me and my generation. When I reminded him of this he replied sternly: 'Maybe, but you know that we do not intend, any of us, to implement Clause Four fully, and I regard it as my duty to say so to the party and the country.' When he considered it was his duty to say or do something nothing could change him. The sharp edge of intellectual integrity would cut through all barriers.[14]

That verdict was more flattering morally than professionally. Gaitskell was a politician too, though a strikingly honest one, and before the inquest on the 1959 defeat he had felt no duty to decide about Clause Four or to share his conclusions with Party and country. When he did so, he presented them very cautiously: 'I do feel that it is necessary to remove what has undoubtedly been a great source of misrepresentation by our opponents and to show that . . . our approach is essentially pragmatic and not doctrinaire. That is all that is at issue.'[15] But in reality Gaitskell sought more than a platitudinous negative with which no one disagreed. He thought the Party was confused between means and ends, and unclear about its real objectives:

Gaitskell said it was important to state the basic aims of public ownership and of the Labour party in relation to the economy . . . What kind of society did they want? . . . How would they achieve it? These were the questions. They had never been properly defined of late and . . . this should be done positively.[16]

All his life he was an educator; a source of both weakness and strength. He spent far too long on precise drafting because he believed that people should say what they meant, even in politics, and would act more coherently if they knew why they were acting. The teacher and not the politician in him was passionate about getting the argument right, and insistent that his followers must tread the right road to the right destination – and for the right reasons. It would often have been far easier to cajole them into swallowing policies they did not understand and would not have approved if they had. Insisting on clarifying comfortable obscurities, and recognising unwelcome necessities, he created great and avoidable difficulties for himself. Many people saw it at the time as utter folly politically, even if admirable intellectually. But we now know that the astute management which buys politicians temporary tranquillity, and the deviousness with which they approach desirable objectives, may prove costly later when illusions can no longer be preserved and confidence is finally shattered.

Two experiences in 1959 thus transformed Gaitskell's attitude to party leadership: the triumphant campaign, establishing him at last as a popular leader appealing to the Party and people; and then the ghastly disappointment when sudden recognition and apparent success turned overnight into humiliating defeat. So far he had kept to Attlee's familiar role of tactfully balancing conflicting forces in the Party; now he feared that that would mean presiding comfortably over its inexorable decline. His personal reception convinced him that he could safely break out of that role to offer advice in good faith to serve the Party and its cause.

So believing, he made several misjudgements. He let his friends open the debate with their own individualistic, tactless, unco-ordinated – and counter-productive – initiatives. He did not foresee the instant revival of factional hostilities; or the hatred of his old enemies, concealed while he seemed about to become Prime Minister; or his opponents' skill in using the blunders of his allies to undermine confidence in himself. Above all he misjudged completely in hoping that a debate on Labour's vague long-term aspirations would minimise conflict. It was an over-rational view, as he quickly discovered.

He said the majority of members had little capacity for real thinking. To them Nationalisation was an emotional issue. This had proved to be the case even more than he had expected. There was depressingly little readiness to think hard about ends and means. The discussion must be got on to that basis. It was not going that way now.[17]

A little later he confessed publicly that he had not foreseen the reaction – and privately that if he had, he would never have raised the issue. For that reaction was strongest in the trade union centre of the Party, so long the foundation of Gaitskell's political strength. The objective of public ownership was written into many union rule-books, and trade unionists, just because their daily activities concentrated their attention on hard practical realities, cherished the distant vision of a bright Socialist horizon. Gaitskell lost the Clause Four battle, and endangered his leadership, by driving most of the trade union centre for the first time into the arms of the Left.

It was a strange mistake. He had himself furiously rejected the very idea of changing the Party's name, with all its emotional links to the romantic attachments and moral commitments of his own youth. That response of his should have made him sensitive and sympathetic to the emotional freight carried by the concept of public ownership.

Idols . , . even when they are so quiescent as to seem almost lifeless, have a capacity for becoming suddenly and violently inflamed . . . No politician can hope to prosper unless he has a weather-sense that warns him in good time what to expect . . . [for] an idol whose worshippers have taken alarm, may threaten him with disaster.[18]

Gaitskell read that passage later, and regretted not having done so in time.

## Blackpool: 'The Biggest Belly-ache'

Gaitskell often expected more from trade union leaders than they could deliver. But over Clause Four in 1959 he was warned at the start by all his staunch friends: Sam Watson, Bill Webber, Jim Griffiths, Charlie Pannell – who found him 'as obstinate as only Hugh knew how'.[1]

Gaitskell had taken very risky solitary decisions in the past, as over the 1951 Budget or the Stalybridge speech. This time, while listening to others he was already eyeing his target. That is not to say that his listening was hypocritical, for he modified many of his ideas. But, once he made up his mind, he would be deterred by neither pressures nor advice. Yet this time his behaviour was different. At Stalybridge he was a prominent front-bencher trying to fight a trend he thought disastrous; now he was leader, trying to persuade his followers. At Blackpool, he said, he would have a three-fold task – the parts of which were incompatible:

1. To guide thinking on the right lines.
2. To keep the party together.
3. To cheer it up.[17]

At Stalybridge he had consulted no one before blasting off. But at Blackpool his tone was conciliatory, and he had talked fairly widely in advance – yet went ahead though most of his friends disapproved.

One very important colleague saw the speech beforehand: Aneurin

Bevan. Pannell on the Thursday before Conference urged him to show Bevan the speech, and Gaitskell told Pannell later that Bevan had said he 'could not fault it in any way'.[19] His reaction was not really surprising. In 1952, when to Gaitskell Clause Four was still unimportant, Bevan had explicitly rejected a wholly publicly owned economy:

It is clear . . . that a mixed economy is what most people of the West would prefer. I have no patience with those Socialists, so-called, who in practice would socialise nothing, whilst in theory they threaten the whole of private property . . . [It does not] accord with our conception of the future, that all forms of private property should live under perpetual threat.[20]

That was precisely the message that Gaitskell intended by his Clause Four speech. But could he rely on Bevan maintaining that view in 1959?

On Saturday morning, 28 November 1959, the leader rose in the Winter Gardens at Blackpool to address his followers in unfavourable circumstances. The prestige won in the election campaign had ebbed. He had arranged no favourable build-up for his own analysis of the defeat and the remedies, while the unofficial discussions in the Party had done only harm. Charges of treachery were being freely hurled about, and Crossman recorded that 'the whole leadership of the Party is now stinking with intrigue and suspicion'.[21]

In this sour mood, Gaitskell's decision to have no agreed lead from the platform was to prove a further handicap. Saying 'it would be an abnegation of democratic evolution of policy if he laid down the line himself at the outset',[17] he trustfully assumed that Conference could act as a candid discussion forum with Executive members putting their individual views.

In the chairman's address, Barbara Castle set the tone, eloquently proclaiming the indispensability of all Labour's traditional attitudes, especially on public ownership. Opening the debate after lunch, Gaitskell said there was no Excecutive view: 'this afternoon I speak for myself alone'. He had not seen the chairman's speech, nor she his. He contended that a third defeat, despite a better programme, better campaign, and better publicity and organisation, showed that 'more fundamental influences' were checking Labour's advance. Great social changes had brought higher living standards and a welfare state. There were fewer and fewer unskilled workers, thanks to technological change. Fear of unemployment declined now that governments were expected to avert future depressions. These changes did not justify the defeatism which preached permanent opposition, for 'The British people . . . do not take kindly, in politics or war, to those who have given up the will to battle.' Three more 'rather desperate remedies'– the Lib-Lab pact, the change of name, the breach with the unions– should go 'out of the window right away'. But Labour must no longer count on old eroding loyalties. It must recognise the changes, continue to defend the underdog, appeal to youthful idealism, and above all try 'to broaden our base, to be in touch always with ordinary people, to avoid becoming small cliques of isolated doctrine-ridden fanatics'.

At last he turned to nationalisation, presenting his own view as a middle way.

We may not be far from the frontier of this kind of giant State monopoly [but] . . . I cannot agree that we have reached the frontier of public ownership as a whole.

At the same time I disagree equally with the other extreme view that public ownership is the be all and end all, the ultimate first principle and aim of socialism.

He set out again seven basic principles: concern for the worst-off; social justice; a classless society; equality of all races and peoples; belief in human relations 'based on fellowship and cooperation'; precedence for public over private interest; freedom and democratic self-government. Public ownership was 'not itself the ultimate objective; it is only a means' necessary for a better distribution of wealth; for controlling 'the commanding heights of the economy' in order to plan; and for ensuring accountability to the people.

We should make two things clear . . . that we have no intention of abandoning public ownership and . . . that we regard public ownership not as an end in itself but as a means . . . to certain ends . . . While we shall certainly wish to extend social ownership, . . . our goal is not 100% State ownership. Our goal is a society in which Socialist ideals are realised . . . The pace at which we can go depends on how quickly we can persuade our fellow citizens to back us.

The party constitution set out Labour's fundamental aims, but it was forty years old and omitted 'colonial freedom, race relations, disarmament, full employment or planning'. Only Clause Four specified domestic objectives and, 'standing as it does on its own', it was obviously inadequate. It confused ends and means, ignored other aims, and

lays us open to continual misrepresentation . . . It implies that we propose to nationalise everything, but do we? Everything? – the whole of light industry, the whole of agriculture, all the shops – every little pub and garage? Of course not. We have long ago come to accept . . . a mixed economy . . . [the] view . . . of 90 per cent of the Labour Party – had we not better say so instead of going out of our way to court misrepresentation?

Hostile interruptions began. Gaitskell responded sharply that an uncontroversial, bromide-laden speech would have brought cheers: 'But I do not conceive that to be my duty today. I would rather forego the cheers now in the hope that we shall get more votes later on.' The enthusiastic Labour workers in the election campaign, he insisted, 'wanted above all that we should win . . . to keep up the spirit of attack . . . again and again and again, until we win'.[22]

Many of his platform colleagues, not all of them left-wingers, conspicuously declined to join in the applause. Then Michael Foot – who had just lost again at Devonport, suffering the third worst swing in the nation – attacked Gaitskell for promoting disunity, said the PLP had no will to battle, and called on the Party to question its leadership. The ovation he received began 'an unbridled personal vendetta from the Left'.[23] On Sunday morning Frank Cousins defended Clause Four, and called for mobilisation of the 'five or six million people who are Socialists in embryo waiting for us to go out and harness them to the power machine we want to drive'.[24]

Then came a great change. First, the NEC election results were announced, and Ian Mikardo had lost his seat. Then Benn Levy was angrily booed from the rostrum for saying that Gaitskell seemed to have been addressing the conference of a different party. Previous speakers had not, after all, spoken for the rank and file. Charlie Pannell denounced them for making Conference 'the biggest belly-ache I have ever come across'. Denis Healey counter-attacked those who were content to

luxuriate complacently in moral righteousness in Opposition . . . who is going to pay the price for their complacency? . . . the unemployed and the old-age pensioners . . . You will have your T.V. set, your motor car and your summer holidays on the Continent and still keep your Socialist soul intact.

Shirley Williams followed with a warning against rancour, and against trying to split Bevan from Gaitskell.[25] So, in the afternoon, Bevan wound up the debate in a new and better atmosphere.

## Aneurin's Mantle

Bevan's mood had changed too. Though he had not objected on seeing the leader's speech on the Friday night, he was angry on hearing it on the Saturday afternoon. 'He was under extreme pressure from some of his old Bevanite friends to go all out for a quick kill, and they tried to press the dagger into his hand.'[23] Bevan decided against them at the last minute, and told Gaitskell so. 'Gaitskell knew at Blackpool what Bevan was going to say in his winding-up speech; and he knew that Bevan couldn't bring himself publicly to follow all the Gaitskell line.'[6]

Bevan talked of variety within unity, ingenuously pointing out that both the leader and the chairman had quoted his own phrase about the commanding heights of the economy:

If Euclid's deduction is correct they are both equal to me and therefore must be equal to each other . . . I agree with Barbara, I agree with Hugh and I agree with myself . . . I am a Socialist: I believe in public ownership. But I agreed with Hugh Gaitskell yesterday . . . I do not believe that public ownership should reach down into every piece of economic activity, because that would be asking for a monolithic society . . . What I do insist upon is . . . a planned economy.[25]

Yet Bevan's only published comment on Blackpool struck a different note: 'the overwhelming majority of the Labour Party will not acquiesce in the jettisoning of the concept of progressive public ownership.'[26] Such ambivalence was not new to Bevan. His generalisations contained no commitments, and different observers attributed to him quite different intentions.

At Blackpool his friendly tones persuaded many people that Gaitskell had escaped only through Bevan's benevolence. Gaitskell did not think so: had there been a vote, he was confident he would have won easily. Bevan would not bid for the leadership, Gaitskell told Hetherington, recalling his split with the unilateralists, since

the Brighton speech . . . was a terrible experience for him. He can't now bring himself to go wholly against the left . . . Bevan knew that if he [Gaitskell] had been dislodged he would have stayed on the National Executive . . . and made Bevan's life exceedingly uncomfortable.[6]

Bevan's friends thought differently about his intentions. He told several people that he would overthrow Gaitskell and take over the leadership, but many did not believe he ever meant it. Crossman concluded after long discussions that Bevan would insist on greater influence within the leadership, not seize it for himself; and even Michael Foot later became convinced that Bevan would have continued the partnership with Gaitskell.[27]

Had he lived, Bevan must have benefited from Gaitskell's difficulties. Probably he approved Gaitskell's speech because, aggrieved at being consulted far too late to have any real say, he felt that the leader should lie in the bed he had made. For himself, he would not (consciously) decide his course till he had to. He could not have overthrown Gaitskell without conciliating the unilateralists, and eating all his words since Brighton. That choice never confronted him, for in December 1959 he had an operation for cancer, and he died in July.

For just ten years his fortunes had been intertwined with Gaitskell's. Before 1950 they had been friendly though not intimate, with the younger man expecting his senior in time to accede to the leadership and the premiership. Then they became bitterly antagonistic rivals over Government policy, and Cabinet power, and the Party's development. To most people Bevan, with his glittering gifts of oratory to which Gaitskell could not aspire, with his roots in the Welsh mining valleys and his devoted following in the local parties, seemed Labour's natural leader. Yet he dissipated his assets as though dominated by a death-wish. (To some people the same affliction, over Clause Four and once or twice afterwards, seemed to grip Gaitskell too.) For both men were moved by passionate emotion—in Bevan instantly visible, in Gaitskell seething deep beneath layers of Wykehamist schooling. So both sometimes chose bad ground to embark on great battles, and were then proudly determined not to retreat or compromise.

Both cared deeply for the Party they led and the country they hoped to lead. Their talents were completely contrasting, and splendidly complementary. Gaitskell thought through his positions with rigorous intellectual honesty, and then clung to them too inflexibly. Bevan derived his from intuition rather than reasoning, inhaling his inspiration from communion with the emotions of great meetings. (He was understandably jealous that the educational system had given his rival, whose mind he felt inferior to his own, a vastly better training.) His Celtic fire excited mass audiences as Gaitskell's carefully argued speeches never yet had, though from 1959 onwards Gaitskell was to develop a new force and passion. Their publics differed as well as their styles, for Bevan responded to the party enthusiasts, Gaitskell to the ordinary Labour voters—and to the others whose confidence had yet to be won. He lacked Bevan's quickness and flexibility in parliamentary debate, and there too displayed real emotional force only in his last years.

Their reconciliation did not come easily in 1957. With their different temperaments, Gaitskell appreciated Bevan's qualities more than Bevan did his; and it was naturally harder for the loser to accept that the outcome was final. Bevan's co-operation was always on terms, and his impeccable public loyalty always concealed private reservations: not surprisingly, for an opposition leader who has never led a government is always on trial until he wins a general election. Yet the two men might not have found it hard to work together in office. For the victory transforms the status and prestige of the new Prime Minister; it enhances his political power and assures his security; it mobilises all the loyal instincts of the Party behind its leaders; and it gives those leaders a common interest, since their reputations depend on the government's success.

Their past records do not suggest exceptional strains threatening their co-operation. Gaitskell as Prime Minister would have been much more radical and acceptable to the party faithful than his detractors believed; he might occasionally have flouted their feelings, but Bevan would have restrained him from doing so too much. Both in office and as Shadow Foreign Secretary, Bevan had shown an acute sense of practical possibilities. Making out his abortive Cabinet list on the Sunday night before the 1959 election, Gaitskell gave a clue to their likely relationship when he told John Harris that a Prime Minister should not try to be his own Foreign Secretary. Bevan's policy preferences would have been closer to Gaitskell's than his admirers supposed, and his ability to win party consent to them far greater than Gaitskell's without him. It was a sad deprivation for the Labour Party and the British people to lose the leadership of either man in facing the problems of the 1960s. To lose both was a major disaster.

### 'A Torment of Misrepresentation'

Though Bevan helped Gaitskell by his last conference speech, the leader emerged from Blackpool badly battered. Observers were astonished by the sudden collapse of his authority in late 1959, and even more by the issue on which he had risked it. His Conservative opponents were first puzzled, later mocking; Iain Macleod said Labour had 'provided us with a mine so inexhaustible but so rich that every Tory candidate can dig with profit in it for ever. I do not understand why they should load us with such golden gifts.'[28] Attlee thought the affair pointless, and even friendly colleagues felt the ground was ill chosen. The leadership's tactics, too, remained appalling, for Gaitskell chose that difficult moment to go abroad – for a business visit to New York, followed by a long-deferred and desperately needed holiday in the West Indies. Bevan's illness brought him back early, but he was not able to see the sick man.

During his absence the critics had kept up their campaign which, as Ian Mikardo explicitly said, was directed not at Gaitskell's actual proposal, but at the imaginary conspiracy which they sniffed behind it, to promote 'acceptance of a public sector hardly differing from the existing one'. Gaitskell's reputation as a skilful compromiser had suddenly become a liability, arousing unjustified suspicions not confined to nationalisation. Knowing it would be damaging to change policies immediately after an election defeat, he had not done so – but was charged with opportunism as if he had. Vicky caricatured him as a doorstep pollster asking a bewildered housewife, 'Which party would you like Labour to resemble?', and as the manager of 'Labour Stores' with notices in the window: 'Gigantic sell out', 'Socialist principles practically given away'. Challenged on TV just after Blackpool, he made himself unmistakably clear:

if you were to say to me ' . . . really we've got to accept the colour bar, because you'll never get into power if you don't', I should say . . . 'Go to hell . . . that's absolutely against my principles'. If you were to say to me 'Don't bother about the old people . . . concentrate on the majority who are well off ', I should say again 'It's no good talking like that to me.' But if you say to me 'I think that your argument for nationalising the machine tool industry . . . is rather weak', I would say 'Well I'll discuss that with you' . . . but don't misunderstand me, I do think . . . public ownership . . . is necessary to achieve the other things that we want.[29]

The charges of opportunism were part of what *The Times* called 'a torment of misrepresentation by those who have . . . [fought] him since at least 1951'.[30] All Gaitskell's old enemies seized their chance to join in. When he arrived back in Britain, his friends were alarmed. Hugh Dalton exploded:

*Is this Labour Party worth leading?* Are its diseases curable? This endless public quarrelling? This wide-open suicide club? This idiot loyalty to an undigested phrase! This built-in personal bitterness by a faction; these built-in sneers; this massive moral cowardice; these pseudo-diplomatic trimmers' silences.[31]

A few unknown young politicians took the risk of speaking out. But more senior – and normally voluble – figures offered only 'calculated public silences'; for half the Shadow Cabinet thought a change in Clause Four either wrong or inexpedient. Harold Wilson, Crossman reported, was 'pouring out his venom against Gaitskell and not concealing his desire to get rid of him'.[32] In public he was more cautious and merely deplored the prospect of a long argument about 'theology', saying that the Party could easily be united on specific nationalisation proposals which could be produced in ten minutes. But the leader was unconvinced.

In less than four months the Labour Party had moved from the unity and fervour of the general election into the worst mood of bitterness and suspicion since the war. But Gaitskell was a very stubborn man, and believed there could be no going back. He wrote to a friend on his return to England: 'the going is rough – very rough . . . I have never been nearer to giving it all up in despair, unhappiness and lack of self-confidence.' But he still thought he would have been wrong to 'have done an Attlee & just doodled.' Anyway, 'it's too late now for regrets. The fight is on and I must see it through.'

## The 'New Testament'

In a major speech to 600 people at Nottingham on 13 February 1960 (largely written by Crosland), Gaitskell repeated that Clause Four was too narrow, in omitting many basic aims; too broad, in hinting at nationalising everything; and unsatisfactory, in not distinguishing public ownership from its least popular form, 'the huge State monopoly'. (Clause Four leaves the specific form open, and the Left justly claimed to have criticised huge state monopolies while Gaitskell was still defending them.) Once again he denied – at length – that he was against extending public ownership: 'I said precisely the opposite of this at Blackpool.' Harm was done not by specific proposals but by the 'vague threat to all private property'. He hit out at all his enemies, beginning with 'the small professional anti-leadership group – the self-appointed opposition to those elected in the party . . . sublimely indifferent to the views of the electorate . . . more and more remote from ordinary people'. Crossman, Wilson and the silent front-benchers were not spared. The constitution, he said, should not be 'a collection of meaningless phrases . . . mere theology'; and he was puzzled by talk of revising a policy which everyone had so recently approved, for that 'really would be cynical surrender for the sake of electoral consider-ations'. The people who had stirred up all the internal controversies were now charging him with dividing the Party; those who said there should be no talk of change until everyone already agreed on it were preaching false unity and permanent stagnation; and those who knew the constitution was out of date, but feared to say so publicly, were 'neither very honest nor very sincere'. It was absurd to reject any change without knowing what the new statement would say.[30]

The audience was actively favourable; and now Labour's heavy guns at last began firing on Gaitskell's side. Trade union MPs like Roy

Mason and Charlie Pannell joined in, though most front-benchers continued to hold their peace. *Tribune* sensed the altered mood, abruptly abandoning frontal attack for the thoroughly misleading assertion 'Mr. Gaitskell changes his tune.' Canvassing of names to replace Gaitskell suddenly stopped. Soon he was writing cheerfully that things were 'going better, and I have little doubt that we shall get a new statement of aims'.[33]

So reassured, he willingly compromised by withdrawing from his maximum objective to his Blackpool view that Clause Four 'standing as it does on its own cannot possibly be regarded as adequate'. He would have preferred the new statement of aims to replace Clause Four, but foreseeing insufficient support from the unions, he settled for unity, by adding the new statement while retaining the old one for its historical associations. The idea of adopting both statements – instantly christened the Old and New Testaments – was pressed by George Brown and Charlie Pannell, the leaders of the trade union group. With Gaitskell's acceptance of it, the air cleared. For no one objected to the new statement of aims – even though the draft itself essentially restated Gaitskell's seven basic first principles. Even Foot approved it. There was as yet no serious expectation that the leader could be overthrown; and so, as soon as the argument shifted from suspicion of his intentions to his actual proposals, the controversy died away.

At the Executive on 16 March 1960, Gaitskell instantly accepted – to the distress of his outright enemies – a series of verbal changes proposed by critics like the NUR member, Crossman, and Jennie Lee. An amendment by Harry Nicholas of the T&GWU, to delete any reference to the place of private enterprise in the economy, was lost by 8 to 16. But the atmosphere was entirely harmonious, and Nicholas cast the only vote against the new statement. The next day, Gaitskell's confidence seemed to have been entirely justified. Most of his friends were satisfied. Pannell wrote that 'you have got most of what you wanted . . . [with] no loss of prestige', and Jay took it for granted that 'now Clause 4 is more or less finished with'.[34] But privately Gaitskell was not so sure, and sometimes thought his success 'very slight. The difficulty with the Party is to get the changes made without such a row in the Party as to vitiate the whole object of the exercise.'[35]

He carefully avoided claiming a victory, leaving the Left to celebrate the frustration of his imaginary conspiracy. At the very worst, the result looked like a draw, for as he had set out to do at Blackpool, Gaitskell had clarified and amplified the historic but inadequate clause. His campaign seemed to many strategically misconceived, and to many more, tactically mishandled; but on 16 March it had apparently attained its purpose with virtual unanimity on the National Executive.

## One Step Forward, Two Steps Back

The election had shown that even with a united party and much improved propaganda and organisation, Labour support was slowly eroding and seemed likely to continue to do so. Gaitskell could have chosen to wait for something to turn up; and hindsight suggests that Britain's gradual economic decline, which he foresaw, might then have brought Labour back to power. But in 1959 that would have been a rash gamble, which he would have seen as an abdication of his duty to his followers for the sake of an easy life for himself. Alternatively, he could have suggested changes of structure not of doctrine. But he was against radical action such as a formal breach with the unions. He might have carried out less drastic changes, strengthening the leadership against its perpetual critics by altering the composition of the NEC as Bevan and Phillips wished; but at the time the benefit of that would have accrued only to the leader and not to the whole party, though in the long run Labour might have gained electorally from it. Instead Gaitskell put forward an expanded version of the Party's long-term aims, assuming correctly that his new statement would be generally acceptable, and mistakenly that the old statement would not be missed.

The acceptability was obscured at the time by Gaitskell's poor tactics. In withholding his own views at the start, in having no lead given by the NEC, and in allowing his friends to make unpopular suggestions, he ensured that his personal impact came in the worst conditions and aroused the maximum suspicion, so that the debate centred on intentions wrongly foisted on him and not on his actual views. Yet though the suspicion of ideological divergence was much and sometimes maliciously exaggerated, it was not wholly unfounded. In 1959 everyone of importance in the Labour Party took it for granted that the mixed economy would last a long time and that the next Labour government would have to manage it. A decade or two later that was no longer true, and the extent and pace of major and irreversible change were again seriously discussed within the Party. In that debate, the survival of Clause Four gave the Left some leverage, and made it rather harder for the leadership to present Labour convincingly to the country simply as a reformist party – whereas in Germany the Social Democrats by their theoretical repudiation of Marxism (simultaneous with the British argument over Clause Four) were by the 1970s to leave their unreconstructed left wing stranded and politically impotent.

Gaitskell's final failure to change the party constitution was not due to the intrinsic strength of the Labour Left. He failed because his approach was over-rational and took too little account of the emotional overtones. It was true that the reputation of wanting to nationalise everything was widespread and damaging to Labour; that, as Mikardo said, nobody wanted to do so in 1959; and that a new statement of aims certainly could be devised (as it was) to which everyone could assent. It was at least plausible to suppose that while changing the policy would have seemed a capitulation, changing the symbolic clause would demonstrate both to the electorate and to the Party itself what its real objectives were. But it was a serious error not to foresee that the emotional revulsion he himself experienced against altering the Party's name would be felt by many loyal trade unionists against taking down the signpost to the promised land. The controversy was studded with biblical terminology: Pannell warned him against tampering with the Tablets of Stone, John Murray against touching the Ark of the Covenant, Attlee and Griffiths against bothering about the 39 Articles. The two statements were christened the Old and the New Testaments, and the defenders of Clause Four were attacked as fundamentalists and idolators. Gaitskell himself once told an old friend that he wished he led a political party and not a religious movement. Yet it was a strength as well as a weakness of the Labour Movement that it shared some of the characteristics of both. And it was a weakness as well as a strength that its leader's commitment to rational discourse sometimes blinded him to the likely emotional reactions of his followers.

Not all his opponents were zealots for whom the revisionist issue was fundamental and who felt that he was seeking to alter the very identity of the Party. They also included pragmatists, fewer but influential, who thought the opposite: that any squabble over 'theology' should have been avoided by silence in opposition until the same ends could be attained, still silently, in practice after coming into power. The leading pragmatists were soon able to put their views into practice, sweeping away a few babies of principle with the bath water of Clause Four nationalisation. When Labour reverted to opposition at the end of the decade, a price was paid for this adaptation by stealth. Never openly challenged, the old shibboleths remained intact and emotionally powerful, while the suspicion of the new leadership had become just as intense, and even more widespread, than in Gaitskell's day.

In March 1960 the pragmatic politicians seemed to have been wrong;

but soon Gaitskell found that he could not achieve his ends in the way he sought. For within four months, four of the six major unions had refused to amend the constitution and, facing certain defeat at Conference, Gaitskell had to downgrade the 'New Testament' to a mere 'valuable expression of the aims of the Labour Party in the twentieth century', while leaving Clause Four intact. Even that face-saving phrase was challenged; it was carried in the NEC by 18 votes to 5. Privately Gaitskell confessed 'rather sadly that if he had foreseen the kind of opposition . . . he would never have raised the Clause 4 issue at all. He admitted that he had erred very much . . . the best thing now was simply to cut his losses.'[36]

No one objected to the content of the new statement of aims but, as Gaitskell wrote, his enemies tried to refer it back mainly 'to damage me personally'.[37] That was said openly in the debate at the 1960 conference; and Cousins supported the move so 'that on at least one issue we should know what it is we are voting about'. Gaitskell in reply protested that his Blackpool speech had been misrepresented: 'I do not think it was entirely my fault [people] were misled.' But he admitted not only that he had quite misjudged the mood but that he had retreated on Clause Four owing to the crisis over defence: 'It was never an issue of principle; it was an issue of presentation . . . we were going to have a major division over defence, and we did not want to add to the divisions in the Party unnecessarily. So we are not discussing amending the constitution.' He went on to stress that in a democratic system, unless 'a programme of extending public ownership seems relevant to the electorate . . . they will not elect you to power.'[38] The new statement was carried by nearly a two-thirds majority.

Though Gaitskell's face was saved, he had lost the battle over Clause Four after all, because of a sudden change in the dynamics of the political conflict. Before the 1959 election, his willingness to compromise was taken to show his concern for unity, and so strengthened his position within the Party. But now his enemies on the Left were uttering cries of triumph, his big trade union battalions were wavering, and his compromise for the sake of unity looked to some like a retreat, encouraging to his enemies and demoralising to his friends – one of whom predicted 'a landslide of questioning which destroys your leadership'.[39] That spring, the Left launched a tremendous new assault against Labour's acceptance of nuclear weapons; and the 'landslide', threatening to sweep away his policy and his leadership together, obliged Gaitskell to abandon any attempt to revise the party constitution.

# 20

# 'Ban the Bomb!' 1960

*'I never like evasions. But I suppose it is necessary this year'*
(HG, June 1960)

*'He can't last long now'*
(Harold Wilson, May 1960)

## The End of Blue Streak

Labour's crisis in 1960 was more than a struggle over a doctrinal point like Clause Four, or over a policy issue like unilateral nuclear disarmament, or over a personality clash concerning Gaitskell's leadership, or even over the location of power within the Party. It was a conflict about its character: whether the Party was to be a protest movement or a prospective government of the country. For one wing, it was or should be controlled from below by its dedicated activists, who expected their parliamentary spokesmen normally to defer to Conference, and feared that the PLP's recognised discretion over tactics and timing might allow the front bench to assert the wrong priorities. For the other wing, Labour must not remain content to witness in the wilderness, impotent but pure: it must seek political power to put principles into practice. In between, a few of the power-seekers crossed the dividing line to form a tactical alliance with the purists.

Throughout Labour history that line has been sharpest over national defence. As a protest movement, the early Labour Party attracted many Christian pacifists who objected to all wars, many minority groups who hated British imperialism, many Socialist Internationalists who loathed national rivalries, many ardent domestic reformers who resented money being freely spent on armaments but begrudged for social improvements at home. In the 1930s, the Opposition's call for resistance to Hitler went unheeded because of its votes against arms estimates; Labour as the alternative government was harmed by the ambivalence which reflected the heritage of Labour as a protest movement.

Whenever driven to decide, the Party had repudiated pacifism and accepted – sometimes reluctantly – the distasteful obligations of national defence. In 1960, however, the issue took a new form: whether Britain or her allies should retain a horrific type of weapon. Its abandonment would leave the country at the mercy of a potential enemy possessing it; its use would mean suicide; the threat of its use seemed, to young people particularly, profoundly immoral. The Campaign for Nuclear Disarmament aroused the largest spontaneous popular movement in post-war Britain. It won much support within the Labour Movement, and indeed attracted attention from many groups hoping to harness the fervour and enthusiasm to their own ends. To the parliamentary leaders who were asking the electorate to entrust them with the government of the country, CND's pressure was doubly threatening. They were sure that renunciation of nuclear weapons by Britain alone would have no effect elsewhere, while her withdrawal from an alliance which retained them would have destabilising and dangerous consequences. But they thought such decisions would never be taken since Labour's leaders would be discredited in the electorate's eyes (and indeed in their own) if their defence policies could be settled in a party conference where votes were distributed irrationally, were often decided before the situation was known or the issue formulated, and above all were cast by people with no responsibility for the consequences.

CND had an explosive impact on the Labour Party. On 1 March 1960, forty-three MPs, led by Crossman and Shinwell, abstained on an official Labour defence motion. Crossman flaunted his dissidence, proclaiming that he meant to continue doing so. The trade union MPs called loudly for discipline. Gaitskell was not eager, but he made it clear that persistent revolt was incompatible with front-bench status. As the NEC assembled for its crucial meeting on Clause Four, therefore, the breach between the two old schoolfellows again yawned widely. Crossman did not 'care a fig' about Clause Four, or disagree with Gaitskell on the merits of the issue;[1] his opposition was a sign that once again he was trying to make life difficult for the leadership.

An external event now intervened. At the end of April the Government announced the abandonment of Blue Streak, the fixed land-based rocket which would have kept for Britain an independent nuclear deterrent wholly under her own control. That change came at a critical moment in the annual cycle of Labour politics. Conference decisions in the autumn are dominated by the big trade unions, each of which casts its vote as a block and may be bound by the mandate settled at its own conference months earlier (where it often had quite different motions before it). Frequently, as at the party conference itself, the activists on the floor try to impose binding commitments on the platform, which seeks a free hand in order to help the party leadership the following October. In times of tension, the decision of one union conference may affect the mood of another; and since two large and unpredictable unions (AEU and USDAW) meet around Easter, that is often the moment when a trend begins.

The nuclear disarmers' Aldermaston march, also at Easter, had in 1960 an exceptional impact on the unions. For, first, the Clause Four controversy had revived old trade union suspicions of Gaitskell as a middle-class intellectual, making it harder for him to convince the leaders and for them to hold their followers; Frank Cousins himself hinted later that but for Gaitskell's line on Clause Four, his own on defence would have been different. Secondly, the Communist Party had belatedly but nimbly leapt on to the rolling CND bandwagon, hoping to upset the Labour leadership; and in trade union policy-making, Communists often played an active part and wielded a substantial minority vote. Thirdly, minds were changing, and in April 1960 the pollsters found the highest support ever achieved by the unilateralists: 33 per cent.

The abandonment of Blue Streak required a decision on whether Britain should try to retain her own strategic nuclear weapon. Labour's policy-making processes were singularly ill-suited for such a problem – which involved technical costs and consequences hard to assess in opposition, which gave rise to passionate emotional conflicts, and which might require premature pronouncements in a fast-changing situation. Gaitskell knew he risked provoking storms by announcing a change of policy without adequate consultation; he did not allow enough for the danger of seeming so to lag behind events that he lost all power to influence them. Thanks to both the man's personal stubbornness and the party leader's awareness of internal differences, he denied himself flexibility and dangerously weakened his own position.

The consequences were sudden and drastic. By March 1960 he seemed to have beaten *Tribune* and won near-unanimous consent to a new statement of aims. But to all his enemies (and some of his friends) that compromise looked like a retreat; and now he was vulnerable on another flank. By the middle of July he had to abandon any amendment of the party constitution so as to concentrate on resisting the Left's campaign to commit the Party to unilateral nuclear disarmament: a commitment which he would not accept, which would put his leadership in jeopardy, and which – owing to the big union votes already decided – seemed pretty certain to be carried easily at Conference in October.

## Gaitskell and the British Deterrent

The decision to abandon Blue Streak was taken in principle by the Cabinet's Defence Committee on 26 February 1960, and ratified a month later by the Cabinet after the Americans had promised to supply an air-to-ground missile, Skybolt, pending later arrangements for a submarine-based one, Polaris. Rumours leaked out, to which Gaitskell referred in the House. In the new situation he would have been wise, while insisting on staying in NATO, to repudiate the independent British deterrent to which he had never given more than tentative support; but Labour's parliamentary spokesmen on defence (George Brown and John Strachey) were committed to it, and he did not do so.

Gaitskell did not stand alone against a united movement, for many Labour people stood well to the Right of him on defence: Shadow Cabinet colleagues, union leaders and old Keep Calmers as well as the trade union Right in the PLP. He did not defend the British bomb out of personal obstinacy, but he did fail for many months to realise the damage he was doing himself in the Party by refusing to repudiate it explicitly. He stressed how little Labour's policy had changed (to appeal to the ordinary voter) rather than how much (to appeal to his own party workers). Opinion in the country was sharply polarised, with a substantial unilateralist minority and a larger number who still favoured a British bomb. (The unilateralists, however, became the smallest group in June 1960 and much the smallest from September onwards.)

Intermediate positions had little public support, but carried weight in informed circles. The Liberal Party had for years opposed the independent British deterrent, and senior Conservative ex-Ministers were already voicing doubts. The far Left in the Labour Party were joined by some conscientious but not left-wing objectors to the nuclear strategy and by its critics on military grounds, like Crossman. Even George Brown was said to be worrying that the Government might renounce the independent deterrent policy while the Opposition still clung to it.

Gaitskell missed these signs. His lieutenants were strongly resisting any change of policy; and Gaitskell was convinced that Brown concurred. Blue Streak was officially cancelled on 13 April – the very day on which Gaitskell told the PLP that the Shadow Cabinet would reassess Labour's nuclear policy, and sent a long memorandum on it to Sir Vincent Tewson the TUC general secretary. But his covering letter showed both that he would maintain his stand on the wider issues of defence and the alliance, to which he attached supreme importance; and that he did not see that he could do so more securely by abandoning the British bomb, to which he attached little importance. In both scope and timing the leadership moved too little and too late. The letter said that he and Tewson agreed that:[2] 'Britain should only abandon her existing independent nuclear weapons in the event of the formation of the non-nuclear club . . . or [for] some similar major compensating advantage.' A new NEC statement could await the eve of Conference, unless the TUC wanted only 'a reaffirmation of last year's statement'. The delay was to prove unwise.

Gaitskell's memorandum set out his own attitude. Unilateral nuclear disarmament (by Britain or the West) would not be followed by other countries. Neutralism would lead not to disarmament, but to the break-up of NATO and Soviet ascendancy in Europe, or alternatively to the replacement of British influence by German – while Britain would be unable either to affect events or to escape a war if it came. For the Party, incidentally, it would mean 'a far greater electoral defeat'. Remaining in NATO meant sheltering under American nuclear weapons and sharing any guilt involved in that: so no new moral issue arose. Gaitskell summed up:

pending comprehensive multilateral disarmament, Britain must remain in N.A.T.O. which must possess the means of deterring a Soviet attack. N.A.T.O. policy should rely more on conventional and less on nuclear arms; the British defence budget should shift in the same direction, short of reintroducing conscription. Labour should be prepared to give up *existing* nuclear weapons to form the non-nuclear club and help stop the spread of nuclear weapons. Instead of producing a British missile, three alternatives were possible: buying from the U.S.A., sharing with the European members of NATO, or leaving all nuclear weapons to the U.S.A.[3]

On May Day at Leeds, he was to repeat the same case publicly. Meanwhile he was out of the country for two weeks, returning on Friday 29 April to find his leadership under very heavy fire.

Both at the Easter conferences and at Westminster, Labour's mood had changed. The Co-operative Party had voted heavily unilateralist, and USDAW narrowly. The House had debated Labour's censure motion over Blue Streak, which Gaitskell unwisely missed, having promised to attend the Socialist International in Haifa. In the leader's absence, George Brown made it clear that once the V-bombers became obsolescent, the failure of Blue Streak would make it impossible to retain our own missiles and means of delivery, and must 'commit the future five or ten years ahead'. Harold Wilson went further: 'From now on, there is no sense in any defence talk about independence.'[4]

Gaitskell heard the news in Haifa, and was very angry. He had always scrupulously defended party policy in public without additions, subtractions or glosses, and his annoyance at this personal policy-making by his lieutenants prevented him from realising that they had done him a service. On his return he told a rally in Leeds that the Labour spokesmen had never suggested 'that they wanted us to disarm unilaterally, give up Nato and become neutralist. They were concerned solely with the future, of what Britain's position was to be in five years' time.'[5]

Many of Gaitskell's associates, as well as his enemies, wrongly thought him – owing to his silence – still attached to the British bomb. But his listing of the long-term possibilities of remaining in the nuclear race shows that he was most unlikely to take up any of them. As soon as he thought it out, he rejected both a British-produced and a joint European missile, and he recognised that one purchased from the United States would give no independence. Yet he weakened his ability to defend policies he cared about by refusing to renounce explicitly the British bomb which he had never thought essential and now thought probably impracticable. After Blue Streak was cancelled, he redrafted the conclusions of his memorandum to favour abandoning the British bomb as a contribution to non-proliferation. His reluctance to speak out in public, in contrast to his willingness to adapt in private, was probably partly because, once he committed himself finally against the British bomb, he would instantly come under pressure to scrap the V-bomber force – which would lose five years of still valid deterrence, give up any leverage to bring others into the non-nuclear club, and publicly change his defence policy under party pressure. He was thinking – yet again – of the mood of the electorate as a whole, not of the active party workers.

Another old inclination helps to explain his attitude: to think as a future Prime Minister rather than as a present Leader of the Opposition. Where many politicians would have cheerfully committed and then reversed themselves, saying circumstances had changed, Gaitskell took pledges seriously. He hated making advance commitments to ease his immediate political problem. That problem, too, was not simple, since most Labour voters, and many political and trade union colleagues, were well to the Right of Gaitskell on this issue.

Such rational considerations account for his reticence, but not his intensity of feeling. He was determined not to let his critics make him feel guilty by, or confine the argument to, their endlessly repeated question, 'Would you press the button?' That was why when CND was launched he wrote to his daughter that it was 'dangerous and nauseating and stupid. For it won't stop war and may indeed encourage it.'[6] Two weeks after he came back to Britain to face savage criticism, he shocked his closest friends by insisting on 'extreme and provocative clarity'. His combative instincts, conscientiously suppressed for years, had been revived in full fury by the injustice, the pettiness, the virulence – and the success – of the attacks on him. He was acclaimed just after the election, reviled a few weeks later. He had given honest advice about the reasons for the defeat, without seeking to pre-empt the Party's decision, and was accused of conspiracy and treason for doing so. He had compromised over Clause Four for the sake of unity, and found the same enemies attacking him still more aggressively. Now he was execrated as though he would welcome a nuclear war. So his blood was up, and publicly he would not recede an inch. A year later Denis Healey was to write of nuclear independence as 'the virility symbol of the atomic age . . . Britain and France both clutched at it in the shock of having their military impotence exposed at Suez'.[7] For one brief moment in May 1960 perhaps Gaitskell too, fearing his political impotence might soon be exposed, was clutching at a symbol rather than defending a policy.

## *Crossman's First Compromise – Accepted in Vain*

Gaitskell's rash absence from the Blue Streak debate provoked a furious personal assault from Michael Foot, who called it 'the bottom – a total declaration of incapacity and unfitness to lead'. The criticism was widespread, and even the *Daily Herald* recorded ominously mixed feelings: 'The view that as leader he ought to have been there was combined with a suspicion that if he had, the situation might not have been handled so well.'[8]

That summer was the low point of Gaitskell's leadership. As Crosland wrote to him on his return from Israel:

In the 7 months since the election we have suffered a major defeat over Clause 4; we are now fighting an unplanned defensive battle over the H-bomb; we have achieved not one single one of the positive reforms . . . your own position is weaker, and you yourself more criticised, than at any time since you assumed the leadership; and the morale of the Right-wing of the Party is appallingly low.[9]

On the same day the national committee of the AEU, the second largest union, voted unilateralist by 38 to 14. Politically, recent by-elections had gone badly for Labour, and press speculation about Gaitskell's chances of remaining leader became general. Grumbles resumed about his remoteness from his back-benchers, and were now endorsed by his friends, like Dalton: 'You've allowed yourself to walk much too much by yourself . . . there's no serious personal challenge for the Leadership but there's very little serious personal support for the Leader – outspoken, continuous and effectively articulated.'[10] It was the only period when Gaitskell really was consorting with the 'Hampstead Set'. For many prominent colleagues had concluded that in the interest of the Party – or of their own careers – they should detach themselves from a leader in decline; and Gaitskell was becoming correspondingly suspicious of the motives of those who disagreed with him. For a short time, too, he behaved like the left-wingers whom he had despised for insisting on purity and principle at the price of political futility.

George Brown was a key figure, both as official defence spokesman and as chairman of the trade union group of MPs. He was also an old T&GWU official, an old friend of Frank Cousins, and a politician with ambitions of his own who meant to save Gaitskell from himself by working with the leader's critics to fix a compromise. At one Shadow Cabinet early in May 1960 he and Gaitskell 'had a flaming row for a long time'.[11] Soon afterwards, Gaitskell told several friends that 'he was very suspicious of Geo. Brown who was paying too much attention to winning Conference'. Gordon Walker noted:

I began to fear that G. has the seeds of self-destruction in him . . . a death wish. He is becoming distrustful & angry with his best friends & wants to take up absolute & categorical positions that will alienate all but a handful . . . G. said it was certain that a pacifist resolution wd. be carried at Conference. . . . G. was not prepared to 'fudge' principles . . . He wanted to say specifically that we should retain and use nuclear weapons as loyal members of the NATO alliance. I said this was madness . . . Crosland said that if G. took this line how many wd. he carry into opposition? He cd not hope for 100. 'Perhaps 10' said G. who became very angry . . . G. kept on coming back to his personal position. He was not going to falter on defence. He must spell things out.[12]

But Gaitskell's intransigence was untypical of him even in that embattled year, and it lasted less than a fortnight. A couple of days later he saw Brown and found his views 'quite satisfactory . . . The thing I most fear at the moment is being urged by those whom I still count as friends to compromise too much so that I am faced with the beastly choice of a break, even with them, or being driven down a slippery slope.'[13] At precisely that moment, too, the world situation changed dramatically for the worse.

The Summit meeting of four heads of state, which Harold Macmillan had spent years promoting, was about to meet in Paris. At the very moment of assembly it was ruined by the Russians' capture of an American U2 espionage plane. It had aroused great hopes, and when it broke down amid bitter recriminations in the middle of May, the prospects for world peace seemed to have darkened catastrophically. Fears of the Soviet threat revived, and support for the American alliance with them. On 19 May Gaitskell wrote to a friend that 'Mr. K is generally thought to have rescued the leader of the Labour Party.'

No longer feeling so beleaguered, Gaitskell again sought an accommodation with his critics, for their difference was now much narrower. Gaitskell wanted to win the vote at Conference, as the others did, but he would rather lose it than sacrifice the substance of the argument. As a prospective Prime Minister he would not give way on what he saw as a fundamental question of national defence – and as a party leader he could look back on past compromises turned sour: the equivocation over tests in 1957, the ambiguity over the 600 companies, his own acceptance of Clause Four alongside the 'New Testament'. Gaitskell felt sure that his critics on the Left would be implacable, so that further concessions would produce not unity, but only harm to his supporters' morale. The danger, he believed, came above all from the man who dominated nearly one-sixth of the vote at Conference: Frank Cousins.

Thus Gaitskell's brief mood of belligerence had passed by late May 1960, and his disagreement with the compromisers turned only on the possibility, the price and the propriety of appeasing Cousins. The argument over that continued intermittently over twelve months, repeatedly distorted by stories fed to the press to create the impression that, but for Gaitskell's individual obstinacy, agreement would be easy. That legend, plausible if he had persisted in his mood of early May, was quite false. In reality, large bodies of embattled opinion existed on both sides; neither Gaitskell nor Cousins was as intransigent as some of their allies, but neither would sacrifice points of real substance to reach agreement; Brown and Crossman hoped to conceal those real differences by ambiguities and omissions designed solely to satisfy Cousins; and they failed because opponents of unilateralism, quite apart from Gaitskell, would not agree.

Even in his difficult mood of early May, Gaitskell – by Crossman's own account – was much less adamant against concessions than some colleagues. At one Shadow Cabinet Crossman learned from Wilson 'that Gaitskell was coming fast my way. But Soskice and Gordon Walker were holding out for the British deterrent'.[11] Then on 11 and 16 May nearly one-third of the whole PLP attended its defence group,[11] and Crossman discovered

that the serious opposition [to his own views] would come, surprisingly enough, from people who used to be the moderate centre of the Party – Michael Stewart, George Strauss, John Strachey – all still believing in the independent British deterrent . . . this was the undoubted mood of the majority of those there.

At the PLP itself on 24 May, a miner, Roy Mason, 'made a tremendous Right-wing attack on any sell-out of Britain's nuclear weapons and got a good deal of popular support . . . Hugh Gaitskell wound up, fairly all right.'[14] Far from taking the side of the right wing, Gaitskell said he 'thought the Party was pretty much in agreement with George Brown' (whose opening Crossman had called 'really admirable'). The vast majority were against unilateral disarmament; we should stay in NATO but it needed reform, to avoid 'too early reliance on nuclear weapons', to improve political control, and to avoid proliferation. 'The Chairman was given an ovation by the majority present.'[15]

The minority felt differently, for the Left scented blood and had no intention of compromising. Victory for Socialism (VFS) put out a violent unilateralist statement; Sydney Silverman hinted that the leader was not far from being a Fascist; Michael Foot telephoned Crossman to say that the latter's latest article on defence 'was OK, as long as no concessions were made to Gaitskell'.[14] But those predictable reactions mattered only if Cousins shared them.

The Labour Party Executive and the TUC General Council were to meet on 31 May. Four days earlier, Crossman had persuaded George Brown and Morgan Phillips 'to prepare our own draft secretly without consulting Gaitskell'. However, Cousins was kept fully briefed in advance; and the draft withheld from Gaitskell was shown to him. He accepted it provided it was not amended. But the other side had become suspicious, and to Crossman's fury, when the two drafting committees met at Congress House on 1 June, Gaitskell was also present. The meeting lasted four hours. The crucial dispute was over stating that the NATO alliance, in which Britain should remain, must retain nuclear weapons as long as the USSR had them. Brown and Crossman of course agreed with that policy themselves, and Cousins was prepared to tolerate it. But his condition was that the draft must not say so; and then, as Gaitskell pointed out, 'the argument which would follow on interpretation would tear the paper in shreds long before the Conference met'.[16] Crossman's draft deliberately omitted the crucial statement; in drawing attention to the omission, the other TUC leaders exposed his semantic shams as hopelessly fragile. In Gaitskell's account:

Both George and Dick were appallingly prima-donna-ish . . . They had clearly prepared their draft, which I had not seen beforehand, with the view to securing Frank Cousins' assent . . . In the event, it was quite useless. So far as Cousins was concerned, after a long interchange in which I myself took no part at all – chiefly between him and Bill Webber – he made it plain that, in his opinion, NATO should have no nuclear weapons at all . . .

Tewson and others . . . are by no means satisfied with the draft because they think it goes too far in the direction of appeasement.[17]

Gaitskell, however, agreed to Crossman's draft of the Labour Party – TUC joint statement, without major changes, for the sake of party unity. To Sam Watson he wrote:

The document is not ideal and, for my part, I never like evasions. But I suppose it is necessary this year, and there is a limit beyond which I cannot press George Brown. The most urgent thing in this field is, of course, to get the support of the miners and, if possible, the railwaymen too.[18]

## Stampede of the Unions

Gaitskell's major speeches on defence all stressed the three issues of principle: support for national defence, for staying in NATO, and for NATO's retention of nuclear weapons while the Russians had them. He thought the USSR was not rashly aggressive like the Nazis, but would expand if it could without cost. A disarmed West would be vulnerable to Soviet threats as well as military action, while an armed alliance would not need to fight to maintain its freedom. NATO without Britain would either break up or fall under German domination. Compared with those crucial questions the British bomb was a minor issue.

The Easter stampede to unilateralism had been temporarily checked, and when the talks began at Congress House, Gaitskell had become more cheerful – hoping to win, but thinking that Conference would probably accept the forthcoming new defence statement even if it carried a unilateralist motion too. He had stubbornly resisted advice from trade union friends to give up the Clause Four battle, where the

Left were proving much stronger, in order to win the more crucial one on defence. But when the AEU and the Yorkshire Miners both voted unanimously to retain Clause Four unchanged, he reluctantly agreed, seeking only to save face by getting his 'New Testament' approved. Many union leaders were giving priority to resisting the unilateralists, and abandoning any effort to persuade their members to vote for the new statement of aims.

The trade union movement has a strong tradition of loyalty to elected leaders and majority decisions, and had always been a reliable bastion. But now there were doubts. Gaitskell had badly misjudged their attitude over Clause Four; and he had handled them clumsily over the defence talks. The ferocity of his opponents, and his own tactical blunders, made even sympathetic trade-unionists wonder whether Labour could ever regain its unity under his leadership. Few general secretaries would risk trouble in their own unions to defend a political leader whose days seemed numbered; and trouble was certain now that the pacifists, neutralists and conscientious objectors to nuclear weapons were reinforced by the Communist Party, which was powerful in several important unions. Harold Wilson told Crossman that the trade union leaders a few weeks earlier had been wishing that there were an alternative to Gaitskell. 'Now they are saying they must get rid of him, whoever takes his place. He can't last long now.'[19] Trade union reticence, and cautious trimming by most prominent politicians, obliged Gaitskell to fight almost alone – not because few agreed with him, but because few had the courage of their convictions. The Left were quite wrong about the division of opinion in the Party, much less wrong in thinking him personally the real obstacle to their victory.

Thinking their hour had come, they overplayed their hand. VFS demanded Gaitskell's resignation; some left-wingers – Zilliacus, Mikardo and Foot – made direct personal attacks on him; the left-wing weeklies trumpeted that he was 'manipulated by a small and much disliked group of anti-Socialist zealots'. It was barely eight months since Crossman had earnestly warned the Party against the 'odious' temptations into which it, and he, so soon fell headlong: 'Too often our Socialist reaction to defeat is the hunt for a scapegoat, we exculpate ourselves by . . . accusing the leadership of sacrificing Socialist principles . . . this will lead first to tensions and then to splits.'[20]

The Left had gone too far, allowing Gaitskell's friends to mount a counter-attack. The NEC passed a vote of confidence in the leader unanimously (after Wilson and Harry Nicholas had failed to substitute a general resolution condemning all personal attacks); and the PLP did so overwhelmingly, though the spokesmen of the trade union group made their support depend on abandoning any revision of the party constitution. On 13 July the Executive agreed to drop the constitutional revision and merely commend the 'New Testament' to Conference. The retreat was inevitable, but so were the headlines ('CLIMB DOWN BY GAITSKELL'). Again his position seemed in serious jeopardy. By late July the settled union votes showed a unilateralist majority of almost a million, which was generally expected – though not by Gaitskell – to be reinforced by most of the million-odd CLP votes. The press gave him only a fifty-fifty chance of surviving Conference; and many of his supporters were completely defeatist. In Lancashire, he was told, Labour leaders felt: 'It's a pity about old Hugh. He's quite right . . .and it's tragic that the Party won't accept his lead. But it won't and there it is . . . So Hugh had better go. God knows who'll follow him but the Party will survive – it always does.'[21]

## Conference and Parliamentary Party

If Gaitskell's policies were defeated at Conference, his fate would depend on the loyalty of the Labour MPs. Their support for his views was not in doubt, but their willingness to defy Conference was far from certain. Bevan had once thought the PLP followed the leadership because too many prominent figures were place-seekers hoping for office; if so, Gaitskell found no help among them. When Gaitskell was a prospective premier who might soon be appointing Ministers, his future challengers like Greenwood, and his critics like Barbara Castle, had been carefully loyal or effusively friendly. But when the storm broke, most senior figures relapsed into a silence of 'spineless expediency – the words are not harsh enough'.[22] Brown and Crossman shared Gaitskell's views over defence, and yet tried to impose on him a defence statement approved by Cousins behind his back. Harold Wilson foresaw the defection of the union leaders and hopefully predicted that Jonah would soon be thrown overboard. George Brown told Dalton that 'ambitious young Parliamentarians were saying: "How long will H.G. last? I don't want to be dragged down with him, if he goes" '.[23] Crossman found Anthony Benn, who six months earlier had been promoted far ahead of his generation, 'full of gaiety and excitement and also pretty clear that Gaitskell couldn't last very long'.[24] Some politicians are easily excited by hopes of new combinations, new vacancies and new opportunities. Rationalisations are never hard to find for those who need them; not all do. In June, one journalist remarked that 'Mr. Gaitskell has suffered more back-stabbing and personal disloyalty . . . than any other political leader' of recent times.[25]

Gaitskell owed his vote of confidence at the end of June 1960 to the solid trade union back-benchers, numbering nearly a hundred out of more than 250 Labour MPs. They had many complaints and grievances against him. But they felt the need for loyalty to the elected leader; they had little hope of office themselves, and no time for those who manoeuvred to acquire it; and they kept in touch with their working–class constituencies and knew how limited was support for the far Left. The vote of confidence was passed by 179 to 7, and the Party–TUC joint defence statement approved by 97 to 15. The Prime Minister ironically congratulated Gaitskell in the House, writing privately – and in contrast to 1957 – 'I should be sorry if he went, for he has ability without charm. He does not appeal to the electorate, but he has a sense of patriotism and moderation.'[26]

Gaitskell's opponents were demanding that he should promise in advance to resign the leadership if he lost at Conference. In reply, a dozen prominent MPs of the second rank – including several of the old Keep Calm leaders, and seven future Cabinet Ministers – were recruited privately by G. R. Strauss late in July to urge on him that resignation 'would be constitutionally wrong and politically unwise'.[27]

A conference vote for unilateralism would at last face Labour MPs with the dilemma inherent in what Crossman called the Party's unworkable constitution. If, despite the conference decision, they backed the leader they had elected and the policies they supported, the Labour Movement would face bitter strife and damage. They would outrage many active Labour workers who believed that great policy decisions should be made by Conference, not by MPs suspected of preferring office to principle. They would in theory risk expulsion by the NEC, in practice trouble from their own management committees. But the alternative was still less appealing. MPs were well known to believe that for Britain to repudiate nuclear weapons and leave NATO would be disastrous for the country's security and dangerous for the peace of the world; if they now said the opposite because Conference told them to, they would be discredited individually and collectively, and the Labour Party with them – less by their new views than by the blatant fact that those views were not their own.

The question of authority in the Party, evaded so long, so cunningly and so often, was at last inescapably posed. A conflict was inevitable because its constitution reflected the circumstances of a time when Labour was essentially an extra-parliamentary movement, part ideological crusade, part trade union pressure-group, without serious claim to govern. That conflict could be postponed as long as the major union leaders wielded their voting power in agreement with the views of the ordinary Labour elector and in support of the parliamentary leadership. For Labour to win power, that leadership had to be seen to make up its own mind on the central issues of policy – subject to ordinary political pressures, but not to directions from industrial potentates or from militants without responsibility to the electorate. Gallup polls in the 1970s found this repeatedly. Asked who *should* have most influence on Labour policy, 51 per cent of respondents in 1977 said the leader or Cabinet; 38 per cent said Labour voters or MPs; 10 per cent said party workers or the NEC; 3 per cent said the unions. (Asked who *did*, the replies were 24, 7, 9 and 61 respectively. There were similar results in 1975 and 1976.)[28] Many politicians, conspicuous for prudence or ingenuity or ambition, sought desperately to escape the conflict. But others, notably James Callaghan, realised that on this issue accommodation to the pressures would be fatal, exposing them to Macmillan's deadly charge: 'as I understand it, the defence policy of the Party opposite depends on the chance vote of a delegate conference of the NUR'.[29]

The Left had hitherto violently criticised the power of the union leaders, but now claimed that the system represented the rank and file; the Right had previously excused it, but now Woodrow Wyatt attacked Cousins as 'the bully with the block vote'. Those were the familiar inconsistencies of politics. The real change was that union spokesmen without responsibility, instead of endorsing the policies decided upon by elected politicians seeking approval from the voters, were now determined to impose on the prospective government major policies it believed wrong and disastrous. Gaitskell and the Parliamentary Party rightly rejected that imposition, causing anguish and fury to many worthy party workers who believed in the right of the 'rank and file' to decide.

Both sides now prepared for the clash. Resolutions were put down seeking to bind MPs to accept policies decided in Conference, while much of the press urged Gaitskell immediately to challenge its authority. That course would, as he knew, risk alienating once more his natural allies in the trade union group. He told an MP who wanted him to make the PLP's stand clear, that it was 'wiser at the moment to keep rather quiet on the Constitution and leave Morgan Phillips to explain the position'.[30]

In July Phillips produced a long report on the state of the Party and a draft on the constitutional position, and the NEC (at Gaitskell's suggestion) unanimously agreed to publish them over the secretary's signature and not as official statements. 'The whole atmosphere', wrote Crossman, ' . . . is now that of . . . trying to get through the day's business without touching on any serious issue for fear it might blow up.'[31] The constitutional statement satisfied Gaitskell, for it argued:

The Parliamentary Party could not for long remain at loggerheads with Annual Conference without disrupting the Party . . . On the other hand, the Parliamentary Party could not maintain its position in the country if it could be demonstrated that it was at any time or in any way subject to dictation from an outside body . . .

A satisfactory relationship between the several elements of the Party can only be based on mutual trust and confidence, not only between the elements but between individual members as well . . . [32]

Annual Conference does not instruct the Parliamentary Party; it does instruct the National Executive Committee . . . The Election Manifesto . . . on which its members are elected, is the one thing to which, under the constitution, the Parliamentary Party is bound.

The press treated that as endorsing Gaitskell's view, and his NEC opponents – Castle, Crossman, Driberg, Greenwood and Nicholas – publicly disowned it.

So, after four years of conciliation, Gaitskell had changed his whole style and challenged all his followers' central myths – over domestic policy, international affairs and the very structure of the Movement. In home affairs he saw that the great majority of Labour supporters and activists accepted the mixed economy in fact (as they did in 1959 though not necessarily a decade or two later); but he did not see that they were none the less (or all the more) reluctant to say so formally. Abroad, the Labour Movement had since the war grudgingly recognised the unwelcome reality of power in international affairs; but natural horror at the H-bomb had revived the pacifist tradition – and the invincible propensity for wishful thinking – which Labour had gradually discarded after 1933. In the former case, Gaitskell had hoped that intellectual honesty about the Party's long-run aims would reassure the uncommitted voter without alienating the faithful; that assumption proved false, but his retreat entailed no unacceptable commitments, though it cost him heavily in personal prestige. In the latter case there could be no retreat; the Party could not dodge or fudge on the main lines of defence policy, and while he strongly opposed a consistent policy of unilateral disarmament and neutralism, he was revolted by 'the basest hypocrisy' – that of renouncing nuclear weapons for Britain, and so claiming moral superiority over the guilty Americans, yet still relying on their bomb to preserve our independence: as he put it, ' "Yank go home, but don't forget us if there is any trouble" . . . the thing I most dislike'.[33]

His insistence obliged the Party to face yet another hateful truth. Its constitutional arrangements, framed for a purely propagandist movement, were odd or unacceptable except to devoted traditionalists or left-wingers with an axe to grind. To Labour as a potential government, they were a grave handicap; for in the eyes of ordinary voters, the most important single quality of a good Prime Minister was the ability to provide strong leadership. Labour's claim to govern conflicted with its revered traditions, and the Party's vocation was at stake.

In all parties, before and since, many a political leader has evaded or postponed such conflicts between myth and reality by putting up a rhetorical smokescreen to conceal his own preferred destination; the more successfully his followers were cajoled during the journey, the more thoroughly they were liable to be disillusioned on arrival. Such politicians open themselves to suspicions which may be quite unjustified but are not hard to understand. But when similar suspicions were directed against Gaitskell, whose passion for explaining in public exactly what he meant kept landing him in trouble, they told much more about the accusers than the accused. In the summer of 1960 his confident enemies were saying openly that the new policy statement was in itself acceptable, but would not do because the untrustworthy leader would interpret it so as to continue the policy – support for the British bomb – to which they wrongly thought him committed. Some people blamed the leader for treating his followers seriously by clarifying what their views would mean in practice, 'when all they needed was a soothing form of words'.[34] But there were unilateralist spokesmen who took a more detached view. A. J. P. Taylor wrote: 'Gaitskell does not try to cheat us. Those who put unity before principle do.'[34]

## The Art of Manipulating Mandates

Most Labour spokesmen were distracted by the furious internal party debate from pressing the attack on the Conservatives. Gaitskell was not, for he felt strongly 'that the right can only win the struggle within the Party by being the most effective spokesmen against the Tories and for the Party . . . And of course, we only do well for the Party by winning the battle within the Party. The two things are mixed up.'[35] His domestic speeches in that summer of 1960 demonstrated once again his commitment to the principles his enemies accused him of betraying. Instead it was they who were now giving the Tories a welcome respite. In Crossman's view, 'if the Opposition hadn't ceased to exist, this Government would be getting into very rough weather at this moment'.[31]

In August Gaitskell escaped with the family to Yugoslovia for a holiday, returning refreshed to plunge back instantly into routine duties and contacts – often reflecting the approaching battles at the two annual conferences: those of the TUC at Douglas, Isle of Man, and of the Labour Party at Scarborough.

Douglas Houghton, an MP who was on the General Council, reported from the TUC:

Cousins would welcome a call from you to meet and discuss the situation. I fear that nothing would come out of it . . . It is not agreement but submission he is after . . . 'The Party leaders', he told me, 'have changed their minds before under pressure from the rank and file; they can change them again' . . .

Cousins I am sure sees himself as saving the soul of the Labour Party on this and other issues . . . He would like to be granted a place in the counsels of the Party which would make him intolerable, quite apart from being bad for us in the country.[36]

The month of September 1960 was a festival of the Labour Movement's arcane art of interpreting and bargaining over conference resolutions. The TUC had two defence proposals before it: the joint statement, and the T&GWU resolution which rejected defence policies based on the threat of using nuclear weapons. It did not explicitly call for Britain to leave NATO; but many resolutions which did so had been withdrawn in its favour. During the debate Houghton asked Cousins whether it was a unilateralist motion, getting no reply and expecting none, since he knew it had been put forward as *not* unilateralist in 1959.

Gaitskell and his supporters were not committed to Britain retaining a nuclear weapon of her own, but were committed to her remaining in an alliance possessing those weapons as long as the Russians did. Three groups opposed that position. The 'fudgers' like Wilson and Crossman agreed with the policy but not with Gaitskell's insistence on spelling out the implications. Unilateralists wanted Britain to renounce the weapons without always specifying that that implied renouncing protection from an alliance which retained them. Cousins agreed personally with the unilateralists, but his union would not say so explicitly though it supported most of their proposals.

The largest union which was explicitly unilateralist was the AEU. Its president Bill Carron was a Gaitskell loyalist, who at the TUC cast its 900,000 votes in favour of both the rival defence motions – drawing ridicule in the press, and saving the platform from defeat. Both motions were thus passed, the joint statement by 4,150,000 to 3,460,000, and the T&GWU resolution by a bigger margin, 4,356,000 to 3,213,000.

Brown now revived the idea of an accommodation with Cousins, urging the NEC to follow Carron's example in supporting both resolutions, and arguing rather tortuously that the motions themselves were compatible if the T&GWU resolution was judged on its wording, not on Cousins's glosses. But Gaitskell, displaying real ruthlessness for the first time, instructed the secretary not to circulate Brown's memorandum. Crossman did so instead, expecting support from the NEC trade unionists; he forgot that the General Council had with Cousins's agreement ruled the two motions incompatible, and was obliged to withdraw the memorandum without a vote.

So strong was the opposition of the other unions to appeasing Cousins that George Brown later attributed Gaitskell's stubbornness not to personal temperament but to his reluctance to abandon his early backers – like Watson, Williamson and Webber – for a new trade union ally. In 1960, however, to accept Cousins's demands under the threat of a conference defeat would have undermined the leader's authority – as 'peacemakers' like Crossman indeed hoped. Gaitskell underlined the point to George Brown, who later recalled:

I was, however, totally unprepared when he abruptly ended the argument about the merits and, walking up and down the room in his characteristic way, quietly and coldly gave me a personal tutorial on politics and the significance of power. He ended it with a comparison. The clash between himself and Bevan at the time of the 1951 Budget was about something much more vital than the issues involved, he told me. 'It was a battle between us for power – he knew it and so did I. And so is this.'[37]

Understandably aggrieved at the way his memorandum had been withheld, Brown sent Gaitskell a furious protest, and on the eve of Conference he went public in the *New Statesman*, arguing that the NEC could accept the T&GWU motion, the T&GWU could accept the official policy as at least an improvement, and both sides should vote, as he would himself, for both motions. Another self-styled peacemaker now emerged. Anthony Benn (who was privately 'discussing quite openly how to get rid of Hugh'[38]) bought 2,000 copies of the *New Statesman* with Brown's article and distributed them to delegates in the train to Scarborough and at Conference. Desperately, even frantically, he tried to build bridges between two determined men who had no time for him at all. At the pre-Conference NEC, Benn proposed a meeting with Cousins, was defeated, and resigned his own Executive seat twenty-four hours before he came up for re-election. That made a poor impression and he lost one-fifth of his 1959 vote and his seat.

Gaitskell's counter-attack began with a speech in Battersea.

If I believed that by giving up our defence we shall [*sic*] be followed by other nations, including Russia and the United States, I should say 'Let us do it'. But I do not believe that. There is not a shred of evidence to show that either Russia or the United States would do any such thing.

If NATO gave up nuclear weapons while Russia did not, 'this is not going to preserve peace and freedom. It is simply handing over the west lock, stock and barrel to any kind of Soviet threat and pressure.'[39] His supporters too had at last found their tongues, and many local parties were switching sides. Yet as Conference convened, everyone knew that for the first time Labour's leaders faced a major defeat. They wanted no bogus compromise, and their jubilant opponents did so still less. On the Sunday afternoon 5,000 demonstrators led by CND's chairman Canon Collins marched outside the Royal Hotel chanting 'Gaitskell must go!' Inside the Royal Hotel neither camp would speak to the other; most people, except the leader's close friends, gleefully or gloomily gossiped about his successor. Observers noted how the Gaitskells were shunned by colleagues fearing association with inevitable defeat. 'Not once have I seen other key Labour Parliamentary leaders talking to Mr. Gaitskell . . . Never before has a party and its leader fallen apart in an atmosphere so devoid of compassion.'[40]

Manoeuvring to the last over the defence resolutions, the rival union leaders that weekend still sought to deny Cousins his victory. Besides the two proposals voted at Douglas – the official policy and the T&GWU resolution – the Scarborough Conference had before it the AEU's own unilateralist motion. Three of the 'big six' unions were mandated to support unilateralism but the Transport Workers were not, having in 1959 most carefully denied any such commitment. But on Cousins's own resolution the three were not bound – and not friendly. (The Railwaymen's executive had been on sour terms with the

Transport Workers since the bus strike of 1958.) So the AEU's motion, for which these three unions had to vote, might lose without T&GWU backing; and the T&GWU resolution might still be defeated owing to this reticence of the other unions. But to prevent that outcome Cousins was quite prepared to treat his mandate just as flexibly as Carron. First he vainly offered to withdraw his own motion and support the AEU's on condition they promised not to vote for the official statement: demonstrating conclusively that he would not compromise as Brown and Crossman had hoped. When Brown reached Scarborough on the Saturday, he at once told Gaitskell he had abandoned his plan.

Sunday 2 October 1960 was a decisive day. That morning Gaitskell, reading the Lesson at the traditional pre-Conference church service, pronounced words which the press found apposite: 'Then there arose a reasoning among them, which of them should be greatest.' In the afternoon the CND demonstrators condemned Gaitskell; and, at the NEC, the trade union members rejected any deal with Cousins. Meanwhile Cousins had ensured Gaitskell's defeat (though not his own victory) by persuading his union to vote, without a mandate, for unilateralism. Everything now turned on the AEU. Its delegation were irritated at the press ridicule for their vote both ways at Douglas; on Tuesday night, 4 October, they decided after some assiduous lobbying to oppose the official statement and support both hostile motions, the T&GWU's and their own. Now the leadership was bound to be defeated on defence.

## Scarborough: Pyrrhic Defeat

Gaitskell's leadership was challenged on two other fronts. One was the party constitution, where he lost a preliminary skirmish but the position was unexpectedly retrieved on the floor. The other was the Left's effort to refer back his new statement of aims supplementing Clause Four.

Two motions asserted the supremacy of Conference over the PLP: an extreme one from Nottingham Central and a milder one from Wednesbury. Several members argued at the NEC that to oppose the Wednesbury resolution would raise the conference temperature so that the Nottingham one might sweep through on angry protest votes. Gaitskell strenuously disagreed, but lost by 12 to 11, and the Executive then voted 15 to 8 to accept the one with qualifications while opposing the other. In the debate the official spokesman recalled that Conference needed a two-thirds majority to include any item in the party programme, and said the NEC accepted the Wednesbury resolution within the normal rule 'that nobody at all has the power to instruct, control or dictate to the Parliamentary Labour Party'. The mover agreed to that interpretation, and his motion passed easily while Nottingham's was overwhelmingly lost.

The third front, the attack on the new statement of aims, was meant as a direct condemnation of Gaitskell personally; and here Cousins was joined by only one other big union, the NUR, supporting old-style nationalisation as it had in 1957. With over 4 million votes cast for the platform, there was plainly no general opposition majority at Scarborough. That made the defence debate on Wednesday 5 October, all the more dramatic. After all the weekend manoeuvres the leadership seemed doomed to heavy defeat on this issue at least, for the latest calculations of committed votes gave the critics a majority of nearly a million.

Sam Watson, who opened, twice asked opponents of the official policy whether NATO (as well as Britain) should give up nuclear weapons which Russia kept. Cousins was as evasive or incomprehensible as ever: 'When people say to me, do I think the Western Alliance should have nuclear weapons whilst the Russians have them, I say that I am not talking for the Western Alliance, I am talking for Britain.' He concluded with a masterpiece of obscurity: 'When I am asked if it means getting out of N.A.T.O., if the question is posed to me as simply saying, am I prepared to go on remaining in an organisation over which I have no control, but which can destroy us instantly, my answer is Yes, if the choice is that. But it is not that.'[41] On television that night Kenneth Harris at last extracted two intelligible phrases from the flood of words:

HARRIS: Would it be fair to say, Mr. Cousins, that what you would like to see is a British Government in NATO, telling NATO to give up the H-bomb?
COUSINS: Of course, of course . . .
HARRIS: Would you get out of NATO if necessary?
COUSINS: If necessary, of course, yes.[42]

In the debate, Cousins alleged quite wrongly that the drafting committee had rejected an item included in both the T&GWU resolution and Labour's 1958 policy: opposition to aircraft carrying nuclear weapons patrolling from British bases. 'If they had agreed that, we could have been nearer agreement now than ever we have been before in our lives.' (Gaitskell replied that as part of previous policy it was reaffirmed in the second paragraph of the official statement; and that no one had ever raised the point in any of the talks.) Cousins had indicated the previous day that his approach over defence would have been different if Gaitskell had never raised Clause Four;[41] but now he claimed 'very proudly' that he and his union had taken their stand against the bomb when the Communists were supporting it. (That was true of himself though not of the union.) He rebutted any suggestion of pacifism:

Sam talks about our being repudiated if ever we were to tell the electorate in this country that we had surrendered the defence of these fair isles. Of course we would, and we would deserve it. But we regard ourselves as the real patriots . . . this is an attempt to make you an expendable base for America.

Shortly before 3 p.m. Gaitskell rose in a tense and crowded hall to make the most important speech of his life. Neither he nor his wife had slept the previous night. He had written the peroration at 4 a.m., and – for the first time since his maiden speech in the House fifteen years before – told her most of what he intended to say. He told her, too, that probably he would lose, retire to the back benches, and carry on the struggle from there. Tense and tired under the glare and heat of the television lights, he began by stressing the areas in which the Party was united: so that he had hoped that the official policy – with the give and take it involved, including 'the decision not to remain an independent nuclear power' – would have been accepted by the overwhelming majority. It had not: and as he turned to his unilateralist critics, the tiredness vanished. It was to CND's credit, he said, that they did not pretend to moral virtue by renouncing Britain's nuclear weapons, while still sheltering for security behind America's; but neither Cousins nor Foot nor the AEU spokesman would say openly that Britain should leave NATO unless it gave up those weapons. Suppose NATO did so:

Are we really so simple as to believe that the Soviet Union, whose belief in the ultimate triumph of communism is continually reiterated by their spokesmen, are not going to use the power you put into their hands? . . . if the Japanese had had atomic weapons in 1945, do you think that President Truman would have authorised the dropping of the bomb? . . . Mr. Khrushchev himself . . . believes that the possibility of retaliation deters the United States . . . why should we not apply the theory the other way round?

So, since the other NATO countries would not give up nuclear weapons:

You cannot escape it. If you are a unilateralist in principle, you are driven in to becoming a neutralist . . . either they [the AEU] mean that they will follow the cowardly hypocritical course of saying: 'We do not want nuclear bombs, but for God's sake, Americans, protect us', or they are saying that we should get out of N.A.T.O. . . .

He could not understand what the T&GWU motion implied about NATO, or what Cousins's explanation meant. 'I leave it to Conference to decide whether we had a clear answer.' Either the differences between it and the policy statement were serious and the Executive had to oppose it, or they were 'almost negligible, as some of my colleagues believe. But if that is the case, how can one explain [Cousins's] determined opposition to the policy statement?'

After speaking for forty-five minutes, he turned to the issue of the leadership. 'It is perfectly reasonable to try to get rid of somebody . . . who you think perhaps is not a good Leader . . . What would be wrong . . . and would not be forgiven, is if, in order to get rid of a man, you supported a policy in which you did not wholeheartedly believe.' Furious interruptions began, especially from the galleries packed with his implacable foes. 'I have been subject to some criticism and attack,' he shouted back, 'I am entitled to reply.' He took up the constitutional issue, no longer in the abstract but as it would soon face the PLP:

It is not in dispute that the vast majority of Labour Members of Parliament are utterly opposed to unilateralism and neutralism. So what do you expect them to do? Change their minds overnight? . . . Supposing all of us, like well-behaved sheep were to follow the policies of unilateralism and neutralism, what kind of an impression would that make upon the British people? . . . I do not believe that the Labour Members of Parliament are prepared to act as time servers . . . because they are men of conscience and honour . . . honest men, loyal men, steadfast men, experienced men, with a lifetime of service to the Labour Movement.

There are other people too . . . who share our convictions. What sort of people do you think they are? What sort of people do you think we are? Do you think we can simply accept a decision of this kind? Do you think that we can become overnight the pacifists, unilateralists and fellow travellers that other people are?

The passage brought continuous boos and shouts, reaching a crescendo at the words 'fellow-travellers'.

He suggested that the system by which most votes were pre-determined before the Executive recommendations were known

is not really a very wise one . . . the result may deal this Party a grave blow . . . but . . . There are some of us, Mr. Chairman, who will fight and fight and fight again to save the Party we love. We will fight and fight and fight again to bring back sanity and honesty and dignity, so that our Party with its great past may retain its glory and its greatness.

He appealed to 'delegates who are still free to decide, to support a policy . . . which yet could so easily have united the great Party of ours, and to reject what I regard as the suicidal path of unilateral disarmament which will leave our country defenceless and alone.'[43]

Gaitskell's speech did not create the division in the Labour Party. But it certainly made the split obviously, physically visible. As he finished exhausted, drenched in perspiration under the hot television lights like an actor after a major performance, he was greeted by cheers from nearly two-thirds of the delegates: 'the biggest ovation of his life . . . He sat down – but they would not let him go. Far more than half were on their feet again singing with great fervour that he was a Jolly Good Fellow.'[44] On the platform where the NEC sat, several trade-unionists joined in enthusiastically, while the middle-class MPs beside them stayed ostentatiously seated like the glum minority in the hall: 'Never have so many matches been struck in such a short time on one small pipeful of tobacco as there were by Mr. Wilson during Mr. Gaitskell's speech. He remained seated in silent demonstration of protest during the standing ovation the leader received.'[45]

Then the votes were announced. The Executive had lost four times. The official policy went down by just under 300,000. Slightly bigger majorities carried the AEU's unilateral motion and defeated a Woodworkers' resolution endorsing the official statement and supporting NATO. Cousins's ambiguous resolution squeaked through but, thanks to the opposition of the NUR, by only a tiny margin.

*Defence Votes at Scarborough, 1960 (in thousands)*

| Motions | NEC | ASW | AEU | T&GWU |
|---|---|---|---|---|
| For the leadership | 3,042 | 2,999 | 2,896 | 3,239 |
| For the opposition | 3,339 | 3,331 | 3,303 | 3,282 |
| Majority | −297 | −332 | +407 | +43 |
| Result | lost | lost | carried | carried |

For the first time the Left had beaten the leadership on a major issue – and Dora was puzzled that they looked so glum at the results, while Hugh sat beaming. For instead of the million-odd votes expected, the majority against him was only a third of that: he had appealed successfully to those 'still free to decide'. The secretary of the Campaign for Nuclear Disarmament herself testified: 'He was extraordinarily effective . . . as he spoke you could feel the Constituency Party votes falling like heavy rain around you . . . it was a hollow victory.'[46]

The figures showed roughly how the constituency parties had voted. In 1960 the local parties were much bigger, more vital and representative than they have since become, and their verdict was trebly significant. Firstly, most of those who decided after hearing the debate were from CLPs; most other votes had been settled months before by people pronouncing on documents they had not seen. Secondly, the CLPs, which could make and unmake MPs, would influence Gaitskell's next vital battle in the PLP. Thirdly, they symbolised the Left's cherished myth: a democratic, struggling rank and file perpetually baffled by an elitist leadership. The very people who had so long been trumpeted by *Tribune* and the Left as the authentic voice of the Movement had come down decisively in Gaitskell's favour. He won about 64 per cent of the CLP votes cast, with perhaps one-fifth abstaining.[47] 'He turned', wrote one journalist, 'what looked like an exultant triumph for his enemies into the hollowest of paper victories . . . It was the greatest personal achievement I have ever seen in politics . . . Everyone in the hall knew that if there had been a straight vote of the delegates Gaitskell would have won overwhelmingly.'[48] As another reporter put it: 'This was no old leader going down; it was a new man rising.'[44]

## A Necessary Struggle

Only a year earlier, Gaitskell had been the unchallenged chief of a united army, acclaimed by his own forces even in defeat; now he was leading a sortie by half those troops against the other half who were besieging his own headquarters. His political style had changed dramatically. Over four years he had earned a reputation for conciliating all Labour factions; for ingenious ambiguity in papering over differences; for giving the highest priority to party unity, and for skill in preserving it even at some cost to its (and his own) public standing. The doyen of industrial reporters wrote that critics as well as supporters saw him as 'more anxious to co-ordinate conflicting views than any previous leader'.[49] But for six months he had been behaving quite differently, insisting on policies clear in substance and presentation which marked out the fault-lines within the Party instead of blurring them. In this

new role he attracted passionate loyalties and aroused bitter resentments which long survived his death.

Two explanations were advanced for the change. One – held by both
admirers and detractors – was that the clash was inherent in his
commitments to intellectual honesty and clarity, to teaching his
supporters that the right thing must be done for the right reasons even
at the risk of a split. That half-truth seizes upon strife-torn and
therefore dramatic episodes – the 1951 Budget, the Stalybridge speech
in 1952, the drive against Bevan in 1955, the crisis of 1960 – and
overlooks long years before, between and after: it does not explain why
those characteristics predominated only for a few brief periods.

Gaitskell was a believer in political teamwork, not individualism. His
loyalty to 'the Party we love' was old and deep and strong, and he never
saw it as merely a vehicle to power. His attachment to the working-class
movement had been firmly rooted since Nottingham; he was
thoroughly at home in the slums and workingmen's clubs of South
Leeds; he drew emotional sustenance from mixing with ordinary
workers on his provincial tours; at the Durham Miners' Gala, 'he was at
his most benign as he watched the banners pass – almost like a teddy
bear in his warmth and spontaneity . . . much loved by the Durham
miners and their wives'.[50] He did not believe (as his opponents
pretended) that the Movement had a left-wing rank and file which must
be manipulated from above through discipline and intrigue by a
handful of middle-class intellectuals and union bosses – but thought
rather that he and not the Left represented the real rank and file: the
ordinary Labour voter and trade-unionist, and the election workers
who had turned out in 1959 in greater numbers than ever. Those
people, he was convinced, believed in his kind of Labour Party – out of
instinctive loyalty, or to achieve practical reforms in an unsatisfactory
society, and not at all for the ends sought by the dedicated ideologues of
the far Left.

A second type of explanation for Gaitskell's new stance was
cherished – or publicised – by his enemies in the Party. At the time of
Clause Four it was fashionable on the Left to suggest that he was
obsessed with winning power for its own sake and not for a purpose: a
view he soon showed to be absurd by risking his own political survival
with reckless courage. He had sought power before 1959 through party
unity, always trying to conciliate and compromise with the Left. In
1957 he had found a formula to conceal the differences about nuclear
testing – and Macmillan's ascent to popularity began with a denunciation of him for that. He had repeated the miracle over nationalisation –

and the Conservatives exploited the ambiguities two years later. He had incurred trade union criticisms, devastating rebuke from Macleod and electoral unpopularity by supporting Cousins in the bus strike; and the union leader promptly repaid the politician's costly sacrifice by a direct political challenge over defence on the eve of a general election. In that election Labour kept its unity despite Cousins, its spirits were better than ever, its prospects seemed good up to polling day; yet it found its popular support had quietly dwindled away.

Gaitskell therefore set out to make the Party adapt its appeal to new social conditions – as the Conservatives had so often done and the Liberals had failed to do. That attempt involved him in a battle on three fronts: Labour's domestic aims, its international stance and its own internal structure. The first front was opened up by his own choice, the second by developments elsewhere, and the third by the battle spilling over on to ground where in October 1959 he had deliberately – if probably unwisely – decided not to engage. He was eventually driven to humiliating withdrawal (short of total defeat) on the first front in order to protect his flank on the second. There, after an initial setback, his counter-attack brought for several years decisive victory on both second front and third. But the struggle left him an object of intense suspicion and even hatred to a large minority of the Party. How far was he responsible for inflicting these deep and lasting wounds? Could they have been avoided? If not, were they justified by the causes for which he fought?

To some extent the disputes arose from misunderstanding; as Gaitskell wrote to one Labour agent, 'The trouble is that people do not read or listen to what one says.'[51] Frequently, they heard only what they wanted to hear. When Gaitskell said he would 'fight and fight again', Anthony Benn whispered to Crossman: 'If only he had said that about the Tories' – quite forgetting that he had, almost in the same phrase, just a year before.[52] Distrust of him fed on misinterpretation, and caused it too. In that Scarborough peroration, the words 'fellow-travellers' infuriated many people. Some of Gaitskell's own friends regretted them. Yet his phrase 'pacifists, unilateralists and fellow-travellers' plainly applied to three groups not one, for no true pacifist can be a fellow-traveller, or vice versa. That night on television he reaffirmed explicitly that he was saying only that some – not all – supporters of unilateral nuclear disarmament were fellow-travellers. So some of them were, and he was just as entitled to say so as they were to point out that the Tory press took his side.

Besides the misunderstanding of words there was misconception –

and misrepresentation – of what Gaitskell stood for. That was most marked over Clause Four, where he was ferociously attacked – not for what he said but for what he was wrongly assumed to mean. His opponents were not totally wrong in reading a little more into his intentions than he said, for though his proposal was only to supplement Clause Four, his private preference was for replacing it. But they were totally wrong in inferring that he was temperamentally a Liberal, without emotional roots in the Labour Movement. George Wigg, who managed both Harold Wilson's leadership campaigns, claimed that the clash at Scarborough arose 'not from conflicts about defence, but from distrust about what Hugh Gaitskell and some of his Right Wing friends would do if they had the power.'[53] Ironically in the light of events only four years ahead, Wilson himself publicly suggested that Gaitskell secretly hoped to resuscitate the independent British deterrent which Labour had officially pronounced to be dead. There was misrepresentation also over the structure of the Party, for it suited Gaitskell's opponents to attack him personally for policies which had emerged from long discussions within the leadership. Yet often the leadership was more willing to compromise than its supporters in the unions, the country or Parliament.

Behind all the misunderstandings lay Gaitskell's sharp policy differences with the unilateralists (if not with all their political allies). Over Clause Four, to many of his followers he seemed to threaten the identity of the Labour Party as they understood it. Over defence, he and his supporters rightly or wrongly felt the same about the unilateralists, who were reverting to the pacifist stance which Labour had abandoned in the 1930s. While that wing were in a minority, said Gaitskell, they would always prefer Labour to the Tories; but if they became a majority the other wing could not defend the new policy and the Labour Party would have been finished.

Vienna and Munich in the 1930s had shown Gaitskell what military defeat and occupation could mean to a working-class movement and a nation, and impressed on him for life the unpleasant realities of power in international affairs which men and women of goodwill are so prone to ignore. The Campaign for Nuclear Disarmament mobilised those people in force, expressing a natural moral revulsion at the horrors of a nuclear war rather than a coherent political argument about the best means of avoiding one. That revulsion harnessed more of the enthusiasm and idealism of the younger generation than any other post-war movement, but Gaitskell was unable to canalise or indeed, it sometimes appeared, to appreciate its achievement – not altogether surprisingly considering how he was vilified by CND spokesmen, and especially by some of their allies who had no place in a democratic movement.

CND sought a moral gesture by Britain in the hope, but not on the condition, that others would follow the example. On that condition, Gaitskell too would have made the gesture. Without it, he was exasperatingly but rightly emphatic that the gesture would be hypocritical, not moral, unless Britain further renounced the protection of the American bomb; but that if she did so, her own security and peace itself might be at risk. Unlike the CND rank and file, the Left politicians preferred to have these unwelcome implications clothed in discreet obscurity – rather as their pre-war predecessors had tried to embrace collective security without quite renouncing pacifism, thus paralysing Labour's opposition to Hitler and denying it either immediate influence or subsequent credit.

Gaitskell was therefore opposed, over defence as well as over Clause Four, by some who disagreed not with his policies but with his tactics – hoping to cover up substantial differences by ambiguous phrases, and to purchase unity by further Danegeld to the Left. They condemned his uncomfortable insistence on speaking out when he might have eased his – and their – political position in the short run by a judicious silence. As one commentator noted:

some M.P.s would much have preferred to discuss other topics with their constituency officers.

The more embarrassed they feel, the more they regard Mr. Gaitskell as the author of their unhappiness . . . [Though] he is only sticking to the policy approved by the National Executive, the Parliamentary Labour Party, the General Council of the T.U.C. . . . other colleagues on these bodies have found it unnecessary to stick so closely to the policy.[54]

Sticking to the policy called for political courage; but when explained, it carried conviction. At Scarborough, Gaitskell's speech was so effective that Crossman, the arch-fudger, said it could satisfy everyone but pacifists and absolute unilateralists, and offered a basis for unity.

Gaitskell found that basis by emphasising the choice between NATO and neutralism: not a provocative side-issue but the real decision facing the country. Some sympathisers have questioned that emphasis, and suggested that the unilateralists could have been satisfied if Britain, like Norway, had stayed in NATO without nuclear arms of her own (relying on those of the USA). That course would have seemed evasive and hypocritical to Gaitskell, and it was also dangerous for him. He would at once have come under pressure to advocate destroying existing stocks and removing existing bases – pressure less easy to resist when the argument of principle had been conceded and his own political authority undermined. In the past he had often acceded – with mixed results – to the call to compromise for the sake of unity. Now he knew it was a dangerous siren song.

His implacable enemies on the Left treated each concession as a sign of weakness: not as a basis for uniting the Party but as a spring-board for demanding more. In March those enemies had sought to refer back the new statement of aims, to which they had no objection at all, solely in order to injure Gaitskell. In June Crossman testified that the new defence statement included only 'the tiniest modifications' to his own compromise but those enemies rejected it, demanding further changes (which would not have satisfied them either). When Houghton put it to Cousins that the leadership had made all the concessions so far, Cousins answered that they should make more.[36] Feeling the wind in their sails, the Left would permit no unity in the Party except on their own terms. But those terms would not have led to unity either, for the other wing would not have accepted them; and even if it had, *Tribune*'s temporary allies from the far Left would at once have broken away to resume the battle.

So if Gaitskell did not stand and fight, he faced ejection or humiliation. Before Scarborough some of his calculating colleagues foresaw him surviving an adverse vote only after ignominious fixing – by a rescue operation purporting to unite the Party, soon to be followed by the *coup de grâce* delivered by a newly elected deputy leader.[31] Suspecting some such plans, Gaitskell knew that concessions made to preserve his nominal leadership would only render it futile, destroying the kind of Labour Party in which he believed and finally alienating the voters.

Of course he made mistakes of judgement. After the 1959 defeat, he had enough personal standing and enough assent from his colleagues to seek structural changes strengthening him for future battles: an appointed parliamentary committee certainly, perhaps even a re-constituted NEC representing directly both the Party in the country and that at Westminster. Instead he chose to assault a cherished myth. 'We were wrong (*all* of us),' wrote Anthony Crosland – tactfully, since he had discouraged the idea – 'to go for *doctrine*; we should have gone for *power*.' The upshot was a retreat, honourable enough since the issue was one of presentation not of principle, but still humiliating and damaging to Gaitskell's leadership. (The retreat caused further loss, but no retreat would have lost more: which is why raising the issue had been an error of judgement.) He replied to Crosland: 'I agree . . . that by going from [sic] doctrine we have lost a lot of power. We have to regain the power and use it more cautiously.'[35]

Nobody had expected the nuclear disarmers' speedy capture of the unions, and Gaitskell admitted in the same candid confession, 'Our great mistake in the last year has been to underestimate the strength of the forces against us within the Party.' That error was not the result of listening too much to a small and unrepresentative clique (in raising Clause Four he listened to them too little). It came from two optimistic beliefs: first that he could once again reach a consensus among conflicting views on the line of adaptation to the new social configuration revealed by the election; and probably also that his former critics sought unity too, and (especially after his triumphant reception in the campaign) would not seek to reopen the old wounds at the first opportunity.

That second assumption, he soon learned, was far too charitable, and instead he found prudent reticence in many quarters, and efforts to exploit his difficulties in some. The experience had a powerful effect in making him wary about his colleagues and dubious of their motives. For a short time he became dangerously isolated, and momentarily almost as over-suspicious as his successor was permanently. His old friend Frank Pakenham sent a worried warning:

I am convinced that you are . . . infinitely the best Leader available . . . But . . . your leadership is in real jeopardy . . . I find a widespread conviction that you expect loyalty without providing the opportunity of consultation which your leading followers might reasonably expect . . . particularly some who are younger rather than older than you and me and who are somewhere near the middle of the road.

Gaitskell took that very seriously, but he was cautious when others encouraged him to develop closer relations in the PLP. Eirene White, just such a representative figure of the Centre, wrote with sympathetic understanding:

That you are by far our best player no one could doubt. But holding a team together is a different job from being a brilliant player and it is asking a great deal from one man to expect him to do both with equal success, especially in the exceedingly difficult position of Opposition, with no real sanctions or benefits at one's disposal. The temptation to work with like-minded men who leave one in peace and don't intrigue must be almost overwhelming. But they are not a sufficient basis for leadership . . . What worries me is the lukewarm loyalty . . . [of] almost all the leading figures in the Parliamentary Party.[55]

Gaitskell replied that he agreed to such co-operation if it did not endanger the line he thought indispensable for the Party's survival. To Anthony Crosland, who also wrote to urge him to consult more with Brown, Callaghan and Wilson, he was blunter:

The timing . . . is very important . . . it would be a bad atmosphere, I think, if the election of deputy leader had not taken place.

The three people cannot really be regarded as just rational human beings, each principally interested in winning the next Election. They are all able and talented, but they are *not* like that! . . . I do not think any 'agreement' which might be supposed to emerge would really be worth anything, though I certainly would not rule it out at a rather later stage – when we are through the rapids.[35]

In the Party as a whole, Gaitskell knew he was far stronger on defence than on Clause Four: with unprecedented support from the CLPs, the supposed fortress of his opponents; a strong majority in the TUC General Council; and almost solid backing from the trade union MPs who knew how working-class voters felt. Strong enough to stand firm as he had not been over Clause Four, he had far more compelling reasons to do so. Defence was not a matter of presentation for the long term but an immediate issue of major policy. It was a decision expressing the whole character of the Party, likely to decide whether Labour could ever regain the voters' confidence, or would rather languish in the impotent purity of perpetual opposition. Besides, Gaitskell's supporters were equally aware of the stakes. Even if he had himself been inclined to further compromise, their strong hostility to it would have driven him to think again.

The Scarborough result brought the issue of power in the Party into the battle. Like Clause Four, defence policy was now entangled with the power struggle, and Gaitskell knew that every retreat and concession now gave momentum and enthusiasm to his enemies, demoralised his supporters, and set his allied chieftains wondering whether the time had come to desert. So, unlike his successor, Gaitskell did not seek to devalue Conference by ignoring the verdict, but to restore harmony between the different sectors by reversing it. Had Conference voted really heavily against him in 1960, he might have felt it wrong, or found it impossible, to organise the resistance as party leader. But the narrow vote banished any thought of resignation from his mind, or of trimming from those of MPs. As one of his chief opponents had once written: 'Conference is . . . wholly unrepresentative of public opinion and . . . [if the leader] concedes to it too far, he will certainly lose the next Election.'[56] Scarborough made it both possible and necessary for Gaitskell to base himself on a representative body of the Movement which was responsible, and therefore responsive, to the mass of Labour supporters in the country: namely, the Labour Members of Parliament.

# 21

# 'Fight and Fight Again' 1960–1

*'The fire of wrangling was hurriedly quenched'*
(Crossman, 1961)
*'A triumph won by fortitude and character'*
(James Griffiths to HG, 1961)

## Challenged for the Leadership

Scarborough transformed Gaitskell's position. Colleagues and out-siders had both written him off. Back in May he had himself doubted if even a hundred Labour MPs would follow him in defying Conference. Few of his senior advisers had believed the PLP would hold. Even afterwards many of his friends were gloomy, including the Chief Whip and George Brown; Denis Healey wondered if the Party could ever be united under Gaitskell; and most of the press still thought the leader would probably be out by Christmas.

Gaitskell, however, at once saw the significance of the narrow conference vote. In the sleepless night just before the debate, he was still telling Dora he might lose, and have to go. But the next night he was sleepless again – planning a campaign throughout the country to 'deal with Mr Cousins'. From Scarborough he went on to loyal South Leeds, where his colleague Alice Bacon found him watching the end of a Western on television; only when the bad men had been rounded up would he turn his mind to doing the same at home. In bed that morning, he said he had begun planning operations at the grass roots to reverse the decision. His sketchy note of his 'Objects' begins 'This year – To consolidate and capture power. Next year – To clean up . . . This year desperately good organization needed. Next year com-pletely ruthless decisions.'[1]

The excesses of Gaitskell's opponents made his task much easier. At the top the amenities were still observed, and Cousins infuriated his wife by inviting Gaitskell to the union's dinner. But in private the critics displayed 'poisonous hatred', and the public debate was conducted with 'incredible venom'. Many unilateralists, being neither sectarian nor vicious, were shocked by their colleagues who were. In one local party, whose MP was chairman of VFS, a careful academic survey found that a third of the members were unilateralists – among whom, half supported Gaitskell's leadership.[2] His opponents never understood that many voters wisely judge a political leader not on policies (which may soon be out of date) but on character (which suggests his response to unforeseen crisis).

Those who agreed with Gaitskell's views naturally reacted still more strongly. Trade-unionist MPs in particular had many grumbles about Gaitskell but felt all their traditions of loyalty outraged by the bitter personal attacks. When Zilliacus called him an 'amateur of genocide . . . making a burnt offering to Pentagon brinkmanship of the British people', the trade union group raised this as blatantly infringing the 1952 rule against personal attacks; those familiar with the Labour Movement and its double standards will at once appreciate, and no one else will ever understand, why it was Mr Gaitskell who felt obliged gently to explain that he felt no personal animosity towards Mr Zilliacus, at whose feet he had sat twenty-five years before. A few weeks later the National Executive suspended Zilliacus from the Party for publishing an article in an official international Communist journal.[3]

The first test of the mood came about because of the death of Aneurin Bevan in the summer of 1960. Since 1959 he had been both party treasurer and deputy leader. For the treasurership, the unions to avoid another political feud settled early on Harry Nicholas, Cousins's deputy in the T&GWU, who was elected unopposed at Scarborough. At Westminster, contests were normal for vacant posts but unheard-of against incumbents. But that precedent was broken in 1960.

Brown, Callaghan and Harold Wilson were the likely contenders for the vacant deputy post (Robens had just left the House to become chairman of the Coal Board). But Wilson, instead, reluctantly stood against Gaitskell in an unprecedented challenge for the leadership itself. His hand was forced by the Left, for if he refused to carry their banner in the major fight, he risked losing their backing in the minor one – and afterwards. On 20 October 1960 he announced that he was standing as an opponent of unilateralism who as leader could unite the Party.

Wilson did not confine himself to the issue of unity; perhaps to conciliate the unilateralists whom he had just rebuffed, he attacked Gaitskell on defence also – particularly over American bases in Britain, where the leader was politically vulnerable since he could not count on one of the two big unions friendly to him, the NUM. Wilson also sought to revive the old unjustified suspicions about Gaitskell and the British bomb, saying:

I believe the crisis of confidence arises from the feeling that some of our leaders do not unequivocally reject the idea of the independent British bomb, and that they are waiting for Skybolt or Polaris to come along, with the idea of returning to the notion of a separate British deterrent, with an American rocket to deliver it. I believe it is essential that the Leader of the party states beyond all doubt that, as the policy statement intended, he accepts that there will be no British H-bomb.[4]

Wilson as leader of the Party certainly did put matters beyond all doubt, for the 1964–70 Government kept the American Polaris submarines, and built a few more of its own.

Gaitskell's majority – out of over 250 Labour MPs – was generally expected to be only 30 to 40, for few people realised how the mood had changed on the back benches since Scarborough. The behaviour of the Left provoked resentment; the debate strengthened members' convictions on the merits; the narrow vote made calculators reassess, as those who shrank from offending their local general management committees found that most CLPs were not on the Left after all, and those concerned about the next election had also to fear a commitment to unilateralism which would lead to a Labour holocaust at the polls.

Above all, most Labour MPs were no longer trying to appease the unappeasable, sensing that in its hopes of deposing the hated leader, the Left had no interest in conciliation except as a manoeuvre to undermine Gaitskell's position still further. The mood of the PLP rank and file had hardened against further concessions; they voted four to one against Barbara Castle's complicated resolution on Polaris bases, knowing that as soon as it was accepted, she would have asked for more. Gaitskell commented that: 'Two or three years ago . . . he would have been under heavy pressure to unite the party by acceding to a reasonable request. There had been no suggestion of that this time.'[5]

This PLP reaction came not mainly from the placemen whom Bevan had so despised, but from the rank and file MPs without much hope of office or flair for publicity. It was not orchestrated by the leaders of the parliamentary Right: for Gaitskell's supporters now included Strauss's group, mainly old Keep Calmers, Jim Griffiths whose career was almost over, and Philip Noel-Baker whose life had been devoted to disarmament. But a few hopeful compromisers still sat in the outgoing Shadow Cabinet: George Brown, Wilson, Fred Lee his running-mate, and Crossman. They had mistaken the mood, and James Callaghan took the lead there in insisting on fighting to reverse the Scarborough decisions.

In such conditions a universally-trusted peacemaker would have faced an uphill task, and Wilson and his friends did not qualify. At Scarborough itself *New Left Review* had cruelly commented in its daily bulletin: 'If the Labour party ends this week facing in two directions, it is certain that the figure of Mr. Wilson will be there, at the end of both of them.' Gaitskell, attending an American election-night party just after the PLP's leadership vote, would not take sides by displaying either a Nixon or a Kennedy button – and when someone suggested wearing both, he replied, 'I can't, they would take me for Harold Wilson.' The critical PLP meeting – held in Committee Room 14 with its large picture of 'The Death of Harold' – further sharpened lines that were clearly drawn. Perhaps disconcerted at his bad reception, Wilson was unusually ineffective, and Brown returned to Gaitskell's side to affirm that no compromise was possible. 'You can't do it, Harold. I know – I've tried . . . Mr. Gaitskell was right, and I was wrong.'[6]

Wilson's friends counted on 20 abstentions to weaken Gaitskell's strength. Instead, only seven of the 254 Labour MPs failed to vote (four Gaitskellites were abroad, and one ill). Wilson had 81, and Gaitskell more than double: 166, nine more – thanks largely to the young newcomers – than when he was elected leader five years before. Other results were as decisive. For deputy leader, Brown won on the second ballot a week later by 146 to 83. Wilson and Lee survived in the Shadow Cabinet, but each dropped more than 40 votes; they came ninth and twelfth (bottom) instead of top and fifth. Harold Macmillan foresaw that Gaitskell's personal position would be stronger by the time of the next election: 'People admire tenacity and courage – and he has shown both.' Hugh Dalton characteristically trumpeted: 'After a month as squalid, ignominious, faithless & ego-ridden as any I can remember in my long political journey, decisive victory at the end, & a strong wind blowing the sheep & goats apart.'[7]

## Crossman's Second Compromise: A House of Marked Cards

The Labour MPs knew Gaitskell's qualities as a leader, and feared that unilateralism might turn the reviving Liberals into dangerous competitors. But for other power centres in the Movement, public opinion was less crucial than feelings (and votes) within the Party itself. Transport House was divided, and the National Executive was properly conscious of its responsibility to Conference.

The role of Conference soon became central to the controversy, partly because unilateralism was losing popular support not gaining it. Party members who had for years opposed conference decisions naturally made the most of their unfamiliar majority status, claiming that Gaitskell was entitled to campaign against the decisions of

Conference only as an ordinary MP, not as leader of the Party, and therefore should not have stood for re-election. At Cardiff on 23 October 1960, just before the PLP voted on the leadership, Gaitskell devoted a major speech to the issue. On that argument, he said, no one with his views should stand – so that the MPs could elect only officers with whom most of them disagreed. Of course the situation of the PLP would become 'extremely difficult' if Conference repeatedly took up a unilateralist or pacifist position by substantial majorities reflecting the views of most of the Party. Instead there had been only a single narrow vote. He believed that Labour supporters were against the decision and that the next conference would reverse it, in which case individual MPs and the PLP would 'look a little silly' adjusting and readjusting.

Privately Gaitskell felt he should, and would have to, resign the leadership if Conference went against him again. But he would not undermine his support by saying so publicly. Instead he reacted to the mass movement's aberration in 1960 by working furiously to win it back in 1961. Symbolically, as his Cardiff audience began to disperse after singing 'Cwm Rhondda' he stopped them to lead them in singing 'The Red Flag'.

The Left had been misled by their own propaganda. They were strong enough among active party workers (notably in middle-class parties in safe Tory seats) and in some unions. But they never recognised that the more strident activists were out of touch with many of the Party's supporters and most of its voters. Gaitskell gave voice and heart to a body of inarticulate but solid Labour and trade union loyalists, and even Crossman admitted that 'Gaitskell is more popular than ever before with the rank-and-file workers.'[8]

Gaitskell's friends at Westminster were helped outside the House by the Campaign for Democratic Socialism, which promoted grass-roots organisation to resist the leftward trend in the Party and reverse the Scarborough decisions. The leader was never personally involved and gave no official blessing; he even told the Chief Whip not to have any dealings with the campaign. CDS won some following in the unions and local parties, and kept as active party workers people who, if isolated, might well have lapsed into apathy and discouragement. It was endorsed by three prestigious figures, R. H. Tawney, Hugh Dalton and Clem Attlee – who wrote quite unexpectedly without being lobbied. Herbert Morrison declined.

On 24 January 1961 the Shadow Cabinet, NEC and General Council set up a drafting committee of four each to compose a new defence policy statement. The Twelve included only two unilateralists, and were predominantly pro-Gaitskell. Crossman, now party chairman by rotation, again sought a formula acceptable to Cousins – working this time only with Gaitskell's opponents, and exploiting the tripartite talks to isolate and destroy the leader.[9]

Gaitskell revealed his private views in a candid letter to a friend: 'Everybody is behaving pretty much as expected – Mr. Cousins impossible – Mr. Crossman petulant and treacherous – Mr. Driberg like a tired snake. On . . . our side [there] has been more loyalty and firmness and successful planning than for a long time.' So the majority rejected Crossman's compromise proposals independently of Gaitskell, who kept in the background. The unilateralists, especially Cousins whom it was Crossman's main aim to placate, were no better satisfied with them. But Cousins, seeing a chance to strike a blow at Gaitskell, suddenly declared that he accepted Crossman's draft as a basis of policy – which he had never said before. Gaitskell wrote to the chairman of CDS: 'I can assure you that during the discussions there was not the slightest indication that Cousins would in fact put the T&GWU behind it. Indeed, I am convinced myself that had we accepted the Crossman draft, Cousins would have most definitely rejected it.'[10] The eight majority signatories publicly rejected Crossman's charge that only Gaitskell's 'obstinacy . . . prevented unanimous agreement' as 'totally untrue' and 'offensive to the rest of us'; and welcomed Cousins's belated conversion, 'particularly the abandonment of his opposition in principle to American bases in Britain'; and Cousins at once upset Crossman's house of cards by retorting: 'I am still opposed completely to American bases in Britain'. The left-wing politicians were no more accommodating, and Crossman himself wrote the last word on his clever manoeuvre: 'The truth is that the Left disliked it even more than the Right.'[11]

## 'The Passion to Stop Wrangling'

In Parliament the maverick Left staged another demonstration over the defence estimates – always a sensitive subject because of the memory of the 1930s. Three times the PLP decided not to oppose them, yet twenty-four unilateralists insisted on voting against the air estimates. The rebels were warned of disciplinary action if they did it again, but on 8 March, five MPs (including Michael Foot) divided against the army estimates. Gaitskell was not keen to penalise them but the Whips and George Brown threatened to resign if nothing was done, and the PLP agreed to withdraw the whip from the rebels.

The carefully cultivated idea that Gaitskell kept Labour MPs under stern discipline is false, for this was the only time sanctions were invoked in his seven years of leadership, and then contrary to his own inclinations. They could never be used against a big revolt, and he knew that they limited the size and frequency of little ones only at the cost of unpopularity outside the House. But renouncing what Michael Foot called 'tinpot totalitarianism' also has its price: namely that some MPs, who fear unpopularity with their local activists if they vote to keep a Labour Cabinet in office, first make absolutely certain that enough of their colleagues will bear that distasteful responsibility to make their gesture quite safe, and then register their ostentatious dissent: a display of fraudulent heroism for the gallery, while the loyalists on whose backs they ride take the heat for betraying the day's good cause.

Outside Westminster, the Campaign for Nuclear Disarmament had lost ground when the new Committee of 100 broke away to organise sit-down demonstrations and challenge the police. The far Left also did themselves harm after Scarborough by provoking the systematic disruption of Gaitskell's meetings and attempting to deny him a hearing – an activity almost unknown in British politics for a generation. It started just after the leadership election, and continued regularly for months and intermittently for the rest of Gaitskell's life. He stood up to it both physically and psychologically, but it added to the already heavy strain. He took on the extra load of these bitter meetings because he thought it his duty, believed in the power of rational argument, and was sure he could persuade ordinary people both of the sincerity of his beliefs and of the cogency of his case. Some politicians positively revel in violent controversy, and rather relish the hatred of the misguided. Gaitskell did not. As Roy Jenkins put it, 'Morally he was in the bravest of all categories: he flinched, but he always went on.'[12] But those months of physical exhaustion and mental stress must have taken a terrible toll.

Gaitskell knew he was gaining ground, but as late as April he was far from sure that the change would come quickly or thoroughly enough. Below the surface, however, the new mood in the Labour Movement was already showing itself in the diminishing scale of parliamentary revolt. In the country, too, after their respective contacts with the rank and file, the reactions of Gaitskell and Crossman were significantly different. The leader wrote to his daughter that, when utterly weary of the enmity at the top of the Party, he was 'revived & encouraged and bound by the response & attitude' he met on his weekend tours.[13] The chairman found no similar support.

The Left is taking a terrible beating . . . up and down the country in the conferences I address . . . [because of] the passion to stop wrangling, combined with a really savage disillusionment against unilateralism. People are seeing more and more that what we need is not merely a protest but a will to power.[14]

Within six weeks of Gaitskell's gloomy comments in April, the campaign of 1961 had been decisively won as suddenly as that of 1960 had been lost.

Over the summer, the union conferences decided the outcome at the party conference as they had done the year before. The swing away from unilateralism was already under way, but those meetings determined that the verdict would go in favour of the leadership's policy and not of Crossman's alternative. Some left-wingers, then and since, have argued that Gaitskell deliberately rejected a compromise which would both have preserved the fundamentals of his policy and united the Party. But Crossman's compromise plan was genuinely supported by only one major politician, Harold Wilson, and by important elements in only two of the 'big six' unions. The Left critics were not satisfied with it, so that it could not have united the Party; and Gaitskell did not need it to defeat them, for it attracted little more support than his own.

Gaitskell understood better than his opponents that in most unions the many delegates who were not intensely political would decide simply to support either the leadership or the unilateralists (now clearly a declining and divisive force in the Party) without caring much about the differences between the official policy and Crossman's alternative. It was different in USDAW, the Union of Shop, Distributive and Allied Workers, where many delegates did care. But being so unrepresentative, it started a bandwagon for Crossman which rolled for Gaitskell instead.

USDAW was a union with an old ILP tradition and a respected president, Walter Padley, who had been one of the Twelve and was against unilateralism, for which the union had voted in 1960. To reverse that decision, Padley resuscitated the Crossman compromise policy which he had seconded in the Twelve – as a policy to unite the Party, which would be submitted to the Labour Party Conference at Blackpool only if other unions accepted it too. If other unions did not back 'Crossman–Padley', then USDAW would vote at Blackpool according to its conference decisions on the other two motions. Those decisions were clear. The unilateralists lost badly, the official policy passed narrowly, and Crossman–Padley sailed through triumphantly by nearly two to one.

One big union joined USDAW: the AEU, where a powerful Communist presence alarmed the other unilateralists into reversing the 1960 unilateralist majority in favour of Crossman–Padley. No others followed; the NUR executive, which in December 1960 had unanimously upheld the Scarborough decisions, now switched to the official policy instead. Westminster felt the draught, and Crossman reported: 'the fire of wrangling was hurriedly quenched when it was felt that the Movement was getting sick of all the leadership, irrespective of Left or Right'.[14] Those colleagues who were less committed to the leader's overthrow drew more cheerful conclusions: 'At last it seems that the long, long quarrel about defence is about to end . . . [soon] we shall at last have an effective Opposition . . . Labour M.P.s are . . . *dreaming once again of the fruits of office*.'[15]

Gaitskell had no reason to abandon the official policy, for Crossman–Padley was presented as restoring unity by knocking the rivals' heads together, rebuking Gaitskell for resisting the policies which it appealed to Cousins to renounce. The ball was now in Cousins's court. His own cause could no longer win, but he could still embarrass Gaitskell by casting the Transport Workers' million votes for the compromise. To do so might avert a humiliating defeat at Gaitskell's hands, but it would entail a worse humiliation: that of visibly preferring tactics to principle, and sacrificing his own beliefs to clutch at USDAW's lifebelt. Cousins was an honest man and a proud one, and he would not do that. So there was no shift in the largest union, and no sign that USDAW's motion would satisfy the unilateralists. It was therefore the leadership and not the compromisers who went on piling up impressive support elsewhere. On 8 June Gaitskell wrote to Sam Watson that 'Things are going fantastically well.' Less than a week later, Padley concluded that without Cousins's backing the Crossman–Padley compromise, designed to unite the Party, could not even be carried; and so the USDAW executive withdrew it. The parliamentary Left, which had disliked it, characteristically accused Padley of betraying them by doing exactly what he had promised. Crossman knew better: 'Walter, probably correctly, calculates that there isn't a majority for it . . . No man has more pedantically insisted on accepting Conference as the final authority . . . and he is bound to accept Conference's support for Gaitskell when it takes place.'[11]

## Principle, Power and Unity

By May 1961 Gaitskell's opponents within the Party had given up hope of ousting him from the leadership; and there was no further serious pressure for unilateralism. His new freedom of manoeuvre reflected the political reality: that MPs and union secretaries must again reckon with him as the prospective tenant of 10 Downing Street. He had ended the acute civil war in the Party, since no one now thought he or his central policies could be overthrown; but he had not genuinely united it, since some of the disappointed losers remained bitterly hostile to him for the rest of his life and beyond.

The advocates of concession, who had mistakenly believed that he could not win, now felt that his success had been too dearly bought. They claimed that he paid, in the resentment of the defeated, a high price for his victory; and so he did. But their other claim is most dubious: that Gaitskell, without capitulation, could have avoided paying that price. Many thought that he could: that he was insensitive to the unilateralists' anxieties, scornful of their character, unfair about their motives. That was quite untrue. But even Denis Healey could say 'he always felt that he was fighting for the right not only against people who were mistaken but who were immorally mistaken.'[16] Hitherto the good intentions of the Aldermaston marchers had protected them from rigorous scrutiny of their policy proposals – or of their dubious political allies. Gaitskell's Scarborough reference to 'fellow-travellers' aroused furious resentment and misinterpretation from critics eagerly seeking grievances to stoke their emotional dislike for the man. Week by week two hostile journals spread the poison, presenting everything Gaitskell said or did (and many things he did not do or say) in the worst possible light – and then pointing to their readers' opposition to him as proof that he could never unite the Party.

Apart from phrasing and tact, there was a problem of political style and approach, especially on the sensitive issue of the American bases. Many people felt that another leader of the Party could better retain confidence among the passionate Left. In the short run that was plainly true. But intentions which can be dissimulated in opposition have to be revealed in power, and we now know that lack of candour may produce a slower but more lasting loss of confidence.

Gaitskell was not needlessly divisive over the Crossman–Padley compromise, because it could not bring genuine harmony to the Labour Party. It was neither essential to attract a decisive majority nor sufficient to reconcile the aggrieved minority. That genuine unity was not to be had, since the Left would accept it only on their own terms, to which others would never agree. Gaitskell's victory did not ensure harmony either, because of the losers' resentment, yet it did end serious hostilities within the Party as a bogus compromise would not have done. That would have repelled the electorate by continuing civil war, compounding the bitterness due to fratricidal strife with that resulting from permanent opposition: a recipe for a party much less harmonious and in much worse spirits than Labour after Blackpool.

By the summer of 1961 the factional strife was ending. Recognising that Gaitskell was unassailable and that the rank and file resented the feud, his moderate critics quickly accepted his victory. As soon as it was assured and long before it was actually achieved, he reverted to his former conciliatory style of leadership; and after he had won, he told Robin Day on television that of course pacifists were still welcome in the Party, though revolutionaries were not.[17]

Labour's Blackpool Conference in October 1961 registered the predetermined victory for the platform on defence, another success on public ownership, and a willingness among all but the irreconcilable Left to reunite under Gaitskell's leadership. It carried the official defence policy by 4,526,000 to 1,756,000, and rejected the T&GWU's by 4,309,000 to 1,891,000. Three of the big six unions and nearly a quarter of the union vote had changed sides over the year. Frank Cousins badly misjudged the mood and faced his first hostile demonstration at a party conference.

The majority supporting the Executive's new statement in 1961 was ten times larger than that which had defeated the old one in 1960. Needless to say, those who had claimed the narrow Scarborough verdict as rigidly binding regarded the massive Blackpool reversal as irrelevant, while emphasising Gaitskell's two setbacks on detail (on Polaris bases and on German troops in Wales), and ignoring the rejection of an explicitly neutralist motion by nearly 7 to 1. (The votes were: Polaris 3,611,000 to 2,379,000; German troops 3,519,000 to 2,733,000; neutralism 846,000 to 5,476,000.) Among the constituency parties, the vote for the leadership increased a little (from about 501,000 to 528,000) in a reduced total; unlike Attlee over German rearmament, Gaitskell retained a substantial CLP majority for his essential objectives. Blackpool brought the unions back into the same camp as the MPs and the CLPs, and reunited the mass of the Movement behind him.

These heavy margins restored his authority as leader despite the two defeats on detail. He had routed a direct attack on his leadership with

no sacrifice of principle. In the Party the outcome left him unquestioned as leader, while in the wider electorate his popularity
soared: in January 1961 only 37 per cent thought him a good leader,
after Blackpool 57 per cent. The struggle, as Macmillan had foreseen,
at last impressed Gaitskell's personality on the country.

For the second time in his career Gaitskell owed a much enhanced
political reputation largely to his opponents on the Left. Bevan's
attacks had given him the stature to become leader of the Party, and
now he had established himself as a national leader by beating off
another bitter assault: not thanks to the plaudits of the press, or even to
the issues at stake, but because adversity brought out his qualities of
character and showed everyone that he would risk his career to fight for
his principles. Old James Griffiths summed up: 'Well Done. Warmest
Congratulations upon a triumph won by fortitude and character and
laurels won with dignity . . . You are now free to get on with the job of
paving the way to victory.'[18]

# 22

# Macmillan in Eclipse 1961-2

*'Gaitskell falling over backwards to be conciliatory'*
(Crossman, 1961)

*'When the showman is shown up . . . it is time for the players to depart'*
(HG to Macmillan, 1962)

## The New Mood of the Party

Early in 1961 Labour's spirits were improved by the course of domestic politics, for the Government's reputation was in decline. Still more important was Gaitskell's handling of the Party once his victory over defence was secure. The Left mistakenly took it for granted that he would purge his opponents by ruthless discipline, and would try to emasculate Labour's domestic policy. In drafting the new statement, *Signposts for the Sixties*, Crossman noted repeatedly 'Gaitskell falling over backwards to be conciliatory'. But on the Left reconciliation, as always, spelt betrayal. Crossman was soon writing: 'on this domestic policy I am sure we shall find Foot and Mikardo will attack it, whatever it says'.[1]

It did not say what the critics expected. Crossman's reports were explicit. At the NEC: 'Here again, very scrupulously, there was no challenge to the policy by Hugh and George . . . Gaitskell and Brown were so careful not to challenge the policy or to talk about watering it down.' At Frognal Gardens for the drafting,

it was clear that Gaitskell was not going to try to go back on the policies we had agreed before his defence triumphs. Most of my Left-wing friends confidently predicted that this would happen . . . But . . . he was scrupulously careful to preserve all the policy decisions.[2]

Gaitskell's main personal contribution was a radical proposal to nationalise all development land, which he later called 'a hobby of mine for a number of years'.[3] He had first raised the subject at Nottingham in February 1960 in his counter-attack against the defenders of Clause Four. During that year he returned to it repeatedly. When he prepared a scheme, Crossman noted: 'Hugh's chapter on building land gets stronger and more radical each time he redrafts it and gets greater interest.'[2] Here was the conception of the Land Commission which, had it not been emasculated before enactment, might have averted the property scandals and speculation of the early 1970s; if not, Gaitskell would certainly have taken more radical measures. As he predicted all too truly: 'It might be said . . . that the horse had bolted. There were, however, many horses still to come.'⁴

*Signposts* went much further on public ownership than the press had expected. 'It takes the party's domestic policy several paces to the Left', wrote *The Times*, 'and puts Labour on the offensive once again.'⁵ Far from being alarmed by that, Gaitskell's friends were enthusiastic. In the Executive the Left were surprised and did not seriously oppose; only Mikardo voted against it. In the PLP their role was not heroic:

It is characteristic that Barbara [Castle], Tony [Greenwood], Tom [Driberg] are all notably absent when a document they have shared in producing, but on which they have agreed with Gaitskell, is being put to the Party. Each is busily preparing a position from which he can say that he did his best valiantly, month after month, but was defeated.²

Introducing *Signposts* on television on 12 July 1961, Gaitskell delivered a prescient warning that current prosperity was precarious and illusory. He had insisted on having Crossman also on the programme to demonstrate unity, and pro-Labour viewers responded favourably both to that impression and to the leader's own sincerity. To one Conservative paper the whole broadcast was 'a gradual build-up towards Mr. Gaitskell, now acknowledged as Labour's dominating personality'.⁶

At Blackpool, Cousins opposed the policy, which Conference accepted more readily in 1961 than its predecessor for which he had voted in 1957. His own electoral strategy was simple: 'Are we trying to get the Tories to vote for us? I thought that we were trying to get the Labour people, the people who are justified in saying that we are the political Party of their faith.' Gaitskell replied by asking Cousins (who was furious) 'Is he sure that every member of the Transport and General Workers Union votes Labour? . . . 3 out of 10 male trade unionists and 4 out of 10 of their wives vote Tory. We had better start by trying to convert them to Labour.'⁷

The public-ownership proposals of *Signposts* were challenged by a resolution with a long 'shopping list' for nationalisation, defeated by nearly three to one; *Signposts for the Sixties* was then adopted by acclamation. Gaitskell in commending it to Conference delivered 'an awesome prophecy'⁸ about Britain's economic future:

[T]his is not just an economic crisis . . . It is rather a crisis of outlook, of temperament, of spirit, a crisis deep in British society today.

Now we could go on as before . . . 'the sick man of Europe' today, we shall become the poor relation tomorrow . . . the whole trend of the past ten years has been in this direction . . . Never has a nation so urgently needed a change of government . . . [to] get out of the valley of sluggishness into which the Tories have led us.[7]

His speeches showed his complete mastery over Conference, and went far to satisfy those who had wondered whether he would bend enough to reunite the Party. For at Blackpool Gaitskell made a major effort to restore confidence as well as to win majorities: in one gesture of reconciliation, winding up the *Signposts* debate, he referred approvingly five times to Harold Wilson's speech opening it. Crossman, in his closing speech as chairman, congratulated delegates on the spirit of the debates: 'the personal rancour . . . has quite disappeared . . . That leadership issue is once for all out of the way.' It was an impromptu phrase, which he found his *Tribune* friends 'regarded as the great betrayal'.[9]

Some of the leader's old enemies did respond, claiming to discover a new, suddenly tolerant Gaitskell: an image which owed a little to his words – for a party leader no longer fighting for his political life could afford gestures now they would not be exploited against him – but mainly reflected the critics' changed perceptions. In 1960 they had magnified or invented grievances against a leader they hoped to depose; having failed, they now sought – and therefore found – what matter for consolation they could. Both the dwindling of the irreconcilable Left and the reconciliation of the Centre contributed to the unity for which the Party yearned. Labour therefore emerged from Blackpool 'more hopeful and more determined to throw out the Tories than at any time for the past ten years'. When a journalist asked where a Labour leader should place himself in the Party, Gaitskell replied that it was the wrong question: 'The question is . . . what will both unify the Party and carry the country. I will endeavour to do both.'[10]

## The Shadow of Economic Decline

No politician could have been more conscious than Gaitskell that with electoral victory his real problems would begin. He was acutely aware of the long-term precariousness of Britain's economy and the risk of a sudden slide downhill. In his TV broadcast introducing *Signposts for the Sixties*, he again gave a chilling but painfully accurate forecast:

[W]e really are at the crossroads in Britain today. We can go on as we have done for the last ten years, and . . . the standard of living will go up a little, but . . . much less . . . than in other countries . . . People will say: oh, the

British, of course they're nice people . . . But when it comes to producing and selling, well somehow or other they haven't got it in them. Now this is a very real possibility . . . [after] another ten or twenty years . . . of the really dangerous complacency in which we've been sunk.[11]

The gradual economic decline could be averted only by a great change of psychological climate – inconceivable under Macmillan, 'the great architect of complacency and the materialist outlook'.[12]

Gaitskell did not disagree fundamentally with the objectives of the Government's pay pause: 'on the basic issue of the need for relating incomes to productivity and production there is no dispute between us'. But he thought it crudely conceived and ineptly handled, saying that while increased productivity was the highest priority, it required agreement with the unions – unattainable by a government whose policies seemed 'unfair and arbitrary'.[13] He heatedly denounced 'the extraordinary behaviour of the government in tearing up the normal procedure of settling industrial disputes in the public service, for the first time, I think, for forty years', and their 'shabby discrimination' against those with enough responsibility not to exploit their power: 'a penalty imposed on virtue'.[14] The audience for that speech was the Confederation of Health Service Employees. We reap what we sow.

Gaitskell knew very well that a Labour government, since its policies would be too costly without faster growth, would be even more dependent on an understanding with the unions, though with Cousins so suspicious of him, he was cautious about discussing it in public. He stressed that the essential problem – that only in Britain did expansion immediately lead to a balance of payments crisis – was a long-term disease which the Government was neither explaining nor tackling: 'The only people who can afford to be complacent are those who are content to see Britain in the 1970s enjoying a lower standard of living than most other industrial nations. This is not a panicky prophecy but a cold appraisal of the prospects.'[15] For years the exports of France, Germany, Italy, Belgium, Sweden, Japan and the United States had all increased more than twice as much as Britain's, whose share of the world market in manufactures was 25.5 per cent in 1950, only 16 per cent in 1960 and down to 9 per cent in 1976, despite exceptionally favourable conditions for trading abroad.

Conservatives had promised that lowering taxes on the rich, and taking controls off private enterprise, would generate expansion, price stability and an export surplus; instead their policy had 'produced industrial stagnation, rising prices and trade deficits'.[16] Gaitskell kept saying that the national lethargy must be shaken, though it was 'the hardest thing of all to create a change in the whole climate of opinion in this country. A great attack has to be made on the soggy complacency of some managements, and the appalling indifference of some workers.'[17] Waking them up would be a tremendous challenge to political leadership, which could not come from the Prime Minister, whom Gaitskell had always thought a fraud.

Privately, Macmillan reacted to Labour's claim to be able to encourage responsibility in the unions by a disreputable effort to use that encouragement for party advantage – urging his colleagues to comb the Communist press for material inciting working-class hostility to the Labour leadership, who were trying to use their influence in the long-term interests of the country and its people.[18] Not knowing that, Gaitskell could still persuasively argue that Macmillan's past doomed his present appeals. His persistent encouragement of selfish material-ism disqualified him from arousing the nation; his sudden repentance was nauseating hypocrisy. 'Having gulled [the people] into com-placency, you cannot galvanise them into action.'[12]

## Commonwealth Immigration, and Southern Africa

Ever since Attlee's day the Labour Party had taken a proprietary pride in the new multi-racial Commonwealth, which largely determined Gaitskell's and the Party's attitude to another political problem: the increasingly controversial issue of coloured immigration. Exclusion of immigrants was, he believed, a crude and cowardly evasion of the real domestic problems, and unnecessary because they came only at times when Britain had work for them. But the Government's restrictive bill, while not needed in Britain, would do great harm in the West Indies.

The Indian sub-continent was a different matter. Gaitskell recog-nised that Britain could not keep an open door in the event of a mass migration, but he thought that 'an utter and complete myth'. If the bill would have kept out those who had come and found work the year before, he told the House, it would 'stop people coming in even when we want them . . . the most crazy kind of Conservative economic planning'; if not (as in the Government's view) it would damage the Commonwealth without touching the problem. The Government had 'yielded to the crudest clamour', and Butler, Sandys and especially Macleod should be ashamed of their failure to stop 'this miserable, shameful, shabby bill' by threatening to resign.[19] Gaitskell's speech won the highest praise, from *The Times* to *Tribune*. It was devastatingly effective because many liberal Conservatives and indeed Tory im-perialists were thoroughly unhappy about the bill – though some

Labour members disliked such strenuous opposition to it. In committee it was drastically amended. But refusal of all control was not tenable in the long run, and Labour policy changed after Gaitskell's death.

The immigration dispute produced an unusual political alignment, in which Labour won much support from liberal-minded opinion outside its own ranks while suffering from some division within them. So did Suez; and so too did many colonial problems. But at first the Central African Federation was a special case, seen by many as a promising solution for the Rhodesian question. Gaitskell had to take care that his commitment to defending African interests could not be presented as an effort to wreck it.

In 1959 the Labour Opposition at Westminster and the Federal Government at Salisbury posed mutually incompatible conditions for joining Lord Monckton's proposed Commission of Inquiry on the constitution of the Federation. Macmillan wanted Labour to participate in order to influence the Africans, but he also needed to carry the settlers, led by the Federal Prime Minister Sir Roy Welensky. By giving them contradictory assurances, Macmillan tried to cajole both into joining and so earned the deep distrust of both. When Gaitskell met Welensky that July, he learned enough of Macmillan's commitments to convince him of the Prime Minister's trickery; he did not yet realise that Welensky was the dupe. That was to become evident only in the next Parliament.

Gaitskell's own view of the conflict was simple. The settlers in Southern Rhodesia must not be allowed to enforce their own rule on the Africans in the neighbouring territories (now Zambia and Malawi). Britain, which would have intervened against a black revolt, must not treat a white one differently. Had he come to power, he would have moved overwhelming forces into the northern territories instantly;[20] and he was already thinking of buying out the settlers as the long-run solution.

Concerned that the constitutional negotiations would fail without African confidence, Gaitskell sought assurances from Macmillan on the membership and terms of reference of the Monckton Commission, to which Welensky flatly refused to agree – with the result that the Africans would not co-operate, and in December Labour therefore declined to serve on the Commission. But several of its members agreed with Labour that it must be allowed to discuss secession by the northern territories, although the Prime Minister was telling Welensky the opposite – leading both the Labour Party and Welensky to believe that secession was ruled out. Instead, in March 1960 when Monckton came home from Africa to say that secession could not be excluded, he found that the Prime Minister agreed; and in October when the Commission reported, it endorsed most of Labour's case. Welensky and Gaitskell now distrusted the Prime Minister equally, but it was the former who had been misled. He began to use overt pressure over Northern Rhodesia (Zambia), and was vigorously supported from the Tory Right.

All the problems of Southern Africa were compounded by the Whites' reaction to the violence nearby, in Angola and the Congo. Gaitskell, in Washington when President Kennedy was inaugurated, found that the new Administration 'will not allow the West to be framed with the charge of colonialism for the sake of Belgian or Portuguese sensitivity'.[21] He told the House of Commons: 'if we believe in freedom in Hungary and in East Germany, then we must believe in it in Angola or Rhodesia'; and he complained that UN resolutions on Portuguese colonialism and on South Africa were always supported by the United States, never by Britain. In reply to Lord Home, the Foreign Secretary, he insisted that 'it would be a disastrous error to try and eliminate the moral and ideological element in the alliance' by neglecting the democratic principles enshrined in the preamble to the NATO Treaty.[22] Without those principles, he said, the Western cause would have no appeal in Africa and Asia; flouting those principles, he knew, multiplied his difficulties within his own party; believing in those principles, he had no sympathy whatever for the defenders of colonialism on the far Right, for the apologists for Communism on the far Left, or for the anti-Americanism characteristic of both.

## Reviving Liberals and Disgruntled Tories

*The Economist* had noted in the summer of 1961 that among Labour loyalists, 'Mr. Gaitskell's personal prestige . . . is mounting skyward like a Russian rocket.'[23] Whenever the Gallup poll asked if he was a good leader, from the autumn of 1961 he never fell far below 50 per cent, which he had very rarely approached before. Blackpool had transformed Gaitskell's position both in the Labour Party and beyond. But if power corrupts, prolonged opposition can demoralise, causing bitter recriminations that poison the atmosphere, and frustrating any politician concerned to achieve results. Gaitskell felt that frustration deeply. When Robens left politics and an old friend said to Gaitskell, 'Alf has got out when the going was good', he provoked the only bitter moment in a long relationship: 'Don't talk like that, Ronnie. You have been fortunate; you have had jobs you wanted; you haven't had to wait for something useful to do, as some of us have had to.'[24]

From the summer of 1961 Gaitskell began to run ahead of Macmillan in the opinion polls. As his own reputation soared ahead of his party's, Macmillan's slumped with that of his Government. In July Conservative losses at last gave Labour the lead, but still with less support than it had had up to 1959. Its sluggish progress at a time of Liberal upsurge provoked press speculation about an electoral pact, which some Labour pessimists began to advocate. Gaitskell had toyed with the idea for a couple of weeks just after the general election, but decided that a pact would be unnecessary to win over the progressive Liberals, and ineffective in winning the others. Perhaps partly because the Liberals in Gaitskell's own West Riding were the most unfavourable of all to Labour, he thought that 'an electoral pact is likely to do more harm than good to us'. Moreover, in 1962 he still felt 'very much under suspicion on the left of the party', and feared to 'do anything to divide the party again'.[25]

Yet his deepest differences with the Liberals were not electoral, reflecting calculations of their prospects of success; nor cerebral, reflecting disagreements over policy: they were visceral. At Scarborough he told a Fabian meeting that he could not stand them because of the snobbery that kept them out of the working-class movement; and two years later he was sceptical of the Liberal revival, seeing it as just a revolt by disgruntled Tories too snobbish to support Labour: 'it's all right . . . to vote Liberal because it's somehow or other respectable, [but] to vote Labour is going down in the social scale . . . [because] the Labour Party is associated with the trade unions'.[26] But if the disgruntled Tories helped Labour win seats on a minority vote, he would cheerfully 'profit by the opportunity . . . People would find, when Labour was actually governing, that a lot of things they thought wrong with Labour were all right.'[25]

In July 1962, after the Conservatives had just lost a humiliating by-election, the 'unflappable' Prime Minister dismissed one-third of his Cabinet in what Lord Butler called 'the Massacre of Glencoe'. Many Tories shared the suspicion of panic in Downing Street. Macmillan justly replied that he had long been reproached for defending colleagues who merited dismissal. Gaitskell stood to gain by either interpretation, since the attack discredited the head of the Government and the defence accredited Opposition criticisms of its policies. The Shadow Cabinet therefore tabled a motion of no confidence in the Government: an occasion which seemed invented for a born Leader of the Opposition. But Gaitskell was not one, and his performance in the House was by no means among his best.

Nevertheless the Prime Minister's appeal was clearly waning at last. A few weeks later the familiar political debate was to be diverted to quite a new topic: the Common Market.

# 23

# The Common Market 1961–2

## Consistency and Evolution

Gaitskell's attitude to the Common Market was consistent throughout. He never felt himself primarily a European, and thought that in a world perspective the EEC enthusiasts over-emphasised a 'parochial' problem. The Common Market was a fact but no cause for rejoicing. In July 1962 he told a Commonwealth audience: 'Whether you and I like it or not the thing is there. In many ways I cannot help regretting it . . . although I see the advantage of Franco-German understanding.'[1] Where some saw a shining opportunity and others a sinister threat, Gaitskell at the height of the controversy told some disappointed supporters of entry that the subject had always been 'a bore and a nuisance.'[2] He thought Britain's economic future would be determined by decisions made at home, not by joining or staying out; and time has shown he was right.

In the early years of the European Communities, the Labour leaders were divided. In 1953 they were at odds over the move to incorporate Germany into a European Defence Community: Morrison favoured British links with it, while Attlee deeply distrusted them owing to his memories of 1940. Soon after becoming leader, when the European Economic Community was just coming into being, Gaitskell said publicly in his Godkin Lectures at Harvard

that most of us felt ourselves not only European but the centre of the Commonwealth, a Commonwealth including very important Asian and African countries, and that we would not want to go in closer with Europe if this meant weakening the Atlantic alliance . . . going into a Federation of Europe was absolutely out of the question . . . [unless] we were somehow cut off from the Commonwealth and left out on our own.[3]

In 1962 he cited these lectures to show that he had not changed his views.

Gaitskell welcomed the Government's effort in 1958 to set up an industrial free trade area. He wanted both to put pressure on France (without saying so publicly) by bringing the future EFTA countries into a 'rival bloc'; and also not to preclude merging the two groups, if ever the Six agreed, into a wider free trade or low-tariff area. He criticised the Government later, however, for delaying talks with the EEC which were now to be begun in an unnecessarily weak position. But whenever in the late 1950s the topic came up at his weekly meetings with the lobby correspondents, 'he never deviated . . . neutral, vaguely uninterested . . . bored by it, he couldn't see what all the fuss was about'.[4]

During 1960 the first serious Shadow Cabinet studies were undertaken by Wilson and Healey. Opinion in the Party was slowly moving against entry, mainly on political grounds. Gaitskell did not concur, but he foresaw all the difficulties of entry. He warned at Scarborough that public opinion would insist on no federation and on fair treatment for the Commonwealth.

Commentators and colleagues all believed that he was privately a cautious supporter of entry. But he resolutely opposed any public declaration, thinking it unlikely to become an electoral issue, and fearing another Labour split.

Macmillan . . . is a very crafty man. This is one reason why I am determined not to let the Party get committed on the Common Market. If we try to reach a decision ourselves I am pretty certain we would remain hopelessly divided while the Tories reluctantly decide to unite behind whatever Macmillan decides to do.[5]

The question became central just as he was winning Labour's defence battle; the wounds had not healed, and internal strife could easily have resumed. The leading parliamentarians agreed with him – but on tactics, not objectives. Wilson and Crossman were both quite hostile to entry, while Gaitskell as always took time to make up his mind – and rejected their efforts to commit the Party to specific terms.

Once the British Government opened negotiations for entry in July 1961, the subject came to the front of the political stage and became fraught with risks for Labour's fragile unity. To most of the Left it meant, said Gaitskell, 'the end . . . [of] an independent Britain . . . sucked up in a kind of giant capitalist, catholic conspiracy, our lives dominated by Adenauer and de Gaulle, unable to conduct any independent foreign policy at all'. To some Marketeers it was a great venture in internationalism which Britain had earlier spurned, but which now gave her a last chance to join a partnership which alone could ensure her economic survival. Gaitskell called the first view 'rubbish' and the second 'nonsense'.[6] In December 1962 he described his motives and aims very candidly in a long memorandum to President Kennedy:

From the start not only the Opposition but the Government as well were *not* in favour of *'going in and trying to get the best possible terms'* but only for *'going in if certain conditions were fulfilled'* . . .

It may be said that in reality the Government had decided to go in whatever the terms and that they only laid down conditions in order to make their new policy acceptable to their Party. I do not know whether this is the case . . . As for the Opposition, we certainly took the conditions very seriously . . . I myself and my leading colleagues all happened to believe and still believe that the arguments of principle were fairly evenly balanced for and against and that the balance would be tipped in favour of our entry only if our conditions were fulfilled. Secondly, this policy of making our final judgment depend on the conditions was the only one which could have been accepted by the Party as a whole. If I had urged [either] unconditional entry [or] . . . outright opposition whatever the terms . . . there would have been a major split in the Party, which, following the great dispute on defence which had only recently been successfully concluded, would have been fatal to our prospects. Both minorities, however, were willing to accept that the issue must be allowed to depend on the terms, nor was there any real disagreement about what the terms must be.[7]

Gaitskell thought that the Six might develop either in the way the Marketeers hoped or in that feared by their opponents, and that the best case for going in was that British entry on the right terms might tip that delicate balance:

If we stay out and the EFTA countries stay out, as they will . . . there would be a greater danger of this State being inward-looking . . . not interested in the rest of the world, nationalistic in outlook, a third force wanting its own nuclear weapons and wanting to break away. The effect of this on the Western Alliance could be serious.

As things are, if we went in we could probably stop that happening, but on the one condition only, that as we go in we maintain our links with the Commonwealth. That is essential.[8]

But he never believed that the 1961–2 negotiations were the last chance, for he felt sure that de Gaulle would prevent any irrevocable federal development. He also privately believed that if the worst came to the worst after entry, no legal text could prevent a country seceding:

supposing the worst fears of people are realised and we become a depressed area off Europe there would be a tremendous urge to get out of it. I do not think that is likely to happen but to avoid that I think the other countries would lean over backwards, and the spirit is likely to be just as important as the letter.[1]

Gaitskell's concept of Europe differed from that of either de Gaulle or the federalists but, it has been said, 'was fairly close to the Europe favoured by much of the Conservative Party as well as by most of the Labour Party'.[9] Substantive policy and party tactics both led Gaitskell to play a waiting game. He thought that the prospects of a Europe developing in the way he wanted depended on the terms. If those proved unsatisfactory, the loss would not be very grave; moreover, the Conservative uncertainty would be too great for the Prime Minister to proceed. Terms good enough to enable Macmillan to carry his own party would also allow Gaitskell to carry his; and without such terms the talks would collapse and Labour could only benefit.

On 22 July 1961 the Cabinet decided to apply, and the House debated it on 2 and 3 August. The committed back-benchers split right across party lines. Gaitskell's careful opening speech was (as Duncan Sandys said, winding up) 'a notable balancing act, ably stat[ing] the case on both sides'.[10] Harold Wilson put forward obviously unobtainable conditions (provoking Roy Jenkins to resign as a front-bench spokesman) – but without Gaitskell's approval.

At the Blackpool Conference this official line was accepted without a card vote; a pro-Market resolution was rejected overwhelmingly, and the anti-Marketeers then prudently agreed to remit their motion to the NEC. Gaitskell did not speak in the debate, and on the air he kept carefully to the agreed compromise. His essential conditions, like the Government's, were to safeguard British agriculture, the Commonwealth and Britain's neutral partners in EFTA. He told a Labour policy conference in December that the Commonwealth was the main worry, and that 'I do not want another internal party row about this.'[11]

From his bitter experiences over Clause Four and the bomb, Gaitskell had learned to time his moves cautiously. To take sides in the abstract for or against British entry seemed to him pointless for the country, for it was a matter of balanced arguments and difficult judgements which need not be final; and dangerous for the Party, which was certain to split over the principle without even knowing what either decision would entail. 'His strategy at this stage', he told Hetherington, 'must be to get a full discussion . . . He had to start from the fact that quite a lot of people in the party were hostile to the

Common Market; and he must not on any account cause another open division . . . Therefore he had to move cautiously.'[12] He warned Roy Jenkins, who wanted him to show some emotional sympathy:

it is not really a matter of what I think; it is a question of carrying the Party . . . if I were to do what you want, we should be more likely to lose control altogether. Certainly the Union Conferences have only gone the way they have because of these conditions which, you say, I am continually stressing.[13]

The lessons of 1960 had left their mark.

### Friendly on the Fence

Twice in early 1962 he himself appeared to be taking a critical line. One occasion was in the United States, where opinion was uncritically favourable to British entry and he characteristically put the other side. The second was private, a meeting on 4 April 1962 of XYZ to which Roy Jenkins had invited Jean Monnet – original 'inspirer' of the supra-national European idea. If the aim was to turn Gaitskell into a 'European', the outcome was catastrophic. Monnet wanted to explain the broad philosophy of the EEC, while Gaitskell tried impatiently to press him over attitudes to the Third World and problems of British entry. It was a characteristic difference between the French and British styles, but in addition Monnet – like Jenkins – thought that the will to solve the subsidiary disputes required precisely that emotional commitment to the principle which Gaitskell would not make. On his side Gaitskell felt that the visitor kept evading his questions about the impact on one or another underdeveloped country; thinking the questions beside the point, Monnet finally protested: 'You must have faith'. Gaitskell was not conciliatory:'I don't believe in faith. I believe in reason and you have not shown me any.'[14]

Jenkins and others concluded that Gaitskell was already moving towards opposition in principle, and feared that he might say so publicly; and Macmillan was privately astonished (and relieved) that he did not. But Gaitskell himself denied it vehemently; and within a week of the Monnet dinner he told Hetherington, who had suggested Labour was hardening against the Market, that 'on the contrary he thought it was moving rather towards support'.[12] He kept faithfully to his line in private as well as in public, writing to his younger daughter at Oxford that the question was 'tricky and complicated' and it would be 'absurd' for the Opposition to decide until the terms and the Government's view were known – adding significantly: 'Provided the terms are reasonable,

I doubt if the country is going to be very anti.'[15] The intellectual fastidiousness, which was later to make him exasperated with shoddy economic arguments for entry, at this stage led him rather to recoil from the political exaggerations of the other side.

His concern for practical details rather than abstract principles was a familiar feature of his political personality. Just at the time of the Monnet dinner, the Labour Party was thoroughly examining the political and economic consequences of entry for both Britain and the Commonwealth, and in March 1962 the half-dozen senior leaders began privately working out minimum terms. They started from a paper by Gaitskell's old Oxford friend Professor James Meade, who favoured joining a liberal-minded and outward-looking Community but not a narrow protectionist one, and thought its terms for the Commonwealth would give a pointer to its likely development. At that time, 'He thought the economic case . . . about fifty-fifty . . . possibly, however, the political argument was decisive. If we left the Six as a close knit unit of their own that would be less satisfactory than broadening, loosening, and leavening it – both with Britain and with the neutrals.'[12]

He disliked the strange anti-Market coalition of a Little-Englander Right with a frequently pro-Russian Left. That distaste emerges strongly from a memorandum he wrote in May 1962 for a group of friendly trade union leaders seeking his advice on dealing with anti-Market resolutions coming up at their conferences. He formally kept to the official line of making the decision depend on the terms – as, formally, he still did at Brighton five months later. But the emotional overtones of the May memorandum were at least as favourable to entry as those of the conference speech were hostile. He dismissed many bogeys which might raise trade union hackles: cheap foreign labour, lower social benefits, losing the freedom to nationalise. Federation was as unlikely as it was unacceptable, so that French or German votes could not decide Britain's foreign policy. He emphasised '*that by not going in we do not prevent the Common Market from coming into existence* . . . If we stay out of it, we run the risk of becoming nothing more than a little island off Europe. We shall be dwarfed politically by the Six.'[16] Without Britain the EEC might fall under German domination (a bogey of his own to make a Labour audience gibber) and might raise tariffs against our engineering goods (another, with which Bill Carron could make flesh creep in the AEU).

Another passage shows that in May he cannot yet have realised he would emerge as a hero of the anti-Marketeers:

Most of the resolutions are . . . almost certainly inspired by Communists. The Communists naturally oppose our going into the Common Market because they believe it would strengthen the democratic forces of the West. They are right in . . . that if we do not go in . . . there could be rather grave political consequences. By going in, on the other hand, we could prevent the formation of a tight, inward-looking federation.

He ended, as he later did at Conference, with an emotional appeal. But whereas in October he was to speak of Vimy Ridge and a thousand years of history, in May he invoked Labour's European Socialist friends who 'are very, very anxious indeed that we should join . . . [seeing it as] a step in the right direction, internationalistic in its approach, and getting away from the narrow nationalism of the past'. He summed up: 'although . . . we should not go in if our conditions are not fulfilled, nevertheless, if they are fulfilled, there is little or nothing to fear and great benefits may well result'.[16]

To some leaders such a great historic decision, about which alarm and enthusiasm both cut across party lines, might have seemed appropriate for an effort at bipartisanship. Macmillan never made the smallest gesture in that direction, for he was planning a crusade to carry the great decision into history – and the Conservative Party back to power. Yet he had no idea whether his public conditions would be met: 'we don't know at all what are the chances of a reasonable offer by the Six . . . Will de Gaulle . . . betray us after all? No one knows.'[17]

Macmillan's shift took Gaitskell by surprise. He assured President Kennedy:

Right up to mid-summer 1962 we remained reasonably hopeful. I myself expected that the terms would be such as to prove acceptable to the Commonwealth Prime Ministers and that my task would be to persuade my Party to accept them . . . I was prepared to do it as being the only course consistent with the line we had followed . . .

We were, therefore, bitterly disappointed and indeed astonished at the provisional agreements reached at the beginning of August.[7]

That reaction affected his immediate decision, not his fundamental attitude. His contacts with Continental leaders convinced him that their political intentions were unacceptable and their economic outlook selfish. While he was never utopian about the Commonwealth, its critical reactions had a profound effect in finally making up his mind. Moreover, he was shocked by what he saw as Macmillan's exploitation of the issue for party purposes, contemptuous of the economic arguments advanced in favour of entry, and exasperated by the overwhelming pressure of the media. His astonishment and resentment were among the reasons for his abandonment of a precise cold-blooded calculating style for opposition with an emotional force and fire which astonished friends and opponents alike.

## The Issues: Politics before Economics

Gaitskell thought that the case for entry rested on political advantage not economic necessity, and that the terms must be assessed in context. He wrote to Kennedy: 'The more enthusiastic one is, the worse the terms which would be acceptable. The more hostile one is, the more one would be inclined to reject any terms – even quite good ones. I have tried on this to take the middle road.'[7]

In deciding that the economic arguments were only fifty-fifty, he followed the experts for whom he had most respect, particularly James Meade, Sir Donald MacDougall and Sir Robert Hall. He was not at all convinced that Continental economic expansion was a consequence of the Community arrangements or would continue after Britain's entry. 'We might find that we got in . . . with all the economic disadvantages and adjustments that were entailed; that there was no expansion after all; and that we were then in the middle of a hideous balance of payments crisis.'[12] But in April 1962 he was reluctant to discuss those economic dangers in public for fear of starting an anti-Market reaction; by October he concentrated on them exclusively.

Gaitskell did not share the Left's fear (and the Right's hope) that entry would prevent a Labour government from planning the economy; even in the event of a flight of capital 'In practice I do not believe this is going to matter a great deal.'[1] The Common Agricultural Policy was 'intolerable', as he said in the House in June. 'Let us have no nonsense about the moral idealism involved in this. This is strict protectionism for European agriculture.' He saw temperate-zone foodstuffs as 'the nub of the problem', for Britain could not accept grave damage to Australia and the ruin of New Zealand.[8] But Gaitskell's priorities were very different from Macmillan's, for whom it was only 'the old Commonwealth' – a polite euphemism for the white dominions – that mattered. The Labour leader said the Six must treat the Commonwealth as favourably as the former French colonies. Privately, he thought Britain could insist on free entry for tropical produce but not for Australian and New Zealand foodstuffs, and could do nothing to help Canadian manufacturers but must protect those of the Asians. But he knew quite well that the Commonwealth could not become an alternative Common Market. He did not take its political survival for granted either, telling the Commonwealth MPs themselves in July:

Supposing the Commonwealth is really gradually going to fall apart – if the ties are going to get weaker . . . if India is drifting apart from us and if Australia and New Zealand [and Canada] are perhaps going to look more and more towards the United States . . . so that we in ten or twenty years' time are just a little island off Europe and nothing more, we are bound to say, 'We had better be in this, too' . . . are you so sure that in ten or twenty years' time the Commonwealth will be there?[1]

On the European side, Gaitskell distrusted the conservative Continental regimes for many reasons. Ever since his time at the Treasury he had loathed their banker-dominated economic policies. He was worried about their strong protectionist lobbies. He strongly opposed any idea of a European nuclear deterrent, which would make checking proliferation impossible; and he warned Kennedy early in 1962 that a European state might well develop in ways damaging to the Western alliance.

One guarantee of the liberal intentions of the EEC would be its willingness to admit the neutrals as associates. But the Americans opposed association for the neutrals, and so did some of the Six including the German Chancellor Adenauer. When Arthur Gaitskell told his brother of Dutch friends who wanted Britain in to liberalise the EEC, Hugh replied that that was hopeless while de Gaulle and Adenauer remained. But that outlook was emotional as well as rational, for Gaitskell strongly approved of James Meade's pamphlet referring disobligingly to what the Continentals (and the United States), in contrast to the white dominions, were doing in 1940.

Gaitskell was clear that Britain was unready to enter a federation for at least a generation: 'there is no question of Britain entering into a federal Europe now . . . I am not saying that we have to commit ourselves for all time, for twenty, fifty or a hundred years hence.'[10] The Continental Socialists wanted British entry in order to tilt the political balance, but feared it might block all progress towards political unity; and they would not endanger harmony among the Six for the sake of satisfying the new applicants and their clients. That attitude gave Gaitskell another reason for wanting Norway and Denmark in, for they were Britain's most likely allies in the Council of Ministers against right-wing tendencies, and unlike the other Socialist parties they were not federalist. Gaitskell therefore counted on them to give Britain an effective veto. With economic arguments so evenly balanced, the shape of the Community's political institutions became crucial, and he was keen for the weighted votes to maintain for Britain plus one Scandinavian ally the blocking power already enjoyed by France plus Belgium.

He was well aware that Britain's position in the world might change radically. In June 1962 he said in the House: 'After ten or twenty years we may find that the Commonwealth . . . declines, and does not count . . . we might find ourselves excluded from a tough, strong, European State, a little island off Europe with nothing else.'[8] He told the Commonwealth MPs in July that such a State 'could be decidedly awkward in all sorts of ways if we were outside it. What is the impact going to be on our relations with America if we do not go in? Are they going to squeeze us out and deal with these people alone?' In private he made it clear that even his hostility to federation was not absolute: 'We could not now accept a Federal solution. Ten years hence, perhaps we might – especially if the Commonwealth had by then broken itself up (but we must on no account do anything to break it up).'[18]

Thus, throughout the first year of negotiations, Gaitskell refused to commit himself in principle until he knew the final outcome. He saw the way the Six treated the European neutrals and the Commonwealth as testing respectively their political outlook and their economic intentions. He thought the Commonwealth's reaction might well determine the outcome in British politics. Gaitskell hoped that in deciding whether the terms were acceptable to it, and therefore to both British parties or to neither, the Commonwealth would resolve his tactical problem for him:

He didn't think Macmillan would sign an agreement that was contrary to the interests of the Commonwealth – the Conservative party would give him so much trouble if he did. If Macmillan signed an agreement that took proper care of Commonwealth interests then Labour would probably assent.[19]

## Summer Hesitation, Autumn Decision

In the summer of 1962 Gaitskell's tactical analysis had not changed. Privately he still thought the Government would probably obtain terms which Labour could support. He did not make enough allowance for Macmillan's eagerness to settle. 'He had never thought that the Government would give way so much. Indeed, they had not done so until they had collapsed at the end of July.'[20]

With those expectations, his objections in the spring were not obstructive ones. His major statement, a party political broadcast on television on 8 May 1962, held the balance fairly even.

You still hear some people speaking as though we could decide whether the Common Market existed or not. Now this, of course, is quite untrue . . . what we have to ask ourselves, looking ahead, is whether . . . we would be better outside it, or . . . inside it . . . To go in on good terms would, I believe, be the best solution . . . Not to go in would be a pity, but it would not be a catastrophe. To go in on bad terms which really meant the end of the Commonwealth would be a step which I think we would regret all our lives, and for which history would not forgive us.[6]

The balance was not quite even, for he did, as he had promised Jenkins, 'get rid of any idea that I am deliberately building up a position in which, whatever the terms, we should be opposed to them'.[13] Both the Labour Common Market Committee and the Conservative press concluded that he was approving entry. Other Labour leaders shifted towards opposition, but as late as July Gaitskell was still determined to keep a free hand, telling Hetherington that he 'wanted to be sure that if Labour had to take a decision it would be taken by the Parliamentary party and not by the conference.'[21] Yet already he was talking for the first time of making the Market an election issue – which in May he had hoped it would not become.

That was not from choice, but because he began to fear that the Government would make it a party matter: he said in private that he would not object to a free vote of the House 'if the Conservative Party were prepared to accept it but I do not think there is the slightest chance they will do so'.[1] He still hoped to see the Tories thwarted, and to escape putting the issue to the Labour Party, if Commonwealth resistance prevented any acceptable agreement emerging.

If . . . Mr. Menzies and Mr. Nehru . . . both say, 'This is intolerable . . . and it means the end of the Commonwealth . . . ' then I am certain we [Labour] would come out against it and I do not think any British Government would dare to go ahead . . . it is up to us to stand out for the terms which will make our entry tolerable.[1]

To Arthur Calwell, the leader of the Australian Labour Opposition, he went further, writing in early August 1962 that

the Prime Ministers' Conference in September will be of decisive importance . . . If the Prime Ministers . . . are satisfied . . . probably we should support entry . . . the leading Prime Ministers [can] stop the whole thing if they want to do so. Whatever the British Government may say, I do not think they could proceed in the teeth of strong opposition from the Commonwealth and from the country at home.[22]

In May, the Commonwealth had been 'really the nub of the whole question' since its treatment would foreshadow Britain's and the EEC's future roles in the world. By July that emphasis had changed significantly, and he was concerned that anti-Market, anti-British reactions in the Commonwealth would break it up and so leave Britain too weak to have any real influence in the Community.

Yet when the House rose that summer Gaitskell was still uncommitted in his own mind, and still left different impressions in the minds of others. Unlike the zealots on both sides, he thought the coming decision – however important – was neither vital nor final. Even if Britain went in, a desperate country could not in the end be prevented from withdrawing. Even if Britain stayed out, that choice could be reversed later – in a year or so if the terms offered were improved, in a decade or so if the Commonwealth disintegrated. In the first case Britain's negotiating position would be weaker because EEC policies would have evolved without her – but it was being weakened still more by the Government's rush to settle. In the second case he himself thought that Britain would urgently need to go in; but that it would be worse still for Britain now to initiate a perhaps avoidable break-up of the Commonwealth by accepting terms intolerable to it.

The political balance depended on how the Community and the Commonwealth each evolved over the next decade or two, and how each would be influenced by Britain's eventual decision: a very difficult judgement, which moreover might be altered when the terms for Britain's associates were known. Economically, the balance sheet for Britain herself was also obscure, for the long-term advantages would be outweighed if bad terms made the short-term drawbacks ruinous. Gaitskell may well have subconsciously exaggerated the difference which the terms could bring about, for the last two years had taught him to worry about tactics and timing, and the wait-and-see attitude was tactically advantageous for the Opposition. But he had never believed that Britain had to enter the EEC at any price, and he still thought the price must be known and reasonable first.

Gaitskell was well aware that the party advantage which the Conservatives counted on obtaining from entry would accrue to Labour instead if the talks failed. He said so in early August to Calwell.

Looking at it from the narrow angle of our own Party political advantage over here, we should, of course, gain rather than lose if the Government fail to get agreement . . . [or] got involved in a major conflict with the Commonwealth. . . . I am assuming that . . . you would regard it as your job to see to it that [Menzies] does not sacrifice Australian interests. This attitude also suits us very well.[22]

That is the first letter in Gaitskell's correspondence to hint that a breakdown might not be unwelcome, or to propose a course of action which might promote one; and it came two weeks after his first call for a general election on the issue if in the end the price of entry proved too high.

The price was known in August, and Gaitskell later told Kennedy:

We were bitterly disappointed and indeed astonished . . . Had such terms been announced at the beginning of the negotiations, they would have been rejected out of hand by the British people . . .

It was perfectly clear that . . . there was no change [*sic*] whatever that the Labour Party would accept them . . . [as] Roy Jenkins . . . [and] George Brown also agreed.[7]

Gaitskell was thus already considering opposing entry when he left England on 16 August for a fortnight's family holiday in Italy, though he made no final decision until mid-September 1962. He had many reasons: his deteriorating relations with the spokesmen of the Six, his shock at the terms, his exposure to the Commonwealth reactions to them, his angry resentment at the Government's conduct and at the pressure of the media in favour of entry. In mid-July the private clash with Jean Monnet had had a public echo in a bitter argument over federalism with Paul-Henri Spaak at the Socialist International. Spaak was also unsympathetic to the Commonwealth, the neutrals and the Scandinavians. Gaitskell found him 'very irritating . . . Spaak's attitude was that Britain had applied to go in – "we didn't ask you".'[2] Though Gaitskell had said nothing new, Spaak rightly sensed a deep psychological gulf between the Continentals, for whom their historic reconciliation was the world's most important political development, and Gaitskell who thought it 'parochial' and felt more in common with North Americans than with Europeans.

In early September Gaitskell met the Commonwealth Socialist parties for three days of talks, which made up his mind. He was impressed by their hostility to the terms; Britain was to give up imperial preferences by 1970, in return for vague offers to discuss world commodity agreements at some future date. A special meeting of the Socialist International followed at once, but to Gaitskell's distress the European mystique of the Continental parties took priority over protecting the interests of underdeveloped countries. The latter's spokesmen, he said, 'had been very bitter about . . . a whole series of specific points . . the European Socialists . . . had hardly a single answer.'²³ Gaitskell felt that the Government had played into French hands by their 'indecent haste', and had failed disgracefully to insist on safeguards for the Commonwealth and EFTA countries; the latter were now unlikely to join.

The first sign that Labour would oppose entry was a critical communiqué by the Commonwealth Labour leaders, fully reported in the *Observer* of Sunday 9 September. Gaitskell maintained that Labour had not changed its attitude, but had simply decided, as it had always intended to, once the general terms were known. Though the shift into opposition had its own momentum, he still claimed that a Labour government would reopen negotiations in 1963 or 1964.

The Commonwealth Prime Ministers' Conference met on 10 September, and the Government's handling of it 'convinced him that the aim was to enter Europe whatever the terms and . . . despite all the undertakings'.² He was furious at the Prime Minister and Government, and indicated to the Labour Marketeers that he felt 'bound constitutionally to adopt the position he had done if only because of the shabby way the Government had behaved'.² Yet he still distinguished his conditional opposition from that of the intransigent anti-Marketeers, whose ultimate aims were quite different from his. He told a friendly correspondent: 'The problem really has been how to maintain our position against going in on the present terms and yet reply effectively to the Government's obvious intention to take us in on any terms.'²⁴ Between July and September, his assessment of that problem had changed. Before the recess he was talking of recalling the Labour MPs rather than putting the question to Conference; later he accepted the risk of stimulating its all-out hostility in order to take full advantage of its mood for his own ends. When Gaitskell committed himself, he did not do so half way.

## Brighton: The Crunch at Conference

On 21 September 1962 Gaitskell replied on television to Macmillan's broadcast of the night before, using the old arguments but now drawing negative conclusions. Britain was to abandon the existing trading system, but the Six offered only 'promises, vague assurances and nothing more'. In return for dismantling imperial preferences the EEC should accept precise agreements for Commonwealth produce: 'this is the acid test of what the Common Market is going to become'. The Government would not insist, since they wanted everything settled before the next election; and that was 'utterly wrong' when the terms were so contentious. He asked if the Prime Minister favoured entering a European federation. If so, it 'means the end of Britain as an independent nation; we become no more than "Texas" or "California" in the United States of Europe. It means the end of a thousand years of history; it means the end of the Commonwealth . . . [to become] just a province of Europe.' The political case for entry was the hope of influencing the EEC's future by

building a bridge between the Commonwealth and Europe; and we cannot do that if we destroy the Commonwealth . . . the present terms do confront us with this choice . . . I have no doubt about what the answer should be. And . . . I don't think the British people . . . will in a moment of folly, throw away the tremendous heritage of history.[25]

Crossman compared the furious Establishment and Fleet Street reaction to a famous occasion six years before:

Not since the Suez crisis has Hugh Gaitskell been so hated outside the Labour Party and so popular inside it as he is today. And the reason is the same as in 1956. At a critical moment, when the Government was reckoning on his tacit support, he has attacked it . . . It was Mr. Gaitskell's unforgivable sin to remind the Commonwealth Prime Ministers on their arrival that, whereas both Government and Opposition had made them clear and explicit promises, it is only the Opposition that intends to keep its word.[26]

Contrary to the Left's view of him, Gaitskell was fortified in his determination by that solid hostility of the Establishment; perhaps it recalled the hated pressure for conformity at school. He had always been exasperated by the bogus economic arguments of those who really wanted to enter on political grounds which they preferred not to stress publicly; now he was equally enraged by 'what I call the hush and mush technique' of the Government publicity machine.[27] He explained his conclusions frankly to Kennedy:

until August I had always assumed and said that we should not have an election on the Common Market. I took the view that either the Government would obtain sufficiently good terms to justify us in supporting them or that the terms would be too bad for them to proceed at all. On this I was wrong – and it is this – their decision to go ahead despite the fact that the terms were in flagrant breach of their pledges and therefore quite unacceptable to us – which has brought this whole matter into the arena of party politics in Britain.[7]

Once he had decided to prepare for a clash with the Government, he had to deal both with his old friends who were still in favour of entry, and his new left-wing allies who would always be against it. The Labour Marketeers, by their earlier acceptance of the conditional policy, had weakened their position when the conditions were not met. They recoiled from voting against entry and so missing what they saw as an opportunity that might not recur. But some of their MPs were wavering, few would refuse to vote against the Government, and all were worried about fighting an election before the legislation was through. The day before Gaitskell's broadcast, they put out a careful statement underlining their points of agreement with him while reaffirming support for entry. But old personal ties with him, political calculation and a long habit of loyalty to the leadership inhibited their resistance.

Gaitskell made a gesture, meeting them privately at the House on 27 September, when he staunchly denied that he was shifting towards hostility in principle. But he did seize the opportunity for reconciliation with some of those in the Party who had fought him for so long. He told his pro-Market deputy: 'do remember, George, that there's six million votes' to win at Conference;[4] and felt he could safely write off the 'small group of [Labour] right-wingers, many of them personal friends of mine, who . . . have been making a little trouble . . . But I am quite convinced that at next week's Party Conference there will be an absolutely overwhelming vote in favour of the official line.'[22] They suspected him of counting on their old loyalty, and they resented it.

His new determination became evident in the week before Conference. At the Shadow Cabinet on 25 September, Gaitskell was 'tough and angry' with his old allies who unsuccessfully opposed his line. When the NEC met at Brighton to approve the policy statement for Conference, the Left for once supported Gaitskell. Just as in 1960–1, Gaitskell, Brown, Crossman and Watson were appointed as a drafting sub-committee; only this time Crossman was Gaitskell's ally against Watson and Brown.

They agreed a draft which, with the Left abstaining, was approved *nem. con.* It reiterated Labour's conditions, stressed the dangerous federalist intentions of the Six, rejected entry on the proposed terms, and demanded precise agreements protecting the Commonwealth countries. It gave no hint that a Labour government would withdraw if it were returned after British entry, saying instead: 'we do not rule out the possibility . . . [of] new and more successful negotiations at a later stage'. Saturday's papers reported, and the Prime Minister at least believed, that Labour was 'back on the European fence' – united for Conference purposes by 'a pretty clever document' to the detriment of

Gaitskell's prestige.[17] Lobbied hard by Watson, the Marketeers prudently accepted the compromise.

George Brown, who was to wind up the debate, wanted to see the text of Gaitskell's opening speech – but Gaitskell kept putting him off. His suspicions aroused, he went to the latter's hotel room at midnight for a last try; Gaitskell covered up the text, but assured his mistrustful deputy that he was not changing the agreed line.[28] Later, Brown's furious sense of betrayal was shared by less explosive characters; an old opponent, Walter Padley, felt it was the only time Gaitskell ever showed 'duplicity'. Yet not all the Marketeers thought the same, and Sam Watson could not budge Gaitskell an inch during a night-long argument.[29]

Shortly before 10 a.m. on Wednesday 3 October 1962, Gaitskell mounted the platform in the overheated hall of the Brighton ice rink to address a Labour Conference for – though no one imagined it – the last time. He had not slept at all the night before; but there was no weariness in his long, carefully structured, highly emotional performance. He began with a quiet plea for tolerance; and he was careful to say he opposed entry into the EEC only on the proposed terms, not on principle. He rejected 'unsound arguments' that economic planning would be hampered; praised the Continental Socialists; and stressed that the Community would continue in any case whatever Britain did. Otherwise balanced judgement gave way to a passionate repudiation of the Government's policy; the emotional overtones were entirely hostile, and Crossman said he had never seen anyone so enjoy his own rhetoric. Even the economic exposition was now entirely one way:

We would gain in markets where we sell less than one-fifth of our exports and lose in markets where we sell about half our exports . . . we are to be obliged to import expensive food from the Continent of Europe in place of cheap food from the Commonwealth . . . You cannot have it both ways. It is either better for industry to have tougher competition – which it will certainly get at home, or better for it to have easier conditions which it will get in the markets of the Six. Both arguments cannot be true . . . it is not mainly because of the Common Market that Europe has had this remarkable growth recently . . . The truth is that our faults lie not in our markets or in the tariffs against us but in ourselves.

Here Christopher Mayhew turned to his neighbour Lord Longford: 'Now we shall have fifteen minutes of the arguments in favour.' Instead, Gaitskell summed up by reiterating that the balance was even – justifying his one-sided approach later by saying he was 'sick and tired of the nonsense . . . on this subject'.

Politically, Western European unity was not an 'outstanding' problem like those of world peace and world poverty: the East–West division and what is now called the 'North–South' division. He admitted 'the force of the argument' (so recently his own) that Britain could best influence the development of the Community from within; it 'must be brought into the balance, but the balancing has not been completed'. For 'there have been evil features in European history too . . . it has its two faces and we do not know as yet which is the one which will dominate.' A European state might develop, seeking its own nuclear weapons. The creators of the Community openly sought federation. 'That is what they mean, that is what they are after'; but even if that was right for them, should Britain become only a Texas or California in the United States of Europe and accept 'the end of Britain as an independent nation state . . . the end of a thousand years of history'? Becoming 'a province of Europe, which is what federation means', must wreck the Commonwealth. A transformed Community, keeping those links intact, would indeed be 'a fine ideal . . . the building of a bridge between the Commonwealth and Europe. But you cannot do that if at the beginning you sell the Commonwealth down the river.'

Having set the stage for rejection, he repeated that 'the arguments . . . are evenly balanced; and whether or not it is worth going in depends on the conditions of our entry'. He protested that the treatment of the neutrals sought 'to convert the Treaty of Rome into a military alliance'. On planning and agriculture, his presentation had become negative. Having stressed in May that nothing in the Treaty threatened Britain's independent foreign policy, he now said: 'The right of veto . . . is imperative and must be maintained.' At last he came to the Commonwealth, citing the military help from the old dominions at Vimy Ridge and Gallipoli, and (less noticed) their economic contribution to Britain's recovery after 1945; and invoking 'this remarkable multi-racial association, of independent nations, stretching across five continents, covering every race . . . potentially of immense value to the world'. He swept aside the Government's terms. The Common Agricultural Policy was 'one of the most devastating pieces of protectionism ever invented'; the abandonment of imperial preferences meant they had 'given away our strongest cards'; the arrangements on Indian tea were scorned. 'It is true we are not obliged – it is very kind of them! – to impose a customs duty on tea over here. We are allowed to drink our national beverage as we like. Very handsome!' The Prime Minister had claimed that the Africans' terms were 'wonderful', ignoring their unhappiness at the political price demanded. 'What a patronising attitude!'

Worst of all was the 'astonishing' and 'odious' contrast with the Government's pledges to the Commonwealth. Duncan Sandys had repeated those pledges in that very hall a year ago; now, in 'a desperate attempt to bulldoze the Commonwealth into accepting what had been done', he warned that Britain was going in anyhow. The Government should instead go back and demand precise agreements before we began the 'irrevocable course' of dismantling preferences and subjecting ourselves to majority rules: 'Let us not underestimate the power of the vested interests in the Community. There are good features of Europe, but there is a very powerful protectionist lobby, and most of the Governments of the Six depend upon it.' No one had said the year before that Britain could not maintain an independent foreign policy or retain reserve powers to protect full employment – and 'Our other three conditions are all Government pledges! . . . Surely they cannot be impossible to meet? . . . The Government have made their pledges; we have made ours. But there is a difference between us. We mean to keep ours.'

Today, Britain's bargaining position had been destroyed by the Government's open eagerness to go in. Tomorrow, we would not 'miss the political boat', for General de Gaulle would protect us against that risk. The Government's haste had been due solely to its determination to enter without an election, which he berated in terms 'as furiously angry as anything [he] has ever said about the Communists and fellow-travellers'.[26] His populist streak emerged in his rage at the respectable press which was denouncing him in chorus: 'We are now being told that the British people are not capable of judging this issue – the Government knows best; the top people are the only people who can understand it; it is too difficult for the rest . . . what an odious piece of hypocritical supercilious arrogant rubbish is this!' Idealist causes in the wider world could be served only in a broad and outward-looking Europe, and that prospect depended on the terms. Those could be improved in a new negotiation later; the conditions could be met; final judgement should await final proposals:

I still hope profoundly that there may be such a change of heart in Europe as will make this possible . . . But . . . if the Six will not give it to us; if the British Government will not even ask for it, then . . . we shall not flinch from our duty if that moment comes.[30]

## Strange Bedfellows

When Gaitskell sat down the wild applause of the delighted Left rolled on and on. A trade union loyalist, very close to the Gaitskells, found Hugh 'radiant . . . with the flowing tide' but Dora worried: 'Charlie, all the wrong people are cheering'.[29] Harold Wilson from the chair said 'this historic speech' should be printed and sent to every member of the Party, and Frank Cousins promised that the T&GWU would pay. Winding up from an impossible position, George Brown dexterously contrived to support the same document from an opposite policy standpoint.

The Left were demanding a general election before any decision was taken: to foil the Government, since it would make the Six wary of British entry; and to blow the Labour Marketeers out of their positions of influence in the Party. Gaitskell therefore called only for an election if the parties differed when the final terms were known – a device to gain time and keep an escape route open. A proposal for an unequivocal commitment to an election was lost on a card vote by well over two to one, so that the intransigent anti-Marketeers were 'resoundingly defeated' as Gaitskell had hoped.[20]

The defeat of Gaitskell's friends was far more resounding. They felt his speech had shown no understanding of their views and no sympathy for their difficulties. He kept telling them that unhappily such a clash was unavoidable, since he had friends committed on both sides. The personal friendships resumed after a brief period of coolness. But he pulled no political punches, for in order to show the Party united he had to isolate and weaken the awkward minority whose dissent could so easily be magnified in the overwhelmingly pro-Market press. He had no wish to weaken or humiliate his old allies, and urged his CDS friends to reply vigorously to the extreme opponents of entry, but to concentrate on pressing for better terms. It was excellent counsel which they could honourably follow, both to keep the Party from going overboard against the Market, and to defend themselves against the Left. Yet the Labour Marketeers by emphasising the conditions now, as previously by accepting them, would weaken their own case for rebelling when the real clash came. Gaitskell's advice would protect them now but neutralise them later – both to his own advantage.

On the other side of the Market fence, he busily looked for allies outside the Labour Party, including even his old enemy Lord Beaverbrook – each of course hoping to use the other, for Gaitskell was without Fleet Street support since both the *Mirror* and *Herald* were now on the other side. Within the Party, Gaitskell exploited the opportunity to consolidate its unity and his own leadership by appealing to the constituency activists. Above all he achieved a genuine reconciliation with his most powerful antagonist, Frank Cousins, whose attitude to the Market was very close to his own, and who offered to pay for printing the speech as a gesture of reconciliation, surprise and pleasure. On 12 November 1962, a month after Brighton, the hatchet was finally buried when Cousins and his wife dined alone with Hugh and Dora at 18 Frognal Gardens. There was no firm proposal or commitment, but Cousins would probably have become Minister of Transport in a Gaitskell Cabinet.[31]

Other union leaders, who had taken big risks to support Gaitskell's policies against Cousins in the past, were understandably alarmed and anxious. Some even feared he was changing sides. His old friends at Westminster were worried too. But Gaitskell had no intention at all of reversing his alliances within the Party, and carefully avoided the trap into which his successor fell headlong ten years later, when the Labour Left were allowed to exploit the Market issue to extend their power in the Party at the expense, initially of their opponents on the pro-Market Right, but eventually of their temporary allies in the leadership. His awareness of the danger made him cautious about the demand for a general election on the EEC issue, in order to avoid committing himself on the next and crucial problem: if he came to power after Macmillan had taken the country into the EEC, would he repudiate the treaty and take her out? That would do the maximum damage to Britain's relationship with her allies – but the threat of it would probably force an election, for the Six might well insist on one before letting Britain join. So the Left sought a pledge to repudiate, to which Gaitskell repeatedly refused to commit himself. But he privately thought that he must reserve the threat in case 'the Government tried to get through impossible terms by the use of the guillotine',[2] and Bill Carron's call for a promise *not* to repudiate was also met with silence. Two months later Gaitskell was still privately stressing his reluctance to Kennedy. 'I have been very careful to say nothing on that. There are circumstances in which I might feel obliged to do so but obviously . . . [only after] the most careful weighing up of all the possible consequences.'[7] He was reserving his heavy weapons to dissuade the Government from behaviour he saw as illegitimate. But he also candidly told a private meeting: 'I won't play that card unless it will win.'[2]

He knew quite well that the Left naturally hoped to make him dependent upon them and then impose their own policies on him. The

Left hoped, and the Right feared, that a successful election campaign alongside the outright anti-Marketeers would so strengthen their influence and his need for their support that a breach with Washington would follow. Yet on two crucial points Kennedy agreed with Gaitskell. He saw no urgency for an immediate settlement and had no sympathy for the intransigence of the Six, insisting privately that the Europeans must be made to show more generosity to Britain and argued out of their protectionism. But the President was as usual more enlightened than American opinion, and Gaitskell warned Kennedy frankly that 'friendship and alliance cannot survive on the basis of threats and pressures'.[7]

Towards the French, he was ambivalent. They were very useful as enemies of federalism but very difficult on all matters of substance; so they made Macmillan's task much harder. Gaitskell was aware of de Gaulle's preference for excluding Britain, not so sure of his ability to do so. In December 1962 Gaitskell went to Paris, deliberately avoiding seeing de Gaulle for fear that Macmillan would make him the scapegoat if the President did keep Britain out.[32] Instead he saw the Prime Minister and Foreign Minister, and also Guy Mollet the Socialist leader; sources close to his French political contacts on both sides promptly began hinting that Britain might become an associate member of the EEC. Back in London, Gaitskell wrote that the talks seemed increasingly likely to fail. 'The French are . . . likely to make as many difficulties for us as they can'.[22] On 11 January 1963, Macmillan was still hoping the negotiations would succeed. De Gaulle pronounced his veto three days later – and four days before Gaitskell's death.

## Community, Commonwealth and Offshore Island

Gaitskell was a party leader who had twice fought battles against many of his own followers and was prudently – and rightly – trying to avoid another. He never concealed that his original 'fence-sitting' policy was adopted partly to keep the Party together. Political advantage and political principle were not in conflict, for that policy was tactically attractive precisely because it corresponded to what he, and most Labour people, felt about the substance. Few were narrow Little England nationalists, but many were suspicious of de Gaulle and Adenauer and concerned about the 'new Commonwealth'; so that, as Gaitskell told Kennedy, the conditions demanded by Labour did outline the kind of Europe they wanted to join.

Until the summer of 1962, Gaitskell assumed that if he could avoid a premature clash within the Party, events would settle his main political problem – and that he would probably find himself leading and winning another battle against the all-out opponents of entry. His assessment had misjudged both the Six and the British Prime Minister. He overestimated the chances of the conditions being accepted, not through having illusions about the French, but because he hoped for too much from the other negotiating partners putting pressure on Paris. Never really appreciating the emotional drive behind the European movement, he expected them to go further than was ever likely both in making concessions to the Commonwealth and in transforming the Community itself. Yet he knew that the Six themselves disagreed about the shape of the future Community. Socialists like Spaak differed from the European Right and shared many of Labour's objectives, but were keen federalists; the Gaullists and the British agreed in opposing federalism, but on very little else; the new military power of which Adenauer and de Gaulle dreamed was a nightmare to both the federalists and the British.

At home Gaitskell, being so wary of Harold Macmillan, suspected the Prime Minister's plan to change the domestic political agenda and so revive flagging Conservative fortunes. But he assumed that the terms would either be good enough for the Opposition to accept, or not good enough for the Government to propose, so that a party clash on the issue was unlikely. Macmillan proved very successful in beating down the Tory rebels, as Gaitskell had come to expect; he also became committed to entry not on party grounds, but as an historic decision for which he ran great political risks. He never forgot how Disraeli had overthrown Peel, and up to 21 August 1962 he feared a revolt led by his most influential colleague, R. A. Butler – which would almost certainly have destroyed either the policy or its architect or both.[33] Once reassured about Butler, Macmillan took a bigger gamble than Gaitskell had expected to achieve the historic objective; for Gaitskell so mistrusted him as to attribute his haste essentially to party political motives, although recognising that he might have broader ones too.

Gaitskell began to suspect in August, and became convinced in September, that the British Government was abandoning many of the original conditions and preparing to enter a substantially unchanged Community. That discovery transformed his whole bearing. From being cool, rational and calculating, he became heated, emotional and passionate. The change was crystallised in his meetings with the Commonwealth Socialist parties: from indignation at the treatment of the Commonwealth, shock at getting no support from the European Socialists, suspicion of imprecise promises by the Six, and anger at

Macmillan's determination to bring Britain into the Community on any terms before the next election – so that Labour would have to reverse a decision already in force instead of questioning a leap in the dark. As Leader of the Opposition Gaitskell felt a political obligation to the British peoples of the old Commonwealth and a moral obligation to the poor nations of the new. Perhaps the passion of Brighton came most of all from his repugnance at defeatism – the claim by some Marketeers that Britain had no future outside the EEC.[29] He saw that not as an economic miscalculation, but as a confession of political bankruptcy; for, in or out, Britain's future would depend on herself, and he loathed the suggestion that she could not get to her feet unless hauled up by foreigners.

His fence-sitting attitude during the EEC talks was therefore transformed by their outcome into furious opposition; and he set about preparing for a campaign which never took place, and which he would not have survived to lead. In doing so he reconciled many left-wing activists within the Labour Party – if not their national spokesmen – to his leadership. That was an intended consequence, but not his motive. Some close friends suspected that he unconsciously recoiled from yet another battle on the old lines; others more plausibly thought that he felt that a party leader should not perpetually fight his own followers. Certainly he made the most of his political opportunity, and certainly he was delighted to find the tide flowing his own way at last. But his course was no tactical necessity, for opponents as well as supporters of entry recognised that Conference would happily have accepted a more balanced line; and by alienating old friends, he risked becoming needlessly dependent on old enemies.[29]

He spoke at Brighton out of conviction not calculation. A fortnight later he told some pro-EEC friends: 'I suppose that I have been all along more emotionally against the Common Market than I realised.'[34] From opposite sides, Roy Jenkins and Peter Shore, both committed and mutually hostile partisans, at least agreed with one another, as against Gaitskell, that the terms mattered far less than the principle – and so may have been more realistic about what the conditions were likely to be. But Gaitskell's basic indifference was not, as with most uncommitted Labour people, a sign of puzzled indecision. He had thought through the alternatives and found them evenly balanced. Even at Brighton, his views did not coincide with those of the delegates who cheered them vociferously. Strong anti-Marketeers suspected the Europeans mainly as militaristic cold warriors; Gaitskell was more worried about their colonialist attitude in Africa and the UN, and about their quarrelling with the United States and weakening the Western alliance.[7] He was more concerned than the Left with the economic policies of the Six – especially with their consequences for the Commonwealth, to which he gave higher priority than his colleagues or most Labour anti-Marketeers did. He never saw it as a long-term alternative to the EEC, but he did insist that Britain had a duty not to provoke its disintegration.

He shared neither the illusion of a few anti-Marketeers, that the Commonwealth could offer a complete alternative, nor their opponents' worry that the great opportunity might never return. He always thought that a negative in 1962 might have to be reconsidered if circumstances changed, and never believed those changes would make reconsideration impossible. Some Marketeers feared that Britain would decline economically outside the Community, who therefore would not welcome her in; but Gaitskell never attributed European economic growth to the Market, and always believed that domestic developments would depend on domestic decisions – notably the quality of British political leadership, and the response to it of the British people.

He would certainly have looked afresh at the new balance of arguments when the Commonwealth lost its cohesion, Britain became a small offshore island with waning influence, and the mirage of a federal Europe receded. His close friends disagree about his likely conclusions. In 1962, Gaitskell had on his side not only the ideologues of the Left, but also many Labour leaders who were men of government, as he was. With the sole exception of Douglas Jay, those colleagues – and his own widow – all changed their minds about the EEC in the next few years: Wilson, Callaghan, Healey, Stewart, Gordon Walker. But whatever his final decision, his approach would not have changed: a cool appraisal of the advantages and drawbacks, quite different from the uncompromising hostility or enthusiastic vision of the zealots on either side. Five years after Britain's entry, and fifteen years after Gaitskell's death, front-benchers and back-benchers in both major parties saw the Community developing as 'a union of consenting national governments . . . working together for limited ends under arrangements many of which should be altered drastically in Britain's interest'.[35] Had he survived, Gaitskell might have found himself close to the centre of gravity of British opinion about the EEC.

# 24

# In Sight of the Promised Land
# 1962–3

---

*'He looked, sounded and was set to be the Prime Minister of England'*
(Obituary of HG by a Tory journalist and MP)

---

## Gaitskell at Fifty-six

Though Gaitskell's political personality was set before he became leader, his last three dramatic years influenced his attitude to other people and led him to reassess his own mistakes. If all politicians are either bishops or bookmakers, Gaitskell the public man sat firmly on the episcopal bench. Yet his seriousness of purpose was tempered with gaiety, even frivolity, so that Malcolm Muggeridge could write: 'Earnestness, [that] disease of the Left in politics . . . only afflicted Gaitskell as a rash, never as a fever.'[1] He emerged from the traumas of 1960–1 fully confident of his capacity to lead the Party back to power, put his principles into practice, and change the course of British politics. 'Last year', he told the 1961 Blackpool Conference, 'our task was to save the Party. This year it is to save the nation.'[2]

During that stormy period he suffered as much violent abuse as any British politician has ever faced, and was more bitterly reviled by his own followers than most party leaders have ever been. There were moments when he wondered if he had made a mistake in ever going into politics. The violence of that conflict turned him into a harder man, and chipped away at some of the amiable traits which made him so attractive as a person but sometimes handicapped him in the political struggle. He wrote to a friend at the worst period of all, early in 1960:

Sometimes I hate it very much – most of all the treachery & disloyalty. I like things that are more straightforward. You sit round a table & discuss a problem calmly & rationally. You reach your conclusions. You act accordingly. But it's not like that at all – at the moment. People seem to be unable or unwilling to do that – except for the few friends you know. Everything is spiced & barbed & the atmosphere is full of suppressed hysteria & neurosis – not so suppressed either! It would be nice like you to treat it as chess. I find that hard.

More than ever he prized courage and loyalty. The courage to take an unpopular line in public, he once said, was the first qualification for political office; and when Roy Jenkins promised to support him whenever he was right, he replied like Disraeli: 'Anybody can do that. I want people who'll support me when I'm wrong.'[3]

In the heat of a bitter struggle, he could judge his opponents harshly – especially the moralisers. Stimulated by a lively conversation among friends, he could become emotional about both people and issues. He assessed his close but not always loyal associates quite without illusions. He rejected a warning that one of them might try to stab him in the back: 'He's a shit and he knows that everybody knows he's a shit. If he stabs he'll stab from in front.' The same man's perpetual pursuit of his own self-interest was, he said, easier to cope with than the unpredictable vagaries of another colleague in search of his. To a friend who wondered in the summer of 1962 how far he could trust a third prominent associate, he replied that he trusted nobody. After so many desertions at critical moments, such resentments were not surprising, however sadly different from his early ambition to prove that there could be friendship at the top after all. But some of his own side also thought him tougher, less free and easy, more often testy and irritable when opposed or criticised. Refractory members summoned to his room in the House sometimes felt it was like going to the Headmaster's study. To his loyal secretary, whatever the strain, 'he never lost his temper, ever – goodness knows he had reason to, but never'. But he 'sweated blood in controversies', and it showed.[4]

Gaitskell knew very well that such emotions were professionally dangerous. He gave a long, candid television interview to Malcolm Muggeridge in the summer of 1961 about his personal outlook, not his views. He told the interviewer that back-stabbing was no less common in journalism than in politics – though less noticed in the press, which lovingly recorded all conflicts but no constructive activities. Muggeridge asked directly whether he felt too bitter to work with those individuals who had led the attacks on him. 'Well,' he replied,

I think it's very important to avoid that if you possibly can, because in politics the situation changes a great deal, and very often you don't understand somebody else's motives, and if you were to sort of be a tremendously unforgiving, ruthless type I don't think again you could do your job properly. I am human and of course one doesn't like it when people, whom you perhaps hoped were on your side, turn against you. But, well, one must just try and get over it, that's all . . . Politics is a very tense sort of existence, people are emotionally excited and roused . . . that is part of the price you pay for a very interesting life.[5]

Nearly all the old friends who found him more difficult in later years were reflecting their first sharp political disagreement with him over the Common Market. They were also reflecting Gaitskell's exceptional earlier standards of patience, tolerance and good humour to both supporters and opponents. At his worst moment at Scarborough, he sought out a left-wing journalist whose father had just died, to express his regrets. After Labour's vote was halved in the Liberal triumph at Orpington in 1962, he asked the humiliated young Labour candidate to lunch at the House to be congratulated on the campaign. A future Conservative Cabinet Minister recalled fifteen years later his astonished delight at receiving a friendly letter of congratulations from the Leader of the Opposition praising his maiden speech – and added wistfully, 'it would never happen now'.

Gaitskell was still concerned about his friends, whether valued henchmen or unknown comrades from his years of obscurity. When his staunch ally Alice Bacon was suddenly taken desperately ill in Yorkshire, he cancelled everything in London to go straight to her bedside. He left early from a PLP discussion on the Common Market to attend the mayor-making ceremony in Chatham of his pre-war friend Mrs Grieveson. Strangers who appealed to him had the same attention; one, not a constituent and with no introduction, wrote to thank him for helping to settle a family problem overseas: 'I am still amazed that a member of the ordinary public such as myself . . . should be able so easily to reach somebody as prominent as yourself in order to bring assistance to a needy relative so far away.'[6]

From goodwill and meticulousness, he accepted far too many commitments. He still prepared elaborately for every speech, and delved thoroughly into quite unexpected subjects: the assistant national agent was understandably amazed at the party leader's concern with bands and styles of jazz for youth concerts. Usually the pressures came the other way, with the machine demanding endless provincial tours to encourage the rank and file. Gaitskell did not resist enough, and took far more interest than Attlee ever had. But when he was worn down by other work, he found it hard to pretend. In Leeds, he was not at home in university circles; often he was obviously weary at the endless arguments with self-righteous critics who would not accept his good faith. Some mistook that mood for elitist indifference to the views of ordinary folk. But Gaitskell always found the workingmen's clubs exhilarating, and wrote to his daughter in 1959: 'I'm glad you went canvassing and liked it. There's a lot that's very tiresome and distasteful in politics but I absolutely agree that working with people for the Party is very satisfying: that's one reason why I like the tours.

One meets so many of the *best* party workers – just *good* people.'[7] Later an American, with long political experience at home, watched Gaitskell mixing easily and naturally with the drinkers at the Belper Labour Club: 'This dignified, elegant, impressive man – I wondered whether he'll just look uncomfortable or will he try to become one of the lads which will embarrass me. He didn't do either. He was friendly, good humoured, exchanged jokes with them – but remained himself.' He was so kind to that visitor that from being 'a convinced Gaitskellite at the start of the tour I became a devoted one at the end'.[8]

With his parliamentary duties, weekend speeches and tours in the recess, he had little time for his family. Dora waited up for him to get back late from the House, and they met – silently – over breakfast. She looked forward eagerly to Labour's return to office, when she could see him at lunch as Molly Butler saw Rab. She went often to South Leeds, and with him at weekends and on tour: 'That's the point of going round the country with my husband. It's a chance to answer back, to argue. And to be together.'[9] Sometimes they were able to take a break for a few hours, as when they went off hunting for antiques during the tour of East Anglia. In one interview on 'turning-points in one's life' Hugh said, moderately as usual: 'More than most jobs, politics imposes stresses and strains which are hard to take without the understanding and companionship of somebody who shares your own fundamental attitudes and interests.'[10]

Otherwise holidays were Gaitskell's main opportunities to see his family. After the children grew up, these were often abroad, especially in Italy and Yugoslavia. Even official foreign trips usually provided an opportunity for non-political relaxation. After the Socialist International met in Oslo, he and his old NEC antagonist Tom Driberg went looking at statues and sculpture, and then gossiped about jazz and ballet over a leisurely dinner: 'one of the most agreeable evenings I've spent with anybody – he was personally so charming, very courteous always and considerate'. Always he detested pomposity, refusing VIP treatment when he took the family to Italy. 'Here is one politician', wrote a normally unfriendly newspaper, 'who does not have an inflated idea of his own position.'[9]

At 18 Frognal Gardens they kept up a comfortable establishment, quite unaltered by Gaitskell's improved financial fortunes. During the booming later 1950s his investments flourished, thanks to skilful friends in the banking world to whom he had committed them. At his death he left £75,000 net; death duties took well over one-third, for he had neglected to take some legitimate precautions. Quite likely he did not know how very well his investments were doing; certainly he did not tell his wife. They wined and dined rather better but made little change in their style of life; they considered having someone living in to run the household, but Dora disliked the idea and they never did. Hugh enjoyed his comforts, but always despised luxury and ostentatious spending.

However, he added a lively round of social engagements to his time-consuming political duties. In 1962 Anthony Sampson called him

relaxed and gregarious, with an extraordinary capacity for enjoyment and no political pomp . . . [and with] a talent for listening which is almost unknown among politicians . . . His circle is large and surprising: he can be seen at Belgravia lunch-parties, at night-clubs, at the celebrations of café society and – more rarely – at trade union socials: he has never found it easy to adapt his social pleasures to political expediency . . . He entertains widely and well, with cosmopolitan scope . . . He talks about almost everything, travels widely and forgets nothing.[11]

The Gaitskells found their relaxation in parties, dinners and dances. He had never been one for what Dora called 'the Great Plains of domestic life' and his friends thought that in his methodical way, he allocated periods off-duty to enjoy himself as he pleased without caring what anyone thought. Never rigidly abstemious, he drank a fair amount; but he knew that alcohol can be dangerous for politicians under strain – from the weight of their responsibilities or the frustration of having none – and he ran no risk of overdoing it.

At home at Frognal Gardens his guests were mostly progressive and few were actively Tory. But he kept up a few personal friendships across the political divide, largely through Anne Fleming and her circle. Crosland chided him about it; but, with his Wykehamist sense of rectitude and distaste for the idle rich, Gaitskell was not in the least worried that he might yield to the embrace of the social Establishment, or might be sourly suspected of doing so. He appreciated its comforts, and its intellectual stimulus still more. But even his taste for that had limits. 'We see a great deal of the Berlins, Stuart Hampshire, Maurice B[owra] and Anne F[leming],' he wrote on one holiday. 'We liked the conversation very much at first but have begun to find it a trifle exhausting . . . you can sit in silence if you are two or even three but not if you are seven or eight. So there is a certain atmosphere of effort.'[7]

His friends, apart from Crosland, were convinced that his active social life had no effect at all on his political views. Indeed, when one Conservative friend wrote rather hectoringly about egalitarianism that it was bad for people to get something for nothing, he referred to her own inherited wealth and rebuked her: 'I don't take your ravings on politics seriously. There's a sort of Bournemouth bellow that comes through – something from a former non-rational existence which you once led.' Occasionally he himself feared that some of his political friends might be unduly attracted by that world, but he never doubted his own immunity to temptation; in an obituary of his old patron Hugh Dalton, he wrote: 'At no time was there the faintest chance that he would be seduced by "society" and for those who showed signs of succumbing to it he had nothing but contempt.'[12] Such complete indifference to the reactions of others was imprudent. But his social life did him less political harm than might have been expected.

Of course his present and prospective status partly explained why he was so much in demand socially; but only partly, for he was still a very pleasant and stimulating companion. 'He was never pompous or self-important, as are most politicians, even the best of them. He tried always to say what he meant and to mean something; likewise an unusual trait among politicans . . . Gaitskell and Aneurin Bevan were . . . the least boring politicians to spend time with.'[1] On first meeting him people felt his charm, notably because each conversational companion of the moment could always count on his undisturbed attention.

Some dedicated political opponents thought that he never understood young people. He did not think youth (or age) made prejudice or irrationality any more attractive; and he once confessed that there was 'nothing I like better than being flattered by the young – very soothing to the bruised ego'.[13] But it was not just political agreement or difference; he would happily argue into the small hours with students who discussed seriously, without slogans or rancour. In March 1962 he spoke – surprisingly – in a funny debate at the Oxford Union, on a motion regretting that no one had succeeded where Guy Fawkes failed. Even for this he prepared elaborately, with material from the House of Commons library on the Gunpowder Plot and its successors. Yet on the night,

his entire speech was composed of refutations of those who had spoken before. His style was . . . dry (even desiccated) but the wit took everyone by surprise. He analysed one by one the political positions being taken by the factions of the day, including (perhaps particularly) those in the Labour party who opposed him. Each section of his speech ended with the conclusion, which became a refrain, greeted with rising gales of laughter, 'So you see, Guy Fawkes was not the man for *you*.'

He showed 'obvious and genuine delight' at the party afterwards, and was one of the last to leave.[14]

Next evening he dined with a college graduate society.

Conversation was relatively lighthearted and spontaneous . . . [his] lack of any pomposity . . . quickly put everyone at ease. Unlike so many politicians Gaitskell was neither a monologuist nor one of those who sit abstracted from mere mortals with weighty matters of state on their minds . . . [he] was a remarkably good listener so one felt there was a real give and take in the conversation. I remember too a wry self-deprecatory humour and a style absolutely lacking in any 'side' . . . some good-natured banter about Hampstead socialism, a couple of funny, slightly malicious anecdotes about Nye Bevan and the temptations of upper bourgeois life.[15]

It was the largest and most enthusiastic meeting for a visitor at the college for at least five years – and the competition included Enoch Powell, Kingsley Martin, Angus Wilson and Stephen Spender. Gaitskell talked for an hour on the intellectual foundations of democratic socialism – with a moving reference to Evan Durbin – and then, in a stiflingly hot room, patiently answered questions for well over another hour, meeting a little mild criticism from nuclear disarmers and more from enthusiastic foreigners wanting Britain in the EEC. 'He received a standing ovation . . . more like a party meeting than a society gathering . . . [he seemed] a warm and likeable man, who had thoroughly enjoyed the evening and who was faintly surprised by the enthusiasm aroused.'[15] That autumn he dined in a Cambridge college where his host had banned any talk of politics, and greatly impressed a Harvard visitor by talking comfortably and knowledgeably about art and Russian literature.

His friends often wondered how he could stand the pace. Worry about his stamina in office was almost certainly misplaced, for he would have been far better staffed, and would not have felt he had to do so much himself; besides, power is an elixir for frustrated politicians. But the physical strain of the life he led, defying all warnings, must have overtaxed even his robust constitution and lowered his resistance to illness. The mental strain told on him surprisingly little, for even at the nadir of his political fortunes he was always able to forget his troubles and relax completely. In the last year those worries were over; he was thought to be, and thought himself, on the threshold of Downing Street. Yet the strain was there, for he was a sensitive man, and beneath the courtesy, good temper and patience was much repressed disgust at the intrigue and the pettiness. At least once those emotions broke the surface; in the early summer of 1962, when things were going well politically, a perfectly trivial incident with George Brown suddenly made him feel he had had enough of it, and he alarmed Alice Bacon by hinting that he would resign and quit politics. The mood did not last long, but it revealed the tensions below.

Gaitskell was no more spoiled by the approach of power than distraught by the proximity of disaster. Malcolm Muggeridge, in his Granada Television interview, interrogated him about ambition, power and the motives and dilemmas of politicians. A couple of years earlier Gaitskell had written to his daughter that there was nothing wrong with ambition in a young man: 'The question is really how far he is a genuine Socialist – i.e. has thought deeply about politics & morals & knows where his sympathies lie . . . if yes I'm not too worried about careerism.'[7] Now in 1961 he was rather pleased to learn that Aneurin Bevan had once privately said that he was not ambitious enough. At once determined to be honest and afraid of sounding priggish, he confessed that

of course I want to be Prime Minister, because being leader of the Labour Party that means a Labour government, but it's not a sort of personal overwhelming desire to be a Prime Minister of Britain . . . there's nothing wrong with ambition, so long as it isn't sort of overriding, I think then it becomes intolerable.

He went on to stress 'one of the great drawbacks of politics . . . the encroachment it makes on your private life, on your privacy . . . it's been almost entirely a public life, and that, I think, is a bore'. He honestly admitted at once that he did not find the limelight altogether unattractive: 'I suppose one would miss it, sometimes one longs to be out of it but . . . in time I think you'd feel you'd had your ration, and would be glad to go back to a quieter life.'[5]

## Kennedy, Gaitskell and Nuclear Weapons

Had he become Prime Minister, Gaitskell could have expected to enjoy close relations with President Kennedy – and therefore to come under fire from the anti-Americans on both Right and Left, a small price to pay for mutual confidence with the new Administration in Washington. The men who had come to power there shared Labour's long-standing worries about official attitudes in the Pentagon, in Whitehall and at NATO headquarters; the affinity between Kennedy's policies and Labour's non-nuclear club proposals of 1959 was marked. With a similar approach to nuclear weapons, and a similar distrust of both hardline cold warriors and wishful-thinking neutralists, Gaitskell's voice was welcome in the White House to counteract right-wing pressures, both domestic and European. It would have carried much further from Downing Street.

When the Russians resumed nuclear testing in August 1961, exploding a gigantic 50-megaton H-bomb in the atmosphere, Kennedy decided with the utmost reluctance that the US must reply. The resumption rekindled the alarm and indignation of the nuclear disarmers, and CND's extreme-Left hangers-on tried to break up Labour's May Day rallies in Glasgow and London. At the former, Gaitskell was speaking quite unprovocatively on Scottish unemployment; after 45 minutes of continuous uproar he shouted to the 300 disrupters, 'Go to the Kremlin and put up your placards there', and told the crowd of 5,000: 'In an election these people . . . are peanuts. They don't count. All they can do is make a noise.' Once again his journalistic traducers used his contemptuous reply to a few deliberate wreckers to pretend that he had scorned all nuclear disarmers; once again Gaitskell had patiently to explain: 'It is a mystery to me why other members of C.N.D. should wear the cap that was not intended to fit them at all.'[16] But he wrote to one friend, linking that affair with his long struggle against neutralism and appeasement before the war: 'if I were to die tomorrow, the one thing I would be remembered for is this particular battle that I have been fighting . . . sometimes rather alone . . . perhaps the thing of which I am most proud in my life'.

Late in 1962 the crisis over the Soviet missile sites in Cuba alarmed the world with the sudden, imminent risk of nuclear war. It evoked the horrifying prospect of nuclear annihilation – in a cause which Gaitskell's critics claimed to be foreign, and over a country towards which the United States had recently put itself in the wrong. Gaitskell pressed the Prime Minister to fly to Washington, believing that the Russians were planning to act in Berlin and that 'we must try to use any opportunity for negotiations and must press the Americans very hard not to go too far'.[17] His instincts were as pro-American as ever, but in public he was cautious, for full support for the USA would have reopened all Labour's old wounds just as they were beginning to heal – a great deal to ask of an Opposition leader whose words could not affect events. Kennedy felt some bitterness at the lukewarm support. It did not last, for his reaction to Gaitskell's death was to regret 'the vanished opportunity of their working together'.[18]

In the parochial sphere of British party politics, the crisis had another significance. If anything could have revived the fears that gave rise to CND, the Cuban missile crisis should have done so. They did not revive. The Labour Left abandoned the cause of nuclear disarmament for many years, and soon their leaders were serving without visible discomfort in a Cabinet which made no move to renounce the bomb. A chapter in Labour's history was over.

## Poised for Power

When the House rose for the Christmas recess, Gaitskell was at the height of his powers. In Parliament he had attained a new stature, and Macmillan's ascendancy was over. In the Party, he had demonstrated that the Left could neither overthrow nor intimidate him – and that he was quite independent of the Right. Now clearly his own man, he was also at last genuinely the leader of his followers, and he had behind him, as a prominent Labour Marketeer put it, 'a Party more united than at any time since 1945–7, poised and prepared for victory, a Moses on the verge of the promised land'.[19] Even before Brighton the doyen of labour correspondents had written: 'Gaitskell stands out like an Everest on the plains against all others.'[9] After Conference another well-known commentator wrote: 'Mr. Gaitskell is now at the peak of his command of the Labour movement . . . Labour . . . for the first time for years seemed to have overcome its obsessional complex about its inner self, appearing more outward-looking and healthy.'[20]

His rising reputation attracted almost as much comment before his death as in the obituary columns. In the opinion polls, those thinking Gaitskell a good leader had been close to 50 per cent ever since the summer of 1961 and went above it (thus outnumbering dissenters and Don't Knows together) in the autumn of 1962. As Macmillan's ratings were slumping, Gaitskell soared ahead. From the election until the summer of 1961 voters had been far less satisfied with him than with the Prime Minister, whose average lead was no less than 20 per cent. In the next year the two men were running neck and neck. But in the last four months the advantage was Gaitskell's, by a comfortable average of 7 per cent.

The Labour Party shared the benefit, winning two of the five by-elections fought on 22 November 1962 – four of them in seats which had been Tory in 1945 – and coming within 1,000 votes in two more. On the Gallup poll, Labour now had a comfortable lead, no longer just due to Conservative weakness: in December it at last began to climb above 40 per cent (Don't Knows included), and led by 5 per cent on the 'casting vote' question: How would you vote in a general election when your vote might decide between five years of a Conservative government under Macmillan or of a Labour government under Gaitskell? Gaitskell's principal Labour critics did not doubt that he would lead the Party to victory at the next election. As Crossman wrote:

one of the most fascinating developments of 1962 was the almost invisible transfer of the nation's confidence, from the man with real power in Downing Street to the man with Shadow power in the Opposition. This has made Hugh Gaitskell one of Labour's main electoral assets. But should a Labour Party be so dependent on a single man?[21]

Four months later, in an obituary, a Conservative journalist and MP wrote of Gaitskell's new authority: 'Probably no Party leader since Parnell has enjoyed [such] unquestioning dominance . . . his House of Commons stature has grown month by month. He . . . looked, sounded and was set to be the Prime Minister of England.'[22]
But that was not to be.

## 'The Abominable Virus'

For some time Gaitskell had suffered from rheumatic pains in his shoulder, supposedly strained while playing tennis. He had physiotherapy at Manor House, the trade union hospital at Golders Green, and seemed to respond. But the symptoms returned; he took to wearing a bangle about which his colleagues teased him, and he became cautious about digging in the garden. On 13 June 1962 he went to Battersea Park to record for the film cameras his opening of the Festival of Labour. When his remarks were played back to him, he protested that that was not what he had recorded and – though everyone else assured him it was – he insisted on a retake. Feeling ill, he sat in his car for some time, and eventually alarmed his companions by driving himself back to Westminster. He had momentarily blacked out, without losing his vision. He would allow no one at all to be told, least of all his wife.

Very few people knew of that episode, but his weariness that summer was obvious to his friends. After one poor speech in the House, Alice Bacon took his diary and crossed out all the trivial engagements. At last, too late, he made a real effort – itself a sign that he was feeling the strain – to reduce his load. He apologised to an MP for not attending an annual constituency dinner: 'I feel not only that I get hardly any rest at all but that there is so little time to do serious reading and thinking.'[23] Even so, during 1962 he worked on two weekends out of three.

By the autumn the shoulder pains were bad enough to make him try to avoid driving his car; and by the end of the session, policemen and secretaries around the House – as well as political friends – were saying that he was looking unwell. At his last dinner party at home on 7 December, he said that he had 'to be careful with his diet that evening as he had picked up something in Paris'.[19] But no one imagined it was anything serious. Dora kept pressing him to see a doctor, which he had not done for years (he had no regular GP). But he refused until the House rose on 14 December.

The following day, feeling quite ill with some tiresome kind of flu, he went into Manor House hospital – partly out of loyalty, partly because, knowing its head Sir John Nicholson, he expected to get much of his own way. Colleagues and friends came in such a steady stream that he might as well have been in his room in the House. He asked Alice Bacon to take some Christmas presents to the Murrays and Gillinsons and Goodwills in Leeds – particularly asking her to visit each house and tell them how he was. Afterwards she thought that he must have been worried about himself, but only George Brown already suspected something seriously wrong. 'They treat me like a piece of ancient porcelain,' Gaitskell wrote to Sir Tom Williamson; and he told Alice Bacon: 'You know, I'm an interesting case. They are quite puzzled about me.' After a few days' rest he felt much better and became an impatient patient, insisting on spending Christmas at home. On 21 December he was writing to friends that he would go to Russia as planned on New Year's Day.

The doctors were not happy about his blood tests but had no adequate grounds to keep him in hospital, though he was told to rest at home. On 23 December he was discharged, and phoned friends saying he was fine and sounding it; but Percy Clark, the Transport House publicity officer, was very worried by his appearance, and once home he felt ill again. A few days later he very apologetically phoned John Harris, who was to have come on the Moscow visit, to postpone it and cancel plans to tour Lancashire in January. On New Year's Eve, feeling better, he wrote several more cheerful letters: 'I am now recovering very well from the second go, although everybody says I have to be rather careful for some time yet.'[24] Already he was thinking of rearranging the Russian trip. But visitors to Frognal Gardens were shocked to see how he looked and how hard he found it even to cross the room. Four days later the illness was back in full force, and he entered the Middlesex Hospital – which the Manor House doctors felt would be quieter – in a room recently occupied by Sir Winston Churchill.

Though he had quite acute symptoms of both pleurisy and pericarditis, there was as yet no public anxiety. The catastrophe came suddenly, and the doctors, especially at Manor House, were much criticised later. But among those taking the early decisions were consultants equally involved later on, and the rare disease Gaitskell had was at that time very obscure indeed, though more has become known about it since.

Lupus erythematosus is an immunological disease, in which a variety of tissues may be damaged by antibodies circulating in the blood. It can follow a mild and relatively minor course, but the systemic form which Gaitskell suffered was then incurable, though it does not often spread so rapidly. Its cause is unknown, and he could not have 'picked it up', as friends believed, in India or Warsaw or Paris. Nor could it have been induced, as the security services suspected at one point, by his being given a drug while he was in Poland. (Almost a year after Hugh's death, they inquired of his brother Arthur and of Dr Walter Somerville, who firmly assured them that there was no question of it. The source of the suspicion was presumably a defector's claim in 1961 that the KGB were planning to kill an opposition leader in the West, later supposed by some CIA officials to have been Gaitskell. Systemic lupus erythematosus can be induced by drugs, but only over a long period and not in the form Gaitskell had. Nor was the theory inherently plausible. It would require a KGB both sophisticated enough to think the successor might not be a Brown but a Wilson, and naive enough to believe that his policies would satisfy them.) But there is some recent evidence of a possible association with viral infection; and it might have been activated by bringing home some other infectious disease. Lupus is not hereditary, though it sometimes affects siblings. It was so little known then that GPs and even hospital doctors might have dealt with only two or three cases in a lifetime. Moreover, Gaitskell was a most unlikely victim, for it is even more unusual among males, and in his age group: at least five-sixths of the known sufferers have been women, and the great majority are under forty. It can lie dormant for years, emerging from time to time in a different organ, or suddenly erupting everywhere as it did with Gaitskell. Since it 'mimics' the characteristic disorders of the particular organ attacked, it is very hard to diagnose in the early stages; the principal study at the time, among patients in New York, found many who had had it for four years – and half a dozen for twenty years – before it was identified. Moreover, pleurisy, pericarditis and unknown fevers appear rarely as the first signs of the disease: only ten times between them out of 200 cases in the New York study. A further complication in Gaitskell's case was the failure of a characteristic laboratory test to detect the 'anti-nuclear factor' – so that even though the doctors quite early suspected systemic lupus erythematosus or something similar, even the post-mortem did not clearly establish it. The evidence from the histology a week later convinced most of them, but the absence of that factor still left some minds in doubt.

As soon as he was in the Middlesex, they saw that both his heart and lungs were affected, apparently by a severe virus infection. Dr Somerville called in appropriate specialists, and four senior doctors saw him twice daily over the weekend. For several days there was no significant change and no real anxiety, though there were disturbing signs in the blood. The doctors were still unsure exactly what was wrong; though correctly suspecting a collagen disease, they dared not risk the normal treatment with steroids, fearing that a virus infection would be made worse by such an approach. As medical knowledge then was, it could probably at best only have delayed the inevitable. Gaitskell was already too ill to see anyone but his brother once or twice, and Dora who sat with him constantly. During the next week he became much worse, developing painful ulcers on the tongue and in the bowel, and the doctors tried heavy doses of one antibiotic after another, vainly hoping that one would produce a response.

Gaitskell faced his condition with the greatest courage, mentally coming to attention the moment he was roused, organising his thoughts clearly, asking sensible questions and firmly telling the doctors to do whatever they thought best – provided they let him know why. But he suffered from insomnia, and he was generally listless and rambling; he recalled popular songs of his childhood, had dreams and saw quite agreeable 'apparitions' (such as a Canaletto on the opposite wall); and regretted a missed opportunity to meet Conor Cruise O'Brien whom he felt he had badly misjudged. By Wednesday 16 January, the doctors' anxiety was acute. The bulletins spoke of installing an artificial kidney; twenty people offered their own, including constituents grateful for past help. The surgery was done next day, but the disease was now rampant, attacking every critical organ at once. On the Friday evening he collapsed, suffering from extreme pulmonary congestion. He died at 9.10 p.m.

The sense of shock was profound. He was only fifty-six. Within the previous year he had become accepted by the public as the right and inevitable next Prime Minister – and, more recently, as indispensable to a Labour Treasury bench which was being called a one-man band. Only for a month had they had any idea that he was unwell; and for less than a week that it was serious. The grief was deep and general and lasting. The tributes poured in from all over the world, from the unknown as well as the famous. An unemotional political colleague reported Labour Party workers weeping that night in a West Country committee room; a young left-wing student was surprised and impressed to see tears flowing in the West Riding working–class pub where he heard the news. In the constituency, Holbeck parish church was packed for the memorial service on a very bleak January evening, but the reporter at the door soon stopped taking names like 'Mr Jones, he were a right good friend to me', or 'Mrs Smith, he helped me through a bit of trouble'. They had no news value, for they were not public men and women paying formal respects, but obscure neighbours saying goodbye to a friend.[25]

To those who had worked closely with Gaitskell the loss went deep, like the unexpected and premature death of a parent. For a generation of politically-minded progressive people, most of whom had not known him personally – teachers, journalists, trade-unionists, civil servants – an inspiration went out of public life which has yet to be renewed. That feeling was not confined to Britain. Some American liberals felt the loss more than the death of any public figure since Roosevelt. Barbara Castle, in Cairo, found every bazaar-keeper next morning wanting to commiserate, not formally but with genuine grief. At home, opponents sensed it too. At Bristol, Iain Macleod stopped a dispersing Conservative audience to be told the news, hear a brief tribute and stand in silence: 'I was surprised to find . . . later how moved I had been.'[26] In a generous gesture, Harold Macmillan moved the adjournment of the House of Commons – for the first and only time for an Opposition leader who had never been Prime Minister. It expressed the feeling of the country at the time. For many people years afterwards, the sense of loss has not diminished.

# EPILOGUE

*'No man is irreplaceable, but some men are unforgettable'*
(Senator Hubert Humphrey on HG)

# 25

# The Last Irony

'He was potentially a world statesman, he had that quality of leadership . . . a man of total honesty, dogged bravery and iron will.'
(Anthony Crosland's broadcast obituary)

The poignancy was sharp. At fifty-six neither Churchill nor Attlee, neither Gladstone nor Disraeli had yet been Prime Minister. Gaitskell had served only a year in a prominent government post, far less than Aneurin Bevan or Iain Macleod, John or Robert Kennedy. He was best known as Leader of the Opposition, a role in which he was not altogether at home. In the immediate outpouring of grief at his death, a Tory journalist wrote of it as Britain's 'most grievous loss of an individual – statesman, scientist, artist or administrator – since the end of World war II'. Labour colleagues like Denis Healey and Anthony Crosland saw their leader developing into 'one of the half dozen greatest statesmen of the world this century'. The sense of loss was lasting. Among his immediate political followers Gaitskell has remained an inspiration for over fifteen years, longer than almost any other politician this century. Beyond their ranks he is still admired and missed by people of different views and backgrounds, not only in Britain. Even before he had led a government, said Senator Hubert Humphrey, Gaitskell 'became the conscience of the Western world'.[1]

## Retrospect: The Road to Leadership

Gaitskell represented a fairly new type of Labour politician: neither a carrier of the aspirations and frustrations of the working-class majority of the Movement, nor a resentful bourgeois in revolt against class or family. In early life he saw little of his parents, but was neither an unhappy child nor an adolescent rebel. As a young man he repudiated the pressures for external conformity that Winchester imposed, but its basic values had marked his character. His personality flowered at Oxford, but his emancipation was slow to take a political turn. In the General Strike he chose his side out of compassion for the underdog; and then went to teach unemployed miners at Nottingham, whose sufferings he never forgot. Those emotional sympathies were underpinned by intellectual exasperation at needless waste, making him as keen to find effective remedies for real social evils, and as impatient with gestures of impotent protest, as the most hard-headed trade-unionist.

Gaitskell was immunised early on against the temptations of purism and irresponsibility which beset inexperienced movements of revolt. The General Strike and then the brutal Viennese repression showed him the danger of playing with revolutionary fire. For the syndicalist myth and the Austro-Marxist tradition had inspired no plans to organise revolution (if they had, the attempts would have failed disastrously). But they had inhibited believers from a realistic appraisal of their own circumstances; and Gaitskell never forgot the terrible consequences for innocent human beings as well as cherished causes. He also learned from Vienna and Munich the price of leaving thugs to monopolise the use of force, and became for life a staunch defender of collective security who could never escape into pacifism. Though never so alarmist as to equate the Russian rulers with the Nazis, and always alert to signs of change in the Communist world, he remained deeply suspicious of Soviet intentions.

The 1930s gave him also his horror of mass unemployment, his commitment to full employment as the primary economic objective, and his faith in Keynesian solutions. (But while he did not question those solutions intellectually, politically he was among the few men of the Left who consistently warned that uncontrolled inflation could undermine prosperity.) His banner was Conscience and Reform, not class struggle. He saw collective action as a means to redress social injustices and to secure for all the opportunities already enjoyed by a minority. He appealed to feelings of equity and compassion, not militancy and greed; like Aneurin Bevan, he would have seen nothing socialist about working-class taxpayers who resented people on social security, or publicity-seeking leaders of middle-class trade unions who aggressively demanded more for their prosperous membership.

A believer in the primacy of private life and personal relations, he looked forward to no collectivist utopia. He gave high priority to securing effective government management of the economy, and regarded public ownership as an instrument not a goal. Where it was relevant, he was keen to use it and believed the voters could readily be persuaded: not elsewhere. A democratic Socialist, convinced that revolutionary dictatorships corrupt Socialist aims, he accepted the constraints upon the pace and scope of change required to convince the electorate – and keep it convinced.

Munich taught him another lesson. Some of his closest friends supported it out of hatred of war, and many right-wing Tories – whom he had deeply distrusted – detested it as much as he did. Opponents, he concluded, were sometimes right and colleagues wrong. Never a good hater, always enjoying social life, he later made a few good friends across the party divide. That had no political importance. He began his leadership of the Opposition by outraging upper-class feelings over foreign policy at Suez, and ended it by defying the consensus over the Common Market. His approach to domestic problems had long been firmly set; and though occasionally he might seem to belong to the conspiracy of gentlemen to keep the country on sound lines, his strong streak of populism separated him from the liberal intellectual Establishment as well as from the conservative social one.

Fitting uneasily into any familiar pattern, he seemed unlikely to enjoy a meteoric rise to leadership. In British politics high intelligence has often caused a man to be shunned, not chosen. By 1955 Gaitskell was known as an excellent administrator who had spent less than a year on the back benches, as a Chancellor controversial within his own party, and as a front-bench spokesman with no record as a rebel and no evident appeal to the ordinary voter: strange qualifications to attract Labour MPs in opposition, seeking a Moses to regain the Promised Land. Gaitskell's success owed much to luck and more to his rivals. The exhaustion of the previous generation of leaders, after eleven exceptionally gruelling years in office, had opened the way for a younger man. Seeking a champion to back against Bevan, the union potentates welcomed an alternative to Morrison, whom they had never trusted on union issues. But it was not just accident that the beneficiary was Gaitskell: his decisiveness over the 1949 devaluation had made him the choice of all his seniors for the Exchequer, and his reckless risking of his career at Stalybridge had brought him the backing of the unions and the leadership of the moderate wing.

Even so, the idea of his supplanting Morrison or Bevan would have seemed ludicrous five years before it happened, and improbable two years before. Both were more experienced and far better known. Neither had as well-trained a mind, but Morrison had great shrewdness, and Bevan a streak of imaginative genius. A party based on the working class might naturally have felt that after twenty years of a public-school leader, his successor should come from a different background. Gaitskell overcame those handicaps because his competitors destroyed themselves. Morrison had made enemies both by ruthless pursuit of narrow objectives and by single-minded ambition; he had failed badly in foreign affairs, and he aged rapidly once out of power. Bevan had convinced his Cabinet colleagues that he was difficult to work with and would be intolerable to serve under. Mistakenly judging the unions to be the decisive arena, he had mortally affronted their leaders without being able to get them replaced. He had neglected and alienated the Labour MPs with whom the choice lay, who feared that he would endanger Labour's chances at the polls, and were convinced by his supreme contempt for them that, should he win, he would ignore the lobby-fodder behind him.

So Gaitskell owed much – including Clem Attlee's somewhat grudging blessing – to good fortune and the blunders of others. But those alone cannot account for the scale of his victory as the only Labour leader ever comfortably elected on the first ballot, with the votes of many former factional opponents. There were also the justified feeling that, unlike his rivals, Gaitskell learned from his mistakes, and the unfulfilled hope that choosing the youngest man would settle the succession for twenty years and so ensure party unity.

## A Man of Government Frustrated

At first, both the feeling and the hope seemed to be justified. From 1951 to 1955, while by no means engaged in continuous warfare within the Party, Gaitskell always assumed that the Left must be defeated if Labour were to regain power: the battles were intermittent – the Budget, Stalybridge, German rearmament, the foolish attempt to expel Bevan – but the priority was constant. In 1955 he revised it. Beginning as a tactical move to benefit from Bevanite divisions, his rapprochement with Wilson and Crossman was quickly extended in 1956 to Bevan himself. Elected as a conciliator, throughout his first Parliament as leader Gaitskell sought not confrontations but party unity, and came as close to attaining it as Labour ever can.

He found that it was not enough. In 1959 a united party went down to its heaviest post-war defeat, and its leader concluded that if Labour was to survive as a potential government it must adapt to uncomfortable realities. At once the hope of a generation of unity under an accepted leadership was dissipated as Gaitskell's few perpetual enemies were reinforced by those who turned against the policies when the opportunity arose to upset the man. But no sooner had the ensuing battles brought the Party back to the threshold of power than Gaitskell promptly resumed his efforts to come to terms with his critics.

The perspective of history does more than his foibles of personality to explain why his career was stormy. Like most men who have reached the top rank in British politics, and like almost all who have left a memorable reputation, he was both a conciliator and a confronter at different stages of his life. After four years of successfully playing Attlee's role, he seemed in 1959 to resume the combative stance which is usually thought to characterise him. Yet neither his past nor his future conduct was provocative by normal political standards. In 1951 he had underestimated the disruption which a difficult Minister could cause once out of office; but so had Bevan's other exasperated colleagues, like those of Joseph Chamberlain and Lloyd George before them. If overruled then, Gaitskell would have resigned (though without trying to split the Party); but most future Prime Ministers have at some point taken such a stand. In his factional battles over the next four years Gaitskell also had many predecessors among ex-Ministers who, once out of office, found their commitments and assumptions challenged by more partisan colleagues.

Once chosen as Labour's leader, and therefore head of Britain's alternative government, Gaitskell was on approval before both party and country; alone among Labour's potential Prime Ministers, he remained so to the end of his life. Each of the rest served eventually in Downing Street, and spent his tenure of the leadership mainly as Premier, ex-Premier or Deputy Premier; so did every Conservative leader in the forty years before Gaitskell's death. Alone among his peers, Gaitskell never won gratitude in his party by bringing it to power, earned prestige in the country by identifying its rule with his personality, or based his reputation on his achievements in government. Alone, he is judged entirely on his performance in a different role, and not the one for which he was best fitted.

After Labour lost in 1959 Gaitskell, like any defeated party leader, had to struggle for survival against his own followers—and from a uniquely weak position as the only Labour leader (and almost the only leader of any party) to lose his first election while still on approval in the post. That occupational hazard operates differently in each of the major parties, like the contrast drawn in Fisher Ames's eighteenth-century simile: 'Monarchy is like a splendid ship, with all sails set; it moves majestically on, then hits a rock and sinks for ever. Democracy is like a raft; it never sinks, but damn it, your feet are always in the water.' The leaders driven out have all been Conservatives—in 1911, 1965 and 1975. But Labour ex-Premiers in defeat have also had a very uncomfortable time. Without enjoying their prestige, Gaitskell nevertheless survived more nearly on his own terms than they were able to do.

The cost for the Party was heavy, but in the long run unavoidable.

Most British party leaders have had trouble trying to reconcile the demands of the faithful with the need to adapt their party to social change. Peel succeeded after 1832 and failed in 1846; Disraeli overthrew him then but emulated him later, after twenty years of purity in the wilderness had given the Tories a lasting preference for office even at the price of compromise. Only Lloyd George repudiated party blatantly and never recovered; even Churchill learned that lesson and returned in the end to the Tory communion – and, in 1951, to office. But that success was due to R. A. Butler modernising a party desperate to regain and retain power.

It was Butler's and not Churchill's style of Conservatism which characterised their rule, presenting Labour with a difficult problem instead of the easy target many of its leaders had expected. Gaitskell never had such illusions. He applied himself to the harder task, circumspectly up to the 1959 defeat, rashly afterwards. In riding the storm which then buffeted him as defeated Opposition leader, he acquired for himself and bequeathed to his successor a new freedom of action. But even that successor, with his strong inherited position and his innate preference for compromise, was before long to find himself in disagreement with most of his followers, and preserved his position only by bending before the storm – with long-term consequences which are still developing.

In response to Macmillan's 1959 triumph, Gaitskell made a different choice – and badly mishandled it. Labour will ultimately have to decide whether it stands for democratic Socialism and the mixed economy, or for total nationalisation as its overriding priority. But in posing the question in that way at that moment, Gaitskell misjudged the mood – failing for understandable reasons to realise that his own influence would be impaired by the 1959 defeat. He misjudged the target, underestimating both the resistance to revising formal doctrine and the damage to his own position if he failed. And he misjudged the timing, twice leaving his critics to make all the running. Driven into a confrontation he had not sought but ought to have foreseen, he soon found he had weakened himself against a really dangerous attack.

Though powerful voices claimed that it too was unnecessary, Gaitskell was justified in feeling that the unilateralist controversy had to be fought out. Early in 1960 he was insensitive to changing moods and inflexible over minor details; but when the conflict reached its height in the summer, he rightly saw that further concession would not only lead to a vulnerable defence policy, but would also weaken the morale of his supporters, the standing of the Party and the authority of its leader. As soon as the foundation for Labour's recovery had been laid by restoring that authority, Gaitskell reverted at once to conciliation. He worked again with the colleagues who had been trying to supplant him, though he never trusted them as he had before 1959.

With his followers the change was more striking. He had always treated them seriously, never regarding Conference as a mere nuisance to be flattered, by-passed and ignored; nor even as a curious anomaly to be kept in line by manipulating the block vote (though like his critics he did his share of that); but mainly as an awkward yet adult body to be persuaded by serious argument on real issues. Now at Brighton in 1962, he was at last discovering also how to evoke from it an enthusiastic emotional response.

Although he became impressive at leading the Opposition, it was never Gaitskell's *métier*. Loathing instant politics and quick decisions based on inadequate information, he was not adroit at seizing tactical opportunities. That weakness was compounded by his reluctance to change his mind and by his concern for consistency. He would not propose in opposition policies he could not carry out in government. He was hampered as a critic by temperamental sympathy for the men in power; thinking always how he would handle their problem, he was quicker to sympathise with their difficulties than to exploit these for his own advantage. Macmillan in a parliamentary obituary of him spoke of the Opposition leader as 'a partner and even a buttress' to the Government in times of national crisis; earlier, he had mocked Gaitskell as missing the fun of opposition by trying to behave like a government when he wasn't one.[2] (When Attlee was Premier, nobody could have accused Macmillan of that.) But as an educated electorate becomes bored with the party dogfight, an Opposition leader who tries to act responsibly may hope to reap a reward later on. Gaitskell showed that a restrained and sober style can do more than virulent polemic to earn the reputation of a potential leader of the nation.

By the time of his death Gaitskell had acquired that reputation. In his first Parliament as Labour leader, he was generally seen as a mere party man – and by Suez enthusiasts as an unprincipled and dangerous one. His public breakthrough began with the 1959 campaign and particularly his dignified concession at the end; it was achieved by his fight to reverse the Scarborough decision on defence. That was not because the Establishment applauded his struggle – for with equal unanimity they condemned his attitude to the Common Market. It was partly because national defence is a sensitive subject, on which the average voter feels that leaders who seek to govern should resist pressure from people without responsibility. Above all it was because Gaitskell put the national interest as he saw it before his own career or the demands of political convenience. By winning that battle he proved himself a strong leader; by engaging in it at all, he demonstrated that he would show in a crisis both high courage and a sense of national duty. The political activist, especially on the Left, often judges leaders by their professed ideology and falls easy prey to calculated rhetoric. But the ordinary voter, less concerned about their views on specific issues, judges on character instead: very wisely, for Ministers must govern and not just legislate, and character is the only guide to how a man will deal with the unpredictable situations which will face him in power.

Within the Party Gaitskell's opponents remained resentful and suspicious. But he was glad to seize the opportunity of reconciliation with them afforded by Macmillan's handling of the Common Market issue. He adopted his policy because of his own convictions and commitments, but in his presentation of it he sought both to underline his independence as leader, and to win over those critics who were willing to bury the hatchet. A few months earlier he had described the need to satisfy the demands of both the activists and the unpolitical voters as 'the greatest challenge to leadership . . . because the enthusiasm is no good without the votes and the votes are not much good without the enthusiasm'. Now in late 1962, as *The Times* political correspondent put it, he was coming to terms with the Labour Party.[3] At that very moment the opinion polls showed him coming to terms with the wider electorate also. With tragic irony, the rare and mysterious disease struck precisely when he was at last resolving his central political dilemma as leader of the Party.

## A Controversial Personality

Gaitskell was resolving his personal dilemmas too. His personality was full of apparent contradictions. In private life he was gregarious and warm-hearted, impressing those he met with his modesty and his interest in other people; but it was not until late in life that he shook off the absurd caricature of the desiccated calculating machine. He was an excellent listener in a profession where they do not abound; but once he had made up his mind he could be infuriatingly stubborn over petty details. For one observer he would analyse appreciatively the strengths and qualities of a bitter political opponent, and explain the conduct of another most charitably; but other people found him touchy, quick to take criticism as a personal affront, and without much understanding for young idealists as inexperienced as he had once been. In his early revolt against the inhibitions of the public-school regime, he was ardent in praise of spontaneity; but in his later years his friends sometimes found him both wary and testy (and once, though only once, felt he had seriously misled them). Thorough, cautious and slow to form his opinions, he was bold and even reckless in advocating them; judicious in weighing the balance of opposing arguments, he committed himself totally to the side he finally espoused; skilful and conciliatory in seeking consensus, he was so combative in a corner that he won the reputation of provoking confrontations; a devotee of reason and enemy of extremism, he defended moderate views with intense passion.

These contrasts led to his being misrepresented by his opponents, misunderstood by the public, and sometimes misjudged by his colleagues. Kenneth Younger, an old critic who by 1955 felt that Gaitskell was the only possible Labour leader, saw his contest with Bevan as a clash of Roundhead and Cavalier. For Gaitskell was, in his daughter's phrase, 'a conscious puritan of the intellect'; and his political style relied upon meticulous preparation and disciplined teamwork where Bevan displayed a Rupert-like impetuosity. But Younger's summary interpretation missed Gaitskell's own Cavalier qualities: the hedonism and libertarianism of the private man, the gambler's streak shown both in some everyday matters and at moments of crisis in the life of the public figure. Indeed he displayed both sets of qualities. He was dedicated to intellectual consistency and integrity, and stubborn about his own point of view. Yet he also saw politics as an activity requiring organisation, co-operation, and mutual accommodation, calling for both loyalty in individuals and solidarity in a team.

Those conflicting commitments were reflected in his own behaviour. Convinced that effective political action required strong, disciplined parties, he was normally punctilious about consulting the appropriate colleagues over policy. Yet at several turning-points in his life he acted entirely alone, without support from his closest friends and sometimes defying their advice: over the 1951 Budget, the Stalybridge speech, Clause Four, the Common Market. In his obituary on R. H. Tawney, whom he so greatly admired, Gaitskell wrote of his friend's combination of strength and humility in terms which applied equally to his own character: 'He never hesitated to lay down the law . . . [but] he never thought of himself in his heart as above or better than other people.'[4] For the genuine modesty of manner co-existed with an extraordinary self-assurance, and in a crisis Gaitskell would suddenly demonstrate boundless confidence in his own judgement and his own star.

That strength of will and self-assurance reinforced a highly intelligent and reasoned outlook on public affairs. In 1959 he told Henry Fairlie: 'I am a rationalist . . . I do not like to think that [people] vote as they do because something appeals to their subconscious.'[5] That approach was basic to his political style almost throughout his life, and was both his principal strength and his principal weakness in projecting his own appeal and that of his party. In some quarters it won solid support founded on understanding, but it quite failed to arouse or excite others, and it left some potent weapons in the political armoury to his opponents – Labour ones as well as Conservatives. It attracted the loyalty and enthusiasm of people who shared his own cast of mind, but it seemed cold to more emotional and passionate types, and even unfeeling to the unperceptive or the prejudiced. Notable among twentieth-century politicians for his lucid and candid public statements, Gaitskell was equally notable for the frequency with which he was misunderstood, especially but not only on the Left – for whom he was neither protected by the prestige attaching to the leaders of 1945, nor recognised as the emotional man he was because he and they were often emotional about different objects.

Gaitskell was a communicator by profession whose meaning was repeatedly mistaken – over his first Suez speech, Clause Four, the British bomb, the Scarborough peroration. Yet far from being to blame for carelessness of expression, he exasperated all his associates by constantly polishing every draft and speech. Much of the confusion was due to unconscious or deliberate misrepresentation by his various enemies, and more to journalistic over-simplification which afforded opportunities for misunderstanding that his detractors eagerly grasped; for, being no phrase-maker, he saw his utterances as a whole, whereas the audience tended to fasten on a headline comparing Nasser to Hitler, or a reference to fellow-travellers in CND, and to forget everything else.

His speeches relied on logical organisation of the argument rather than on colourful wording to tickle the emotional palate. They were based on carefully gathered information, thorough analysis and a persuasive deployment of his case. There is rarely anything in them to haunt the memory, but read in retrospect they show an impressively detailed and realistic grasp of a wide variety of subjects, with little mere point-scoring. They meet in advance many common objections to his views: his Suez policy did not rest on a naive confidence in the United

Nations, or his opposition to joining the EEC on seeing the Commonwealth as a permanent alternative, or his criticism of immigration controls on any commitment to the open door for ever. Yet in the rough and tumble of controversy, even attentive observers easily missed far-sighted qualifications about possible future changes modifying his position. Clarity and foresight and candour did not always ensure even that his meaning was fully grasped; and it was only towards the end that he appealed to the emotions as well as the intelligence. For most of his life he was a teacher not an orator, strong on rational argument rather than moralising fervour, speaking to the mind rather than to the heart.

His private warmth was not always appreciated. He was genuinely interested in the feelings of others. But he took on far too much and left himself too little time to reflect and relax; and he could occasionally behave as insensitively as Attlee did habitually. (Being unexpected, it was held against Gaitskell – whereas in his predecessor it was taken for granted and not resented.) More seriously, he was often misunderstood because his own rationalism made him misjudge the irrational responses of others. Far better equipped for national leadership than most men in the front rank of recent British politics, he was not an ideal party leader in opposition, since his antennae were not finely tuned. He was generally shrewd about the long-term preferences of the British people, but less clear-sighted about their spontaneous outbursts of emotion. He failed to foresee the patriotic reflex when the troops went ashore at Port Said. He knew that elderly trade-unionists no longer believed in nationalising all the means of production, distribution and exchange – and so was taken aback when they clung to Clause Four which symbolised the dreams of their radical youth. He was irritated by the emotionalism, born of desperate worry about nuclear war, which channelled all the fears and frustrations of a generation into CND. He recognised but never comprehended the distant vision of the enthusiastic Europeans, who believed they must seize a unique opportunity for practical internationalism.

That approach, and those failures, help to explain why for so long his personality was not easily projected. They were failures of imagination, not of conviction. Contrary to the legend spread by his opponents late in 1959, Gaitskell was no trimmer. The middle of the road appealed to his reason, but half-measures were alien to his temperament: over Munich, the blockade, nationalisation, devaluation, 'responsible finance', rearmament, Suez, the American alliance, the Commonwealth Immigration Act, the Common Market. Especially in his last few years, his appeals were delivered with a force and passion which bred misunderstanding. For with Labour in opposition the impact of the wholehearted final commitment led commentators to look only at the direction in which he was leading his followers. Had he been in office they would have had to attend also to the careful, balanced assessment which preceded decision, and on which the policy would depend. But the capacity to evoke so stirring an emotional response developed too late in Gaitskell's short life to help propel him and his cause to power.

Part of his problem was that many of his followers were ambivalent about power. Comfortable middle-class idealists without responsibility find it easy to keep their consciences spotless, preaching principle in the wilderness, while the price is paid by poorer people whose grievances go unheard by the men in government; yet the professional politician who rationalises his conduct by that legitimate argument, comes easily to pursue power so single-mindedly that he forgets or compromises away his original aims. Gaitskell never did that. But many Labour people were misled by their historic suspicion that insistence on workable policies, and on getting into government so as to apply them, is only a convenient screen behind which careerists without principles can manoeuvre. The brilliant cartoonist Vicky shared and spread a grotesque illusion in portraying Gaitskell as a politician eager to win votes by any means, and power without caring how to use it. But few of those who met him or heard him speak were deceived by that caricature. For while he was not a man to keep digging up his philosophy to investigate its roots, his principles were firmly fixed; and he was as determined not to betray them as he was willing to adjust the means of achieving them. He was untainted by the temptations of careerism – and by those of self-righteous and impotent purity.

Where Gaitskell's conduct was ruled by Max Weber's 'ethic of responsibility', many of his followers acted on the alternative 'ethic of ultimate ends'. Often, too, they had a strong propensity to wishful thinking with which he was impatient and scornful. Mutual suspicion and misunderstanding thus grew all too easily. When Clause Four was a sleeping idol, Gaitskell did not anticipate the fury he would arouse by disturbing it. When CND was in full flood, he seemed to its adherents to show scorn for their deep feelings. His own commitments reflected his temperament and preference for clear-cut solutions, together with his strong Wykehamist sense of public duty and of the need for leadership; they earned him at times the bitter dislike of people who violently differed from him or felt misjudged by him. Many Conservatives over Suez, many unilateralists after Scarborough detested him cordially and would never forgive him.

In part, that was simply because people became indignant when he broke the rules by which they had conveniently chosen to assume the game should be played. For Tories, Labour's middle-class moderates were supposed to support the Government when it unilaterally proclaimed a national crisis. For the Left, a Labour leader was expected to genuflect before the noble motives of his attackers – not to refer contemptuously to their own calculations and manoeuvres. So on the Right Gaitskell's enemies reviled him for betraying his class and even his country, and on the Left for deserting Socialism and ignoring the horrors of nuclear war. Both sets of bitter critics, hot for action and scornful of compromise, had been led by passionate emotion to clamour for policies whose consequences they did not thoroughly examine. Both were quite annoyed at the cool and critical dissection of those consequences, but absolutely furious at the challenge to their claim to a moral superiority which they took for granted. Their resentments did not vanish when the crisis was past. Instead, wounded self-esteem made people whom he had criticised prone to adopt discreditable interpretations of his words and actions.

In fact Gaitskell was himself a man of powerful passions, but harnessed to realistic objectives. He felt keenly about translating the demands of 'conscience and reform' into practical measures; he had little time for dramatic protests which assuaged the indignation of the demonstrator not the condition of the sufferer. So he looked to a limited horizon, stretching beyond the present but not into the indefinite distance. Never obsessed by the next week's tactical problem (perhaps not enough so), he always sought policies valid for the foreseeable future. But, rightly thinking it unreal to look more than a decade ahead, he did not bother much about what might lie beyond.

That did not make him indifferent to new ideas: for a practising politician he was quite far-sighted in spotting future issues like consumer grievances, environmental problems, changes in youth culture, and even (despite his early disillusionment with syndicalism) looking for practical plans for workers' control. It did not make him a tame devotee of the reigning orthodoxy: he fought the Establishment over Europe as he had fought the predominant views of the 1930s or the Treasury's liberal doctrines in the 1940s. But he was a man of his time and his time was not ours. He was the standard-bearer of Attlee's post-war consensus, labelled and misinterpreted as Butskellism: the mixed economy, the Keynesian strategy, full employment, strong but not overweening trade unions, the welfare state, the Atlantic alliance, decolonisation, and a tacit understanding that governments, whether moderate Conservative or democratic Socialist, would not strain the tolerance of the other side too violently. That legacy makes him a natural hero for social democrats.

When economic decline sapped the foundations of that consensus, Gaitskell the realist would have adjusted accordingly; but like everyone else he failed to foresee its imminence. He was no seer, and he lacked the broad imaginative sweep of General de Gaulle or even Aneurin Bevan. He was a man to handle issues as they arose, to look ahead for forces modifying the existing scene, rather than to try like a Joseph Chamberlain or even a Lloyd George to transform the whole political landscape. But he knew that the politician must work with the materials available and deal as best he can with the current tensions threatening the fabric of society. He would have done so, in office, in a manner to command public confidence: for the qualities in which he excelled were far better deployed in government than in opposition.

Being a man of high moral courage, who chose his course only after careful thought, Gaitskell was most reluctant to change it under pressure. During the bitter quarrel with many of his own side in 1960, a Conservative MP whom he had known since boyhood asked how he could stand the hatred of his assailants; he replied that when he had decided on the right thing to do, he just went ahead and did it without worrying about the criticism. He would have been a poor politician if he had really worked by that rule all the time, and we have seen that he did not; but he did try harder than most to apply it on matters of major principle, demanding to be convinced by arguments from reason, not expediency. To Gaitskell, that outlook was frequently a short-term handicap. Since his death, British public life has often shown how in the long run its absence corrodes public respect for politics and trust in politicians.

Partly because of that outlook, even more because of his style of expressing it, Gaitskell had rarely aroused enthusiasm among the utopians and visionaries who naturally find their home in a party of the Left. Intellectually he knew they were necessary to it, but emotionally he never really appreciated them – still less they him. But in his last few months he was overcoming that weakness too. In 1962, more than ever before, he aroused the enthusiasm of Conference by appealing to its emotions as well as its reason. It was not a political skill which he had previously exhibited. Once he had written, revealingly, that revulsion against exploiting it had inhibited his old mentor Douglas Cole from ever entering electoral politics.[6] Gaitskell's temperament and his whole career suggest that he too felt that distaste, and overcame it only at the end of his life. He was developing to the last: not merely resolving his political problem by finding how to appeal at once to his active followers and to the wider electorate, but also integrating the intellectual and emotional sides of his own character. Only close colleagues, said one of them, fully appreciated 'his extraordinary capacity to learn. He was always widening and deepening his personality as a politician.'[7]

## Prospect: The Government that Never Was

Friendly or hostile, no one who knew him doubts that Gaitskell was a natural Prime Minister rather than a natural Leader of the Opposition. He would not have continued long in the latter role. Had he lived and lost again in 1964, he would probably have felt obliged to resign the leadership without waiting to be repudiated. Had he won with the same tiny majority as Wilson, he would doubtless have handled that difficult situation less well, for day-to-day tactics were not his forte. But probably he would have won that election by a bigger margin. At the time of his death, Labour was at last beginning to run ahead of the Conservatives by attracting support on its own account, not just because Tories were defecting to the Liberals. For when the Liberals fell back again in the polls, it was now Labour which sharply improved its position. Gaitskell's personal rating was comfortably ahead of his party's, and like Harold Wilson he would assuredly have soared much further ahead in 1963. He too would have profited from the collapse of the Government's reputation, and would, for the first time against the Prime Minister, have enjoyed extraordinary favour from a Fleet Street furious with Macmillan for having two journalists imprisoned over the Vassall case. Wilson was a new face as Opposition leader, welcomed by the opinion-makers as the next tenant of No. 10; but Gaitskell was accepted already in that role, which the good publicity would have consolidated in the public mind. Labour's lead might have slipped in 1964 as the approach of the election drew disillusioned Tories reluctantly back to the fold: but very likely by less than it did, since his reputation as fit for the Premiership was firmly founded at last.

In the 1959 campaign Gaitskell had proved far more formidable than anybody expected; and in 1964 he (like Heath in 1970) would have reaped the benefit of vainly exposing at the previous election the hollowness of the Government's boasts of prosperity. Facing Sir Alec

Douglas-Home, Gaitskell like Wilson would have been obviously superior on the domestic front; while because of the recent past he would have enjoyed much more confidence than Wilson on the very foreign and defence issues where the new Prime Minister was most credible. These electoral conclusions, if not necessarily the arguments, were shared by most politicians interviewed from the Labour mainstream, though with several Don't Knows; and by nearly every Liberal and Conservative asked. Dissenters were almost all from the Labour Left, though a couple of distinguished spokesmen in each of the last two groups disagreed with their fellows.[8]

It is fruitless to imagine how Gaitskell might have acted in a radically different political world; but not absurd to speculate on his handling of problems he already foresaw. Any incoming Prime Minister enjoys goodwill (and patronage) at Westminster, and a new prestige among his followers in the country. If, as seems likely, he had had a majority of 25 to 40, he would have been able to think strategically, which was both his inclination and his strength.

A Gaitskell government in October 1964 might well have looked quite similar to Wilson's. The latter had inherited and then gave office to the old Shadow Cabinet, few of whom had supported him for the leadership; they were elected by the PLP, and Gaitskell would have selected much the same people, for he thought highly of almost all. Wilson was generous in appointing and later promoting talented Gaitskellites; Gaitskell might have moved them up faster, though in the past he had often treated his friends less well than merit would have dictated.[9] Without sharing Wilson's obsession with the factional balance of his appointments, he would have tried as he did with Cousins to reconcile old opponents – and would have succeeded, for no left-winger but Cousins ever resigned over an act or omission of Wilson's government. Some who stood high in Wilson's confidence thought that they would have had very inferior offers from his predecessor; but those who earned preferment would doubtless not have been denied it on account of the past. Some Ministers who were appointed or survived because of their personal loyalty to the new leader might not have been chosen, and would not have been retained, by the old one. For Gaitskell would have been as relentless as Attlee in removing dead wood; he could justly claim that fear of having able men around him was not among his faults.[3]

After thirteen years in opposition few members of the incoming government were familiar with the official machine. Half Wilson's Ministers had never held office; only two – Griffiths and Gordon

Walker – had served in a Cabinet. That situation would have obliged any Prime Minister to play a dominant role, and tempted Gaitskell to intervene too much. Some of his intimate friends doubt whether he would have delegated enough, but his record does not bear them out. Both at Fuel and Power and at the Exchequer he had given responsibility to his juniors; and the love of detail which appalled his civil servants and irritated his Opposition colleagues had good reasons then (different in the two cases) which would not have applied in Downing Street. There he would have been both in unquestioned command of an efficient advisory machine which he knew how to use and how to control; and the central figure in a political team where individual reputations depend largely on collective success. Able to delegate more confidently, politically strong and personally secure, he would neither have needed nor hungered for constant public interventions to establish his authority. In one retirement tribute to Attlee, Gaitskell said: 'One of his great qualities was his capacity for devolving work and for trusting his colleagues to get on with the job on their own. This is nowadays almost a "must" for a Prime Minister.' In another, he praised Attlee as a Prime Minister who never tried 'to cut a dash or to make an impression himself. What he was concerned with from start to finish was the success of the team.'[10]

In 1961 and 1962, Gaitskell was looking ahead to the problems of taking office. Conscious of his own limited experience when he became a Minister, he took much trouble to ensure that the leading Shadow Ministers were better prepared. There may have been a 'power book', perhaps similar to the 'war book' in which, before 1914, Whitehall tried to anticipate impending problems. Gaitskell persistently pressed his Shadow Chancellor for studies on the central problems of the economy; and with the help of Desmond Hirshfield and others, he very discreetly compiled a panel of friendly industrialists from whom a Labour government could seek experienced business advice. He had always been keen on relating science to public policy, and on becoming leader in 1956 he had set up an advisory group of quite senior scientists. But he was never at ease with them, and did not trust their political judgement, partly no doubt because so many of them were left-wing unilateralists. They felt (correctly) that he looked to them for specialist advice, not to run the country; and in November 1962 they protested by collectively threatening to resign. But scientists in whom Gaitskell had confidence, like Zuckerman, would certainly have played a major role.

Gaitskell's main priority as Prime Minister would have been to tackle

Britain's long-term economic difficulties: partly because the viability of Labour's programme and the credibility of the government depended upon doing so, mainly because of his long-standing alarm at the gradual decline. He was better equipped to analyse its causes than any post-war Prime Minister, and his solutions would have been radical. Very likely, too, he would have taken early steps to phase out the sterling area as Roy Jenkins, a close friend and probable financial adviser, had long advocated; he was himself an expert on the subject, unsentimental, self-confident, and sceptical of bankers' advice.

To secure a breathing-space before slow-acting measures could affect the major problems of insufficient investment, low productivity and a precarious external balance, he would probably have devalued early. He had been accused a few years earlier of having a penchant for devaluation; and he would no more have seen it as morally iniquitous like Heath, or as politically fatal like Wilson, than as a remedy in itself. Such a decision might have avoided the deep disillusionment of both Labour and uncommitted voters at the mounting unemployment figures. Even the mood of militancy and revolt within the unions might not have developed so fast or so far in a better economic climate, making it easier to act on the long-term problems while they were still relatively manageable.

Gaitskell would have sought the co-operation of the unions through some kind of social contract, while tolerating neither the reality nor the appearance of union dictation. His legendary stubbornness would have been very valuable – perhaps even indispensable – in dealing with the Civil Service; for instance in arguing with the Inland Revenue over tax reform, and in tackling the problem of urban land against the resistance of a formidable Permanent Secretary.

In education, Gaitskell foresaw the danger, which Labour's Secretary of State had himself predicted, that to attack selection for the grammar schools while leaving the public schools alone would end by narrowing the educational ladder and widening the gap between classes. There can be few more striking cases of a policy frustrating its original purposes than that by which the educational egalitarians drove the direct grant schools *en bloc* into the independent sector. Gaitskell would have sought to avoid that by a policy on public schools which might have been contentious. But for the education of the vast majority of schoolchildren his approach could well have proved acceptable to the moderate Conservatives who were then in the ascendant, and might have pointed the way to a stable bipartisan consensus instead of the now familiar sharp lurches in policy and disruption of young lives.

He would probably have retreated on one major domestic issue: coloured immigration. Had Labour continued to oppose all controls, it seems unlikely that it could have won in 1964. Being a very stubborn man, especially where he saw a principle at stake, Gaitskell would have been reluctant and slow to move. But his principle was not unconditional free entry, which he had never endorsed and for which he would not have been likely to risk all his other aims. He would have preferred defeat to accepting a colour bar; but he probably would have accepted controls on entry, compensating by early and effective measures to require equal treatment for coloured people already here, and by special treatment in housing for the areas most affected.

In the defence field he would not have evaded a difficult choice by trying to preserve both a frontier on the Himalayas and an expenditure ceiling incompatible with it. Having in 1957 presciently condemned Western military intervention against popular left-wing movements in Asia, and reaffirmed that view over Laos in the spring of 1962, it is plain that he would have disapproved of American policy in Vietnam. If any foreign advice could get a hearing in Washington, or among the American public, Gaitskell's – coming from a proven friend who had risked his political life for the Atlantic alliance – had the best chance; a number of politically experienced Americans even thought that President Johnson would have listened to him. But he would never have reaped an easy harvest of left-wing cheers by strident denunciation of US imperialism (as General de Gaulle did, while escaping all publicity or opprobrium for his own imperialist activities in sub-Saharan Africa). In this area the Left would have been less tolerant of Gaitskell than of Wilson, with his odd reputation as one of themselves.

The most speculative question of all is the Common Market. Gaitskell would have been reluctant to change his mind, but he would have followed carefully all new developments in Britain and throughout the world. With his cosmopolitan tastes and sympathies – so different from many of his friends and early mentors – he was not in the least vulnerable to the charge of Little Englander insularity. In time, all but one of the other pragmatists of Labour's Right and Centre came round to support entry; perhaps he would have done so too. If so, he would not have switched back in opposition.

Curiously, the Left would have preferred Gaitskell on the point of external policy where he would most certainly have differed from Wilson. He never thought that the Rhodesian settlers would be amenable to mere persuasion. Long before David Owen and Andrew Young, he talked of buying them out as the likeliest solution. But he also thought pressure would be needed, and said twice – once just before the 1959 election and again late in 1962 – that his very first act on arriving in Downing Street would be to move troops to Lusaka[11]. His policy might have led to early violence and a 'left-wing Suez'; it might have avoided a bloodier confrontation later on; it would unquestionably have changed the history of Southern Africa for good or ill.

There may be some exaggeration in the common assumption that a Gaitskell government would have faced endless harassment from the Left. Firstly, any Labour Prime Minister before the 1970s could – patronage apart – count on intense loyalty from the rank and file both in and out of Parliament. Secondly, Gaitskell was acutely conscious that back-bench opinion could be 'extremely powerful' and that if Ministers took its unconditional support for granted, the results could be disastrous.[3] Finally, office transforms political attitudes both to men and to issues. In opposition, Labour leaders are assessed by their rhetoric; the Left is very credulous about those who strike its cherished emotional notes and very suspicious of those who do not. Within six weeks of Gaitskell's death his successor was making speeches which 'religiously copied out the Party policy' but, as Wilson's ally Crossman wrote, 'sounded astonishingly left wing . . . no one had any idea until that weekend that the Labour Party had quite radical policies on every subject under the sun'. Similarly, an American academic interviewer found that just before Gaitskell's death Labour activists were critical of the presentation of policies rather than the content, and that just after it they would say: 'Now that Wilson is leader, I'm satisfied with the policies as they are.'[12]

In government, those people would have worried less about how policies were advertised and more about whether they were implemented. They would have recognised the importance of problems like the exchange rate, which had no ideological significance and so were wholly ignored in opposition. Thus Wilson's government went through many crises, but they rarely aligned Left against Right and frequently found Gaitskellites and left-wingers combining against the pragmatists of the Centre. Wilson's past had given him a left-wing reputation (though not among Gaitskellites) which enabled him to pursue unexpectedly cautious policies with relative impunity; conversely, Gaitskell might have benefited from taking action much more radical than the critics had anticipated. In that wholly different climate, the man who had aroused less sweeping hopes might well have fulfilled more of them, and left much less disillusionment behind.

## The Promise Unfulfilled

Outside Labour's ranks, Gaitskell on taking office would have been recognised as a potential leader of the nation. Some Conservative goodwill would have vanished as they found him more of a Socialist than their own myth had painted him; Rhodesia would have brought him real hatred from the far Right (incidentally helping him with his own back-benchers). But moderate Conservatives would have opposed in the same spirit as Gaitskell himself had done. To Liberals, he would have appealed more than most other Labour leaders: more than Attlee because there were few radical Liberals in 1945–51, more than Wilson because of his record and his less partisan style. (As a student, the future Liberal leader David Steel was ready to join a Gaitskellite Labour Party at the end of the 1950s.[13]) Had his economic management proved successful, he would have attracted uncommitted voters too, and changed the face of British politics. For the kind of practical undoctrinaire Socialism which Gaitskell proposed – the tradition of 'conscience and reform' – has a strong appeal in a country which has hardly ever given a majority of votes to a Conservative Party undisguised. He believed that a Labour Party which followed that tradition, seeking real solutions to real problems, would by adhering to its own principles and not by compromising them establish itself as Britain's natural party of government.

Harold Wilson also wanted to make Labour the natural party of government, and also believed it could be done only in office. Many of their policies might have been similar, but their style was quite different. In 1957 Wilson is said to have told a Tory editor that Macmillan was 'a genius . . . holding up the banner of Suez . . . [while] leading the Party away from Suez. That's what I'd like to do with the Labour Party over nationalisation'.[14] Gaitskell, however, wrote to a friend in 1960, about Macmillan's skill at dissembling and his own incapacity for it: 'no doubt in politics the corkscrew is really what you need. It's no use being superior & goody goody about this, when it's really just that you can't do it that way.' If he was sometimes too careless of political constraints, of tactics and timing, yet he was always learning from those mistakes; while the proven commitment to principle convinced opponents as well as friends in the last year or two that he was not just another party politician but a genuine national leader, and led the spokesman of American liberalism to say of him: 'No man is irreplaceable, but some men are unforgettable'.[1]

A recent American scholar has identified seven qualities of the successful political executive: willingness to take responsibility for hard decisions, audacity and zest for combat, sense of proportion and perspective, capacity to withstand unfair criticism, skill in judging men, ability to inspire confidence and loyalty, political sensitivity and timing.[15] With minor qualifications Gaitskell excelled on the first four characteristics. He was competent on the next count; on the sixth, he evoked hostility as well as devotion; he fell below average only on the last. No leader is perfect, and few have combined so many qualities so superbly, or developed hidden new capabilities so regularly.

A Gaitskell premiership would not have been without risk. There was a streak of recklessness in his make-up, and a sometimes dangerous self-confidence. The increased prestige and power of the highest office, making it easier for him to win acceptance for his policies, might also have tempted him to plunge into hazardous enterprises. As Leader of the Opposition he was always conscious (as his opponents never understood) of his duty to his party as he saw it; as Prime Minister he would unquestionably, in case of a clash, have subordinated that duty to his duty to the whole nation. There can be no certainty that a Gaitskell government would have accomplished its ends: only that he would have pursued them boldly and openly, and that even his failures would have marked British politics profoundly.

Always a 'do-er not a be-er', Gaitskell would have used the premiership as an opportunity for teaching and for leadership, for which there was far wider scope before a deteriorating economic and political situation undermined governmental authority and trust in politicians. He would not have shown great creative imagination, and might have been slow to adapt to the changes of the 1970s in British society and particularly in the Labour Movement. But he combined a wider range, a deeper understanding and a more straightforward approach than any post-war Prime Minister. He identified major issues, faced difficult decisions, and built public confidence by explaining what he was doing and why. He attracted able followers and made them proud to work with him. He appealed to the best in others, not the worst. He sought the consent of ordinary people – both in the Labour Movement and in the country – by treating them as adults capable of intelligent judgement, and by arguing a serious case on great controversial issues. His style of leadership would have raised the tone of public debate and respect for public men, and the country would have been the richer for it. Many men of less promise, in Britain and elsewhere, have performed unexpectedly well in the highest office.

Gaitskell, whose capacities had expanded and whose reputation had grown with every broadening of his responsibilities, might have been the great peacetime leader that twentieth-century Britain has badly needed, and sadly failed to find.

# Notes

Letters quoted are from Gaitskell's papers (HGP) or supplied by the correspondent. Publication details for books are given where first cited, or in the bibliography if the author is quoted in more than one chapter: references in the notes are then limited to the author's or editor's surname and the date of publication, e.g. Rodgers (1964). Frequently quoted unpublished sources are abbreviated thus:

Diary  Hugh Gaitskell's Diary (to be published shortly)
AHD  Alastair Hetherington's diary (memoranda of off-the-record talks with HG by the editor of the *Guardian*)
HDD  Hugh Dalton's diary (at LSE)
HDP  Hugh Dalton's papers (at LSE)
HGP  Hugh Gaitskell's papers (at UCL)
RCD  Richard Crossman's back-bench diary (manuscript at Warwick University)

## CHAPTER 1

1. In Rodgers (1964), pp. 23, 25.
2. Lucille Iremonger, *The Fiery Chariot* (Secker and Warburg, 1970); Hugh Berrington's review in *British Journal of Political Science* IV, pp. 345–69; *The Times*, 3 December 1975, on Dr Pierre Rentchnick's work.
3. Diary, 1 October 1948. (He kept it from 1945 to 1956, with gaps.)
4. To the Royal Scottish Academy, 27 April 1951: HGP.
5. To J. P. O'Donnell, 5 November 1958, for a *Saturday Evening Post* profile: HGP.
6. To HG 22 October 1950: HGP.
7. By A. J. P. Taylor (on HG) in the *Sunday Express*, 25 September 1960.
8. To his mother Mrs Wodehouse, 29 September 1926.
9. J. B. Orrick, interviews and letters to the author.
10. Quoted in his obituary in *The Draconian*, no. 226, Easter 1963.
11. Cyril Robinson to Alan Wood, quoted in the latter's profile of HG in *Picture Post*, 7 April 1951: in HGP.
12. *The Wykehamist*, nos. 633, 639, 643.
13. HG to his cousin George Martelli, 29 June 1959.
14. HG, 'At Oxford in the Twenties', in Briggs and Saville (1967), pp. 6–7.
15. Interview, Professor M. M. Postan.
16. To Arthur Gaitskell, 4 June 1932.
17. To his mother, 15 December 1926.
18. Ibid., 4 and 11 January 1927.

19. To Julie Gaitskell, 7 June 1959. (His italics.)
20. Bowra (1966), pp. 177, 179.
21. HG to Alan Wood for his profile (see n. 11), 2 February 1951; HGP.
22. To Julie, 16 February 1958.
23. To Cressida Gaitskell, 5 November 1962.
24. To Arthur, 18 November 1928.


## CHAPTER 2

1. Interview, J. B. Orrick.
2. To his mother, 5 May 1926.
3. In Briggs and Saville (1967), pp. 9–12, 14, 16.
4. Bowra (1966), p. 179; and in Rodgers (1964), pp. 20, 25.
5. Dalton (1953), p. 164.
6. HG on Tawney: n. 12 below. Tawney on HG: interview, Professor M. M. Postan.
7. To his mother, 11 January 1927 (probably quoting back a phrase from a letter of hers).
8. To his mother, 3 June 1926.
9. Interview, George Martelli; HG to profile writers (Ch. 1, notes 5 &21).
10. HG's essay on socialist ideology in Britain (see below, Ch. 3, n. 25).
11. HG to Julian Symons, 28 November 1955: HGP.
12. To his mother, 20 May 1926. (His worry about 'the working classes being encouraged not to think but to enjoy the cinemas and the football matches which the Capitalist likes them to enjoy' shows a surviving Wykehamist puritanism which he was later to shed completely.)
13. To his mother, 3 November and 15 December 1926.
14. To his sister 'Bunty', 11 January 1927; also to his mother, same day.
15. Cole to HG, about to start his first job: n.d., HGP.
16. Interview, Dame Margaret Cole.
17. *The Tablet*, 24 January 1959 (memoir of Cole).
18. To his mother, 4 January 1927.
19. To his sister, 16 July 1926.
20. M. M. Postan in Rodgers (1964), pp. 55, 62.
21. Interview, Sir Hubert Ashton.
22. 'The Battle of the Unions', *Manchester Guardian*, 16 April 1928. (The Spencer Union lasted ten years.)
23. HG to his brother Arthur, 9 December 1927.
24. Interview, G. V. Keeling.
25. HG to his mother, 17 October 1927.
26. To Arthur, 8 May 1928. (His emphasis.)
27. Interview, Lady Longford.
28. To Arthur, 4 June 1932.

29. To J. P. O'Donnell, 5 November 1958: HGP.

30. From his lecture on the same subject in Minnesota in 1952: HGP.

31. To his mother, 17 and 31 January 1928. (His emphasis.)

32. Keeling to Alan Wood, in *Picture Post*, 7 April 1951.

33. Hansard, 20 May 1946, 57.

34. HG to Seymour Cocks MP, 28 October 1950; at the London Old Students' Club supper of the Workingmen's Club, December 1958: HGP.

35. Dalton (1962), pp. 426-7.

36. To his mother, 5 March 1928. (His emphasis.)

37. Ibid., 15 February 1928 – after asking some other advice but before receiving it.

38. Ibid., n.d. but spring 1928.

## CHAPTER 3

1. Richard Cranford, *East Anglian Daily Times*, 14 January 1956.

2. Interview, Professor Herbert Tout.

3. To his mother Mrs Wodehouse, 15 February 1928. Her second husband was Graham Wallas's nephew.

4. HG's preface to Durbin (1954), p. 10.

5. From Egypt, probably June 1945: HGP.

6. To Arthur Gaitskell, 6 May 1932.

7. In an interview with George Gale, *Daily Express*, 12 and 13 December 1955.

8. Interview, Dr John Bowlby.

9. HG to Arthur Gaitskell, 17 July 1930.

10. Margaret Cole in Rodgers (1964), p. 42.

11. He appears as Pussy, in *We Have Been Warned*.

12. HG to G. D. H. Cole, 17 September 1928.

13. HG to Arthur Gaitskell, 4 June 1932.

14. He told the story often. (Half a crown was $12\frac{1}{2}$p., 5s. was double.)

15. HG to Arthur, 13 November 1928 and 27 December 1928. (His emphasis.)

16. HG to his mother, 11 January 1927.

17. HG in Briggs and Saville (1967), pp. 14, 16 (his omission marks), 18.

18. Note by E. A. Radice in Fabian Society Papers, Box N. 24.

19. *Chatham News*, 18 November 1932.

20. Ibid., 20 January 1933.

21. Ibid., 6 October 1933.

22. 'Socialism and Wages Policy': Cole Papers, Box N. 12.

23. *Chartism* (WEA, 1929) pp. 85-7; he went on to say that the alliance policy implied middle-class leadership – an obvious truth in the 1840s, from which critics persistently drew false inferences about his views on working-class strategy a century later.

24. M. M. Postan in Rodgers (1964), pp. 55–8.
25. Essay on the ideology of British democratic socialism: *Socialist International Information* 24 November 1955, pp. 930–1.
26. MS notes in HGP. (His emphasis.)
27. In G. D. H. Cole, ed., *What Everybody Wants to know about Money* (Gollancz, 1933).
28. In G. E. G. Catlin, ed., *New Trends in Socialism* (Lovat Dickson and Thompson, 1935).
29. Williams (1970), pp. 112–13.
30. HG to James Meade, 20 June 1932: Meade Papers.
31. Les Ellis to HG, 16 June 1929: HGP.
32. Dexter to HG, 12 October 1932: HGP.
33. Interview, Mrs B. Grieveson.
34. Interview, Lord Willis.
35. Macey to HG, 8 May 1933, in reply.
36. HG to Harold Barger, 1 December 1933.
37. Professor Howard S. Ellis to the author.
38. HG to Arthur, 3 December 1933.
39. Ibid., 9 December 1927.
40. John Gunther, *Inside Europe* (Hamilton, 1936 ed.), p. 314.
41. Mrs I. Polanyi to the author.
42. Interviews with his Austrian friends, particularly Dr Gertrud Wagner.
43. F. S. (Scheu) in *Arbeiter Zeitung*, Vienna, 16 December 1955.
44. Interview, Naomi Mitchison.
45. Paper on Labour foreign policy (see above, pp. 69–70), 2 October 1935: HGP.
46. *Chatham News*, 28 December 1934. (There was a Nazi putsch in July.)

## CHAPTER 4

1. Memorandum of 7 December 1934 in HGP: 'social justice' inserted in HG's handwriting.
2. M. M. Postan in Rodgers (1964), pp. 60–3.
3. Beatrice Webb's diary, 15 February 1936, in Passfield Papers.
4. HG to Arthur Gaitskell, 3 December 1933.
5. MS notes for a lecture on 3 February 1935: HGP.
6. *Plebs*, May, July and August 1935.
7. Interview, Lord Willis.
8. Paper of 2 October 1935: HGP.
9. NFRB conference reports 18–19 January 1936, 27–8 June 1936: Fabian Society Papers, Box N. 29.
10. Williams (1970), p. 111.
11. Durbin to Dalton, 26 December 1936: Dalton (1957), p. 124 n. Gaitskell

certainly agreed, for they had no major difference from 1934 to Munich.

12. *Daily Herald*, 11 August 1939.
13. *South Leeds Worker*, December 1937.
14. Notes (1938) in HGP.
15. Notes for two lectures in 1935: HGP.
16. HG to Margaret Cole, 12 March 1962: HGP.
17. Dalton (1962), pp. 426–7.
18. From HG's preface to Durbin (1954), p. 9; and from HG to Alan Wood (see n. 22).
19. *Chatham News*, 28 December 1934.
20. HG to George Martelli, 23 July 1959: HGP.
21. Interview, Dr John Bowlby.
22. Assistant Secretary to HG, 16 November 1936 (HGP); HG to Alan Wood, 2 February 1951 (HGP) for *Picture Post* profile, 7 April 1951.
23. *The Uses of Literacy* (Penguin, 1957).
24. Brett to HG, 20 October 1950: HGP.
25. Hansard (Lords), 18 December 1975, 1617.
26. HG to Harold Barger, 7 July 1937.
27. Interview, Sir Noel Hall.
28. HDD, 24 April 1945.
29. Gordon Petter in *Victoria Times* (Canada), 6 December 1955.
30. Interview, Professor Paul Rosenstein-Rodan.
31. Interview, Professor W. A. Robson.
32. His Diary, 6 April 1949.
33. Interviews, Lord Roll, Lady Brook.
34. 'Watchman' (Vyvyan Adams), *Right Honourable Gentlemen* (Hamish Hamilton, 1939), p. 215.
35. HG to Julie Gaitskell, 21 January 1959.
36. Leonard Woolf, *Downhill All the Way* (Hogarth Press, 1968), p. 248.
37. To Harold Beale, 1 July 1938: HGP.
38. HG to Dalton, 21 May 1957: HGP.
39. HG–Durbin, correspondence and memorandum just after Munich.
40. HDD, 19 October 1938.
41. *The Beeston Democrat*, November 1938.
42. Douglas Jay in Rodgers (1964), pp. 83–5.

## CHAPTER 5

1. HG to George Martelli, 23 July 1959: HGP.
2. HG to George Brett, 14 September 1939: HGP.
3. Ibid., 8 September 1939.
4. HG to Alan Wood, 2 February 1951: HGP.
5. HG in the *Listener*, 20 March 1952, reviewing W. N. Medlicott, *History of*

*the Second World War: the Economic Blockade*, Vol. I (HMSO and Longmans, 1952).

6. Medlicott, I.17.
7. Dalton (1957), p. 296.
8. HDD, 17 March 1940.
9. Dalton (1957), p. 305.
10. Ibid., p. 318, cf. p. 381.
11. Interview, E. A. Radice.
12. HDD, 30 October 1941.
13. Dalton (1957), p. 334.
14. HG's draft obituary of Dalton: HGP. Published in the *Guardian*, 14 February 1962.
15. Interview, Mrs M. Durbin. Her husband was present.
16. Interview, Miss K. M. Elliott.
17. HG to Brett, 23 September 1940.
18. Dalton (1957), pp. 378ff.
19. Churchill's phrase for the Ministry which dealt with propaganda and subversion.
20. R. H. Bruce Lockhart, *Comes the Reckoning* (Putnam, 1947), pp. 155–6.
21. HDD, 15 August 1940.
22. Dalton to Attlee, 25 September 1941: HDP.
23. HDD, 27 December 1941.
24. Dalton (1957), p. 381.
25. HG in George Gale interview, *Daily Express*, 12 and 13 December 1955.
26. Both in HDP.
27. Dalton (1957), pp. 389–93; HDD, 11 and 19 March 1942. Sir Evan Williams had led the owners since 1919.
28. HDD, 7 April and late May 1942.
29. W. H. B. Court, *Coal* (HMSO and Longmans, 1951), pp. 160–1.
30. Dalton (1957), p. 391; Bevan, Hansard, 11 June 1942, 1298–9.
31. HDD, 12 June 1942.
32. Interview, Sir Raymond Streat.
33. HDD, 7 September and 2 October 1942; 7 April 1943.
34. Douglas Jay in Rodgers (1964), p. 88.
35. HG to Christopher Mayhew, 22 September 1943.
36. Eady memorandum to Sir Richard Hopkins, 12 October 1943, in the Public Record Office.
37. Interview, Professor G. C. Allen – his fellow-draftsman.
38. HG to Brett, 16 January 1944: HGP.
39. HDD, 9 November 1944.
40. HG's phrase, quoted in Arthur Gaitskell to HG, 15 June 1944: HGP.
41. Harold Cowen to HG reminding him, 25 October 1950: HGP.
42. HG to Brett, 19 February 1944.

43. Brett to HG, 13 January 1941 and August 1942.
44. HG–Brett correspondence, April-June 1945.
45. Interview, Lady Bacon.
46. HG–Brett correspondence, July 1945.


CHAPTER 6

1. HG's Diary, 6 and 13/24 August 1945: HGP.
2. Diary, 12 August 1947, covering his 15 months in office.
3. William Pickles, European Service, 9 October 1947: BBC Archives.
4. Diary, 14 October 1947.
5. Dalton (1962), p. 203. (My italics.)
6. Richard Cleaver to the author.
7. Dr F. E. Budd to the author.
8. *Star*, 5 February 1947.
9. Interviews with civil servants.
10. Their next-door neighbour Harold Albert in the *People*, 28 December 1947.
11. HG to James Langham, 7 March 1946: BBC Archives.
12. *Yorkshire Post*, 8 October 1947, on his appointment.
13. Diary, 22 October 1947.
14. Harold Wilson was President of the Board of Trade, and Russell Strauss Minister of Supply.
15. Fergusson to HG, 8 October 1947: with HG's Diary.
16. Interview, Sir Goronwy Daniel.
17. Diary, 18 June 1948.
18. Quoted by Douglas Jay in Rodgers (1964), p. 92.
19. Hansard, 28 October 1947, 709.
20. Diary, 30 January 1948.
21. Diary, 28 October 1948.
22. Fergusson to HG, 26 December 1947: HGP.
23. Diary, 23 April 1948.
24. Hansard, 16 June 1948, 534. Diary, 1 June 1948 (on Reid's resignation).
25. HG to (Sir) D. N. Chester, 1 February 1954: HGP
26. Diary, 8 October 1948.
27. HG's memorandum to the Cabinet Committee on Socialised Industries: S.1(M)(49)38 of June 1949, paras. 3 and 11.
28. Press, 9 July 1948.
29. Durbin to HG, 5 May 1948: HGP.
30. Diary, 4 December 1947.
31. Diary, 16 February 1948.
32. Diary, 5 August 1948.
33. Diary, 29 July 1949.

34. HDD, vol. 36; 'end of 1948' – on the views of Stafford Cripps, Ernest Bevin and Aneurin Bevan.

35. Diary, 17 January and 2 February 1949.

36. Diary, 6 April 1949.

37. Diary, 20 September 1948.

38. HG to Dr John Bowlby, 28 October 1950: HGP.

39. To a Labour student conference at Dorking, 13 April 1949: HGP.

40. Diary, 21 June 1949.

41. Diary, 12 July 1948.

42. HG to Morrison, January 1949: HGP.

43. HG to Michael Young, Research Secretary of the Labour Party, 21 January 1949: HGP.

44. HG memorandum (see note 27) para. 9: quoted Sir Norman Chester, *The Nationalisation of British Industry 1945–51* (HMSO, 1975), pp. 548–9.

45. Diary, 26 October 1949.

46. HG memorandum (see note 27), para. 10.

47. Diary, 27 January 1950.

48. HG memorandum (see note 27) S.1(M) (49)33 of 30 May 1949: Chester, pp. 995–8.

49. Ibid., para. 11.

50. Diary, 17 March 1949.

51. Diary, 12 August 1948.

52. HG to Morrison, 15 May 1950: HGP.

53. Vickers to HG, 7 March 1950: HGP.

54. HDD, 22 August 1948.

55. Various sources in the Press, 20 February 1950: speech at Barnsley.

56. James Margach, *The Abuse of Power* (Allen, 1978), p. 86.

57. Diary, 2 February 1949.

58. Interviews, J. R. L. Anderson, J. H. Lawrie.

59. Press, 9 March 1949.

60. *Daily Mail* (Leslie Randall), *Daily Express* (Trevor Evans), 7 July 1949.

61. HG to Michael Young, 6 December 1948: Fergusson's minute attached: HGP.

62. Sir George Legh-Jones to HG, 12 June 1950: HGP.

63. Diary, 3 August 1949.

64. Diary, 1 February 1950.

65. Interview, C. Plumb, who was present.

66. HG to Alan Wood, 2 February 1951: HGP.

67. HDD, 27 January 1950.

68. G. L. Watkinson to HG, 11 June 1949: HGP.

69. Alderman Ed Porter MP to HG, 3 March 1950: HGP.

CHAPTER 7

1. Douglas Jay in Rodgers (1964), p. 95.
2. Diary, 21 June 1949.
3. Diary, 29 June 1949.
4. Diary, 3 August 1949 (covering several weeks). The '(*sic*)'–quoted on p. 145–is in the original Diary.
5. HDD, 'end of July 1949'.
6. Diary, 21 September 1949 (covering several weeks).
7. HDD, 12 September 1949. (His italics.)
8. To be published with HG's Diary.
9. W. Wyatt, *Turn Again Westminster* (Deutsch, 1973), pp. 179–82; quoting Cripps.
10. Diary, 26 October 1949.
11. HDD, 12 and 13 October 1949.
12. Diary, 21 November 1949.
13. Diary, 1 February 1950.
14. Diary, 27 January 1950.
15. Diary, 21 March 1950.
16. HDD, 27 January 1950.
17. Granada TV interview, 28 July 1961.
18. HG to Evelyn Hewitt, 8 March 1950. Sebastian Haffner, *Observer*, 22 October 1950, and Haffner (1954), p. 68.
19. Hansard, 6 April 1949, 2084, 2093.
20. Seventh Report, paras. 44, 56 (2).
21. Hansard, 9 December 1949, 2263; Wyatt, p. 148n.
22. Public Accounts Committee, Fourth Report, 1950–1, para. 55.
23. Hansard, 14 March 1950, 937–8.
24. Foot (1973), pp. 292–4.
25. Hansard, 18 April 1950, 59–60.
26. Diary, 26 May 1950.
27. Diary, 11 August 1950 (covering several weeks).
28. Obituary of HG, *Sunday Times Weekly Review*, 20 January 1963.
29. HG's obituary of Cripps, BBC North American Service, 22 April 1952: HGP.
30. Hansard, 24 April 1950, 631–2.
31. HDD, 24 January 1950, on HG's paper to the Cabinet's Economic Policy Committee.
32. J. C. R. Dow, *The Management of the British Economy 1945–60* (Cambridge University Press, 1970), p. 152.
33. HG to Harriman, 24 June 1950: HGP.
34. On 5 September 1950 (HDP) in reply to Dalton to HG, 2 September (in HGP).
35. Diary, 3 November 1950.

36. Hansard, 12–14 September 1950, 959, 965, 1130, 1145, 1150.
37. His memorandum on these talks, kept with his Diary (they are to be published together).
38. Diary, 10 January 1951.
39. *Observer*, 8 October 1950.
40. All quotations on his trip are from his Diary, 3 November 1950.
41. Interview, R. L. Sharp.


CHAPTER 8

1. James Callaghan MP to HG, 14 November 1950: HGP.
2. Diary, 3 November 1950.
3. Diary, 5 January 1951.
4. Wilfred Sendall, *Daily Telegraph*, 2 October 1950.
5. Foot (1973), pp. 300–1, with Attlee's reply.
6. HDD, 18 January 1951, reporting Bevan.
7. Brittan (1964), p. 155.
8. Hansard, 2 November 1950, 350–2.
9. Diary, 24 January 1951.
10. Diary, 10 January 1951.
11. Diary, 2 February 1951.
12. These alarms may not have been imaginary. A defecting official Communist historian produced apparent confirmation years later from Czech archives: *The Times, Le Monde*, 6 May 1977.
13. HDD, 4 February 1951.
14. Interview, Lord Strauss.
15. Sir Kenneth Younger's diary, 13 May 1951.
16. Hansard, 15 February 1951, 739–40 (Bevan), 644 (Gaitskell, repeating Attlee on 29 January, 583).
17. Diary, 16 February 1951.
18. Hunter (1959), p. 158.
19. Shinwell in the *Sunday Times*, 30 July 1961.
20. Diary, 30 April 1951 (covering several weeks).
21. Diary, 4 May 1951. Unattributed quotations in this chapter come from these two long entries.
22. HDD, 5 and 9–12 April 1951.
23. Interview, Lord Armstrong.
24. Joan Mitchell, *Crisis in Britain 1951* (Secker and Warburg, 1963), p. 100.
25. *Tribune*, 6 April 1951.
26. R.R. Jones, ed., *Chips* (Weidenfeld and Nicolson, 1967), p. 458. (The diary of a Tory MP).
27. Foot (1973), p. 324.

28. Hansard, 10–12 April 1951: S. Evans (1109), J. McGovern (918), R. Maudling (1122). Press of 11 April.

29. HDD, 19 and 20 April 1951.

30. Ibid., reporting Chuter Ede who saw it.

31. Duff (1971), pp. 29, 48, 76. She was then its business manager.

32. A. J. P. Taylor, *Beaverbrook* (Penguin ed., 1974), p. 764.

33. Cripps to HG, 31 March 1951; Lady Cripps to HG, 24 April 1951: HGP.

34. Both letters in Foot (1973), pp. 372–3.

35. Sir Kenneth Younger's diary, 13 May 1951.

36. According to Freeman and Callaghan (HDD 17 and 20 April 1951), supported by Foot (1973), pp. 333–4.

37. Hansard, 23 April 1951, 35–43.

38. Foot (1973), pp. 334.

39. Freeman to HG, 12 April 1951: HGP.

40. HDD, 24 April 1951.

41. Callaghan to HG, 10 April 1951: HGP.

42. Interview, L. J. Callaghan.

43. Diary, 11 May 1951.

44. Lord Gordon Walker's diary, 16 April 1951.

45. HG to Evelyn Hewitt, 7 May 1951. (His emphasis.)

46. Brown in the *Spectator*, 24 January 1964.

47. HDD, 22 March 1951.

48. Dalton to Attlee, 15 April 1951: HDP.

49. Douglas Jay in Rodgers (1964), p. 100; he named Ede in interview.

50. Dalton (1962), p. 365.

51. Diary, 10 August 1951.

## CHAPTER 9

1. Hansard, 26 July 1951, 674.

2. Diary, 10 August 1951.

3. *Report*, 1951, pp. 363–71.

4. Diary, 11 May 1951.

5. Diary, 9 August 1951.

6. HG to John Strachey MP, 15 February 1954: HGP.

7. Diary, 9 November 1951.

8. HDD, 27 September 1951.

9. HDD, 24 September 1951. (His emphasis.)

10. Dean Acheson, *Present at the Creation* (Macmillan, 1970), pp. 559–60.

11. Diary, 16 November 1951.

12. His Cabinet paper, summarised in Douglas Jay MP to HG, 26 September 1951: HGP.

13. Hansard, 7 November 1951, 192.

14. Diary, 23 November 1951.

15. Hunter (1959), p. 40.
16. HG to F. C. Evennett, 10 November 1952 (HGP) and in *Tribune*, 28 December 1951. Minister of Supply, Hansard, 23 July 1951, 60–2.
17. Memorandum on anti-Americanism in Britain, probably June 1952: HGP.
18. Sir Kenneth (Lord) Clark to HG, 5 October 1954: HGP.
19. Interview, Sir Arthur Snelling.
20. Lord Roberthall to the author, and interview.
21. Attlee to HG, 3 November 1951: HGP.

## CHAPTER 10

1. Jennie Lee, *This Great Journey* (McGibbon and Kee, 1963), p. 116.
2. HG in the *New York Times Magazine*, 5 October 1952.
3. At Newcastle, 23 March 1952.
4. *Daily Mirror*, 26 February 1952: heavily emphasised.
5. HDD, 29 January 1952.
6. To NUGMW conference at Whitley Bay, 16 June 1952.
7. HG to Wallace Phillips, 22 November 1951: HGP.
8. Diary, 6 October 1954 (covering two years).
9. Hunter (1959), p. 123.
10. Lord Gordon Walker's diary, 22 June 1952.
11. Ibid., 30 July 1952.
12. Henry Fairlie in the *Spectator*, 11 December 1955. HG to Hilary Marquand MP, 7 October 1952: HGP.
13. At Stalybridge on 6 October 1952: full text in the *Leeds Weekly Citizen*, 10th.
14. His own estimate was one-twentieth: HG to Desmond Donnelly MP, 10 October 1952, HGP.
15. Correspondence in HGP.
16. Foot (1973), p. 388; RCD, 23 October 1952, reporting Attlee; Griffiths in the *Daily Herald*, 15 October 1952.
17. RCD, 14 and 15 October 1952.
18. HDD, 24–8 October 1952.
19. At the Festival Hall, 11 October 1952.
20. RCD, 23 and 27 October 1952.
21. Ibid., 2 and 3 December 1952.
22. Interviews with his constituency workers.
23. HG to his agent George Murray, 7 October 1953: HGP.
24. Butler (1973), p. 162.

## CHAPTER 11

1. HG in the *Daily Herald*, 14 October 1952.
2. Memorandum on anti-Americanism, HGP: probably June 1952.

3. Foot (1973), pp. 430-2.
4. Diary, 6 October 1954.
5. HDD, 14 April 1954. The 'tape' is the ticker-tape machine in the House.
6. Hunter (1959), pp. 78-9, quoting Crossman.
7. RCD, 3 and 6 May 1954.
8. Ibid., 28 April 1954.
9. HG to Solly Pearce, 5 July 1954: HGP.
10. RCD, 8 July 1954.
11. HDD, 4 September 1951.
12. HG to Wilfred Fienburgh MP, 22 November 1954: HGP.
13. At Saltburn-on-Sea, 27 June 1954
14. Foot (1973), p. 450.
15. RCD, 1 February 1957.
16. HG to Geoffrey (Lord) Crowther, editor of the *The Economist*, 22 November 1954: HGP.
17. 'In Defence of Politics', the Birkbeck Foundation Oration, 2 December 1954.
18. Diary, 9 November 1954.
19. RCD, 1 November 1954.
20. Ibid., 22 February and 3 March 1955.
21. Crossman to Ted Davies of Coventry, 7 March 1955 (with his diary).
22. This account is from HG's Diary, 19 and 25 March and 2 April 1955; so are unattributed quotations in this chapter.
23. RCD, 16 March 1955.
24. Letter in HGP.
25. RCD, 24 March 1955.
26. Interview, Lady Brook.
27. Croccman to Bevan, 31 March 1955 (with his diary). Foot (1973), pp. 482-3.

## CHAPTER 12

1. Diary, 9 November 1954.
2. *The Times*, 21 May 1955.
3. HG in *Socialist Commentary*, July 1955. (His italics.)
4. HG to Alma (Lady) Birk, 3 June 1955: HGP.
5. *Observer*, 16 October 1955.
6. *Report*, p. 175.
7. Hunter (1959), p. 143.
8. *Tribune*, 14 October 1955.
9. Irving Kristol, *New Leader* (New York), 16 October 1955.
10. RCD, 15 October 1955.
11. Hansard, 20 April 1955, 204.

12. Ibid., 26 July 1955, 1016.
13. Cf. ibid., 27 October 1955, 406–7. Also in the *Daily Herald*, 7th; at Margate, 10th.
14. Hansard, 27 October 1955, 393, 399, 408.
15. Hunter (1959), pp. 135, 138.
16. Jenkins (1974), p. 172.
17. RCD, 16 March 1955.
18. Leslie Smith, *Harold Wilson* (Hodder and Stoughton, 1964), pp. 174–6.
19. Interview, Roy Jenkins. (His emphasis.)
20. Hunter (1959), p. 164.
21. HDD, 28 April 1955.
22. Viscount Stuart of Findhorn, then Secretary for Scotland, *Within the Fringe* (Bodley Head, 1967), p. 144.
23. Griffiths (1969), p. 145.
24. Tawney to HG: HGP.
25. Interview, Lord Pannell.
26. RCD, 16 December 1955.
27. Interviews, D. Healey, Lord Pannell, P. Rosenstein-Rodan.

## CHAPTER 13

1. Williams (1970), p. 308.
2. To Susan Barnes: *Sunday Express*, 30 September 1962.
3. On 'Press Conference', 21 September 1956 (BBC Archives). The transcript shows his embarrassment.
4. To Jim Orrick, 21 October 1954, HGP.
5. Interview, Lady Brook.
6. HG to Julie Gaitskell in 1958 and early 1959; and 28 February 1961 on the New Left. (His emphasis.)
7. L. Lyle of the wartime Board of Trade to HG, 6 November 1950: HGP.
8. Peter Lewis in the *Yorkshire Evening Post*, 26 September 1954; Shinwell quoted in Haffner (1954), p. 67; Grimond in Hansard, 22 January 1963, 48.
9. Interviews, Mrs Jane Page, Lady Donaldson.
10. Hunter (1959), p. 219, confessing the terms might be wrong: 'bobop' is.
11. Francis Williams in the *Daily Herald*, 19 November 1957.
12. To Nell Summerscale, 23 June 1955: HGP.
13. 'In the News', 9 December 1955, on Attlee: BBC Archives.
14. Younger to HG on 4 April (his emphasis) and reply 8 April: HGP.
15. Harold Hutchinson in the *Daily Herald*, 22 September 1959.
16. HG to Anthony Crosland, 16 January 1957: HGP.
17. *Spectator*, 9 December 1955; *Observer*, 21 July 1974.
18. RCD, 16 December 1955.
19. *New Statesman* profile, 13 February 1954.

20. On 14 October 1955 (HGP), criticising the Socialist Union's manuscript *Twentieth Century Socialism* (Penguin, 1956).
21. *Financial Times*, 12 January 1973.
22. Quoted by Drew Middleton in the *New York Times*, 19 January 1963.
23. *Daily Telegraph*, 16 January 1959.
24. To the ETU educational college at Esher, 28 June 1962.
25. *Socialist International Information*, 24 December 1955.
26. To John Murray, 3 January 1955, HGP; interview, P. Morris; to the New Democratic Party's founding convention in Ottawa, 4 August 1961. (An experiment was tried in the Post Office twenty years later.)
27. AHD, 10 May 1961.
28. RCD, 19 March 1959.
29. Interview, Lord Willis.
30. To Henry Fairlie: *Daily Mail*, 10 May 1957; 30 July 1959.
31. RCD, 26 March 1953.
32. To Sir Vaughan Berry, 24 July 1962 (HGP); and interview, Christopher Mayhew MP.
33. Elaine Burton MP to HG, 2 April 1955; HG to Peter Shore, 14 December 1962: HGP.
34. To Dr Barnett Stross MP, 7 November 1958: HGP.
35. Published as *The Challenge of Co-existence* (Methuen, 1957). Quotations are from pp. 51–2, 54–5, 71–2, 77–8, 89.
36. HG to Crossman, 28 May 1958: HGP.
37. HG in *Challenge*, pp. 59–62, and in *Reynolds News*, 3 February 1957.
38. To John Murray, 9 March 1955: HGP.
39. Allen to HG, 1 January 1958: HGP.

## CHAPTER 14

1. *Birmingham Post, Financial Times, Daily Telegraph* (R. T. McKenzie): all 15 December 1955.
2. Hunter (1959), p. 8.
3. Tom Hutchinson, *Illustrated*, 15 March 1958.
4. On 'Press Conference', 2 August 1957: BBC Archives.
5. In *Tribune*, 3 January 1958. (His italics.)
6. Henry Fairlie, *Daily Mail*, 6 February 1958.
7. *Daily Telegraph*, leader, 24 January 1956.
8. Robert Edwards, *Sunday Express*, 27 March 1959.
9. *Chartism* (WEA, 1928), p. 39.
10. HG to Julie Gaitskell, n.d. (November 1958, his emphasis) on democracy; 7 June 1959 on ambition.
11. To the ETU educational college at Esher, 28 June 1962.
12. On Granada TV, 28 July 1961: HGP.

13. HG's characterisation of Dalton in his obituary: *Guardian*, 14 February 1962.
14. Foot (1973), pp. 500–1.
15. Fairlie in the *Spectator*, 10 February 1956. On Bevan, HG called this article 'an almost verbatim account of my views' (n. 16 below).
16. Diary, 14 February 1956.
17. Diary, 21 January 1956.
18. Diary, 23 February 1956.
19. RCD, 21 March 1956.
20. Diary, April 1956, on which this account of the Soviet visit is based.
21. RCD, 6 November 1957.
22. Diary, 9 October, 1956.
23. RCD, 4 July 1956.

## CHAPTER 15

1. Hansard, 16 May 1957, 680.
2. Diary, late July 1956.
3. Diary, August 1956.
4. Hansard, 2 August 1956, 1609–17.
5. HG to Lance Mallalieu MP, 10 August 1956: HGP.
6. HG to Cyril Robinson (his old housemaster), 1 July 1958.
7. HG to Eden, 3 August 1956: HGP.
8. Anthony Eden (Earl of Avon), *Full Circle* (Cassell, 1960), p. 492.
9. Diary, 5 September 1956.
10. *Reynolds News*, 26 August 1956. (His heavy emphasis.)
11. Hansard, 12 September 1956, 15–32.
12. George Thomson MP, *Forward*, 21 September 1956.
13. Diary, 14 September 1956.
14. RCD, 28 September 1956.
15. *The Economist*, 6 October 1956.
16. *Report*, pp. 76–7. (His emphasis.)
17. RCD, 26 October 1956.
18. Butler (1973), p. 190.
19. Randolph Churchill, *The Rise and Fall of Sir Anthony Eden* (MacGibbon and Kee, 1959), pp. 291–2.
20. Quoted by HG (in n. 6 above).
21. Hansard, 31 October 1956, 1454–62.
22. Ibid., 3 November 1956, 1862.
23. *Listener*, 8 November 1956.
24. *New Statesman*, 10 November 1956.
25. Monckton's undated memorandum in Lord Birkenhead, *Walter Monckton* (Weidenfeld and Nicolson, 1969), pp. 307–8.
26. Interviews, Arthur Allen, Sir Hubert Ashton, Lord Butler.

27. Sir Edward Boyle MP to HG, 30 January 1957; Lady Violet to HG, 4 November 1956: HGP. *National Newsletter*, 5 December 1956.
28. Interview, Sir Arthur Gaitskell.
29. HG to Chuter Ede MP, 4 December 1956: HGP.
30. Macmillan (1971), p. 185.
31. His diary, 16 September 1956.


## CHAPTER 16

1. Jenkins (1974), p. 175.
2. To John Beavan (Lord Ardwick), 19 April 1961: HGP.
3. Lord Pakenham (Lord Longford), *Observer*, 6 October 1957.
4. *Daily Telegraph*, 30 September 1957; *Sunday Times*, 6 October 1957.
5. *Socialist Commentary* editorial, October 1957.
6. RCD, 17 September 1957.
7. HG to Douglas Jay MP, 6 September 1957; transcript of taped Labour Party discussion, September 1957: HGP.
8. HG to John Murray, 9 October 1957: HGP.
9. Macmillan (1971), p. 235: from his diary.
10. HG to Kenneth Younger MP, 8 April 1957: HGP.
11. HG to John Murray, 10 April 1957: HGP.
12. RCD, 3 May 1957.
13. Jennie (Baroness) Lee, *Observer*, 10 December 1972.
14. *Report*, pp. 181–2.
15. RCD, 4 October 1957.


## CHAPTER 17

1. Macmillan (1971), pp. 713–14 from his diary, p. 719.
2. HG to Julie Gaitskell, 1 May 1958 (Cousins); 21 January 1959 (TV).
3. Hansard, 8 May 1958, 1452–3.
4. RCD, 11 July 1958, reporting HG.
5. *Report*, p. 170.
6. Foot (1973), p. 609.
7. *Observer*, 5 October 1958.
8. *Spectator*, 1 August 1958.
9. Francis Williams in the *Daily Herald*, 18 and 19 November 1958.
10. To Christopher Mayhew MP, 7 November 1958: HGP.
11. *The Times*, 21 July 1958.
12. *Daily Telegraph*, 9 June 1959.
13. Roy Jenkins in Rodgers (1964), p. 124.
14. Interview in the *Daily Mail*, January 1959.
15. 'Crossbencher', *Sunday Express*, 10 August 1958.

16. To Ronald Harker, 28 April 1959: HGP.
17. To Alan Rodway, 12 February 1959: HGP.
18. Macmillan (1971), p. 419; from his diary, 5 October 1957.
19. HG to Arthur Blenkinsop MP, 24 October 1957: HGP.
20. HG to Arthur Woodburn MP, 25 February 1958: HGP.
21. AHD, 9 July 1959.
22. At Workington, 11 July 1959.
23. 'At Home and Abroad', 17 July 1959: BBC Archives.
24. On BBC television, 10 July 1959.
25. RCD, 2 February 1959.
26. Ibid., 29 June and 3 July 1959.
27. *Daily Mail*, 30 July 1959.


CHAPTER 18

1. Brittan (1971), pp. 224–6.
2. RCD, 3 July 1959.
3. Denis Healey's obituary of HG, 18 January 1963: BBC Archives.
4. Interview, John (Lord) Harris, then HG's personal assistant.
5. Macmillan (1972), p. 8: from his diary.
6. RCD, 24 September 1959.
7. Ibid., 9 and 27 October 1959; AHD, 29 October.
8. Report by Morgan Phillips (general secretary of the Party) to the NEC, 22 October 1959, which analysed the experience of 200 Labour candidates: HGP and Labour Party Archives.
9. 1959 Conference *Report*, p. 83; and HGP.
10. *New Statesman*, 17 and 24 October 1959.
11. Don Cook, *New York Herald Tribune*, 9 December 1959.
12. *Daily Mail*, 12 October 1959.


CHAPTER 19

1. Interviews with participants.
2. HDD, 11 October 1959.
3. RCD, 19 October 1959.
4. Interview, Lady Gaitskell.
5. Interview, Sir Harold Wilson.
6. AHD, 10 December 1959. (Hetherington was editor of the *Guardian*.)
7. *Observer*, 15 November 1959; *The Times*, 23 November.
8. HG to Stephen Spender, 27 October 1959: HGP.
9. 'General Election Round-up', 9 October 1959: BBC Archives.
10. HG to J. B. Battle, 10 November 1952: HGP.
11. To the 1951 Society, Manchester, 31 October 1955 (BBC Archives);

R. T. McKenzie in the *Daily Telegraph*, 15 December 1955.

12. On 'At Home and Abroad', 4 October 1957: transcript in HGP.

13. Janosik (1968), p. 31.

14. Griffiths (1969), p. 135.

15. HG to George Thomas MP, 26 January 1960: HGP.

16. AHD, 29 October 1959.

17. Ibid., 12 November 1959.

18. F. S. Oliver, *The Endless Adventure* (Macmillan, 1930), pp. 46–8.

19. Interview, Lord Pannell; confirmed by Lord Harris and by Richard Crossman.

20. *In Place of Fear* (Heinemann, 1952), p. 118.

21. RCD, 25 November 1959.

22. *Report*, pp. 105–14.

23. *Sunday Times*, 6 December 1959.

24. *Report*, pp. 127 (Cousins).

25. Ibid., pp. 136–7 (Pannell), pp. 143–4 (Healey, Williams), pp. 151–5 (Bevan).

26. Foot (1973), pp. 641–51.

27. Interview, Michael Foot.

28. *Daily Telegraph*, 22 March 1960.

29. On 'Panorama', 30 November 1959, BBC Archives; *The Times*, 1 December.

30. *The Times*, 15 February 1960.

31. Dalton to HG, 31 January 1960 (his emphasis): HGP.

32. RCD, 12 February 1960.

33. HG to Dalton, about 1 March 1960: HGP.

34. To HG, 19 and 23 March 1960: HGP.

35. HG to Arthur Gaitskell, 14 April 1960: HGP.

36. AHD, 14 July 1960.

37. HG to Sam Watson, 23 September 1960: HGP.

38. *Report*, pp. 218–21.

39. John Murray to Dora Gaitskell, 28 March 1960: HGP.

## CHAPTER 20

1. Reported in HDD, 4 May 1960.

2. HG to Tewson, 13 April 1960: HGP.

3. Memorandum for the Shadow Cabinet, sent also to several trade union leaders: HGP.

4. Hansard, 27 April 1960, 226, 329.

5. *The Times*, 2 May 1960.

6. HG to Julie Gaitskell, 8 March 1958.

7. *Commentary* (New York), May 1961.

8. Foot in *Tribune*, 29 April 1960 ('John Marullus'). *Herald*: Deryck Winterton, 5 May 1960.

9. Crosland to HG, 4 May 1960: HGP.

10. Dalton to HG, 4 April 1960: HGP.

11. RCD, 11 May 1960 (mostly reporting Wilson).

12. Lord Gordon Walker's diary, 12 May 1960.

13. Letter to a friend, 15 May 1960.

14. RCD, 11 and 26 May 1960.

15. Minutes in HGP.

16. HG to Crossman, 13 June 1960: HGP.

17. HG to Sam Watson, 3 June 1960: HGP.

18. HG to Watson, 23 June 1960: HGP.

19. RCD, 12 May 1960.

20. *New Statesman*, 17 October 1959; 25 June 1960.

21. John Murray to HG, 31 July 1960: HGP.

22. *The Economist*, 19 March 1960.

23. HDD, 12 May 1960.

24. RCD, 26 May 1960.

25. *Daily Mail*, 9 June 1960.

26. Macmillan (1972), p. 232, from his diary.

27. Strauss *et al.* to HG, 26 July 1960: HGP.

28. *Sunday Telegraph*, 2 October 1977.

29. Hansard, 14 July 1960, 1610.

30. HG to Lance Mallalieu MP, 23 June 1960: HGP.

31. RCD, 4 August 1960.

32. Morgan Phillips, *Constitution of the Labour Party* (August 1960). Here, HG noted in the margin: 'all the difficulty!'

33. To the NUGMW conference at Great Yarmouth, 23 May 1960.

34. Apparently a quotation from Wilson: in Andrew Roth, *Sir Harold Wilson–Yorkshire Walter Mitty* (Macdonald, 1977), p. 249. Taylor letter in *New Statesman*, 9 July 1960.

35. HG to Anthony Crosland MP, 4 September 1960 (HGP); replying to Crosland's letter of 1 September. (His emphasis.)

36. Douglas Houghton MP to HG, 12 September 1960: HGP.

37. *Spectator*, 24 January 1964.

38. RCD, 20 September 1960.

39. *The Times*, 26 September 1960.

40. *Financial Times*, 5 October 1960; and interviews.

41. *Report*, pp. 178–80 (and p. 156 on Clause Four).

42. 'Labour Party Conference Report': BBC Archives

43. *Report*, pp. 195–201.

44. William Barkley, *Daily Express*, 6 October 1960.

45. *Sunday Times*, 9 October 1960.

46. Duff (1971), p. 191.
47. Evidence in *Political Quarterly*, July 1962.
48. Harold Hutchinson, *Daily Herald*, 6 October 1960.
49. Trevor Evans, *Daily Express*, 3 October 1960.
50. Sam Watson, in Rodgers (1964), p. 113.
51. HG to C. Shopland, 10 March 1960: HGP.
52. In his concession speech after the general election.
53. Lord Wigg, *George Wigg* (Michael Joseph; 1972) p. 231.
54. Francis Boyd, *Guardian*, 4 October 1960.
55. To HG, 20 June (Pakenham), 18 October (White): HGP.
56. RCD, 26 October 1956.


## CHAPTER 21

1. Undated note in HGP, probably written at Scarborough.
2. F. Bealey, J. Blondel and W. P. McCann, *Constituency Politics* (Faber, 1965), pp. 285, 287: referring to Newcastle-under-Lyme.
3. *Daily Herald*, 10 October 1960 ('genocide'). Zilliacus had been expelled in 1949 but was readmitted in 1952. For his pre-war contact with HG see above p. 63.
4. *Guardian*, 26 October 1960.
5. AHD, 5 November 1960.
6. *Daily Telegraph*, 27 October 1960.
7. Macmillan (1972), p. 256 from his diary; Dalton to HG, 4 November 1960, HGP.
8. RCD, 26 October 1960.
9. This interpretation is based on Crossman's diary; the evidence is set out in the hardback edition of this biography.
10. HG to W. T. Rodgers, 1 March 1961: HGP.
11. Press of 28 February and 11 March 1961; and RCD, 14 June 1961.
12. In Rodgers (1964), p. 119.
13. HG to Julie, 28 February 1961.
14. RCD, 4 and 17 May, 1961.
15. Derek Marks, *Evening Standard*, 9 May 1961. (His italics.)
16. Interview, Denis Healey.
17. 'Panorama', 2 October 1961: BBC Archives.
18. 'Jim G.' to HG, 8 October 1961: HGP.


## CHAPTER 22

1. RCD, 24 April and 17 May 1961.
2. RCD, 14 and 29 June 1961.
3. To Alderman George Hodgkinson of Coventry, 11 April 1962: HGP.

4. AHD, 10 May 1961.
5. *The Times*, 29 June 1961.
6. *Daily Telegraph*, 13 July 1961.
7. *Report*, pp. 148–9, 153–4.
8. John Cole, *Guardian*, 4 October 1961.
9. RCD, 28 November 1961.
10. Sydney Jacobson in the *Daily Mirror*; HG to Geoffrey Goodman on 'Ten O'Clock' (BBC Archives): both 6 October 1961.
11. Party political broadcast, 12 July 1961: HGP.
12. Hansard, 7 November 1961, 822.
13. Hansard, 9 April 1962, 1019–22.
14. To Robin Day on 'Panorama', 2 October 1961 (BBC Archives); to COHSE at Torquay, *Guardian*, 19 June 1962.
15. At Derby on 14 January 1961.
16. At the Durham Miners' Gala, 15 July 1961.
17. Hansard, 18 July 1961, 1080.
18. Macmillan to Selwyn Lloyd, 3 October 1961: Macmillan (1973), p. 542.
19. Hansard, 16 November 1961, 792–803.
20. Patrick Keatley in his *The Politics of Partnership* (Penguin, 1963), p. 493, and in the *Guardian*, 3 November 1967: quoting conversations with HG in 1959 and 1962.
21. *Daily Herald*, 24 January 1961.
22. Hansard, 5 July 1961, 1466; 17 October 1961, 47–8; 5 February 1962, 51.
23. *The Economist*, 5 August 1961.
24. Interview, Sir Ronald Edwards.
25. AHD, 6 February, 10 and 17 April 1962.
26. HG to Anthony Sampson, 13 November 1961: HGP.

## CHAPTER 23

1. Private speech to the Commonwealth Parliamentary Association, 12 July 1962: HGP.
2. To a private meeting with supporters of CDS on 21 October 1962: W. T. Rodgers's note.
3. His own summary on his return: *Manchester Guardian*, 21 January 1957.
4. Interview, Harold Hutchinson (deputy editor of the *Daily Herald*).
5. HG to Solly Pearce, editor of the *Leeds Citizen*, 21 June 1961: HGP.
6. Party political broadcast, 8 May 1962: HGP.
7. Memorandum to President Kennedy, 11 December 1962: HGP.
8. Hansard, 6 June 1962, 521–7.
9. Miriam Camps, *Britain and the European Community 1955–63* (OUP, 1964), pp. 423–4. The fullest account.
10. Hansard, 2–3 August 1961, 1501–2 (HG), 1768 (Sandys).
11. At Blackburn, *Observer*, 10 December 1961.

12. AHD, 10 and 17 April 1962.

13. HG to Roy Jenkins, 8 May 1962: HGP.

14. Interviews, Sir Robin Brook, Lord Diamond, Douglas Jay.

15. HG to Cressida Gaitskell, 25 January 1962.

16. Memorandum for Fred Hayday and others, May 1962: HGP.

17. Macmillan (1973), from his diary: p. 65 (de Gaulle), p. 139 (Labour Party).

18. AHD, 3 May 1962.

19. Ibid., 30 November 1961.

20. Ibid., 27 September 1962.

21. Ibid., 10 July 1962.

22. To Arthur Calwell, 3 August, 26 September, 6 December 1962: HGP.

23. AHD, 11 September 1962.

24. HG to Colin Gray, 17 October 1962: HGP.

25. Party political broadcast, 21 September 1962: HGP.

26. *Guardian*, 14 September 1962 (Crossman); 4 October (John Cole).

27. HG to Mrs J. P. Cannon, 26 September 1962: HGP.

28. (Lord) George Brown, *In My Way* (Penguin ed., 1972), pp. 211–12.

29. Interviews.

30. *Report*, pp. 154–65.

31. Geoffrey Goodman, *The Awkward Warrior – Frank Cousins* (Davis-Poynter, 1979), p. 340.

32. Interview, Lord Harris.

33. Macmillan (1973), pp. 121, 125.

34. Longford (1964), pp. 240–1.

35. *Sunday Times*, 10 December 1977.

## CHAPTER 24

1. Muggeridge in the *Evening Standard*, 21 January 1964.

2. *Report*, p. 194.

3. Jenkins (1974), p. 173.

4. The first and fourth sections (*Gaitskell at Fifty-six* and '*The Abominable Virus*') are largely based on interviews; those quoted here are his secretary Mrs Skelly, and James Griffiths on 'controversies'.

5. Granada TV, 28 July 1961: HGP.

6. A. E. Skerry of Plymouth to HG, 8 February 1960: HGP.

7. HG to Julie Gaitskell, 18 May 1959 on canvassing (his emphasis); 7 June 1959 on careerism; 24 August 1962 on holiday.

8. Interview, Professor Austin Ranney.

9. *Daily Express*, 20 June 1962 (Dora); 19 August 1962 (VIP); 26 September (Trevor Evans on Brighton).

10. *Sunday Express*, 28 September 1961.

11. Anthony Sampson, *Anatomy of Britain* (Hodder and Stoughton, 1962), p. 97.

12. HG in the *Guardian*, 14 February 1962.
13. HG to Mr and Mrs Jack (Lord and Lady) Donaldson, n.d.
14. Hugh Stephenson (then president) to the author.
15. Neal Blewett (the chairman) to the author.
16. *Tribune*, 11 May 1962; *New Statesman*, 25 May and 1 June; HG to Miss E. A. Strachan of Cheltenham, 26 June, HGP.
17. AHD, 23 October 1962, reporting HG an hour before he met Macmillan.
18. Arthur Schlesinger jr., *A Thousand Days* (Fawcett Crest ed., 1965), p. 806.
19. Longford (1964), pp. 242–3.
20. James Margach, *Sunday Times*, 7 October 1962.
21. In the *Guardian*, 11 January 1963.
22. Charles Curran, *Evening News*, 19 January 1963.
23. HG to John Robertson MP, 9 October 1962: HGP.
24. HG to James Griffiths MP, 31 December 1962: HGP.
25. The then Vicar of Holbeck (Archdeacon W. H. S. Purcell) to the author.
26. Macleod in the *Sunday Telegraph*, 19 January 1964.

## CHAPTER 25

1. Obituaries in the *Sphere*, 2 February 1963 (John Connell); *Leeds Weekly Citizen*, 1 February (Healey); on BBC television (Crosland); *Congressional Record*, 21 January, pp. 690–1 (Humphrey).
2. Hansard, 21 January 1963, 42; *Daily Mail* interview in January 1959.
3. Transcript of HG's address (on the PLP) to the ETU's educational college at Esher, 28 June 1962; interview, David Wood.
4. *WEA News*, November 1962.
5. *Daily Mail*, 13 July 1959.
6. In Briggs and Saville (1967), p. 19.
7. Denis Healey on 'Panorama', 18 January 1963: BBC Archives.
8. Of 70 politicians asked, 29 had been Cabinet Ministers; 53 were Labour, 12 of them from the Left. Only nine thought Gaitskell would have lost (two were Tories, six left-wingers); nine (all Labour) were Don't Knows.
9. He once told Julian Amery he would have four new men in his Cabinet: Crosland, Donnelly, Jenkins and Wyatt.
10. At Attlee's retirement dinner on 10 February 1956, and at the PLP's Golden Jubilee rally in Leeds Town Hall on 19 February.
11. Above, Ch. 22, n. 20.
12. RCD, 5 March 1963; Janosik (1968), p. 29n.
13. John Mackintosh MP in *The Times*, 22 July 1977.
14. Paul Foot, *The Politics of Harold Wilson* (Penguin, 1968), p. 127: quoting John Junor.
15. Joseph Kallenbach, *The American Chief Executive* (Harper and Row, 1966), pp. 257–67.

# Select Bibliography

Only authors quoted in more than one chapter are listed in this bibliography. Publication details for other books are given in full at the first mention.

Bowra, Sir Maurice, *Memories* (Weidenfeld and Nicolson, 1966).

Briggs, Asa, and J. Saville (eds), *Essays in Labour History in Honour of G. D. H. Cole* (Macmillan, 1967 ed.).

Brittan, Sam, *The Treasury Under the Tories 1951–64* (Penguin, 1964).

—— *Steering the Economy* (Penguin, 2nd ed. 1971).

Butler, Lord, *The Art of the Possible* (Penguin ed., 1973).

Dalton, Hugh, Memoirs I: *Call Back Yesterday* (Muller, 1953).

—— Memoirs II: *The Fateful Years* (Muller, 1957).

—— Memoirs III: *High Tide and After* (Muller, 1962).

Duff, Peggy, *Left Left, Left* (Allison and Busby, 1971).

Durbin, E. F. M., *The Politics of Democratic Socialism* (Routledge, 1954 ed.).

Foot, Michael, *Aneurin Bevan*, I (Four Square, 1966); II (Davis-Poynter, 1973).

Gaitskell, Hugh, *Chartism* (WEA, 1929).

—— *The Challenge of Coexistence* (Methuen, 1957).

Griffiths, James, *Pages from Memory* (Dent, 1969).

Haffner, Sebastian, ed., *Observer Profiles* (*Observer*, 1954).

Hunter, Leslie, *The Road to Brighton Pier* (Barker, 1959).

Janosik, E. G., *Constituency Labour Parties in British Politics* (Pall Mall, 1968).

Jenkins, Roy, *Nine Men of Power* (Hamish Hamilton, 1974).

Longford, Earl of (Frank Pakenham), *Five Lives* (Hutchinson, 1964).

Macmillan, Harold, Memoirs IV: *Riding the Storm* (Macmillan, 1971).

—— Memoirs V: *Pointing the Way* (Macmillan, 1972).

—— Memoirs VI: *At the End of the Day* (Macmillan, 1973).

Pakenham, see Longford

Rodgers, W. T. (ed.), *Hugh Gaitskell 1906–63* (Thames and Hudson, 1964).

Williams, Francis, *Nothing So Strange* (Cassell, 1970).

# Index

### USING THE INDEX

In a few long entries, main references are in **bold** type.

Organizations indexed by their initials come *first* in the relevant letter, e.g. 'AEU' before 'Acheson'.

Relationships specified are to HG. Except for living persons, titles are normally those used during HG's career.